MW00588573

RETHINKING
PUBLIC
INSTITUTIONS
IN INDIA

RETHINKING
PUBLIC
INSTITUTIONS
IN INDIA

edited by

Devesh Kapur
Pratap Bhanu Mehta
and
Milan Vaishnav

OXFORD
UNIVERSITY PRESS

OXFORD
UNIVERSITY PRESS

Oxford University Press is a department of the University of Oxford.
It furthers the University's objective of excellence in research, scholarship,
and education by publishing worldwide. Oxford is a registered trademark of
Oxford University Press in the UK and in certain other countries

Published in India by
Oxford University Press
YMCA Library Building, 1 Jai Singh Road, New Delhi 110001, India

© Oxford University Press 2017

The moral rights of the authors have been asserted

First Edition published in 2017

All rights reserved. No part of this publication may be reproduced, stored in
a retrieval system, or transmitted, in any form or by any means, without the
prior permission in writing of Oxford University Press, or as expressly permitted
by law, by licence, or under terms agreed with the appropriate reprographics
rights organization. Enquiries concerning reproduction outside the scope of the
above should be sent to the Rights Department, Oxford University Press, at the
address above

You must not circulate this work in any other form
and you must impose this same condition on any acquirer

ISBN-13: 978-0-19-947437-0
ISBN-10: 0-19-947437-0

Typeset in Berling LT Std 9.5/13
by The Graphics Solution, New Delhi 110092
Printed in India by Replika Press Pvt. Ltd

CONTENTS

TABLES AND FIGURES

Tables

Figures

ACKNOWLEDGEMENTS

No edited volume is possible without the help of a large cast of characters. As the editors, we would like, first and foremost, to thank all of the contributors to the book. When we first set out to re-examine many of the issues first raised in the 2005 volume *Public Institutions in India: Performance and Design*, edited by two of us (Devesh Kapur and Pratap Bhanu Mehta), we reached out to the best scholars and practitioners we could think of who had a unique grasp of the workings of the Indian state. We were honoured and delighted that—to a person—they agreed to contribute their insights.

We are grateful to the Rockefeller Foundation for hosting a four-day book workshop at the Bellagio Center in July 2013, where we had a chance to discuss initial drafts of the chapters included here. We would like to thank Rob Garris and Joel Santana at Rockefeller for making the workshop possible and Laura Podio in Bellagio for her bountiful hospitality. We would also like to thank the Think Tank Initiative of Canada's International Development Research Centre (IDRC) for additional support. David Malone, IDRC's former president, was extremely supportive of the project. Milan Vaishnav is also grateful to the Carnegie Corporation of New York for its generous support of a research project on India's state capacity.

The Bellagio conference was a joint effort of four institutions: the Center for the Advanced Study of India (CASI) at the University of Pennsylvania, Philadelphia, United States of America, the Centre for Policy Research, New Delhi, India, the Carnegie Endowment for International Peace, Washington, DC, United States of America, and the University of Pennsylvania Institute for the Advanced Study of India (UPIASI), New Delhi, India. We owe E. Sridharan, S.D. Gosain, and Ruchika Ahuja of UPIASI our gratitude for their tireless help in organizing and managing the conference logistics. Juliana Di Giustini of CASI deserves special thanks for making the conference such a success; her good cheer, attention to detail, and *buon Italiano* were indispensible. At Bellagio, we had the good fortune of learning from several experts who shared their insights and experience working in and studying India for many decades. Rajiv Lall, Pradnya Saravade, and Ronen Sen graciously lent their time, as did Marshall Bouton, who also serves on CASI's International Advisory Board.

When the time came to prepare the manuscript for publication, Saksham Khosla provided excellent editorial assistance. Aidan Milliff provided many useful inputs during the final stages of the editing process. The team at Oxford University Press in New Delhi was extremely enthusiastic about the project from the start. It has been a pleasure working with them on every aspect of the book. We also benefited enormously from the detailed comments of two anonymous reviewers, whose suggestions greatly improved the final manuscript. Ananth Padmanabhan was a great help in carrying out the initial formatting of the chapters. We would be remiss if we did not acknowledge the special contribution made by Madhav Khosla, who went out of his way to make sure that this project was a success. We are also grateful that Madhav and Ananth agreed, at a late date, to jointly author the chapter on the Supreme Court.

Last, but certainly not least, we would like to extend a special thanks to our colleagues, friends, and families for their unending support.

Devesh Kapur
Pratap Bhanu Mehta
Milan Vaishnav
February 2017

ABBREVIATIONS

AAP	Aam Aadmi Party
ACD	Anti-Corruption Division
ADR	Association for Democratic Reforms
AERO	Assistant Electoral Registration Officer
AG	Auditor General
AGMUT	Arunachal Pradesh, Goa, Mizoram, and Union Territories
AIS	All India Services
AMRUT	Atal Mission for Rejuvenation and Urban Transformation
AoR	Advocates-on-Record
APTEL	Appellate Tribunal for Electricity
AQMF	Annual Quality Management Framework
ARC	Administrative Reforms Commission
AS	Additional Secretary
ASEAN	Association of Southeast Asian Nations
ASOSAI	Asian Organization of Supreme Audit Institutions
ATR	Action Taken Report
BJP	Bharatiya Janata Party
BLO	Booth Level Officer
CAG	Comptroller and Auditor General
CBI	Central Bureau of Investigation
CBLO	Collateralized Borrowing and Lending Obligation
CCIL	Clearing Corporation of India Ltd.
CDR	Central Deputation Reserve
CEC	Chief Election Commissioner
CEO	Chief Electoral Officer
CGA	Controller General of Accounts

CIC	Central Information Commission
COPU	Committee on Public Undertakings
CPI	Consumer Price Inflation
CPSMS	Central Plan Scheme Monitoring System
CSO	Civil Society Organization
CSPMS	Central Sector Plan Monitoring System
CSS	Centrally Sponsored Scheme
CVC	Central Vigilance Commission
CVO	Chief Vigilance Officer
DA	Divisional Accountant
DEO	District Election Officer
DoPT	Department of Personnel and Training
DoT	Department of Telecommunications
DP	District Panchayat
DRDA	District Rural Development Agency
DRSC	Departmentally Related Standing Committee
EC	Election Commissioner
ECB	European Central Bank
ECI	Election Commission of India
EIN	Expenditure Information Network
ENA	École Nationale d'Administration
ERO	Electoral Registration Officer
EVM	Electronic Voting Machine
FDI	Foreign Direct Investment
FPI	Fund for Public Investment
FRBM	Fiscal Responsibility and Budget Management
FSLRC	Financial Sector Legislative Reforms Commission
G-20	Group of 20
GAO	Government Accountability Office
GDP	Gross Domestic Product
GIS	Geographic Information System
GoI	Government of India
GP	Gram Panchayat
GPOD	Gram Panchayat Organizational Development
GST	Goods and Services Tax
HRD	Human Resource Development
IAAD	Indian Audit and Accounts Department
IAAS	Indian Audit and Accounts Service

IAS	Indian Administrative Service
ICAS	Indian Civil Accounts Service
iCED	International Centre for Environment and Audit of Sustainable Development
ICS	Indian Civil Service
ICT	Information and Communication Technology
IDI	International Organization of Supreme Audit Institutions Development Initiative
IDMA	Independent Debt Management Agency
IEO	Independent Evaluation Office
IFS	Indian Foreign Service
IGL	Indraprastha Gas Limited
IIDEM	India International Institute of Democracy and Election Management
IMF	International Monetary Fund
INCOSAI	International Congress of Supreme Audit Institutions
INTOSAI	International Organization of Supreme Audit Institutions
IPS	Indian Police Service
IRC	Independent Review Committee
IRDP	Integrated Rural Development Program
IRS	Indian Revenue Service
IT	Information Technology
JBIC	Japan Bank for International Cooperation
JNNURM	Jawaharlal Nehru National Urban Renewal Mission
JPC	Joint Parliamentary Committee
JS	Joint Secretary
LFA	Local Fund Audit
LG	Local Government
MBA	Master of Business Administration
MCC	Model Code of Conduct
MDG	Millennium Development Goal
MGNREGA	Mahatma Gandhi National Rural Employment Guarantee Act
MGNREGS	Mahatma Gandhi National Rural Employment Guarantee Scheme
MKSS	Mazdoor Kisan Shakti Sangathan

MLA	Member of the Legislative Assembly
MoPR	Ministry of Panchayati Raj
MoU	Memorandum of Understanding
MP	Member of Parliament
MPC	Monetary Policy Committee
NAO	National Audit Office
NDA	National Democratic Alliance
NDC	National Development Council
NDS-OM	Negotiated Dealing System-Order Matching
NGO	Non-Governmental Organization
NITI	National Institution for Transforming India
NJAC	National Judicial Appointments Commission
NPM	New Public Management
NRHM	National Rural Health Mission
NRI	Non-Resident Indian
OBC	Other Backward Class
OERC	Orissa Electricity Regulatory Commission
OPD	Old Public Discipline
P and T	Post and Telegraph
PAC	Public Accounts Committee
PC	Prevention of Corruption
PDS	Public Distribution System
PEM	Public Expenditure Management
PFM	Public Financial Management
PFMA	Public Financial Management Accountability
PIL	Public Interest Litigation
PMO	Prime Minister's Office
PNGRB	Petroleum and Natural Gas Regulatory Board
PPP	Public–Private Partnership
PRI	Panchayati Raj Institution
PWD	Public Works Department
RBI	Reserve Bank of India
RFD	Results Framework Document
RO	Returning Officer
RPA	Representation of the People Act
RTI	Right to Information
SAI	Supreme Audit Institution

SARFAESI	Securitization and Reconstruction of Financial Assets and Enforcement of Security Interest
SC	Scheduled Caste
SDG	Sustainable Development Goal
SE	Superintending Engineer
SEB	State Electricity Board
SEC	State Election Commission
SERC	State Electricity Regulatory Commission
SES	Senior Executive Service
SGFF	Second Generation Fiscal Federalism
SGL	Subsidiary General Ledger
SLR	Statutory Liquidity Ratio
SSA	Sarva Shiksha Abhiyan
ST	Scheduled Tribe
SVEEP	Systematic Voters' Education and Electoral Participation
TDSAT	Telecom Disputes Settlement Appellate Tribunal
TELPE	Technology Enhanced Learning Process Enabler
TG&S	Technical Guidance and Supervision
TRAI	Telecom Regulatory Authority of India
UNGA	United Nations General Assembly
UPA	United Progressive Alliance
UPSC	Union Public Service Commission
VAT	Value Added Tax
WPI	Wholesale Price Index
YPP	Young Professionals Program

INTRODUCTION

Devesh Kapur, Pratap Bhanu Mehta, and *Milan Vaishnav*

Over the past quarter century, India has witnessed multiple transformations that have fundamentally reshaped its economy, foreign policy, politics, and society. Nearly a quarter century after liberalization, the Indian economy is today more market-oriented and integrated with the world economy. These economic changes, along with the demise of the Soviet Union, have also reoriented India's external posture to a deeper engagement with the United States (US) and Japan. With respect to politics, an era of Congress party–dominance in New Delhi as well as in the states first gave way to an era of coalition politics at the centre. The coming to power of the Bharatiya Janata Party (BJP) government in 2014 may mark yet another profound shift in Indian politics: it has positioned the BJP as a potential centre of gravity for Indian politics. The rigidities of social hierarchies in Indian society persist, but are showing signs of erosion. Many (but not all) hitherto marginalized social groups have acquired at least some degree of voice, and new social alliances are challenging old social permutations.

However, despite the strides India has made in these domains, its public institutions have not undergone a commensurate transformation. Indeed, India's multiple transformations are increasingly buffeted by strong headwinds of deep institutional malaise. The integrity and responsiveness of the Indian state to the multiple challenges facing the country—ranging from its rapid urbanization to low agriculture productivity, from security threats to weak human capital, and from widespread corruption to environmental degradation—will fundamentally determine India's future. While the broad outlines of India's governance challenge are well known, there are few analytical studies on their institutional underpinnings. And although much work has been done on the juridical and normative frameworks in this regard, studies on how institutions actually *work* (or not work, as is often the case) are few and far between.

The principal goal of this book is to examine the institutional foundations of the Indian state and the organizational and institutional context in which it operates. It is our hope that this understanding will help build a more capable Indian state suited for the unique challenges of the twenty-first century. By the 'Indian state', we are referring to the country's core federal institutions, as opposed to its subnational 'state' entities.

The 'institutionalist' focus of the social sciences in recent decades, most commonly associated with the work of Nobel laureate Douglass C. North, has been the primary lens to understand the mechanisms by which institutions produce specific outcomes.[1] This focus has meant that institutions are largely treated as a bundle of rules that shape incentives in contexts that are exogenous to them. But institutions are also complex organizations with internal norms, cultures, financial wherewithal, patterns of hiring and firing, and leadership selection. The neglect of institutions qua organizations has meant that the inner workings of specific institutions are for the most part a black box, an outcome variable as well as a causal variable.

One Decade On

To address this lacuna, more than a decade ago, two editors of the present volume (Kapur and Mehta) organized a conference on 'Public Institutions in India', focusing on the key federal institutions of the Indian Republic. The resulting volume, *Public Institutions in India:*

---

[1] According to North, institutions are 'the rules of the game in a society or, more formally, the humanly devised constraints that shape human interaction'. Douglass C. North, *Institutions, Institutional Change and Economic Performance* (New York: Cambridge University Press, 1990).

Performance and Design, made institutions the object of explanation, with a focus on the ways in which the micro-incentives *within* institutions helped explain certain features of the institution itself.[2] While that volume did well and has undergone multiple printings, India's public institutions, sadly, fared less well. In the interim period, the travails of many public institutions have been all too manifest. It is hard to think which of India's critical public institutions—be it Parliament, the judiciary, bureaucracy, police and other investigative agencies, or the myriad regulatory agencies—are on a path to regeneration. Equally worrying, as one of us has argued, the challenges of development that India faces, 'from urbanisation to the environment, technology to education, require institutions to mediate complex forms of knowledge and elicit widespread social acceptance. The biggest question mark over India is the ability of its institutions to do just that. It could be argued that in significant ways, the quality-of-life gains of growth are being severely constrained by this deep mismatch between institutional design, politics and developmental needs.'[3]

This, along with considerable changes unfolding in India's political economy, motivated us to go back to the drawing board in order to take a fresh look at India's key public institutions. In July 2013, we organized a successor conference titled 'Building an Indian State for the 21st Century'. The cumulative result of this initiative are the chapters in the present volume, which not only help us understand the variation in institutional performance of the Indian state, but also provide a window to the evolution of the state itself and its capacity to adapt to a rapidly changing economic, political, and social environment.

It is our contention that improving the capacity of India's public institutions is the single biggest challenge that India faces in the twenty-first century. If India can successfully rejuvenate its core public sector institutions, it will go a long way towards realizing its developmental objectives at home and ambitions abroad. If, however, the gap between popular aspirations and the quality of governance is not remedied, this

---

[2] Devesh Kapur and Pratap Bhanu Mehta, eds, *Public Institutions in India: Performance and Design* (New Delhi: Oxford University Press, 2005).

[3] Pratap Bhanu Mehta, 'The Coming Storm', *Indian Express*, 19 December 2015.

mismatch will imperil the substantial transformations India has experienced in other domains.

There is no better example than the economy. If the dizzying transformation of the Chinese economy has been the defining story of economic development in the last three-and-a-half decades, economic changes in India—while considerably less dramatic—have also been transformative. However, India's recent success masks deep underlying challenges whose import will only multiply in the foreseeable future. While it has been argued that in many ways India's improved economic performance has been *despite*, not because of, the state—epitomized by epigrams such 'India grows at night while the government sleeps'— continued welfare gains, better distributional outcomes, and the resilience and sustainability of rapid economic growth are in considerable doubt in the absence of better-performing public institutions.[4]

To get a sense of the looming challenges, consider this. In the two decades after the onset of economic liberalization, India added 364 million people to its population—more than the stock at the time of Independence, which itself was accumulated over millennia. India's democratic success and this 'demographic dividend' mean that tens of millions of young people will be joining India's workforce with aspirations that previous generations could not even dream of, but without the jobs commensurate with their skills and aspirations. The ranks of those who live in India's urban cities and townships are rising at a rapid clip, so swift that even the government's own agencies have difficulty adequately measuring India's changing demographics.[5]

A booming population and growing economy are stressing natural resources, and contestation over land, energy, and water are only going to become more severe. If the pessimistic predictions of the effects of climate change on India come to pass, the prognosis is even grimmer. With about a million people entering the working-age population every month—a group that will be increasingly urban, interconnected,

---

[4] Gurcharan Das, *India Grows at Night: A Liberal Case for a Strong State* (New Delhi: Penguin, 2012).

[5] The World Bank estimates that India's urban population will swell by 250 million between 2014 and 2030. See World Bank, *Urbanization beyond Municipal Boundaries: Nurturing Metropolitan Economies and Connecting Peri-Urban Areas in India* (Washington, DC: World Bank, 2013).

and informed—providing capable and responsive governance to manage these new expectations will be no mean task.[6]

Capacity Gaps

Even a casual observer of the Indian state would be struck by its limitations. The most obvious manifestation of this is its relatively small size. Contrary to popular belief, the Indian state is one of the smallest among major nations on a per capita basis. While India's population increased from 846 million to 1.2 billion between 1991 and 2011, total public sector employment actually decreased from 19.1 to 17.9 million. Over this period, the absolute size of the elite Indian Administrative Service (IAS) dropped by 10 per cent; by 2010, the total strength of the IAS and the Indian Police Service (IPS) was less than 11,000, while the vacancy rate stood at 28 per cent. In foreign affairs, the strength of the Indian diplomatic corps is less than that of Sweden's. India's judicial system presently has a backlog of more than 31 million cases. Government estimates suggest that as many as 10 per cent of all cases have been pending for a decade or more.

Even in the high-stakes realm of national security, there is a pattern of endemic weakness. The Indian Army is facing a serious shortage of officers—more than 9,000 in 2015, when it recruited 1,900 and those who retired stood close to 1,000. Despite major internal security concerns, 8,000 posts are lying vacant in the Intelligence Bureau, while 8 of the mere 10 Assistant Commissioner posts for the Maharashtra State Anti-Terrorism Squad remain vacant—this after a deadly, humiliating terrorist attack on Mumbai against which the Indian state's feeble response was manifest. Compounding the fact that India has one of the lowest per capita police rates among major countries (1.3 constables per 1,000 citizens), official estimates of police vacancies stand around 23 per cent (0.5 million of 2.2 million posts vacant).[7]

[6] As of 2015, the Ministry of Labour estimates that 12.8 million Indians are entering the labour force each year. See Ministry of Labour and Employment, *Annual Report, 2014–2015* (New Delhi: Government of India, 2015).

[7] Praveen Swami, 'India's Spy Agencies More Toothless than Ever', *Indian Express*, 1 December 2014; Mateen Hafeez, 'Shortage of Manpower Hounds ATS', *Times of India*, 11 July 2015. Law and order is a state subject under the Indian Constitution and, hence, states exhibit dramatic variation in terms of

But while the state might be undermanned in terms of adequate personnel, it is most certainly as over-bureaucratized as it is under-staffed. Consider, for example, the well-known indicators compiled by the World Bank that capture the ease of doing business in nearly every country in the world. According to the 2016 edition of the 'Doing Business' indicators, India ranks 130 out of 189 countries in the overall ease of doing business, 155 in ease of starting a business, 178 in enforcing contracts, and 183 in getting a construction permit—a sad testimony to the state of the Indian state, especially for a country that is a member of the Group of 20 (G-20) and which aspires to be a global power.[8]

Unfortunately, all this makes painfully evident that the Indian state is struggling to perform even the most basic functions of a sovereign state. While much of the attention on the manifold shortcomings of the Indian state has focused on high levels of corruption and venality in public life, an equally compelling limitation is the lack of competence, both at the policy design and formulation levels, and the even larger challenge in effectively implementing these policies. The latter, of course, is much more the responsibility of state governments, an issue which is not the focus of this volume.

This 'state capacity'—the ability of the state to effectively design and implement public policies—varies greatly across India. The Indian state is not failing but is seen to be only too often 'flailing'.[9] It can successfully manage highly complex tasks, but fails in executing relatively simple ones. On the one hand, India can organize elections for 850 million eligible voters, conduct a census for 1.2 billion people, and run a highly effective space programme. Yet, on the other hand, its

performance and personnel. With regard to vacancy rates, for instance, 60 per cent of the police force in Uttar Pradesh stands vacant, while only 4 per cent of positions in Maharashtra are unfilled. See National Crime Records Bureau, Ministry of Home Affairs, *Crime in India 2013* (New Delhi: Government of India, 2014).

[8] World Bank, *Doing Business 2016: Measuring Regulatory Quality and Efficiency* (Washington, DC: World Bank, 2015).

[9] Lant Pritchett, 'A Review of Edward Luce's *In Spite of the Gods: The Strange Rise of Modern India*', *Journal of Economic Literature* 47, no. 3 (September 2009): 771–80.

record in providing basic public services, from health to education and water to sanitation, ranges from modest to dismal. The persistence of a stubborn Maoist insurgency and the sporadic resurgence of communal violence in certain pockets speak to its patchy law and order prowess, while chronic power shortages are a stark testimony to the quality of its regulatory institutions.

The underlying institutional weaknesses of public institutions in India stand in contrast to relatively dynamic private and civil society organizations. According to a 2012 government report, India was home to 144,000 registered non-profit societies as of 1970; by 2008, that number had grown by a factor of nearly 8 (1.14 million).[10] In 1957, fewer than 30,000 companies with a paid-up capital of barely 1,000 crore rupees (1 crore is equal to 10 million Indian rupees; 1 lakh is equal to 100,000 rupees) were operational in India. Fast-forward to 2014, and India boasts nearly 950,000 firms with a paid-up capital of 21 lakh crore.[11] Undoubtedly, the expansion and growth of India's private sector and vibrant civil society will substitute for some of the short-comings of the public sector in the foreseeable future. Nevertheless, there is a wide range of core functions, from regulation to security, from social inclusion to public goods provision, where the state is—and will be—indispensable. This is particularly true for India's vulnerable population—such as its 265-million-odd poor or members of histori-cally marginalized minority groups—who rely on public assistance to meet their most basic needs.[12] These vulnerable populations, unlike India's middle and upper classes, do not have a viable 'exit' option from the public sector and its myriad deficiencies.[13]

In turn, the ability of the Indian state to adequately respond to the multiple challenges facing the country will have a broader regional

[10] Central Statistics Organisation, Ministry of Statistics and Programme Implementation, *Final Report on Non Profit Institutions in India: A Profile and Satellite Accounts in the Framework of System of National Accounts* (New Delhi: Government of India, 2012).

[11] Ministry of Corporate Affairs, *58th Annual Report on the Working and Administration of the Companies Act, 1956* (New Delhi: Government of India, 2014).

[12] The poverty figures are from 2011 and come from the World Bank, which uses a poverty line of $1.90 purchasing power parity.

[13] Devesh Kapur, 'Exit', *Seminar* 677 (January 2016): 110–14.

and global impact. The momentous shifts in the locus of global economic power towards Asia mean that a range of key actors—including Australia, Japan, the US, and the Association of Southeast Asian Nations (ASEAN)—seeks to partner with India on a broad spectrum of issues to add ballast to regional stability and confront global challenges such as climate change and terrorism. However, India's ability to be an effective partner and take on a leadership role in all of these realms rests on its capacity to generate inclusive economic growth, while maintaining political stability. This is unlikely to occur if its governance weaknesses persist.

Analytical Framework

While the broad outlines of India's governance challenge are well known, there are few in-depth studies on these issues. Few subjects elicit more boredom in high-powered academia than the nuts-and-bolts of public administration. Even more unfortunately, public administration reform has received lesser attention from successive governments, notwithstanding professed statements from the highest level of government and innumerable commission and task force reports dissecting the state's myriad governance failures. Indian intellectuals and activists have always pressed the state to do more, be it through legal or policy mandates. Few, however, have engaged with improving state capacity with the sort of detailed analysis and understanding that this complex subject requires.

Indeed these gaps in understanding are even more pronounced, thanks to the numerous changes that have reshaped India's governance landscape since the launch of our first volume on India's public institutions.[14]

First, civil society has become much more active, as evident in its role in passing landmark 'rights based' legislations such as the Right to Information (RTI, 2005), Right to Education (2009), and Right to Food (2013) Acts, and a bill to revise the 1894 Land Acquisition Act (Land Acquisition, Rehabilitation and Resettlement Act, 2013). The rapid growth of non-governmental organizations (NGOs) has provided a buffer against the state's weaknesses and also helped to improve

---

[14] Kapur and Mehta, eds, *Public Institutions in India*.

accountability in some cases. For instance, Amitabh Mukhopadhyay's chapter on financial accountability in this volume (Chapter 8) argues that the introduction of social audits by community-based organizations can act as a force multiplier when the government's own auditing agencies are badly stretched. Similarly, the chapter by E. Sridharan and Milan Vaishnav on the Election Commission of India (ECI) (Chapter 10) points to the pivotal role civil society organizations have played in using Public Interest Litigation (PIL) to compel the courts and the ECI to enhance transparency in elections.

Yet, the rise of the civil society and the 'rights agenda' have not been unambiguously positive. All legally enforceable rights require resources and all resources have opportunity costs.[15] These realities are rarely addressed by civil society groups other than at the banal level of the need for more aggregate resources. The absence of a commensurate increase in state capacity has sabotaged these innovative efforts. The RTI Act is one such example. Less than a decade after its establishment, the RTI's ultimate appellate body, the Central Information Commission (CIC), faced a serious backlog of RTI cases with thousands of fresh cases being sent its way each month. In November 2015, it came to light that the agency was so severely overwhelmed that it literally had not opened its mail in months, with more than 10,000 pending requests gathering dust.[16] As Madhav Khosla and Ananth Padmanabhan point out as well in their chapter on the Supreme Court (Chapter 3), the growth of PIL has also taken its toll on the apex court, which spends increasingly less time deciding important questions of a constitutional nature and more on populist posturing.

Furthermore, civil society has not been uniformly transparent or accountable either. While many NGOs that engage in legitimate work are hampered by the weakness of public infrastructure as well as capricious and oversensitive state organizations, there is little transparency in the operations of many civil society organizations, some of which are little more than money laundering operations (often fronting for politicians) with little accountability of their own.

---

[15] Stephen Holmes and Cass R. Sunstein, *The Cost of Rights: Why Liberty Depends on Taxes* (New York: W. W. Norton & Co., 1999); Devesh Kapur, 'The Wrongs of Rights', *Business Standard*, 7 July 2013.

[16] 'Central Information Commission Has Not Opened 10,000 RTI Envelopes Since August-end', *Economic Times*, 19 November 2015.

Second, Indian politics has become significantly more decentralized as the primacy of national politics has lost ground to regional politics. While the 2014 general election, in which the BJP earned the first single-party majority in three decades, represents a shift back towards centralized power, it is not clear whether this is the harkening of a new trend or merely a temporary hiatus. Indeed, despite the BJP's dominant electoral victory, 37 parties claim representation in the Lok Sabha (the lower house of the Indian Parliament), while the Rajya Sabha (the upper house) remains deeply divided. As M.R. Madhavan discusses in his chapter on Parliament (Chapter 2), the rise of coalition politics and the fragmentation of political power have adversely affected the functioning of Parliament, resulting in a greater number of disruptions and fewer sittings, undermining the critical deliberative role of a parliament in any democracy.[17]

The regionalization of politics reflects the decline of national parties and a greater salience of states in the federal polity. This trend has empowered regional political leaders who have grown increasingly assertive in countering attempts (real or perceived) by federal authorities to exert undue influence on state prerogatives. State governments, however, are no paragons of virtue. As Nirvikar Singh demonstrates in his chapter on expenditure institutions (Chapter 5), while the centre has been reluctant to devolve the purse strings to state capitals, states in turn have rejected calls to give more financial autonomy to the third tier of government. However, following the acceptance of the recommendations of the Fourteenth Finance Commission, the centre has increased the share of central taxes flowing directly to the states from 32 to 42 per cent. This historic shift, although not free of implementation issues, along with the Goods and Services Tax (GST, once it becomes operational), will markedly shift India's fiscal federalism in ways that are likely to significantly remake India's political economy. But, if further fiscal decentralization to the third tier (local governments) does not occur, the Indian body politic will have an expansive middle bulge and weakened head and feet.

Third, economic liberalization, while reducing the state's role in direct production, has simultaneously enhanced its regulatory role.

---

[17] A broadly similar case is made by Mahendra Prasad Singh, 'The Decline of the Indian Parliament', *India Review* 14, no. 3 (2015): 352–76.

As Navroz K. Dubash relates in his chapter on regulatory institutions (Chapter 6), the state is not so much receding as changing the locus of its activities. This transition has been an uneasy one. Many regulatory bodies across India suffer from a common set of problems stemming from congenital birth defects reflected in their design: insufficient authority; circumscribed financial autonomy; weak human resources; multiple, overlapping mandates; a lack of legitimacy; and, unsurprisingly, political interference that is both the cause and consequence of their multiple weaknesses. Some regulatory bodies, such as those in the domain of electricity, which were designed to insulate them from politics, have lacked the personnel with the judgement and expertise to operate in an increasingly 'deals-based' environment.

As one of the government's primary economic institutions—with key regulatory functions as well—the Reserve Bank of India (RBI) is widely recognized as one of the country's better-functioning federal institutions. Yet, as Errol D'Souza writes in this volume (Chapter 4), many of the functions the RBI performs—such as debt management—represent a conflict of interest with its core function of overseeing monetary policy. Attempts to shift this function out of the RBI have opened new fissures in the relationship between the central bank and the Ministry of Finance, indicative of the difficulties in undertaking institutional reform even in the better-run institutions.

What Is—and Is Not—Covered

This volume explicitly seeks to build on the work of our previous volume and attempts to fill the gaps in our knowledge of the actual working of the Indian state. In 2002, we sought to provide an analytical and empirical foundation for the study of state capacity in India through a careful analysis of federal institutions—the core institutions of the Indian state—and interactions among them, while situating them in India's broader societal context. The first objective of our earlier work was to use positive analysis to address a critical normative concern: how do we make public institutions more effective to their members and society at large? The second was to provide a much-needed catalyst to researchers, policymakers, and civil society actors to seriously begin thinking through the complex and multidimensional problems of state capacity in India.

In our second attempt at providing such a catalyst, we focus, as before, on the core institutions of the Indian state. We have identified three pillars to guide our inquiry: recruitment of human capital, internal organizational features that motivate performance, and the interaction of agencies with one another and the conditions in which they reinforce or undermine each other. Our aim is to understand the specific political economy operating in each area and within each institution. These three pillars need to be addressed in tandem because each is inexorably linked to the other. For instance, human resources cannot be understood outside their organizational context. Organizational performance, on the other hand, occurs within a complex web of larger institutional dynamics and interrelationships.

Before introducing readers to greater detail about what is in the present volume, we would like to clarify what they will *not* find in the subsequent pages. For starters, this volume is focused on India's core federal institutions. As such, it does not delve deeply into state-level institutions and/or policies that are constitutionally under the jurisdiction of India's federal units. This might strike some readers as anachronistic as much of day-to-day governance takes places in the states, as opposed to New Delhi. The decision to focus on India's core federal institutions was, in part, compelled by analytic coherence; covering state-level institutions, and the large variation in performance that lies therein, is a daunting task for any group of researchers.

But there is a second reason for narrowing our sights: to compare trends over time. The predecessor volume to the present compendium also focused primarily on national-level institutions. Returning to these institutions a decade later allows us to understand what has and has not changed. This book, however, is not simply an update of the previous volume; we also shed new light on institutions, such as the ECI, that were not the explicit focus of chapters in the 2005 book. Finally, this book does not scrutinize India's security institutions. This again is not because of lack of interest; indeed, numerous scholars have raised alarm bells about the institutional and organizational challenges facing India's diplomatic, military, paramilitary, civil police, and intelligence agencies. Our hope is that other researchers will take up the task of extending our analysis to these institutions in the domain of national security and foreign policy.

In broad terms, the institutional analyses that follow can be roughly grouped into four clusters. The first, institutions of oversight and restraint, focus on three premier arms of state power: the presidency, Parliament, and the Supreme Court. The second cluster comprises economic institutions: the RBI, India's institutions of expenditure governance (namely, the erstwhile Planning Commission and the Finance Commission), and new regulatory institutions. The abolition of the Planning Commission in 2014 and the advent of the National Institution for Transforming India (NITI Aayog), a successor entity, provide us with an opportunity to take stock of the lessons learnt from the former's experience in order to extract lessons for the latter. The third cluster involves India's accountability institutions. Our exploration focuses on institutions of internal accountability—such as the Central Vigilance Commission (CVC) and Central Bureau of Investigation (CBI)—as well as the Comptroller and Auditor General (CAG), an important agent of external accountability. The fourth and final cluster delves into the critical institutions of implementation: the civil services, the ECI, and local government institutions—the last representing the frontlines of the state where multiple federal mandates, from rights to centrally sponsored schemes, face their acid test.

Key Themes

Given the extensive reach of the Indian state, it is difficult to adequately capture the richness of diversity of India's institutional scene with a few summary points. Nevertheless, there are significant commonalities we can identify when scanning across the core federal institutions this book examines. We choose to highlight six in particular that are especially salient.

Personnel Failures

The most basic reality of India's public institutions is the acute talent crunch they face. This crunch has a quantitative—in terms of endemic vacancies and personnel shortages—as well as a qualitative dimension—in terms of a paucity of adequately skilled, trained, and equipped personnel.

In terms of quantity, which we have already alluded to earlier, the November 2015 report of the Seventh Pay Commission, which sets salaries for central government employees, provides a set of useful figures. As of January 2014, according to the commission's findings, the 56 ministries and departments of the Union government had nearly 729,000 vacancies (the gap between the number of sanctioned positions and those actually filled), or a shortfall of 19 per cent.[18] This disjuncture is, in part, the result of a purposive slowdown in direct recruitment that began in the early 1990s and was intended to slash the size of government payrolls. Furthermore, it does not capture the large shift towards temporary workers contracted by the central government, on which the centre spends around 300 crore rupees each month, according to the commission's estimates. Whatever the case may be, the chapters in this volume uniformly highlight debilitating staff shortfalls.

For instance, Mukhopadhyay comments (Chapter 8) on the severe shortfall in qualified government auditors, an outcome he deems the result of powerful staff unions successfully lobbying for expanding internal promotion rather than fresh recruitment—an affliction common to all public institutions, be it the higher judiciary, the civil services, or the RBI. The situation in the CAG is compounded by the fact that, even within the existing bureaucracy, just 17 per cent of the employees are dedicated to conducting performance audits. The outcome of these twin realities, Mukhopadhyay argues, is highly uneven audit appraisals.

Other accountability institutions suffer from similar maladies. As R. Sridharan notes in his chapter on internal accountability institutions (Chapter 7), that although the sanctioned strength of the CVC modestly increased from 288 to 296 officials in 2013, the actual number of positions remained at 230. Even then, the CVC lacks a dedicated investigative agency, instead relying on the already overburdened Chief Vigilance Officers (CVOs) and the highly politicized CBI to follow-up on inquiries and undertake investigations.[19]

---

[18] It should, however, be emphasized that we do not have any independent measure of vacancies, just what the government reports.

[19] Indeed, as Sridharan notes, the number of sanctioned CBI positions has grown from 5,961 in 2009 to 6,674 in 2013, yet vacancies continue to hover between 12 and 15 per cent.

The issue of shortage of personnel is not simply about aggregate numbers, it is also about their spatial allocation. As K.P. Krishnan and T.V. Somanathan's chapter on the IAS amply documents (Chapter 9), there are large variations in the size of IAS cadres with respect to total state populations. As a result, the IAS cadre in India's most populous state is more than 40 per cent smaller than it should be, while the corresponding number of officers in Sikkim is 15 per cent larger than it should be, based on population alone. There are also distortions in the extent to which officers are placed on central deputation in New Delhi, which means that many small states have much better representation in central ministries and departments than their larger peers.

Of course, even if shortcomings in the allocation and quantity of personnel were immediately remedied, the issue of competence would remain. Krishnan and Somanathan, in their analysis of the IAS, find this to be an equally troubling infirmity.[20] Changes in the design of official recruitment policies have led to an apparent reduction in the quality of entrants to the IAS, perhaps the result of an increase in the maximum age and number of attempts needed to pass the exam.

In his analysis of India's prime expenditure institutions (Chapter 5), Singh finds a clear lack of specialized expertise in key agencies, especially among those of sufficiently senior rank. This gaping hole would be less noticeable, perhaps, if the largely generalist staff systematically consulted with outside domain experts; lamentably, Singh notes, this is all too infrequent an occurrence, given the present incentives bureaucrats face.

Another place where the lack of domain expertise is particularly striking is in India's regulatory institutions. As Dubash notes, the country's regulatory bodies have become the vanguard of the 'sinecure state', in which prized postings have become routine opportunities for dispensing political patronage. This reality, in turn, has two obvious impacts: first, it ensures that many bureaucrats and judges who vie for

---

[20] Interestingly, an internal exercise carried out by the Ministry of Personnel and all state governments found that out of the 1,089 IAS officers who had completed at least 15 years of service (both direct recruits and those who had come up the ranks), only 2 were deemed unfit and asked to opt for premature retirement. Subhomoy Bhattacharjee, 'Only 2 of 1,089 IAS Officers Inept', *Business Standard*, 22 April 2016.

plum post-retirement positions as regulators have few incentives to
take politically unpopular decisions in the final stages of their careers
lest they fall out of favour with the government of the day; and, second,
it stacks the deck with regulators whose credentials are primarily political or personal in nature, rather than professional—further hampering
the agencies they oversee.

Legal Ambiguity

Although ambiguities surrounding the legal and constitutional mandates
of various federal institutions are not necessarily new, it can be argued
that the negative consequences of such muddled mandates have grown.
Part of this lacuna can be attributed to constitutional design; for instance,
when it comes to the 'third tier' of government, the expenditure responsibilities of local government overlap to a great extent with the subjects
enumerated on the state list of the Constitution. As Singh writes, this
confusion—coupled with states' reluctance to devolve financial autonomy—results in local governments that are given mandates without
commensurate resources (both financial and human) or authority. The
engineered failures then become the excuse to recentralize.

The divergent fortunes of the CAG and ECI, two constitutional bodies, also illustrate the importance of clear mandates. Article 324 of the
Constitution grants the ECI clear authority over the 'superintendence,
direction and control of the preparation of the electoral rolls', while
subsequent articles provide the apex body with supreme authority over
the conduct of elections, including insulating the agency even from
judicial interference while elections are ongoing. This firm constitutional framework was further enhanced by the twin Representation of
the People Acts of 1950 and 1951. The result, while far from perfect
(as Chapter 10 by E. Sridharan and Vaishnav makes clear), is one of
the most autonomous and widely praised election agencies the world
over. However, the ECI's role in addressing three severe challenges facing India's electoral democracy—curbing runaway election expenses,
regulating the actions of political parties, and mitigating the nexus of
crime and politics—demonstrates that institution's need to constantly
adapt if it is to retain its vitality.

Like the ECI, the CAG was also underpinned by a constitutional
mandate. However, as R. Sridharan points out in Chapter 7, the latter's

mandate was far less robust. Article 149 of the Constitution only states that the duties of the CAG will be prescribed by an act of Parliament with the pre-Independence legal foundations guiding the chief auditor in place until then. Unfortunately, for the CAG, it took two decades (until 1971) for authorizing legislation to materialize. Thus, in a sense, the CAG's constitutional 'mandate' is actually a misnomer; the Constitution more or less states that Parliament, when it sees fit, will deliver the CAG with a mandate when it chooses to act. Although the CAG is often discussed as having its origins outside of the three major branches (executive, legislative, and judicial), R. Sridharan contends that it is really 'an extended outreach agency of the legislature'. And if the legislature chooses to ignore reports from the CAG, the latter has very little recourse.

In other cases, it is not the Constitution per se that is to credit or to blame, but subsequent action undertaken by the executive and/ or legislative branches. For instance, the government established the CVC in 1964 in response to the Santhanam Committee Report, charged with providing advice on how to curb corruption in public life. Yet, the CVC was hamstrung from the outset; it could only take up inquiries on the basis of 'files'. In other words, unless officers have left an incriminating paper trail in official government correspondence, the CVC has no basis to recommend an investigation. Even in such rare cases where a paper trail can be discerned, the CVC must rely on agencies like the CBI to take cases forward. The CBI, in turn, is hamstrung in its own ways. Under the Delhi Special Police Establishment Act,1946, the CBI must obtain permission of India's states if it wants to carry out an investigation into wrongdoing occurring within states unless, for instance, the central government's equities are directly affected or central employees are implicated. Arguably, the CBI's greatest weakness is its malleability. The apparent ease with which it can be manipulated by the political executive has rendered it a 'handmaiden' of the government and the sobriquet 'Compromised Bureau of Investigation'. The reality is that governments of the day have used CBI corruption investigations to reward and/or punish key politicians from opposition parties depending on the prevailing winds. Unfortunately, this has meant that even when its cases are bonafide, accused parties can scream 'political vendetta' to undermine the case in the public eye.

The 2013 creation of a *Lokpal*, or anti-corruption ombudsman, was meant to address the structural weaknesses of the CBI. Instead, it is likely to end up further muddying the waters. Its creation epitomizes a trend highlighted in our earlier volume, namely, the tendency to address institutional weaknesses by setting up new institutions rather than addressing the reasons for failure of existing institutions head-on and reforming them. The result is a multiplicity of institutions, competing for scarce resources and battling for turf, while providing a modicum of an institutional 'safety net'.[21]

While it is too early to tell how this new agency will function, the mandate question appears tricky in this case as well. For instance, while the authorizing legislation empowers the Lokpal with superintendence over the CBI in those cases the latter has referred to it, the Lokpal has limited powers to actually direct the actual course of the investigation itself—rendering these supervisory powers moot.

Economic and political change has also raised new questions about mandates once widely perceived to be clear-cut. The growth in the breadth and depth of capital markets and financial services has, as D'Souza notes in his chapter, highlighted the inadequacies and conflicts inherent in the mandate of the RBI, one of the most highly respected public institutions. Indeed, the 2013 report of the Financial Sector Legislative Reforms Commission (FSLRC), a two-year initiative launched by the Ministry of Finance to propose revisions to the sector's legal and regulatory framework, offered a thorough reimagining of the existing architecture. Among the commission's most controversial recommendations were calls to create a unified financial regulator, an independent public debt management agency, and a monetary policy committee (MPC) that will set policy interest rates, with extensive representation selected by the executive.

All three have significant implications for the RBI and, unsurprisingly, have proved to be highly contentious. Of the three, the only one where there has been a satisfactory resolution has been the composition of the MPC, where the government conceded and agreed to a six-member

[21] Devesh Kapur, 'Explaining Democratic Durability and Economic Performance: The Role of India's Institutions', in *Public Institutions in India: Performance and Design*, eds Devesh Kapur and Pratap Bhanu Mehta (New Delhi: Oxford University Press, 2005), 28–76.

committee with three members from the RBI, including the governor, who would have a casting vote. While the creation of the MPC has finally brought the RBI in line with other major central banks, this has not been the case with debt management. In principle, creating a public debt management agency would imply taking powers away from the RBI and handing them to an independent agency, thus relieving the central bank of a conflict of interest between public debt management and monetary policies. However, opponents of the move cite a lack of expertise outside the RBI as well as the likelihood of an increased cost of government borrowings. According to D'Souza's analysis, both objections are red herrings. There is no reason why the debt management personnel in the RBI could not be part of a new agency, and the increased cost of government borrowing might actually be desirable from a deficit reduction perspective. Instead, this tussle points to a pathology of all public institutions in India—a deep reluctance to let go.

Political trends have also raised new concerns about public institutions that have been largely dormant until recent years. James Manor's chapter (Chapter 1) on the presidency is perhaps the most acute example of this. During the first several decades following Independence, the Congress party dominated electoral politics—especially at the centre—obtaining clear parliamentary majorities in every election from 1952 to 1989 (the post-Emergency election in 1977 serving as the lone exception). This meant that the role of the president as head of state (but not government) was relatively circumscribed. In the post-1989 era of coalition politics, however, prevailing conditions have created greater opportunities for the president to assert his (and in one case, her) authority for the purposes of government formation. Paradoxically, as Manor points out, those very opportunities also generate strong reasons *not to act*, as doing so creates risks that the office—considered to be above the partisan fray—gets coloured by everyday politics. For instance, when a general election does not produce a party with a clear majority, it is the president who must exercise discretion in initiating the process of government formation. By norm, the president would turn to the single largest party, but must he or she always do so? Might there be circumstances under which the president turns to, say, the second-largest party because s/he believes it is more likely to produce a sustainable majority? And, either way, should there be clear rules or procedures codified to guide the president? Manor raises a similar concern regarding the presidential use of 'pocket vetoes', whereby the president either questions advice from the Council of Ministers or fails to act (thereby vetoing the proposed action by deliberate inertia).

Manor's perceptive points raise another issue: the importance of prudent leadership, an attribute that is difficult to quantify. Indeed, if we return to the comparison between the powers enumerated to the ECI versus the CAG, it is clear that leadership—not constitutional foundations alone—matters a great deal in determining performance. Even in the case of the ECI, which has been blessed by relatively robust legal underpinnings, it was not until the tenure of T.N. Seshan in the 1990s that the agency fully came into its own. Beginning in the 1960s, electoral abuse in India began to gain ground as the links between crime and politics grew in the shadow of political fragmentation, institutional weakening, a growing influx of illicit money in elections, and the rise of identity politics. This toxic brew gathered strength in subsequent decades, calling the very legitimacy of the democratic process into question. Seshan, building on his agency's broad constitutional remit and exploiting a fragmented polity, leveraged his bully pulpit role and consolidated the ECI's control over the timing and conduct of elections, especially through the rigid enforcement of the Model Code of Conduct. The ECI's institutional renewal is an instructive example of institutional change as punctuated equilibria, where changes in the external environment can provide space for creative agency and drive institutional change.

Coordination Dilemmas

Another cross-cutting theme revolves around the issue of coordination. This, in turn, can be assessed on two dimensions: horizontal coordination between government agencies and vertical coordination between levels (or tiers) of governance.

As Singh's chapter argues, a central irony with regard to the former is that at the same time ministerial decision-making is highly fragmented—pointing to the weakness of another key institution, namely the cabinet—and power within ministries is highly centralized. Take an issue like energy. India currently has separate ministries for coal; environment, forest, and climate change; mines; new and renewable energy;

petroleum and natural gas; and power.[22] This fragmentation complicates both policy formulation as well as implementation. Within ministries, however, an excessive concentration of power and responsibility rests with the minister, which can crowd out dissenting voices within the government and ideas emanating from outside. This issue exists on top of routine turf struggles that are endemic to large bureaucracies around the world. Unsurprisingly, India has its fair share of tussles within the bureaucracy over institutional and policy equities—as the previous example from D'Souza's chapter on the RBI illustrates.

As India moves to address new complex challenges such as climate change or national security, the need for better and more creative coordination mechanisms is obvious. The obvious existing mechanisms— the Prime Minister's Office (PMO) and the Cabinet Secretariat—are only as effective as the authority of the prime minister and the quality of personnel manning these bodies, and can very easily become overcentralizing bodies.

The issues plaguing vertical coordination are in a state of flux. One of the Modi government's first acts was to abolish the Planning Commission, which over the years had morphed into both an advisory council as well as a financial conduit for central funds. In its stead, the government established the NITI Aayog, a government think tank intended to foster greater cooperation between the centre and the states. Two institutions—the Finance Commission (discussed in Nirvikar Singh's chapter) and the Pay Commission—play a coordinating role, explicit in the first case and implicit in the second. As a constitutional body, the Finance Commission has played a stabilizing role in coordinating fiscal federalism. And while the Pay Commission's recommendations have coordinated salaries horizontally across different central government organizations, they have also established benchmarks that have, in effect, coordinated public sector salaries vertically in states as well.

With centrally sponsored schemes projected to decline and substantially greater spending by states, the transmission mechanisms from

[22] The Modi government has partially addressed this issue by giving one minister of state (Piyush Goyal) responsibilities for the power, coal, and new and renewable energy portfolios. In principle, this should mitigate challenges of horizontal coordination.

the federal government to the local level seem tenuous. The record of decentralization vis-à-vis panchayat and urban local bodies—or the third tier of government—is widely known and highly discouraging. Here, it is states—rather than the centre—that are primarily culpable for the 'stop-start nature of the devolution of functions, funds and functionaries' to local government bodies, as T.R. Raghunandan argues in Chapter 11. Although there is significant variation across states, many state governments have been reluctant to devolve powers to the local level, lest they cede their levers of local control and patronage. Central authorities are partly to blame; over the past decade and a half, a plethora of parallel structures have sprouted up around the proliferating number of centrally sponsored schemes that regularly attach one-size-fits-all strings to key social programmes initiated by New Delhi. A central cause of these vertical coordination failures is the misalignment between the expenditure and revenue stream. While changes brought about by the Fourteenth Finance Commission will likely contribute to greater autonomy at the level of states, local governments will continue to be beholden to their state capitals for transfers. Without significant avenues for resource mobilization, local governments continue to have limited options.

External Accountability

The transparency of government functioning is one area where there has been notable progress in the time that has elapsed since the last volume. Transparency has been an area where the government has responded creatively, thanks to the pressure imposed by strong external actors—namely civil society and the media—that led to the passage of the landmark RTI Act. As alluded to earlier, there are serious concerns about the government's capacity to adequately respond to the demands imposed on it by opening up its activities to external scrutiny.

Globally, regulatory institutions have come under fire for operating in technocratic bubbles relatively free of popular scrutiny and lacking a culture of openness. In India, in several instances, regulatory institutions have been at the forefront of improving the visibility of their deliberations to a broader set of stakeholders beyond the government. As Dubash argues in his chapter, opening up administrative hearings and document access to a wide diversity of civil society actors has infused regulatory bodies—especially in the electricity sector—with a newfound culture of sharing. Dubash finds that some regulators in this domain threw open their documentation to the public even prior to the passage of the RTI Act. Dubash goes so far as to argue that establishing guidelines to enhance accountability and transparency 'may be among the most significant contributions of regulatory agencies to the challenges of infrastructure governance'.

Other agencies of the government, typically those involved in service delivery (such as health or a variety of entitlement transfers), have been nudged by civil society and a growing number of citizens' groups conducting social audits. As Mukhopadhyay discusses, social audits entail citizens investigating the reasons for their own subjugation, which is expected to galvanize social pressure and bureaucratic adjustment to programmatic failings. This expectation is only sometimes realized; empirical research demonstrates that these audits as well as related information dissemination campaigns often suffer from concerns about the very lack of transparency that motivates their existence.[23] An analysis of social audits carried out under the Mahatma Gandhi National Rural Employment Guarantee Act (MGNREGA) 2005 found that while audits resulted in a significant decline in complaints related to the non-provision of work, they were 'accompanied by an increase in more sophisticated and harder to detect material-related irregularities'.[24] In other words, while audits may be effective in detecting irregularities, they appear to have limited deterrent effect, since information by itself has little effect on sanctions on public officials.

If it is surprising that regulatory institutions, often constructed such that they are relatively insulated from politics, can be relatively open agencies, it is equally counter-intuitive that Parliament—which has a direct popular mandate—lags behind with regard to external-facing accountability. For starters, the practice of 'question hour' is deeply flawed. As Chapter 2 by Madhavan outlines, fewer than 15 per cent

[23] Sandip Sukhtankar and Milan Vaishnav, 'Corruption in India: Bridging Research Evidence and Policy Options', *India Policy Forum* 11 (July 2015): 193–276.

[24] Farzana Afridi and Vegard Iversen, 'Social Audits and MGNREGA Delivery: Lessons From Andhra Pradesh', *India Policy Forum* 10 (July 2014): 297–341.

of questions listed are actually answered orally in Parliament. This is largely a function of time constraints, which are felt even more acutely given that so much time allotted for questions is lost due to frequent disruptions. Furthermore, unlike the British Parliament, there exists no separate question time reserved for the prime minister to address concerns brought forward by members of the House. A second issue concerns basic norms of transparency on parliamentary voting; presently, there is no way for ordinary citizens to learn how Members of Parliament (MPs) vote on any given bill or motion. It is difficult to construct an argument for why citizens should not be given ready access to this level of information (with the caveat, of course, that India's anti-defection law typically ensures partisan bloc voting when a party whip is issued).

The parliament's shortcomings with regard to transparency also extend to the Public Accounts Committee (PAC), a select body that audits the expenditure of GoI (in conjunction with the CAG). Mukhopadhyay reports that, while there is no established rule forbidding discussion of PAC reports in the House, such a norm does exist. This absence of discussion around audits is further compounded by the fact that all of the PAC's deliberations take place in private, closed off to both the media and ordinary Indians. Indeed, this latter fact applies across the board to all parliamentary committees since their deliberations are held *in camera*.

The Supreme Court, as Khosla and Padmanabhan note in their chapter, also has been criticized for a lack of transparency, particularly in regard to judicial appointments. The current collegium system, whereby the five most senior judges (including the Chief Justice of India) control appointments to the Supreme Court and the various high courts, has come under harsh criticism for being highly opaque. A constitutional amendment establishing a National Judicial Appointments Commission (NJAC) that would replace the collegium passed both houses of Parliament and was ratified by a majority of state legislatures. Nevertheless, the Supreme Court ruled the NJAC unconstitutional on the grounds that it violated the basic structure of the Constitution. While views diverge as to whether the NJAC was the right solution to the problem of appointments, most observers believe that the judiciary's attempts at self-regulation have not fared well.

Internal Accountability

If evidence of improved external accountability represents a positive trend, the same cannot necessarily be said of internal accountability. There are several reasons for this. First, as pointed out earlier, ministries remain highly over-centralized, with little internal competition for ideas or checks on the power of the top brass. Second, few agencies have successfully adopted outcome-based budgeting or performance evaluation that would link agency objectives to a clear set of measurable metrics. The health ministry, for example, could in theory condition fiscal transfers on measurable progress on reducing infant mortality. Its reluctance to do so is partly a reflection of weak capacity; but it is also a testament to the resistance put up by bureaucrats and politicians in efforts to curb discretionary authority.

In general, the entire design of government programmes is based on inputs and processes to transform those inputs into outputs. In a sense, this was what the entire planning process did. And accountability mechanisms have followed suit, focusing primarily on process and procedures. Unless the design of government programmes puts the onus of accountability on outcome-based measures, it is hard to see why public officials will behave any differently.

When it comes to strengthening internal accountability mechanisms, one straightforward remedy is more effective decentralization. Singh notes in his chapter that India's initial experience with local government in the wake of the 73rd and 74th Amendments to the Constitution tends to support the notion that both accountability and effectiveness increase with decentralization. The empirical evidence on this score is ambiguous, but the additional external accountability created by decentralizing power can, in turn, boost levels of internal accountability.

Political Interference

The ability of politicians to manipulate the workings of core central institutions is perhaps the most disturbing of trends present in nearly all chapters. Some of these tendencies are well known. For decades, scholars have commented upon the ease with which politicians transfer bureaucrats to punish or reward them on the basis of criteria unrelated to their performance. Indeed, Krishnan and Somanathan lament the widespread nature of personally disruptive transfers of IAS officers in their chapter. What is more troubling is that the issue extends far beyond transfers to a broader set of concerns over postings. For instance, politicians have often resorted to arbitrary demotion, which involves authorities unilaterally downgrading a post without any clear appeal to what is in the public interest, as a 'stick' with which to sanction officers. On the other hand, politicians have also deployed 'carrots' with equal aplomb. The authors cite service extensions and promises of post-retirement employment (typically working with a regulatory or appellate government agency) to reward pliant IAS officers who are due to retire.

The issue is not restricted to the IAS alone. Indeed, D'Souza notes that the terms of the RBI governor and deputy governor have been a source of constant tension between the agency and the Finance Ministry. In the 2005 Kapur and Mehta volume, Deena Khatkhate had pointed out that few governors appointed after 1969 successfully completed their full tenure of five years in office.[25]

The ECI is the rare agency that, thanks to its constitutional mandate, has experienced relatively few instances of overt political interference. Of course, there have been instances in the past when various ruling parties of the day have curbed the authority of the Commission. Although such infractions have grown increasingly rare, E. Sridharan and Vaishnav note that this is no excuse for complacency. Indeed, without additional safeguards, a future government could move to 'pack' the Commission with officers it favours or, given the paucity of protections, remove commissioners other than the Chief Election Commissioner (CEC).

In some cases, it is inaction—rather than action—on the part of the government that constitutes interference. Take the example of the CBI. A hotly contested issue, as discussed by R. Sridharan (Chapter 7), is the repeated absence of action on the part of the CBI when politically powerful individuals are accused of wrongdoing. Quite often, this inertia is deliberate; in fact, it might even be instinctual in settings where political reprisals are commonplace. A common feature

---

[25] Deena Khatkhate, 'Reserve Bank of India', in *Public Institutions in India: Performance and Design*, eds Devesh Kapur and Pratap Bhanu Mehta (New Delhi: Oxford University Press, 2005), 320–50.

of India's public institutions (and the public sector in general) is how frequently senior positions remain unfilled despite full ex ante information on when individuals are going to retire. Again, the inertia is often deliberate, as delays mean that possible contenders also retire, clearing the way for the political favourite.

The Larger Picture

The chapters in this volume are rich in describing the micro-dynamics of institutions. But it is important to point out that there are several big-picture transitions at stake in these institutional battles. To put it somewhat schematically, Indian institutions are struggling to accomplish the transition from what one might call 'old order' institutions to 'new order' institutions while maintaining formal continuity. The key elements of this transition are summarized in the following pages.

Transition from Discretion to Accountability and Public Reason

Traditionally, Indian public sector institutions have had wide scope for discretion, which they exercised in numerous ways. They exercised discretion in allocating state resources, prioritizing services, negotiating and renegotiating contracts, and, generally, granting all manner of favours to different groups of citizens. To a certain extent, discretionary power is inevitable in institutions; without it, robots could perform the jobs of public servants. But increasingly, as a result of anti-corruption movements and greater scrutiny by various branches of government, such as the judiciary, there is a growing clamour to either reduce discretion or to hold the exercise of discretionary power accountable to norms. But what normative, practical, and legal standards officials should be held accountable to is a matter of deep contestation. Nevertheless, there is no question that the exercise of power cannot hide behind discretionary authorities vested in different offices. In a highly mobilized, mediated society, such sweeping discretion is no longer possible. The exercise of state power has to be publicly justified in terms that all those affected by the exercise of those powers can freely accept. But the struggle between the demands of robust public justification and the temptation to hold on to discretion marks all the institutions scrutinized in the pages that follow.

Transition from Secrecy to Information

In part, wide discretion was sustained by the fact that the practices of the state remained relatively opaque to most citizens. But there has been a dual revolution that has completely upended the knowledge relationship between state and society. On the one hand, legal instruments like RTI have empowered citizens; indeed, many chapters detail the various ways in which RTI has reshaped institutional decision-making. On the other hand, civil society now produces far more knowledge than the state does—and it can use that knowledge to make demands on the state. At the risk of over-simplifying, in the old order, the state could often get away with excessive secrecy. It could also disproportionately control the agenda because the balance of knowledge production was not (yet) so skewed in favour of non-state actors.

Public institutions can no longer govern on the presumption that their decisions will remain secret for too long. And they can no longer govern on the presumption that they can control the knowledge agenda, and therefore control what institutions should do. Many Indian institutions are struggling to adapt to this new knowledge order, where the state has to be more open—both from the inside-out (it will be hard to keep secrets) and from the outside-in (knowledge produced outside will set the agenda to an ever greater extent). Institutions will also have to develop the capacity to mediate between contending modes of knowledge.

Transition from Low-Capacity to High-Capacity State

Many of the authors in this volume agree that India has historically been a low-capacity state. 'Capacity' in this context does not simply refer to the intrinsic capabilities of the state; it also relates to the state's capabilities in responding to demands put on the state by the citizenry. On the demand side, the pressures on the state have increased manifold, as a result of social mobilization, the 'rights' revolution, economic transformation, globalization, and the nature and gravity of collective risks posed by phenomena such as climate change. These are familiar facts, and they impact all institutions. Almost all the chapters in this volume touch upon one fundamental question: can Indian institutions be transformed into high-capacity institutions?

Transition from Centralization to Decentralization

A more mobilized citizenry demands inclusive governance. But the central question of what functions should be performed at what level of government has never been easy to settle in India. This question applies not simply between levels of government, as many of the chapters that discuss federalism amply demonstrate, but it also applies within institutions—what is the appropriate degree of delegation versus centralization in a hierarchical organization? India has historically been an immensely centralized state. Today, there is no question that there is greater political consensus in favour of decentralization than ever before. To be sure, the drive towards decentralization has been more episodic than linear; nevertheless, the trend towards greater devolution is unmistakable.

But the contemporary decentralization debate now comes with two new twists. First, what is the relationship between political, administrative, and fiscal decentralization? Under the compulsion of coalition government, India's states have become more important. The slogan of 'cooperative federalism', promoted by the Modi government, further promises to grant the states enhanced room for experimentation. But can this kind of fiscal and administrative decentralization really work if political party structures actually become more centralized? What would administrative decentralization mean in a context where chief ministers are more dependent on the centre for their political power? Conversely, chief ministers can be politically independent, but stymied by fiscal centralization.[26] Or perhaps most worryingly, what does administrative decentralization mean when chief ministers act in a highly personalized, Bonapartist manner? The same questions apply to decentralization to local government. But the broad contest over decentralization, and the fact that fiscal, administrative, and political inclusiveness do not go in tandem, pose immense challenges for inclusion.

The second twist is the degree of centralization within institutions. Do chief justices have inordinate power within the judiciary?

---

[26] For instance, the proposed GST might reduce states' discretion with respect to taxation authorities.

Does the PMO's control over the rest of government run the risk of over-centralization, thereby distorting the relationship between civil servants and the political executive? Regardless of how one answers these specific queries, there is no question that, within institutions, many actors are trying to hold on to more centralized power while the demands of democracy require more devolved institutional architecture where the roles and autonomy of each level of the hierarchy are more clearly secured.

Transition from Upward to Downward Accountability

In historical practice, the Indian state was often institutionalized in terms of upward vertical accountability, or the idea that officials will be held accountable to and by their superiors, not by either the public or by independently defined standards of performance. One of the subtler shifts in institutional discourse has been the demand to institute more downward accountability. This is the idea that state officials should satisfy some independent standards of performance, or what they do for citizens, rather than simply for their superiors in a hierarchical order. Institutions are struggling to initiate new practices of performance evaluation that are more citizen-focused and outward-looking.

In a way, these different elements have been linked; wide discretion, low capacity, high centralization, secrecy, and upward vertical accountability created a self-reinforcing loop of a low-performing state. Can India transition to a new equilibrium—a virtuous cycle of an accountable, high-capacity, decentralized, information-based state that is responsive to citizens rather than superiors? In their own ways and at their own pace, all of the institutions covered in this volume are struggling with this dilemma.

***

The following chapters in this book lay bare the notion that India's core federal institutions are badly in need of an overhaul. The story is not uniformly negative, however, and bright spots do exist. Compared to its developing country peers—not to mention several advanced democracies—India's highly respected elections body consistently delivers high-quality polls, especially in more recent years. The RBI, which does face internal capacity issues, not to mention a spate of newfound external challenges, has emerged as a highly credible voice on issues of monetary policy, banking, and finance. Even from within the ranks of the much-beleaguered bureaucracy, one can identify talent that is comparable to the best anywhere in the world.

Institutional change is always difficult, no matter what context. And indeed, that should be the case. Institutions are 'sticky' and, hence, change is inevitably gradual in the absence of major exogenous shocks. At the same time, institutions are always 'incomplete' in the sense that their design reflects conditions and an external environment at the time they were created. Consequently, there will always be a tension stemming from the need for change to reflect the changing external environment and institutional 'stickiness'. But institutions are always vulnerable and their stability cannot be taken for granted.[27]

The challenge for policymakers is to take whatever 'pockets of efficiency' do exist, to borrow a term from the sociologist Peter Evans, and find ways of expanding their coverage.[28] There are a number of low-cost, relatively easy-to-implement policy solutions that can do just this. For instance, removing the ease with which politicians can interfere in the postings and transfers of IAS officers can go a long way towards improving performance. If the Supreme Court were to insist on strict limits on courts granting adjournments, it would reduce delays in trial proceedings. Not all fixes are so easy; indeed, many require revisiting first principles of legal and institutional design. There is no magic wand, for instance, that can be waved to get the CBI's house in order.

In India, to borrow a phrase from former minister and noted journalist Arun Shourie, when all is said and done, much more is usually said than done. However, the silver lining is that there are ongoing experiments which, if they bear fruit, can be the basis for a new push to reform India's public institutions. Technocratic solutions, while they have their place, also have their limitations. Active coalitions are required to underpin institutional stability, and change will emerge

[27] James Mahoney and Kathleen A. Thelen, *Explaining Institutional Change: Ambiguity, Agency, and Power* (New York: Cambridge University Press, 2010).

[28] Peter Evans, *Embedded Autonomy: States and Industrial Transformation* (Princeton, NJ: Princeton University Press, 1995).

from coalitional shifts. For effective institutions to emerge, there will have to be a political consensus around what it takes to build such a state. Is there a possibility of such a consensus? Historically, it is difficult to build high-capacity states without a commitment to raising one's tax-to-gross domestic product (GDP) ratio. After adjusting for its low per capita income, India is not a significant outlier when it comes to tax revenue as a share of its overall economy. Nevertheless, compared to its fellow long-standing democracies, India has consistently under-performed, most notably when one focuses on direct taxation (such as income tax).[29] As such, India is in danger of being locked into a vicious circle: a low-performing state also reduces citizens' appetite to finance the state. But if citizens do not pay, the capacity constraints will only grow further. It is a sobering lesson of history that the popular appetite for taxation increases only in times of crisis or war—neither of which are outcomes to be wished for.

In the Indian case, these coalitions are likely to emerge from civil society selectively aligning with specific political parties and elements of the bureaucracy. But as India's challenges mount, the need for institutional reform is vital if the country is to build and sustain an Indian state for the twenty-first century. It is not a matter of choice, but of survival.

[29] Ministry of Finance, *Economic Survey 2015–16* (New Delhi: Government of India, 2016), Chapter 7.

1

THE PRESIDENCY

*James Manor**

The President of India is the head of state but not the head of government. Like heads of state in other parliamentary systems, s/he is
required by the Constitution to act on the advice of ministers. All
actions of the Government of India (GoI) are undertaken in the name
of the president—and reported as such in the media—but in reality
they are the actions of ministers and not of the president.

This subtlety is not always clear to citizens or even to some media
commentators. We might have expected this misperception to diminish over time but, as we shall see, it lives on. It poses dangers to the
presidency in two ways. It threatens to enmesh presidents unfairly in
partisan controversy when they are supposed to stand above it as a
symbol of the nation's unity. It also creates confusion about who should
be accountable for government actions.

There are, however, times when a president cannot be subordinate
to ministers—when no prime minister is in place who commands the
confidence of the lower house of Parliament, the Lok Sabha. There are
also times when the authority of a prime minister to demand certain
crucial actions from the president is open to doubt. Such occasions

* The present chapter is a substantial update, revision, and enlargement of J.
Manor, 'The Presidency', in *Public Institutions in India: Performance and Design*,
eds. D. Kapur and P.B. Mehta (New Delhi: Oxford University Press, 2005),
105–27.

have often arisen since 1989, when it became impossible for any single party to win a majority of Lok Sabha seats (2014 serving as the sole exception). There are no rules to guide presidents in such situations. The absence of rules is beneficial in that it gives presidents great flexibility to exercise their judgement in the teeth of vexing dilemmas. But it also threatens to entangle presidents in unwelcome controversy.

These and other problems that surround the presidency have received very little attention from scholars. More has been written about the role of state governors within India's federal system, and even about an executive presidency as a potential alternative to the present institution, than about the institution itself. This chapter provides a detailed assessment of this great office.

The presidency is first situated amid changes that have occurred in the political system since 1950. This chapter then considers presidential assertiveness in the period before 1989, when individual parties consistently obtained parliamentary majorities. Then, changes that occurred after 1989, an era in which no party achieved a majority (until 2014), are examined. In this period, massive powers have flowed away from the once-dominant Prime Minister's Office (PMO) to other institutions and forces at the national and state levels. All those institutions have become stronger, and most have been more assertive than before. Against that background, this analysis assesses increased assertiveness by some presidents since 1989. The last two sections discuss new evidence on presidents' room for manoeuvre after 1989. The first of them explains that precedents place very few constraints upon the actions of presidents. The second focuses on presidents' rights to question formal advice from ministers, on presidents' 'pocket vetoes', and on a largely unnoticed—and as yet unused—ultimate weapon that is available to presidents when profound disagreements with ministers arise.

Recent History and the Presidency

To grapple with these issues, a little background in India's recent political history is needed. I have authored four previous studies on the presidency.[1] On most of those occasions, I felt that I was examining

[1] These studies are: J. Manor, 'Seeking Greater Power and Constitutional Change: India's President and the Constitutional Crisis of 1979', in *Constitutional*

a comparatively marginal institution—or at least an institution which achieves immense political importance only rarely. In parliamentary systems, that usually happens when no party commands a legislative majority.[2] That occurred only twice between 1950 and 1989: after splits in the Congress party in 1969, and in the Janata Party in mid-1979. In both cases, presidents became crucial players. During the latter episode, ferocious controversy arose. But since parliamentary majorities existed at all other times in those years, Indian presidents almost entirely avoided public controversy—although, as we shall see, President Zail Singh (who held office from 1982 to 1987) courted it, and a few other ructions took place behind the scenes.

However, changes since 1989 have increased the importance of the presidency—and both the *need for* and the *risks of* presidential intervention—because no single party has gained a parliamentary majority. It took time for the two major political parties (the Bharatiya Janata Party or BJP, and the Congress) to adjust their strategies to this new reality. Four parliamentary elections—in 1989, 1991, 1996, and 1998—passed before they set about forming multi-party alliances capable of commanding Lok Sabha majorities. In the three subsequent elections—in 1999, 2004, and 2009—the two major parties did succeed in creating stable, multi-party alliances.

In 2014, for the first time in three decades, a single party—the BJP—managed to secure an absolute majority in the Lok Sabha. At present, it is not clear whether the most recent general election heralds the

Heads and Political Crises: Commonwealth Episodes, ed. D.A. Low (London: Macmillan, 1988), 126–41; J. Manor, 'India', in *Sovereigns and Surrogates: Constitutional Heads of State in the Commonwealth*, eds D. Butler and D.A. Low (London: Macmillan, 1991), 144–70; J. Manor, 'The Prime Minister and the President', in *Nehru to the Nineties: The Changing Office of Prime Minister in India*, ed. J. Manor (London: Hurst; New Delhi: Penguin, 1994), 115–37; and J. Manor, 'The Presidency', in *Public Institutions in India: Performance and Design*, eds D. Kapur and P.B. Mehta (New Delhi: Oxford University Press, 2005), 105–27.

[2] In India, there has been one exception to this generalization: in June 1975, when President Ahmed hastily agreed to sign a declaration of a state of emergency at the request of Prime Minister Indira Gandhi. We still do not have a satisfactory analysis of that incident, and it will probably remain impossible to explain, unless the Ahmed family opens the president's diaries which are reliably reported to exist.

dawn of a new era, or is simply an aberration. Given the confluence of economic and political circumstances surrounding the 2014 poll, not to mention the unique figure of BJP prime ministerial candidate Narendra Modi, one expects it is more likely the latter.

Coalition governance greatly enhances the importance of the president because s/he is the referee in the game of government formation, and s/he decides whether to grant prime ministers' requests for dissolutions of Parliament or not. Since 1989, the former task has become more difficult, and the latter is a potential problem. This makes it more likely that presidents will be ensnared in heated disputes which may occur even if they seek to avoid controversy, as they usually do.

Political institutions have passed through three phases since the establishment of the Republic of India, and thus the office of president, in 1950.

1. 1950 to the late 1960s: In this era, the Congress party dominated politics at the national level and in almost every state. This had a paradoxical impact on formal institutions of state. It spared them most of the stresses which wrecked such institutions in many other emergent nations, so that they could take root and acquire institutional substance. But formal institutions were subordinate to the dominant Congress party, and that stunted their growth somewhat.

2. 1971 or so to 1989: During most of this era, power was radically centralized in the PMO. Whatever substance and autonomy most formal state institutions had acquired was systematically undermined, and this de-institutionalization caused them to atrophy.[3] Prime ministers often abused their power.

3. 1989 to the present: Between 1989 and 2014, a period in which no single party managed to win a majority in the Lok Sabha, massive powers have flowed away from the PMO to other formal institutions at the national level—the courts, Parliament and its committees, the Election Commission of India (ECI), and the Comptroller and Auditor General's (or CAG's) office, among others—and to state governments in the federal system and forces operating mainly at the state level. This redistribution of power has enabled many

[3] There were two exceptions to this generalization: the armed forces and the ECI.

formal institutions to acquire greater substance and autonomy than ever before—to regenerate and to play their assigned roles in the constitutional order more effectively, free of the subordination to a dominant party seen in Phase I, and to the overweening power of de-institutionalizing prime ministers seen during most of Phase II. Newly empowered institutions have checked the power of the PMO. India since 1989 has witnessed fewer abuses of power by prime ministers than the United Kingdom experienced under either Margaret Thatcher or Tony Blair.

The history of the presidency during these three phases differs somewhat from the history of other formal institutions. In Phase 1, Prime Minister Jawaharlal Nehru, supported by the cabinet, prevailed in a dispute with India's first president, Rajendra Prasad, about presidential prerogatives. That established (in conformity with the Constitution) the subordination of the president's actions to ministers—in contrast to the subordination of other formal institutions to Congress dominance, which retarded both their growth and the emergence of the kind of interplay between institutions which the Constitution intended.

In Phase 2, controversy arose when Prime Minister Indira Gandhi persuaded President Fakhruddin Ali Ahmed to declare a state of emergency around midnight on 25–6 June 1975. Cabinet ministers were only informed of this a few hours later, after many of Mrs Gandhi's opponents had been arrested. An intimidated cabinet accepted the fait accompli. In 1978, the Janata government, which had taken power after a post-emergency election that dealt Indira Gandhi a crushing defeat, passed the 44th Amendment to the Constitution, stating (among other things) that an emergency could be declared by the president only after s/he had received written confirmation of cabinet approval. After Indira Gandhi returned to power in 1980, she dealt contemptuously with the presidency. But the 44th Amendment remained in force and provided that office with some protection[4] in

---

[4] The amendment also permitted presidents to seek advice on certain matters from central government institutions other than ministers (variously, the Supreme Court, the ECI, and the CAG). This somewhat diluted the influence of ministers over presidents but, since it also made the advice that was received binding upon presidents, it did not enhance their power.

an era in which de-institutionalization was the predominant trend. So in Phase 2 the presidency experienced less change—and somewhat less damage.

In Phase 3, when other formal institutions were undergoing substantial regeneration, the presidency gained in importance but again experienced less change—for two main reasons. First, that office had enjoyed some protection and had even undergone some regeneration during part of Phase 2, thanks mainly to the 44th Amendment. Second, in Phase 3, as other institutions gained power and became more assertive, the constitutional requirement that presidents should acquiesce to the will of ministers implied that greater assertiveness was inappropriate.

Presidents have therefore tended to restrain themselves from greater assertiveness since 1989. They have done so despite their awareness of more assertive behaviour by actors in other central government institutions like the ECI and the CAG's office. They may have been concerned that certain actions proposed by ministers had gone beyond the restraint that conditions in Phase 3 should impose on governments, but they have rarely made such views public. There are exceptions to that generalization, discussed later, but their assertiveness was inspired less by the redistribution of power after 1989 than by presidents' personal proclivities.

But is greater assertiveness by presidents *advisable*? This chapter argues that, for the most part, it is not—although that could change if future prime ministers seek to abuse their powers. It has not, so far, been advisable because the changes that have occurred since 1989 present presidents with a curious paradox. They have more opportunities to assert themselves. But since the president embodies the unity and dignity of India, it is particularly important that s/he avoid controversy and the appearance of partisanship—things which usually come with greater assertiveness.

This chapter also argues that—because post-1989 changes inevitably require presidents to intervene more often—people in India must adjust their attitudes to what constitutes appropriate behaviour by presidents. They must begin to develop a higher tolerance for presidential activism during the process of government formation—of the kind extended to heads of government in political systems where parliamentary majorities are seldom achieved, such as some in continental

Europe.[5] If such an adjustment is not made, Indian presidents will be unjustly accused of partisanship.

Presidential Powers

The powers listed subsequently are those which can, arguably, be exercised by the president independently—that is, without 'advice' from the council of ministers which guides the great majority of presidential actions. The word 'arguably' in the previous sentence is important because some of the points below are open to dispute. Some presidential powers are derived from the Constitution, while others are not.

Formal Powers Rooted in the Constitution

The first section below lists powers which the Constitution provides to presidents, explicitly or by implication. After each item in that section, the part of the Constitution which addresses the issue is cited.

1. The president must decide whom to appoint as prime minister. [Article 75(1).]
2. The president may decide whether to accept a request from a prime minister for dissolution of the Lok Sabha (which will lead to a general election). [Article 75(2).]
3. If a prime minister loses the confidence of the Lok Sabha and refuses to resign—something that has not yet occurred in India—the president may dismiss him. [Article 75(2).]
4. When a bill—except a 'money bill'—that has been passed by both houses of Parliament is sent to the president, s/he may assent to it (whereupon it becomes an Act and acquires the force of law), or s/he may return it to Parliament with suggestions for amendments. If the bill is passed without amendments, the president must give assent. [Articles 74 and 111.]
5. The president may refer any matter, on which a question of law has arisen or is likely to arise, to the Supreme Court for its opinion. The

[5] For an introduction to some of these, see V. Bogdanor, 'European Constitutional Monarchs', in *Sovereigns and Surrogates* eds, Butler and Low (Houndmills, Basingstoke, Hampshire: Macmillan, 1991), 274–97.

court is not required to respond, and the president is not bound by
the opinion of the court. [Article 143.]

6. The president may 'require' the prime minister to submit for the
consideration of the council of ministers any matter on which a
decision has been taken by a minister without the council of ministers considering it. [Article 78.]

Informal Powers Not Derived from Constitutional Provisions

In addition to the aforementioned list of officially designated powers, there is a second set of informal powers not derived from the
Constitution. When the president receives advice from the council of
ministers with which s/he disagrees, s/he may take no action—and not
refer it back to the council since a reiteration of the advice would compel assent (the 'pocket veto'). *In extremis, the president may also refuse
assent even after such reiteration—a drastic step not yet taken in India,
which would trigger a constitutional crisis.*

Presidential Assertiveness before 1989

Since the chapter's focus is mainly on events since 1989, this discussion
on the period before that is rather brief. More detailed assessments
of those earlier years, when governments almost always had solid Lok
Sabha majorities, can be found elsewhere.[6]

The limitations on the power of presidents in that earlier era were
established during the term of office (1950–62) of the first president,
Rajendra Prasad. He disagreed with Prime Minister Jawaharlal Nehru
on several issues and twice sought privately to resist decisions by the
Nehru government. On both occasions, it required threats of resignation from the prime minister to persuade Prasad to yield. But when he
gave way, it confirmed in practice what the Constitution made clear
on paper—that while presidents can advise and warn ministers and ask
them to reconsider intended actions, they cannot defy the will of a
government with a parliamentary majority.

Prasad made occasional public statements that amounted to veiled
criticisms of the government (as some of his successors have also done).

[6] See, in particular, Manor, 'India', 144–70; and Manor, 'Prime Minister',
115–37.

But these were largely tolerated, except on one occasion when he said, in effect, that a president need not conform to the line laid down by the government. This was, understandably, sharply rebuffed. This left Prasad feeling powerless.[7]

Most of the other six presidents who served before 1989 were far more restrained. President Ahmed has been rightly criticized for being *too* restrained when he acceded to Indira Gandhi's demand for an emergency declaration. However, two later presidents in this period sought quite forcefully to assert themselves. N. Sanjeeva Reddy (in office, 1977–82) enjoyed less success than he hoped for. On 15 July 1979, four days after losing his majority in the Lok Sabha, Prime Minister Morarji Desai of the Janata Party offered his resignation to Reddy without requesting dissolution. The president then invited the leader of the opposition, Y.B. Chavan, who headed the non-Indira Congress party, to form a government. When he failed to secure adequate support, the president turned to Charan Singh, who led a small breakaway group from the old Janata Party. He initially appeared likely to obtain a majority, thanks to support from Indira Gandhi's Congress party, but when its backing was abruptly withdrawn, Charan Singh resigned and formally asked the president to dissolve the Lok Sabha and call an election.

Since Singh had never obtained a vote of confidence, he had little justification for making such a request. His purpose in doing so was to prevent an invitation to the main body of the Janata Party, which was now led by Jagjivan Ram, a leader from the (ex-untouchable) Scheduled Castes (SCs), who appeared likely to gain majority support. President Reddy apparently preferred to deny Ram the premiership and acceded, very controversially, to Charan Singh's request. Many observers believed—rightly in this writer's view—that Reddy expected a fresh election to produce a hung parliament in which he could exercise more influence than the Constitution intends. In the event, it yielded a sizeable majority for Indira Gandhi's Congress, so that whatever ambitions Reddy may have harboured were thwarted. But he was far more assertive than any of his predecessors and most of his successors.[8]

---

[7] For more details, see Manor, 'Prime Minister', 115–37.

[8] This is discussed in greater detail in Manor, 'Seeking Greater Power', 126–41. For Reddy's unconvincing account of this episode, see N.S. Reddy, *Without Fear or Favour: Reminiscences and Reflections of a President* (New Delhi: Allied Publishers, 1989).

The other example of presidential assertiveness before 1989 occurred when a prime minister had a solid (indeed, a four-fifths) majority in the Lok Sabha. Rajiv Gandhi had obtained this in a landslide election victory at the end of 1984, soon after the assassination of his mother and predecessor in office, Indira Gandhi. The president at that time, Giani Zail Singh, had been hand-picked for that post by Mrs Gandhi in 1982, in part because he appeared likely to do her bidding.[9] If Rajiv Gandhi had handled him sensitively, the president would probably have proved amenable. But Prime Minister Gandhi, who came from a highly anglicized background, found Zail Singh's rough and ready ways distasteful. As Granville Austin put it, 'he and Rajiv Gandhi were oil and water'. He, therefore, shunned President Singh. He failed to meet his constitutional obligation 'to furnish such information ... as the president may call for'.[10]

This was not a first for the Indian presidency, but it caused Zail Singh intense irritation.[11] He was dissuaded by Congress party emissaries from confronting Rajiv Gandhi, but in 1987, he made his feelings plain—by withholding assent from a bill passed by Parliament,

[9] Prior to his selection, Zail Singh—the then home minister, and a man of limited education—had informed the Lok Sabha that he had developed great admiration for one Adolf Hitler. The house predictably erupted, which came as a shock to Zail Singh since he had not understood that the *fuehrer* was widely scorned. He was utterly humiliated. In most governments, this would have disqualified him from the highest office in the land, but Indira Gandhi saw that if she raised him to the presidency, he would be entirely her creature. So in her drive for personal dominance of every possible power centre, she chose him.

[10] Article 78(b) The Constitution of India, 1950. See Granville Austin, *Working a Democratic Constitution: The Indian Experience* (New Delhi: Oxford University Press, 1999), 513. There have been *no* meetings at regular intervals between presidents and prime ministers at least since the late 1980s. Meetings are 'need bound', in the words of Gopalkrishna Gandhi who served under two presidents. So in times of crisis they meet often. At other times, weeks may pass between meetings. They meet very often on ceremonial occasions during state visits by foreign leaders which now occur practically every month, even in the hot weather. But discussions between them scarcely occur then. Gopalkrishna Gandhi (former Governor, State of West Bengal), in discussion with the author, 1 March 2013.

[11] President Reddy had suffered similar treatment from Prime Minister Morarji Desai in the late 1970s. Reddy, *Without Fear*, 17–20.

and by voicing exasperation in press interviews. During the ensuing controversy, it emerged that the prime minister had largely ceased to communicate with the president.[12]

Zail Singh later stated that, out of the public eye, gravely serious actions were contemplated on both sides of this dispute. The president considered dismissing the government for 'irresponsibility and corruption over the Bofors arms purchasing scandal'—which would have triggered a full-scale constitutional crisis and probably a general election. He also claimed that Rajiv Gandhi instructed an advisor to draw up documents to impeach him.[13] In the end, neither man took these drastic actions, and the matter ended in 1987 when Zail Singh left office. But he came close to a spectacular act of presidential assertiveness.

The incidents involving presidents Prasad, Reddy, and Zail Singh were exceptions to the predominant trend in the pre-1989 period. In those years, presidents tended to restrain themselves—as was only natural, given the prevalence of decisive election outcomes and Lok Sabha majorities. Since 1989, however, things have changed and presidents have had to operate in very different circumstances. Let us now consider the implications of these changes.

Since 1989: The Dispersal of Power and Assertiveness by Extra-Parliamentary Institutions

Presidents are elected to five-year terms indirectly, by members of both houses of Parliament and the state legislatures. If a president dies in office (which happened in 1969 and 1977), a fresh election is held soon thereafter. All presidents since 1977 have served full terms, so presidential elections have occurred in the second and seventh years of recent decades. But since 1969, they have not occurred at the same time as parliamentary elections. Table 1.1, a timeline, details the staggered

---

[12] See the discussions on the postal bill and of presidents' 'pocket vetoes' later in this chapter.

[13] See, in this connection, Madhu Limaye's comment carried in *Times of India*, 20 March 1987. On the dubious attempt by presiding officers in the two houses of Parliament to bar discussions on this matter, see A.G. Noorani, *Indian Affairs: The Constitutional Dimension* (New Delhi: Stosius Inc/Advent Books Division, 1990).

Table 1.1   Presidential and Parliamentary Elections[1]

Presidential Elections	Parliamentary Elections
1952 (Rajendra Prasad)[2]	1952 (Jawaharlal Nehru)
1957 (Rajendra Prasad)	1957 (Jawaharlal Nehru)
1962 (S. Radhakrishnan)	1962 (Jawaharlal Nehru)
1967 (Zakir Hussain)	1967 (Indira Gandhi)
1969 (V.V. Giri)	
	1971 (Indira Gandhi)
1974 (Fakhruddin Ali Ahmed)	
1977 (N. Sanjiva Reddy)	1977 (Morarji Desai/Charan Singh)
	1980 (Indira Gandhi)
1982 (Giani Zail Singh)	
	1984 (Rajiv Gandhi)
1987 (R. Venkataraman)	
	1989 (V.P. Singh/Chandra Shekhar)
	1991 (P.V. Narasimha Rao*)
1992 (Shankar Dayal Sharma)	
	1996 (H.D. Deve Gowda/I.K. Gujral)
1997 (K.R. Narayanan)	
	1998 (Atal Bihari Vajpayee)
	1999 (Atal Bihari Vajpayee*)
2002 (A.P.J. Abdul Kalam)	
	2004 (Manmohan Singh*)
2007 (Pratibha Patil)	
	2009 (Manmohan Singh*)
2012 (Pranab Mukherjee)	
	2014 (Narendra Modi)

Source: Author's compilation.

Notes: [1]Asterisks next to the names of prime ministers in the period following 1989 indicate that the ruling party or alliance had a reliable majority on its own in Lok Sabha.

[2] Rajendra Prasad became the president when the Republic of India came into being on 26 January 1950, but the first formal election to this office (which he won) occurred only in 1952.

timings of presidential and parliamentary elections, with the names of presidents and prime ministers in parentheses.

As mentioned earlier, parties or alliances of post-1989 prime ministers had a reliable majority—on their own—in the Lok Sabha. This has been the norm since 1999. But during the decade before that, major parties had not yet comprehended the need to forge broad multi-party alliances to ensure majorities.[14] The 2014 general election results notwithstanding, the post-1999 'norm' may cease to prevail, complicating matters for presidents.

We should also note that in the hung parliaments between 1989 and 1999, some governments were closer to majorities than others. That influenced the dilemmas faced by presidents. Narasimha Rao's Congress won a large minority of seats in the 1991 election, and no other party had anything like its total tally of seats. This enabled it to make numerous difficult decisions, especially in the field of economic liberalization. In 1993, Members of Parliament (MPs) from a regional party were induced to support the government, which gave it a working majority. It saw out its full five-year term.

By contrast, the parties that took power after the parliamentary elections of 1989, 1996, and 1998 were far less securely placed. In 1989, the party with the largest minority of seats (Congress) preferred not to assume power, so President Venkataraman summoned Janata Dal (the next largest party) to form a government, which it did with outside support from the BJP and the Left. In mid-1990, however, Prime Minister V.P. Singh sought to appeal to disadvantaged voters by announcing his intention to implement the Mandal Commission report which recommended reservations in public sector employment and education for such groups. This caused the BJP to withdraw support and Singh's government fell. It was replaced by another with a precarious hold on power, led by Chandra Shekhar, which lasted only a few months. The 1991 election duly followed.

In 1996, the largest single party (BJP) was invited to form a government but lasted only 13 days because it failed to obtain majority support in the Lok Sabha. A minority government was then formed by H.D. Deve Gowda of the Janata Dal which was dependent on the Congress party, which did not join it. After just under a year, Congress refused to continue backing him, whereupon another Janata Dal leader (I.K. Gujral) became prime minister with continued dependence on

[14] The Congress government of P.V. Narasimha Rao obtained a working majority (in fact though not in name) in 1993 by bribing MPs from the small Jharkhand Mukti Morcha to help in defeating a no-confidence vote.

Congress. His government lasted less than a year, and thus another parliamentary election occurred in 1998.

That election brought in a government led by Atal Bihari Vajpayee of the BJP, which depended for its very tenuous majority on an alliance with a large number of smaller, mainly regional parties that engaged in very public squabbling. His government lasted only until early 1999, but then collapsed when Congress machinations with one alliance partner deprived it of a majority. After several months in which Vajpayee headed a caretaker government, the general election of 1999 gave his expanded alliance a solid majority.

The point of all of this is that, except for the period between 1993 and 1996, no government in the decade after 1989 was securely placed in the Lok Sabha. This inspired people occupying senior posts in institutions that stood beyond the supervision of government ministries to begin asserting themselves to a degree that had been unthinkable before 1989. But did the advent of hung parliaments, and the ensuing dispersal of power away from prime ministers and their cabinets, fully explain this increased assertiveness? The evidence indicates that it did not. Other things mattered too.

Not all the institutions which were beyond the control of central government ministries became more assertive. The judiciary and the ECI plainly asserted themselves, and so did state governments in the federal system. The CAG has followed suit since about 2010. But some other institutions did not do so. It appears that these variations are mainly explained by key personalities within these institutions. Certain activist judges, certain chief ministers in state governments (whose number included both allies and opponents of ruling parties in New Delhi), and the irrepressible Chief Election Commissioner T.N. Seshan were plainly more inclined to act forcefully than were senior figures in some other institutions.

Presidential Assertiveness and Restraint since 1989

President R. Venkataraman had an apt metaphor for the role of the president in India, and of heads of state of all parliamentary systems: 'The office of the President is like an emergency light. It comes on automatically when there is a crisis and goes off automatically when the crisis passes away.'[15] The dispersal of power since 1989 has increased the number of occasions when the emergency light must come on. So presidents have been forced by circumstances to become more assertive, but this does not imply that all or even most have *chosen* to assert themselves. Their proclivities have varied, and so have the circumstances that they faced.

For seven of those years (1989–93 and 1996–9), neither single parties nor multi-party alliances had reliable Lok Sabha majorities. But between 1993 and 1996, Congress had a working majority, and since 1999, multi-party alliances led first by the BJP (1999–2004) and then by the Congress (since 2004), and then by the BJP again (2014–present) have had dependable majorities.

Several questions arise. Did post-1989 presidents—like senior figures in some other central government institutions—become more assertive? Did the weakness of governments for seven of those years help to persuade presidents to become more assertive? Did the more reliable majorities that governments achieved in other years inspire greater presidential restraint? Have various presidents' personal proclivities, including their attitudes to the risks posed by controversy, been more important that the strength of sitting governments in determining whether they were assertive or restrained? When we consider assertive actions, is it important to distinguish between occasions when they were justified because governments proposed to act inappropriately, and occasions when that was not true?

India has had six presidents since 1989. Did they become more assertive? The answers vary. The answer for R. Venkataraman (1987–92) is 'maybe, but probably only when the need arose'. For K.R. Narayanan (1997–2002), it is 'yes'. But it is, for the most part or entirely, 'no' for each of the other four: Shankar Dayal Sharma (1992–7), A.P.J. Abdul Kalam (2002–7), Pratibha Patil (2007–12), and Pranab Mukherjee (2012 to the present, but see the penultimate paragraph in this chapter). We shall see below that there is an intriguing twist in Kalam's story, but let us examine these presidents in a little detail.

[15] R. Venkataraman, *My Presidential Years* (New Delhi: HarperCollins, 1994), 434.

Presidents Venkataraman and Sharma

In his memoirs, President Venkataraman (1987–92) takes pains to show that he behaved with great restraint. It is clear that on many occasions, he was indeed restrained, but two episodes require comment. In 1991, after Prime Minister Chandra Shekhar had resigned and no alternative could be found, Venkataraman intervened to ensure that certain vital legislative and administrative actions could be taken—an example of judicious assertiveness. It has also been alleged that earlier, in 1989—either before the parliamentary election or just after it produced an inconclusive result—he tried to get himself selected as prime minister at the head of a government of national unity.[16] This is said to have been inspired both by his own ambition and by the widespread anxiety that no leader or party in the Lok Sabha elected in that year could provide a stable government. These allegations, which are implausible, were mostly expressed verbally by people who held prominent posts in various parties, and few have appeared in print.[17] This writer has stated previously that there is insufficient evidence to substantiate these charges.[18] That argument gains further credence from Venkataraman's discussion on the events of 1989 in his memoirs, but since he does not address the issue squarely, he leaves the field open for alternative views.[19]

For the most part, President Shankar Dayal Sharma (1992–7) showed great restraint, but he asserted himself constructively on one occasion. In 1996, he returned (and thus thwarted) two ordinances to the cabinet: one extending SC reservations to new groups, and the other reducing the period of election campaigns. The problem with these measures was not their content but their timing. He regarded them as inappropriate because they had been issued just before a parliamentary election.[20]

---

[16] Venkataraman, *My Presidential Years*, 481–92; F.S. Nariman, *The State of the Nation: In Context of India's Constitution* (New Delhi: Hay House, 2013), 174.

[17] But see M. Limaye, *Decline of a Political System: Indian Politics at the Crossroads* (New Delhi: South Asia Books, 1992), 119. However, I do not regard Madhu Limaye as a thoroughly reliable source.

[18] Manor, 'Prime Minister', 115–37.

[19] Venkataraman, *My Presidential Years*, 314–26.

[20] Nariman, *State of the Nation*, 174; Janak Raj Jai, *Presidents of India: 1950–2003* (New Delhi: Regency, 2003), 250.

The Narayanan Tenure

Sharma was succeeded by K.R. Narayanan (1997–2002), clearly the most assertive of these six presidents. When he took up his post, he announced that he intended to be a 'working president', which suggested that he would be proactive. His subsequent actions confirmed that impression. Some observers believe that he went beyond the constitutional limitations of his office. This needs careful consideration.

The first clear sign that he intended to assert himself came in 1998. He was asked by the Janata government, headed by I.K. Gujral, (whose hold on power was quite tenuous) to endorse the imposition of president's rule in the state of Uttar Pradesh. President's rule is a device provided by the Constitution whereby a democratically elected state government is removed from power, and is replaced by direct rule from New Delhi. It is to be used only 'in case of failure of constitutional machinery in States' or when ' ... a situation has arisen in which a Government of the State cannot be carried on in accordance with the provisions of this Constitution'.[21]

President Narayanan concluded that the proposal was unwarranted and sent it back to the cabinet with a request that they reconsider it. He was fully entitled under the Constitution to do this, but this was the first time that a president had asked ministers to think again about the imposition of president's rule—which had been frequently abused by prime ministers between 1971 and 1989. The cabinet backed down partly because a Supreme Court of India ruling in 1994 had set out objections to the abuse of this device, and partly because Narayanan had won plaudits for his action, since there was widespread disenchantment with the excessive use of president's rule for partisan purposes.

On that occasion, his assertiveness was clearly justified because the government's proposal was inappropriate. He then said publicly, 'I am not a rubber stamp'. If narrowly interpreted, that statement was an accurate description of his office, since a president has the right to advise and warn ministers. But it raised questions about his willingness to follow formal 'advice' from ministers, which the Constitution plainly required him to do.

---

[21] Article 356, The Constitution of India, 1950.

The next election in 1998 brought in a coalition government led by the BJP, again without a firm grasp on power. Thereafter, Narayanan provoked greater controversy on several occasions. The first occurred in August of that year. Presidents traditionally address the nation on 14 August, the eve of Independence Day. By convention, the president sends the text of his speech to the government to be vetted—and there have been occasions (notably in the time of President Zail Singh) when such texts were altered on ministers' advice. In 1998, Narayanan gave not only the usual address but also an extensive interview with a leading journalist. Its content could not be vetted in advance. During the interview, he subtly made clear his discomfort with the Hindu nationalist ideology of the ruling BJP.[22] An eminent journalist, Kuldip Nayar (no supporter of the BJP), observed that even though the government felt too weak to raise objections, Narayanan had been 'institutionally wrong' to take this action.[23]

The next day, at a meeting in the central hall of Parliament to mark the end of independent India's fiftieth year, the president gave an address that had not been vetted in advance by the government. Early in the speech, he noted that the BJP-led government had been in power for five months. Then later, he criticized people holding public office who saw it as 'an opportunity to strike gold'. The reference can of course be read to refer to politicians of all parties, but coming after the mention of the existing government in New Delhi, it was seen by some to be directed at that government. This provoked Nayar to say that Narayanan had engaged in 'violation(s) of precedent ... twice in two days'. He added that in earlier public statements, the president had 'challenged the entire direction of the new economic policy'[24] to which most major parties were largely sympathetic.

In early 1999, when one of the larger parties in the BJP's coalition exited from it, the government appeared to have lost its majority. At that point, President Narayanan requested Prime Minister Vajpayee to establish, through a vote in the Lok Sabha, that he still had majority support.

[22] K.R. Narayanan (former president of India), interview by N. Ram, 14 August 1998, Doordarshan and All India Radio.

[23] Kuldip Nayar, 'Two Incidents: Were They Deliberate', *Deccan Herald*, 27 August 1998.

[24] Nayar, 'Two Incidents'.

The president was within his rights in making this request; the Constitution lays down next to no detailed guidelines for presidents in such situations. But three objections might be raised nonetheless. First, Indian and Commonwealth precedents (for the most part) strongly suggest that in such circumstances, inaction is the convention. (Note however, [i] that India's Constitution explicitly states that the president is not bound by precedents or conventions from other countries; [ii] presidents have ignored *Indian* precedents established by their own predecessors often enough to make them, in practice, non-binding;[25] and [iii] would-be prime ministers, but not prime ministers like Vajpayee who had previously enjoyed majority support, had been asked to obtain majority votes in the Lok Sabha.)

Second, President Narayanan might have expected opposition parties in Parliament to seek an early vote of no confidence—a further reason for inaction. Third, BJP sympathizers argued that the prime minister was entitled to continue in office until a vote of no confidence succeeded. In their view, until that happened, the president remained bound by advice from the government which obviously would not have asked him to act as he did. This is to say that Narayanan was pushing his powers to the limit.

There is, however, another dimension to this. The differences between President Narayanan and the two Vajpayee governments (before and after the 1999 election, since differences did not end in 1998) have been exaggerated. Many newspapers overplayed them, slightly or extravagantly, and opposition parties went about this very aggressively.[26]

Clear differences emerged in January 2000 between the president and the prime minister over the government's decision to review the Constitution—differences which were set out by Narayanan in another unvetted speech at the celebration of the fiftieth anniversary of the Constitution. Press reports indicated that he believed that because this was not a formal address such as the one presidents give at the opening

[25] See the discussion on precedents in this chapter. See also the discussion on precedents in connection with the dissolution of the Lok Sabha prior to elections in Manor, 'Prime Minister', 133–4.

[26] See the criticism of other publications in an editorial in the *Hindustan Times*, 24 March 2000.

of a session of Parliament, he need not submit it to the government. He was probably right since there are no clear rules for such occasions. But predictably, the speech triggered strong, positive reactions from opposition parties. The Congress party hailed the president's 'wise words' as 'a lamp unto our feet and light unto our path'. A Communist Party of India-Marxist leader stated that he had adopted the 'correct position'.[27] The following month, after the ruling BJP's journal had accused the president of being 'partial' and of having 'descended into politics', a Congress spokesman protested at what he regarded as 'a vituperative act of calumny' intended to 'besmirch' the president's reputation.[28]

The point here is that any president who is as assertive as Narayanan should expect such exaggerations—and he was canny enough to understand this. (Presidents should also be aware of one other thing which compounds this problem—when so-called 'constitutional experts' provide instant commentaries to newspapers on episodes involving the presidency, their views are usually intended to serve the interests of one or another party.) Are these inevitable exaggerations and political controversies good either for the presidency or for the polity? President Narayanan obviously concluded that he could live with this, but numerous observers—including many who are not true believers in the Hindu right—had misgivings.[29]

Finally, in March 2000, US President Bill Clinton visited India. At a state banquet in Clinton's honour, President Narayanan departed from the text of a speech prepared by the Ministry of External Affairs—which, again, he was apparently free to do. After several positive references to the US, he said that (as one newspaper paraphrased him) 'globalisation was fast reducing the world to a global village but one that did not need a "headman"'. He alluded to the Cold War mentality that still influenced American policy, and emphasized the continuing relevance of the non-aligned movement, although that had gone unmentioned in the government's National Agenda for Governance.[30]

[27] 'Cong.(I) Hails President's Wise Words', *The Hindu*, 28 January 2000.

[28] 'Cong.(I) Condemns "Attack" on President', *The Hindu*, 18 February 2000.

[29] See, for example, the editorials in *Times of India* and *the Hindu*, both on 29 January 2000.

[30] Editorial, *Hindustan Times*, 24 March 2000. A subsequent attempt to play down differences between the president and the government on these

This speech offended the Americans and caused intense anxiety in the Ministry of External Affairs. It provoked rebukes even from newspaper editors who had supported Narayanan's earlier outspokenness. The issue was not whether he was free to depart from the Ministry's text, but the things that he said when he did so. The *Hindustan Times* argued that '[e]lementary courtesy dictates that when you are hosting a man for dinner in your house, you do not sternly lecture him or make vaguely insulting remarks'. It asked of Narayanan, 'should he be flying solo in the complex area of foreign relations?'[31]

Let us consider the *ideas* that appear to have inspired Narayanan to act in this way (which will tell us more about the effect of the changed conditions in the post-1989 era on the actions of presidents), and then the *implications* of his actions for the presidency and the wider polity in that era. His assertiveness appears to be explained mainly by two or perhaps three ideas, each of which is probably more important than the changed character of the national party system since 1989.

First, like many others, he apparently believed that the legitimacy of government in India was in some doubt, and that new approaches to development were needed to restore it. Such questions about legitimacy did not arise because of the inability of single parties to obtain Lok Sabha majorities. The problem was that the government had come to be perceived as insufficiently responsive and inclusive. There was thus a need to find ways to open the government up to previously excluded groups, to ensure that diversity was respected, and to seek greater synergy between state and society.

This writer should come clean and say that he agrees with these views, and thus regards this motive for acting more assertively as admirable. It is also worth stressing that presidents have not just the option but a responsibility to raise moral and constitutional concerns. But we shall see later that even when constructive motives and concerns inspire presidential assertiveness, it can do unintended damage.

The second thing that appears to have inspired the president's actions was closely linked to the first. Narayanan comes from a severely

---

issues was unpersuasive. See K.K. Katyal, 'The President & Foreign Policy', *The Hindu*, 27 March 2000.

[31] Editorial, *Hindustan Times*, 24 March 2000.

disadvantaged community, and felt—again understandably—that he, therefore, had a special responsibility to do all that he could to catalyse change that might help such excluded groups.

He *may* also have been inspired by a third idea, which is a potential cause for concern. This is the notion that he had been elected by a wider constituency than that which supported the ruling coalition headed by the BJP. That party had yielded so many seats to allies at the previous general election that both the total number of seats that it won and its share of the popular vote were somewhat limited. It would not have been entirely illogical for Narayanan to have concluded that, despite the fact that he was *indirectly* elected, the number of MPs and state legislators who supported him constituted a broader political base than the BJP possessed. If that was in his mind, and it may not have been, it might have made him feel justified in acting more assertively.

This is potentially worrying for reasons that were set forth, very perceptively—long before anyone imagined an era of hung parliaments—by Jagjivan Ram. In an interview with Pran Chopra in the late 1960s, he expressed the following concern. A president who chooses to play politics can in fact make himself a formidable power because the only constraint which Parliament can exercise upon him is impeachment, which requires a three-fourths majority, and a president who has played his political game with skill can never fail to obtain sufficient support in Parliament to prevent this.[32]

Ram was mistaken about one detail: impeachment requires a two-thirds majority of the total number of both houses of Parliament (not just those present and voting). But his basic point is valid and important, and in an era in which no party can win a majority in the Lok Sabha, it acquires greater force. If no majority were obtainable, an ambitious president might seek to assist someone to become prime minister on the understanding that the latter would permit the head of state greater influence over the government than the Constitution intends. Such a president might even seize effective control of the government by issuing orders without taking advice from ministers.

[32] Pran Chopra, 'After Charisma: A Study of the Evolution of the Office of Prime Minister in India' (unpublished manuscript, 1970–1), part I, 4 (interview with Jagjivan Ram). I am grateful to Pran Chopra for sharing this material with me.

The Indian president's orders do not need to be counter-signed by the prime minister or others, as is the practice in some other systems.[33] President Narayanan intended no such thing, but President Reddy appears to have attempted to acquire great leverage over a government in mid-1979 in just this way. So this is a concern that deserves greater attention.

Presidents Kalam, Patil, and Mukherjee

Narayanan's successor, President Kalam (2002–7), may have been too restrained in giving assent to the Bihar Dissolution Bill in 2005, although it should be noted that he was on a state visit to Moscow at the time. The Supreme Court later struck that law down. But Kalam then turned assertive when he returned an office of profit bill for reconsideration. Parliament examined his arguments and returned the bill to him without amendments—and he duly signed.[34] Kalam's successors—Pratibha Patil (2007–12) and Pranab Mukherjee (2012–present)—have, for the most part, been quite restrained.

In assessing the merits of assertiveness and restraint in the post-1989 era, one needs to recognize that, in the foreseeable future (and leaving 2014 aside, once more), huge numbers of voters are likely to support state-based parties in such a manner that the larger national parties will continue to fall well short of Lok Sabha majorities. If their seat totals in Parliament shrink much further, it may even become difficult to construct multi-party coalitions that can provide stable governments. Looking out into the future, one can thus expect a significant degree of uncertainty and instability at the national level. Such a climate will require presidents to become more proactive and, if you like, assertive—even *if* they do not wish to do so—because there will be more occasions in which the refereeing that only presidents can perform will become necessary.

If that happens, it will be more important than ever that the ultimate referee is perceived to be non-partisan since without that, the

[33] Chopra, 'After Charisma', Chapters 9, 15.

[34] See the account of this in P.M. Nair, *The Kalam Effect—My Years with the President* (New Delhi: HarperCollins, 2008), 110–13. See also Kalam's use of a little-noted device which enhanced his room for manoeuvre, discussed subsequently.

legitimacy of the outcomes of that refereeing (that is, national governments) will be open to question. Thus, there are more compelling
reasons now than before 1989 for presidents to do their utmost to
avoid perceptions (and indeed, misperceptions) that they are partisan.

In sum, even though post-1989 conditions create greater opportunities—and often the necessity—for presidents to act assertively, they
also generate strong reasons for presidents not to do so, because assertiveness tends to foster suspicions of partisanship even when there is
no such intention.

It is only fair to add that in the current era, people in India need to
become more tolerant of legitimate presidential interventions, because
the changed circumstances will inevitably require more of these. People
need to develop the kind of willingness—to see their head of state seek
to foster sustainable governments in fragmented parliaments—shown
by citizens in, for example, the Netherlands. But it is unrealistic to
expect this change to happen swiftly. So, over the medium term, Indian
presidents need to take great care to ensure that their interventions
are—and are seen to be—legitimate.

Room for Manoeuvre: Presidents and Precedents

Evidence has recently emerged which indicates that Indian presidents
have somewhat more room for manoeuvre than most scholars had
previously assumed. There are two themes to consider here. Let us first
focus on the question of whether precedents constrain presidents when
they receive requests from prime ministers to dissolve the Lok Sabha,
and when they are deciding how to proceed after general elections fail
to give any party a majority.

A clarification is necessary here. In an earlier study, this writer stated
that the president's office in New Delhi apparently did not keep systematic records of previous presidential decisions, and of the calculations that
shaped them.[35] Fresh evidence indicates that this was inaccurate. Such
records have been kept and filed, quite systematically, so that a president
who wishes to inspect them can gain access to them 'in a moment'.[36]

[35] Manor, 'Presidency'.
[36] Gopalkrishna Gandhi, in discussion with the author, 1 March 2013. He
served in senior posts under Presidents Venkataraman and Narayanan.

So, presidents cannot be said to be free from constraints imposed by precedents because they have no (or inadequate) information about them.

Several key details are worth adding. These records focus only on previous *Indian* episodes. No assessments are maintained of similar decisions by heads of state in other countries with parliamentary systems. This is consistent with India's Constitution which explicitly frees presidents from precedents elsewhere. The records do not include material on decisions by state governors in India's federal system, since the position of governors differs from that of a president. The records only cover decisions by presidents.[37] In addition, the records do not cover every possible eventuality. Unprecedented dilemmas often arise. Certain actions by previous presidents may be deemed injudicious. President Ahmed's agreement to declare a state of emergency in 1975 and President Reddy's actions in mid-1979 fall into this category. There is nothing in the Constitution that requires a president to follow the example of a predecessor when making a decision. Records of predecessors' deliberations are kept only to suggest possible courses of action.

Presidents, thus, have immense flexibility. They are free to take whatever actions they consider appropriate, even in circumstances that differ little from those faced by their predecessors. And yet, despite all of this, complications remain. The best way to illustrate them is to examine comments made by President Venkataraman in interviews after he left office. He was a perceptive man, formidably learned in the law.

One interview focused on his decision in 1991 to accept Prime Minister Chandra Shekhar's request, when the latter submitted his resignation, for a dissolution of the Lok Sabha. When Venkataraman was asked whether a president must accept such a request, he replied 'I don't say he has to. He should. That is the Constitutional position if you follow the British Constitution.' But as his first sentence indicates, British precedents are not binding. He adds, 'This question has not been settled in India'. He then says that he agreed to Chandra Shekhar's request not because he was bound to do so, but because no other party in that Lok Sabha 'was prepared to shoulder the responsibility

[37] Gopalkrishna Gandhi, in discussion with the author, 1 March 2013.

of forming the government'. His decision was determined not by precedent, but by the political realities of the moment.[38]

A similar message emerges from a second interview. Venkataraman
initially appears to argue that certain precedents (or at least conventions) are in fact binding—but then he retreats from that assertion.
He first says that when a president has invited one party in a hung
parliament to form a government, and then it either declines to try or
fails to obtain a majority, the president cannot call that party again. But
then he shifts his focus to the political realities of any given moment.
He explains that a president must understand the subtle details of
parties' inclinations in the Lok Sabha because his main responsibility is to respond to them in ways that facilitate the establishment of
a stable government. He then acknowledges that parties' inclinations
may change as events unfold and adds, crucially, that in 1990—when
a stable government was proving difficult to achieve—he might have
been justified in issuing a second invitation to the Congress party to
form a government, even though it had previously declined his invitation. That would have been justified if he had thought that enough
had changed to enable Congress to muster a stable government. So
the convention barring a president from summoning a party more than
once can be set aside if the political realities of the moment require
this—and so may all other conventions and precedents. Indian presidents face no constraints in such situations.[39]

That point is echoed in another comment. On the question of the
order in which parties in hung parliaments should be invited by a president to form a government, he says 'Normally, he should ask the parties
according to their strength'. But the use of the word 'normally' indicates
that this principle is not binding in all circumstances. This has assumed
greater importance since governments in New Delhi began, in 1998, to
be formed not by single parties but by multi-party coalitions. It is quite
possible that the single largest party might not lead the largest coalition. In those circumstances, a president in search of a stable government might be justified in turning first to the latter. Venkataraman then
refers to his decision in 1989 to summon the largest party (Congress)

[38] Interview with *Rediff on the Net*, 4 April 1997. Available at www.rediff.
com/news/apr/o4cong.htm.

[39] Interview with *Rediff on the Net*.

and then the second largest (the BJP), even though he knew in advance that they would both decline to form governments. But he treats this as a matter of propriety and not as a response to a binding precedent. It was something which should 'normally' be done—but those norms are not binding constraints.[40]

President Venkataraman liked to say that he was a 'copy book' president. But there is nothing in any 'copy book', or in the records maintained in the president's office, to constrain his actions in such situations. There is plenty of guidance there, but no constraints. This is worth remembering when so-called 'constitutional experts' write articles in the Indian press that explain what a president 'must do' in moments of uncertainty. Their comments are often influenced by their enthusiasm for a particular party, and even when they are non-partisan, their arguments are inaccurate. There is nothing at such moments that a president 'must' do.

A further question arises here. Should formal rules and procedures be established which would affect the Presidency—on two fronts? First, presidents might be required to follow certain procedures in deciding whom to summon first from a hung parliament to form a government. The problem here is that much depends upon the distinctive dynamics that exist at any given moment—the coherence or fragility of differ- ent multi-party coalitions, good or abrasive relations between larger and smaller parties, and other such factors. In some situations, a stable government (the main priority for presidents) is more likely to emerge if a particular coalition is invited. In others, that is more probable if the largest party is summoned. Because different dynamics prevail in different circumstances, a codification of procedures (which would reduce presidents' room for manoeuvre) could cause more problems than it solves.

Codification has also been suggested to tackle a second bundle of issues which relate to the selection of presidents. Should rules and pro- cedures be created to ensure that a president is competent and capable, or that s/he is not excessively partisan, or that s/he is not vulnerable to blackmail by politicians who have evidence of past misdeeds? It is difficult to see how a formal code could ensure these things. A far more reliable means of achieving that goal has existed since 1989. So many

[40] Interview with *Rediff on the Net*.

parties now loom large in Parliament and the state assemblies—from which votes in presidential elections come—that it is difficult for one large party to insert incapable, partisan, or blackmail-able candidates into the presidency. It is safer to trust this *in*formal reality than to rely on formal rules and procedures which are unlikely to succeed.

Room for Manoeuvre: Questioning Formal 'Advice', 'Pocket Vetoes', and a President's Ultimate Weapon

Finally, let us turn to a second set of issues, which emerge when a government with a Lok Sabha majority tenders formal 'advice' to a president to undertake action which s/he finds ill-considered or objectionable. S/he has the option of returning the proposal to ministers, with a request that it be reconsidered. If the advice is reiterated, the president is legally bound to give assent. We have seen that President Narayanan referred a proposal for president's rule back to the cabinet, which then abandoned the idea. That case was unusual but not unique.

In 1986, both houses of Parliament passed a postal bill which empowered state and central governments to intercept, detain, or dispose of any items sent through the post which were deemed to endanger national security. This triggered a huge, angry public outcry. The bill was then sent to President Zail Singh who was already at odds with Prime Minister Rajiv Gandhi. He took no action on it for the remaining half-year of his tenure.[41] He later wrote that his inaction was explained by his view that the bill compromised fundamental freedoms, but some analysts suspect that he may have been exhibiting discontent with the prime minister.[42] In July 1987, Venkataraman became president. He had strong reservations about the bill and returned it to the government, to seek a review by the Attorney General.[43] It was eventually

[41] Austin, *Working a Democratic Constitution*, 512–13.

[42] Giani Zail Singh, *Memoirs of Giani Zail Singh: The Seventh President of India* (New Delhi: Har-Anand Publications, 1997), 276.

[43] In his memoirs, Venkataraman uses mild words: '[M]y feeling that the Bill was *not* necessary at all'. Venkataraman, *Presidential Years*, 42. But Granville Austin was told by a close associate of the President that he 'disliked much of the bill'. See Austin, *Working a Democratic Constitution*, 513.

referred by the next government to the upper house of Parliament where, in effect, it died.[44]

It is not just bills that have been returned to ministers by presidents. More often, ministerial advice to presidents on mercy petitions from people condemned to death has also been returned. To say only that is to oversimplify a more complicated story which calls attention to a little-known device that some presidents have used to enhance their room for manoeuvre. For that reason, and because controversies over mercy petitions loomed large in media reports in 2012 and 2013, and gave rise to serious misunderstandings, they warrant detailed attention.

This issue attracted media attention after Pranab Mukherjee assumed the presidency in mid-2012. He rejected a number of mercy petitions and several executions were duly carried out. Article 72 of the Constitution gives presidents the power to commute death sentences. Some reports in the press in 2012–13 compared the varied responses to mercy pleas during different presidencies, and gave the impression that presidents' proclivities had played decisive roles. This is partially misleading.

Decisions on such petitions are made not by presidents but by ministers. The evidence clearly contradicts some media reports which attributed decisions to presidents and the view of one Supreme Court judge that the president's personal views should prevail in such matters.[45] When a mercy petition comes to a president, s/he usually refers it to the Home Ministry for comment. After consideration, it sends the petition to the president with its recommendations. Then both the president and the presidential secretariat study it. They may also take legal advice on certain issues.[46] The president may then return the recommendations to the Ministry with a request that it be reconsidered, sometimes indicating specific points for review. If the file is then sent

[44] Austin, *Working a Democratic Constitution*, 512–14.

[45] V. Venkatesan, 'Death Penalty: A Presidential Dilemma', *Frontline* 22, no. 23 (November 2005), 5–13.

[46] Such advice may come from government lawyers, other legal experts, or the Supreme Court. On the last of these, see R. Vakil, 'Advising the President', *Seminar* 642 (February 2013), 59–63.

to the president a second time with unchanged recommendations, s/he must accept them.[47]

The president's views, capabilities, and work habits always matter when this issue arises.[48] They usually engage, but to varying degrees, in dialogues with ministers, or sometimes, lesser officials. Some presidents examine mercy petitions in great detail while others do not.[49] Presidents and ministers also take public opinion into account, although most of them understand that in India (as in many countries), the enthusiasm for death penalty among citizens exceeds that among senior politicians, civil servants, and jurists.

Presidents appear to have influenced ministers and officials in some cases but not all, which is not surprising, given the variations in the personal chemistry between these leaders over the years. But the key point to reiterate here is that decisions on the death penalty are always made by ministers, although a crucial exception apparently emerged in January 2017 (see the penultimate paragraph in this chapter). Presidents' views have seldom been decisive.[50]

Another complication arose in mid-2013, when the Supreme Court challenged President Mukherjee's decision to reject a mercy plea. The

[47] These processes usually work quite smoothly, but the Supreme Court alleged that President Patil was 'kept in the dark' about a recommendation for clemency in one death row case by her predecessor, President Kalam. See J. Venkatesan, 'Pratibha was Kept in the Dark about Kalam's Note to Commute Death: SC', *The Hindu*, 4 May 2013. This is a serious charge, since it implies perfidy on the part of the Home Ministry and (apparently) incompetence on the part of President Patil's staff.

[48] One report claims unkindly that, unlike other presidents, Pratibha Patil 'had little interest in any substantive aspect of statecraft or was incapable of dealing with such issues'. K.P. Nayar, 'The President at Home: Tradition and Change at Rashtrapati Bhavan', *The Telegraph*, 31 July 2013.

[49] President Narayanan, who did not oppose the death penalty in principle, studied the facts of each case very intensively. He sent some files back to the Home Ministry with questions and recommendations—in most cases, his views were respected. Gopalkrishna Gandhi, in discussion with the author, 1 March 2013.

[50] These comments are based on an article by Gopalkrishna Gandhi, 'The Power to Pardon', *The Hindu*, 18 April 2013; on an interview with him dated 1 March 2013; and on a communication from him dated 12 May 2013. See also Venkatesan, 'Death Penalty'; and Venkataraman, *Presidential Years*, 157–8.

government reacted by stating that a president's decision in such a case was 'a sovereign act', and that the court had overstepped its authority.[51] At this writing, that dispute remains unresolved (again, refer to the penultimate paragraph of this chapter).[52]

Even if we set that aside and consider only interactions between presidents and ministers, the comments above indicate that presidents have quite limited room for manoeuvre in dealing with mercy petitions. That is not quite the full story, however. A further intriguing dimension emerges when we consider the handling of a mercy petition during the presidency of A.P.J. Abdul Kalam. It was submitted to his office on 11 July 2005 by the Home Ministry, with a recommendation that it be rejected. He exhaustively studied details of this case (and numerous others) and concluded that the petition should be accepted. He might then have sent it back to the Ministry stating his case, but he knew that if they insisted that it be rejected, he would have to comply. He therefore did nothing—or as the journalist V. Venkatesan put it—he 'saw merit in using his pocket veto against the government'.

It is unclear how often 'pocket vetoes'—on death sentences or other issues—have been exercised by presidents. President Narayanan may have decided not to refer twelve mercy petitions to ministers to avoid receiving formal advice to reject them, since President Kalam (his successor) inherited them upon taking office. There are reportedly numerous other examples of this.[53] The 'pocket veto', which enhances the president's room for manoeuvre, has gone largely unnoticed.[54] It

[51] Venkatesan, 'Kalam's Note'.

[52] See also, on Supreme Court involvement in mercy petitions, the editorial in *The Hindu*, 29 July 2013. In a 2009 commentary on the Constitution, P.M. Bakshi argued that as a result of several Supreme Court decisions, 'the courts exercise a very limited power of judicial review, to ensure that the president considers all relevant materials before coming to his decision'. P.M. Bakshi, ed., *The Constitution of India* (Delhi: Universal Law Publishing Co., 2009), 99. But the Supreme Court's intervention in 2013 went beyond that, to consider whether long delays after death sentences were passed might warrant the acceptance of mercy petitions.

[53] Venkatesan, 'Death Penalty'.

[54] In comments on presidents' room for manoeuvre, Fali Nariman does not speak of pocket vetoes, but he makes one important observation. He discusses the 44th Amendment—introduced after Indira Gandhi's emergency to counter

must be said, however, that this term is misleading. A genuine 'veto' is permanent. 'Pocket vetoes' are temporary; they last only until the end of a president's five-year term, when they may be reversed. So this device has serious limitations.

One further, potentially crucial theme needs attention, and it applies not just to mercy petitions but to other issues. When a president questions advice from ministers, or remains inert in order to exercise a pocket veto, s/he is stopping short of drastic action. Questioning advice does not produce a full-scale constitutional confrontation and pocket vetoes lapse when a president's term ends. There is, however, a further (drastic) option which represents a president's ultimate weapon. It has never been used—or rather, it appears to have been used only once in January 2017—and it has hardly ever been discussed, but it must not be ignored. It was suggested not by a hot-headed radical, but by a president who is respected for measured judgement.

After President Narayanan had returned the central government's request for the imposition of President's Rule in Uttar Pradesh for reconsideration, former President Venkataraman gave an interview. He first said that he believed that Narayanan was correct to return the request because, despite violent acts by certain legislators in Uttar Pradesh, a vote of confidence in the state government had been obtained—so there had been no political breakdown. When asked whether Narayanan would have had to accede to the government's request if it had been reiterated, Venkataraman quietly provided a potentially sensational answer: '[O]ne cannot be sure what the president would have done'. He then elaborated:

> If the president is asked to do something against the Constitution, then the mere fact that the Cabinet has reiterated its earlier decision may not be binding upon him ... I am not sure whether the president is

---

the 42nd Amendment passed during the emergency, which had reduced the president to what Nariman calls 'a titular functionary'. He reminds us that although the 44th Amendment explicitly affirmed the president's right to 'require' ministers to reconsider their advice, with the proviso that the president 'shall act in accordance with' reiterated advice, he adds that it set down 'no constitutional prescription as to the time when he/she should so act'. This leaves the door open to pocket vetoes. Nariman, *State of the Nation*, 172.

bound to act on a reaffirmation by the cabinet if it is totally contrary to the Constitution. Because the president has given an oath that he will defend the Constitution. Therefore if anything goes against the Constitution, he has to defend it.[55]

Herein lies political dynamite. But what action might a president take in such a situation? Four drastic possibilities present themselves. S/he might resign. That, however, could be self-defeating since a successor might be more acquiescent. S/he might dismiss the government and either seek out other leaders in the Lok Sabha who could form a new one, or dissolve Parliament and call a fresh election. But either action would appear dangerously radical, and might produce unwelcome outcomes.

A president might refer the government's proposed action to the Supreme Court for a view on its constitutionality. This might avoid a confrontation with Parliament because since the Court's ruling in 1973 in the *Kesavananda Bharati* case, it has been recognized that the Constitution, rather than Parliament (and ministers), is supreme. But a prime minister and cabinet might nevertheless be disinclined to accept the relevance of that case to their dispute with a president, and obdurately proceed with a confrontation.[56]

It is, therefore, most likely that a fourth action would be taken: s/he might simply refuse to comply with the government's request. That would trigger a constitutional crisis, but it would force the government to bear the onus associated with rash action against a president who could argue that s/he is defending the Constitution. Ministers might seek to impeach the president.[57] But impeachment could prove

[55] 'The Rediff Interview/R. Venkataraman', *Rediff on the Net*, 23 October 1997. Available at: www.rediff.com/news/oct/23rvhtm.

[56] In 1973, the Supreme Court of India ruled in *Kesavananda Bharati* v. *State of Kerala*, (1973) 4 SCC 225, that Parliament does not have unlimited power to amend the Constitution, and that no amendment which undermines its basic structure is permissible. However, if the Supreme Court supported a president in a confrontation with ministers, the latter might argue that fundamental rights and the 'basic structure' were not at issue, and refuse to back down. I am grateful to the other contributors to this book for raising this issue.

[57] The president's decision was first reported in the *Indian Express*, 22 January 2017.

impossible because, as Jagjivan Ram noted, the huge majority of both houses of Parliament required for impeachment might be unobtainable. So, ministers might instead decide to seek a general election. But since the outcome would be unpredictable, that would also be an unpalatable choice.

One further event which might have sparked a confrontation between ministers and a president deserves comment. On 1 January 2017, President Pranab Mukherjee commuted death sentences passed on four men who had been convicted of murder during a 1992 inter-caste conflict. He apparently acted contrary to reiterated advice from ministers. He based his decision on a 2014 Supreme Court ruling which permitted commutations when there had been long delays in disposing of mercy petitions. Supreme Court rulings are 'law declared': that they are binding upon presidents and governments. President Mukherjee apparently concluded that this ruling freed him from the requirement that he accept reiterated advice from ministers—when considering mercy petitions, but not in other matters. The Modi government may have disagreed, but at this writing soon after the commutation, it has taken no action against the president.[58] A confrontation has thus been averted in this case, but the potential for a constitutional crisis remains.

As this final comment indicates, the presidency may not at first appear to be a topic to set our pulses racing, but the potential is there— *in extremis*—for a compelling drama rooted in the very fundamentals of a democratic order.

---

[58] The president's decision was first reported in the *Indian Express*, 22 January 2017.

2

PARLIAMENT

*M.R. Madhavan**

Parliament is the apex legislative body in India. Modern legislatures in India evolved from the nineteenth century when legislative councils were formed through various Acts of the British Parliament. Legislative bodies were made more representative and progressively more power was devolved through the Government of India Acts of 1919 and 1935. The framers of the Constitution decided to follow the Westminster model, and the first Parliament of the Indian Republic was formed in 1952.[1]

At a broad level, Parliament is one of the key governmental institutions to secure to all citizens the ideals of justice, liberty, equality, and fraternity, as resolved in the preamble to the Constitution. At a more functional level, the mandate of Parliament is as a representative body that makes laws, holds the executive accountable, and sanctions and monitors public expenditure. Individual Members of Parliament (MPs)

* I thank Chakshu Roy and Mandira Kala for discussions on this topic and Kusum Malik for collating the data. I also thank the participants of a workshop on 'Building an Indian State for the 21st Century', held in July 2013 at the Rockefeller Foundation Centre in Bellagio, for their comments, which helped shape this chapter.
[1] For a detailed narration of the evolution of the Indian Parliament, see S. Kashyap, *History of the Parliament of India* (New Delhi: Shipra, 1994), vols I–VI.

are also expected to raise issues of public interest, which may also be issues that affect the interests of their constituency. In this chapter, we discuss the following two questions. How well has Parliament functioned in these roles? Are there design issues that need to be addressed to improve the effectiveness in fulfilling these roles?

This chapter is structured as follows. We briefly describe the structure of Parliament, and examine how the representation has changed over the years. Then we look at the performance of Parliament. First, we discuss the decline in the frequency of sittings of Parliament and increase in disruptions, as well as the possible reasons for this behaviour. Then, we look at various functions and mechanisms of Parliament, such as question hour (when parliamentarians hold the government accountable), legislative process, financial oversight, and the committee system. For each of these, we examine their performance and discuss whether any structural changes can be made for improving outcomes. Finally, we discuss a few core structural issues that impede better functioning: the anti-defection law, lack of recorded voting as a standard norm, and dearth of resources for MPs.

Structure of Parliament

India has a bi-cameral Parliament. The lower house, Lok Sabha or the House of the People, has 545 members, of which 543 members are directly elected and 2 members are then nominated by the president (on the advice of the government) to represent the Anglo-Indian community. The upper house, Rajya Sabha or the Council of States, has 233 members elected by state legislators, and 12 members nominated by the president for their contributions to science, literature, arts, and public service.

Similar to the British Parliament, the lower house has a larger role in the division of powers. The executive government, headed by the prime minister, is formed by the person who enjoys the confidence of the majority of MPs in Lok Sabha; the Rajya Sabha has no say in this matter. Similarly, money bills need the support of the majority of members voting in the Lok Sabha, while the Rajya Sabha has only a recommendatory role.

The two houses have equal powers on other legislative business. Every ordinary bill has to be passed by a majority of each house. Any amendment made by one house needs the concurrence of the other. That said, even in the case of legislation, the lower house may hold an edge. If the two houses cannot agree on a bill, the president may call a joint sitting of the two houses. As each MP has one vote and Lok Sabha outnumbers Rajya Sabha by a factor of 2.2, the parties that have a majority in the Lok Sabha can get their way. This is not a common occurrence, with only three instances—spread over four decades— when a joint session was called to determine the fate of a bill.[2]

The Constitution prescribes the process by which it can be amended. All constitutional amendments need the support of a two-thirds major- ity of members who are present and voting and a simple majority of the total membership of each house (and, for some types of amendments, ratification by half of all state legislative assemblies). There is no provi- sion for a joint session if an amendment to the Constitution does not get the required majority. Therefore, the two houses have equal powers when they sit as a constituent body.

On issues of accountability, with the exception of a no-confidence motion (which may be moved only in Lok Sabha), both houses have similar powers. Both have a question hour in which individual mem- bers may ask questions of ministers. MPs may also raise and discuss issues of national importance during zero hour, or as full debates (with or without a vote) on any issue that the house may permit. Members of either house can move a resolution to amend or reverse any executive rule or regulation that has been made as part of delegated legislation. Oversight of the government is also exercised through parliamentary committees. All departmentally-related standing committees and finance committees have memberships from both houses.

Representation

The Lok Sabha is directly elected by all adult citizens as their represen- tative body. Any Indian citizen over 25 years of age is eligible (subject to a few disqualifications such as conviction for certain offences, being declared as being of unsound mind, insolvency, and others) to contest

---

[2] Joint sessions were held to pass the Dowry Prohibition Bill, 1961; the Banking Service Commission (Repeal) Bill, 1978; and the Prevention of Terrorism Bill, 2002.

elections. The Lok Sabha reserves nearly one-quarter of seats for people belonging to Scheduled Castes (SCs) and Scheduled Tribes (STs) (the number of seats reserved is in proportion to their share of population in each state).

It is interesting to see how the composition of the house has changed over the years. Figures 2.1 to 2.4 show the evolution of the composition of Lok Sabha on four parameters: gender, age, educational qualification, and profession. These data are based on self-declarations by members, either to Lok Sabha or to the Election Commission of India (ECI).[3]

A few trends are evident. The proportion of women has crept up, from 5 per cent in the first Lok Sabha to 11 per cent in the sixteenth (elected in 2014). There have been several attempts to amend the Constitution to reserve legislative seats for women. The last such bill, introduced in 2008, was passed by Rajya Sabha but lapsed upon the dissolution of the Lok Sabha in 2014. This bill sought to reserve 33 per cent of seats in Lok Sabha and state legislative assemblies for women for the next 15 years, with reserved seats rotating every five years (Figure 2.1).

The Lok Sabha has been getting older. In the first Lok Sabha, there was just one member above the age of 70 years, and none over 75 years. The sixteenth Lok Sabha has 46 members who are at least 70 years old, with 15 of them being over 75 years of age. The percentage of young MPs, that is, those in the age group of 25 years to 40 years, has declined from 26 per cent in the first Lok Sabha to 13 per cent in the sixteenth (Figure 2.2). The educational profile of MPs has been improving, with a more sizeable share of graduates now. The first Lok Sabha had 23 per cent MPs without a matriculation certificate (tenth grade in school), which has declined to 4 per cent now. The percentage of MPs with at least an undergraduate degree has risen from 58 to 77 per cent (Figure 2.3).

---

[3] The data for the first to the twelfth Lok Sabha have been obtained from http://parliamentofindia.nic.in/jpi/MARCH2000/CHAP-5.htm. The data for the thirteenth to the fifteenth Lok Sabha have been collated from the individual member pages on the Lok Sabha website. The data for the sixteenth Lok Sabha are collated from the affidavits of candidates for election, available on the website of the ECI.

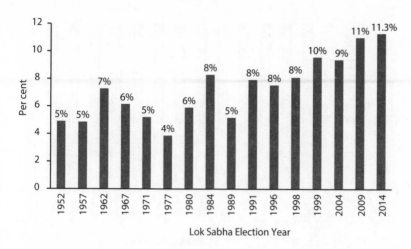

Figure 2.1 Share of Female Members of Parliament, 1952–2014
Sources: Journal of Parliamentary Information; Lok Sabha website; and candidate affidavits found on the website of the Election Commission of India.

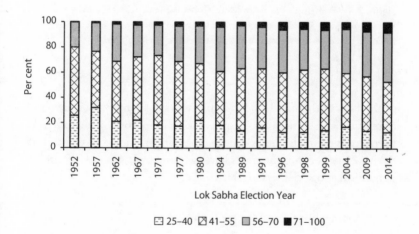

⊟ 25–40 ⊠ 41–55 ☐ 56–70 ■ 71–100

Figure 2.2 Age Profile of Members of Parliament, 1952–2014
Sources: Journal of Parliamentary Information; Lok Sabha website; and candidate affidavits found on the website of the Election Commission of India.

MPs have also declared their professions. Whereas 36 per cent of the members of the first Lok Sabha were lawyers, this figure has declined to 7 per cent in the sixteenth Lok Sabha. The percentage who claimed to be farmers has increased from 22 to 27 per cent. Interestingly, none

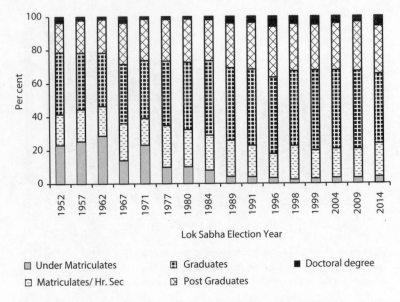

Figure 2.3 Education Profile of Members of Parliament, 1952–2014
Sources: *Journal of Parliamentary Information*; Lok Sabha website; and candidate
affidavits found on the website of the Election Commission of India.

of the MPs in the first Lok Sabha had marked themselves as involved
in political and social work, despite a large proportion of them having
been involved in the Independence movement. In the sixteenth Lok
Sabha, 24 per cent of members have declared their primary profession
as political and social service (Figure 2.4).

Performance and Design Issues

In recent years, the inability of Parliament to transact business in an
orderly manner has been a matter of concern. Not only have the number of sittings decreased over the decades, but Parliament has also not
been able to function smoothly during the scheduled time. We examine two metrics to judge the progression in the overall functioning of
Parliament: the frequency of meetings and the amount of time that is
lost due to disruptions by some members. We also discuss some possible ways to tackle this issue.

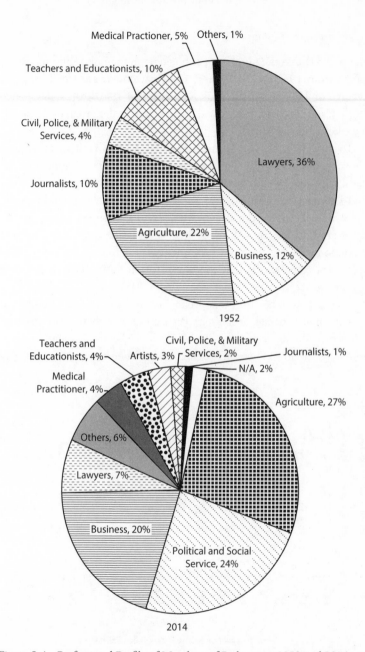

Figure 2.4 Professional Profile of Members of Parliament, 1952 and 2014
Sources: Journal of Parliamentary Information; Lok Sabha website; and candidate affidavits found on the website of the Election Commission of India.

Frequency of Sittings

Figure 2.5 shows the number of sitting days in the Lok Sabha and Rajya Sabha from 1952 to 2012. There is a clear downward trend, from an average of 127 days in the Lok Sabha in the 1950s to 71 days since 1990. Can this trend be reversed by a change in design, that is, amending rules and procedures?

To answer this issue, it is vital to understand how Parliament sessions are scheduled currently. For starters, there is no pre-set annual calendar. Parliament usually has three sessions a year: budget session from mid-February to mid-May, monsoon session during July and August, and winter session from late November to Christmas. However, the dates are not determined in advance; the president, on the advice of the union cabinet, summons Parliament with a three-week notice. The only hard constraint is that the Constitution limits the gap between sessions to six months.

This structure can lead to a progressive reduction in the number of parliamentary sittings every year. Parliamentary debates and question hours provide the opportunity to MPs to hold the government accountable for its actions. There may be occasions when the government may

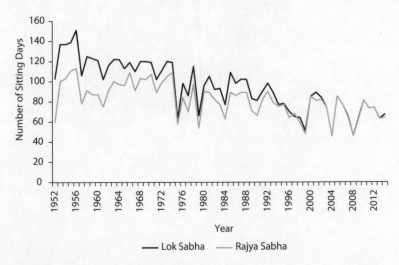

Figure 2.5 Number of Sitting Days in Parliament, 1952–2015
Source: PRS Legislative Research.

be uncomfortable in defending its actions, and may prefer not to have debates on various issues (see the next section for a discussion of this point). As the government can decide the dates of Parliament sittings, it can decide to have fewer sittings when it may be under pressure to justify its actions.

There have been various attempts to ensure a higher number of days. In 2009, the Rajya Sabha discussed a private member's bill to amend the Constitution to require that Parliament sit for at least 100 days every year. However, the government, while accepting the spirit of the bill, said that it would be impractical to include this in the Constitution.

One way to fix the issue is to require that Parliament be summoned if there is a written notice by a pre-determined number of members. As the government, by definition, has the support of a majority of MPs in Lok Sabha, the number should be set at lower than 50 per cent. For instance, the threshold for admitting a no-confidence motion is set at 10 per cent of the membership of Lok Sabha. It is worth noting that the 1916 proposal of the Indian National Congress and the Muslim League to establish an Imperial Legislative Council (within the British Empire) included a provision for a special session on the requisition of one-eighth of the members.[4]

Another (and perhaps, an easier to implement) way is to announce the calendar of sittings in advance, soon after the Lok Sabha elections. Many parliaments, including the British Parliament and the US Congress, announce their annual calendar at the beginning of each year.[5] This process not only helps MPs prepare their schedules better, but also makes it difficult for the government to avoid facing Parliament when it faces accusations of impropriety.

---

[4] 'The Congress-League Scheme, December 1916', Chapter III, Article 7, reproduced in B. Shiva Rao, *The Framing of India's Constitution* (New Delhi: Universal Law Publishing Company, 2004), vol. 1.

[5] See 'Days in Session of the U.S. Congress', Congress.gov. Website, 6 May 2016. Available at http://thomas.loc.gov/home/ds/index.html#senate; and 'House of Commons Recess Dates', UK Parliament. Website, 6 May 2016. Available at http://www.Parliament.uk/about/faqs/house-of-commons-faqs/business-faq-page/recess-dates/.

Disruptions of Proceedings

In Figure 2.6 we show the time lost to disruptions as a percentage of scheduled time for the period from 1962 to 2015. It can be seen that the fifteenth Lok Sabha has been the worst performer. That is, not only has there been a significant decline in the number of sitting days over the years, but also the time lost in those sitting days has increased.

One casualty of parliamentary time being disrupted is the time being spent deliberating on bills. We have seen many bills passed without any discussion. An extreme example was 23 December 2008, when the Lok Sabha passed eight bills within 17 minutes. Examples of bills passed without any discussion in recent years include the Competition (Amendment) Bill, 2006 (which created the framework for regulating anti-competitive behaviour) and the Sexual Harassment of Women at the Workplace Bill, 2010. Figure 2.7 shows the time spent discussing bills in Parliament in the fifteenth Lok Sabha; over one-fourth of all bills were passed in less than 30 minutes.

What are the proximate causes of disruption? A former leader of the opposition in the Rajya Sabha argued that disrupting Parliament is a legitimate tactic:

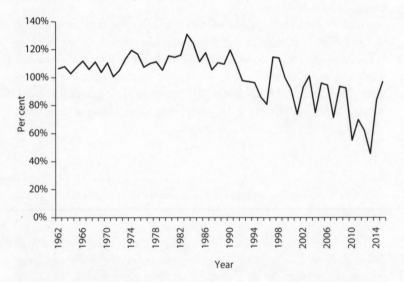

Figure 2.6 Sitting Time as a Percentage of Scheduled Time in Parliament, 1962–2015
Source: PRS Legislative Research.

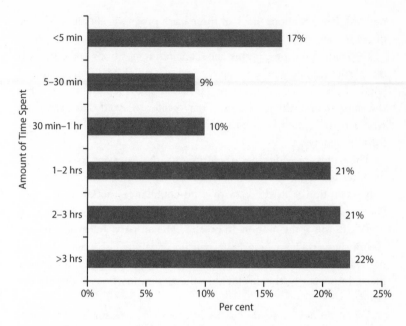

Figure 2.7 Time Spent per Bill Passed in Parliament, 2009–14
Source: PRS Legislative Research.

Parliamentary obstructionism should be avoided. It is a weapon to be used in the rarest of the rare cases. Parliamentary accountability is as important as parliamentary debate. Both must co-exist. If parliamentary accountability is subverted and a debate is intended to be used merely to put a lid on parliamentary accountability, it is then a legitimate tactic for the Opposition to expose the government through parliamentary instruments available at its command.[6]

The argument is that there are occasions when the only method by which the government can be held accountable is through disruptions. Is there merit in the argument? If so, can we tweak the design of parliamentary proceedings to address the underlying issues?

At present, there are various accountability mechanisms available to MPs. Other than question hour, there are four types of debates through which substantive issues may be discussed. These include a discussion under Rule 193, a motion under Rule 184, adjournment motion, and

---

[6] A. Jaitley, 'Defending the Indefensible', *The Hindu*, 28 August 2012.

no-confidence motion.[7] Each of these has a progressively higher degree of consequence for the government.[8]

Depending on the circumstances, including positions taken by various parties (including those that are part of a ruling coalition or support it), the opposition parties may prefer debate under a particular rule. For the same reason, the government may prefer to avoid that debate. So who gets to decide whether the issue will be debated, and under which form of debate?

The rules provide the discretion to the speaker to determine whether to admit a discussion, and if so, then under which form. The only exception is in the case of a no-confidence motion in the Lok Sabha, where the rules state that it is obligatory to debate the motion if 50 MPs move the motion. In practice, the all-party business advisory committee decides which issue will be debated. This means that all parties have to agree on a discussion (and the form) before it takes place. Importantly, this means that the government has a veto on the issue.

When there is an issue that could cause embarrassment to the government, opposition parties—which are pressing for a debate under a

---

[7] These are the Rules of the Lok Sabha. The Rajya Sabha has similar procedures, with the exception of the no-confidence motion.

[8] The difference between these forms is as follows. Rule 193 provides for a general discussion without a vote. MPs debate the issue, and the minister replies on the various points that are raised. The government prefers this type of discussion as this will not result in a losing vote and consequent embarrassment. Rule 184 is similar but crucially differs in the sense that there is a formal motion that is voted upon. This would force each MP (and the political party) to reveal their positions unambiguously. In some instances, in order to avoid embarrassment, the government may agree to such a motion only if it is worded in a particular manner. For example, in August 2011, opposition parties had raised the issue of rising prices of essential commodities and insisted on a discussion under Rule 184. The motion that was moved called upon the government 'to take immediate effective steps to check inflation that will give relief to the common man'. Who can object to such a demand? An 'adjournment motion' requires the house to adjourn. If the government loses this motion, it is not required to resign. However, the motion is seen as a severe censure of the government. Finally, a no-confidence motion has the most serious consequence. A government that loses such a motion has to resign from office.

particular rule—are not allowed to do so. Having been rebuffed, these parties then claim that the only way they can ensure accountability is to block all other business until that particular issue is resolved. The resultant disruption and loss of working hours is usually resolved by the government eventually backing down. There are several examples of this behaviour; for example, the winter session of 2012 saw heated wrangling on whether the debate on permitting foreign direct investment in retail trade would be followed by a vote. Parliamentary work was disrupted until the government agreed to a motion with a vote under Rule 184. Perhaps, the most extreme instance took place during the winter session of 2010, when the government refused to accede to the demand for a Joint Parliamentary Committee to examine the issue of allocation of 2G spectrum licences. The entire session saw no work, and the government finally conceded to the demand just ahead of the next session.

What are the possible design tweaks that can improve the process? One possibility is to claim that the speaker need not follow the decision taken by the business advisory committee. However, this formulation could lead to an even higher level of dissatisfaction in some situations. The speaker is elected by the house, and is usually a member of the ruling party or coalition. Usually, the speaker does not give up his or her party membership. As the speaker is a member of the party in power, his decision may not be always perceived as non-partisan.

The trick to resolving this tangle would be to reduce the discretion of the speaker and the business advisory committee. There are two possible approaches towards this goal, which are not mutually exclusive. One would be to give opposition members the say to decide Parliament's agenda for a certain number of days. For example, the House of Commons in the British Parliament has reserved 20 days per year during which the agenda for discussion can be decided by the opposition—17 days of which are reserved for the main opposition party and three for the next largest opposition party.[9]

The other approach is to require a discussion if a significant minority demands this. Parliament already has similar rules in some cases. For

---

[9] Order No. 14(2), Standing Orders of the House of Commons, September 2012. Available at http://www.publications.Parliament.uk/pa/cm201213/cms tords/614/614.pdf.

instance, a no-confidence motion has to be scheduled if 10 per cent of the membership of Lok Sabha demands one. One parliamentarian has suggested that if one-third of the membership asks for a voting debate, it should take place.[10] Indeed, the Congress-League Scheme, drafted in 1916 as a reform of the Imperial Legislative Council, asked for an adjournment motion to be taken up if supported by one-eighth of the membership.[11]

Question Hour

The first hour of proceedings each day is reserved as question hour. This process provides a key instrument for MPs to hold the government accountable. Ministers have to answer questions asked by MPs on the working of their ministries. All ministries and departments are allocated a particular day of the week, and the minister is expected to be present in the house to answer questions. MPs are required to submit their questions at least 10 days ahead of the date. Only a few questions (20 in the Lok Sabha, 15 in the Rajya Sabha) are selected for oral answers (starred questions) and a larger number (230 in the Lok Sabha, 155 in the Rajya Sabha) for written replies (unstarred questions). This selection is made through a ballot of all questions. In the case of starred questions, the MP who had asked the question has the right to ask a supplementary question. Other MPs may also be permitted by the speaker to ask supplementary questions.

There are two significant shortcomings with the current system: the number of questions that are actually orally answered and the quality of questions. First, the number of questions that are actually answered orally with supplementary questions and answers is less than 15 per cent of the total number of questions listed. Two factors contribute to this: there is barely enough time to take up five to six questions in an hour, and a significant part of question hour time is lost to disruptions. For example, in the fifteenth Lok Sabha, 61 per cent of the time allocated for question hour was wasted. That is, on average, the house convened for just 25 minutes during question hour. For other business, Parliament often sits late to make up for time lost to disruptions;

---

[10] B. Panda, 'Restoring the House', *Indian Express*, 6 December 2011.
[11] Congress-League Scheme, 1916.

however, questions are not taken up during this extra time, and the loss of time during question hour is not made up.

There have been attempts to mitigate some of the adverse factors. In the budget session of 2011, the Rajya Sabha decided to start the day with zero hour to provide time for MPs to raise their grievances, and moved question hour to the afternoon. There was little improvement in the performance, and this experiment was abandoned in the very next session. The Rajya Sabha again tried the same experiment from the winter session of 2014, but the question hour remained hostage to disruptions; it functioned for just 2 per cent of the allocated time in the monsoon session of 2015.

This issue can be resolved if one successfully addresses the issues discussed in the earlier sections. If Parliament meets for a larger number of days, and if MPs do not disrupt the proceedings, then they would have more opportunities to ask questions as well as supplementaries. The second significant factor is the quality of questions and answers given. Most questions are related to data and information, which can be asked through a query under the Right to Information Act, 2005 (RTI). An analysis of the starred questions in the fifteenth Lok Sabha indicates that about 70 per cent of them were of this nature.[12] There is no systemic barrier for changing this situation. Members of Parliament need to plan their strategy to maximize their opportunity to ask relevant questions through various channels, including question hour and the RTI route.

A structural problem arises from the fact that the minister who is in charge of a ministry responds to the questions. This implies that there is no avenue for asking broad policy questions that may span more than one ministry. The British Parliament has resolved this issue through creating the prime minister's question hour, during which the prime minister's schedule is tabled, and any policy question can be asked as a supplementary. This enables detailed questioning of the government's policy and implementation on issues that involve several ministries.

---

[12] Each question was evaluated on two criteria: (a) whether it was purely asking for some information, and (b) if so, whether such information could have been asked under the RTI. It was found that 70 per cent of the questions passed this filter.

Legislation

A key function of Parliament is to make laws on subjects on the union and the concurrent lists of the Seventh Schedule to the Constitution. The laws made by Parliament on the union list subjects apply to the whole of India. In case of a concurrent list item, state legislatures can also make law, but a law passed by Parliament will override the state law if there is a contradiction.

The process of enacting a law is as follows. Bills may be introduced on behalf of the government by the relevant minister. These bills are called government bills. Any other MP may also introduce a bill. These are called private member bills. If a private member bill is passed in one house, another MP who is a member of the other house will have to pilot it in that house.

The introduction of a bill in the house is called the first reading. At this stage, there are only two permitted grounds for objections: (a) that the bill violates some provision of the Constitution; or (b) the item is in the state list and, therefore, Parliament does not have jurisdiction to make law on the issue (which, in essence, is a constitutional violation). After introduction, the speaker may refer the bill to the relevant departmentally related standing committee (DRSC); this step is discretionary. After the committee's report is tabled, the bill may be taken up for consideration. At this stage, the provisions of the bill are discussed in detail. A clause-by-clause discussion takes place, and amendments may be moved. Each clause is voted upon. This comprises the second reading. Then the bill is taken up for a final vote (third reading). There is no discussion at this stage—only an up or down vote. Following passage, the bill is transmitted to the other house (first reading), and the other two stages are followed. After the bill is passed by the second house, it is sent to the president for his assent. At this point the bill becomes an act.

The standing committee system for considering bills was created in 1993. However, referral to the committee is not mandatory. There are several important bills that bypass this step. For example, the Criminal Laws Amendment Bill 2013, which made several significant changes to the Indian Penal Code, Indian Evidence Act, and the Code of Criminal Procedure in relation to violence against women, was not referred to the relevant committee. Similarly, the National Investigation Agency

Act, which was passed soon after the November 2008 terrorist strike in Mumbai, was passed without scrutiny by the committee.[13] This process differs from the British system. In the British Parliament, the committee examines all bills after the second reading in each house, and the next step can take place only after the committee's report is presented.[14]

One way to measure how well Parliament is performing its legislative role is to look at the number of bills passed (see Figure 2.8). However, this number does not give any indication of the quality of the bill passed. There could be ways to judge whether an act is a robust one—whether it clearly enunciates the objectives, makes the relevant provisions in a coherent manner, is written in unambiguous and simple language, and so on. We do not go into those details in this chapter but use two simple proxies. First, does Parliament devote sufficient time to debate bills? During the fourteenth and fifteenth Lok Sabha, discussions on legislative business took up 20 per cent of the total time spent. However, as we saw in Figure 2.7, 28 per cent of bills were not discussed in any detail. A second measure is to count the number of acts that were amended within three or five years of enactment. While any legislation may need to be amended to cater to changing circumstances, an amendment shortly after passage indicates that some key factor was missed or an imminent change in circumstances was not foreseen. In the period since 1993, about 1 per cent of all laws enacted have been amended within three years of their passage, and a further 2 per cent in three to five years since their being passed.

There can be several improvements in the process. First, the pre-legislative process of drafting bills can be strengthened.[15] Second,

[13] We discuss several other design issues related to committees in a later section on committees.

[14] 'Passage of a Bill', UK Parliament. Web. 6 May 2016. Available at http://www.Parliament.uk/about/how/laws/passage-bill/.

[15] The erstwhile National Advisory Council had made several recommendations. These include that draft legislation be kept in public domain, feedback be solicited, and a summary of the feedback and the ministry's response be published.

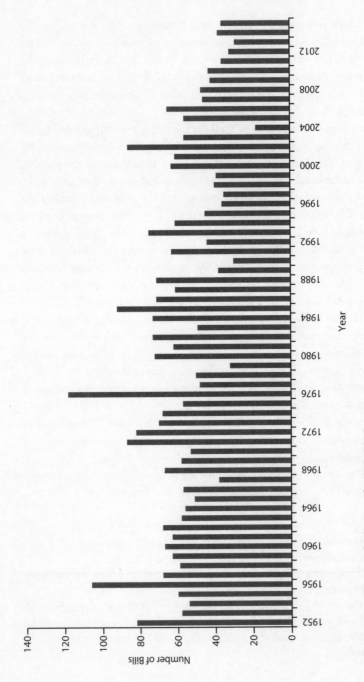

Figure 2.8 Number of Bills Passed, 1952–2015
Source: PRS Legislative Research.

the standing committee process can be made mandatory, with a provision for fast-tracking urgent bills. Third, the support system for MPs and committees to better examine bills could be enhanced (see section on 'Resources for MPs'). Fourth, the anti-defection law could be amended to enable a free discussion on the various issues of a bill and to find a reasonable balance across conflicting objectives (see section on the 'Anti-Defection Law'). Fifth, greater interest and accountability of MPs could be encouraged by requiring a division on every bill and major clauses and amendments (see section on 'Recorded Voting').

Private Members' Bills

Any legislation that is initiated by a private member (that is, by an MP who is not a minister) is called a private member's bill. Historically, such bills have not been given much importance. Even in the early days, few private member bills were passed; only fourteen such bills were enacted in the first two decades. The significance has declined even further: not even one private member bill has been passed since 1970. Indeed, just two-and-a-half hours are allocated every alternate week for this activity. In the fifteenth Lok Sabha, a total of 372 private member bills were introduced. Of these, only 11 were discussed in Parliament, and none was passed.

The Constitution states that a financial bill may not be introduced or considered by Parliament unless the president, acting on the advice of the council of ministers,[16] has recommended that it may be introduced or considered.[17] Therefore, the government has a veto on introduction of any financial bill by a private member.[18]

[16] Constitution of India, Article 74.

[17] Constitution of India, Article 117.

[18] Lok Sabha Secretariat, 'Rules of Procedure and Conduct of Business in Lok Sabha' (New Delhi: Government of India, 2014), rule 65(2). Interestingly, rule 65(1) says that the speaker may revise the statement of objects and reasons appended to a bill by a private member.

Financial Oversight

Any expenditure of the central government needs parliamentary approval.[19] All taxes may be imposed only through law made by Parliament (only the Lok Sabha needs to approve these items, and the Rajya Sabha has only a recommendatory role).[20] Thus, one of the important roles of Parliament is to allocate resources through the budgetary exercise.

Every year, the central government presents its budget to Parliament. The budget includes detailed demand for grants of each department and ministry. These are usually referred to the DRSCs (see the section on Committees). Parliament discusses the general thrust of the budget. After the DRSCs submit their report, the Lok Sabha discusses the demands of a few ministries in detail. The demands of other ministries are clubbed together and voted upon (this process is called the 'guillotine'). Tax changes in the budget are effected through amendments to various tax laws clubbed together as a finance bill.

Ex post financial oversight of budgetary provisions is carried out by the Public Accounts Committee. Parliament may also choose to discuss any budgetary issue on the floor of the house. However, this process often does not play out in full. For starters, committee referral is not mandatory. For example, in 2011, demands for grants were not referred to the committees. The reason given was that senior MPs were busy campaigning for their parties in elections for five state assemblies. On other occasions, the committee report has been submitted just a few hours before the demand was discussed in the house.[21] There are also occasions when Parliament does not discuss the demand for grants on the floor of the house, usually when proceedings are disrupted for some other cause. For example, both the 2013 demand for grants and the Finance Bill were passed without discussion. Figure 2.9 shows the time taken for discussing the union budget, while Table 2.1 shows the number of departments for which the demand for grant was discussed and the percentage of demands guillotined.

[19] Constitution of India, Article 266.
[20] Constitution of India, Article 265.
[21] For example, on 20 April 2010, the DRSC on External Affairs presented its Report on the Demand for Grants of the Ministry of External Affairs at 12 p.m. and the discussion on the demand started at 2:05 p.m. that day.

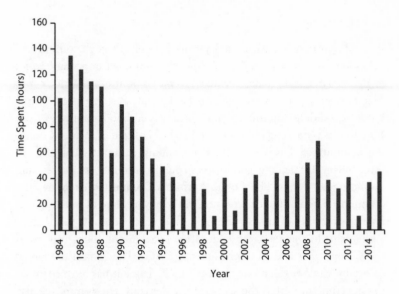

Figure 2.9 Time Spent on the General Budget in Parliament, 1984–2015
Source: PRS Legislative Research.

Table 2.1 Percentage of Budget Discussed (amounts in Rs crore)

Year	Total	Discussed	Guillotined	% Guillotined	Ministries Discussed
2004	339,300	–	339,300	100	0
2005	384,844	57,217	327,626	85	4
2006	448,109	74,053	374,057	83	3
2007	547,020	29,017	518,003	95	3
2008	597,662	223,734	373,928	63	4
2009	887,194	187,495	699,699	79	6
2010	982,483	157,911	824,572	84	3
2011	1,119,732	209,113	910,620	81	4
2012	1,292,455	107,872	1,184,583	92	4
2013	1,400,396	–	1,400,396	100	0
2014	1,452,312	81,405	1,370,908	94	4

Source: Compiled by the author from Union Budget documents and 'Bulletin-I' of Lok Sabha.

Committees

A significant part of parliamentary work happens through committees. Parliament is too large and unwieldy to examine all important issues in detail. Therefore, it has formed several committees that look into specific issues and report back to Parliament. Parliament has three types of standing committees and can form ad hoc committees from time to time. Standing committees may be classified as financial standing committees, DRSCs, and other standing committees. There are three financial standing committees: public accounts, estimates, and public undertakings. The Public Accounts Committee examines the accounts related to the expenditure of the government of India, annual finance accounts of the government, and other accounts laid before Parliament. In this task, the committee takes into account reports of the Comptroller and Auditor General (CAG). The committee has to ascertain whether the money granted by Parliament has been spent by the government within the scope of the demand. The committee also examines cases involving losses and financial irregularities. Since 1967, this committee has always been chaired by a senior opposition MP.

The Estimates Committee deliberates on ways to effect economies, improvements in organization, efficiency, and administrative reforms consistent with the policy underlying financial estimates. It may also recommend alternative policies to improve efficiency and economy in administration, examine whether the money is well laid out, and suggest the form in which estimates may be presented to Parliament.

The Committee on Public Undertakings examines the reports and accounts of public undertakings, the reports of the CAG on these, examines whether prudent commercial practices and sound business principles are being applied in managing the undertakings, and exercises such functions vested in the public accounts committee and estimates committee in relation to public undertakings, as allotted by the speaker (Table 2.2).

Since 1993, Parliament has also constituted DRSCs, each of which oversees one or more ministries or departments. Currently, there are 24 DRSCs, each consisting of MPs from Lok Sabha and 10 consisting of MPs from Rajya Sabha. These committees have three main functions: they examine bills referred to them; they examine demand for grants; and they can look into various policy issues.

Table 2.2 Reports Prepared by Financial Committees

	Fourteenth Lok Sabha			Fifteenth Lok Sabha		
	Original	ATR	Total	Original	ATR	Total
Public Accounts Committee	43	41	84	54	46	100
Estimates Committee	11	9	20	19	17	36
Committee on Public Undertakings	24	16	40	10	23	33

Source: Lok Sabha and Rajya Sabha websites, accessed on 5 November 2014.
Note: ATR: Action Taken Report.

The committee's recommendations on bills, while not binding on the government, function as inputs to MPs while they are considering the bill on the floor of the house. The government may accept some of the recommendations and bring in suitable amendments, but there is no obligation to justify why it is or is not accepting other recommendations. However, MPs may ask the government its reasoning for rejecting the committee's recommendations.

In turn, the government's decision on whether to accept the committee's recommendation may depend on various factors such as whether it agrees with the recommendations and/or its assessment of its ability to pilot the bill through Parliament. When the government does not have a majority in the Rajya Sabha, it may tend to defer to the committee. For example, in 2011, the Standing Committee on Finance rejected the National Identification Authority of India Bill, 2010, which the government chose not to pursue. A year earlier, the government chose to ignore the recommendations of the Standing Committee on Human Resource Development on the Educational Tribunals Bill, 2010, and got it passed by the Lok Sabha, but had to defer the second reading in the Rajya Sabha after the general discussion on the bill as several MPs raised objections; the bill was never brought to Parliament for further consideration.

When the committee examines any policy area or the working of a department (subject), it acts as an oversight body. The government is bound to report back on its actions on the recommendations and justify its decision to reject or partially reject any recommendation. The same principle applies when the committee examines demand for grants. The final action taken (or not taken) is summarized in an action taken report (ATR) prepared by the committee. In a majority of instances, the government tends to accept the committee's recommendations or to provide a response that satisfies the committee. During the period of the fifteenth Lok Sabha, the committees were satisfied by the government's response to 67 per cent of all recommendations, and unhappy in 21 per cent of the cases (the government had not given a final reply to the remaining 12 per cent of recommendations). In Table 2.3, we tabulate the committees' reaction to the responses of the government. We can see that there is significant variation across committees on this matter.

A look at Table 2.4 shows some interesting trends in the law-making priority of the government. During the fifteenth Lok Sabha, four DRSCs—finance, human resource development, personnel and law, and home—accounted for more than half of all bills considered by the committees. This reflected the focus on financial sector reforms, higher education reforms, anti-corruption issues, and security concerns. Also, the Committees examined fewer demand for grants during the fifteenth Lok Sabha than the fourteenth Lok Sabha, as this process was bypassed in 2011. That year, the budget session was curtailed to enable MPs to campaign for their party candidates in the state assembly elections; however, some committees examined the demands after they were passed by Parliament.

Other standing committees include the Business Advisory Committee (which determines the daily agenda), the Committee on Government Assurances (which keeps track of the assurances given by ministers), Privileges Committee, Rules Committee, Petitions Committee, Committee on Welfare of Scheduled Castes and Scheduled Tribes, Committee on Private Members' Bills and Assurances, Committee on Salaries and Allowances of MPs, Committee on Empowerment of Women, and others.

Parliament may also form ad hoc select committees to look into specific issues or bills (for example, Rajya Sabha formed a select committee in 2012 to examine the Lokpal Bill, which had earlier been examined by a DRSC and passed by the Lok Sabha). It can also form joint committees, such as the joint parliamentary committee that was formed in 2011 to examine issues related to the allocation and pricing of the 2G telecom spectrum.

Table 2.3 Acceptance of Departmentally Related Standing Committee (DRSC) Recommendations

	Number of Recommendations	Accepted by Government	Committee Accepted Government's Response	Committee Rejected Government's Response	Final Response Awaited
Agriculture	866	547	37	212	70
Chemicals and Fertilizers	315	199	6	51	59
Coal and Steel	544	323	21	127	73
Defence	377	219	19	104	35
Energy	375	266	26	65	18
External Affairs	251	155	9	22	65
Finance	446	362	7	76	1
Food, Consumer Affairs	334	234	51	28	21
Information Technology	797	445	18	181	153
Labour	401	262	5	75	59
Petroleum and Natural Gas	311	157	25	80	49
Railways	393	245	71	60	17
Rural Development	673	483	26	72	92
Social Justice and Empowerment	415	246	13	62	94
Urban Development	309	184	17	87	21
Water Resources	302	238	23	34	7

(Cont'd)

Table 2.3 (Cont'd)

	Number of Recommendations	Accepted by Government	Committee Accepted Government's Response	Committee Rejected Government's Response	Final Response Awaited
Commerce	346	89	136	55	66
Health and Family Welfare	976	323	231	382	40
Home Affairs	704	347	143	144	70
Human Resources Development	323	11	197	111	4
Industry	386	45	125	106	110
Personnel, Public Grievances, Law and Justice	488	169	143	93	83
Science and Technology	314	220	0	92	2
Transport, Tourism, and Culture	781	377	130	95	179
TOTAL	11,427	6,146	1,479	2,414	1,388
Percentage	100%	54%	13%	21%	12%

Source: Lok Sabha and Rajya Sabha websites, accessed on 30 April 2016.
Note: Data compiled from various ATRs of the fifteenth Lok Sabha. These include: 43rd report of the DRSC on health and family welfare; 179th report of the DRSC on home affairs; 213th, 214th, 215th, 216th, 217th, 218th, 219th, 232nd, 233rd, 234th, 235th, 236th, 237th, and 238th reports of the DRSC on science and technology, environment and forests; and 184th, 185th, 186th, 187th, 212th, and 213th reports of the DRSC on transport. Tourism and culture do not spell out these categories, and have been omitted from this analysis.

Table 2.4 Trends in Legislative Activity

	Fourteenth Lok Sabha (2004–9)					Fifteenth Lok Sabha (2009–14)				
	Bill	Subject	ATR	DfG	Total	Bill	Subject	ATR	DfG	Total
Agriculture	5	2	20	20	47	5	9	27	20	61
Chemicals and Fertilizers	0	5	14	10	29	1	6	22	15	44
Coal and Steel	1	4	19	15	39	2	12	24	15	53
Defence	2	14	15	5	36	1	3	12	5	21
Energy	1	6	14	10	31	0	12	22	10	44
External Affairs	0	1	12	10	23	2	2	11	10	25
Finance	20	6	29	24	79	24	6	29	25	84
Food, Consumer Affairs	5	2	12	10	29	5	4	14	10	33
Information Technology	3	9	36	20	68	4	5	24	20	53
Labour	10	8	12	10	40	8	7	21	10	46
Petroleum and Natural Gas	1	8	11	5	25	1	6	11	5	23
Railways	2	15	20	5	42	1	7	12	5	25
Rural Development	3	2	21	20	46	2	6	24	19	51
Social Justice and Empowerment	5	6	19	11	41	4	7	19	16	46
Urban Development	0	13	18	10	41	4	1	15	10	30
Water Resources	0	1	5	5	11	1	5	10	5	21
Commerce	2	9	6	10	27	2	6	9	6	23
Health and Family Welfare	10	1	10	13	34	8	6	19	12	45

(Cont'd)

Table 2.4 (Cont'd)

	Fourteenth Lok Sabha (2004–2009)					Fifteenth Lok Sabha (2009–2014)				
	Bill	Subject	ATR	DfG	Total	Bill	Subject	ATR	DfG	Total
Home Affairs	13	5	7	12	37	14	6	11	4	35
Human Resources Development	14	11	20	20	65	23	2	12	12	49
Industry	4	12	31	19	66	0	20	19	9	48
Personnel, Public Grievances, Law and Justice	16	5	3	10	34	18	4	9	6	37
Science and Technology	2	4	39	34	79	7	2	21	21	51
Transport, Tourism and Culture	15	9	23	25	72	8	15	26	15	64
TOTAL	134	158	416	333	1,041	145	159	423	285	1,012

Source: Lok Sabha and Rajya Sabha websites, accessed on 5 November 2014.
Notes: ATR: Action Taken Report; DfG: Demand for Grants.

One of the major successes of these committees is that they usually work in an objective manner, without being led by party whips. Indeed, in most cases, committees deliver a consensus report, though in some cases, there are a few notes of dissent. This behaviour has come under stress in a couple of recent instances, both related to the 2G issue: the Public Accounts Committee that examined the issue failed to give a report (there were two versions, after the members from the treasury and the opposition could not reach an agreement); the 30-member joint parliamentary committee also saw walkouts by some opposition members and the report was finally submitted with a 16–11 vote, with three abstentions.

Another feature is that these committees provide a forum for engaging with various stakeholders and experts. They invite written feedback and may also invite a few stakeholders for oral testimony. In this, the performance of committees is mixed. A few examples will illustrate this point. The DRSC on human resource development examined the Copyright (Amendment) Bill, 2010. It called over 25 groups, representing a wide variety of stakeholders, to present their views before making its recommendations. On the other hand, the DRSC on food, consumer affairs, and public distribution examined the National Food Security Bill, 2011. The committee reports that it received over 150,000 memoranda and examined 'representatives of central ministries, associations, women organisations, child welfare associations/experts/individuals and Members of Parliament etc.', but 'not a single objection was raised on the National Food Security Bill per se'.[22] It is pertinent to note that the committee invited only those persons who had publicly supported the bill; a number of experts who had critiqued the bill (including some within the government) were not invited as witnesses.[23] Indeed, appearing before the committee, one witness (also an MP) said that

---

[22] Standing Committee on Food, Consumer Affairs and Public Distribution (2012–13), *Twenty Seventh Report* (New Delhi: Government of India, January 2013), http://www.prsindia.org/uploads/media/Food%20Security/SC%20Report-Food%20Security%20Bill,%202011.pdf.

[23] For example, see A. Gulati *et al.*, 'National Food Security Bill: Challenges and Options' (Discussion Paper No. 2, Commission on Agricultural Costs and Prices, New Delhi, 2012), http://cacp.dacnet.nic.in/.

there was a 'need to ensure truthfulness of the Financial Memorandum to avoid serious consequences in the implementation of Bill'.[24]

It is evident from this description that committees have a significant amount of work, including that of a technical nature, to perform. One of the major drawbacks is that they do not have any expert staff to assist them. Typically, these committees, including the financial standing committees and DRSCs, have a few office staff (five to ten persons), all of whom are from the Parliament Secretariat's administrative service. This office assists the committee with logistics support—identifying and summoning witnesses, keeping transcripts and minutes of meetings, drafting and writing reports, and so on—but does not have the technical background to provide expert support. Bridging this gap can make a significant improvement in the effectiveness of committees to examine issues including government bills, financial demands and accounts, and policy proposals and decisions.

All committee meetings are held *in camera*. While the minutes are made available to the public at a later date, these may not capture all the details of the discussion. Given that Parliament's sessions are open and telecast live and that committees are parliamentary bodies carrying out the same functions, the question has arisen, whether parliamentary committee meetings should also be made open hearings. One school of thought believes that the objectivity/neutrality of committees would be spoilt if the proceedings were made open to the public.[25] There have been some concerns that MPs have been grandstanding more often in Parliament from the time proceedings started being telecast live. Perhaps, the middle-ground between transparency and preserving the neutral nature of committees could be reached by opening the meetings to the public and the media, but not telecasting them live. Another option is to make the transcripts of the committee proceedings public (except for any internal deliberation of the committee) when the committee presents its report to Parliament.

[24] See minutes of the sitting of DSRC on Food, Consumer Affairs and Public Distribution on 18 October 2012 with N.K. Singh, MP, appearing as a witness.

[25] Comments by S. Bal Shekhar, Additional Secretary, Lok Sabha, at the second Commonwealth Parliamentary Seminar, New Delhi, organized by Commonwealth Parliamentary Association, November 2011.

Some Structural Issues

The Anti-defection Law

India enacted an anti-defection law by amending the Constitution and adding the Tenth Schedule in 1985. The law, which has been amended a few times, says that any MP can be disqualified from Parliament if he leaves the party from which he was elected, or does not vote in accordance with the party whip on any issue. In effect, the MP has no freedom to vote on any bill or on any other issue according to his perception of national interest; he has to vote in accordance with the diktat issued by the party.

It is pertinent that the Constitution of India does not have any mention of 'political party', with the exception of the issue of defections in the Tenth Schedule. It is interesting to note that no major country in North America or Western Europe has an anti-defection law. New Zealand enacted a law in 2001 that expired in 2005. Indeed, even most of the 40 countries that had an anti-defection law on the books restricted the application to the resignation or expulsion from the party by a member. In making the law applicable for voting against the party line, India has five countries for company: Pakistan, Bangladesh, Guyana, Zimbabwe, and Sierra Leone.[26]

The anti-defection bill was introduced in the context of a number of defections that made governments unstable. The state reasoning for the law was: 'The evil of political defections has been a matter of national concern. If it is not combated, it is likely to undermine the very foundations of our democracy and the principles which sustain it.'[27] However, the bill did not limit its application to defection but extended it to all votes.

The argument for having an anti-defection law is as follows. A given candidate is elected on a party ticket. His electors voted not just for him but also for the party. Therefore, he should be bound to follow the party line. However, this argument reduces every MP elected on

[26] Csaba Nikolenyi, 'Constitutional Sources of Party Cohesion' (Working Paper, Oslo-Rome Workshop on Democracy, The Norwegian Institute in Rome, Rome, 2011).

[27] Statement of Objects and Reasons, Constitution of India. (Fifty-Second Amendment) Bill, 1985.

a party ticket to a mere number to be counted in favour of the party line on every vote. It ignores the fact that political parties are coalitions of interests, and its members may share a broad philosophy but hold differing opinions on several specific issues. It also ignores the theory that MPs are expected to discuss issues from their own perception of national interests and reach common ground.

The anti-defection law also impinges on the issue of separation of powers (as pointed out in a Rajya Sabha debate).[28] The government of the day is formed by the party (or parties) having a majority in the Lok Sabha. We have seen that the Lok Sabha has a significant numerical advantage over the Rajya Sabha in case of a joint sitting. In light of the anti-defection law, every MP of the ruling coalition can be compelled to vote in accordance with a decision taken by the cabinet. This means that the executive has control over Parliament on all votes, including any legislative bill.

In practice, the anti-defection law has several other drawbacks. It reduces the incentive for MPs to consider the merits of various arguments since they are bound to toe the party line. It also reduces their accountability to their constituents as they can avoid defending their actions in any parliamentary vote by stating that it was not their personal view but that of the party. It may also require them, in some instances, to vote against the interests of their constituency.

Ironically, this law has failed to curb defections on several occasions when the stability of the government was at stake. Political parties may offer incentives (including ministerial positions) to defectors. For example, the government moved a confidence motion in 2008, and in the ensuing vote, 21 MPs defied the whips issued by their parties.[29] There were also allegations of large sums of cash being offered by the ruling coalition.[30]

[28] B. Jalan, Rajya Sabha Debates, 27 July 2006.

[29] '21 MPs Cross-voted During Parliament Trust Motion', *Economic Times*, 23 July 2008.

[30] Some Bharatiya Janata Party (BJP) MPs brought in bags of cash to Lok Sabha, which they claimed were offered to them. A parliamentary committee rejected the allegations (with notes of dissent). The committee report is available at http://164.100.47.132/LssNew/Committees/R-I-INQUIRE-ENG. pdf. Also see 'Going Rate of MPs at Rs. 25 Cr: Bardhan', NDTV.com. Web. 6 May 2016. Available at http://www.ndtv.com/video/player/news/going-rate-of-mps-at-rs-25-cr-bardhan/33778. The clip shows the General Secretary of the

The 2008 confidence vote episode also highlighted another implication of this law. Parliament is home to a large number of parties, and all governments between 1996 and 2014 were formed by coalitions of parties. Though the 2014 elections resulted in one party gaining a slight majority (52 per cent of the seats), the remaining seats were split between 36 parties, with the largest among them possessing 8 per cent of the membership of the Lok Sabha. As the anti-defection law considers political parties as units, the stability of a coalition government can be at risk if some of the constituent parties decide to leave the ruling coalition. The combination of a lack of inner party democracy, the whip system, and the anti-defection law is a possible reason for splintering of political parties. That is, any political leader can have greater influence if he controls a small party than if he is a senior member (but not the final decision maker) of a large party. This may result in him leaving the parent party to form his own party. A two-pronged solution has been suggested to address the issue. One proposal is to get rid of the anti-defection law. But if this first solution is not possible, a second solution would be to extend the anti-defection law to pre-poll alliances.[31]

Is there a way to balance the desire for stability with providing independence to MPs to vote according to their conscience? A private member bill (now lapsed) had suggested a formula.[32] The proposal would restrict the application of this law to votes of confidence, adjournment motions, and financial and money bills—or areas where the loss of the vote would be a censure of the government or require it to resign. On all other issues, MPs would be free to vote. They could still be subject to any disciplinary action by the party but they would retain their parliamentary membership.

Recorded Voting

Most motions in Parliament have a voice vote. The chair decides the outcome. If any MP disputes the decision of the chair, he can ask for a 'division'. This results in a recorded vote.

Communist Party of India alleging at a public rally that the going rate for 'buying' an MP was Rs 25 crore.

[31] See 'The Jalan Solution', *Business Standard*, 10 June 2010.

[32] Manish Tewari's private member's bill introduced in 2010 is available at http://164.100.24.219/BillsTexts/LSBillTexts/asintroduced/411ls.pdf.

The advantage of a recorded vote is that there is a track record of voting for each MP. This leads to greater accountability to the electorate as the MP could be asked to justify the way s/he voted. The Indian Parliament rarely exercises this option. During the five years of the fifteenth Lok Sabha, only 78 divisions related to 22 topics were called. This includes 27 occasions related to five constitutional amendment bills which required a recorded vote. Lok Sabha passed 175 ordinary bills (including money bills) during this period, of which only 11 bills had any division vote. In other words, 94 per cent of the bills were passed by voice vote, and we do not have a record of how each MP voted on these bills. Given that Parliament has the infrastructure (voting buttons on each MP's desk), implementing a recorded vote requirement is not a difficult task. This change can be achieved by a few MPs who can insist on a division on every occasion.

Resources for MPs

As the discussion in this chapter has shown, MPs have to undertake a number of functions. Every year, they have to consider 50 to 60 bills and study budgetary demands from ministries; they raise questions, bring important issues to the notice of the house, and, if so moved, introduce private member bills. They also have substantial committee work. For example, in the year 2010–11, the DRSC on Agriculture held 40 meetings, totalling 83 hours; the material presented to them for consideration totalled 4,300 pages.[33] MPs also have to consider various documents tabled in the house—committee reports, annual reports, CAG reports, and delegated legislation, among others—that total over 4,000 documents per year.[34]

It is a remarkable fact that Indian MPs have limited resources to fulfil their duties. The Parliament library has an excellent reference service but there is no research unit similar to those in some western democracies.[35] Therefore, they do not have an independent service

---

[33] Computed from data given in Lok Sabha Secretariat, *Departmentally Related Standing Committees: Summary of Work 31st August 2010 to 30th August 2011* (New Delhi: Government of India, 2011).

[34] Author's calculations based on daily bulletins of the Lok Sabha.

[35] For example, the Library of Congress in the US has the congressional research service, which provides detailed analysis on various bills and other

within Parliament that can provide non-partisan analytical research on bills and other issues that MPs may want to raise.

On an individual basis, each MP is allocated Rs 30,000 per month for his staff. This amount is insufficient to hire even one competent secretary, let alone a researcher. Contrast this with the US, where a senator is provided sufficient funds to hire 30–40 staff members, including over a dozen researchers, and the UK, where each MP has four to five support staff.[36] Indeed, the mistaken priorities are evident when one notes that MPs are allocated housing in New Delhi but do not have office space. Some of these issues—office space and research resources—need to be addressed if we wish MPs to be more effective in their parliamentary duties.

***

At the core of Parliament's role as an oversight body is the need for it to be able to act independently of the executive. There are two measures that could be taken, and both require an amendment to the Constitution. Article 85(1) of the Constitution states that the president shall summon Parliament at such time and place as he thinks fit, and fixes the maximum interval between two sessions at six months. An amendment to this article could be made, that requires Parliament to be summoned if a significant minority of members give a written notice. As the threshold value for moving a no-confidence motion is 50 MPs (about 10 per cent of the strength), it may be appropriate to set a similar threshold. The second suggestion relates to the anti-defection

issues. The British Parliament also has similar research groups within the Commons Library and the Lords Library.

[36] In 2013, the US provided an average funding of about $4 million per year to each Senator, of which about $3 million is for staff salaries; see 'Committee Reports—112th Congress (2011–2012)—Senate Report 112–197', Thomas.loc.gov, 6 May 2016, Accessed at http://thomas.loc.gov/cgi-bin/cpquery/?&sid=cp112N9Aoi&r_n=sr197.112&dbname=cp112&&sel=TOC_61782&. In the British Parliament, from April 2014, London Area MPs are reimbursed up to £145,500 per year and other MPs up to £138,600 per year for office staff; see Independent Parliamentary Standards Authority, 'Annual Review of the MPs' Scheme of Business Costs and Expenses 2014', HC 1122 (London: The Stationery Office).

law, which negates the very concept of an MP being a representative who weighs the merits of each issue and then decides his position on it. This should be reversed by omitting Article 102(2) and the Tenth Schedule of the Constitution. An intermediate solution could be to amend the Tenth Schedule so that an MP is disqualified only if he votes against the party whip on a no-confidence motion or a money bill.

A number of changes can be made by altering rules as well as by evolving conventions that lead to better practice. For example, announcing an annual calendar of sittings would not only help MPs plan their schedule, but also put pressure on the government to adhere to the schedule even when it faces the possibility of being asked tough questions. Changing the rules to give greater weight to the opposition parties would also help them keep the government in check.

Given that parliamentary committees examine issues in detail, there could be a case for strengthening their role. This includes providing them with dedicated research staff and consultant experts, making it mandatory for the government to respond to their recommendations, and requiring ministers to appear before them. The working of the committees could be made more transparent and accessible to the public by permitting media coverage of their meetings.

It is easy to tweak the rules to require that the final vote on any bill or motion needs a division. This change will enable citizens to learn how their MPs voted on various issues, and will build greater accountability of the representatives to their voters. Such a result can also be obtained if a few MPs decide that they would demand a division on every motion.

The composition of Parliament has changed after the 2014 general elections. For the first time since the eighth Lok Sabha (1984–9), a single party holds the majority in the house, albeit only a slight majority. However, in the Rajya Sabha, the ruling party (even including its allies) does not have a majority of seats. Given that about one-third of the members of the Rajya Sabha are elected every two years and the results depend upon the membership of state legislative assemblies, the ruling alliance cannot obtain a majority in that house before 2018. This configuration implies that there is no risk to the government of losing a confidence motion, but that it also needs the support of a few opposition parties to pass bills in Rajya Sabha. As we have discussed earlier, the government does have the option of calling for a joint session if it is unable to pass a bill, but this method has been rarely used in the past.

It would also need the support of other parties in both houses to pass an amendment to the Constitution.

How does this configuration affect the chances of reform to the procedures of Parliament? The key question is whether the government would want to make such reforms. Any change that increases the power of Parliament over the executive should find support from the opposition parties. The exception is the anti-defection law, which would be opposed by party bosses across the spectrum as it dilutes their power over their party MPs. Indeed, even the government is unlikely to modify this law as such a move would reduce its ability to get bills passed, and a repeal of the law could even threaten its stability.

The Indian Parliament has much to be proud of as a key institution of the Indian republic. From the early days of the republic, when some scholars predicted that the Indian union would not survive for long, it has provided a channel for negotiating competing interests and holding the country together. It has made many laws that have attacked entrenched social inequalities and helped usher in social change. It has adapted to changes in economic thinking. And on several occasions, it has held the government accountable for its actions and has successfully removed incumbent governments through parliamentary processes.

Having said that, there are several ways in which the performance of Parliament can be improved in its key roles as a law-making body, as an institution of accountability, and as the allocator of financial resources. This chapter identifies some of the factors that have impaired the effectiveness of the institution and suggests some measures to address these issues.

3

THE SUPREME COURT

Madhav Khosla and *Ananth Padmanabhan**

Even a bare perusal of news from India on any given day captures
the extraordinary place that the Indian Supreme Court has come to
occupy within public life. Yet, outside of careful and important legal
analyses of the Court and its doctrine, the institution (and the broader
judicial system) remains surprisingly understudied. The crucial contributions in various areas of Indian law have been largely written by
and for the legal community. Their attention has been devoted towards
legal doctrine and practice; it has been to unpack and demystify the
conversations that cover judicial hallways. But the Supreme Court is
not alone. It is situated in a broader political and social universe, and to
better understand the institution we must engage with that universe.
This chapter hopes to plug some holes in this regard and consider the
Supreme Court as a *public institution*. The Supreme Court has a dual
identity. It is both a legal institution—a court of law that has appellate
and constitutional powers—and a public institution that is required to
engage with, respond to, and negotiate the political pressures and social
expectations that surround it. The relationship between both these
roles is complex, and one beyond the scope of this chapter, though one
might note that in principle the Court could be a powerful political

* We are grateful to Saksham Khosla and Aidan Milliff for their valuable
search assistance and to the editors for helpful feedback.

institution, in the power and public legitimacy that it enjoys, and yet be a rather weak legal institution, in its capacity to both enforce justice and also in its internal doctrinal coherence and vision. Indeed, the current status of the Indian Supreme Court might not be too far from this picture. This chapter begins by considering the relationship between the Supreme Court and Indian democracy. It first examines the Court's practices of judicial review and the way in which the use of its power, say through developments like public interest litigation, have shaped the form of adjudication it performs. It then turns to the question of judicial appointments, especially recent controversies on how accountability and independence are to be secured within the higher judiciary. The chapter then explores the inner working of the Supreme Court, that is, its structure and functioning. This involves examining the rules that determine how the Court is approached, its bench structure, the management of case load, and so on. We also explore the topics of legal aid, a crucial component in assessing access to the institution, and the legal fraternity, whose organization and role has had major, if unexplored, consequences for judicial power and functioning in India.

The Supreme Court and Indian Democracy

The Practice of Judicial Review

The formal powers of the Supreme Court of India—the nature of its jurisdiction and authority—are the familiar stuff of legal scholarship. The Court's power to enforce fundamental rights, the range of its jurisdiction (from the authority to issue writs to admit appeals), and so forth have been subject to careful legal analyses.[1] However, the Supreme Court's place within the larger democratic framework in which it resides has invited markedly less attention. Both contemporary historical accounts as well as studies by political scientists reveal scant interest in the relationship between the Supreme Court and Indian democracy.

---

[1] See R. Vakil, 'Jurisdiction', in *The Oxford Handbook of the Indian Constitution*, eds S. Choudhry, M. Khosla, and P.B. Mehta (Oxford: Oxford University Press, 2016), 367; A. Padmanabhan, 'Rights: Breadth, Scope, and Applicability', in *The Oxford Handbook of the Indian Constitution*, 581; G. Subramanium, 'Writs and Remedies', in *The Oxford Handbook of the Indian Constitution*, 614.

In other words, there has been surprisingly limited scholarship on the Supreme Court as a public institution, in contrast with an institution that is simply a neutral arbiter of legal disputes.

If such disinterest may have been justified in the early years of the Indian republic—and that very much remains an open question—it seems impossible to justify today. It is hard to imagine any major issue in Indian political life which has not become the subject of legal contestation. The Supreme Court is today a crucial actor within Indian politics. It intervenes in even the most ordinary of political matters; its voice has become a fixture in the daily rituals and drama of democratic life. How can we account for this fact and how might we make sense of the Court's journey through the course of independent India?

There are two aspects to the Supreme Court's emergence as one of India's most significant public institutions. The first has to do with an enlarged understanding of what falls within the Court's ambit. Since the late 1970s, India's representative institutions—namely the legislature and the executive—have weakened. This weakening has been linked to both the ineffectiveness and the corruption associated with these institutions. The Court's emergence in Indian politics occurred against the backdrop of this decline. It positioned itself as an institution that was responsive and capable, as well as one that was committed to larger substantive socio-economic goals. This repositioning of the Court was noticeably distinct from its identity in the 1950s and 1960s. To be sure, in these years the Court made a range of powerful decisions and hardly acquiesced to the other branches of government. A notable example would be the protection of private property. Yet, the Court's ambit was narrowly defined, and its self-conception was clear.

Scholars have taken note of the Court's reinvention through the 1970s, some paying attention to changed practices of constitutional interpretation over time, with others highlighting the importance of political events like the Emergency.[2] But it is important to notice that the Court's reinvention occurred through two legal developments, which took place by and large simultaneously. One was an enlargement

---

[2] See S.P. Sathe, 'India: From Positivism to Structuralism', in *Interpreting Constitutions: A Comparative Study*, ed. J Goldsworthy (New York: Oxford University Press, 2006), 215; G. Austin, *Working a Democratic Constitution: A History of the Indian Experience* (New Delhi: Oxford University Press, 1999).

of the subjects considered fit for judicial resolution. In the early 1970s, the Court put forth the basic structure doctrine, by which it placed limits on Parliament's power to amend the Constitution.[3] A subsequent development was the emergence of substantive due process. This principle, which the Supreme Court had previously rejected in *A.K. Gopalan*, became a constitutional guarantee in *Maneka Gandhi*.[4] The Court now declared it suitable to judicially consider the fairness of a range of legislation (like preventive detention laws) on non-procedural grounds. Another crucial instance of the broadening of judicial matters was a reinterpretation of the word 'life' in Article 21 of the Constitution. The right to life was interpreted to guarantee an astonishingly wide range of socio-economic goods, an interpretation which effectively made the explicitly unenforceable directive principles of state policy enforceable. There were now, through these interpretive moves, a host of questions and topics and concerns which acquired *legal* significance. A range of matters that had been part of political life, from the substantive character of constitutional amendments to the social welfare policies, were transformed into matters of law.

These developments in the substantive character of the guarantees which the Constitution offered were accompanied by procedural developments. Through 'public interest litigation', which diluted standing requirements and allowed petitioners to approach the Court even though they themselves had suffered no legal injury, the Court made itself readily available for redressing a host of public grievances. The relaxation of *locus standi* occurred alongside other procedural changes in the judicial process. Interim orders emerged as a form of ordinary judicial relief, proactive steps were taken to reach out to different

---

[3] See *Kesavananda Bharati v. State of Kerala*, (1973) 4 SCC 225; R. Dhavan, *The Supreme Court of India and Parliamentary Sovereignty: A Critique of Its Approach to the Recent Constitutional Crisis* (New Delhi: Sterling Publishers, 1976); M. Khosla, 'Constitutional Amendment', in *The Oxford Handbook of the Indian Constitution*, 232.

[4] See *A.K. Gopalan v. State of Madras*, AIR 1950 SC 27; *Maneka Gandhi v. Union of India*, (1978) 1 SCC 248; T.R. Andhyarujina, 'The Evolution of Due Process of Law by the Supreme Court', in B.N. Kirpal *et al.* eds, *Supreme but Not Infallible: Essays in Honour of the Supreme Court of India* (New Delhi: Oxford University Press, 2000), 193.

interest groups, it became standard practice for the Court to assume a kind of supervisory role, and so forth. If an expansive interpretation of constitutional guarantees altered the character of disputes, public interest litigation and its associated process-based developments changed the nature of litigation and adjudication. The Supreme Court became accessible and involved in hitherto unseen ways—even if such access and involvement was very much mediated by an elite set of lawyers and activists—and made its decisions through negotiation, compromise, and interaction between different stake holders as if it were an overarching omnipotent body supervising the unravelling of Indian democracy.[5]

These substantive and procedural developments were crucial to the Supreme Court's repositioning,[6] but a second crucial feature of the Court's emergence relates to the internal doctrinal character of its decisions and its approach towards legal reasoning. The Court's framing of legal questions, its determination of fault, and its awarding of remedies all made it a 'player' in Indian democracy—an actor in an ongoing set of political interactions. The Court's routine involvement has made it extremely active, but this activism, as it were, has taken place alongside considerable conformism in terms of the merits of particular decisions. At the very least, what this means is that in substantive terms, the Supreme Court does far less than its visibility and self-proclaimed narrative might suggest. In the case of socio-economic rights, for example,

---

[5] On public interest litigation and its associated developments, see U. Baxi, 'Judicial Discourse: Dialectics of the Face and the Mask', *Journal of the Indian Law Institute* 35, no. 1 (January–June 1993): 1–12; U. Baxi, 'Taking Suffering Seriously: Social Action Litigation in the Supreme Court of India', *Third World Legal Studies* 4, no. 6 (June 1985): 107; C.D. Cunningham, 'Public Interest Litigation in the Indian Supreme Court: A Study in Light of American Experience', *Journal of the Indian Law Institute* 29, no. 4 (January 1987): 494–523; P.P. Craig and S.L. Deshpande, 'Rights, Autonomy and Process: Public Interest Litigation in India', *Oxford Journal of Legal Studies* 9, no. 3 (Autumn 1989): 356.

[6] These developments can also be studied as part of a larger global trend towards the enhanced presence and influence of the judiciary in politics, a trend appropriately branded the 'judicialization of politics'. See R. Hirschl, 'The Judicialization of Politics', in *The Oxford Handbook of Law and Politics*, eds G. A. Caldeira, R.D. Kelemen, and K.E. Whittington (New York: Oxford University Press, 2008), 119–41.

while the Court has recognized rights such as the right to education, the right to health, and so on, this recognition has not been matched by the awarding of strong remedies.[7]

The modesty of specific remedies has been witnessed across the spectrum. On corruption, for example, the Supreme Court has done little to truly ruffle political feathers and challenge the state. The more serious consequence of the Court's form of legal adjudication, where law is not developed through the parsing of texts and principles but instead through the perceived interests of different groups, has been its implications for the rule of law. As Pratap Bhanu Mehta has argued, 'the Court's concern for its own authority has meant a reading of the political tea leaves as it were; the judicialization of politics and the politicization of the judiciary have turned out to be two sides of the same coin'.[8] The rise of the Supreme Court, as Mehta notes, should not be confused with the rise of constitutionalism. The Court's legitimacy has been closely linked to its ability to satisfy different agendas and to intervene through affirmance of the prevailing gestalt, rather than reshaping public opinion. In doctrinal terms, this has meant that the courtroom is hardly what Ronald Dworkin once famously termed as 'the forum of principle'.[9] In a sense, the remarkable achievement of the Supreme Court in Indian politics has been its capacity to be openly political—not in the way that Western judiciaries are often thought to be (where judges are often alleged to have clear associations with specific political interests), but rather in the sense that its adjudicatory techniques guide and intervene in a set of compromises between different players rather than ruthlessly settle questions of right and wrong in

[7] See M. Khosla, 'Making Social Rights Conditional: Lessons from India', *International Journal of Constitutional Law* 8, no. 4 (October 2010): 739.

[8] P.B. Mehta, 'India's Judiciary: The Promise of Uncertainty', in *Public Institutions in India: Performance and Design*, eds D. Kapur and P.B. Mehta (New Delhi: Oxford University Press, 2005), 158, 171. See also P.B. Mehta, 'The Rise of Judicial Sovereignty', *Journal of Democracy* 18, no. 2 (April 2007): 70; P.B. Mehta, 'The Supreme Court and the Art of Democratic Positioning', in *Unstable Constitutionalism: Law and Politics in South Asia*, eds M. Tushnet and M. Khosla (New York: Cambridge University Press, 2015), 233.

[9] R. Dworkin, 'The Forum of Principle', *New York University Law Review* 56, nos 2–3 (May–June 1981): 469.

strong rule of law terms. Many of the fears that were once voiced with regard to group litigation in the UK—that is, a jettisoning of the values of independence, rationality, and finality—have come to be true in the Indian context.[10]

Such an approach has been central to the Court occupying a seat in the front row of Indian politics, but it should not be viewed as simply an attempt to preserve its own power. Often, the departure from rule of law characteristics occurs out of a concern for the viability of judicial outcomes. In other words, the Court has no option but to work in a universe of dysfunctional public institutions; any attempt to ignore that would only mean the irrelevance of its decisions. The cloud of state failure hangs over Indian constitutionalism. Indians have turned to the Supreme Court as the saviour of their democracy—as the institution which can bring integrity into politics, which can enable social justice and welfare policies—out of a lack of other alternatives. On certain specific issues, such as in the areas of accountability and governance or in the daily workings of welfare schemes, the Court's interventions have often been crucial and, at the very least, they have highlighted matters which the ordinary political process has been able to avoid. But the entry into lands where judiciaries rarely traverse has meant a significant departure from ordinary practices of judicial review. In addition to the issue of constitutional legitimacy, such departures also prompt the all-important question of whether judges of the Supreme Court possess the competence and expertise to enter such unconventional terrains. Over the long term, it remains to be seen whether such departures mark a positive development not simply for Indian democracy but also for Indian constitutionalism.

Judicial Independence and Accountability

The Supreme Court's emergence and place within Indian democracy has been made possible through its practices of judicial review. A second crucial factor in preserving the Court's position has been the procedure for the appointment of judges. Judicial independence has many facets—the financial autonomy of the judiciary, the mechanism for the

---

[10] See C. Harlow, 'Public Law and Popular Justice', *Modern Law Review* 65, no. 1 (January 2002): 1.

transfer of judges, post-retirement norms for judges, and so forth—but above all, it is secured by the way in which judges are appointed.[11] Under Articles 124 and 217 of the Constitution, appointments to the higher judiciary are to be made by the executive in consultation with the judiciary. In what are now known as the Three Judges Cases, the Supreme Court interpreted these provisions to hold that the collegium of the Supreme Court (the five most senior judges, including the Chief Justice of India) would have control over appointments to the Supreme Court and High Courts.[12]

The collegium system for appointments emerged out of executive interference with the judiciary during and after the Emergency. Judicial independence was regarded as central to India's separation of powers scheme, and control over appointments to the judiciary was considered to be the chief means for securing this independence. Despite the fact that the *Three Judges Cases* seemed difficult to reconcile with the bare text of Articles 124 and 217, the collegium system managed to survive because of the legitimacy enjoyed by the judiciary, in comparison with the legislature–executive. There were few reasons to believe that appointments by the representative organs of the state would not suffer from corruption and nepotism, corroding the judiciary in the same fashion as other public institutions had been corroded. Thus, although there were regular political calls and even formal attempts to create a new system for appointments, none led to any tangible change.

In 2014, a change was finally witnessed with the enactment of the 99th Amendment to the Constitution and the National Judicial Appointments Commission Act. These enactments took place amid growing concern with judicial accountability in India. In sharp contrast to the independence concern which had motivated and secured the collegium system, judicial accountability now acquired prominence. The collegium system's opaque character and its lack

---

[11] For an excellent empirical and historical study on the factors that have shaped the appointment of judges to the Supreme Court, see A. Chandrachud, *The Informal Constitution: Unwritten Criteria in Selecting Judges for the Supreme Court of India* (New Delhi: Oxford University Press, 2014).

[12] *SP Gupta v. Union of India*, (1981) Supp SCC 87; *Supreme Court Advocates-on-Record Association v. Union of India*, (1993) 4 SCC 441; *Re Special Reference No 1 of 1998*, (1998) 7 SCC 739.

of transparency were attacked amid growing discontent with the Indian judiciary. Incidents of mismanagement and internal conflict, episodes of corruption and professional impropriety, increasing doctrinal uncertainty and incoherence, and an incapacity to deliver tangible outcomes had all contributed to growing dissatisfaction with the judiciary. Two decades after its creation, it became politically feasible to replace the collegium system.[13] The judiciary's attempt at self-regulation was thought to have failed and external regulation was necessary. The 99th Amendment to the Constitution and the National Judicial Appointments Commission Act put in place a federal commission for the appointment of judges. Expectedly, such changes were challenged, and a four-to-one majority of the Supreme Court held that the impugned measures violated the basic structure of the Constitution.[14]

An interesting feature of the Supreme Court's decision was its clarification of the existing appointment scheme. This scheme, as laid down by the *Three Judges Cases*, was alleged to give the Court exclusive and complete control over the appointment process. Instead, the Court argued that the government's own memoranda for Supreme Court and High Court appointments, issued in 1999, showed that the executive did, in fact, have a role to play in appointments. These memoranda were drafted after the *Three Judges Cases* to provide clarity on the precise mechanism of how appointments were to be made. On the specific issue of the executive's role, the memorandum for Supreme Court appointments specifies that the opinion of the members of the collegium and the relevant High Court judge would be transmitted to the executive. The final recommendation of the Chief Justice would be sent to the Union Ministry for Law, Justice, and Company Affairs, who would forward the same to the prime minister, who in turn would

[13] The Constitution (99th Amendment) Bill that replaced the collegium system met with unanimous support in both the Lok Sabha and the Rajya Sabha. At the time of voting, only the All India Anna Dravida Munnetra Kazhagam abstained from voting on the Bill in the Lok Sabha. There were no dissenters. The Bill was also ratified by 16 of the state legislatures.

[14] *Supreme Court Advocates-on-Record Association* v. *Union of India*, 2015 SCC Online SC 964. The following analysis draws on M. Khosla, 'Pick and Choose: Judicial Appointments in India', *ConstitutionNet*, 30 October 2015.

advise the president as regards the appointment.[15] In the case of the High Courts, the memorandum states that once the Chief Justice of India has sent the recommendation to the Union Minister of Law, Justice and Company Affairs, the minister would then obtain the views of the concerned state government and subsequently submit the proposal to the prime minister, who would in turn advise the president.[16]

A simple reading of these memoranda does not seem to indicate any special role for the executive; that is to say, the role seems to be formal. Yet, the Supreme Court's reliance upon them for the claim that the allegation of judicial exclusivity in appointments was false indicates the extent of opacity in the appointment process: both the judiciary and the executive did not even have a common understanding of how appointments are in fact made, regardless of the merits of the process. The Court's reliance on the memoranda reframed the question posed by the impugned measures. Rather than judicial exclusivity, the question was whether judicial independence required judicial *primacy* in the appointment process.

The Court argued that the composition of the proposed National Judicial Appointments Commission violated judicial independence. The Commission was to include six members: the Chief Justice of India, two senior Supreme Court judges, the Union Minister for Law and Justice, and two 'eminent persons'. Under the scheme outlined, Justice Khehar noted that the two eminent persons could reject all recommendations by themselves; the vesting of such powers in persons unconnected with the administration of justice was declared arbitrary. The role of the Union Minister for Law and Justice was similarly attacked by the bench. His inclusion was thought to raise major conflict of interests, given the extent of government litigation before the Court. Justice Lokur noted further that entrusting the Union Minister with such a role would tamper with the principle of cabinet responsibility. The Court noted that the constitutional scheme of mandatory consultations between the president and

---

[15] Memorandum showing the procedure for appointment of the Chief Justice of India and judges of the Supreme Court of India, http://doj.gov.in/ sites/ default/ files/ memosc.pdf, accessed January 2016.

[16] Memorandum showing the procedure for appointment and transfer of Chief Justices and judges of High Courts, http://doj.gov.in/ sites/ default/ files/ memohc.pdf, accessed January 2016.

chief justice was made a sham exercise through the impugned measures, with the Commission as an intermediary.

A large part of the Court's reasoning was based upon a perceived belief about how the Commission would work. Concerns were voiced by the Court over the bargaining between different actors that the impugned scheme would bring out, and the kinds of pressures that were likely to be at work. The state suggested that the judiciary should view the proposal with some degree of trust, and that the process had the potential to be deliberative. But the Court's response was similar: the collegium system too had the potential to be deliberative. In the end, which reasoning we find persuasive turns on whether we would rather trust the judiciary or the executive, and whether we see more dangers emerging from a lack of judicial independence or a lack of judicial accountability.

However, at least two observations may be made about this recent development and the road ahead. First, the legislature–executive seem to have lost a genuinely worthy opportunity to replace the collegium system. Two decades on, the system's charm had expired, but the 99th Amendment to the Constitution and the National Judicial Appointments Commission Act were riddled with a number of concerns. These range from poor drafting, like in the case of undefined 'eminent persons', to the structure of the Commission, which offered several opportunities for undue executive influence. A more carefully constructed proposal, which may have given the judiciary primacy but had a genuine, meaningful role for the executive, would have been very hard for the Court to strike down. Second, by striking down the measure and reinstating the collegium system, the Court has only increased further scrutiny of its decisions. In its decision, the Court acknowledged the failures of the collegium system and vowed to improve the process. Although it has commenced consultations with the bar and the executive over how the collegium system might be reformed, it remains to be seen what such improvements would be. Importantly, however, the Court is no longer in the position that it was two or three decades ago. Over the past decade, it has lost much of the comparative institutional legitimacy that it once enjoyed. Unless it can look inward, tackling both doctrinal incoherence and administrative mismanagement, not to mention major concerns regarding corruption and accountability, its time in the sun is unlikely to last.

The Supreme Court: Structure and Functioning

A knowledge of the structure and design of the Supreme Court is crucial to the study of its efficacy. As Nick Robinson has shown, different structural approaches promote different conceptions of a highest court's functions and values.[17] The study of structure extends to all operational aspects of the Supreme Court's functioning, the most important of these being the jurisdiction of the Court, its work allocation across benches, the norms and practices governing admissions, final hearings, adjournments, and urgent motions, and the supervisory role it plays in the functioning of the High Courts and the lower judiciary.

Of these, the jurisdiction of the court is detailed in the Constitution but the remaining aspects are covered sketchily, if at all. Article 145 of the Constitution of India leaves most operational aspects to be worked out through the rules framed by the Court, with presidential approval. Recently, the Supreme Court Rules 2013 came into effect, repealing the earlier 1966 rules. These rules, like the repealed set, are comprehensive, covering a whole gamut of matters integral to the functioning of the Court. These include the format of the various petitions and appeals, the professional standards governing advocates and advocates-on-record, the registry of the Court, summons and notices to parties, and so on. Aspects of these rules feature in the following discussion.

Pathways to the Supreme Court

Table 3.1 enumerates the different procedural pathways through which a case can reach the Supreme Court. Of these, the most important is the appellate route, and within the appellate route, the appeals that come up before the Court by way of special leave under Article 136 of the Constitution.

Interestingly, Article 136 was originally intended by the drafters of the Constitution to be minimally used. They apprehended that a wide exercise of the discretionary power contained here would eventually result in flooding the Court with too many appeals.[18] Moreover, when

[17] N. Robinson, 'Structure Matters: The Impact of Court Structure on the Indian and U.S. Supreme Courts', *American Journal of Comparative Law* 61, no. 1 (Winter 2013): 173–208.

[18] Vakil, 'Jurisdiction'.

Table 3.1 Jurisdiction of the Supreme Court

Type of Jurisdiction	Description
Appeals under the Constitution	(i) **Article 132**: Appeal to the Supreme Court from any judgement, decree, or final order of a High Court, whether in civil, criminal, or other proceedings, if the High Court certifies that the case involves a substantial question of law as to the interpretation of the Constitution.
	(ii) **Article 133**: Appeal to the Supreme Court from any judgement, decree or final order in a civil proceeding of a High Court if the High Court certifies that the case involves a substantial question of law of general importance and in its opinion the said question needs to be decided by the Supreme Court.
	(iii) **Article 134**: Appeal to the Supreme Court from any judgement, final order, or sentence in a criminal proceeding of a High Court if (a) it has on appeal reversed an order of acquittal of an accused person and sentenced him to death, or (b) has withdrawn for trial before itself, any case from any Court subordinate to it and has in such trial convicted the accused and sentenced him to death, or (c) it certifies that the case is a fit one for appeal to the Supreme Court.
	(iv) **Article 136**: Supreme Court may, in its discretion, grant special leave to appeal from any judgement, decree, determination, sentence, or order in any case or matter passed or made by any Court or tribunal in the territory of India except the Court or tribunal constituted by or under any law relating to the armed forces.
Statutory Appeals	(i) **Section 379 of the Code of Criminal Procedure, 1973**: Appeal from any judgement, final order, or sentence in a criminal proceeding of a High Court, if the High Court (a) has on appeal reversed an order of acquittal of an accused person and sentenced him to death or to

(*Cont'd*)

Table 3.1   (*Cont'd*)

Type of Jurisdiction	Description

imprisonment for life or to imprisonment for a period of not less than ten years; (b) has withdrawn for trial before itself any case from any Court subordinate to its authority and has in such trial convicted the accused person and sentenced him to imprisonment for life or to imprisonment for a period of not less than ten years.

(ii) **Section 130E of the Customs Act, 1962**: Appeal from any judgement of the High Court on a reference made under Section 130, in any case which the High Court certifies to be a fit one for appeal to the Supreme Court, or any order passed by the Appellate Tribunal relating to the rate of custom duty or the value of goods for the purpose of assessment.

(iii) **Section 35L of the Central Excise and Salt Act, 1944**: Appeal from any judgement of the High Court delivered on a reference made under Section 35G, in any case which the High Court certifies to be a fit one for appeal to the Supreme Court, or any order passed by the Appellate Tribunal relating to the rate of duty of excise or the value of goods for purposes of assessment.

(iv) **Section 23 of the Consumer Protection Act, 1986**: Appeal from orders made by the National Commission.

(v) **Section 19(1)(b) of the Contempt of Courts Act, 1971**: Appeal, as of right, from any order or decision of Division Bench of a High Court in exercise of its jurisdiction to punish for contempt.

(vi) **Section 38 of the Advocates Act, 1961**: Appeal from an order made by the Disciplinary Committee of the Bar Council of India.

Table 3.1   (Cont'd)

Type of Jurisdiction	Description
	(vi) **Section 116A of the Representation of People Act, 1951**: Appeal on any question, whether of law or fact, from every order passed by a High Court under Section 98 or Section 99 of the said Act.
	(vii) **Section 10 of the Special Court (Trial of offences relating to Transactions in Securities) Act, 1992**: Appeal from any judgement, sentence, or order not being interlocutory order, of the special court, both on fact and on law.
	(viii) **Section 18 of the Telecom Regulatory Authority of India Act, 1997**: Appeal against any order not being an interlocutory order, of the Appellate Tribunal (TDSAT), on one or more of the grounds specified in Section 100 of Code of Civil Procedure.
	(ix) **Section 15(z) of the Securities and Exchange Board of India Act, 1992**: Appeal from any order or decision of the Securities Appellate Tribunal on any question of law arising from such order.
	(x) **Section 261 of the Income Tax Act, 1961**: Appeal from any judgement of the High Court made on reference or appeal, upon certification by the High Court as a fit case for appeal.
	(xi) **Section 53T of the Competition Act, 2002**: Appeal against any decision or order of the Competition Appellate Tribunal.
Original Jurisdiction	(i) **Article 32**: Writ jurisdiction for enforcement of fundamental rights.
	(ii) **Article 131**: Jurisdiction over disputes between the Centre and one or more States or between the States themselves.
	(iii) **Article 71**: Jurisdiction over disputes relating to the election of a President or Vice-President.

(Cont'd)

Table 3.1 (*Cont'd*)

Type of Jurisdiction	Description
Transfer Jurisdiction	(i) **Article 139A(1)**: Power to transfer to itself cases pending either before the Supreme Court and one or more High Courts, or before more than one High Court.
	(ii) **Article 139A(2)**: Power to transfer a case from one High Court to another.
	(iii) **Section 125 of the Code of Civil Procedure, 1908**: Power to transfer a suit, appeal, or other proceedings from a High Court or other civil court in one State to a High Court or other civil court in any other State.
	(iv) **Section 406 of the Code of Criminal Procedure, 1973**: Power to transfer any case or appeal from one High Court to another, or from a criminal court subordinate to one High Court to another criminal Court of equal or superior jurisdiction, subordinate to another High Court.
Advisory Jurisdiction	(i) **Article 143(1)**: Opinion of the Court offered in cases where the President seeks such opinion because the case involves a question of law or fact of an expedient nature and public importance.
	(ii) **Article 317**: Opinion of the Court offered in cases where the President seeks such opinion, involving the merits of an enquiry for removal of the Chairman or any other member of a Public Service Commission on the ground of misbehaviour.
Statutory References	(i) **Section 257 of Income Tax Act, 1961**: The Income Tax Appellate Tribunal can, through its President, refer to the Supreme Court, any question of law on which there is difference of opinion between different High Courts.
	(ii) **Section 14(1)/17(1) of the Right to Information Act, 2005**: President of India/Governor of a State refers to the Supreme Court to conduct

(*Cont'd*)

Table 3.1   (*Cont'd*)

Type of Jurisdiction	Description
	enquiry and report on the question of removal of Chief Information Commissioner/State Chief Information Commissioner or any Information Commissioner/State Information Commissioner on the ground of proven misbehaviour or incapacity.
Review Jurisdiction	**Article 137:** Supreme Court has the power to review any judgement pronounced or order made by it.
Curative Petition	As held in *Rupa Ashok Hurra* v. *Ashok Hurra*, (2002) 4 SCC 388, even after dismissal of a review petition under Article 137 of the Constitution, the Supreme Court may entertain a curative petition and reconsider its judgement/order, in exercise of its inherent powers in order to prevent abuse of its process, and to cure gross miscarriage of justice.

Source: Based on *Supreme Court of India Practice & Procedure: A Handbook of Information* (3rd edition, 2010), available at http://supremecourtofindia.nic.in/handbook3rdedition.pdf.

the Court, in its first two decades, liberally granted leave to appeal, Parliament responded by enhancing the criminal appellate jurisdiction of the Supreme Court,[19] and removing the pecuniary limit for civil appeals that required the dispute to be above a particular value to merit the Court's consideration.[20] These measures were introduced to ensure that in cases involving substantial questions of law or those where the stakes were high, appeals would automatically lie without the need for a separate admissions hearing. However, despite these efforts to widen the Court's normal appellate powers, and thus indirectly nudge towards self-regulation of its discretionary appellate power, the Court has continued expanding the scope of Article 136 to the point where it is unclear what is excluded from its purview.

[19] Supreme Court (Enlargement of Criminal Appellate Jurisdiction) Act, 1970.
[20] Constitution (30th Amendment) Act, 1972.

This move has, in turn, led to a rapid rise in the admission matters instituted before the Court at a scale much higher than the regular hearing cases, thereby moulding the court's identity in a particular direction. In the mere five-year period from 1976 to 1981—the crucial Emergency and post-Emergency years—the number of admission matters went up five fold.[21] This number has again nearly tripled over the present post-liberalization phase.[22] Between 2005 and 2011, the number of cases appealed to the Supreme Court increased by 44.8 per cent and the number of cases the Court accepted for regular hearing increased by 74.5 per cent. However, the number of cases disposed of by the subordinate courts increased marginally by about 7.8 per cent during this timeframe, indicating that litigants were bypassing the subordinate judiciary and appealing to the Supreme Court wherever possible. The increasing acceptance of such appeals by the Court was also signalling them in this direction.[23]

The admission-heavy character of the court's weekly docket— Mondays and Fridays are now almost exclusively devoted to admission hearings—has resulted in three significant problems. The first is the arrears or pendency problem in the Supreme Court because of the sheer number of appeals arising from all over the country against orders—interim or final, passed by courts or tribunals—involving criminal, civil, regulatory, and commercial disputes. While the total arrears do not appear so alarming when contrasted with the pendency in the High Courts and lower courts, two factors are worth noting. First, the fact that Supreme Court arrears are spread over a total judicial strength of a mere 31 judges, unlike the pendency figures for the other courts, makes it all the more difficult for the Court to reduce its pendency in the coming years. This is particularly so because increasing judge strength in the Supreme Court is not an easy process, requiring as it

[21] N. Robinson, 'A Quantitative Analysis of the Indian Supreme Court's Workload', *Journal of Empirical Legal Studies* 10, no. 3 (August 2013): 570–601.

[22] 20,435 admission matters were filed in 1992. The figure for 2014 (through the end of November) was 67,965. See *Supreme Court Annual Report, 2014–15*, available at http://supremecourtofindia.nic.in/annualreport/annual-report2014-15.pdf.

[23] N. Robinson, 'India's Judicial Architecture', in *The Oxford Handbook of the Indian Constitution*.

does a parliamentary enactment.[24] Moreover, the Court, as a matter of convention, does not function through resort to retired Supreme Court and High Court judges appointed on an ad hoc basis for disposal of arrears.[25]

Second, that the pendency is disproportionately higher with regular hearing cases as compared to admission hearings seriously hampers the court's role as a legal institution.[26] To illustrate this further, consider the latest available figures for initiation and pendency of admission and regular hearing cases. In 2014, till the month of November, 67,965 admission cases were instituted, as opposed to 13,618 regular hearing cases. However, the pendency figure for admission cases is at 35,284, while that for regular hearing cases is at a disproportionately high 29,635. A possible explanation for this is that the high institution of admission cases has considerably reduced the time available for conducting regular hearings, thus clogging the disposal of final hearing cases. This is also borne out by some of the data, which shows that while 7 per cent of regular hearing matters had been pending for more than five years in 2004, the percentage had shot up to 17 per cent by 2011, that is, within a short span of seven years.[27] In 2011, 41 per cent of five-judge-bench matters and 67.8 per cent of three-judge-bench matters were pending for more than five years,[28] a particularly telling fact because a good many cases before such benches involve questions of constitutional significance. The more parties are made to wait for the final disposal of their cases, the lesser would be their perception of the Court as an effective legal institution.

[24] Article 124(1), Constitution of India.

[25] Technically, under Article 128, authority vests with the Chief Justice of India to request specific individuals from the pool of retired Supreme Court and High Court judges to serve on an *ad hoc* basis with prior presidential approval.

[26] Regular hearing cases include both (a) cases where the Court has to mandatorily hear and dispose the appeal under law, and (b) where the Court has applied its discretion and admitted the appeal, thus expressing willingness to hear the appeal on its merits.

[27] N. Robinson, 'A Quantitative Analysis of the Indian Supreme Court's Workload'.

[28] Robinson, 'Quantitative Analysis'. The monthly statements issued by the Court after 2011 do not contain this detail.

The allied problem with an admissions-heavy system is that the serious responsibility of the higher judiciary—declaring and refining the law on a case-by-case basis—suffers. Regular hearings are the mainstay of a common law system, with the apex court at the top of the judicial edifice, laying down precedents for courts below to follow. Unless regular hearings are actually conducted on a timely basis, appeals will not get finally disposed of, resulting in parties to a dispute losing faith in the legal process itself. Even when regular hearings take place, the Court has very little control over the time allotted for such hearings. While it is common practice for the bar to justify prolonged hearings on the ground that adjudicating complicated legal issues cannot be time-bound,[29] it is time the Supreme Court led by example and started imposing rigid timelines for completion of oral hearings. This reform could lead to much faster disposal of cases by the Supreme Court, adoption of a similar mechanism by High Courts to curb prolonged oral hearings, as well as drastic improvement in the quality of written briefs and arguments filed before courts in India.

Moreover, the irregularity in regular hearings can lead to ineffective response mechanisms on the part of the Court to refine or correct poor precedent. This is striking in the case of commercial litigation, as seen from the example of the Arbitration and Conciliation Act, 1996, and case law governing the scope of judicial intervention in both domestic and international arbitrations. The Court's precedents have resulted in virtual paralysis of the arbitral panel appointment process, and confusion regarding the enforcement of international arbitral awards. Yet, each subsequent response from the Court to the problem has taken several intervening years, with the matter getting stuck before larger benches. In the interim, courts below are befuddled as to the correct approach, and divergent views emerge from multiple lower courts, contributing to confusion in the minds of commercial actors who look to the law to organize their affairs in advance. Litigation relating to higher education offers a similar story. Both higher educational institutions and prospective students are left to the mercy of the Court finally

[29] This is an almost baseless claim, considering similar issues of deep constitutional or legal significance are disposed of by the US Supreme Court through oral hearings that last for hours, not days or months as is the norm with the Indian Supreme Court.

getting down to slot time for the actual hearing of the case, and must perforce rely on piecemeal orders in the interim that offer little regulatory guidance.

Despite the surge in admission matters, and the consequential pendency problem, the Court has unfortunately been unwilling to exercise its discretion carefully or frame clear guidelines to curtail unbridled resort to Article 136. In its own words, this provision is 'an untrammelled reservoir of power incapable of being confined by definitional bounds',[30] which can be deployed to fix 'grave injustice'[31] or redress conduct 'shocking the conscience of the court'.[32] The irony of the situation is that the Court, after almost six years since a larger bench reference was made by a two-judge bench seeking broad guidelines for the exercise of its discretion under Article 136, recently declined to frame any guidelines.[33] The Court held that 'in the interest of justice', it would be better to exercise its discretionary power 'with circumspection, rather than to limit the power forever'.[34] There can be no clearer invitation to parties to partake in the lottery that the special leave petition (SLP) admission process has become. This verdict will further clog the wheels of the regular hearing system. It would be arguably more effective, therefore, to experiment with novel ways to tackle the admission process itself, especially on the lines of replacing oral hearings with in-chamber deliberation on the drafted petitions. The Court already operates differently in the case of curative petitions,[35] a novel form of judicially crafted relief, listed in Table 3.1. The Court could also consider creating a separate pool of judges, selected on rotating basis, who are exclusively dedicated to deciding on admissions, thus guaranteeing that the others can devote their time and expertise exclusively to

---

[30] *Kunhayammed* v. *State of Kerala*, (2000) 6 SCC 359.

[31] *Pritam Singh* v. *The State* AIR 1950 SC 169; *State of Madhya Pradesh* v. *Ramkrishna Ganpatrao Limsey* AIR 1954 SC 20; *Gian Singh* v. *State of Punjab* (1974) 4 SCC 305.

[32] *Haripada Dey* v. *State of West Bengal*, AIR 1956 SC 757; *Hindustan Tin Works* v. *Employees*, (1979) 2 SCC 80.

[33] The reference was made in *Mathai* v. *George*, SLP (C) No.7105/2010, vide order dated 19 March 2010.

[34] Order dated 11 January 2016, in *Mathai* v. *George*.

[35] See Or. XLVIII, R.4 of the Supreme Court Rules, 2013.

the authoring of well-reasoned judgements in regular hearing cases all through the working week. However, there is a political economy built around the admissions system. The incentive structure, particularly for the senior advocates at the bar, is such that they earn much more, for likely less effort, from a short SLP admission matter on a Monday or Friday rather than by way of a regular hearing on other days. As Pratap Bhanu Mehta points out, Justice Krishna Iyer's remark in *Easwara Iyer* v. *Registrar, Supreme Court*,[36] that many oral arguments could be replaced with written submissions, provoked a strike that continued till the government of the day stepped in to declare that no such change would be introduced.[37]

The Supreme Court's last published annual report of 2014 lists several initiatives taken by the Court to boost up regular hearings. Most of the solutions mentioned, however, only address the symptom and not the cause. For instance, taking up cases for final disposal rather than first granting leave, increasing the number of matters listed before each bench on miscellaneous days, reducing the numerical requirement for listing identical cases as group matters from ten to five, or listing expedited regular hearing matters separately, do not perform the impossible task of adding time or the difficult one of freeing the time of the Court for regular hearings. They only offer an illusory comfort to parties that their case is featured in the cause list. The situation in which the Court finds itself today is tricky. It is one that steadily weakens its identity as an effective legal institution meant to resolve questions of law in a clear and efficacious manner.

Finally, the Supreme Court's approach towards the admission of cases was motivated in part by the poor state of affairs in the High Courts and lower judiciary. But by hearing cases which should ordinarily not be reserved for the apex court, the incentive to reform the High Courts and lower judiciary has diminished. The Court has only made matters worse by decreasing the significance of the High Courts and lower judiciary (about which we say a little more subsequently). In

[36] AIR 1980 SC 808.

[37] P.B. Mehta, 'India's Judiciary: The Promise of Uncertainty', in *Public Institutions in India: Performance and Design*, eds D. Kapur and P.B. Mehta (New Delhi: Oxford University Press, 2005).

short, by attempting to do more, the Court actually appears to be doing much less than expected of an apex institution.

Supreme Court Benches

Article 145(2) leaves it to the Court, by way of rules, to fix the minimum number of judges sitting for any purpose, and to provide for the powers of single judges and division courts. The sole stipulation—often breached—is contained in Article 145(3), which provides that five shall be the minimum number of judges deciding any case involving a substantial question of law as to the interpretation of the Constitution. The *proviso* to this clause is instructive: this provision can be operationalized by referral to a constitutional bench of any appeal involving such questions, by the division bench currently hearing such appeal. Decisions delivered by a larger bench are binding on smaller benches of the court. As laid down in *Dawoodi Bohra Community* v. *State of Maharashtra*,[38] a bench of lesser quorum cannot doubt the correctness of any view on law taken by a larger bench. The smaller bench can only invite the attention of the Chief Justice and request for the matter to be placed for hearing before a bench of larger quorum than the bench whose decision had come up for its consideration. Only a bench of coequal strength can express an opinion doubting the correctness of the view taken by an earlier bench of coequal strength. In the event of such expression of doubt, the matter may be placed for hearing before a bench consisting of a quorum larger than that of the bench whose decision is doubted.

Constitution benches have played a key role in shaping the identity of the Court as a public institution, often asserting its independence and authority as the final voice on all matters legal. They have also distinctively shaped the law of the land in the field of constitutional law. Yet, over the years, they have become a less common occurrence.[39] Even larger benches, expressly constituted to resolve conflicting legal

---

[38] AIR 2005 SC 752.

[39] A. Agarwal, A. Goel, K. Kakkar, N. Robinson, R. Muthalaly, and V. Bhandari, 'Interpreting the Constitution: Supreme Court Constitution Benches since Independence', *Economic and Political Weekly* 46, no. 9 (26 February 2011): 27–32.

principles enunciated in verdicts by benches of equal strength, have featured less over time in the litigation landscape. Moreover, many such benches constituted through the process of referral by the lower bench to the Chief Justice finally get to hear the issue in question after inordinate delay and postponements, and in some cases, do not ever get to adjudicate the referred issue.[40]

This is a direct consequence of the rising backlog, which in turn leads the Court to spread itself thin across more cases. Data reveals that the post-Emergency period, when the Court clearly felt the need to reassert itself as a strong institution in the political space, saw a drastic increase in writ petitions addressing diverse public-interest causes and a rapid decrease in the constitutional benches deciding important questions of constitutional law.[41] This period also witnessed the rise in the two-judge bench system, as backlog and the relaxation of *locus standi* compelled the Court to transform the prevailing norm of three-judge benches into an exception. Individual benches, in turn, started focusing on fixing the issue before them rather than crystallizing legal principles and providing a cohesive structure to the judge-made law. Benches started involving themselves with the detail of issue-specific guidelines, and wielded authority in a discretionary manner in matters ranging from grant of special leave to awarding of death penalty. This, in turn, has lent a polyvocality—the ability of an institutional actor to speak in multiple voices—to the Supreme Court's identity as a public institution. Chief Justices of India, enjoying significantly lesser tenures on average when compared with their counterparts in the United States (US) or the UK,[42] have been more concerned with the daily administration of justice than with lending coherence to the multiple voices emerging from these benches. The proliferation of chief justices calls

[40] Nick Robinson points out that by the 2000s, just 27 per cent of constitution bench references were decided within two years of being filed in the Court, and 39 per cent took eight years or more. See footnote 31 for more information.

[41] A. Agarwal, A. Goel, K. Kakkar, N. Robinson, R. Muthalaly, and V. Bhandari, 'Interpreting the Constitution: Supreme Court Constitution Benches since Independence', *Economic and Political Weekly* 46, no. 9 (26 February 2011): 27–32.

[42] The US Supreme Court has had 17 chief justices from 1789 to the present, while the Indian Supreme Court has already had 43 chief justices over a much shorter time span of 66 years.

for a rethink in the system of automatically appointing the senior-most judge as the Chief Justice, without factoring in the number of years (or months, as has been the case with many of India's past Chief Justices) of service left for the judge in question. The common practice followed in the case of the senior bureaucracy, of appointing only those with a minimum of two years of service left in them to key positions, must be adopted when appointing Chief Justices of the Supreme Court. Today, lawyers are more likely to reference a particular bench than the Supreme Court as a whole, when proffering legal advice. This takes a heavy toll on the value ascribed by the public to the 'law laid down' by the Court. It can thus be posited that the Court's dual identities have worked at cross-purposes here, and when its identity as a political institution assumed significance, its identity as a legal institution started taking a turn for the worse.

Arrears and Case Management in the Lower Courts

The top-heavy character of the judicial system has unfortunately resulted in huge pendency and a consequent lack of faith in the lower courts. A recent Law Commission report on arrears innovated upon the usual methods of calculating court arrears, and came up with a rate of disposal formula to measure pendency.[43] The results are alarming, especially in the case of the lower judiciary (Tables 3.2 and 3.3).

These tables reveal that the present situation demands heavy infusion of judicial manpower in the lower judiciary—both higher and subordinate judicial services—to resolve the pendency problem. The Supreme Court, while aware of this, has failed to unequivocally support one initiative that was empirically shown to have worked: the setting up of fast-track courts.[44] These courts, which by 2011 had disposed of nearly 33 lakh cases at a clearance rate of nearly 84 per cent of the total cases referred to them,[45] were sought to be closed down in

---

[43] Law Commission of India, *Report No. 245—Arrears and Backlog: Creating Additional Judicial (Wo)manpower* (New Delhi: Government of India, 2014).

[44] 'Despite 1,000 Fast Track Courts, 32 Million Cases Still Pending', *The New Indian Express*, 23 December 2013.

[45] P. Salve, '1,200 Fast Track Courts in India but 600,000 Cases Still Pending', *Indiaspend*, 18 January 2013.

Table 3.2 State-wise Arrears in the Lower Judiciary: Higher Judicial Service

State	Cases Pending for More Than One Year (as on 31 December 2012)	No. of Judges Required for Clearing This Backlog in		
		1 Year	2 Years	3 Years
Andhra Pradesh	98,072	121	61	41
Bihar	184,746	928	464	310
Delhi	45,669	103	52	35
Gujarat	267,853	255	182	85
Himachal Pradesh	11,477	9	5	3
Jammu and Kashmir	25,152	34	17	2
Jharkhand	40,603	193	97	65
Karnataka	98,970	148	74	50
Kerala	152,175	126	63	42
Punjab	43,769	47	24	16
Haryana	54,041	56	28	19
Sikkim	243	1	1	1
Uttarakhand	14,061	21	11	7

Source: Based on data in *Law Commission Report No. 245*.

Table 3.3 State-wise Arrears in the Lower Judiciary: Subordinate Judicial Service

State	Cases Pending for More Than One Year (as on 31 December 2012)	No. of Judges Required for Clearing This Backlog in		
		1 Year	2 Years	3 Years
Andhra Pradesh	472,656	799	400	267
Bihar	1,038,598	4,871	2,436	1,624
Delhi	231,452	208	104	70
Gujarat	1,122,354	1,843	922	615
Himachal Pradesh	85,307	64	32	22
Jammu and Kashmir	83,431	67	34	23
Jharkhand	187,939	573	287	191
Karnataka	657,058	658	329	220
Kerala	459,911	171	86	57
Punjab	252,973	231	116	77
Haryana	252,736	215	108	72
Sikkim	216	1	1	1
Uttarakhand	87,419	79	40	26

Source: Based on data in *Law Commission Report No. 245*.

2005, just about five years after they were initially set up. The central government, quite inexplicably, chose to starve this initiative of funds. Unfortunately, the Supreme Court, instead of directing continuation of funds, as it did in 2005,[46] permitted the Union of India to shut down the project in 2012.[47] About 1,500 judges were left in the lurch, as the Court sided with the Union to hold that they were ad hoc judges with no right to regularization.[48] The fast-track scheme, at least in its initial period, provided some indication of how trials could possibly be concluded if judges were specifically allocated to this task and given a free hand in shutting the loopholes for adjournment present in the current law. The scheme was beset with several problems, but its closure indicated how litigation policy works in India—the decision was ad hoc without any substantial engagement with data and reform proposals.

The Supreme Court has called upon lower courts to be hard-nosed when granting adjournments and to ensure that delay does not defeat justice. The spate of amendments to the Code of Civil Procedure, 1908, carried out in 1999 and 2002, provided inter alia that adjournments shall not be granted to a party more than three times during the hearing of a suit, and made mandatory the imposition of costs occasioned by the adjournment as well as higher costs in appropriate situations.[49] When interpreting this provision, the Court chose to read it down and hold that the three-adjournment policy is not a hard and fast rule.[50] While one cannot find fault with the Court's concern for the instances in which a litigant was hapless enough to have suffered an emergency necessitating more than three adjournments, its interpretation has only resulted in encouraging clever lawyers to play fast and loose with the three-adjournment policy. The Court could have reshaped the law more purposively, stipulating the imposition of exponentially rising costs—borne by the party seeking adjournment—for every subsequent adjournment after the third. Leaving the grant of additional adjournments in the hands of the lower judiciary without much guidance for

---

[46] *Brij Mohan Lal* v. *Union of India*, (2007) 15 SCC 614.

[47] *Brij Mohan Lal* v. *Union of India*, (2012) 6 SCC 502.

[48] See C. Gonsalves, 'When India had 1500 Fast Track Courts', *The Hindu*, 11 January 2013.

[49] Or. XVII, R.1.

[50] *Salem Advocate Bar Association* v. *Union of India*, AIR 2005 SC 3353.

the exercise of such grant has weakened the amendment to an extent. Even so, the Court's caution that adjournments in excess of the third must not be granted except for situations beyond the control of the applicant has had a signalling effect on lower courts, with the more earnest judges adhering to the three-adjournment policy.

An overarching adjournment policy may not, however, resolve the pendency problem without a serious look at the actual stages of a hearing when a case is most likely to get stalled. A more nuanced policy, addressing grants and denials of adjournments during specific stages of a hearing and based on the type of case involved, would work better. The Supreme Court is best placed to facilitate such categorized policymaking using its supervisory powers. For instance, the adjournment problem in the Supreme Court, which mainly hears questions of law as an appellate forum, is different in its impact and possible resolution from that affecting the lower courts of first instance. One of the crucial stages of a trial identified by the Court for immediate redressal is that between the examination in chief and the cross examination of a witness. During this phase, it is very likely that the witness would be compelled to compromise. Lawyers can facilitate this process by buying time for their clients, time that can then be used to 'get to the' witness. Adjournments at this stage can, therefore, completely wreck the fairness of the trial process. The Supreme Court has, therefore, identified this stage of the trial as one demanding strict scrutiny of adjournment requests. The Court, resorting to strong language, branded adjournments as an 'ailment' and held that it is imperative that the cross-examination be completed the very same day as the examination-in-chief of any witness. The Court also directed circulating copies of this verdict to the High Courts, and through them, to the trial courts.[51]

There is another important, if under-recognized, dimension to the adjournment problem: the fact that it severely affects the learning curve of the profession and its ability to plan in advance. The Supreme Court is the only institution that can infuse this thinking into the current debate on adjournments, which is heavily focused on the impact of adjournments on litigants. For litigation to hold as a promising career for fresh law graduates, the Court has to initiate reform measures built around the recognition that professionally oriented lawyers are as much

[51] *Vinod Kumar v. State of Punjab*, (2015) 3 SCC 220.

victims of the adjournment crisis as litigants. A good step initiated
in this direction, which also recognizes the reality that adding more
judges may not necessarily work unless the process is itself altered, is
the Court's suggestion to introduce a case management policy.[52] The
Committee set up in pursuance of this suggestion has come out with a
consultation paper which, if implemented, can potentially revolution-
ize the way cases are conducted in India. The most important shift
in thinking ushered in by a case management policy is a proactive
approach on the part of the judge and his staff to fix timelines for the
completion of a case, rather than leaving it to the advocates for the
parties, as happens to be the scenario presently.[53]

Another important area where the Supreme Court has signalled
legal reform is the imposition of costs in civil cases. The Court has consistently maintained that the present system of levying meagre costs in
civil cases is 'wholly unsatisfactory'[54] and has only resulted in a 'steady
increase in malicious, vexatious, false, frivolous and speculative suits'.[55]
At the same time, it has been aware that mere transposition of systems
in foreign jurisdictions that devote considerable time to the compu-
tation of costs will only worsen the pendency problem.[56] Correctly
reasoning that attempts to reduce pendency or encourage alternative
dispute resolution methods would be futile in the absence of 'actual
realistic costs'[57] suited to the Indian conditions, the Court has called
for the Law Commission's consideration of this issue. Subsequently,
the Law Commission came out with its report, recommending changes
to the Code of Civil Procedure that bring about the awarding of actual
costs so as to indemnify successful litigants, deter vexatious litigation,
and encourage early settlement of disputes.[58] However, the bar is

[52] *Salem Advocate Bar Association* v. *Union of India.*

[53] See Law Commission of India, 'Consultation Paper on Case Management',
Paper presented at International Conference on ADR and Case Management,
Ministry of Law and Justice, Government of India, New Delhi, 3–4 May 2003.

[54] *Ashok Kumar Mittal* v. *Ram Kumar Gupta*, (2009) 2 SCC 656.

[55] *Vinod Seth* v. *Devinder Bajaj*, (2010) 8 SCC 1.

[56] *Sanjeev Kumar Jain* v. *Raghubir Saran Charitable Trust*, (2012) 1 SCC
455.

[57] *Salem Advocate Bar Association* v. *Union of India*, AIR 2005 SC 3353.

[58] Law Commission of India, *Report No. 240—Costs in Civil Litigation* (New
Delhi: Government of India, 2012).

infamous for its resistance to any civil procedure reform, as borne out by the spate of strikes instigated by the earlier amendments of 1999 and 2002. Therefore, the Supreme Court will have to take it upon itself to compel suitable amendments to the law as proposed by the Law Commission.

Legal Aid and Access

The Supreme Court has placed considerable emphasis on access to legal services in general, and to its own jurisdiction in particular, through its rulings and administrative machinery. The Supreme Court Legal Services Committee was established as the successor to the erstwhile Supreme Court Legal Aid Committee, vide the set of regulations issued by the National Legal Services Authority in 1996. The primary function of the Committee is to administer and implement the Supreme Court's legal services programme, and to maintain the panel of advocates who give legal advice in the Supreme Court. Forty-six senior advocates are also part of this panel, lending their assistance in murder cases, convictions under the Narcotic Drugs and Psychotropic Substances Act, 1985, and other serious offences where the sentence awarded to the accused is more than ten years. From 2005 to 2014, over 10,500 applicants have benefited from this service. The Committee has also been instrumental in organizing continuing legal education programmes for its panel advocates and national *Lok Adalat*s for settling disputes under the guidance of Supreme Court judges.[59] Realizing the potential of alternate dispute resolution methods to make the law more accessible and expedite conflict resolution, the Court has taken welcome baby steps in this direction, including the running of a mediation centre.[60]

The complex issue of access to the Supreme Court brings into sharp relief the conflict between the dual identities—political and legal—assumed by the institution. As a political institution, the Court's solitary presence in New Delhi makes perfect sense. Having more than one venue for the court—in the form of additional benches—can potentially expose it to higher political intervention in its functioning. Moreover, the signalling effect served by the Court speaking in one

[59] *Supreme Court Annual Report, 2014–15.*
[60] *Supreme Court Annual Report, 2014–15.*

voice, from one building, is diluted when more benches are created. On the other hand, because the Court has, over time, spread itself thin and entertained appeals on a discretionary basis, and in a wide variety of cases from all over the country, there is a legitimate expectation on the part of the public that locational disadvantages do not hamper the hearing of their appeal. Unfortunately, some of the recent empirical work indicates that many more appeals are referred to the Supreme Court from orders passed by high courts near Delhi—mainly the Delhi High Court and the Punjab & Haryana High Court—as compared to the rest of the country. This is despite the other High Courts, including the Madras, Bombay, and Calcutta High Courts, hearing many more cases than the aforementioned courts.[61]

When evaluating the Supreme Court as a legal institution, one is, therefore, sadly forced to admit that its location in New Delhi makes it less accessible to litigants from other regions. Aware of this, the Law Commission of India has come up with an interesting proposal: a Constitution Bench in Delhi to deal with constitutional and other allied issues, and four Cassation Benches in the northern, southern, eastern, and western regions of the country to deal with all appellate work arising out of the orders/judgements of the courts in these respective regions.[62] Though this proposal may never be taken up because of a strong resistance to its implementation by the present Supreme Court bar, the splitting up of constitutional and appellate work may well enable the Court to cement its identity as a strong legal institution.

The Supreme Court's effort to improve its registry, particularly through the use of technology, deserves special mention as a positive step enhancing litigant access. The Court registry, though a vital part of its administrative machinery, has several independent powers and functions that place it in a position of authority over litigants and lawyers. In

---

[61] N. Robinson, 'A Quantitative Analysis of the Indian Supreme Court's Workload'.

[62] As explained by the Commission, a court of cassation is the judicial court of last resort and has power to quash or reverse decisions of the inferior courts. See Law Commission of India, *Report No. 229—Need for Division of the Supreme Court into a Constitution Bench at Delhi and Cassation Benches in Four Regions at Delhi, Chennai/Hyderabad, Kolkata and Mumbai* (New Delhi: Government of India, 2009).

several situations, the registry can actually play foul with the fate of a client who is desperate for an interim order or an order copy. This 'living law' presents an unhealthy scenario as it breeds favouritism towards certain law offices and a culture of unprofessional discharge of duty by officials in the registry. The Court appears to be trying to weaken the ill-effects of the strong inter-personal bonds festered between the bar and the registry by deploying technology and facilitating litigant-friendly measures such as e-filing of petitions, maintenance of an exhaustive website, and online accessibility to daily orders and judgements. It would be even better if the Court were to expand its experience with modernizing and professionalizing the registry to courts all over the country through a national policy for the revamp of court registries.

The Bar and Legal Fraternity

In order to function effectively, the Supreme Court also requires support from the bar. Two important constituents of the bar have been integral to the evolution of the Court as a competent and independent institution: senior advocates and advocates-on-record (AoRs). Order IV, Rule 2 of the Supreme Court Rules, 2013, provides that an advocate may be designated by the Chief Justice and other judges as a senior advocate if, in their opinion, he is deserving of such distinction by virtue of his ability, standing at the bar, or special knowledge or experience in law. Once so designated, these senior advocates cannot represent clients directly, and have to necessarily appear along with an advocate-on-record before the Supreme Court. Even senior advocates designated by the various High Courts and practising before the Supreme Court are bound by these constraints against directly advising or representing clients. Anecdotally, it appears that senior advocates have found ways to bypass the bar on them directly engaging with clients by routing the client through junior advocates who work in their chambers.

Apart from appearing on behalf of private parties and obtaining favourable outcomes, senior advocates have contributed significantly to the growth of the law, particularly in the first three decades when the Constitution was being tested regularly in the Supreme Court and many legal principles were yet to be fully settled. Eminent counsel such as Nani Palkhivala, M.C. Setalvad, Fali Nariman, Ram Jethmalani, and others have assisted the Court in shaping and defining the boundaries of the law across various substantive areas of practice. Many of them have also lent invaluable assistance to the court as *amicus curiae*, particularly in public law matters where rights violations have been at issue.

But the system of the chosen few has also created, more so in recent times, an unhealthy incentive structure built around the discretionary lottery spawned by the grant or denial of special leave to appeal. In a recent study of the senior advocate system in the Supreme Court, Marc Galanter and Nick Robinson attribute the success of such advocates to the 'extensive human capital they have developed within the court system and their nuanced knowledge of both formal and informal judicial procedure'.[63] Indeed, one of the key insights offered by this study is that this cult of legal superstars—individuals who at times tower over even Supreme Court judges in stature and personality—manages to sustain and thrive because the Court is hard-pressed for time to dive deep into questions of law; success before the Court is much more about control in the interim and much less about outcomes at the end of a long, drawn-out hearing process. Research also indicates that a special leave petition argued by a senior advocate has roughly double the chances of being heard by the Supreme Court, compared with cases without a senior advocate.[64] Given this, it is unlikely that the Supreme Court's senior advocates will allow any real reforms to the admissions stage of hearings.

The other crucial tier in the bar consists of AoRs, a class of lawyers who are specially qualified to plead before the Supreme Court. As a collective body, they have been influential in shaping the practice of the Court, and were instrumental in their capacity as the lead petitioner in bringing about the collegium system of judicial appointments.[65] Order IV, Rule 1(b) of the Supreme Court Rules, 2013, makes it clear that no advocate other than the AoR for a party shall appear, plead, and address

[63] M. Galanter and N. Robinson, 'India's Grand Advocates: A Legal Elite Flourishing in the Era of Globalization', *International Journal of the Legal Profession* 20, no. 3 (November 2013): 241–65.

[64] A.P. Kumar, 'The True Worth of a Senior Advocate', *LiveMint*, 16 September 2015, available at http://www.livemint.com/Politics/FFgFOFnz N8rqvRNWTTgugM/The-true-worth-of-a-senior-advocate.html.

[65] *Supreme Court Advocates-on-Record Association* v. *Union of India*, (1993) 4 SCC 441.

the Court unless such advocate is so instructed by the AoR. Rule 5 stipulates important preconditions to qualify as an AoR, including a minimum of four years of practice, training of one year with an AoR, and an office in Delhi within a radius of 16 kilometres from the court house. Despite all of this, the AoR system has, in reality, become one in which many AoRs are mere name- and signature-lenders to the petition and the real work is done by some other advocate who has a more direct relationship with the client. This practice came to the attention of the Supreme Court in a recent contempt action, when the Court observed that mere signature-lending on the part of the AoR, without assuming any responsibility for conduct of the case, would defeat the very purpose of this special class of advocates.[66] Subsequently, an explanation was inserted in Order IV, Rule 10 of the Supreme Court Rules, clarifying that mere name-lending by an AoR without further participation in the proceedings of a case would amount to misconduct or conduct unbecoming of an AoR.

The Court also makes use of specially constituted commissions for various purposes that facilitate its adjudicatory role, the most common of these being fact-finding or fact-gathering missions. The composition of such bodies often varies depending on the nature of the task at hand, and their membership includes district judges, journalists, lawyers, mental health professionals, bureaucrats, technocrats, and expert bodies. In environmental matters, the Court has issued commissions to the Central Pollution Control Board and the National Environmental Engineering Research Institute to propose remedial solutions and monitor their implementation. Resort to such commissions is arguably effective when the Court is adjudicating on a public interest petition where the petitioner may have approached the Court with an important grievance but without sufficient facts to support the claim. However, the Court must be careful to check its commissions from lending an aura of technocratic influence over its decision-making process and the grant of final relief, in order to prevent the weakening of its identity as a legal institution.

Finally, formal law-clerk appointments are an important initiative by the Supreme Court to involve the legal fraternity in the making of

---

[66] In *re: Rameshwar Prasad Goyal, Advocate*, (2014) 1 SCC 572.

law. This system, started in the early 2000s, has sought to tap into the potential of law graduates from India's leading law schools. Although over a decade has passed since this system began, there seems to be no set of uniform norms that have developed over the exact functions and responsibilities that law clerks are to perform.

***

This chapter has aimed to provide an assessment of how the Supreme Court functions—both with regard to other public institutions and also internally. As we make clear, the Court presently faces a range of challenges. Current debates on legal reform in India have a tired quality to them, and blindness towards these challenges is bound to impact the Court's legitimacy and efficiency. The Court's performance will, in part, be improved by further studies on the Court as a public institution, by social science research and data-driven analyses that can shed light on its operation. The first step to improving the Court's performance as a public institution might be to begin studying it.

4

RESERVE BANK OF INDIA
The Way Forward

Errol D'Souza

The Reserve Bank of India (RBI) was set up on 1 April 1935, and over the years its monetary policy objectives have been to maintain price stability and ensure an adequate supply of credit to assist the process of economic growth.[1] It is entrusted with the management of foreign exchange reserves, and its founding statute requires it to be the manager of the public debt of the Government of India and to be the banker to the government. The Union Government is, as per the Reserve Bank of India Act, 1934, allowed to give such directions to the RBI after consulting its Governor 'as it may consider necessary in the public interest'. Other than this, the management of the RBI lies with its central board of directors. The governor, deputy governors, and directors of the central board—comprising 14 eminent persons from different walks of life—are appointed by the government, which also has the power to remove them.[2] The balance of the annual profits of the RBI, after making provisions and transfers to its reserves, is transferred to the government.

---

[1] The RBI was set up as a private shareholder bank and was nationalized in 1949 by the Government of India.

[2] The secretary dealing with economic affairs in the Ministry of Finance is also a director on the board of the RBI, but has no vote.

This chapter begins by providing a brief history of the RBI's monetary operations in the context of economic developments and its relationship with the fiscal authority over the past 20 years. Next, it evaluates the RBI's statement of its monetary policy objective in terms of balancing price stability and economic growth while safeguarding financial stability. Following this, it discusses the Financial Sector Legislative Reforms Commission (FSLRC) report on objective setting for monetary policy and the criteria to be considered when appointing MPCs. It is in this context that the chapter next examines the recommendations of the RBI's own Expert Committee (Urjit Patel Committee) to revise and strengthen the monetary policy framework. As macroeconomic stability requires coordination between monetary, fiscal, and debt management policies, an appraisal of the RBI's management of government debt follows. The financial crisis brought out starkly that even when the output and inflation gaps are stable, there could be pressures building up in the financial system. In this regard, the chapter also deliberates on the use of macro-prudential policy to manage systemic risk. The RBI's quantum of holding of foreign exchange reserves places it among the top five country holding of reserves among emerging and developing economies. Hence, the management of these reserves in terms of the objectives of capital preservation and liquidity is worthy of review. In a developing country, a central bank has the additional responsibility of developing markets and financial institutions as well as allocating credit towards priority activities. The RBI's involvement along this dimension of central bank activity is also explored. The chapter concludes with a discussion on the human resource organizational structure of the RBI and its capacity to respond satisfactorily to changes in the financial environment.

Parsimonious History of Recent RBI Policy

Until 1997, the financial independence of the RBI was compromised as the government had automatic access to central bank credits to finance its expenditure. This phasing out of automatic monetization of fiscal deficits in 1997 was an important landmark in providing a measure of autonomy to the RBI to conduct monetary policy without being subordinated to fiscal policy. Another important milestone in the last couple of decades was the enactment of the Fiscal Responsibility and

Budget Management (FRBM) Act in 2003, prior to which the RBI did not participate in the primary issuance of government securities. In 2005, the RBI decided to constitute a technical advisory committee on monetary policy. This committee is chaired by the governor and includes the four deputy governors, two non-official directors of the board of the RBI, and five independent outside experts. The committee was constituted by the RBI so as to benefit from outside expertise on the framing of monetary policy, and its role is strictly advisory.

A central bank's conduct of monetary policy is usually assessed with respect to its ability to manage economic cycles. Figure 4.1 depicts the quarterly inflation rate and the output growth rate gap—the difference between realized gross domestic product (GDP) growth rate and trend or potential GDP growth rate—in the Indian economy between 1997 and the end of the financial year of 2012.[3] Output growth rate gaps above the 5.5 per cent level in Figure 4.1 represent positive (negative) gaps where realized GDP growth is above potential GDP growth. The main monetary policy rates set by the RBI for this period are depicted in Figure 4.2.[4] These three policy rates—cash reserve ratio, repo rate, and reverse repo rate—affect the amount of liquidity and the balance sheet of the banking system. During this period, it is evident that the RBI was behind the curve between the second quarter of 2003 and the fourth quarter of 2004, when it reduced policy rates though the output growth rate gap had risen significantly and inflation (though below its target of 5.5 per cent) was rising. This was the beginning of a phase of large capital inflows into the Indian economy, and it is possible that the RBI had a 'recognition lag' which caused it to change policy rates

[3] The output growth gap has been rescaled in Figure 4.1. Thus, a zero output growth gap is represented as an output growth gap of 5.5 per cent. In effect, output growth gaps above (below) the 5.5 per cent level represent positive (negative) gaps.

[4] In Figure 4.2, monetary policy rates within any quarter are the average of policy rates set by the RBI in that quarter. The repo rate is the rate at which banks can borrow from the RBI in the overnight cash market, and the reverse repo rate is the rate at which banks can park their surplus cash with the RBI. The cash reserve ratio is the fraction of deposits that a commercial bank cannot lend out and which is required to be kept as funds in an account with the central bank.

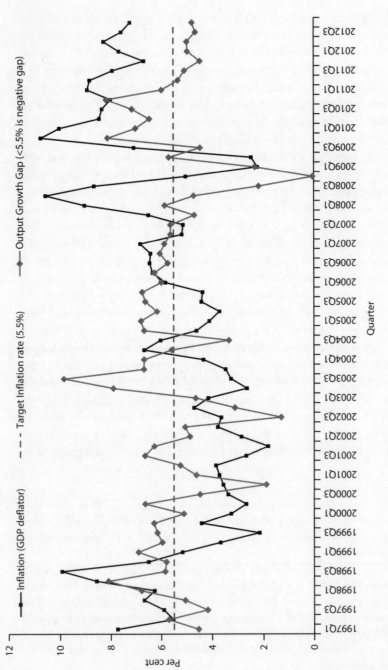

Figure 4.1 Inflation and Output Growth Gap, 1997–2012
Source: Database on Indian Economy, Reserve Bank of India.

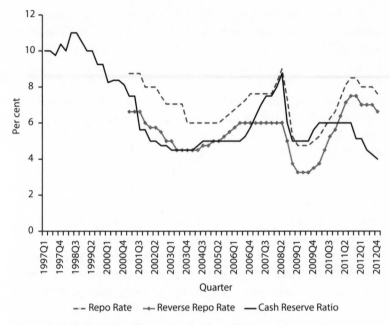

Figure 4.2 Major Monetary Policy Rates, 1997–2012
Source: Database on Indian Economy, Reserve Bank of India.

later than warranted.[5] However, during the period between the fourth quarter of 2009 and the fourth quarter of 2011, the RBI was behind the curve again as policy rates were lower than the inflation rate and there existed a positive output growth rate gap for most of this period. This was also a period of extensive fiscal deficits, and many market agents were also of the view that the RBI was accommodating the Finance Ministry, which was responsible for these deficits, by keeping policy rates low.

The RBI's actions to influence the course of the economy are reflected on the assets side of its balance sheet in terms of changes in its domestic assets (net bank credit to the government plus net claims on banks and the commercial private sector) and changes in net foreign

[5] A recognition lag in monetary policy is the time period it takes policy-makers to recognize that there has been a change in the economy that requires them to act so as to stimulate or restrain aggregate spending through a change in monetary policy rates.

assets.[6] Khatkhate demonstrates how the RBI had no control over the net bank credit to government since Independence, and this continued until 1997, when it forged an agreement with the Ministry of Finance to replace ad hoc funding of government debt with ways and means advances provided by the RBI within specified limits to meet temporary mismatches between government receipts and expenditures. This resulted in what Khatkhate calls a watered-down version of the previous system as the government, in many instances, devolved its debt on the RBI rather than in the debt market by arguing that the debt eventually would reach the market through the RBI's open market operations.[7]

The monetization of fiscal deficits changed after 1997, however, due to the arrival of heavy capital inflows on Indian shores. The RBI absorbed the inflows by purchasing foreign exchange and sterilizing the monetary impact by selling government securities. This process accelerated from 2003 with the surge in capital inflows. As depicted in Figure 4.3, the RBI, in response to capital flows, replaced its domestic assets with foreign exchange assets. By 2004, the RBI experienced a shortage of government securities from the heavy sterilization it was resorting to, and the government had to issue market stabilization bonds to mop up the surplus liquidity due to capital inflows.[8] Through the end of the 1990s, the RBI was powerless to deal with the large government borrowings—which were reflected in the net bank credit to government on its balance sheet—that crowded out its net claims on banks and the private commercial sector.[9] Subsequently with the phase

---

[6] The availability and cost of money is affected by changes in reserve money, defined as the sum of domestic assets and foreign assets less net non-monetary liabilities.

[7] D. Khatkhate, 'Reserve Bank of India: A Study in the Separation and Attrition of Powers', in *Public Institutions in India: Performance and Design*, eds D. Kapur and P.B. Mehta (New Delhi: Oxford University Press, 2007).

[8] The proceeds from market stabilization bonds were parked in a separate identifiable cash account operated by the RBI. The RBI decreased the net RBI credit to government in response to the proceeds into this account and thereby nullified the expansionary impact of the increase in foreign exchange assets.

[9] For the decade of the 1990s, domestic assets comprised 78.2 per cent of the asset base of the RBI on average. Within the components of domestic assets, the net bank credit to government was 5.3 times the net claims on banks and

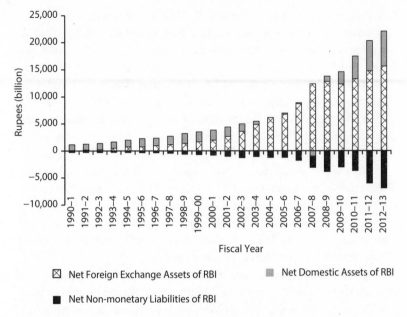

Figure 4.3   Major Components of Reserve Bank of India Assets, 1990–1 to 2012–13
Source: Database on Indian Economy, Reserve Bank of India.

of capital inflows, the action moved from substitution within these two domestic assets by the RBI to the conduct of monetary policy in order to manage the external account by substituting foreign assets for domestic assets.

The easy liquidity from capital inflows fuelled the more than 8 per cent growth rate of GDP in India between 2003 and 2008. With a 'sudden stop' of capital following the collapse of Lehman Brothers in 2008, it was inevitable that growth would slow down as well. Fiscal policy responded to the slowdown with an even larger fiscal deficit. The fiscal deficit/GDP ratio of the central and state governments, which had averaged 5.9 per cent between 2003 and 2007, increased to 7.9 per cent on average over the next five years. This large replacement of net exports with fiscal expenditures did manage to sustain the momentum

the private commercial sector. In other words, net bank credit to government was 65.9 per cent of the asset base of the RBI.

of economic growth until the end of 2010–11, after which corruption scandals resulted in a slowdown. However, monetary policy played an accommodative role starting from the third quarter of 2009, when the RBI raised policy rates by less than warranted in the face of a large positive output growth gap and high inflation (Figures 4.1 and 4.2). Inflation on a quarterly basis averaged 7.7 per cent between 2008 and the end of fiscal year 2012, in contrast to 5 per cent in the preceding five-year period. The slow reaction of monetary policy to rising prices resulted in a phase of persistently high inflation and inflation expectations in the economy despite the output growth gap turning negative from the second quarter of 2011 (Figure 4.1). From 2009 to 2011, the RBI shifted from accommodating capital inflows to accommodating the government deficit. The RBI's accommodative stance has often been interpreted by financial markets as an indication of its limited independence in conducting monetary policy.

Major monetary policy announcements by the RBI were made on a quarterly basis until recently. In addition, there were four mid-quarter policy announcements.[10] From March 2014 onwards, monetary policy announcements became bi-monthly in frequency. Monetary policy is decided on internally by the governor with the help of inputs from the deputy governors and the technical staff of the RBI, after taking into account the suggestions made by an external committee of experts who form part of the technical advisory committee on monetary policy. This technical advisory committee is not a decision-making body and has no legal mandate. The monetary policy objective of the RBI has been described by Mohan as follows: 'In essence, Indian monetary policy aims at maintaining a judicious balance between price stability and economic growth, while also ensuring financial stability. The relative emphasis between the three is governed by prevailing circumstances at a particular point of time, and consequently, there is an ongoing re-balancing of priorities'.[11]

---

[10] Of course, the RBI is free to make monetary policy changes according to changed circumstances at any time other than during the periodic quarterly and mid-quarterly calendars.

[11] R. Mohan, *Growth with Financial Stability: Central Banking in an Emerging Market* (New Delhi: Oxford University Press, 2011), 61. Further, it is widely accepted that monetary policy has a short-run impact on unemployment (the

With respect to financial stability, there has been a steady deterioration in the asset quality of banks in India. From 2009 to the end of 2013, the stressed advances of the banking system more than doubled to a significant 10.2 per cent of total advances.[12] Public sector banks have a dominant share of stressed advances, with such advances at 12.3 per cent of total advances. The new private banks in India have had much better asset quality relative to the public sector banks. Stressed assets have grown because of the slowdown in the economy and also because public sector banks changed their compliance after a lenient RBI relaxed the asset classification of restructured advances following the onset of the financial crisis.[13] Twenty-nine state-owned banks wrote off a total of Rs 1.14 lakh crore of bad debts between financial years 2013 and 2015, much more than they had done in the preceding nine years.[14] Banks' credit appraisal also may have become less stringent in the fast growth period up to 2008, as they competed for credit disbursal with the surplus funds available to them from the reduction in the statutory liquidity ratio (SLR).[15]

---

size of which is uncertain) but is neutral in the long run. Monetary authorities are thus required to anchor expectations by choosing a target inflation rate and output, and the instruments of policy should be set so that inflation and output stay near those targets. Even when the economy is close to its inflation and output targets, the recent financial crisis has shown how financial imbalances build up and result in instability. The objective of monetary policy, due to the learning from such phenomena, is essentially price stability and financial stability, with the ultimate aim of achieving stable economic growth.

[12] Stressed advances as per the international definition include gross non-performing assets and restructured standard advances. A non-performing asset is an asset that ceases to generate income—interest or instalment of principal—for the bank over a specified past period, which in India is 90 days. Restructured standard advances occur when a bank changes the terms of a loan to prevent it from becoming non-performing.

[13] These revised classification norms were in place till April 2015.

[14] These are the figures from a Right to Information (RTI) request, as reported in Utkarsh Anand, 'Rs. 1.14 Lakh Crore of Bad Debts: The Great Government Bank Write-Off', *Indian Express*, 9 February 2016.

[15] The SLR declined from 30.5 per cent of total assets in 2005 to 22.5 per cent in 2008 and was accompanied by an increase in the growth of loans disbursed.

Public sector banks have concentrated credit disbursal, which has the potential to affect their asset quality if there is deterioration in the financial health of the borrower.[16] Five sectors are responsible for 51 per cent of stressed advances and thus have contributed significantly to this phenomenon—infrastructure, iron and steel, aviation, textiles, and mining.[17] A large exposure to a sector that is loss-making has the potential to cause distress to the bank that had disbursed credit to the sector, as well as result in contagion due to the effect on the distressed bank. Such risks are usually minimized by the prescription of exposure limits by banking regulators. The rule in India is that a bank may have exposure of up to 25 per cent of its total capital for a single borrower, and its exposure to a corporate group can go up to 55 per cent of total capital. India defends such regulation as required for the purpose of funding the country's growth. However, India's financial sector assessment programme, conducted by the International Monetary Fund (IMF) and World Bank in 2011–12, argued that such large exposure limits are significantly higher than the limit of 25 per cent, which is the norm in international practice.

The high concentration of loans can be construed as a form of cronyism and can conceivably result in the default of a group borrower to cause a large loss of capital in a bank. The RBI was among the earliest central banks to impose higher-risk weights on bank lending to selected sectors that seemed in danger of overextension in 2004. It has recognized the problem of credit quality and imposed a higher provisioning coverage ratio for banks, which is to be eventually replaced by a dynamic provisioning practice. Exposure limit regulations, however, require a reconsideration so as to enhance the stability of the banking system.

Objective of Monetary Policy

There is a view about central banking that the objective of monetary policy should be specified by the government and that this objective

[16] Their lending has been to Air India and Kingfisher in the aviation sector for instance, both of which have doubtful viability for repayments.

[17] See RBI, *Financial Stability Report—Issue No. 8* (Mumbai: Reserve Bank of India, December 2013), 31.

should be a quantitative, monitorable one.[18] A quantitative, monitorable objective can be given for price stability but not for financial stability. Work on a widely acceptable macro-prudential framework for financial stability is still at an early stage, and quantitative targets have not been established yet.[19] A price stability target specified by the government is good for a central bank as it amounts to an anti-inflationary pre-commitment by the government and enables the central bank to resist any pressure from the government to accommodate inflation. In India, the FSLRC envisaged the price stability target to be set by the central government in consultation with the governor of the RBI.[20]

Even when specifying the target and horizon for price stability, however, there are important considerations that must be kept in mind in the case of a country like India. First, it is well known that monetary policy has long and variable lags. Since the effect of monetary policy on prices has a lag of over 18 months, one can only assess the action a long time after it is taken. This makes accountability difficult to explain to the public, as current policy is to be assessed by comparing it with inflation performance a year or two in the future. To assist in this process, monetary authorities are required to set up a method for inflation forecasting that uses indicators containing information about future inflation. Intermediate targets are generally used to convey future inflation developments in terms of contemporary variables that are observable. Central banks that have price stability as a goal usually announce intermediate targets such as the exchange rate, credit, or monetary aggregates, depending on their operational association with the price level or inflation. When price level or inflation targets are set, the existence of intermediate targets enables economic agents to

[18] In India, this view has been propounded recently by the FSLRC. See FSLRC, *Report of the Financial Sector Legislative Reforms Commission* (New Delhi: Government of India, March 2013).

[19] Macro-prudential policy aims to prevent and mitigate systemic risks. This is dealt with in a subsequent section of the chapter.

[20] This is common practice in many countries such as Australia, Brazil, Canada, New Zealand, South Korea, and Thailand. In some countries, such as the United Kingdom (UK) and Israel, the government sets the inflation target, while in others, such as Switzerland, Sweden, and the Czech Republic, the central bank sets the target.

monitor how the central bank is fairing with regard to its objective. Targeting requires a good understanding of the monetary transmission mechanism and estimates of the time lag between the adjustment of the monetary instruments and their effect on prices and output. In India, it is difficult to suggest variables that are closely associated with future price developments, and this needs to be kept in mind when setting inflation targets.

Second, central banks can only affect long-run inflation that has its antecedents in monetary phenomena, as the FSLRC recognizes.[21] However, there are temporary deviations from price stability which the central bank cannot be held accountable for—those arising, for instance, from changes in labour costs, or sudden international rise in coal prices that raise the cost of power. Unsustainable fiscal deficits by the government that aim to stimulate the economy are an additional non-monetary source of inflation that affects the time horizon for achieving price stability. No central bank can be held accountable for such temporary deviations from price stability. This means that it is important to explicitly specify and communicate escape clauses in the mandate for price stability. Specifying a clear mandate for the central bank is important so as to make it possible to assess whether it has stayed true to its specified intent.

These are related to the important point about how to empirically define price stability. Should it be in terms of a headline measure or a core measure that excludes the prices of certain goods and services? The US Federal Reserve System does not provide a definition of price stability, and the Bank of England expresses it in terms of headline inflation. In India, the RBI has been referring to headline inflation as measured by the wholesale price index (WPI) because it is released in a timely manner, has national coverage, and is available in a disaggregate format.[22] The RBI has also been referring to a measure of WPI core inflation in its monetary policy statements—essentially excluding the prices of energy and food, over which it has no control, in order to downplay temporary fluctuations in prices. In India, the measures of consumer price inflation

---

[21] FSLRC, *Report*, Chapter 11.

[22] D. Mohanty, 'Measures of Inflation: Issues and Perspectives', Speech at the Conference of Indian Association for Research in National Income and Wealth, Centre for Development Studies, Thiruvananthapuram, 9 January 2010.

(CPI) were available historically with reference to specific segments of the population, such as agricultural workers and industrial workers. It was only in February 2011 that the Central Statistical Organisation of the Indian government released a new all-India CPI without reference to specific classes of the population. Going forward, it is important that the RBI uses the new CPI to indicate the headline inflation in India. This is because the WPI ignores the services sector prices which comprise more than half of India's GDP and constitute a significant share of the expenditures in the country.

Apart from empirical factors, there is also another fundamental reason as to why a central bank should focus on a measure of inflation that is related to the prices that consumers pay. Since consumption is the final objective of economic activity, a measure of the cost of consumption should also be an objective of monetary policy. CPI is also the measure of inflation that most economic agents are familiar with and can relate to. For some time, CPI—which is what the common man associates with the cost of living—has been consistently higher than WPI inflation in India. This has increased the risk that a central bank focused on a subset of the basket of goods that a common man consumes is perceived as out of touch with reality, especially when there are persistent movements in the prices of commodities that have been excluded from the core measure of inflation. Central bank accountability is sacrificed in such instances unless the bank is an aggressive communicator about the benefits of the measure it has adopted.

Process of Arriving at Monetary Policy Decisions

Is the current practice of deciding on monetary policy within the RBI appropriate? Currently, the governor is responsible for decision-making, and he relies on the views of a mix of internal experts and the external members of the technical advisory committee on monetary policy. Recently, the FSLRC recommended a move to a predominantly external expert committee. The literature on monetary policy has emphasized that decisions made by a group of professionals in a committee are better than those made by an individual. There is disagreement, however, as to which range of committee approaches (internal versus external) and decision-making practices (consensus versus majority) are best suited to achieving the objectives of central banking. The FSLRC recommended that the monetary policy committee (MPC) have eight members. In addition to the governor and an executive member of the board of the RBI, there were to be five external members, two to be appointed by the central government in consultation with the governor, and three by the central government. In addition, a representative expressing the views of the Ministry of Finance would participate but not have voting rights. The reason provided for having so many external members was to avoid the possibility of 'groupthink' within the central bank.

The FSLRC does not consider the possibility that the five external members have other occupations and may provide insufficient attention to the details that need to be considered while focusing on steering the course for monetary policy. Also, what are the incentives of independent MPC members? Are their incentives solely to provide public service? Why should the MPC rely on the altruism of its members? These issues are especially important when the recommendation is to move monetary policy formulation with the involvement of experts from outside the RBI from the current advisory role to a role in which they have to vote.

When conferring a vote in what is an important decision, it is necessary to ensure that the person with the vote has a stake in the decision. This also requires much more involvement of the MPC members with the central bank. For instance, in the Bank of England, MPC members continuously receive comprehensive briefings from Bank staff and there is also a pre-MPC meeting on the Friday before the interest rate setting meeting, where data and analysis of issues about the economy are shared. The MPC interest rate setting meeting that follows is a two-day meeting, held monthly. MPC members are considered to be employees of the bank, appointed on a part-time basis averaging three days a week, and are paid a remuneration equal to roughly 42 per cent of that of the governor and 50 per cent of that of the deputy governors.[23]

[23] This is calculated as the salary plus benefits. External members of the MPC, for instance, received a salary of £101,362 in 2011–12 and a supplement of 30 per cent of this in lieu of membership of the Bank's pension fund. They are also entitled to coverage under the Bank's group medical insurance scheme. See Bank of England, *Annual Report 2012* (London: Bank of England, 2012), 44–6.

In India, it is difficult for experts to be released in a timely fashion from their prior commitments to organizations they work in. In such a situation, only those who are retired will qualify for membership in a voting committee. Besides, the RBI has information about the future course of the economy and about the banking system that is an important input into monetary policy formulation. Excluding the deputy governors from the formulation of policy is akin to not directly using that valuable information and expertise.[24] Besides, the top echelons of the RBI are constantly interacting with the market and the public and have the right incentives in place to establish credibility, which is a much-required prerequisite for effective monetary policy. In the Bank of England, MPC members have to go through the Bank's Press Office for making speeches and media contributions and must keep it informed of events, whether public or private, where it is likely that MPC matters could be discussed, so as to align the communication with the MPC policy.[25] Similarly, in the US, the Federal Open Market Committee (FOMC) is constituted by a majority of members (seven) hailing from the Board of Governors of the Fed, who are appointed for 14-year terms, and five voting members from among the presidents of the 12 federal reserve banks that constitute the operating arms of the central bank.[26] All members of the FOMC, thus, have a significant stake in the monetary policy decisions they vote on. Similarly, for the European Central Bank (ECB), the governing council that formulates monetary policy comprises fifteen governors of the euro area national central banks and the six members of the executive board of the ECB.

[24] The governor always has access to the views of the deputy governors and can bring these to the MPC. However, this is an indirect use of information and does not align with the incentives of the deputy governors, besides putting the entire onus of the RBI's take on the policy rate on to the shoulders of the governor.

[25] They are also required to circulate at least 48 hours in advance their articles to the governor and other members of the Bank's Press Office to provide them an opportunity to comment.

[26] The president of a regional Federal Reserve Bank is nominated by the directors of the Reserve Bank, subject to approval of the Board of Governors of the Federal Reserve system. A director's term is usually staggered three-year terms, generally limited to two terms of three years each.

Each of them, thus, has a considerable involvement with the issues that have a bearing on monetary policy matters. In practice, the governing council of the ECB strives for consensus, but each member has one vote and a monetary policy decision is legitimate if voted for by a simple majority.

The advantage of external members, as recognized by the FSLRC, is that they bring in new perspectives and are not prone to the groupthink that may be present among the officials of the central bank. However, their attention to matters of monetary policy is not complete as they are gainfully occupied elsewhere, and the flip side of groupthink is that there may be a lack of coherence in the way a decision is arrived at or communicated, which could affect the credibility of the central bank. For instance, how is the public to decipher a policy statement where the voting displays dissent on the policy that has been announced?

There is always a risk of confusing the markets about the monetary policy in such a situation, which is an important consideration for a central bank in an emerging market that is seeking to establish credibility. Another disadvantage of a committee is that the formal accountability of the institution and the governor is weakened, especially when the decision is taken by a majority. The major advantages of an MPC, then, are that groups make better decisions than individuals and there will be continuity in policy when there is a change of governor. The disadvantages are that it enhances the risk of communicating monetary policy strategy and might weaken institutional accountability.

When individuals are on a committee and their incentives to make the investments of time and effort to process large amounts of information that are relevant to the decision are not aligned with their individual daily interests, then they would tend to free ride and rely on the data and analysis that is being provided by the central bank. This is not beneficial for decision-making by committees. It has been suggested that publication of the discussions along with the names of persons who contribute can be a deterrent to persons who free ride. However, this has the associated cost that members of the MPC may be reluctant to make the kind of frank statements that emerge when there is confidentiality, which then reduces the productivity of the discussion.

In January 2014, the RBI released a report of the Expert Committee to revise and strengthen the monetary policy framework.[27] The Committee recommended that inflation as measured by the new headline CPI be the nominal anchor for monetary policy, as it reflects the cost of living and influences inflation expectations. The target for inflation suggested by the Committee is four per cent with a band of +/− 2 per cent, so as to accommodate external and supply shocks that affect the predictability of inflation.[28] The time horizon for achieving this target is suggested as two years so as to balance the long lags with which monetary policy affects output with the shorter warranted horizon, so as to anchor inflation expectations and establish the credibility of the monetary authority. Significantly, the Expert Committee also sought to de-emphasize the overnight guaranteed bank specific access windows for liquidity management and to progressively expand the market's general access to term repos from the RBI. This change to term repos which the RBI has begun implementing will improve the transmission of monetary policy across the interest rate spectrum.

The core of what credible monetary policy does is to anchor inflation expectations around a known low level.[29] The Committee, however, does not distinguish between short- and long-term inflation expectations, which is fundamental to the literature on credible monetary policy. Short-term inflation expectations, those up to two years ahead, should vary with the business cycle and shocks to the economy. Longer-term inflation expectations of three to five years or more are considered as anchored if the variations in short-term expectations do not affect their level significantly, because it indicates that public belief about the commitment to price stability by the monetary authority is

[27] The Chairman of this committee was Dr Urjit Patel, the serving deputy governor in charge of monetary policy in the RBI. See RBI Expert Committee, *Report of the Expert Committee to Revise and Strengthen the Monetary Policy Framework* (Mumbai: Reserve Bank of India, 2014).

[28] The Expert Committee suggested that since the current inflation and inflation expectations in India are elevated at 10 per cent, there should be a transition path that brings down inflation to the target zone of 6 per cent before the target of 4 per cent with a band of +/- 2 per cent is adopted.

[29] See L. Svensson, 'Inflation Targeting', in *Handbook of Monetary Economics*, eds B.M. Friedman and M. Woodford (North Holland: Elsevier, 2010), vol. 3b, Chapter 22.

stable. By setting a target for inflation which anchors inflation expectations, a central bank gains the flexibility to respond to shocks and obtain the effect of less persistence of any deviation of inflation from its expected long-term level.[30] The central bank should thus aim to anchor long-run inflation expectations by setting the target for inflation around a long-run level. The credibility of a central bank is in question if long-term inflation expectations follow movements in short-term inflation expectations.

The RBI has been assessing inflation expectations through surveys such as the Inflation Expectations Survey of Households, and the Survey of Professional Forecasters.[31] The household survey captures inflation expectations of the near future with three-month and one-year expectation periods. The professional forecasters' survey is more varied and captures quarterly, annual, 5-year and 10-year forecasts of inflation.[32] Historically, the professional forecasters defined inflation in terms of the WPI and the CPI for industrial workers, and this survey is now reoriented to collect data on short-term forecasts for the new combined CPI. This should be supplemented with data on long-term forecasts of inflation.

The Expert Committee also recommended that decision-making for monetary policy be vested in an MPC of five members. The governor of the RBI is to be the chairman of the MPC, the deputy governor in charge of monetary policy the vice chairman, and a third member would be the executive director in charge of monetary policy. Two external full-time members of the MPC will be decided on by the chairman and the vice chairman. The MPC is to take decisions by majority voting.

---

[30] This return of inflation to its long-term level occurs because the credibility of the monetary authority means the public will expect the monetary authority to do what is necessary to return inflation to its target level over the medium term.

[31] The other two surveys are the Industrial Outlook Survey of about 1,600 manufacturing companies with a three-month future horizon and the Consumer Confidence Survey across six metro cities with a one-year future horizon.

[32] This survey covers forecasters that bring out periodic updates on the economy, which include investment banks, commercial banks, stock exchanges, international brokerage houses, research and educational institutions, credit rating agencies, and asset management companies.

With restricted goal independence when the target for inflation is set in consultation with the government, it makes sense to give operational independence to the RBI to select the members of the MPC.[33] In that way, the government will be seen to be delegating responsibility and the RBI can also be held accountable by the requirement to explain its stance if it is unable to achieve the inflation target over a given time horizon. Majority voting is not a necessary requirement for an MPC constituted in such a manner as three of the members are from within the hierarchy of the RBI and the two external members, being chosen by the RBI, will most likely have some affinity for the views of the RBI. Such an MPC will be a version of an advisory MPC as currently practised. Its decision-making, to borrow a term used by Blinder, would be 'collegial' as the governor and his internal team would seek to elicit the views of the external members which they would deliberate on before arriving at the final policy statement.[34] The low likelihood of differences in the MPC would help the RBI to build credibility of its monetary policy statements and enhance its transmission. As credibility gets established, the MPC could have more external members and take decisions by voting.

The credibility of a central bank is achieved not only by making the MPC accountable for its decisions but also by insulating it from political pressure. The Expert Committee recommends a three-year term for the MPC, which is an insufficient period for the MPC to keep its focus on the long-term nominal anchor and also to establish its credibility. This is best achieved by giving the governor and deputy governor in charge of monetary policy long terms in office. The terms of the governor and deputy governor at the RBI have been a huge source of friction with the Ministry of Finance and a source of the un-anchoring of inflation expectations in India.[35] The consideration here should be that

[33] Fiscal dominance is addressed by having the central bank set the inflation target for the next five years in conjunction with the Ministry of Finance so that any fiscal adjustments within this timeframe have to take into account the inflation target.

[34] A. Blinder, 'Monetary Policy by Committee: Why and How?' Working Paper No. 92, De Nederlandsche Bank NV, Amsterdam, 2006.

[35] Khatkhate points out that in the period prior to 1969, there was a healthy convention of appointing the governor for five years. Since then, only four governors have completed their full term of five years, with one of these being

the appointment term of the governor and deputy governor should be longer than the term of the body that appoints them.[36] Since a government has a five-year term, it is important that the terms of the top functionaries of the RBI be set at seven years.[37] Such a long term in office can give these functionaries independence as well as the incentive to think about monetary policy over the long term, over which it is known to have an impact on the economy. The terms of the external members of the MPC who will be appointed by the central bank could be set at three years with the possibility of reappointment.[38]

In March 2016, the government announced its plan to appoint a committee to be headed by the cabinet secretary to select three members of the RBI MPC. The other three members will consist of the governor of the RBI, the deputy governor in charge of monetary policy, and one official of the RBI to be nominated by the central bank. This seems to be a negotiating compromise between the position of the FSLRC and the RBI Expert Committee recommendations, rather than a coherently thought-out way of establishing membership to such a committee. Once the goal of the MPC has been decided on—targeting inflation within a band—the task of achieving that goal is best delegated

---

extended after an initial term of two years. See Khatkhate, 'Reserve Bank of India'.

[36] Appointment procedures for central bankers significantly affect the conduct of policy. Chappell, Havrilesky, and McGregor show how policy votes by members of the Federal Reserve Board of Governors are affected by the President by whom they were appointed. See, H.W. Chappell Jr., T. M. Havrilesky, and R.R. McGregor, 'Partisan Monetary Policies: Presidential Influence through the Power of Appointment', *Quarterly Journal of Economics* 108, no. 1 (2013): 185–218.

[37] The Banco de Mexico, for instance, before adopting inflation targeting, modified the institutional framework so as to break the political cycle of the monetary authority given fiscal dominance. The central bank was made more independent by allowing the governor to be chosen in the third year of the current presidential administration, which lasts for six years. The governor cannot be replaced until the third year of the next administration.

[38] Expert Committee, *Report to Revise Monetary Policy*, January 2014. The Expert Committee of the RBI recommends no renewal prospects of the term in office for a member of the MPC.

to the RBI to achieve with clauses requiring it to be accountable by providing reports whenever it is unable to achieve the inflation target. It is superfluous for the government to both set the inflation target and then to decide on the membership of the MPC as it affects the operational flexibility with which the RBI approaches how to achieve the inflation target.

Management of Government Debt

Macroeconomic stability requires a coordination between monetary, fiscal, and debt management policies. The interconnection between these policies is portrayed in Table 4.1 below:

Table 4.1 Coordination between Monetary, Fiscal, and Debt Management Policies

Policy Coordination Due to Government Budget Constraint		
Fiscal Policy	Debt Management	Monetary Policy
D_t $=$	$B_t - B_{t-1}$ $+$	$M_t - M_{t-1}$

Source: Author's compilation.

The expression in the table states that budget deficits (D_t) must be financed by taking out loans through the net sales of bonds $(B_t - B_{t-1})$ or by the central bank's credit to the government which results in the growth of money supply $(M_t - M_{t-1})$. In reality, in most countries, money supply is not created exclusively through the central bank's credit to the government. However, in many countries (India included), the central bank is responsible for public debt management. Historically, this has been because central banks are involved with financial markets in their daily interventions so as to affect liquidity and so have more market expertise than government departments such as the Finance Ministry. This does give rise to a number of conflicts of interest.

A conflict arises when a central bank that attempts to be an effective debt manager would have an incentive to sell bonds at high prices, which would lead to a downplaying of its monetary policy role of being concerned with the control of inflation.[39] An implication of this

[39] These conflicts have been highlighted in India in the *Report of the Internal Working Group on Debt Management* chaired by Jahangir Aziz in 2008, and

conflict of interest is that a central bank that is concerned with the smooth issuance of public debt would be induced to provide more credit to the financial system when that debt is not favourably received by the market. In some limiting cases, the central bank may act as a residual buyer when the market exhibits an aversion to exposure to the auction of public debt. Since a central bank can always issue currency to buy unsold government securities, it has led rating agencies to give the highest local currency rating to government paper.

The implication is that once an independent debt management agency (IDMA) is established, the government should lose some of that high credit rating. The cost of an IDMA is a deterioration of government creditworthiness. The creditworthiness of government-issued securities by an IDMA will be determined by the projected flow of tax revenues and expenditure. This will, particularly with a fiscally profligate government, raise the interest cost of government debt and the cost of capital in the economy.

Another rationale for an IDMA is that a central bank that issues government securities has an incentive to mandate that banks hold large amounts of government paper. In turn, it is often alleged that this makes it difficult to develop a liquid market in government securities and inhibits the development of a corporate bond market. Unlike in the past, government securities are now issued at market rates of interest, and even though the statutory liquidity ratio has declined, banks continue to hold more government paper than is mandated. This is due to problems associated with doing business in the real economy and not due to issues in the financial markets. Banks find it difficult to secure the credit they offer because potential borrowers do not have assets that can be efficiently collateralized, or because they cannot enforce lending contracts and security provisions at low costs in the courts, or because of the weak infrastructure of the market that does not assist

---

by the FSLRC's own Working Group on Debt Management Office, chaired by M. Govinda Rao. These working groups overlook the implication of this conflict for government creditworthiness that is discussed in this chapter. See Internal Working Group on Debt Management, *Establishing a National Treasury Management Agency* (New Delhi: Ministry of Finance, 2008); and Working Group on Debt Management Office, *Report* (New Delhi: Ministry of Finance, 2012).

in reducing informational asymmetries. In such circumstances, banks prefer to offset the credit risks that are a characteristic of lending to the private sector with public debt that has low credit risk. In fact, it could be argued that depositors' willingness to put their savings into banks that are intermediating in risky assets increases if the financial intermediary has sufficient government debt on its balance sheet. The advantage of holding large amounts of public debt even when there is no regulatory requirement to do so is because it is easy to pledge as collateral in wholesale security markets and repo markets and there is a liquid secondary market that provides a reasonably stable resale value for it. Banks would continue to hold a large portfolio of government securities even if SLR requirements were to be reduced.

The prudent management of public debt is then very important for the health of the banking system, as banks hold this debt to facilitate their credit intermediation to the private sector. For instance, the FSLRC has correctly argued that unifying the public debt management function and linking it with the cash and investment management functions will improve information and decision-making. Within the Finance Ministry, priority is given to budget preparation and the analysis of expenditure proposals and ensuring that debt and cash management are not high-profile activities. And within the central bank, there is a conflict of interest between debt management and monetary policy. Thus, it is best to have an independent debt management agency in place while recognizing the interconnections between debt management and fiscal and monetary policy.

Objectives of Debt Management Agency and Monetary Policy

The FSLRC has stated that the objective of debt management is to minimize the costs of meeting the government's financing needs over the long term while taking into account an acceptable level of risk. Here, it ought to be added that the objective for cash management is to minimize the cost of offsetting the government's net cash flows over time, keeping in mind the risk acceptable to the Finance Ministry. Two factors need to be flagged here. First, the objective of debt management should explicitly be long term and not tied to the annual remits given by the Finance Ministry that would specify the planned annual sales of government securities and their split by maturity band. It should be concerned with the long term to ensure that market participants are confident the IDMA does not take tactical decisions which exploit legal or informational constraints faced by them.[40] It is important to recognize that an IDMA should not look for short-term opportunistic benefits as the government's financing needs have costs that have long-term implications arising from the interest payments on the debt, and the associated costs of borrowing again in the future. It is also important for an IDMA to develop a liquid and efficient secondary market since it is going to repeatedly borrow in this market.

Second, debt management should be consistent with the aims of monetary policy. It is often forgotten that the independence of a central bank from fiscal institutions is shaky because the arithmetic of the government's budget constraint requires interdependence. Each period, the government budget constraint states that the real value of government expenditures plus interest payments on government debts plus retirements or repayments of outstanding debts must be financed. Part of this is financed through tax collections and disinvestment. The deficit of the government is then funded by proceeds from issues of new interest-bearing government debt. Then, if the monetary authority were to raise the interest rate with the aim of controlling inflation, the expenditure side of the government budget increases from the increase in interest payments on government debt, and in addition, the government must issue new debt to finance this expenditure. As monetary policy is working to contract the level of economic activity, the budget would be working in the opposite direction. The fiscal effort of the government must, then, be consistent with monetary policy in the sense that the fiscal deficit must be adjusted to ensure that it is in sync with the objective of monetary policy. An important part of the objective of debt management, then, is that it is consistent with the aims of monetary policy.

How can this be achieved in practice? First and foremost, it requires the government to set out a fiscal policy objective. With a view towards debt management and consistency with monetary policy, fiscal policy must have an objective of promoting equity across generations, which means that the government budget must be sustainable. A mandate

---

[40] The FSLRC recognizes this aspect of debt management.

of sustainable public finances must be joined with the objective that, while stabilizing business cycles, fiscal policy is supportive of monetary policy and improves its effect on the economy. A sustainable fiscal policy requires the government to set targets for the debt and the deficits and, in the process, set targets for growth and inflation. Having posted targets for these macro variables, it should give full operational independence to the central bank to set monetary policy with the aim of achieving those targets. Since one of the objectives of fiscal policy is sustainability, which is a long-run objective, and since fiscal policy must be consistent with monetary policy, the objective of debt management should be to minimize over the long run the costs of meeting the government's financing needs, taking into account the government's appetite for risk, and also that debt management policy is consistent with the aims of monetary policy. Many countries that have established IDMAs stipulate such an objective of consistency with monetary policy.

At present, RBI participates actively in the cash forecasting process and uses ways and means advances to smooth out mismatches in revenue and expenditure. The discussions between the budget division of the Ministry of Finance and RBI on cash management, as RBI is the banker to the government, should be associated with a requirement that RBI and the budget division will supply to the IDMA forecasts of the government's net cash requirement and exchequer cash flows. This will help the IDMA to ensure that the government does not have surplus cash on hand while it is borrowing unnecessarily on the capital markets and incurring debt servicing costs.

An IDMA should legally be part of the Ministry of Finance but operate at arm's length from it, as part of its brief of being an executive agency. More importantly, from the perspective of the financial markets, prospective bondholders would be apprehensive that government debt managers are using inside information to manipulate the price of bonds. To allay this concern, it is important that debt managers be operating in an institutional set-up where there is no possibility of inside information being shared on changes in fiscal or monetary policy. There ought not be any formal membership of the Finance Ministry or RBI in the debt management committee, which should be accountable to Parliament for its performance.

Macro-prudential Policy

The recent financial crisis has made policymakers realize that even
when the output gap and inflation gap are stable, all may not be well
in the background of the economic arena. There could very well be
pressures building up in the financial sector, which results in financial
instability that eventually transforms into setbacks to economic activity. Since financial imbalances can build up due to the under-pricing
of risk, moral hazard in the presence of implicit safety nets, and herd
behaviour, it is important to mitigate such systemic risk. When imbalances unwind, shocks rapidly propagate through the financial system as
a result of the high degree of interconnectedness. To maintain financial
stability, then, it is important to use macro-prudential policy that aims
to prevent or mitigate systemic risk. It is the task of macro-prudential
policy to identify and counter the build-up of financial imbalances in
order to address the inappropriate incentives that trigger or strengthen
herd-like behaviour or excessive risk-taking.

Financial stability has a time-series dimension and a cross-section
dimension. In the time-series dimension, the focus is on the build-up
of financial imbalances over time—for instance, in good times agents
tend to underestimate risk and over invest. Such over-investment is
driven by credit. In bad times the opposite occurs: agents become more
risk averse and are unwilling to invest. Banks also hold back credit for
new investment. The cross-section dimension of systemic risk stems
from externalities in the financial system. Spillovers arise from the
underlying interconnections in the financial system, such as interbank
exposures via the interbank market or counterparty exposures between
financial institutions. Spillovers also take place due to common exposures when financial institutions invest in the same asset and are then
simultaneously hit by a shock to the price of that asset.[41]

Various time-varying instruments and mechanisms to internalize
externalities have been suggested for stabilizing financial imbalances
that trigger systemic risks to the stability of the financial system.[42]

[41] This has been the case when financial institutions in many countries have
invested in housing.

[42] For time-varying instruments, capital buffers, loan-to-value ratios, and
liquidity charges have been suggested. For internalizing externalities, capital

There are strong interconnections between monetary policy and macro-prudential policy.[43] An expansionary monetary policy that keeps interest rates low can lead to the underestimation of risk and risk-taking. This would require the use of macro-prudential tools. For instance, policymakers may require higher loan-to-value ratios that have a negative effect on housing investment, which in turn reduces the output of the economy. Macro-prudential policy in such an instance requires a balanced monetary policy that sets policy rates above that consistent with flexible inflation targeting.[44] In that case, monetary policy also affects financial stability in addition to its standard output and inflation stabilization objectives. In a period when risks are building up and financial imbalances growing, monetary policy rates should be higher than the neutral level that is required by flexible inflation targeting. Similarly, policy rates should be cut sharply whenever a crisis emerges.

The wisdom until the occurrence of the financial crisis had been that central banks should do nothing until asset price bubbles burst. That is valid so long as the only instrument available to a central bank is the policy rate. With macro-prudential tools available to a central bank, there is a need to coordinate policy rates with these tools so as to maintain economic stability and support economic growth.[45]

---

surcharges on systemically important financial institutions, collateral-based tools that value collateral based on constant margins and haircuts so as to avoid fire sales, and measures to improve the resilience of large-value payments and settlement systems, such as real-time gross settlement, have been suggested.

[43] O. Blanchard, 'Monetary Policy in the Wake of the Crisis', in *In the Wake of the Crisis: Leading Economists Reassess Economic Policy*, eds O. Blanchard, D. Romer, M. Spence, and J. Stiglitz (Boston: MIT Press 2012), 7–14.

[44] Under flexible inflation targeting, central banks allow the inflation target to be achieved over a longer time horizon so as to stabilize the output gap.

[45] The tasks of macro-prudential policy are not easy. Since monetary policy is forward-looking by nature, central banks will have to focus on the identification of latent future risks brought about by current developments in the financial sector. This is not easy in good times when default rates drop, and banks report fewer credit losses and allocate less towards provisioning. The most promising forward-looking indicators have been found to be deviations of current values of credit-to-GDP or the ratio of real estate prices to income from their long-term trends.

Monetary policy that responds to economic recessions by extending liquidity or lowering interest rates has the potential to promote moral hazard and excessive risk-taking and contribute to the amplification of the financial cycle, as the recent financial crisis has demonstrated. Thus, prudential supervision of the financial system and macro-prudential policy should be located in the central bank. With a responsibility for systemic stability, the central bank has to strike the balance between inflation and output stabilization and financial stability. The central bank should then be formally charged with the responsibility and the tools to conduct macro-prudential policy.

This is not a new feature of central banking. A major historical motivation for the creation of central banks in the mid-nineteenth century was to manage the payments system and stabilize banking systems. The German Reichsbank (1875) and the Federal Reserve System of the United States (1914) were set up with this purpose. It was only later, with the advent of fiat money, that central banks began to be concerned with the problem of price stability. However, so far independence for central banks has been granted only for the maintenance of price stability in countries where this has been explicitly stated as an objective. Holding central banks accountable for this is made easy by the availability of benchmarks or a numerical goal (inflation between 0 and 2 per cent, for instance) against which the public or its representatives can measure the performance of the central bank. The same is not true of financial stability. At best, a country can mandate periodic reporting requirements to the government indicating how the central bank is pursuing its mandate regarding financial stability. But the absence of an explicit nominal anchor such as for inflation makes it difficult for the central bank to be convincing in this regard.

Moreover, whereas the setting of the monetary policy rate is perceived as being fairly neutral as between various sections of society and sectors of the economy, in the case of financial stability, it is often a particular sector that is being targeted (as in the case of loan-to-value ratios set for housing and real estate). Finally, macro-prudential policy aiming at curbing the excess build-ups in the financial system is still at an early stage of development, and success in macro-prudential policy is still ill defined. Since there are many trade-offs involved in macro-prudential policy and it could involve the cooperation of other institutions or ministries of the government, the governance arrangements for this may involve more political oversight and less independence for the central bank. This is a difficult situation for a central bank to be in, but in the process of setting up the governance and oversight mechanisms by which this function will be held accountable, it is important that fragmentation of the supervisory structure be avoided.

One reason monetary policy is viewed as being neutral is because its capability of affecting inflation (and in the short run, economic activity) has been emphasized over its impact on the distribution of income and wealth. Monetary policy does have an impact on distribution because different sections of society are holding different levels of debt and the real value of this debt could be reduced or increased by the inflationary or deflationary pressures stemming from changes in policy rates. Recipients of fixed incomes such as from wages and interest payments (creditors) would always have an interest in a strong currency. However, by focusing on price stability and delivering on it and achieving credibility that it will not act opportunistically, central banks have been able to maintain that they are neutral about the distributional outcomes arising from monetary policy measures. In a similar vein, it is important going forward for macro-prudential policy to be perceived as credible even when it is known to have differential impacts across sectors of the economy.

Fortunately, in the Indian context, the regulation of the financial sector has historically been entrusted to the RBI, and it has used prudential measures to curb the build-up of financial imbalances.[46] When high credit growth was observed in sectors such as real estate and the stock markets, specific sectoral measures were embarked on with the tightening of provisioning norms and risk weights. On witnessing a sharp rise in house prices and high credit growth to the real estate sector in 2010, the loan-to-value ratio was capped at 80 per cent for loans above Rs 2 million and 90 per cent for loans up to Rs 2 million, which was a variable that had never been regulated before. Such measures did have the effect of moderating credit growth and restricting the gradual

[46] The Preamble to the RBI Act of 1935 states the organization's basic objective as being to 'regulate the issue of bank notes and keeping reserves with a view to securing monetary stability in India'.

accumulation of housing loan exposures of the banks.[47] This was made possible because bank supervision is under the auspices of the central bank and that enabled information flows within the organization, from the banking supervision department to the monetary policy department, and supported the making of central bank decisions which promote a stable economic system. Such measures not only had the impact of mitigating the steady accrual of financial imbalances at an early stage, but also had the beneficial consequence of increasing credibility for the central bank. Just as credibility is important for managing expectations in monetary policy, the credibility of the central bank and its ability to influence expectations is important for financial stability. Once it becomes known by agents that the central bank will intervene to stabilize the implied volatility from excessive risk and irrational exuberance, such risks may not even build up in the first place. The promotion of financial stability in India so far has been ad hoc,[48] and going forward, the RBI needs to adopt more systematic approaches (see note 28 in this chapter) so that agents in the economy may conduct economic transactions after taking into account the likely trajectory of policy. This will temper the underlying volatility of the economic process.

In the realm of financial stability, it is imperative for central banks to establish a fine working relation with their governments as it is not always the case that central bank funds are sufficient to manage a financial stability measure. The New York Fed's 'Maiden Lane' vehicles, for instance, that were set up to acquire the assets of Bear Stearns or provide financial support to AIG, were backed by the US Treasury in the event of losses being realized.[49] Similarly in India, the large capital inflows from 1993–4 onwards resulted in a stress on liquidity management as continuous sterilization by the RBI led to a shortage of government securities on its balance sheet.[50] Since the RBI Act, 1934 prohibits the

---

[47] Other prudential regulations that the RBI introduced were an overall ceiling on bank access to external borrowings in the wake of large capital inflows, and interest ceilings and minimum maturity requirements on Non-Resident Indian (NRI) deposits. See Mohan, *Growth with Financial Stability*, 271–346.

[48] Mohan, *Growth with Financial Stability*, 43–81.

[49] The Swiss National Bank's Stabfund set up to bail out UBS was supported by the Swiss cantons through a SFr 6 billion subscription to mandatory convertible notes.

[50] See Figure 4.3 in this chapter.

issuance of securities by the RBI, the government issued short-term treasury bills and medium-term dated government securities that it did not need for borrowing purposes because the RBI required it for liquidity management. This market stabilization scheme was introduced on 1 April 2004, and the proceeds from the securities were parked in a separate identifiable cash account maintained and operated by the RBI.[51] The RBI was thus able to nullify the expansionary impact of the increase in net foreign exchange assets from the capital inflows. In times of crisis and when dealing with financial stability issues, central bank policy often gets tied up with the domain of a government institution. Such instances can undermine the credibility and independence of a central bank, and it is important for the central bank to share openly with the government the dilemmas it faces, and yet to ensure that the government gives significant weight to the assessments about policy made by the RBI. The RBI can ensure this if it is always apolitical and takes a long-term view of macroeconomic management.

Foreign Exchange Reserves Management

Unlike many other emerging markets, India's increased reserves in the last decade were driven by a capital account surplus and were due to portfolio flows rather than debt flows.[52] The RBI responded to the capital inflows by accumulating foreign exchange reserves so as to provide confidence to the markets that external obligations can always be met, and to enhance its capacity to intervene in foreign exchange markets to reduce volatility and to limit external vulnerability. India's reserves are the fifth-highest among emerging and developing economies as of the end of 2012, and the eleventh-highest in world economy.[53] As reserves

---

[51] Interest payments on these securities are borne by the government, and such securities can only be used for redemption. During capital outflows, such as just after the failure of Lehman Brothers, these securities are redeemed and liquidity is injected into the banking system.

[52] E. D'Souza, 'Globalization's Underbelly: Capital Flows and Indian Economy—V.C. Padmanabhan Memorial Lecture', *Economic and Political Weekly* 43, no. 35 (2008): 34–8.

[53] The top five countries are China (reserves of US $ 3.3 trillion), Saudi Arabia (reserves of US $ 662 billion), Russia (US $ 537 billion), Brazil

grow, there is bound to be a shift from viewing reserves as an insurance policy that provides a level of comfort about managing external obligations and volatility to a view that reserves should be viewed as a source for a national investment fund. As foreign exchange reserves grow, they attract the attention of the media and politicians who think of 'excess' reserves as an opportunity to pursue projects that may have little benefit for the economy. Central banks, including the RBI, have to engage with politicians so that the establishment of a sovereign wealth fund does not result in a loss of control over reserves. Central to this engagement is the requirement to develop a consensus as to what the goals of reserve management are, so that there is mission clarity for central bank reserve managers who face an increasing demand to seek additional yield to offset the negative carry of holding increasingly larger amounts of foreign exchange reserves. The trend has been for the managers of such reserves to slowly move away from investing in deposits to short-term fixed income securities, and recently also to inflation-linked securities on the expectation that developed countries may resort to inflation to handle their large debt burdens that have resulted from the financial crisis.[54]

Foreign exchange reserve managers are increasingly struggling with defining whether their primary objective is capital preservation or liquidity. In this connection, the RBI has earlier flagged the possibility of having tranches of reserves, with each tranche having a different combination of safety, liquidity, and return.[55] This idea must be made more explicit. For instance, with the aim of defining separate tranches, each with a different objective, risk tolerance level, and benchmark, a step-wise method to reserve management could be developed. The first tranche of reserves could be purely for the meeting of liquidity with instruments denominated in the US dollar, which is the principle currency used for intervention. As reserve targets satisfy the demand for insurance, a second tranche could be activated that stipulates a greater risk appetite such as

(US $ 371 billion), and India (US $ 287 billion). See 'World Economic Outlook Database', Statistical Appendix to 'World Economic Outlook Report 2012', IMF October 2012, IMF Publication Services, Washington, DC.

[54] G. Smith, 'Held in Reserve', *Central Banking* 22, no. 2 (2012): 75–9.

[55] Y.V. Reddy, *India and the Global Financial Crisis: Managing Money and Finance* (New Delhi: Orient BlackSwan, 2011), 261–72.

investing in higher yielding assets like agency mortgage-backed securities. Regulations would have to be put in place indicating how the risk appetite of a higher tranche is detached from the management of a lower tranche so as to insulate the reserves from negative performance. Rather than having to constantly guard against the expropriation of reserves by politicians, especially when there are low yields on their primary asset (US government securities), developing guidelines on managing reserves allows them to justify the time horizon of their investments and the returns associated with them that match with the need to hold reserves for insuring against external vulnerabilities.

Financial Policies

Apart from regulating financial markets, central banks in developing economies are involved in two other types of financial policies: developing markets and financial institutions, and allocating or directing credit towards priority activities. The RBI realized that for monetary transmission to take place, efficient price discovery is essential, which requires deep and liquid financial markets. Ever since the economy gravitated towards market determination of interest and exchange rates along with current account convertibility and gradual capital account convertibility, the RBI and the government took many initiatives to develop financial markets. In the banking sector, for instance, during the early phase of liberalization, public sector banks required capital infusion from the government. Over time, such banks were allowed to issue their shares on the market, subject to maintaining public ownership of 51 per cent. This contributed to a diversified ownership, and banks today are in a position to meet Basel III capital rules. Over time, the classification of non-performing assets was tightened, and yet, the share of non-performing assets in total assets has been declining since the middle of the 1990s. A landmark regulation was the promulgation of the Securitization and Reconstruction of Financial Assets and Enforcement of Security Interest (SARFAESI) Act of 2002, which assisted in the resolution of non-performing loans. Greater competition has been introduced in the banking sector with the entry of new-generation private sector banks. The productivity and performance of the Indian banks have also improved as they resort to technology to manage their assets. Despite these changes, the reach of the banks has

improved and the goal of extending credit facilities to the disadvantaged sections of society has continued.

It is in the development of the money markets that the RBI has played
a large role in initiating far-reaching institutional changes. Specifically,
the call money market has been altered into an interbank market from
August 2005. To facilitate price discovery and bring liquidity to the
market, new money market instruments were enabled to manage
short-term liquidity requirements. The repo market outside the liquidity adjustment facility[56] of the RBI, for instance, was broadened by
allowing non-bank financial companies, mutual funds, housing finance
companies, and insurance companies that did not hold Subsidiary
General Ledger (SGL) accounts to undertake repo transactions from
March 2003.[57] Settlement was handled through a delivery-versus-
payments system. A new instrument in the form of collateralized borrowing and lending obligations (CBLO) was introduced in 2003, along
with the institutionalization of the Clearing Corporation of India Ltd.
(CCIL) as a central counterparty. [58] These resulted in the development
of the interbank market. Similarly, the RBI has initiated many measures
in the government securities market, such as introduction of auctions
for the issuance of these securities, the widening of the investor base
with the introduction of primary dealers, and the development of the
technological infrastructure via an anonymous platform for trading in
the form of Negotiated Dealing System-Order Matching (NDS-OM)[59]

[56] This is a monetary policy tool that allows banks to resolve any short-term
cash shortages by borrowing money through repurchase agreements from the
RBI by using eligible securities as collateral.

[57] Government Securities are held in demat form to the credit of the holder
in the SGL maintained in the books of RBI. This account gets debited or credited with the sale or purchase of securities.

[58] This is a discounted instrument in electronic book form for a maturity
period ranging from 1 to 90 days. The eligible securities are central government securities and the CCIL is the counterparty and guarantees settlement of
transactions. The CBLO segment of the repo market has participation by banks,
insurance companies, mutual funds, non-bank finance companies, primary dealers, non-government provident funds, corporates, and so on.

[59] The NDS-OM system, which is owned by the RBI, was introduced in
August 2005 as an electronic, screen-based, anonymous, order-driven system for
dealing in government securities.

and settlement mechanism through the CCIL.[60] The weak point in the debt markets has been the near absence of the corporate debt market in India. Indian corporates use private placements to issue small amounts of bonds and rely on external borrowings which tend to be much cheaper than domestic borrowing.[61] In addition, the lack of a dependable system for resolving financial distress also makes investors unwilling to purchase unsecured bonds of risky corporates.

The RBI has also been involved in regulating banks so that credit is directed to priority sectors in accordance with social objectives. Financial penetration has been adequate in India, as evinced by the fact that in a cross-country plot of credit-GDP ratios and per capita income levels, India is above the trend line,[62] suggesting that credit penetration is higher than expected, given its level of income.[63] Identifying whether there has been success or failure of a directed credit programme is not easy as there is no way of knowing whether access to credit at affordable rates of interest by the target groups would have been higher or lower in the absence of such programmes. After bank nationalization in 1969, however, bank branches opened in approximately 30,000 rural locations (as of 1990) where no prior formal credit and savings institutions existed. The RBI had announced a branch licensing policy in 1977 (that remained until 1990) which required that for a license to open a branch in a banked location, the bank must open branches in four eligible unbanked locations. Branch expansion was significantly higher in financially less developed states and led to a reduction in rural poverty.[64]

[60] CCIL is a joint stock company owned by major banks and financial institutions. It is the exclusive clearing and settlement agency for the government securities market and acts as the central counter party for all secondary trades in the market. The RBI regulates the CCIL.

[61] High Level Committee on Financial Sector Reforms (CFSR), *Report: A Hundred Small Steps* (New Delhi: Sage Publications, 2009), http://planning-commission.nic.in/reports/genrep/rep_fr/cfsr_all.pdf. The CFSR, chaired by Raghuram Rajan, submitted its report to the Government of India in 2009.

[62] Per capita income is in purchasing power parity US dollar terms.

[63] Mohan, *Growth with Financial Stability*, 3–42 (especially Figure 1.3).

[64] R. Burgess and R. Pande, 'Do Rural Banks Matter? Evidence from the Indian Social Banking Experiment', *American Economic Review* 95, no. 3 (June 2005): 780–95.

After 1990, with the advent of economic reforms, banks were required to clean up their balance sheets, and credit expansion to agriculture and the small-scale sector did slow down. At the same time, credit from non-institutional sources began to expand in the 1990s.[65] However, since 2002, this trend has been reversed with access to formal financial institutions improving. To increase bank penetration in the economy, the self-help group-bank linkage programme and the *kisan* credit card scheme were introduced in 1992 and 2001, respectively. In 2005, the RBI counselled banks to open 'no-frill' accounts with low or zero-minimum stipulated balances and charges to expand their outreach to larger sections of the population. In recent years, microfinance has also been promoted. However, the spatial distribution of banking services is still lopsided, with the share of deposits and credit in metropolitan areas increasing. The RBI has been spending a lot of effort on promoting financial inclusion, which requires supporting innovations that introduce mobile technologies and establish credit information bureaus on a platform that will extend the reach of formal institutions.

Human Resources and Organization Structure

The RBI has been reorganizing its various internal departments over the years in order to respond to the various changes in the financial environment. For instance, as monetary management began to increase in complexity, the Credit Planning Cell was transformed into the Monetary Policy Department. The RBI set up the Board of Financial Supervision in 1994 to guide banking supervision and regulation, and more recently the Financial Stability Unit and Risk Monitoring Department in response to the growing vulnerabilities in the financial system. However, departments were rarely rationalized along functional lines, and the decision as to which deputy governor they were to report to was taken rather so as to equalize the administrative burdens of the deputy governors. A few years ago, the RBI rationalized the reporting structure, leading departments to be organized according to the following clusters: (1) Monetary Policy and Research, (2) Regulation and Risk

---

[65] RBI, *The Banking Sector in India: Emerging Issues and Challenges*, vols IV and V, *Reports on Currency and Finance, 2006–08* (Mumbai: Reserve Bank of India, 2008), https://rbi.org.in/Scripts/PublicationsView.aspx?id=11269.

Management, (3) Supervision and Inclusion, (4) Financial Markets and Infrastructure, and (5) Human Resources Operations. With five clusters and four deputy governors, the RBI should now move towards having an additional deputy governor. However, this requires an amendment to the RBI Act which allows for a maximum of four deputy governors. Similarly, with one executive director looking after two to three departments in a cluster, the number of executive directors required would grow from the existing nine to eleven to as many as twelve. After this revamp, the recruitment of officers to clusters is to be done via a common entrance exam, following which there would be a period of initial training where an overall view of the bank would be provided, and then officers would be encouraged to specialize in their initial years in a couple of clusters. The RBI is developing an Assessment Centre that would assess staff aptitude and a new Performance Evaluation System along with careful job profiling as part of the promotion and development of employees. There are plans to create an RBI Academy that will hone the higher-order skills of officers and staff, and there is a shift in incentives towards rewarding high performers with more challenging assignments.

Contemporary important units have been set up in the past couple of years, such as the Forecasting and Modelling Unit within the Monetary Policy Department and the Market Intelligence Unit within the Financial Markets Regulation Department—an indication of organizational responsiveness to the ever-changing financial landscape. The RBI is finally channelling some of its energies towards human resource development—a long overdue requirement. Significantly, the number of employees has declined by 53 per cent from 35,500 in 1981 to 16,700 today. However, with 44 per cent of these belonging to Class I staff, the organization has too many assistant, maintenance, and service staff.

The RBI has been actively engaged in keeping abreast of recent trends that have a bearing on its functioning. Its officers are provided incentives to upgrade their skills, with several sent to training programmes in different parts of the world as well as e-learning via the Financial Stability Institute. About one hundred officers have been sent for a year's training at some of the foremost academic institutions in the world such as Harvard, Stanford, London School of Economics, and so on.

The officers of the RBI have also been involved in many multilateral working groups such as at the Bank of International Settlements Financial Stability Forum, and some are sent on deputation to these institutions, which increases their exposure to best practices. RBI staff produce many technical papers and reports, such as the RBI occasional papers series. Expertise from outside the organization is brought in with the Development Research Group at the RBI funding studies from scholars in other institutions, in collaboration with the staff of the central bank. The RBI has supported the growth of markets by promoting bodies like the Primary Dealers Association of India and the Fixed Income Money Market Dealers Association of India, and it interacts frequently with industry bodies such as the Indian Banks' Association. Finally, the RBI gains from external know-how by including academics, representatives of industry associations, and market participants on its working groups and committees. The nurturing of a high level of technical expertise compared to that available to the government is an important component that enables the RBI to define and retain its independence and to choose appropriate monetary and financial policies, as well as to resist those that are not favourable for the course of the economy.

The RBI, as an institution, was set up to conduct monetary policy, manage public debt, be a banker to the government, and manage the foreign exchange reserves of the country. Its top management is appointed by the government, and to insulate them from political pressure as well as enable them to take a long-term view which is essential to monetary policy, it is advisable that the governor and deputy governor in charge of monetary policy be given a seven-year term. In order to align fiscal and monetary policy and to pre-commit economic policymakers it is advantageous that the government, in consultation with the central bank, also specify a price stability target. As of now, the RBI defines inflation with reference to the WPI. Since the last couple of years, with the publication of a CPI that applies to the whole population, the RBI should use this index to indicate headline inflation in India. The government has set up FSLRC that has recommended the institution of an MPC with voting rights. However, when members of an MPC are not employees of the central bank, their incentives to provide the public service required at the MPC are blunted. While they do bring in new perspectives and can negate some of the groupthink that officials of the central bank may be subject to, they could also free ride and rely on the data and analysis that is provided by the officials of the bank. Making their decision visible by publishing the discussions of the MPC in order to deter free riding has the flipside that the lack of confidentiality may result in chilling frank discussion. In an emerging market, it is also important to keep in mind that dissent in voting on the policy rate can affect the coherence of the policy and affect the credibility of the central bank. The incentives to communicate with the market and to establish credibility currently lie with the top management of the RBI, and monetary policy should continue to be their responsibility, after taking inputs from an advisory MPC that alerts them to other perspectives.

The RBI has been the debt manager to the government, which involves a conflict of interest, as when it sells bonds it would like interest rates to be low whereas monetary policy that is concerned with inflation would focus on a higher interest rate policy. Setting up an IDMA will come with associated costs; since the issuing of government paper will no longer be connected with the central bank, the creditworthiness of government securities will have to be determined by the projected flow of tax revenues and government expenditures. This does mean that the cost of debt could go up. However, setting up an IDMA has the benefit that the government will have to think of debt management as a long-term activity and of government budgets as sustainable. But it requires that fiscal efforts should be consistent with monetary policy. An IDMA should, then, have the objective of minimizing the long-run costs of meeting the government's financing needs, taking into account the government's appetite for risk, and ensuring that debt management policy is consistent with the aims of monetary policy with respect to the price stability target.

Since the 2007–8 financial crisis, the monetary policy goal of central banks of price stability has been compounded with a macro-prudential goal of financial stability. Both price stability and financial stability are intermediate targets that contribute to the ultimate goal of a central bank—which is to promote a stable economic system that spurs growth. The RBI has pursued the goal of financial stability in an ad hoc manner thus far. It is important that the RBI takes a more systematic approach to this issue so as to reduce the volatility in the economy. Financial stability is not as well-developed an area of expertise as monetary policy and involves the cooperation of other institutions that could affect the autonomy of the RBI from political interference. Thus, it is important that the RBI and government work closely to avoid opportunistic behaviour with regard to prudential policies that enhance financial stability.

This is possible if they share a healthy relationship where they give significant weight to one another's assessments about policy and take a long-term view of macroeconomic management.

With India among the top foreign exchange reserve holding countries, there is always a danger that reserves will come to be viewed at some point not so much as an insurance for managing external obligations and exchange rate volatility but rather as a source for a national investment fund. Again, the RBI must engage with politicians and the government to ensure that it does not lose control over reserves. At the same time, it is imperative that the objective of reserves management be defined in terms of capital preservation or liquidity. This requires defining separate tranches, each with its own objective and risk tolerance level. The first tranche could be used to meet liquidity while a second tranche could invest in higher yielding assets and be subject to higher risk. RBI guidelines should articulate the time horizon of reserve investments, and the trade-offs between insuring against external vulnerabilities and higher returns should be carefully considered.

***

The RBI has been effectively engaged in developing financial markets in conjunction with the government so as to strengthen the monetary transmission process. Greater competition among banks, new regulation strengthening debt recovery, increasingly stringent classifications of non-performing assets, the development of the CBLO segment of the money markets, and auctions for government securities have all helped to increase the resilience of the financial markets. Importantly, the RBI has also been involved with the social and distributional goal of directing credit towards priority activities.

Central banks evolve with economic conditions; most central banks have been designed. A well-designed central bank must always consider the implications of its decisions on fiscal policy and debt management, which requires it to have a healthy relationship with the government in which assessments for macroeconomic policy are taken with a view to promoting sustainable economic growth over a long-term horizon.

Operationally, however, the central bank should be independent and not be under pressure from the government. Even when the setting up of India's central bank was being contemplated, none other than Keynes insisted that it be operationally independent so as to avoid government pressures for lending. Keynes also insisted that it would be better if the central bank be situated not in Delhi but at a geographical distance from the seat of government, so as to lessen the influence of government on it.[66] Today, it is as essential that the RBI have operational independence.

---

[66] F. Capie, 'Some Scattered Thoughts from History on Evolution and Design in Central Banking', in *Designing Central Banks*, eds D. Mayes and G. Wood (London: Routledge, 2008), 18–33.

5

REFORMING INDIA'S INSTITUTIONS OF PUBLIC EXPENDITURE GOVERNANCE

Nirvikar Singh

From the time of Independence, the majority of India's political leaders have conceived of a significant role for the government in promoting economic growth, as well as for fostering development more broadly. This has translated into an active role in regulating private sector economic activity, as well as direct government participation in many aspects of the economy, including production, distribution, and finance, that might otherwise be performed by the private sector. The case for this degree of government control of the economy was built on a combination of conceptual and empirical foundations, including ideas about market failure (especially coordination failures but also inefficiencies and inequities created by private sector monopolies) and the apparently successful example of Soviet-style central planning. In 1947, government-led modernization of India's economy (and its society as well) was by no means an implausible path.

India's own experience and global events combined to lead to a reorientation of economic policy thinking, and, certainly from 1991—if not somewhat earlier—the government has embarked on a slow, fitful process of removing some constraints on private sector economic activity, as well as opening the economy to the rest of the world. The precise nature, timing, and impact of this historical shift are still being debated. Even without definitive answers to questions about past experience, there is also a vigorous debate on the appropriate role of government in the economy going forward—in India as well as across the globe.

At one level, there is now greater conceptual clarity about the role of government, in the sense that theoretical advances in economics and related disciplines have given us a better understanding of the working of markets and the sources of market failure. In addition to classic arguments for government action based on the existence and realities of public goods and externalities, there are also justifications based on the presence of information asymmetries and of incentives for strategic behaviour. While these theoretical arguments provide a richer rationale for government intervention in the workings of the economy, they also introduce complexities that make it harder to assess the empirical experience of the past and also to design effective future policies. On the latter front, in particular, paying attention to information and incentives raises issues of institutional design; the government is no longer a unitary, wise, and benevolent ruler, but a complicated amalgam of rules, norms, individuals, and motivations.[1]

In the Indian case, one can elucidate several facets of the current debates about economic policy. One continuing strand of argument is that the government must continue giving more space to the market in order to promote economic growth and employment generation.[2] A different line of argument, quite widely held in India, is that the government has retreated from its proper task of providing relief to

---

[1] In fact, foregrounding the role of institutions extends to the design of market institutions (for example, stock markets, auction markets) as well, and to the structure of private sector organizations, ranging from conventional for-profit corporations to a diversity of non-profits, cooperatives, and voluntary organizations. Institutions have been given more attention in recent empirical attempts to explain the history of economic development and growth as well, going beyond earlier emphases on property rights, to encompass other measures of institutional quality. For a discussion on the Indian case in this context, see N. Singh, 'Some Economic Consequences of India's Institutions of Governance: A Conceptual Framework', *India Review* 3, no. 2 (April 2004): 114–46.

[2] See, for example, J. Bhagwati and A. Panagariya, *Why Growth Matters: How Economic Growth in India Reduced Poverty and the Lessons for Other Developing Countries* (New York: Public Affairs, 2013).

those citizens who are deprived in essential ways—whether it is food, healthcare, education, livelihoods, or general purchasing power.[3] These two perspectives are not polar opposites: the real issues, often not clearly surfaced, have to do with the trade-offs that exist and that policymakers are willing to make with respect to economic growth and equality, growth and broader measures of well-being, and short-run versus medium- or long-run gains in the different dimensions of positive achievement. Disagreements about trade-offs can be positive in nature (for example, what are the trade-offs in practice?) or normative (for example, what are the best choices along a frontier of possible combinations of growth and equality?).

However, there is a more basic question that transcends these debates about Indian economic policymaking. Whatever the government does, or should do, how can it do those things better? This general question then translates into specific issues of institutional design. Of course, one cannot address institutional design of government independently of considerations of objectives and trade-offs. For example, how one envisages the proper role of government in providing higher education will have implications for how the education ministry or relevant department is organized, what kinds of skill sets are needed by the relevant government employees, and so on. Nevertheless, some questions of institutional design can be posed where the premises and the answers will be agreeable to a wide spectrum of opinion. For example, if there is a broad consensus that the government should directly provide some extent of primary healthcare, while there may be differences of opinion with respect to its proper scope, there can also be broad agreement that public sector doctors should work the hours they are paid for, in the location they are expected to serve. An institutional reform that achieves this better than the current situation (at appropriate cost and without other negative consequences) should also, therefore, find broad support.

Accordingly, my focus partially transcends some of the debates about the precise role of government.[4] The question I pose is even

---

[3] See, for example, J. Drèze and A. Sen, *An Uncertain Glory: India and Its Contradictions* (Princeton, NJ: Princeton University Press, 2013).

[4] Those questions will inevitably be in the background; in particular, my presumption is that the government has a role to play in the economy that

narrower than 'how can the government be better at doing what it does?' Instead, I ask, 'how can the government spend its money to achieve its desired results better?' This excludes many important issues of regulation—regulation does involve government expenditure, but the amounts are trivial compared to spending on salaries for large numbers of government employees, transfer payments, delivery of health and education, and various kinds of public infrastructure.

So far, I have spoken of 'government' as a unified, somewhat abstract entity, but as was indicated earlier in this introduction, government is a complex, multifaceted institution. To understand its working and the potential for reform, one has to unpack 'government'. Three important aspects of this unpacking are: (a) the horizontal divisions of government across functional responsibilities (external affairs, home affairs, agriculture, industry, health, education, etc.), (b) the structures of the bureaucracy, that is, the individuals whose careers are bound up with carrying out the functions of government, and (c) the vertical division of government across different jurisdictions (national, state, and local, in the case of India). In thinking about institutional reform of government, it is natural to focus on the first two of these dimensions, since the third, in some ways, simply acknowledges that those issues of internal organization have to be addressed at multiple levels of jurisdiction. However, one of the main arguments of this chapter will be that paying close attention to this third dimension is crucial in improving the efficacy of public expenditure in India.

To understand how the government can spend its money better, this chapter considers four potential areas of institutional reform. First, it examines possibilities for the improved functioning of individual ministries and departments, at the central and state levels. The answer here is not surprising, having to do with basic improvements in information gathering, decision-making, and so on, but also with some consideration of structural changes in the bureaucracy. In some ways, this is a relatively generic prescription, and the stuff of detailed discussions on public financial management.

---

consists of enabling markets, regulating markets, and directly making up for their deficiencies. Therefore, institutional reforms should be prioritized based on the 'proper' role of government.

The second area is the possibility of better coordination across individual ministries and between the centre and states. An important institution in this potential coordination role was the central Planning Commission, which, as it operated in India, was quite specific to that country in its history and evolution. In 2015, the Planning Commission was abolished and replaced with a successor institution, the National Institution for Transforming India (NITI Aayog). My discussion on the change will be somewhat tentative, given the newness of the NITI Aayog. However, I will argue that political realities that limited the coordination possibilities that the Planning Commission could achieve will constrain the NITI Aayog as well.

The third area for institutional reform is more significant, being structural in nature: the possible reassignment of expenditure responsibilities across levels of government. In particular, I argue for reassignment of responsibilities downward, from centre to state and state to local governments. Formal expenditure responsibilities are broadly determined by the union, state, and concurrent lists in the Indian Constitution and for local governments by schedules introduced by the 73rd and 74th Amendments that strengthened the status of the local government level. Arguably, de facto expenditure authorities do not match these constitutional assignments, being effectively much more centralized, and I discuss this issue too.

Finally, I discuss and argue for a complementary reform to the decentralization of expenditure responsibilities, namely a reassignment of tax authorities that better aligns with those expenditure requirements. I argue that this will provide improved incentives for expenditure governance through electoral accountability. As noted earlier, changes in assignments across levels of government also require internal reforms at each level, but I seek to make the case that internal reforms are more likely to be successful when there is pressure that comes from better assignments of expenditure and revenue authority.

The four areas of potential institutional reform are discussed in the sections below. As a prelude, the next section provides an evaluative overview of some of the main features of India's institutions of public expenditure management, including a discussion on different types of accountability. Ultimately, I argue, it is external accountability to citizens, however imperfect, that provides the foundational incentive mechanism for improving the governance or management of public expenditure, and this drives the nature of reforms posited in this chapter. The final section provides a summary conclusion.

Institutions Governing Public Expenditure

The broad contours of India's public institutions are well known, including the constitutional framework, the structures of parliamentary democracy (with the true executive being combined with the legislative branch, and the president chiefly a symbolic post), and a relatively strong judiciary. A federal system is embodied in elected state legislatures and, to some extent now, elected rural and urban local governments. The local level (also known as the third tier of government) is still weak, however, while state governments have gained some autonomy and power at the expense of the centre in recent years, for reasons including national party fragmentation, the rise of regional parties, and some decentralization of economic controls.

The Constitution explicitly recognizes a national Indian bureaucracy. There are also provisions for independent bureaucracies in each state. The key component of the bureaucracy is the Indian Administrative Service (IAS), whose members are chosen by a centralized process and trained together. They are initially assigned to particular states, and may serve varying proportions of their careers at the state and national levels. The dominant post-Independence economic policy approach vested the bureaucracy with considerable discretion in such matters, that is, in granting industrial licences. At the local level, IAS members are also vested with some judicial authority.

Turning specifically to public expenditure management, budgetary procedures for the central- and state-level legislatures are also detailed in the Constitution. Budgeting is the responsibility of national- and state-level finance ministries. Bureaucratic support and monitoring are also provided through specialized cadres of the civil service. For example, members of the Indian Civil Accounts Service (ICAS), under the expenditure secretary of the central Finance Ministry, oversee and maintain central government accounts, and there are similar state-level cadres. Members of the Indian Audit and Accounts Service (IAAS), under the independent Comptroller and Auditor General (CAG), are responsible for the auditing of central- and state-level government accounts. At the centre, accounting procedures are relatively strong, with reasonably good detection of certain types of malfeasance. However, corruption in various forms does exist, and poor (as opposed to illegal) use of funds is not well detected under the current system.

Over the last decade or more, the central government, with inputs from the World Bank and other agencies, has attempted to document, evaluate, and improve budgetary practices. These attempts are part of a global effort to improve public financial management (PFM), and an elaborate methodology has been developed. PFM studies typically include broader considerations of fiscal management, including aggregate fiscal discipline and policymaking and efficacy, in addition to budgetary and expenditure control process improvements. I provide some examples here, and return to the issues in more detail in subsequent parts of this chapter. Typically, these studies are outsourced by international organizations to Indian experts.

K.B.L. Mathur uses the public expenditure management (PEM) framework of the Japan Bank for International Cooperation (JBIC), which identifies the stages of the PEM cycle as policy, plan/programme/activity, budgeting execution, evaluation, and feedback (with sub-stages or components of each of these).[5] He gives a qualitative assessment of strengths and weaknesses at each stage, a quantitative assessment using a different checklist approach from the World Bank's PEM handbook, and recommendations for action to support better integration of policy and budgeting, as well as better monitoring and feedback with respect to expenditures.[6] Basic improvements such as the use of accrual accounting and more effective cash management also feature in this study.

A subsequent World Bank analysis surveys the literature, and has a somewhat broader scope, engaging with issues of legislative oversight, the performance of public enterprises, controls on the voluntary sector (which receives government funds), and the quality of procurement procedures, in addition to the issues raised in Mathur.[7] This study

[5] K.B.L. Mathur, 'India: Fiscal Reforms and Public Expenditure Management' (JBIC Research Paper No. 11, Research Institute for Development and Finance, Japan Bank for International Cooperation, Tokyo, 2001).

[6] World Bank, *Public Expenditure Management Handbook* (Washington, DC: World Bank, 1998).

[7] World Bank, 'A Study of Recent Literature on Public Financial Management and Accountability (PFMA) System of the Government of India' (Working

highlights developments such as the Ministry of Finance's assignment of financial advisors to individual ministries, and the push for greater transparency, including creating a 'right to information'. Processes of revenue administration, intergovernmental transfers, and auditing mechanisms are also discussed in detail—close to 400 pages, the report illustrates the breadth of issues encompassed within the PFM framework.

P.R. Jena produced a recent PFM report following the latest World Bank framework: this involved examining 28 categories (with multiple dimensions in some cases) spread across three broad areas: the credibility of the budget, comprehensiveness and transparency, and the budget cycle.[8] This last area has four components: the policy basis for budgeting; predictability and control on budget execution; accounting, recording and reporting; and external scrutiny and auditing. Each of the 28 categories is assessed either quantitatively (for example, deviations of actual from budgeted expenditure) or qualitatively (for example, meeting norms of organizational separation, or minimum standards of reporting), and a grade is assigned, from A to D, with 'pluses' used in some cases. Somewhat surprisingly, given the common impression that India's central government does a relatively good job of PFM, there are only 11 As and Bs, versus 15 Cs and Ds, with two categories not rated for lack of information. It is difficult to distil such a wide-ranging and detailed analysis into one or two key points, but one conclusion from the exercise is that relatively routine tasks are carried out reasonably well, while aspects of PFM that involve judgement, evaluation, and effective feedback loops, especially across different components of government, are weaker.

Jena, building on the World Bank report, subsequently offered a summary evaluation that lists five areas as crucial for reforms to strengthen the PFM system.[9] These are:

Paper, Financial Management Unit, South Asia Region, Washington, DC: World Bank, 2005).

[8] P.R. Jena, 'India: Public Expenditure and Financial Accountability', *Public Financial Management Performance Assessment* (New Delhi: National Institute of Public Finance and Policy, 2010).

[9] P.R. Jena, 'Improving Public Financial Management in India: Opportunities to Move Forward', *International Journal of Governmental Financial Management* 12, no. 2 (2012): 1–15.

1. producing suitable performance measures to influence budgetary decisions;
2. continuing with existing efforts to expand accrual accounting;
3. modernizing internal audit and control;
4. improving the effectiveness of external audit; and
5. introducing an exclusive procurement law.

This list focuses more on the (important and necessary) nuts and bolts of budget management, and while Jena discusses issues such as problems with some types of central government transfers to the states, the role of the Planning Commission, and some aspects of weakness in accountability, the main message from this approach is that incremental improvements in processes are needed in many areas of the core PFM system. On the one hand, such incremental reforms within existing institutional structures may be the most feasible. On the other hand, they may not tackle the areas where institutional reforms can have the most positive impacts.

The first item on Jena's list is, however, important for some of the subsequent discussion in this chapter. Jena, in both works cited above, traces the history of performance budgeting in India, starting in the 1970s, and points out its relative ineffectiveness. He briefly discusses the introduction of outcome budgeting in the mid-2000s, outlines the process, and notes the difficulties and the potential of this approach. This chapter takes up these issues in subsequent sections. Outcome budgeting seeks to get to the crux of the problem of ineffective service delivery. By documenting the results of spending, it seeks to contribute to creating an effective feedback loop from outcomes to programme design and the policy basis for budgeting. One caveat comes from the work of A. Shah,[10] who, following another line of World Bank efforts on fiscal management,[11] emphasizes the distinction between outputs of

---

[10] See A. Shah, 'Governing for Results in a Globalised and Localised World', *Pakistan Development Review* 38, no. 4 (November 1999): 385–431; and A. Shah, 'A Practitioner's Guide to Intergovernmental Fiscal Transfers', in *Intergovernmental Fiscal Transfers: Principles and Practice*, eds R. Boadway and A. Shah (Washington, DC: World Bank, 2007), Chapter 1.

[11] In this context, see also A. Shah, ed., *Fiscal Management* (Washington, DC: World Bank, 2005).

public spending and final outcomes. For example, spending on schools may lead to more school buildings, more textbooks, and higher enrolments—these can all be considered outputs of public spending. The true outcome of education may, however, depend on other factors that are beyond the control of government.

This is an appropriate point at which to discuss the issue of quality of public service delivery. In an earlier work, I suggest that the poor quality of public service delivery in India can be directly observed from the poor use of inputs (for example, absenteeism by teachers, doctors, and nurses who are government employees), observed in deficient outcomes (erratic electricity and water supplies), or inferred from other outcomes (for example, large losses by public sector enterprises) or the behaviour of citizens as consumers (for example, even the poor paying for private education when free government schooling is available).[12] Pritchett has discussed examples of corruption, absenteeism, and poor quality of service in detail, and termed India a 'flailing' rather than a failing state.[13] The essence of Pritchett's view is that poor public service delivery in India is not the result of a lack of financial or human resources, but has other roots, in societal structures. A slightly different view is found in a recent World Bank country strategy document which, while acknowledging absolute failures, also characterizes the problem as one of a 'failure of public services to keep up with people's expectations'.[14] These and other studies make the argument for government failure on case-study-type evidence, which is abundant for India. On the other hand, following the approach of Afonso *et al.* for several other countries,[15] Lalvani attempts to create quantitative indices of efficiency

---

[12] N. Singh, 'Expenditure Governance and IT: Assessing India's Situation and Potential', *India Review* 9, no. 2 (May 2010): 107–39.

[13] L. Pritchett, 'Is India a Flailing State? Detours on the Four Lane Highway to Modernization' (HKS Faculty Research Working Paper Series RWP09–013, Cambridge, MA: John F. Kennedy School of Government, Harvard University, 2009).

[14] World Bank, 'Country Strategy for the Republic of India for the Period FY2009–2012' (WBG Report No. 46509–IN, India Country Management Unit, South Asia Region, Washington, DC: World Bank, 2008).

[15] A. Afonso, L. Schuknecht, and V. Tanzi, 'Public Sector Efficiency: An International Comparison', *Public Choice* 123, nos 3–4 (June 2005): 321–47.

and effectiveness of public expenditure (focusing on inputs and out-puts rather than outcomes), and applies it to data for India's states, constructing indices of expenditure adequacy and effectiveness.[16]

In fact, much of the discussion on PFM for India has focused on the national or central level, although the three studies (Mathur, World Bank, and Jena) considered earlier also examine state-level performance. Problems of poor budgeting and expenditure practice are greater at the level of the states. Some states have better governance traditions than others, but all states came under fiscal stress in the 1990s. Budget prac-tices deteriorated in this situation of intensified political competition, increased uncertainty, looser hierarchical controls, and new complexi-ties of governance. Examples of problems in budgetary and expenditure practices include unrealistic projections, poor tracking of spending and outcomes, unclear assignment of responsibilities among different state government departments and agencies, lack of transparency, and inap-propriate degrees of control—too lax in some parts of the process and too stringent in others.[17] However, there has been a gradual effort to

[16] M. Lalvani, 'Public Expenditure Management Reform in India via Intergovernmental Transfers', *Public Budgeting & Finance* 30, no. 3 (September 2010): 98–133. I will not discuss this analysis here, but note that it has some conceptual and technical shortcomings, unsurprising for a relatively innovative exercise. Alternatively, rather than comparing public expenditure effectiveness across states, Fan, Hazell, and Thorat compare different categories of public expenditure, focusing on a specific outcome, namely, reducing rural poverty. Their econometric analysis suggests that additional investments in rural roads, agricultural research, and education have the largest impact on rural poverty per additional rupee spent. However, this focuses on outcomes, and does not address the issue of whether the result is tied to differences in efficiency of expenditure across categories. See S. Fan, P. Hazell, and S.K. Thorat, 'Impact of Public Expenditure on Poverty in Rural India', *Economic and Political Weekly* 35, no. 40 (October 2000): 3581–8.

[17] See International Monetary Fund, 'India: Selected Issues and Statistical Appendix' (IMF Staff Country Report 03/261, Washington, DC: International Monetary Fund, 2003), Chapter 4; World Bank, *State Fiscal Reforms in India: Progress and Prospects* (*A World Bank Report*) (New Delhi: Macmillan India, 2005), Chapter 2. For three additional useful examples of detailed analy-ses of state-level public financial management and accountability, see World Bank, 'India—Punjab: Note on the Workings of the State Public Financial

reverse negative trends and fix longstanding problems at the state level
as well as the centre, and some states have made significant improvements in budget practices. I discuss these developments subsequently.

I conclude this part with a brief discussion on accountability. That
term has taken on a life of its own, and covers a variety of circumstances. I distinguish between two fundamental types of accountability in the context of government: external and internal. External
accountability refers primarily to the answerability of elected officials
to citizens. The main mechanism for this accountability is through the
ballot box, but the media, civil society, and even avenues such as public
interest legislation can serve to create collective mechanisms that push
the behaviour of politicians toward the interests of their constituents.
In this context, the mechanism of 'exit' does not provide as direct an
avenue for achieving accountability—if a citizen moves jurisdictions, or
switches to private providers, there is no obvious feedback mechanism
to improve the behaviour of politicians.

Internal accountability refers to the chains of accountability built
into the institutional structures of government: these may be conventional vertical chains, or horizontal links of checks and balances.
In the context of internal accountability, the links between politicians
and bureaucrats are of particular importance—bureaucrats derive their
legitimacy from serving elected politicians, but if there are problems
with the behaviour of politicians, the mechanisms of internal accountability become problematic rather than beneficial. In this context, the
observation of N.C. Saxena is useful:

> [B]etween the expression of the will of the State (represented by politi-
> cians) and the execution of that will (through the administrators) there
> cannot be any long-term dichotomy. In other words, the model in which
> the politics will continue to be corrupt, casteist, and will harbour crimi-
> nals whereas civil servants will continue to be efficient, responsive to

Management System' (Report No. 36327–IN, Washington, DC: World Bank,
2006); World Bank, 'India—Jharkhand: Public Financial Management and
Accountability Study' (Report No. 70425, Washington, DC: World Bank, 2007);
and World Bank, 'India—Himachal Pradesh: Public Financial Management and
Accountability Assessment' (Report No. 48635–IN, Washington, DC: World
Bank, 2009).

public needs and change agents cannot be sustained indefinitely. In the long-run political and administrative values have to coincide.[18]

In other words, ultimately it is the effectiveness of external accountability that matters. This theme will be developed in detail in this chapter.

Individual Ministries

Individual ministries are, of course, encompassed within the general discussion on public financial management, as outlined previously. I develop some of those themes with specific examples, as well as general observations. O.P. Agarwal and T.V. Somanathan provide an insightful analysis of public policymaking in India that is very relevant for the current discussion.[19] They begin by noting that problems can arise in formulation of policy as well as implementation. They identify several key weaknesses in policymaking which are of first-order importance, and would seem to require attention before one is likely to see major benefits of the many process improvements surfaced in the World Bank-type PFM analyses.[20]

The first weakness they highlight is excessive fragmentation of decision-making, which is a consequence of dividing sectoral responsibilities (for example, transportation) across several ministries. Unfortunately, this phenomenon is driven by the political realities of India, where numerous powerful politicians or political groups (for example, regional factions within a party or smaller parties that are pivotal in a ruling coalition) have to be given ministerial titles with their accompanying

[18] N.C. Saxena, 'Improving Programme Delivery', *Seminar* 541 (September 2004).

[19] O.P. Agarwal and T.V. Somanathan, 'Public Policy-Making in India—Issues and Remedies' (Working Paper, Centre for Policy Research, New Delhi, 2005).

[20] The focus of their analysis is on the working of central ministries, but the ideas carry over to state governments as well. This kind of analysis also provides a corrective to the view of Pritchett, commenting on the elite central bureaucracy: 'The brains of the Indian state can formulate excellent policies and programs in nearly every domain'. Pritchett's own tentative reason for poor government functioning in India is the depth and pervasiveness of identity politics centred on caste.

rewards (monetary and non-monetary). Potentially, of course, there are institutions for coordinating in such cases, including cabinet meetings and—until recently—the Planning Commission. Why these institutions do not work well is dealt with in the next part of the chapter. In any case, one probably has to accept the current degree of fragmentation across ministries as mostly beyond any agenda of institutional reform.

The second weakness seems to be a critical issue for policymaking in India, and is not really surfaced in analyses by outsiders: Agarwal and Somanathan, on the other hand, have an insider perspective. They argue that there is over-centralization in the decision-making structures of each individual ministry. Within each ministry, the bureaucrat with secretary rank (that is, most senior) is the minister's 'policy-adviser-in-chief', and makes or advises on decisions that can have cross-cutting impacts. However, much of these top bureaucrats' time is spent on routine administration, leaving inadequate time for policy formulation in an environment that has become increasingly complex.

A related weakness is the inadequacy of inputs from outside the government, and a lack of informed debate. A better process for obtaining and evaluating information and ideas that are pertinent to policy design would substitute, to some extent, for the shortage of time at the top. In other words, centralization is exacerbated by isolation. Agarwal and Somanathan make an exception in the case of the budget formulation process, where there is a tradition of outside consultation.[21] Another example, not discussed by these authors, is the use of expert committees on areas such as various aspects of financial sector reform or tax reform.[22] In this context, the Finance Ministry probably stands out as one where these processes are used often and are better developed, whereas some other ministries do not have such strong traditions.

A final identified weakness is also a variant of the previous two: a lack of systematic analysis and integration. On this issue, Agarwal and

[21] This positive evaluation is within the constraints imposed by the planning process and the plan–non-plan distinction in budgeting: that issue is taken up in the next part of this chapter.

[22] See N. Singh, 'The Dynamics and Status of India's Economic Reforms', in *The Oxford Handbook of the Indian Economy*, ed. Chetan Ghate (New York: Oxford University Press, 2012), 499–525, for a discussion on the role of expert committees in influencing policy formulation and policy reforms.

Somanathan suggest that specialists are not consulted enough, while the generalists (the senior IAS bureaucrats) who should be capable of the integrated analysis ultimately required are not properly trained in this skill. One is tempted to suggest that the problem lies elsewhere than the inadequate training or expertise of the top bureaucrats; I would instead argue that the weaknesses come from a lack of adequate numbers of specialists with sufficiently high status within the ranks of government, as well as the political pressures that come from many of the politicians heading the ministries.

In any case, some reforms are possible. Agarwal and Somanathan suggest that the number of secretaries be reduced (currently there can be several in each ministry), that more responsibility for implementation be pushed one or two levels below the secretary, that policy advisory groups be created within each ministry, that the career trajectory and training of the IAS be modified, and that there be more lateral entry. In 2012, the central government took a step in the direction of reform by amending the rules for the IAS to permit earlier career evaluations than previously, with possible early retirements in the case of inadequate performance (either with respect to competence or integrity).

It is important to focus, as Agarwal and Somanathan do, on the incentives and competencies of the key bureaucratic decision-makers within ministries. How does the typical PFM framework relate to this focus? Much of the PFM analysis, beyond the policymaking stage, deals with tracking implementation in the sense of flows of funds. Most of this financial tracking, monitoring, and evaluation is performed by specialists, rather than the generalist policy advisers of the IAS. Outcome budgeting can be thought of as providing parallel tracking tools for physical activities, as well as outputs or outcomes. Indeed, in some cases, outcome budgets mainly achieve an enumeration of what would be best classified as inputs rather than outputs, let alone outcomes. Outcome budgets, even if they do not live up to their name, therefore, provide one tool to address weaknesses of information gathering and evaluation that exist in Indian public policymaking.

In this context, it is important to distinguish between the roles of outcome budgets in different ministries. For example, the Ministry of Finance and the Ministry of External Affairs both produce detailed outcome budgets, but neither is heavily responsible for public service delivery (except to the extent that they provide national public goods such as diplomacy and fiscal prudence).[23] At the same time, the high-level objectives of each ministry are not easily aggregated up from the detailed lists of activities and achievements that constitute the outcome budget in each case. On the other hand, ministries such as health and family welfare, human resource development (HRD), and rural development have large administrative responsibilities for areas such as health, education, and rural infrastructure, where large quantities of money are allocated, transferred, and spent all across the country—increasingly through what are known as centrally sponsored schemes (CSS). In the standard language of public finance, these are essentially categorical matching grants, but with a host of institutional features peculiar to the Indian case, which will be explored in subsequent parts of the chapter. In these cases, creating a useful outcome budget is both more difficult and more valuable.[24] This point was recognized by the then deputy chairman of the Planning Commission in public remarks made in 2009, four years after the beginning of the current outcome budgeting effort, though his take on the prospects for usefulness was more pessimistic, leaning towards giving up the exercise. To the contrary, outcome budgeting has continued and expanded.

A review of the efforts of some of the key ministries that matter for public service delivery provides a sense of where the effort currently stands. The HRD Ministry, for example, produces an integrated annual report, and the two major departments—of school education and literacy and of higher education—each have a results framework document

[23] However, one important example of a traditional 'public service' at the individual citizen level is the issuing and renewal of passports by the Ministry of External Affairs.

[24] Chakraborty *et al.* perform a useful exercise in estimating how much central expenditure can be ascribed to categories that are spatially dispersed, and the shares of different ministries in these categories. Excluding Finance, Defence, and Home, the ministries which spend the most are (2008–9 percentages follow each name): Rural Development (5.65), Human Resource Development (5.15), Consumer Affairs, Food and Public Distribution (4.44), Chemicals and Fertilisers (4.20), Shipping, Road Transport and Highways (2.47), Health and Family Welfare (2.41), and Agriculture (1.93). See P. Chakraborty, A.N. Mukherjee, and H.K. Amar Nath, 'Interstate Distribution of Central Expenditure and Subsidies' (Working Paper No. 2010–66, National Institute of Public Finance and Policy, New Delhi, 2010).

(RFD) and an outcome budget. The outcome budgets and RFDs follow standardized templates, with detailed quantitative measures used wherever possible, grading of different possible levels of achievement, and mappings from outlays to physical outputs and outcomes. There are also summaries of the various programmes, schemes, and missions under which the outlays are allocated. Clearly, there are shortcomings in these documents, since there is not necessarily a high degree of confidence in numbers aggregated up from possibly thousands of field reports; indeed, this was one concern of the former deputy chairman of the Planning Commission. In many cases, the connection between the physical outputs and the outcomes that matter is weak or non-existent. This is a point made forcefully by Muralidharan in his survey of the learning outcomes in Indian schools, which are either poor, failing to improve, or not being measured, while large sums are spent on various schemes to provide 'education', or at least teachers, school buildings, and other potential educational inputs.[25]

On the other hand, one can argue that outcome budgets and related documents provide a necessary first step in understanding how money is spent. They may not directly lead to better policymaking, but they provide information in an integrated, accessible form that was not previously available. This information can be useful to those inside and outside government in evaluating the effectiveness of certain kinds of spending. This is not to say that outcome budgets cannot be improved; a comparison of HRD Ministry documents with concise evaluations produced by an organization such as the Accountability Initiative[26] reveals some of the trade-offs of completeness versus comprehensibility—but they represent a new level of transparency for government.[27]

[25] K. Muralidharan, 'Priorities for Primary Education Policy in India's 12th Five Year Plan', *India Policy Forum* (2013): 1–46.

[26] The website of this organization is http://www.accountabilityindia.in/, and it includes several studies on the accuracy of government data as well as the effectiveness of programmes ('From Outlays to Outcomes'). Ministry-level outcome budgets can provide inputs into such non-governmental studies, in addition to those studies providing independent checks on performance.

[27] Prajapati Trivedi, who served as Secretary, Performance Management, in the government, provides an excellent overview of India's efforts on performance monitoring and evaluation systems, including the recommendations

Coordination Institutions

Unlike many of the other institutional features discussed so far, such as legislative and bureaucratic structures, the central Planning Commission was not mandated in the Constitution. Instead, it was established by a resolution of the central cabinet in March 1950, within three months of the adoption of the Constitution. Membership of the commission was determined by appointment at the prime minister's discretion, and could include former bureaucrats, politicians, and technical specialists. Following the central model, state governments appointed their own planning commissions or boards later on. The Planning Commission began making grants to states in support of their five-year plans (which the commission formally approved). Its activities in this realm were seen as justified in terms of constitutional provisions for discretionary transfers. When central ministries began making their own grants in support of CSS to be implemented by the states (also covered by the same article of the Constitution), the Planning Commission took on the task of coordinating and overseeing these funds, though with the ministries still playing a leading role in administering the schemes. It

---

of the tenth report of the Second Administrative Reform Commission in 2008 and the Sixth Pay Commission report in the same year. See P. Trivedi, 'India: Performance Monitoring and Evaluation System (PMES)', *Proceedings of Global Roundtable on Government Performance Management, December 11–12, 2013* (New Delhi: United Nations Development Programme). Periodic Pay Commissions are another constitutional institution that impact government expenditure management. They are charged with making recommendations on pay adjustments for government employees, as well as on a range of issues relating to recruitment, promotion, performance, and incentives. In practice, every commission since at least the fourth has made detailed recommendations with respect to the latter set, which mostly get sidelined, while pay increases are readily implemented. This lack of connection between pay and performance, the infrequency of pay commissions, and the spillovers to a range of other public institutions represent major problems with current practice: these were recognized at the very beginning of the report of the Fifth Pay Commission, which nevertheless awarded large pay increases. The report also alluded to international best practices as alternative institutional designs, but little has changed since then. See *Report of the Fifth Central Pay Commission*, vol. I (New Delhi: All India Railwaymen's Federation, 1997): 1.

was formally wound up and replaced by the new NITI Aayog—discussed later in this part—in January 2015.

The commission also made grants and loans for implementing development plans. Before 1969, plan transfers were project-based. After that, the distribution was proposed to be made on the basis of a consensus formula decided by the National Development Council (NDC). The NDC was chaired by the prime minister, and its members included selected central cabinet ministers, chief ministers of the states, and members of the Planning Commission. The NDC played an important role in plan formulation, serving as a forum for political bargaining (as did the commission itself, though less explicitly). In practice, discretionary transfers did not disappear, and, more recently, as central and centrally sponsored schemes expanded, formula-based transfers were far outstripped in aggregate amount by these project- or mission-based funds.

The role of the Planning Commission, while it existed, was often questioned. The constitutionality of plan transfers was challenged by some legal scholars, but affirmed by the Supreme Court.[28]

The Eleventh Finance Commission recommended a reassessment of plan transfer formulae, with this task to be brought within the scope of the Finance Commission, which is itself a constitutional body charged with guiding all aspects of the process of centre–state transfers. This report (as well as numerous other analyses, including some of the PFM reports discussed previously) noted the conceptual muddle with respect to Planning Commission transfers, with economically meaningless distinctions between plan and non-plan categories of expenditure. It recommended reform of the financing of the plans so that plan revenue expenditure was financed from available revenue receipts after meeting non-plan expenditure, with borrowing used only for investments. The next two Finance Commissions (Twelfth and Thirteenth) echoed the recommendations of the Eleventh Finance Commission with respect to the categorization of expenditures, but significant change came with the Fourteenth Finance Commission, discussed later in this chapter.

---

[28] This occurred in its decision in *Bhim Singh* v. *Union of India* in 2010, where the Court provided a very expansive view of central transfers to the states under the provisions of Article 282 of the Constitution.

Despite the demise of the Planning Commission, reports of other committees on its functioning are still of relevance. A committee set up by the Planning Commission and chaired by C. Rangarajan to examine the efficient management of public expenditure called the plan-non-plan distinction in expenditure 'dysfunctional and an obstacle in out-come-based budgeting'.[29] That report proposed a unified approach to budgeting (keeping the necessary revenue versus capital expenditure[30] distinction), managed by the Ministry of Finance, and the most recent Union Budget, for 2016–17, adopted this approach as a complement to the Planning Commission's closure.[31]

[29] Planning Commission of India, *Report of the High Level Expert Committee on Efficient Management of Public Expenditure* (New Delhi: Government of India, 2011).

[30] Even here, there can be conceptual difficulties when investments are in people, but it seems that there is still a case for the traditional distinction based on the nature of tangible, long-lived physical capital.

[31] Earlier, Singh and Srinivasan questioned the need for a Planning Commission in a market-oriented economy, suggesting an alternative system in which richer states would use market borrowing for capital projects, and poorer ones would receive grants for capital spending: see N. Singh and T.N. Srinivasan, 'Indian Federalism, Globalization and Economic Reform', in *Federalism and Economic Reform: International Perspectives*, eds T.N. Srinivasan and J. Wallack (Cambridge, UK: Cambridge University Press, 2006), 301–63. They later put forward an alternative set of reforms, with the centre taking full responsibility for financing, operation, and maintenance of projects where it has a compelling reason for central intervention, such as spillovers across states. They suggested that the Planning Commission be reconstituted as a Fund for Public Investment (FPI) for both the centre and states, with the state and central governments as shareholders. This Fund, much like a multilateral development bank, would appraise the projects proposed for their economic and social returns as well as feasibility and soundness of proposed financing, from the centre or state's own resources, borrowing from domestic and foreign sources and capital transfers from the centre, if relevant. See N. Singh and T.N. Srinivasan, 'Federalism and Economic Development in India: An Assessment', in *Economic Reform in India: Challenges, Prospects and Lessons*, eds Nicholas C. Hope, Anjini Kochar, Roger Noll, and T.N. Srinivasan (Cambridge, UK: Cambridge University Press, 2013), 33–95. As will be seen later in this part, NITI Aayog does not fulfil such functions, and it is not clear how these assessments are done within the government.

In 2010, the then prime minister announced a goal of transforming the Planning Commission into a strategic thinking group. Subsequently, the Rangarajan report stressed the Commission's potential role in providing technical assistance to individual ministries for their budgeting, and in coordinating expenditure plans across ministries, working with the Ministry of Finance to monitor and evaluate expenditures related to 'planned' development. In 2014, after the election of a new government, the Planning Commission was effectively suspended; in 2015, it was replaced by a new 'think-tank'-type body, the NITI Aayog.[32]

NITI Aayog does not have the same kind of allocative functions that the Planning Commission possessed. Planning and plan transfers are continuing for the moment, but their role and details are likely to evolve relatively quickly. Indeed, the Fourteenth Finance Commission, appointed under the previous government, gave its report in December 2014, the month before the creation of NITI Aayog, in which it recommended significant changes in the allocation of central transfers to the states. The headline number has been that the Finance Commission recommended an increase of the share of the states in the central divisible pool from 32 to 42 per cent. However, M. Govinda Rao, a member of the Commission, has explained clearly that the actual increase in devolution was about 3 to 4 per cent of the divisible pool. In his words:

Unlike the 13th Commission, which made its recommendations to meet non-Plan revenue expenditure needs of states, this Commission has taken into account the total requirements in the revenue account, without making a distinction between Plan and non-Plan. This implies the recommendation subsumes the normal Central assistance given by the Planning Commission (the Gadgil formula for grants), other Central assistance for Plan, Special Plan assistance, special Central assistance and grants for items like the backward region grant fund (state and district components) given by the Planning Commission.[33]

---

[32] This was done through a cabinet resolution, explicitly superseding the resolution that created the Planning Commission 65 years earlier. NITI is an acronym for National Institution for Transforming India, but also is Hindi for 'policy'. Aayog means 'commission' in Hindi, giving 'Policy Commission' as an interpretation of the name.

[33] See I. Bakshi and J.P. Upadhyay, 'Misleading to Compare Devolution Suggestions of 13th and 14th Commissions: M. Govinda Rao', *Business Standard*, 25 February 2015.

The institutional import of this is that the Fourteenth Finance Commission achieved more closely what had been intended in the constitution: a comprehensive assessment of and recommendations for state government fiscal needs, which had earlier been confounded by the separate operations of the Planning Commission. In terms of timing, the Finance Commission's report also fit well with the abolition of the Planning Commission.

Aside from losing control or influence over certain transfers to states, how else does NITI Aayog differ from its predecessor? It is difficult to ascertain much that is specific from the cabinet resolution that created it, which is very broad in vision and scope. It does emphasize 'cooperative federalism', interpreted as giving state government leaders more of a say, but how that will play out in practice is hard to predict. Certainly, NITI Aayog, like its predecessor, is the brainchild of a strong prime minister who also recognizes the importance of regional political leaders, though in the current instance he has also been such a regional leader. A brief progress report after NITI Aayog's first year of existence suggests that it is tackling, naturally, questions related to initiatives emanating from the prime minister, such as skill development, sanitation, ease of doing business, and innovation and entrepreneurship. The use of committees of state chief ministers for some issues is a nod to cooperative federalism. There are several completed and ongoing monitoring and evaluation studies, and a grab bag of projects related to regulatory and legal reforms, international economic ties, and data availability. The impression is of an institution mostly still finding its way, and its stated plan of seeking several dozen new professionals for the staff is an indicator of at least one still-missing ingredient for a think tank: human capital.

With respect to aspects of public expenditure management such as technical assistance, coordination, and evaluation, why was there so little improvement in the efficacy of the Planning Commission over the decades? And can NITI Aayog do better? Part of the problem may have been that the Planning Commission was subject to the same structural weaknesses as individual ministries, as discussed earlier, including over-centralization and lack of sufficient high-quality inputs for policy-making.[34] The difference was that the Planning Commission had little

---

[34] This view might seem to be contradicted by the number of committees and taskforces under the aegis of the Planning Commission. When it closed,

control over implementation, governance of which lies mostly with the ministries. Hence, there was not the same problem of misallocation of organizational resources between routine implementation tasks and those requiring high-level judgement or analysis, as seems to exist in line ministries. An Independent Evaluation Office (IEO) was set up and became operational in 2013–14, to assess expenditure effectiveness for plan and related developmental expenditures, but it was quickly disbanded by the new government. Similar tasks are being performed within NITI Aayog, but the Planning Commission had done that too, albeit somewhat ineffectively.

The real causes of the Planning Commission's limited effectiveness may have lain in the political economy of the internal workings of the government. The short existence of the IEO is perhaps an example of the various political economy factors at work in determining how important categories of public funds are spent and how that expenditure is evaluated. The commission initially was a tool of a strong prime minister, providing discretionary control over government expenditure outside the line ministries. Over time, for a variety of reasons, the office of the prime minister had lost power. Instead, individual ministers who commanded the political support of critical factions or groups of Members of Parliament (MPs) (and who were often ministers for precisely that reason) had a greater say in how funds were allocated and spent.[35] When Planning Commission transfers were made formulaic,

---

its website was comprehensive and well-organized, listing, for example, 26 categories of working groups or steering committees for the Twelfth Plan, defined mostly by sectoral focus (available at http://planningcommission.nic.in/aboutus/committee/index.php?about=12strindx.htm). One category, human resource development, had nine working groups and four steering committees listed. The steering committee on Higher and Technical Education had 33 members. The corresponding working group had 46 members. Perhaps the conclusion from these numbers is that quantity and quality of inputs are not the same thing.

[35] With NITI Aayog lacking the Planning Commission's role in allocation and budgeting of funds, it is freed up from political bargaining to focus on providing higher-quality technical inputs, but that might reduce the weight given to those inputs by central ministries. Presumably, the job of exercising political bargaining power within the government will rest more with the Finance Ministry.

the response over time was to expand alternative discretionary modes of transferring funds to different states or for different kinds of expenditure through the CSS. These schemes were much more under the control of individual line ministries, and the Planning Commission's supposed coordination role could only be nominal in such circumstances, although it contributed to recurring attempts to rationalize the CSS. The latest of these attempts is a major report from a committee of chief ministers under the auspices of NITI Aayog. This committee was able to build on the changes made by the Fourteenth Finance Commission, as well as earlier committees, to propose prioritization and consolidation of such schemes.[36]

Does this political economy argument mean that no progress is possible? One feasible avenue for improvement may lie precisely in the development of outcome budgets by individual ministries. These would provide information in a reasonably standardized framework for the NITI Aayog and/or the Finance Ministry to provide a more systematic analysis of the performance of various central and centrally sponsored schemes, including the overarching 'missions' that have been conceived for tackling areas such as primary education, rural health, sanitation, and urban infrastructure. The quantification in individual ministry documents, discussed earlier, represented an advance on the Planning Commission's own sometimes ad hoc and qualitative analysis

---

[36] A report by B.K. Chaturvedi, then a member of the Planning Commission, gave a detailed history of the CSS as well as recommendations such as consolidation, increased flexibility, and greater evaluation and accountability. See Planning Commission of India, *Report of the Committee on Restructuring Centrally Sponsored Schemes* (CSS) (New Delhi: Government of India, 2011). The union government did implement some restructuring of CSS in 2013, but it was perceived as insufficient. A significant recommendation of the Rangarajan Committee concerned how CSS and related funds are channelled. Following Dikshit *et al.*, a case was made for such central transfers to flow through state government treasuries, and from there directly and without blocking options to beneficiaries, rather than going through assorted district, block, or village government agencies, or through NGOs and para-governmental societies. See A. Dikshit, R. Viswanathan, and T.R. Raghunandan, 'Efficient Transfer of Funds for Centrally–Sponsored Schemes', *Economic and Political Weekly* 42, no. 23 (2007): 2159–63.

of how money should be spent, and its limited analysis of the impacts of spending.[37]

One can also argue that an approach to expenditure management that tracks the results of spending has to be foundational to the potential role of the NITI Aayog, including strategic thinking. The last deputy chairman of the Planning Commission fulfilled the latter role well, but much of the rest of the organization appeared to lag in complementing strategic thinking with nuts and bolts analysis of data. It is also possible that political economy considerations would work against even minor improvements in analysis and decision-making since these improvements could reduce political discretion or rent-seeking opportunities. My argument in this chapter is not that improvement is guaranteed, but that a PFM-type process-based approach with specific incremental improvements has the best chance of getting the ball rolling with respect to positive institutional reform.

Expenditure Assignments

In the previous parts of this chapter, I have focused on the institutional structures of the central government that pertain to expenditure management and governance, noting only briefly that similar institutions, of varying quality, exist at the state level. A key theme has been the possibility of improving the structures and processes of expenditure management within a level of government. I now turn to considering

---

[37] The recommendation being made here is different from the role of the Central Plan Scheme Monitoring System (CPSMS), which is a web-enabled management information system. The CPSMS improves tracking of financial flows, and provides a comprehensive picture of these flows across different plans or other centrally initiated schemes. This can help avoid problems such as allocating additional funds when the initial allocation lies unutilized. The CPSMS represents an important improvement in the vertical dimension of PFM, and has the potential to force improvements in state (and eventually local) government expenditure tracking. However, it neither yields information on the physical outcomes of spending, nor is it meant to. Hence, it does not deal with the fundamental problem of monitoring and evaluating the results of spending. Further discussion on the CPSMS and recommendations for its use and extension can be found in the Rangarajan and Chaturvedi Committee reports.

change across different levels of government, examining expenditure in this part and revenue in the next.

The Indian Constitution, in its Seventh Schedule, assigns the powers and functions of the centre and the states. The schedule specifies the exclusive powers of the centre (the union list) and the states (the state list), and those under joint jurisdiction (the concurrent list). All residuary powers are assigned to the centre. Over time, through various amendments, these three lists have been altered in the direction of greater centralization, by expanding some powers in the union list, and shifting some items from the state to the concurrent list. The nature of the assignment of expenditure functions remains fairly typical of federal nations, and broadly fits with economists' theoretical rationale, though the breadth of the concurrent list, in some cases, creates problems of lack of clear responsibility.

The state list includes health, agriculture, water (except for inter-state rivers), land, and local government; education and 'social and economic planning' are in the concurrent list. The latter assignment, by virtue of its breadth, provides tremendous latitude to the centre, as well as scope for conflicts of authority.[38] Nevertheless, the formal assignments of expenditure responsibility appear to give the states considerable scope with respect to public service delivery. In practice, the states' performance on this front was less than desirable. Lack of resources may have been one cause, particularly in the poorer states, but the thrust of central planning, and the mechanisms of intergovernmental transfers that sometimes were designed to fill perceived 'gaps' in state resources, contributed to the problem. Essentially, state government decision makers focused on influencing the central government, rather than making spending decisions to enhance electoral prospects.[39] In this view of the world, voters also failed to tie electoral support to public service delivery, instead being driven by group identities and loyalties. A key point to make here is that the centre exercised considerable influence on state expenditure priorities, both through the planning process and through political bargaining and control, so that

[38] Education, excluding higher education, was, in fact, on the state list until 1971, when it was moved to the Concurrent List by a constitutional amendment.

[39] See M. Govinda Rao and N. Singh, *The Political Economy of Federalism in India* (New Delhi: Oxford University Press, 2005).

real and formal expenditure authorities have diverged, to the detriment of efficiency of expenditure.

The initial decade of economic liberalization also saw a strengthening of regional political power, and one can make the case that the central government responded to this challenge to its control by expanding the scope of its categorical transfers such as the large new CSS (for example, Sarva Shiksha Abhiyan [SSA], National Rural Health Mission [NRHM], and Jawaharlal Nehru National Urban Renewal Mission [JNNURM]). Other possible reasons for the central government's shift could be the global demonstration effect of the Millennium Development Goals (MDGs), and growing worries that liberalization was undercutting the political and fiscal ability of the states to direct adequate expenditure towards economic and human development. In any case, the new millennium saw the rise of large central government schemes that provide funds to the states for implementation in areas such as education and health, but constrain the states in the process.[40] I have noted attempts to rationalize the CSS through consolidation and redesign, and through improving information systems for flows of funds, but the problem is deeper, and may require a more fundamental solution. In the last part, I argued that there is scope for the NITI Aayog to do a better job than its predecessor of monitoring, evaluating, and perhaps coordinating across states and schemes. A more fundamental reform would be to make categorical (block or matching) grants for areas such as health or education, or even just to provide the states with more untied funds (for example, through the Finance Commission) and allow them to choose how to spend the money.[41] The approach taken by the Fourteenth Finance

---

[40] For example, the NRHM created separate new bureaucracies in each state, bypassing the consolidated fund of the state, as well as much of the state government bureaucracy (although senior bureaucrats and ministers end up exercising control in any case).

[41] The World Bank Country Strategy document states, 'Accountability for service delivery is recognized as weak, as a result of entrenched bureaucracies, systemic corruption, and an incomplete process of decentralization. Moreover the public financial management system has not kept pace with the rapid growth, and is therefore not able to provide relevant and in-time information for decision-making. These issues are particularly acute in Centrally Sponsored Schemes, which are designed and funded by the central government but implemented by the states and lower tiers of government.'

Commission, described in the last part of this chapter, is a significant step in this direction, but may not be enough, as is discussed in the next part.

The incentives for state government decision-makers with greater freedom of expenditure choices would come from meeting the expectations of their constituents. This line of reasoning is based on the assumption that external, electoral accountability works, as outlined earlier. How true has this been in India? Some theoretical models of the democratic political process predict politicians' efficient responsiveness to voters' preferences, driven by their own preferences for getting re-elected.[42] However, the existence of interest groups can lead to lobbying or other political pressure and therefore to biased outcomes. Politics in India, at all levels, seems to have been characterized by such 'rent-seeking', evidenced in subsidies, overstaffing of government, and distortion of expenditure plans. On the one hand, it has also been argued that rent-seeking in India increased over time.[43] On the other hand, state-level expenditure policies have been influenced by intra-state competition for political power, as one would expect if electoral accountability is operative.[44] Furthermore, Khemani compares national

[42] See, among others, A. Downs, *An Economic Theory of Democracy* (New York: HarperCollins, 1957).

[43] For example, Chhibber explains the deepening of rent-seeking and the persistence of laws that made it possible in terms of intensifying needs of political competition. Powers of patronage for electoral support became more important in the 1970s and 1980s, swamping possible concerns about the inefficiency; see P. Chhibber, 'Political Parties, Electoral Competition, Government Expenditures and Economic Reform in India', *Journal of Development Studies* 32, no. 1 (November 1995): 74–96. Also, both Rao and Singh and Kapur and Mehta have argued that large payments were directed by the centre in the late 1990s to the states of origin (Andhra Pradesh and Punjab) of regional parties that were key central coalition partners. See M.G. Rao and N. Singh, 'The Political Economy of Center–State Fiscal Transfers in India', in *Institutional Elements of Tax Design and Reform*, ed. J. McLaren (Washington, DC: World Bank, 2002), 69–123; and D. Kapur and P.B. Mehta, 'The Indian Parliament as an Institution of Accountability, Democracy, Governance and Human Rights' (UNRISD Programme Paper No. 23, Geneva: United Nations Research Institute for Social Development, 2006).

[44] See M.G. Rao, 'Ideological Factors, Political Stability and Tax Revenue Determination: A Case Study of Four Indian States', *Public Finance/Finances*

and state elections, and finds evidence that voters reward (punish) governments for good (poor) economic performance more at the state than the national level.[45] At the same time, the central government tries to influence state-level policy choices, and indirectly, voters, through fund transfers to states.[46]

Prior to the last national election, the situation was one in which the centre, with a coalition headed by a quasi-national political party, competed with regional parties for votes, and this is still partly true with the new government. Delivery of public services through CSS allows the national government to claim more credit for delivering these services, as well as for making transfers through subsidies. Given this structure, I have argued earlier in this chapter that there are specific micro improvements that can be made in organizational processes and structures. Here I suggest that a more effective institutional reform, albeit a more difficult one, would be to provide states with clearer expenditure authority. This would, of course, increase the need for internal reforms at the state level, but supporting those reforms is precisely the kind of public good that the centre should be providing to the states. Electoral accountability will operate more effectively in such a situation.[47]

Publiques 34, no. 1 (1979): 114–27; M.G. Rao, *Political Economy of Tax and Expenditure Determination in Indian States* (New Delhi: Allied Publishers, 1981); and B. Dutta, 'Fragmented Legislatures and Electoral Systems: The Indian Experience', in *Institutions, Incentives, and Economic Reforms in India*, eds S. Kahkonen and A. Lanyi (New York: Sage Publications, 2000), 77–100.

[45] S. Khemani, 'Decentralization and Accountability: Are Voters More Vigilant in Local than in National Elections?' (Policy Research Working Paper 2557, Washington, DC: World Bank, 2001). This result is consistent with survey evidence that voters look mainly to state governments for provision of many public goods. For example, see P. Chhibber, S. Shastri, and R. Sisson, 'Federal Arrangements and the Provision of Public Goods in India', *Asian Survey* 44, no. 3 (May/June 2004): 339–51.

[46] W. Arulampalam, S. Dasgupta, A. Dhillon, and B. Dutta, 'Electoral Goals and Center–State Transfers in India', *Journal of Development Economics* 88, no. 1 (January 2009): 103–19. See also Rao and Singh, 'Political Economy of Federalism in India'.

[47] The argument is not complete, since the revenue side also has to be considered, and I do that in the next part of this chapter.

This argument for clear decentralization of expenditure authority does not stop at the level of the states, but extends to the local level. As it is, the district is already effectively the pivot point for implementation of many types of government expenditure, having been a crucial administrative unit at least since the Mughal period. The IAS structure also works to make administering a district a key step in the career path.[48]

Local governments in India were given formal constitutional status through the passage of the 73rd and 74th Amendments in 1993, which assigned new expenditure responsibilities to the local level and mandated regular local elections. Guidelines for assignments of local subjects were added to the Constitution, in the eleventh and twelfth schedules. Precise assignments were made through individual states' legislations, and there was considerable variation among the states in the extent to which the functions in the two new constitutional schedules were transferred,[49] particularly for rural governments. In many

[48] The linkage between senior IAS officials in Delhi and their junior colleagues in the districts is a parallel channel of communication and influence, though formal authority is meant to flow from the centre through the federal structures of state legislatures and cabinets, not purely through bureaucracies. Of course, there are senior IAS officers in every state capital as well, and they also serve as links in this chain. There is a complicated institutional process whereby bureaucrats and politicians engage with each other: this includes the location and nature of assignments, and the frequency and types of transfers. See L. Iyer and A. Mani, 'Traveling Agents: Political Change and Bureaucratic Turnover in India', *Review of Economics and Statistics* 94, no. 3 (August 2012): 723–39. However, district-level development bodies are typically controlled by IAS officials or state-level politicians, and this works against effective local spending authority. In this context, the Thirteenth Finance Commission stated, 'Ideally, development authorities should be dissolved and their functions taken over by the local bodies in whose jurisdiction they operate'. Finance Commission of India, *Thirteenth Finance Commission Report 2010–15* (New Delhi: Government of India, 2009), 182.

[49] See M.G. Rao and N. Singh, 'How to Think about Local Government Reform in India', in *Economic Reform and the Liberalisation of the Indian Economy: Essays in Honour of Richard T. Shand*, ed. K.P. Kalirajan (Northampton: Edward Elgar, 2003), 335–90; and S. Chaudhuri and P. Heller, 'The Plasticity of Participation: Evidence from a Participatory Governance Experiment'

cases, states chose to hold back in devolving the full list of functions from the eleventh schedule.[50] A significant problem with the new local expenditure responsibilities has been the overlapping of the 'local lists' with the state list of the Constitution. Combined with the lack of effective decentralization of funds and personnel, this gives the states the ability to overawe local governments completely, if they wish.

Despite these severe limitations, the local government 'experiment' in India provides new evidence on electoral accountability. At the local level, the measurement of local public good delivery can potentially be more precise, through geographically concentrated survey data. Regular direct local elections have the potential to increase the accountability of local government by providing more direct and refined incentives to please constituents. The counter-argument is that interest groups or powerful individuals will instead have more influence at the local level.[51]

(Working Paper 03–01, New York: Columbia University: Institute for Social and Economic Research and Policy, 2003).

[50] They also capped village-level authority to directly approve expenditures, often at very low levels. In general, even states which devolved significant responsibilities to local governments subsequent to the amendments retained control over the requisite funds, as well as over the bureaucrats or functionaries who would be responsible for implementation.

[51] Concerns about elite domination of elected rural local bodies have existed since Independence and heavily influenced India's federal design. Pre-reform qualitative studies of local government found examples of interest group capture, but also positive impacts of local democratic processes. For example, Dash gave examples of the Puri Municipal Council in Orissa providing reductions in or exemptions from octroi taxes to specific commercial products, benefiting local interest groups. See Gokulananda Dash, *Municipal Finance in India: Based on Orissa* (New Delhi: Concept Publishing, 1988), 223. See also A. Dasgupta and D. Mookherjee, *Incentives and Institutional Reforms in Tax Enforcement: An Analysis of Developing Country Experience* (New Delhi: Oxford University Press, 1998). Other case studies note the reluctance of local governments to impose taxes, being responsive to their constituents in this respect. See, for example, A. Aziz, 'Income Structure of Rural Local Governments: The Karnataka Experience', in *Local Government Finances in India*, ed. Konrad Adenauer Foundation (New Delhi: Manohar, 1998). Bardhan and Mookherjee provided a post-reform analysis of 'local capture.' See P. Bardhan and D. Mookherjee, 'Capture and Governance at

Interestingly, as long ago as 1965, Andre Béteille countered the pessimistic view of elite domination in local government, observing in his study of a rural area of Tamil Nadu, 'Adult franchise and Panchayati Raj have introduced new processes into village society', and 'political and legislative changes have altered the bargaining positions of the old economic classes'.[52] He argued that local elections increased the power of those who were worse off but were in greater numbers, rather than perpetuating or increasing domination by the traditional rural elite. In another early example, the Shiv Sena (often better known for other aspects of its ideology) built some of its success as a political organization on its attention to ward and municipal constituencies in Mumbai. It achieved electoral rewards by being responsive to those near the bottom of the economic ladder.[53]

There is significant evidence that local electoral participation is beginning to influence outcomes, often positively. For example, Chaudhuri[54] found that decentralized resource allocation in Kerala improved *perceived* delivery of roads, housing, and child development

Local and National Levels', *American Economic Review* 90, no. 2 (2005): 135–9. Banerjee and Somanathan found that local heterogeneity distorted the pattern of public service delivery. See A.V. Banerjee and R. Somanathan, 'Caste, Community and Collective Action: The Political Economy of Public Good Provision in India' (Working Paper, Department of Economics, MIT, 2001); and A.V. Banerjee and R. Somanathan, 'The Political Economy of Public Goods: Some Evidence from India', *Journal of Development Economics* 82, no. 2 (March 2007): 287–314. Kochar, Singh, and Singh provide an analysis of institutional features of rural spending. To explain some of these results in more depth, see A. Kochar, K. Singh, and S. Singh, 'Targeting Public Goods to the Poor in a Segregated Economy: An Empirical Analysis of Central Mandates in Rural India', *Journal of Public Economics* (2009): 917–30. See P. Keefer and S. Khemani, 'Why Do the Poor Receive Poor Services?', *Economic and Political Weekly* 39, no. 9 (February/March 2004): 935–43, for an overview of some of this literature.

[52] A. Béteille, *Caste, Class, and Power: Changing Patterns of Stratification in a Tanjore Village* (Berkeley: University of California Press, 1965), 221–3.

[53] V.S. Naipaul, *India: A Wounded Civilization* (New York: Alfred Knopf, 1975).

[54] S. Chaudhuri, 'Building Local Democracy: The People's Campaign for Decentralized Planning in the Indian State of Kerala' (presentation, South Asia Decentralization Series, Washington, DC: World Bank, 2005).

services, with the decentralization involving devolution of budgetary authority to elected rural local governments.[55] Initial social conditions such as education and caste, as well as the precise structure of political institutions, do matter for outcomes, but these may be unavoidable and acceptable limits on the efficacy of the political process.[56]

---

[55] Other examples include T. Besley, R. Pande, and V. Rao, 'Political Selection and the Quality of Government: Evidence from South India' (Working Paper, London School of Economics, 2006); T. Besley, R. Pande, and V. Rao, 'Participatory Democracy in Action: Survey Evidence from South India' (Working Paper, London School of Economics, 2006); and T. Besley, R. Pande, L. Rahman, and V. Rao, 'The Politics of Public Good Provision: Evidence from Indian Local Governments' (Working Paper, London School of Economics, London, 2006), for southern India. P. Bardhan and D. Mookherjee, 'Pro-poor Targeting and Accountability of Local Governments in West Bengal', *Journal of Development Economics* 79, no. 2 (April 2006): 303–27; and P. Bardhan and D. Mookherjee, 'Ideology vs. Competition in Redistributive Politics: An Analysis of Land Reforms in West Bengal' (Working Paper, Department of Economics, Boston University, MA, 2006), are similar examples for West Bengal in eastern India. Local government may not be the only avenue for political voice. Jha, Rao, and Woolcock found that informal governance structures arose within Delhi slums, and in turn provided more general access to public services through their leaders' links to elected local politicians. See S. Jha, V. Rao, and M. Woolcock, 'Governance in the Gullies: Democratic Responsiveness and Leadership in Delhi's Slums', *World Development* (2007): 230–46. Other studies of southern India suggest that participation in village assemblies (*gram sabhas*) is driven by constituents' self-interest, but is amenable to being changed through policy interventions. Thus, participation in this new avenue of direct democracy has also been encouraging, despite initial concerns about its efficacy.

[56] For example, for positive impacts of seat reservations at the local level, see R. Chattopadhyay and E. Duflo, 'Impact of Reservation in Panchayati Raj: Evidence from a Nationwide Randomised Experiment', *Economic and Political Weekly* 39, no. 9 (28 February–5 March 2004): 979–86; A. Dongre, 'Female Political Leadership and Prevalence of Water Borne Diseases: Evidence from a Natural Experiment in India' (Working Paper, UC Santa Cruz, January 2010), http://papers.ssrn.com/sol3/papers.cfm?abstract_id=1697107; and K. Deininger, J. Songqing, and H.K. Nagarajan, 'Can Political Reservations Affect Political Equilibria in the Long-Term? Evidence from Local Elections in Rural India' (Research Paper No. 59, Proceedings of the German Development Economics Conference, Berlin, 2011).

While I cannot precisely compare outcomes of state and local electoral accountability, it appears that the experience of decentralization to the local level in India has had many positive outcomes, and has not been subject to extremes of local capture.

The positive results on local electoral responsiveness are emerging *even though* the institutional structures are generally far from being supportive. Besides lacking independent revenue authority, local governments are still subject to control and interference from state-level bureaucrats and politicians over their entire domain of expenditure authority. Furthermore, local governments are often restricted in key areas such as land use, where state governments retain control. A final problem has been low levels of human and organizational capital in local government, typically summarized as 'lack of institutional capacity'. This lack has been somewhat of a self-fulfilling expectation of higher-level decision-makers, since local governments were denied the resources and authority to make meaningful decisions.[57] It is well understood that building local capacity in areas such as budgetary management is critical, but there have been problems in getting the states to pursue this objective effectively.[58] For example, grants made by the Eleventh Finance Commission to improve the databases and accounts of local bodies (urban and rural) were found to be 70 per cent unutilized when the next commission examined the situation almost five years later.[59] The report of the Fourteenth Finance Commission

[57] One might also argue that the use of information technology and standardization of production allow for greater centralization, by expanding the span of control. However, the case for decentralization is not simply based on technical efficiency considerations, but on how well incentives work. The argument is that internal, hierarchical accountability for public service delivery is difficult to achieve, and that external, electoral accountability has more potential to improve efficiency. Hence, elected local officials have to clearly bear the responsibility for good or bad performance. They can still outsource some functions, or get technical assistance from those with greater expertise.

[58] Finance Commission of India, *Report of the Twelfth Finance Commission 2005–10* (New Delhi: Government of India, 2004).

[59] Finance Commission of India, *Twelfth Finance Commission Report*, paragraph 8.43.

makes clear that many of the problems and issues with respect to local governments that were outlined above persist.[60]

I end this part by briefly noting the efforts in institutional capacity building, tying these back to the previous discussion. A synthesis report on PFM (augmented by the new condition of Accountability, so PFMA) for urban local bodies by a consulting firm, submitted to the World Bank,[61] provided an important summary of the situation at the time. The report described and analysed weaknesses in legislative frameworks, planning and budgeting, budget execution, accounting procedures, cash and fund flow management, procurement, internal control and audit, asset and liability management, reporting, external audit, and external oversight. In other words, every possible dimension of the effective organization of these bodies needed attention, though there was naturally considerable variation across different local governments, by region and by scale.[62]

The magnitude of the task is enormous, and recent documents of the Planning Commission and the JNNURM indicate only slow progress in capacity building, with efforts still being made to professionalize urban management and provide the requisite skill training. The JNNURM had started to produce score cards similar to those in outcome budgets, identifying whether specific cities have adopted double-entry accrual accounting, for example, but the data were presented for only 12 states, suggesting that progress has been quite

[60] See Finance Commission of India, *Fourteenth Finance Commission Report 2015–20* (New Delhi: Government of India, 2014), as well as M.G. Rao, 'For a Truer Decentralisation', *The Hindu*, 2 November 2015.

[61] Infrastructure Professionals Enterprise, 'Public Financial Management and Accountability in Urban Local Bodies in India' (Synthesis Report, Fiscal Management Unit, World Bank, New Delhi, 2006).

[62] All of these issues apply to rural local bodies, and are briefly discussed in the reports of the Thirteenth and Fourteenth Finance Commissions. See Fourteenth Finance Commission (2014) and Finance Commission of India, *Thirteenth Finance Commission Report 2010–15* (New Delhi: Government of India, 2009). One weak link in this chain is the low status and poor quality of work of many of the State Finance Commissions, which is another dimension of lack of institutional capacity.

incomplete.[63] Furthermore, a process of replacing the JNNURM with a new Smart City Mission and Atal Mission for Rejuvenation and Urban Transformation (AMRUT), begun in 2015, has put the brakes on municipal capacity-building efforts of the states under the old JNNURM.[64]

Revenue Authorities

To achieve effective accountability, decentralization of expenditure responsibility must be matched by some degree of decentralization of revenue or tax authority. The reasons are twofold: first, an over-dependence on intergovernmental transfers has the potential to soften budget constraints; and second, reliance on transfers weakens the connection for constituents between benefits and costs (called the Wicksellian connection) and makes lines of accountability more difficult to establish.[65] However, just as on the expenditure side, decentralization does not guarantee efficiency: there can be interest group capture, inefficient tax competition, and problems of government credibility that can make revenue raising politically difficult. I address these issues after laying out the current situation and recommendations.

The initial constitutional assignment of tax powers in India was based on a principle of separation, with tax categories being exclusively assigned either to the centre or to the states. Most broad-based taxes were assigned to the centre, including taxes on income and wealth from non-agricultural sources, corporation tax, taxes on production

[63] This assessment is based on material on the JNNURM website, and is subject to change over time, of course. For examples of conceptual exercises with respect to capacity-building efforts for urban local governance, see Ministry of Urban Development, *Report of the Working Group on Capacity Building, Urban Development Management for the Formulation of the Twelfth Five Year Plan (2012–2017)* (New Delhi: Government of India, 2011); and Ministry of Urban Development, *Toolkit for Comprehensive Capacity Building Programme* (New Delhi: Government of India, 2013).

[64] See M. Jeelani, 'Centre Puts the Brakes on JNNURM Research Projects, Capacity-building', *The Hindu*, 25 September 2015.

[65] The term comes from the writings of Knut Wicksell: see A. Breton, *Competitive Governments: An Economic Theory of Politics and Public Finance* (New York: Cambridge University Press, 1996).

(excluding those on alcoholic liquors), and customs duty. These were often taxes where the revenue potential was greater, as a result of relatively lower collection costs and higher elasticities with respect to growth. The centre was also assigned all residual tax powers.

Initially, the central government followed principles that emphasized extreme progressivity and narrow targeting, resulting in a very inefficient tax structure, and tax administration that was highly susceptible to corruption. Economic reform has led to a substantial rationalization of the central government tax structure, in terms of lowering marginal rates, simplification of the rate structure, and some degree of base broadening. In the realm of tax administration, also, some progress has been made, through the use of information technology.

At the subnational level, a long list of taxes was constitutionally assigned to the states, but only the tax on the sale of goods has turned out to be significant for state revenues. This is largely a result of political economy factors (for example, rural landed interests were initially quite powerful in government at the state level) that have eroded or precluded the use of taxes on agricultural land or incomes (and also of user charges for public irrigation and electricity) by state governments. In addition, the separation of income tax powers between the centre and states based on source (agriculture versus non-agriculture) created avenues for evasion, since the states chose not to tax agricultural income.

The greatest inefficiencies arose in indirect taxes. Even though in a legal sense taxes on production (central manufacturing excises) and sale (state sales taxes) were separate, they taxed the same base, causing overlapping and cascading, and leaving the states less room to effectively choose indirect tax rates. Also, the states were allowed to levy taxes on the sale and purchase of goods (entry 54 in the state list) but not services. This also provided avenues for tax evasion, and delayed the design and implementation of a comprehensive value added tax (VAT). These issues have been a major subject of recent policy and institutional reform initiatives, with the VAT having been successfully introduced, and now being transitioned into a relatively comprehensive goods and services tax (GST).[66]

---

[66] Under the United Progressive Alliance (UPA) government, the GST was blocked by the opposition, which is now the ruling party and seeking to proceed with it, as of this writing in April 2016. Technical and economic issues

Through a combination of tax assignments and choices by the states, their revenues are well short of their expenditure responsibilities, and the difference is made up by constitutionally mandated tax sharing, guided by the Finance Commission, but also other channels discussed earlier. Several of these transfer channels involve responding to states' projected revenue gaps. These features encourage unrealistic budgeting to try and enhance transfers, and make clear budgeting and proper tracking of spending and outcomes difficult. The previous discussion on Planning Commission transfers and those under various central schemes and missions is pertinent here. Note that the abolition of the Planning Commission and the new approach of the Fourteenth Finance Commission do not completely solve the problem of transfer mechanisms in India. For example, it appears that the Finance Ministry has sought to impose conditions on grants recommended by the Finance Commission that were intended to be untied, and the government continues to impose cesses and surcharges as ways of collecting revenue that is not constitutionally shareable with the states.[67] Only greater revenue authority for the lower-level government can counter such manoeuvres by the higher level.

For local governments, the new constitutional amendments provided no explicit guidelines for revenue authority. The language of the amendments simply leaves such assignment up to the states, which are supposed to decide which taxes local bodies may levy themselves, and which state-collected taxes are to be assigned to local governments.[68]

---

have been overcome, and it appears that political manoeuvring is the final source of resistance.

[67] See Seetha, 'Finance Comm Gives More Power to States but the Finmin Just Watered Down Co-operative Federalism', *FirstPost*, 25 February 2015; as well as P. Chakraborty and M. Gupta, 'Evolving Centre–State Financial Relations: Role of the New Framework for Grants', *Economic and Political Weekly* 51, no. 16 (April 2016): 43–6.

[68] Even before the constitutional changes, local governments had a number of taxes assigned to them by individual states. Rural local governments had as many as 27 different taxes (20 exclusive, 7 concurrent with the state government) available to them—see A. Datta, 'Local Government Finances: Trends, Issues and Reforms', in *State Finances in India*, eds A. Bagchi, J.L. Bajaj, and W.A. Byrd (New Delhi: Vikas Publishing House, 1992)—but with great variation across states. Exclusive taxes included terminal taxes and octroi; property

Thus, tax assignments remain unclear, and states do not provide assistance or guidance to local bodies in implementing tax collection. Rural local governments, in particular, do not have adequate sources of revenue assigned to them, although for both rural and urban governments, the problem is also one of inadequate revenue effort. Even so, revenue authority may be the dimension of decentralization where local governments are most constrained. The state finance commissions have generally failed to do an effective job of making transfers to local governments, reflecting the states' political reluctance, and their own budget constraints.

Turning to non-tax revenue (from user charges and fees),[69] this was on average less than tax revenue for rural and urban governments, though the ranking was reversed in many states.[70] Poor delivery often creates a situation where the imposition of user charges is politically difficult, because the benefits are not clear to the payers: a low-level equilibrium persists.[71] In many cases, unclear or overlapping assignments of expenditure responsibility compound problems of accountability and implementation of fees.

---

and building taxes; oil engine, food, timber, fishery, and produce taxes; and profession and labour taxes. Concurrent taxes included those on commercial crops and on land. For the lowest rural government level in some states, land revenue was a significant proportion of revenue, though absolute amounts were small in all cases: no rural local tax was a significant source of revenue. Twenty different taxes were available to urban governments, nine exclusively to them and 11 concurrent with state governments. In contrast to rural governments, several of these were significant revenue sources, particularly octroi and property taxes, but also entertainment taxes in some cities.

[69] The most common fees are user charges for water and lighting. These are typically collected at the lowest rural level and, in the absence of monitoring ability, are flat fees. On the other hand, charges for sanitation, or for public events such as fairs and festivals, are rarely assigned or employed. Panchayats (village-level councils) are usually not empowered to levy user charges on health and education (with some states being exceptions), even though aspects of these functions are assigned to them. User charges in urban areas are often extremely low, not just for goods consumed by the poor, but also services such as land development. See M.G. Rao and N. Singh, 'Local Government Reform'.

[70] Finance Commission, *Twelfth Finance Commission*, Annexures 8.1 and 8.4.

[71] See M.G. Rao and N. Singh, 'Local Government Reform'.

At both the state and local levels, therefore, the revenue authority falls short of what would allow each level to independently meet its expenditure responsibilities. To some extent, this is a natural outcome of the different driving forces for assigning revenue authority and expenditure responsibility. Most significantly, mobility across jurisdictions increases as the size of the jurisdictional unit decreases, and a tax base that is mobile may shrink dramatically in response to a tax, making it harder for smaller jurisdictions to raise revenue from taxes. If this factor implies that more taxes should be collected by the centre, there will be a tendency for there to be a mismatch between revenues and expenditures for subnational jurisdictions, to the extent that subnational governments are relatively better able to respond to diversity of preferences.[72] This is certainly true in India, and is dealt with through large intergovernmental transfers, including tax sharing but also the other channels discussed earlier. The argument here is that large transfers create problems for expenditure efficiency, and that this argues for decentralizing revenue authority along with expenditure responsibilities.[73]

---

[72] The problem of tax competition can be avoided to some extent by coordination of taxes among subnational jurisdictions. For example, different states might agree to charge the same minimum sales tax rate or income tax rate. The centre can also impose this coordination of minimum rates, to reduce cheating.

[73] Singh and Srinivasan, in 'Federalism and Economic Development', analyse issues of incentives with respect to intergovernmental transfers. In addition to arguing for redesigning the formulaic part of the intergovernmental transfer system to directly improve marginal incentives, they also suggest that reducing the magnitude of transfers can decrease the scope for political influence effects that distort subnational behaviour, as well as directly improve subnational political incentives—constituents of subnational jurisdictions can more clearly identify the Wicksellian connection between their costs and benefits in voting on taxation when transfer revenues do not dominate lower-level government budgets. Since there is no reason for centralizing expenditure decisions more than the status quo, reducing transfers requires further decentralization of tax authority. This can be done through allowing subnational jurisdictions to piggyback on some of the same tax bases that are used for centre–state tax sharing. For example, allowing states and local governments to impose income tax surcharges would not only improve their marginal retention, but it could reduce the need for tax sharing. Piggybacking, combined with a removal of the

The last dimension of revenue institutions, after statutory assignment and imposition, is collection. Collection of taxes and user charges is relatively poor at all levels of government. Even the mechanisms for collection of charges between governments or government-owned enterprises function poorly, although India has reasonably well-defined institutions and organizational structures for collection. Of course, corruption is a major problem at all levels, so that illegal payments substitute for tax or fee collection. Designing administrative systems to control corruption is not easy, but can be done, following certain conceptual guidelines.[74] In many cases, the design of tax systems is poor, hindering collection and encouraging corruption; however, progress has been made in areas such as the national income tax and state sales taxes.

However, particularly at the state and local levels, design problems remain. Sometimes rates or fees are trivially low, making collection inefficient. In other cases, tax rates are prohibitively high, encouraging corruption. Assessment of tax liabilities is often done poorly, especially for cases such as the property tax.[75] Exemptions of various kinds narrow tax bases, reduce fairness, decrease allocative efficiency, and also encourage evasion.

Poorly designed tax systems and fee schedules make collection more difficult, contributing to poor collection rates. For some taxes, such as the urban property tax in many cities, collection rates have been abysmally low, but problems have also existed for national taxes such as the personal income tax. Poor collection rates at the local level are also a reflection of poor accountability, both in delivery of public services that are meant to be funded from these taxes and fees, and

---

distinction between non-agricultural and agricultural income, would represent a change in tax assignments that could increase efficiency as well as reduce the states' fiscal problems. Paralleling the suggestions for centre–state tax coordination, small piggybacking taxes can also be introduced at the local level at the point of last sale to replace octroi, giving local governments a chance to benefit from the new GST infrastructure.

[74] Dasgupta and Mookherjee, *Incentives and Institutional Reforms*.

[75] World Bank, 'India: Urban Finance and Governance Review, Volumes I–II' (Energy and Infrastructure Unit, South Asia Region, Washington, DC: World Bank, 2004).

in the collection agencies and their political superiors. Poor revenue collection is, therefore, another aspect of the low-level political equilibrium analysed by Rao and Singh.[76] Formal institutions such as the bureaucracy and public enterprises function below their potential in this kind of equilibrium.

A final point to emphasize is with respect to the political economy of the three tiers of government in India. Centre–state relations have long been viewed as contentious, with the central government seeking to impose political and economic control on the states, for reasons ranging from fears of disintegration to individual egos and insecurities. Economic liberalization in the 1990s coincided with the beginning of local government reform, and also problems of fiscal management at the state level. In a sense, this was the least auspicious time for trying to push expenditure and revenue authority down to the local level, in order to improve the delivery of local public goods and services. The states, in some cases, even viewed local-government strengthening as driven by a desire of the centre to do an end-run around them. From this perspective, the structure of centre–state fiscal relations continues to be a barrier to local government reform. The politically feasible way to improve local government functioning may, therefore, be to increase the revenue authority of the states, giving them the fiscal room to support urban governments in particular, where infrastructure needs and growth will create the greatest pressures.

***

[76] See M.G. Rao and N. Singh, 'Local Government Reform'. Their model of government–citizen decision-making is adapted from Inman, in analysing tax limitations imposed by voters in some states in the US. The relevance in this context is the observation for Indian local governments that their decision-makers are reluctant to impose higher taxes, or to collect existing taxes, because they fear voters' displeasure; indeed, one hears the argument that taxation should be determined at a distance from the taxed. At the same time, as has been the main concern of this chapter, the level of local public services is perceived as too low. The model displays this type of equilibrium. Importantly, it also shows that increasing efficiency, even slightly, may lead to a very different equilibrium, with higher levels of provision and higher welfare. See R.P. Inman, 'The "New" Political Economy', in *Handbook of Public Economics*, vol. 2, eds A. Auerbach and M. Feldstein (Amsterdam: North Holland, 1985).

India's government works very well in some ways (functioning democracy, stability, responsiveness, and so on) but is maddeningly inept in others, especially in improving the provision of basic public services, ranging from health and education to water and electricity supplies. Lant Pritchett's term of a 'flailing' state for India uses a bodily metaphor:

> *[A] nation-state in which the head, that is the elite institutions at the national (and in some states) level remain sound and functional but ... this head is no longer reliably connected via nerves and sinews to its own limbs.* In many parts of India in many sectors, the everyday actions of the field level agents of the state—policemen, engineers, teachers, health workers—are increasingly beyond the control of the administration at the national or state level.[77]

It may be debatable whether the deterioration is in absolute terms, or relative to expectations and aspirations, but the question, is what can be done to change this situation?

Pritchett's solution to the problem that so many have identified, and which he has so picturesquely named, is unclear. He suggests that India's 'administrative modernism' is out of step with the country's politics and society. He argues that political competition focuses on loyalty to identity groups, rather than provision of effective public services. He suggests that India will eventually muddle through with incremental reforms and learning by doing. This chapter offers some different perspectives on the problem and the possible solutions.

Ultimately, as Pritchett and others have recognized, a major issue is that of weak accountability of government employees. Accountability can be internal, within an organization (for example, to one's boss), or external, such as to citizens as voters. There are a variety of ways in which accountability can be improved. Agarwal and Somanathan, themselves senior bureaucrats, suggested some structural changes for decision-making within central ministries, including letting more policy implementation be managed below the top level, providing better

---

[77] L. Pritchett, 'Is India a Flailing State?: Detours on the Four Lane Highway to Modernization' (HKS Faculty Research Working Paper Series RWP09–013, John F. Kennedy School of Government, Harvard University, Cambridge, MA, 2009).

career incentives for performance by elite bureaucrats, and broadening the input of expertise into policymaking.[78]

The suggested changes can, in fact, be thought of as embodying two fundamental principles, those of decentralization and competition. Decentralization allows for better matching of skills and tasks, at least when training is appropriately provided. Competition provides incentives, sometimes pecuniary, but sometimes non-pecuniary, for better effort. The interesting idea here is that relatively small structural changes at the very top may have significant impacts—the decentralization envisaged is modest, just pushing some decisions one or two levels down the hierarchy. The competition envisaged is also modest—slightly more in the way of performance expectations and appraisals, plus potential and actual competition from outsiders to the bureaucracy.

Such micro reforms can, of course, be copied at the level of each state government, and would need to be. A second set of reforms, which are much more macro in nature, apply the principles of decentralization and competition at a different scale. This chapter has argued that India's so-called flailing state is very much a result of over-centralization with respect to the different tiers of government. It has argued that more expenditure authority needs to be pushed down to the level of state governments, and from there to local governments, particularly city and town governments. Currently, the states appear to have considerable responsibilities for expenditure, and there is a view that they have failed to meet these responsibilities, necessitating more central government control through transfers with strings attached. In this chapter, I have developed a case that state governments instead need to be given more autonomy, and that more revenue authority needs to be delegated to state governments, who must then delegate further to local governments. Decentralization is essential for creating effective external accountability, which in turn can drive internal accountability.

Of course, in decentralizing, there are issues of inequity, of corruption, and of capacity. However, each of these can be addressed directly. None of these problems are solely associated with decentralization, and none of them have to be a necessary difficulty of decentralization. The

---

[78] Agarwal and Somanathan, 'Public Policy Making in India'.

initial evidence from India's massive local government reform supports the idea that accountability and effectiveness can increase with decentralization, even as mechanisms are needed to deal with the adverse consequences mentioned. And this has happened without giving local governments even a semblance of appropriate revenue authority.

The two suggestions for government reform presented here—decentralization and competition within top-level government organizations, and across tiers of government—illustrate the problem with Pritchett's metaphor. There is not just one brain that controls nerves, sinews, and limbs. Government is made of individuals with skills that can be better utilized, and that can be improved. Democratic governments ultimately serve at the pleasure of citizens, and government workers need to make that connection more explicitly, through appropriate incentives and institutional arrangements. A focus on these possibilities can make the government work better more rapidly than pessimists might believe.

6

NEW REGULATORY INSTITUTIONS IN INFRASTRUCTURE
From De-politicization to Creative Politics

*Navroz K. Dubash**

Independent regulatory institutions in India are no longer in their infancy. Widely associated with the economic liberalization period of the early 1990s, regulatory institutions are often understood as a necessary institutional adjunct to emergent private-sector involvement in sectors prone to monopolistic market structures, such as infrastructure. Consequently, many new regulatory institutions have emerged in infrastructure sectors over the last two decades, and these are the focus of this chapter.

Viewed through an economic lens, regulators substitute for, or mimic, competitive markets in a context where scale economies, network externalities, or information asymmetries are present. There is an important political corollary to this perspective. In order for economic regulators to focus on economic efficiency-oriented outcomes, regulators have to be insulated from addressing political, particularly redistributive, concerns and this insulation is to be achieved by hewing

* I am deeply grateful to Anirudh Burman for research assistance in putting together this chapter, and also to Jafar Alam for compiling exhaustive sectoral literature reviews.

to technocratic decision-criteria.[1] Based on a somewhat casual acceptance of this received wisdom, Indian regulatory discussions have been
dominated by practitioners debating questions of design: how does
one design a regulatory agency to best mimic competitive markets in
a given sector?

There is good reason for thinking that this narrow framing of the
institutional problem is incomplete at best, and misleading at worst.
Consider the following impressionistic observations, for which further
evidence is provided in the body of the chapter:

1. Electricity: Electricity regulators have been created in almost all
   states in the context of persistent state ownership, but with little
   evidence that they have successfully led to tariff rationalization or
   attracted private investment. They have, however, led to a robust
   culture and practice of public engagement and transparency in the
   regulatory process.
2. Telecom: The establishment of the Telecom Regulatory Authority
   of India (TRAI), often considered a success story, has coincided
   with the development of a highly competitive telecom market in
   India, even though the causal relationship between the two may be
   complicated. Over its history, TRAI has also been embroiled in long-
   standing disputes with the executive and has been shaped strongly
   by judicial intervention. The telecom sector as a whole has been
   rocked by the spectrum allocation scandal.
3. Petroleum and Natural Gas: The Petroleum and Natural Gas
   Regulatory Board (PNGRB) has been riven with conflict since its
   inception over the scope of its pricing powers and charges of internal
   dissension, and the entire sector has by no means solved its problems
   of credible price signals to the private sector.
4. Coal: A coal regulator is under active consideration, but in the
   course of debate, its powers—particularly regarding pricing—have
   been considerably limited.
5. Other sectors: Several other sectors have recently established or are
   actively considering creation of regulators, including airports, ports,
   education, and real estate.

---

[1] G. Majone, 'The Rise of the Regulatory State in Europe', *West European
Politics* 17, no. 3 (1994): 77–101.

These vignettes by no means support a story of regulators proliferating because they provide a successful institutional design to
compensate for absent markets. Instead, the empirical record suggests:
imperfect performance at best; complex and ongoing interactions with
other branches of government, notably the executive and the judiciary;
and regulators as providing a deliberative space for public engagement
in infrastructure governance rather than being technical bodies alone.
Above all, given the mixed record, what explains the enthusiasm of
ministries to delegate control to unproven bodies over which they lack
control?

This is not to claim that the creation of independent regulators is
to blame for all the ills of the respective sectors, or even that their creation has led to less effective sector governance in all cases. It is, however, to argue that this mixed, but also very intriguingly multifaceted
empirical record calls for further explanation. In other words, there
are unexplored questions associated with the emergence, persistence,
and functioning of independent regulatory agencies that have been
inadequately addressed and that are salient to an understanding of how
these institutions can contribute to governance in India.

These issues have been raised in the Indian literature, but to a surprisingly limited extent. Srinivasa-Raghavan, for example, asks where
the regulator fits into an overall governance context and what happens
if regulatory decisions operate at cross-purposes with various social
objectives being pursued by the government of the day.[2] Bhattacharya
and Patel suggest that, in the Indian context, the prevalence of powerful
incumbents and the reluctance of the government to relinquish control
have been important contributors to the varied performance of regulators.[3] More than a decade after the first infrastructure regulators were
established, the Planning Commission of India put out an approach
paper asking, among other things, where regulators fit in India's constitutional framework.[4] Exploring questions such as these usefully shifts

[2] T.C.A. Srinivasa-Raghavan, 'Regulatory Independence in Indian Context',
The Asian Journal 8 (April 2001): 1–10.

[3] S. Bhattacharya and U.R. Patel, 'New Regulatory Institutions in India:
White Knights or Trojan Horses?', in *Public Institutions in India*, eds D. Kapur
and P.B. Mehta (New Delhi: Oxford University Press, 2007): 406–56.

[4] Planning Commission of India, *Approach to Regulation of Infrastructure*
(New Delhi: Government of India, 2008).

the discussion away from a universal design question—how to build an institution to mimic competition in monopoly sectors—and towards an exploration of specific contexts, both national and sectoral, within which regulators function.

Attention to local context also emerges as a central theme in much of the international literature on regulatory agencies. A classic study on regulatory governance argues that the potential for regulatory institutions needs to be understood in the context of existing political and social institutions.[5] Sociological explanations point to institutional emulation as the reason for the spread of regulatory agencies,[6] but conditioned by a process through which the 'rationalising myth' of regulatory agencies then goes through a process of embedding in local context.[7] A study on the spread of developing agencies in the 'south' suggests that this process is shaped by three common structural features: the transplant of the regulatory model without adequate thought given to its suitability and adaptability to local context; the heightened prevalence of redistributive politics; and lower levels of state capacity.[8] The common theme is that a newly created regulatory institution, whether developed through rational design or institutional emulation, inevitably follows a process of accommodation and adjustment to local context. The result is a diversity of regulatory outcomes that varies both by sector and country.

This chapter suggests that the role that Indian infrastructure regulatory agencies plays is shaped by the process through which they are embedded in a local context. This perspective helps explain the diverse

[5] B. Levy and P.T. Spiller, 'The Institutional Foundations of Regulatory Commitment: A Comparative Analysis of Telecommunication Regulation', *Journal of Law, Economics, & Organization* 10, no. 2 (October 1994): 201–46.

[6] J. Jordana, D. Levi-Faur, and X.F. Marin, 'The Global Diffusion of Regulatory Agencies: Channels of Transfer and Stages of Diffusion', *Comparative Political Studies* 44, no. 10 (May 2011): 1343–69.

[7] N.K. Dubash, 'Regulating through the Back Door: Understanding the Implications of Institutional Transfer', in *The Rise of the Regulatory State of the South*, eds N.K. Dubash and B. Morgan (New York: Oxford University Press, 2013).

[8] N.K. Dubash and B. Morgan, eds, 'The Rise of the Regulatory State of the South', in *The Rise of the Regulatory State of the South* (New York: Oxford University Press, 2013).

empirical realities of regulatory functioning and also, therefore, the potential of regulators as a new feature of India's institutional landscape. The empirical record suggests that while regulatory creation was driven by an effort to insulate decision-making from undue political influence by delegating powers to technocratic agencies, this effort has largely been unsuccessful. But, the chapter argues that conceptualizing the regulatory process as one to be re-made around technical rules was probably too simple; the Indian context requires regulators to also engage with and make more orderly the inevitable negotiation that occurs over regulatory decisions. For this reason, rather than regulatory agencies alone, the idea of a regulatory space is a more appropriate construct, one that includes, at minimum, the judiciary and civil society.

The chapter begins with an examination of the context within which regulatory agencies in various sectors were introduced in India, their formal objectives, and the early issues they faced. The next section delves deeper into the process of embedding, trying to understand the evolution of the regulatory agency in each case as an outcome of the complex of political forces and institutional circumstances with which it was forced to engage. The discussion draws primarily on electricity and telecom regulators, on which there is a substantial literature, and to a more limited extent on the petroleum and natural gas regulator, and a proposed coal regulator.

Regulatory Transplant: The Importance of Local Context

The introduction of regulatory agencies into infrastructure in India occurred as part of a much larger global trend. In a sample of 15 sectors in 48 countries from 1966 to 2007, Jordana and colleagues. find that the annual rate of addition of new regulatory agencies rose from less than 5 a year between the 1960s to the 1980s, to 15 a year in the 1990s through 2002, with more than 20 agencies a year coming into existence between 1995 and 2001.[9] Notably, this peak coincides with the substantial increase in private infrastructure investment in much of

[9] J. Jordana, D. Levi-Faur, and X.F. Marin, 'The Global Diffusion of Regulatory Agencies: Channels of Transfer and Stages of Diffusion', *Comparative Political Studies* 44, no. 10 (October 2011): 1343–69.

the developing world during the 1990s, suggesting a possible relation-ship between the two trends.

While the establishment of infrastructure regulators in India and the origins of that process in the mid-1990s was part of a global trend, I argue in this section that any effort to understand its implications requires considerable attention to the local context. Specifically, it is necessary to understand the governance problem the establishment of a regulator was supposed to solve, and the outcomes arising from the establishment of regulators. To enable a discussion across so many sec-tors with complex histories, Table A6.1 provides a snapshot of these regulators along several dimensions: context for their creation, objec-tive of creating the regulator, primary design elements, and a glimpse of its functioning. Any such synoptic account is necessarily partial; additional points are outlined in the subsequent discussion.

Sectoral Dysfunction and the Requirement of Political Insulation

An examination of the immediate context and objectives for establish-ment of regulators in Table A6.1 suggests that sectoral dysfunction, the imperative of attracting private capital, and a desire to promote market competition are strong and common themes. In each case, creation of a regulator was a part of a sectoral transformation strategy aimed at a deepening of markets. In electricity, for example, promoting private investment was an explicit objective. For telecom, easing concerns of private investors and signalling credibility of reforms, in particular the intent of checking the monopoly power of the incumbent, was a driver. In coal, ending the monopoly of Coal India Limited and creating a level playing field was the intent, as was bringing about some degree of insu-lation of decision-making from overt political interests. Indeed, this has become the primary rationale for creation of regulators. As Table A6.1 suggests, this was to be accomplished by hiving off an insulated arena of technocratic decision-making in which economic logic could operate unencumbered by redistributive pressures and the consequent messi-ness of politics. Thus, in electricity, the objective was to distance the government from tariff setting, and in telecom, to separate policy mak-ing and regulatory functions. These themes are reinforced by a slightly more detailed look at each sector.

The experience of the electricity sector most clearly illustrates the anticipated role of a regulator as an agent of de-politicization. In the early 1990s, the context for sector reform was growing shortages of power, exacerbated by rising losses that provided a deterrent to new investment. Globally, and especially in Asia, the power sector was attracting record levels of investment, but little of it was coming to India. In this context, reform in the form of a global model of electricity restructuring, mid-wifed by the World Bank, began in the states (electricity is a concurrent subject under the constitution), in particular in Orissa, in 1995.[10] The World Bank's loan document for Orissa baldly states the expected contribution of the regulator was 'to insulate Orissa's power sector from the government and ensure its ... autonomy'.[11] In particular, by doing so, it would ' ... ensure the sustainability of tariff reform ... inter alia to attract sufficient private investment and protect the interests of consumers'.[12] The expected impact of the regulator is clear from these statements: the regulator would insulate decision-making, particularly on tariffs, from what had been government populism, which would lead to greater credibility and increased confidence on the part of private investors.

In the telecoms sector, the concern once again was with attracting a greater share of the surge of private investment evident in the 1990s, but the concerns of political interference focused on the potentially anti-competitive role of state incumbents in the telecoms industry. The need for a regulator—the TRAI was established in 1997—was driven by the requirement of signalling that the government, in its policy-making role, would maintain a distance from its service delivery arm.[13] Although the investment climate had cooled off considerably by the time the PNGRB was established in 2006 and the Coal Regulator

[10] N.K. Dubash and S. Chella Rajan, 'Power Politics: Process of India's Power Sector Reform', *Economic and Political Weekly* 36, no. 35 (September 1–7, 2001): 3367–90.

[11] World Bank, 'Staff Appraisal Report: Orissa Power Sector Restructuring Project', Annex 5.3, 2. (Washington, DC: World Bank, 1996).

[12] World Bank, 'Staff Appraisal Report', 7.

[13] R. Mukherji, 'Regulatory Evolution in Indian Telecommunications' (Working Paper, Institute of South Asian Studies, Singapore, 2006).

was approved by the Union Cabinet in mid-2013, the motivation for their creation was substantially similar to telecoms: bringing in private investors into non-performing sectors, and assuring those investors that incumbents would not be unduly favoured.

Regulatory Agencies as Agents of De-politicization in Practice

Was this expectation of regulatory agencies as a political buffer justified, and was there adequate consideration of how to best design regulators to play this role? A glance at Table A6.1, particularly the columns on design and functioning, suggests there is mixed evidence of any explicit effort to design regulators to effectively perform the function of political insulation.

This is particularly evident in the case of the electricity sector, the first infrastructure sector to experiment with a regulator. Interviews with those involved in the Orissa process suggest that while the World Bank had a clear idea of the regulator's role, their domestic interlocutors saw the electricity regulator merely as a necessary hurdle—a costless diversionary tactic imposed by donors.[14] The legislation to craft Orissa's electricity regulator was drafted by international consultants with inputs from Indian lawyers, with very little attention to how the regulator would be embedded within the context of Indian governing institutions, and in particular whether it was feasible for the regulator to act as an agent of de-politicization.

In its early years, the Orissa Electricity Regulatory Commission (OERC) showed little sign of playing its intended role of defending against populism. The OERC followed a nuanced approach to tariff setting, by deciding against raising tariffs substantially, and certainly by less than reform designers thought necessary to attract investment. Instead it quite reasonably ruled that the public should not be made to suffer for past mismanagement. As a reaction, in the next state to privatize electricity distribution, Delhi, the tariff decision was embedded within a form of regulation by contract for the first five years, rather than being left to the regulator entirely. Neither case demonstrated the value of the regulator as a de-politicizing agent.

[14] Dubash and Rajan, 'Power Politics'.

Despite these unconvincing results, the model of regulatory agencies for electricity, and the assumption that they would be able to depoliticize tariff setting, spread rapidly through states and was enshrined in two central acts, the Electricity Regulatory Commissions Act, 1998, and the Electricity Act, 2003. As the next section discusses, the inability of electricity regulators to deliver on their original design intent continues to plague electricity governance, and calls into question the original conception of the role regulatory agencies should play in Indian electricity.

Almost two decades after the introduction of regulatory agencies, the electricity sector remains in a state of disarray—Table A6.1 documents official reports of the state of the sector from 2012, describing it as being as bad as during the early days of regulatory agencies in 1998, with the finances of distribution companies remaining under stress. While this state of affairs cannot by any means be laid entirely at the door of regulatory agencies, it is notable that the core function of regulatory agencies, tariff setting, remains at the heart of sectoral dysfunction.

The context for creation of TRAI was quite different and, as Mukherji argues, the sector-reform motivation was substantially home-grown.[15] While there was significant opposition to private participation in telecom, strong backing from the Prime Minister's Office (PMO) and the Finance Ministry were essential to the creation of TRAI as a counter-weight to the influence wielded by the Department of Telecommunications (DoT), which originally, and successfully, had managed to block its creation. The Telecom Regulatory Authority of India Act was passed in 1997 after initially coming into existence through an ordinance, which was then re-issued twice more.[16] This is not to suggest that TRAI was immediately able to play its role as an effective counter-weight. For example, while TRAI did have tariff fixation responsibility, control over inter-connection between providers, responsibility for consumer interests, and ensuring compliance with license conditions, it did not have other key powers, notably jurisdiction over disputes between the DoT and service providers, or the power to issue or cancel licenses. Moreover, TRAI faced overt hostility from the

[15] R. Mukherji, 'Managing Competition: Politics and the Building of Independent Regulatory Institutions' (Working Paper, Center for the Advanced Study of India, University of Pennsylvania, Philadelphia, PA, 2004).

[16] Mukherji, 'Managing Competition'.

DoT in the form of several cases challenging the legality of TRAI's actions.[17]

Mukherji plausibly describes 'a gradual process of conflict resolution' through which institutional change led to the emergence of new interests, which in turn led to further institutional layering, leading to a credible regulatory regime. There have been some notable problems in telecoms regulation, particularly the 2G scam, that are tied to continued uncertainty over TRAI's advisory role and the extent to which TRAI has, in fact, been able to play a balancing role between incumbents and entrants.[18]

The impact of creating PNGRB on the petroleum and natural gas sector is hard to assess, in part because it is of more recent vintage and because less has been written on PNGRB. However, as compared to either telecom or electricity, the PNGRB seems to be a far more toothless body. PNGRB's responsibilities are limited to the downstream end of the sector, with control over the lucrative upstream sector, which has recently aroused much debate over the basis for pricing decisions, remaining in the hands of the Directorate General of Hydrocarbons.[19] Moreover, the PNGRB has no jurisdiction over pricing of petroleum or petroleum products. The Petroleum and Natural Gas Regulatory Board Act, 2006 is designed to require case-by-case notification of products to be placed under the jurisdiction of PNGRB. Indeed, the relatively short history of the PNGRB seems to have been dominated by jurisdictional battles with the Ministry of Oil and Petroleum. In one case, the PNGRB sought to exercise powers over city gas, while the Ministry and the retailer in question claimed the relevant section delegating the necessary authority had not been notified.[20] In another case, the Ministry

---

[17] A. Thiruvengadam and P. Joshi, 'Judiciaries as Crucial Actors in Regulatory Systems of the Global South: The Indian Judiciary and Telecom Regulation (1991–2012)', in *The Rise of the Regulatory State of the South*, eds N.K. Dubash and B. Morgan (New York: Oxford University Press, 2013).

[18] R. Mukherji, 'Interests, Wireless Technology, and Institutional Change: From Government Monopoly to Regulated Competition in Indian Telecommunications', *Journal of Asian Studies* 68, no. 2 (May 2009): 491–517.

[19] E.A.S. Sarma, 'Natural Gas Price Hike: Subsidising Producers' Profits?', *Economic and Political Weekly* 48, no. 28 (13 July 2013): 12–14.

[20] 'No Retrospective Implementation of Current Order to IGL: L Mansingh, Ex-Chairman, PNGRB', *Economic Times*, 10 April 2012; 'PNGRB Entitled to Fix Tariffs, Says Centre', *India Today*, 23 May 2012.

requested the PNGRB to determine the marketing margin that could be charged on natural gas.[21] The PNGRB stated it did not have the authority to do so (as natural gas had not been notified), seemingly to make a point about its attenuated powers. The Ministry further replied calling for the PNGRB to act under a different subsection under which it is required to perform any other function as entrusted to it by the central government, perhaps in an effort to reaffirm the existing pecking order. The PNGRB experience suggests the executive has decided it is important to hedge bets with regard to delegating important pricing power to independent regulatory agencies.

The most recent experience with a coal regulator suggests that the lesson has now become accepted wisdom. Discussions over the establishment of a coal regulator have been underway at least since 2009, largely following the received wisdom that an independent regulator is an important element in signalling credibility to private investors, and ensuring that commercial terms are obtained in the sector. However, in the intervening years, circumspection seems to have prevailed. The Coal Regulatory Authority Bill, approved by cabinet in late June 2013, provides only recommendatory powers to a new coal regulator on principles and methodology for determining coal prices, and does not grant powers to issue licenses.[22] According to news reports, these decisions were taken explicitly to 'avoid conflict with the functions of the coal ministry'.[23] If, indeed, one important challenge to a rational coal sector is correcting what is currently a distorted pricing mechanism, it is hard to see how the creation of a new regulator, shorn of pricing power out of deference for the ministry that has caused the distortions to begin with, will move the sector in this direction.

These sectoral snapshots do not lend much confidence in regulatory agencies as rationally designed institutions carefully aimed at solving governance problems. The problem diagnosis of key sectors continues to revolve around the need to de-politicize decision-making, particularly

[21] 'PNGRB Refuses to Fix Gas Marketing Margin', *Press Trust of India*, 8 May 2012.

[22] 'Cabinet Approves Setting up of Coal Regulatory Authority', *Press Trust of India*, 27 June 2013.

[23] P. Siddhanta, 'EGoM Votes for Coal Regulator Empowered to Recommend Guidelines, not Regulate Prices', *Indian Express*, 8 May 2013.

to avoid perpetuation of distorted pricing structures, and to attenuate the powers of entrenched state monopolies. Regulatory institutions are still the institutional mechanism of choice to solve these problems of governance, but the design of those institutions demonstrates a trend towards delegating ever less powers, particularly critical powers over prices and licenses. Given these contradictory trends, why do regulatory agencies continue to proliferate?

One answer might be the sociologically informed notion of the 'rationalising myth'—the idea that the very creation of regulatory agencies helps send signals of credibility through adoption of an institutional form that carries with it powerful overtones of technocratic rationality. This narrative may indeed have been powerful during the heyday of infrastructure privatization in the 1990s. However, the unconvincing empirical evidence of regulatory performance over the succeeding decades should surely, by now, have reduced the salience and currency of any such rationalizing myth. The persistence of regulatory institutions, and the reason they continue to be created now, likely has to do with how they are embedded over time within the institutional substrate of economic governance, how they transform this landscape, and in doing so, the interests they serve.

The Process of Embedding: Regulators as Institutional Irritants in a Broader Regulatory Space

The ideal of an apolitical regulator whose credibility rests on technocratic ability arises out of the European Union experience, which has dominated the last two decades of regulatory literature.[24] This approach presumes that the political and economic content of decisions can be separated, and that the economic issues can be handed to regulators, while political concerns are dealt with by the legislature and executive. More generally, it assumes a sufficiently large set of issues that are amenable to technocratic intervention, to which there is a uniquely correct answer, obviating the need for the exercise of judgement.

In this version of the regulatory story, the regulator operates in what Pritchett calls a 'rules' world, where the only governance challenge is

---

[24] Majone, 'Regulatory State'.

the application and monitoring of agreed-upon rules.[25] What if, however, as Pritchett argues is the case in much of the developing world where deal-making rather than 'rule-following' is the norm: '[T]he deep underlying problem is a government administrative (and juridical) apparatus that expects deals?'[26] As Dubash and Morgan explain, in many developing countries, even when rules are created, they are often insufficiently 'owned' by domestic constituencies because, as with regulatory agencies, they are often introduced through an externally led programme of reform. Moreover, in developing countries, redistributive pressures tend to be greater, placing rules under stress, and institutional capacities and norms through which to support rules are insufficiently developed.[27] For all these reasons, the regulatory environment in developing countries may retain some irreducible element of negotiation.

However, the term 'deals' should not be understood to connote a free-for-all environment where only relative power settles decisions and there is no scope for institutional constraints. Instead, the intent is to recognize that many regulatory decisions, particularly in developing countries, may involve the exercise of judgement because technical virtuosity alone cannot provide a definitive and unique answer.

For example, tariff-setting decisions in Indian electricity are complicated by high levels of electricity theft as well as by entrenched patterns of subsidies and consequent loss making for utilities. Under these conditions, it is unclear if the cost of investing in technical and institutional capacity to reverse these patterns should be front-loaded on consumers, or whether the sequencing should take into account the need to demonstrate system improvement prior to raising tariffs.[28] Similarly, recent fraught decisions over spectrum allocation in telecom in India, in addition to being bound up with complex technical and economic details, are also confounded by lack of clarity on the objective: maximizing

[25] L. Pritchett, 'The Regulatory State Goes South in the South', in *The Rise of the Regulatory State of the South*.

[26] Pritchett, 'Regulatory State', 234.

[27] N.K. Dubash and B. Morgan, 'The Embedded Regulatory State: Between Rules and Deals', in *The Rise of the Regulatory State of the South*.

[28] N.K. Dubash and D. Narasimha Rao, *The Practice and Politics of Regulation: Regulatory Governance in Indian Electricity* (New Delhi: Macmillan, 2007).

resources or ensuring rapid roll-out of networks.[29] And, in the face of recent controversies about gas pricing, the calls for an independent regulator to solve the problem take insufficient account of the fact that there is no objective benchmark for gas prices in India, and that cost-plus based calculations come with their own problems of asymmetric information and incentives to gold plate.[30] As these examples suggest, if in some cases (not all) technical rationality alone does not provide a basis for a unique outcome, the resultant space for negotiation lends the regulatory decision a deal-making character. Put differently, the line between what is a policy decision and a regulatory decision is often blurred. If, as suggested above, many regulators face situations that require the exercise of judgement, then credible regulation needs ways of functioning beyond the technocratic application of rules.

To address this need, regulatory agencies can serve as another pole of interaction between multiple agencies, inject new information into debates, provide new opportunities for voice, or restructure or shift expectations around outcomes. However, these possibilities, and the vision of regulation they imply, require broadening the landscape of analysis beyond the focus on an agency to a larger 'regulatory space' that includes the judiciary, civil society organizations, and industry groups.[31] Another metaphor that helps capture this broader role of regulators is Levi-Faur and Jordana's description of regulators as a 'policy irritant', a new entrant to a system that provokes a range of different and often unpredictable responses.[32] Viewing regulators thus may yield more insight than searching for a simplistic shift from a politicized decision-making space to a sanitized rule-bound regulatory space.

But adopting this approach means accepting that regulatory outcomes are deeply contingent, and depend on how regulators become

[29] P.G. Thakurta and A.R. Ghatak, 'TRAI Recommendations: The Next Round of Tussles', *Economic and Political Weekly* 47, no. 22 (2 June 2012): 51–7.

[30] Sarma, 'Natural Gas Price Hike'.

[31] L. Hancher and M.J. Moran, 'Organizing Regulatory Space', in *Capitalism, Culture and Economic Regulation*, eds L. Hancher and M.J. Moran (Oxford: Clarendon Press, 1989), 271–300.

[32] D. Levi-Faur and J. Jordana, 'Regulatory Capitalism: Policy Irritants and Convergent Divergence', *Annals of the American Academy of Social and Political Science* 598, no. 1 (March 2005): 191–9.

embedded within country and sector-specific circumstances. At worst, regulators can provide one more institution through which to obfuscate the making of 'deals'; at best, they can serve to restructure the negotiation space, to constrain it, make it more transparent, and legitimize certain forms of negotiation that contain public safeguards. Below, I discuss three aspects of that embedding: interaction with the judiciary, including the regulatory appeals process; provision of space for public participation and voice; and evolution of internal capacity and staff.

Role of the Judiciary in the 'Regulatory Space'

Of the various additional actors in the Indian regulatory space, the judiciary has perhaps been the most important. Given the limited experience with infrastructure regulatory agencies when they were first introduced in the mid-1990s, it is perhaps unsurprising that regulation in practice has evolved through the layering of practices and norms, often through judicial intervention.

Thiruvengadam and Joshi make a strong case that the judiciary has played a particularly important role in Indian telecoms regulation.[33] Indeed, they argue that even the establishment of a regulator was, in part, due to the Supreme Court's insistence on the need for an independent regulator in the context of privatization, in *Delhi Science Forum* v. *Union of India*.[34]

Subsequently, in the COAI case,[35] the Court overruled a judgement of the Telecom Disputes Settlement Appellate Tribunal (TDSAT), which was founded on the reasoning that the TDSAT could not interfere with policy decisions of the government, particularly that of a high-level government committee. In overruling this decision, the Supreme Court reminded the TDSAT that it had the authority to decide on the legality of an executive decision, a decision interpreted by Thiruvengadam and Joshi as defending the jurisdiction of the regulatory apparatus vis-à-vis the executive and tutoring the TDSAT on its role.

[33] Thiruvengadam and Joshi, 'Judiciaries as Crucial Actors'.

[34] (1996) 2 SCC 405.

[35] *Cellular Operators Association of India* v. *Union of India*, (2003) 3 SCC 186.

The Supreme Court's intervention in the 2G Spectrum Case[36] is somewhat more complicated to interpret. The Court noted that TRAI's recommendations have been applied selectively, even while critiquing TRAI for the nature of its recommendations. Ultimately, the Supreme Court turned back to TRAI, emphasizing that new recommendations should emanate from TRAI in the first instance due to its expertise. Thiruvengadam and Joshi see in these judgements a larger pattern of the Supreme Court buttressing the telecom regulatory structure, including by upbraiding TRAI and TDSAT when they fall short, thereby working toward a well-functioning regulatory system.[37] Whatever the merits of this argument, the accumulated case law on telecoms suggests that the functioning of TRAI and TDSAT bear considerable imprint of interaction with the judiciary.

Assessing the role of the judiciary in the electricity sector is hampered by a lack of equivalently systematic analysis. However, it is worth mentioning one curious case that potentially shapes the practice of electricity regulation in deeply counter-intuitive ways. The case in point is a decision at the Appellate Tribunal for Electricity (APTEL) on *suo moto* tariff revision (11 November 2011). This case is based on a letter from the Ministry of Power to the APTEL, requesting the latter to take action to direct state electricity regulatory commissions (SERCs) to, in turn, take *suo moto* action on the determination of tariffs if the regulated utilities do not file for tariff increases on an annual basis. The context for the request is the poor financial health of state distribution utilities, which the Ministry of Power attributes in part to the failure to seek tariff revision.

By agreeing with the Ministry of Power, and directing SERCs to undertake *suo moto* proceedings for tariff revision if necessary, the APTEL turns on its head the normal roles of regulator and regulated. A great deal of regulatory literature focuses on the challenges a regulator faces in limiting approved costs given the incentives for a regulated entity to inflate costs in a cost-plus regulatory regime, and in the face of asymmetric information, where the regulated entity inherently

---

[36] *Centre for Public Interest Litigation and Others* v. *Union of India*, (2012) 3 SCC 1.

[37] Thiruvengadam and Joshi, 'Judiciaries as Crucial Actors'.

knows more than the regulator about its activities. However, in this case, the Ministry of Power's request, and the APTEL's endorsement of it, places regulators in the strange position of seeking to *inflate*, not limit, costs, and therefore also increase tariffs, in the face of utility reluctance to raise costs (presumably under political direction). But if asymmetric and private information gets in the way of the regulator holding costs down, presumably it can also obstruct a regulator that seeks to raise tariffs; there is nothing to stop a utility from under-reporting costs. Quite aside from whether this approach will serve the instrumental ends of the Ministry of Power—to regularly raise tariffs—this approach fails to ignore the underlying issue, ironically the same issue that led to creation of regulators in the first place: tariff hikes are politically unpopular and state-owned utilities are subject to being used as instruments of populist policies. That the Ministry of Power has to resort to oblique and counter-intuitive tactics suggests the failure of the larger project of de-politicizing electricity decision making, of which the regulators were intended to be the lynchpin. It also points to the ongoing interaction between courts and regulators in shaping regulatory outcomes.

The extent of this interaction is indicated by the track record of the dedicated appeals process set up as part of the regulatory system, which also serves as an important indicator of regulatory functioning. While no systematic and careful study of this exists, a fairly straight-forward quantitative analysis of the proportion of orders that are appealed before the electricity and telecom appeals bodies over the period January 2009 to December 2012 reveals some interesting patterns (see Table 6.1). First, the proportion of telecom cases appealed is a startlingly high 62 per cent, while the weighted (by share of orders) average for electricity cases across all state regulators is a much more reasonable 8 per cent. Second, there is considerable variation across state electricity regulators. While Maharashtra and Haryana exhibit appeal rates of 23 per cent and 27 per cent, respectively, the corresponding numbers for Tamil Nadu and Andhra Pradesh are 3 per cent and 5 per cent. While it is difficult to defend any particular range as a reasonable rate of appeals, it is clear that towards the higher end of this range, the credibility of the regulator as an effective decision maker is likely to be called into question.

Table 6.1 Regulatory Orders Appealed before the Appellate Tribunal for Electricity (APTEL) and Telecom Disputes Settlement and Appellate Tribunal (TDSAT)

	(a) APTEL: Percentage of Orders Appealed from SERCs (January 2009–December 2012)			
Rank	State	APTEL Cases	Total ERC Orders	Percentage of Orders Appealed
1	Maharashtra	94	416	23
2	Haryana	31	114	27
3	Delhi	29	412	7
4	Odisha	24	453	5
5	Gujarat	17	203	8
6	Kerala	16	NA	NA
7	Madhya Pradesh	16	297	5
8	Karnataka	15	173	9
9	Punjab	20	213	9
10	Himachal Pradesh	13	94	14
11	Rajasthan	12	85	14
12	Tamil Nadu	11	401	3
13	Andhra Pradesh	9	173	5
14	Jharkhand	9	102	9
15	West Bengal	9	NA	NA
16	Uttar Pradesh	8	553	1
17	Bihar	8	56	14
18	Chhattisgarh	6	254	2
19	Uttarakhand	4	134	3
20	Meghalaya	2	11	18
21	Assam	4	6[1]	67
22	Sikkim	1	NA	NA
				Weighted Average = 8%

Source: Author's analysis of data collected from APTEL and SERC websites.
Note: The weighted average is computed by weighting the percentage of orders by each state's share of total orders. The overall average of cases appealed (from 22 states) is 11.12 per cent (from 2009 to 2012). This is higher due to the high proportion of cases appealed from Assam. Without including Assam, the overall average drops to 8.47 per cent (for 21 states). Out of 22 states covered here (with data for 19 available so far), seven states have a higher appeal rate than the average, with Assam, Haryana, and Maharashtra having the highest.[2]

(*Cont'd*)

Table 6.1   *(Cont'd)*

[1] Assam ERC's website does not contain information on general orders passed by the ERC. This may be skewing the data and leading to a disproportionately high percentage of cases appealed.
[2] Some states tabulate details of orders based on the date on which the petition was filed, rather than when the case was decided. This does not make any difference for our study.

TDSAT: Total Numbers	
(b) Comparison of TRAI Orders, Directions, and Rulings and TRAI Cases in TDSAT (January 2009–December 2012)	
Total TDSAT cases	73
Total Orders, Directions, Guidelines by TRAI	117
Percentage appealed	62

Source: Author's analysis of data collected from TDSAT and TRAI websites.
Note: The information in this table is based on manual estimation of orders, directions, and guidelines listed on the TRAI website since consolidated information on TRAI orders, directions, and rulings is not available on the TRAI website.

Accountability through Public Participation and Voice

If, in fact, regulation involves much more than the technocratic application of rules, but also the exercise of regulatory discretion and negotiation, what keeps the regulatory process from descending into one more arena for insider dealing? What prevents wholesale capture of the regulator by private interests, as laid out many decades ago by Stigler,[38] or indeed, the use of regulation to further the interests of public elites?[39]

In response, a substantial body of theory suggests that regulatory legitimacy lies at least as much in wide participation in decision-making

[38] G.J. Stigler, 'The Theory of Economic Regulation', *The Bell Journal of Economics and Management Science* 2, no. 1 (Spring 1971): 3–21.
[39] P. Cook, C. Kirkpatrick, M. Minogue, and D. Parker, 'Competition, Regulation and Regulatory Governance: An Overview', in *Leading Issues in Competition, Regulation and Development*, eds P. Cook, C. Kirkpatrick, M. Minogue, and D. Parker (Cheltenham: Edward Elgar Publishing Limited, 2004), 3–35.

as in technical expertise.[40] Participation increases the information basis
for a regulatory decision, an approach that Palast *et al.* view as the
lynchpin of the American electricity regulatory process,[41] and when
tied to appropriate procedures such as reason-giving and review, provides a mechanism for accountability.[42] While a technocratic view of
regulation places the emphasis on the regulatory *solution*, a stakeholder
view of regulation emphasizes the regulatory *process*. Specifically, the
integrity of the regulatory process needs to be safeguarded by carefully
developed procedures, such as access to information, open hearings,
and a requirement of reasoned orders, which help ensure democratic
legitimacy.

There have been various efforts to examine the existence and
use of administrative procedures in electricity sector regulation, but
unfortunately, no similar analysis for other sectors. In electricity, such
procedural safeguards are prominent in the various Acts under which
electricity regulators have been created, starting with the OERC. For
example, the OERC Act, 1995, includes notice and comment procedures for licensing and passing of orders, and subsequent regulations
detail procedures that guide hearings.[43] These administrative procedures appear to have been imported whole cloth as part of the regulatory transplant process, apparently with the idea of providing investors
a defence against arbitrary administrative action.[44]

[40] A. Hira, D. Huxtable, and A. Leger, 'Deregulation and Participation: An
International Survey of Participation in Electricity Regulation', *Governance: An
International Journal of Policy, Administration, and Institutions* 18, no. 1 (January
2005): 53–88; and T. Prosser, 'Theorising Utility Regulation', *Modern Law
Review* 62, no. 2 (March 1999): 196–217.

[41] G. Palast, J. Oppenheim, and T. MacGregor, *Democracy and Regulation:
How the Public can Govern Essential Services* (London: Pluto Press, 2003).

[42] Select Committee on the Constitution, *The Regulatory State: Ensuring
its Accountability* (Report No. 6 of Session 2003–04, House of Lords, London,
2004).

[43] An assessment of such administrative law procedures in the Indian electricity sector has been published in S. Mahalingam *et al.*, *Electricity Governance
in India: An Analysis of Institutions and Practice* (New Delhi: Centre for Policy
Research, 2006).

[44] N.K. Dubash, 'Regulating through the Back Door'.

However, these procedural safeguards have been used to create a new political space for a whole slew of civil society actors, who have enthusiastically stepped into the breach, and, somewhat ironically for institutions often considered distant and technocratic, imbued them with a robust democratic culture.[45] A review of usage of these procedures in three states illustrates that: regulatory agencies were among the first to allow access to their documentation prior to the passage of the Right to Information Act; that participants in hearings include a broad range such as labour groups, consumer groups, political parties, individuals, industry associations, farmers, large consumers, and other public entities; and in some cases, these participants come armed with detailed analysis of tariff orders and with specific queries and questions on regulatory decisions and procedures.[46] For example, the 2006–7 tariff order in Andhra Pradesh attracted a total of 330 objections filed by 46 different individuals or institutions. In 2004–5, Delhi received 212 objections from 69 objectors. Interestingly, in both states, industry groups, which might be expected to be better resourced, by no means dominated hearings.

Interpreting the use of these procedures is challenging and highly contingent on particular contexts. In Andhra Pradesh, for example, there is some evidence that public engagement led to more stringent scrutiny of new power purchase approvals, with possible gains to consumers. In Delhi, regulatory participation took on a more partisan tone, with the debate dominated by local resident welfare associations. While the outcomes are far from predictable, the vibrancy of engagement around regulatory commissions suggests that the addition of these institutions to sector governance has certainly increased the democratic quality of decision-making in the sector, and provided a partial forum for more structured negotiation around entrenched issues in the sector. More specifically, it has changed the nature of political engagement in the electricity sector. While in the past, interest groups could only mobilize around large and blunt demands (such as free power to farmers), the

[45] N.K. Dubash, 'The New Regulatory Politics of Electricity in India: Embryonic Ground for Consumer Action', *Journal of Consumer Policy* 4, no. 6 (December 2006): 465–87.

[46] For details on electricity regulation in Delhi, Andhra Pradesh and Karnataka, see Dubash and Rao, *Practice and Politics*.

regulatory arena has provided access to specific knowledge (detailed surveys of actual power use by farmers) and enabled mobilization around finer-scale decisions (approvals of particular plants, schema for categorization of tariffs) that enables a structured and somewhat more orderly negotiation around the distribution of costs and benefits.

Regulators as a structured site for political contest are an inversion of the original conception of regulators as agents of de-politicization. But, given the prevalence of substantial interests in sectoral outcomes and complex issues not amenable to technocratic solutions, the need for political engagement is inevitable. The careful and consistent use of procedures for accountability and voice, and the consequent creation of legitimate political spaces for negotiation may be among the most significant contributions of regulatory agencies to improved governance of Indian infrastructure.

Human Resources and Staff Capacity

A third issue salient to the embedding of regulatory agencies is the relatively mundane, but relevant, issue of human resources and staff. Two distinct issues are important: the appointment of the regulator and the size and quality of the staff.

The professional background, expertise, and character of the regulator get disproportionate attention in public debates over the performance of regulatory agencies. The presumption of many participants in these debates appears to be that the regulatory challenge can be boiled down to appointing the right person for the job, one with suitable technical expertise, and the ability and intent to exercise independence from the government. In particular, the perceived dominance of former government employees in regulatory positions is seen as under-cutting independence.

Empirically, the limited material that does exist suggests that former government employees do, indeed, occupy most regulatory positions. A 2003 Prayas survey of state electricity regulators found that 10 of 21 regulators were drawn from the Indian Administrative Service.[47] Table 6.2 reinforces this impression, with respect to a wider range of

[47] Prayas, 'A Good Beginning but Challenges Galore: A Survey Based Study of Resources, Transparency, and Public Participation in Electricity Regulatory Commissions in India' (Research Study, Prayas Energy Group, Pune, 2003).

Table 6.2 Background of Members of Independent Regulatory Agencies (inception to March 2012)

Regulatory Body	Year of Establishment	Members Directly from Nodal Ministry/Department	Members from Related Departments/PSUs	Other Ministries Departments/PSUs	Non-government Members
TRAI[1]	1997	4	1	5*(1)	6*(1)
TDSAT	2000	1	1	4	–
CERC	1998	9	2	5	1
APTEL	2003	1	5	–	–
PNGRB	2006	–	2	5	1
AERA[2]	2008	–	-	1	–
SEBI	1992	3*(1)	6	8	–
SAT[3]	1998	–	2	8	–
CCI[4]	2003	–	2	1	1
IRDA	1999	1	9	5	–
Total		19 (19%)	30 (30%)	42 (42%)	9 (9%)

Source: Author's compilation.

Notes: Data for this table have been collated based on publicly available information on the websites of the regulators as well as news sources. In the case of each regulator, the information is compiled from inception until March 2012. Only the member's last designation is being taken into account. Judges are classified as non-government members since they are from outside the executive. With respect to CERC, members from SERCs are being classified as 'Members from related departments/PSUs'. Examples of 'Related departments/PSUs' are MTNL/BSNL for TRAI or the Central Board of Direct Taxes (CBDT) for SEBI. For SEBI, only whole-time members have been taken into account because the SEBI Act mandates inclusion of part-time members who do not perform executive functions. If the person's last designation is not available, the penulti-mate designation is used. All such numbers are marked with a '*', and the number of such members are mentioned in the bracket next to the *.

[1] There was no information on the background of two members. Six members were from a non-government background (including one from the judiciary).

[2] Only one member's details are available on the AERA website.

[3] Details of one member were not available.

[4] Information is only available on four members. CCI does not have a nodal ministry and its jurisdiction overlaps with the Ministry of Consumer Affairs, Ministry of Corporate Affairs, and also other sectors.

sectoral regulators examined over the lifetime of each regulator. The data suggest that 91 per cent of regulators have a government background, and of these, 49 per cent have been with the nodal ministry or a closely related department immediately prior to their appointment as regulator.

But interpreting this data is not so straightforward. The predominance of government officials as regulators is, in part, because of a legacy of state ownership in many of these sectors, as a result of which the pool of skills outside government is shallow. More generally, a direct causal relationship between a government track record and a lack of independence from government is hard to establish. There have been a sufficient number of cases of former government officials, such as T.N. Seshan (former Chief Election Commissioner) and Vinod Rai (former Comptroller and Auditor General), whose track records suggest vigorous independence.

At the same time, the high proportion of former government officials in regulatory positions does arouse an even larger concern. Given the lack of a compelling explanation of why ministries and departments are keen to establish regulators given their relatively thin track record as agents of improved sectoral governance, it is hard to rule out the prospect of post-retirement employment as a compelling reason for creation of regulators. Indeed, the trend over time has been for regulators to have ever fewer powers, but for regulators to proliferate. Regulatory agencies as the vanguard of a 'sinecure state' provide at least one plausible explanation for their persistence and spread.[48]

The ability of the individual regulator to avoid government capture is only a portion of a larger canvas of Indian regulatory issues. As discussed earlier, the challenges of regulation go far beyond regulatory selection issues, and are rooted in fundamental inconsistencies in expectations about the extent to which regulators can de-politicize decision-making, and how. While expertise is useful, many regulatory decisions do not have one unique answer revealed through technocratic means. Independence is indeed essential, but perhaps not of the quasi-judicial sort, which emphasizes maintaining detachment. The discussion here suggests that, in addition to expertise and independence, effective regulators need to also be able to engage multiple players to garner

[48] I thank Devesh Kapur for suggesting this phrase.

information and credibly facilitate agreement, even while maintaining credibility buttressed by robust procedure. In an evocative phrase, Prosser suggests that in fraught regulatory environments, regulators have to adopt a stakeholder model of regulation, to be 'government in miniature'.[49] From this perspective, the salient question is less regulatory selection and more the understanding of the job that regulators, once selected, bring to their work.

A second, and related consideration is the numbers and quality of regulatory staff. If regulation is not only about the relentless exercise of technocratic virtuosity, but also about the ability to engage complex situations and multiple actors, then an important precondition is the necessary staff numbers and capacity. Table 6.3 summarizes the available

Table 6.3 Staffing across Selected Regulatory Agencies

A. Telecoms[1]

Year	Sanctioned Posts	Posts Filled	Vacant Posts (% of Total)	Major Posts Lying Vacant
2011–12 (as of 31.3.2012)	239	190	49 (21%)	Principal advisor (2), Jt. Advisor/Dy. Advisor (10), Sr. Research Officer (9)
2010–11 (as of 31.3.2011)	240	188	52 (22%)	Jt. Advisor/Dy. Advisor (14), Sr. Research Officer (9)
2009–10 (as of 31.3.2010)	237	177	60 (25%)	Principal advisor (5), Jt. Advisor/Dy. Advisor (14), Sr. Research Officer (12)
2008–9 (as of 31.3.2009)	194	169	25 (13%)	Jt. Advisor/Dy. Advisor (3), Sr. Research Officer (7)

(Cont'd)

[49] Prosser, 'Theorising Utility Regulation'.

Table 6.3 (*Cont'd*)

B. Electricity

CERC[2]

Year	Sanctioned Posts	Posts Filled	Vacant Posts	Major Posts Lying Vacant
2010–11 (As of 31.3.2011)	80	59	21 (26%)	Secretary (1), Chief (2), Jt. Chief (1), Dpty. Chief (3), Asst. Chief (6)
2009–10 (As of 31.3.2010)	80	60	20 (25%)	Chief (2), Dpty. Chief (5), Asst. Chief (6)
2008–9 (As of 31.3.2009)	83	52	31 (37%)	Chief (2), Dpty. Chief (8), Asst. Chief (7)
2007–8 (As of 31.3.2008)	83	53	30 (36%)	Secretary (1), Chief (1), Jt. Chief (1), Dpty. Chief (6), Asst. Chief (7)

C. Petroleum and Natural Gas PNGRB

Year	Sanctioned Posts	Posts Filled	Vacant Posts	Major Posts lying vacant
2011–12 (As of February 2012)	45	34	9	Only 2 officer level vacancies existed as of February 2012.

D. Sample of State Electricity Regulatory Commissions

State	Years	Average Vacancy (%)
Rajasthan	2007–8 to 2011–12	30%
Maharashtra	2008–9 to 2012–13	29%
Tripura	2010–11 to 2011–12	53%

Source: Data compiled by the author based on information from the relevant agency's website.

Notes: This information is purely illustrative and not representative, as states were picked based on availability of information, rather than from a deliberate sample.

[1] Data collected from TRAI Annual Reports from 2008–9 to 2011–12.

[2] Data collected from CERC Annual Reports from 2007–8 to 2010–11.

information for TRAI, Central Electricity Regulatory Commission (CERC) and SERCs, and PNGRB. While the data is uneven and inconsistent, a few themes emerge. First, there remain substantial numbers of vacant posts in all regulators, in the range of 15–30 per cent vacancies. Several of the posts lying vacant are more senior posts. According to a report by the Forum of Regulators, 41 per cent of the posts meant for professionals are lying vacant in the electricity regulators.[50]

Second, a comparison across categories of staff in electricity regulators (Table 6.4) suggests that (with the notable exception of Maharashtra) permanent employees occupy a relatively small slice

Table 6.4 Comparison of Staff Categories across State Electricity Regulatory Commissions (SERCs)

State ERC	Permanent Employees	Employees on Deputation	Employees on Contract Basis	Consultants	Total Officers
Karnataka (2011–12)	4	20	23	3	50
Kerala (2007–8)	–	1	7	2	10
Himachal Pradesh (2010–11)	6	23	–	–	29
Rajasthan (2007–8)	10	27	–	–	37
Maharashtra (2012–13)	40	5	–	9	54
West Bengal (2011–12)	N/A	N/A	N/A	N/A	58
Tripura (2011–12)	1	8	–	–	9

Source: Author's analysis of annual reports of SERCs from these states over various years.

[50] Forum of Regulators, *Staffing of Electricity Regulatory Commissions* (Report, Central Electricity Regulatory Commission, New Delhi, 2008).

of the staff strength. Instead, a large proportion of employees are on deputation. Third, in its report, the Forum of Regulators goes on to identify inflexibility in salaries, and disincentives for staff from other agencies to come on deputation due to losses in benefits such as accommodation, health, and benefits as the main reasons for the difficulty in filling positions. Under-staffing and a lack of institutional memory are deeply unhelpful attributes in addressing the complexities of India's regulatory environment.

This pattern of staffing is unlikely to change soon and certainly not without deliberate effort. In all these sectors (with the possible exception of telecom), the largest pool of skilled human capacity resides in the public sector regulated entities. This explains also the high levels of deputation. But as a smaller entity, with fewer opportunities for upward mobility, and less ability to provide additional benefits such as accommodation, the regulator is frequently a less attractive destination than its corresponding public sector entity. Regulation, with its own employment culture, and ideally with overtones of merit, is yet to emerge as a distinct career pathway.

***

From their inception, Indian infrastructure regulators have been intended as a way of sidestepping, insulating, and bracketing political pressures that are perceived to have undermined effective operation of a sector. This institutional project has, by and large, not gone well. The underlying politics—redistribution in tariff setting, or rent allocation—have not gone away. They have simply manifested in other ways, through regulatory efforts to deflect tariff pressures, and through antagonism between the executive and the regulator. Setting up regulators as if they operate in a strictly rules-based world, and seeking to judge them by that benchmark, appears a quixotic enterprise.

This is not to argue that Indian regulators are powerless to prevent a slide into chaotic decision-making driven only by positions of relative power. Rather, it is to suggest that the regulatory role could fruitfully be re-conceptualized as one that constrains and shapes the space for negotiation, increases its transparency, and generates norms around negotiation. In other words, Indian regulators need to also develop the ability to provide order to what is a deals-based space. To do so would require combining technical ability and independence with a deliberate effort to build a legitimate set of institutions that are fully engaged with the range of actors that occupy India's complex regulatory spaces.

Two particularly important actors in these spaces are the judiciary and broader civil society. The somewhat thin conception of Indian regulators at the time of transplant is successively fleshed out through the judicial process in several sectors. In many cases, the ratio of appeals to decisions remains high, suggesting this interaction is still a work in process. The establishment of procedures that guide public participation in regulatory hearings, and the accountability possibilities that these procedures confer, may be among the most significant contributions of regulatory agencies to the challenges of infrastructure governance.

Sectoral factors are an important determinant in understanding the nature of the governance challenge faced by a regulator. In sectors such as electricity, managing redistributive politics around the end-user is the primary challenge. In sectors with powerful incumbents, such as coal or telecoms, ensuring a competitive playing field for new entrants is an issue. A fruitful future research agenda would be to explore regulatory functioning across different sectors, notably infrastructure and finance.

Finally, it is worth returning to the questions of why regulators persist, and indeed proliferate, despite thin evidence that they are effective agents of improved sector governance, and why executive agencies continue to relinquish a sub-set of their powers to regulators? In their early days, the adoption of the regulatory agency model could credibly be understood as a 'rationalised myth', a relatively low-cost way of signalling improved governance to fulfil a condition necessary to attract foreign investment. But uneven performance and a trend towards reduced powers for every new regulator created have called into question the continued salience of this explanation. Notably, a review of the functions and powers of infrastructure regulators suggests a trend towards ever more miserly delegation—from the early days of electricity and telecom regulators to the substantially more hollow petroleum and natural gas, and coal regulators. While it may be simplistic as a complete explanation, the idea of regulatory agencies as an important component of an emergent 'sinecure state'—the provision of continued employment for retiring senior government officials in relatively toothless regulators—certainly grows in plausibility with the creation of each new disempowered regulator.

However, as the complicated history of existing regulators has shown, design and intent at origin is only a portion of the picture. The process of being embedded in the economic and political landscape, particularly through interventions of the judiciary and civil society, can yield surprising outcomes. Whether these are good or bad surprises depends a great deal on the details of each case. Nearly two decades into India's experiments with infrastructure regulation, further proliferation of regulatory agencies as a means of sidestepping political pressures seems a futile exercise. But regulatory agencies created as an instrument of creatively engaging politics is worthy of further exploration.

APPENDIX

Table A6.1 Comparison of Infrastructure Regulators

Regulator	Year	Context (reason for creating regulator)	Issues		
			Objective (what were the 2–3 clear objectives the regulator was intended to perform?)	Design (whether powers given to the regulator allowed it to meet its objectives)	Functioning (what issues have been highlighted in the functioning of the regulator vis-a-vis its objectives and design)
Electricity Central Electricity Regulatory Authority (CERC) and State Electricity Regulatory Authorities (SERCs)	1998 (CERC) Various years (SERCs)	Deterioration of the Indian power sector owing to poor health of SEBs caused by irrational tariff structure, and '…heavy shortfall in the planned capacity in the power sector during the Eighth Five Year Plan'.[1]	Rationalize tariffs (ERC Act was enacted to distance government from tariff regulation).[2] Increase accountability of State Electricity Boards.[3]	CERC: regulate the tariff of power generating companies. Also: promote competition, efficiency and economy in the activities of the electricity industry.[5]	The CERC and the Ministry of Power agree that the state of SEBs is almost as bad as it was in 1998. Both blame it on the non-rationalization of tariffs, which were among the primary reasons for the CERC Act, 1998 and the Electricity Act, 2003.[7]

(Cont'd)

Table A6.1 (Cont'd)

Regulator	Year	Context (Reason for creating regulator)	Issues		
			Objective (What were the 2–3 clear objectives the regulator was intended to perform?)	Design (Whether powers given to the regulator allowed it to meet its objectives)	Functioning (What issues have been highlighted in the functioning of the regulator vis-à-vis its objectives and design)
			Promote private investment into the electricity sector.[4]	SERCs: – determine the tariff for generation, supply, transmission and wheeling of electricity within the state. – regulate electricity purchase and procurement process of distribution licensees. – promote generation of	'The VK Shunglu Committee Report attributed the losses of DISCOMS to the poor managerial and operational performance of DISCOMs as well as irrational tariffs set by SERCs ... Delays in receiving subsidies, coupled with delays in tariff revision and a high level of AT&C losses, put the finances of DISCOMs under severe stress.'[8]

				- electricity from renewable sources of energy. - adjudicate disputes between the licensees, and generating companies. - specify or enforce standards with respect to quality, continuity and reliability of service by licensees. - advisory functions with respect to the state governments.[6]	The CAG pointed out a huge loss in revenue arising from the improper issue of 2G licenses in 2008. One of the irregularities pointed
Telecom Regulatory Authority of India	1997	Creation of an independent regulatory authority in the telecom sector was to ease any concerns private investors may have regarding the liberalization	Enable creation of a competitive market in the telecom sector.[12] To separate policy-making and regulatory	Regulate telecom services. Fixation/revision of tariffs for telecom services.[14] Fair and transparent	

(Cont'd)

Table A6.1 (Cont'd)

Regulator	Year	Issues			
		Context (Reason for creating regulator)	Objective (What were the 2–3 clear objectives the regulator was intended to perform?)	Design (Whether powers given to the regulator allowed it to meet its objectives)	Functioning (What issues have been highlighted in the functioning of the regulator vis-à-vis its objectives and design)
(TRAI) and Telecom Disputes Settlement and Appelate Tribunal (TDSAT)		programme initiated by the government.[9] 'The reason for creating TRAI by ordinance was that we were facing difficulties in attracting private investment without an authority like the TRAI. Private investors, including foreign investors were hesitant to sign contracts, as they were not convinced about our ongoing processes of privatization and liberalization.'[10]	functions then being conducted by DoT.[13]	policy environment, which promotes a level playing field and facilitates fair competition including broadcasting and cable services.[15] TRAI Fund: The TRAI Fund had not been formed as of 2000 even though the Amended TRAI Act provided for it. The funding of	out was the DoT disregarding the TRAI's recommendations on the manner of allotment.[17] TRAI has only recommendatory powers in this regard.

'The regulator ...was to generate an even playing field for private capital. Private capital would need regulatory independence to check the excesses of the incumbent arising from its monopoly position. Second, the synergy between the government's dual role, that of policy-maker cum service provider, reinforced the monopoly position of the incumbent, which was invariably the state-owned telecom company in most countries. The three daunting tasks for the regulator would be to secure independence from the telecom department; to ensure that government

TRAI's total operations could be through this fund, that is, by taking a certain fee that it could charge from all those who were regulated by this body.[16] The TRAI Fund is important since it ensures the financial independence of TRAI from the executive.

(Cont'd)

Table A6.1 (Cont'd)

Regulator	Year	Context (Reason for creating regulator)	Issues		
			Objective (What were the 2–3 clear objectives the regulator was intended to perform?)	Design (Whether powers given to the regulator allowed it to meet its objectives)	Functioning (What issues have been highlighted in the functioning of the regulator vis-à-vis its objectives and design)
		as policy-maker was not unduly favorable towards its own service providers; and, to push the government as policymaker to establish itself as a separate entity from its service provision functions...."[11]			
Petroleum Petroleum and Natural Gas Regulatory Board (PNGRB)	2006	The bill creating the PNGRB was intended to set up a single super regulator with wide-ranging powers to facilitate uninterrupted and adequate supply of petroleum and petroleum products in all parts of	Promote competition and fair trade. Protect interests of consumers. Monitor prices and take corrective measures to prevent restrictive trade practices.[20]	Protect the interest of consumers by fostering fair trade and competition among the entities. Register entities to market petroleum	Reports of internal dissension.[22] Some commentators have stated that PNGRB has appropriated more powers than given to it under the PNGRB Act. For instance, PNGRB has

the country, including remote areas, at fair price, and promote competitive markets and access to monopolistic infrastructure in the nature of common carrier on non-discriminatory basis by all entities.[18]	and petroleum products, establish LNG terminals, create storage facilities for petroleum, petroleum products or natural gas exceeding specified capacity.	been authorizing city gas developers across cities, whereas the government has stated that the PNGRB does not have the power to do so. The section concerned was finally notified by the Petroleum Ministry while a case pertaining to this power was pending in the Supreme Court.[23]
PNGRB does not include powers to regulate upstream sectors. The stated reason was 'the merging of upstream sector with the downstream sector and constitution of unified regulatory authority... was considered too radical. There is no such tested model in the world.' Exploration and production	Authorize entities to lay, build, operate, or expand a common carrier, or local LNG distribution network.

Monitor prices and take corrective measures to prevent restrictive trade practices. | There is also a lack of clarity in the regulator's powers. This is most clearly seen in the dispute between PNGRB and Indraprastha Gas |

(Cont'd)

Table A6.1   (*Cont'd*)

Regulator	Year	Issues			
		Context (Reason for creating regulator)	Objective (What were the 2–3 clear objectives the regulator was intended to perform?)	Design (Whether powers given to the regulator allowed it to meet its objectives)	Functioning (What issues have been highlighted in the functioning of the regulator vis-à-vis its objectives and design)
		involve activities altogether different from refining, marketing and distribution. Accordingly, the regulation of upstream sector has been excluded from the present Bill.'[19]	Secure equitable distribution for petroleum and petroleum products;Monitor transportation rates and take corrective measures to prevent restrictive trade practices.[21]		Ltd. (IGL) over the regulator's decision to cut tariffs being charged by IGL with retrospective effect: 'A few months back, the government said the regulator will decide the marketing margin charged by IGL and now they have gone and cut network tariff and compression charges. It's not clear whether all the three tariffs—network tariff, compression charges and marketing

margin—will be controlled.'[24]

The government has remained the de facto controller of prices of petroleum products even though 'the theoretical position since October 01, 2006 is that all entities are free to price their products and the PNGRB is to regulate anti-competitive behaviour like predatory pricing.'[25]

Inability to streamline city gas networks: 'Long established CGD companies authorised by the government—and in some cases owned by

(Cont'd)

Table A6.1 (Cont'd)

Regulator	Year	Issues			
		Context (Reason for creating regulator)	Objective (What were the 2–3 clear objectives the regulator was intended to perform?)	Design (Whether powers given to the regulator allowed it to meet its objectives)	Functioning (What issues have been highlighted in the functioning of the regulator vis-à-vis its objectives and design)
					it—have been at the receiving end of the regulator's wrath while illegal entities have been allowed to continue with their squatting operations. Instead of the network expanding in a significant way, no new projects have come up in the last two years; on the other hand, expansion of existing projects was brought to a standstill for long periods although authorisations are now being accepted in some cases.'[26]

| Proposed Coal Regulator | Not set up yet | The objective of the regulator is to end the monopoly of Coal India Limited in the coal sector, and to ensure level playing field between government players and captive block allotees who go into mining.[27] The 'sector is characterised by acute shortages, poor quality, inefficient mining practices and distorted pricing mechanisms.... Many of these issues have been ascribed to the virtual monopoly enjoyed by the state-owned Coal India.'[28] | To facilitate more standardized operational norms. Establishment of benchmarks in safety standards, performance, and productivity through adoption of best mining practices. It would also deal with issues such as mining authorization, production and supply of coal. Specify and determine the grades/quality of | Initial indications suggest the regulator will not in fact have pricing powers: 'An empowered group of ministers (EGoM) on Tuesday decided that the proposed regulator in the coal sector should have no pricing powers and its say would be limited in recommending the guiding principles of pricing the fuel.'[30] 'The regulator is also expected to oversee coal |

(Cont'd)

Table A6.1   (*Cont'd*)

Regulator	Year	Issues			
		Context (Reason for creating regulator)	Objective (What were the 2–3 clear objectives the regulator was intended to perform?)	Design (Whether powers given to the regulator allowed it to meet its objectives)	Functioning (What issues have been highlighted in the functioning of the regulator vis-à-vis its objectives and design)
			coal, and price of coal, and adjudicate disputes amongst producers and consumers.[29]	supplies from Coal India to consumers such as power producers. It could also independently monitor the progress made by state-run and private companies in extracting coal under government allocated mining licenses."[31]	

Source: Author's compilation.

(Cont'd)

Notes:

1. Lok Sabha debate on 'Disapproval of Electricity Regulatory Commissions Ordinance and Electricity Regulatory Commission's Bill, 1998 (Concluded). Statutory Resolution—Negatived Motion for Consideration—adopted', 12th Lok Sabha Debates, 9 June 1998.

2. Rajya Sabha debate, 'Disapproval of Electricity Regulatory Commissions Ordinance and Electricity Regulatory Commission's Bill, 1998', 9 June 1998, available at: http://parliamentofindia.nic.in/lsdeb/ls12/ses2/1709069801.htm.

3. Ibid.

4. Ibid.

5. S. 79, Electricity Act, 2003.

6. S. 86, Electricity Act, 2003.

7. Oral evidence of Chairman, CERC to Standing Committee on Energy in its 30th Report on 'Functioning of Central Electricity Regulatory Commission (CERC)', August 2012.

8. A. Chitnis, S. Dixit, and A. Josey, 'Bailing Out Unaccountability', *Economic and Political Weekly* 51, no. 22 (22 December 2012), 22–5.

9. Parliamentary debate on 'The Telecom Regulatory Authority of India Bill, 1997', 12th Lok Sabha Debates, 20 March 1997.

10. Minister of Telecom Shri Beni Prasad Verma (in Hindi), Parliamentary debate on 'The Telecom Regulatory Authority of India Bill, 1997', 12th Lok Sabha Debates, 18 March 1997.

11. R. Mukherji, 'Regulatory Evolution in Indian Telecommunications', ISAS Working Paper, January 2006.

12. T.H. Chowdary, 'Telecom Demonopolization: Policy or Farce?', *Economic and Political Weekly* 6, no. 5 (5 February 2000), 436–40.

13. Ibid.

14. S. 11, TRAI Act, 1997.

15. Ibid.

16. Thirteenth Report of the Standing Committee on Information Technology, Functioning of Telecom Regulatory Authority of India (TRAI), November 2000.

17. Comptroller and Auditor General, 'Performance Audit on the Issue of Licenses and Allocation of 2G Spectrum', 2010–11, p. iv, http://cag.gov.in/html/reports/civil/2010-11_19PA/Telecommunication%20Report.pdf.

18. Standing Committee on Petroleum and Chemicals, 'Report on the Petroleum Regulatory Board Bill', 13th Lok Sabha, 8 May 2003.

19. Ibid.

Table A6.1 *(Cont'd)*

20 S. 11, 12 PNGRB Act, 2006.

21 S. 11, 12 PNGRB Act, 2006.

22 'Majority Members of Oil Regulator Revolt against Chairman', Press Trust of India, 11 July 2008.

23 A.S. Mahajan, 'Gas Distribution: Fits and Starts', *Business Today*, 6 January 2013.

24 S. Hussain, 'Out of Gas', *Outlook Business*, 12 May 2010.

25 M. Kacker, 'Will the Petroleum Regulator Stand Up?', *Business Standard*, 24 December 2009.

26 L. Jishnu, 'Gas and the City: Far Apart', *Business Standard*, 10 September 2009.

27 Press Information Bureau, 'Setting Up of Coal Regulatory Authority', 3 May 2010, http://www.pib.nic.in/newsite/erelease. aspx?relid=61336; M. Williams and J. Dash, 'Reforms to See Regulator Monitoring Coal Sector', *Business Standard*, 9 June 2009.

28 'Coal Regulator Will Help Overhaul Coal Sector: India Ratings', Press Trust of India, 9 July 2013.

29 Press Information Bureau, 'Setting Up of Coal Regulatory Authority', M. Williams and J. Dash, 'Reforms to See Regulator Monitoring Coal Sector.'

30 P. Siddhanta, 'EGoM Votes for Coal Regulator Empowered to Recommend Guidelines, Not Regulate Prices', *Indian Express*, 8 May 2013.

31 S. Chaturvedi, 'India Approves Setting Up of Coal Regulator', *Wall Street Journal*, 27 June 2013.

7

INSTITUTIONS OF INTERNAL ACCOUNTABILITY

R. Sridharan[*]

Institutions of internal accountability are essentially about ensuring the accountability of the executive. In his review, former Indian Administrative Service (IAS) officer S.K. Das discussed three such institutions: the Comptroller and Auditor General (CAG), the Central Bureau of Investigation (CBI), and the Central Vigilance Commission (CVC).[1] Of these three institutions of internal accountability, the role of the CAG is much larger than those of the other two. Anti-corruption activities largely define the roles of the CBI and the CVC; in this task, their functions are complementary. The CVC's domain is the more limited even among these two; it only exercises original jurisdiction over Group 'A' officers, or those who occupy the senior-most positions in government. The CAG, on the other hand, has a broader mandate

---

[*] The views expressed in this chapter are purely the personal views of the author and should not in any way be construed as representing the views of the organization to which the author belongs. Nothing in this chapter is, or is intended as, or should be construed as, criticism of the Government of India, or any constitutional authority in India, or of any state government.

[1] S.K. Das, 'Institutions of Internal Accountability', in *Public Institutions in India: Performance and Design*, eds D. Kapur and P.B. Mehta (New Delhi: Oxford University Press, 2005).

that can be described as one of ensuring financial propriety as well as value for money; control of corruption is but one task that is subsumed within this broad mandate.

As far as the CAG is concerned, Das concluded that the impact of audit has been marginal.[2] This was found to be so despite the Constitutional mandate of the institution, its statutory independence from the executive, the high quality of its personnel, its knowledge resources, its diligence, and its enviable organization culture.

The primary reason for the lack of impact of the CAG's labours was diagnosed as the inadequate response of other institutions in the state structure; while the financial committees of Parliament were found to have been negligent in assisting it, departments of government were seen to be doing their best to thwart it.

Das found that the CVC has been ineffective as an anti-corruption institution, largely because personnel and institutions such as the Chief Vigilance Officers (CVO) and the CBI, which have been designed to support it, have not done so adequately. Furthermore, he argued that the CBI itself was too close to the political executive to be uncompromised and to do a professional job.

In more than a decade since Das's work was published, there have been momentous developments in the matter of ensuring accountability. Many instances of alleged impropriety and financial misdemeanour have been reported, rendering civil society considerably exercised. There has been a sustained effort over the recent past to look closely at the mechanisms that have been set up to improve the accountability of public institutions in order to ensure that they function better. The CAG, CVC, and CBI are at the centre of this intense scrutiny.

The Setting

An understanding of what constrains these institutions and what needs to be done to make them more effective requires an analysis of the larger canvas against which these institutions operate. Any discussion on the accountability of the executive has to concern itself with the questions of accountability to whom, and to what standards.

[2] Das, 'Institutions of Internal Accountability'.

The executive is accountable to the judiciary for ensuring that it stays within the bounds of the law. It is accountable to the legislature on a continuous basis for its policies, its performance, and the general standard of service delivery. The legislature and the judiciary represent the checks and balances designed to ensure that the executive adheres to the straight and narrow path. The executive is also directly responsible to the people through the need to obtain a fresh electoral mandate at prescribed intervals.

In a parliamentary democracy such as that of India, the executive is chosen from among the legislature and holds office only as long as it enjoys the latter's confidence. The Indian Constitution was heavily influenced by the British connection and the legacy of constitutional evolution in India—so much so, the choice of parliamentary democracy over a presidential system was almost automatic and instinctive. While introducing the draft constitution in November 1948, Dr B.R. Ambedkar—the father of India's Constitution—summarized the pros and cons of both systems.[3] A democratic executive had to be both stable and responsible, he said; he saw difficulties, however, in ensuring both in equal measure. Ambedkar felt that a non-parliamentary executive tended to be less responsible to the legislature than a parliamentary executive.

Moreover, he said, while the assessment of the responsibility of the executive under a non-parliamentary system is periodic (say once in four years), and by the electorate, the assessment of the responsibility of the executive under a parliamentary system is both daily and periodic. He felt that the daily assessment of responsibility would be far more effective than a periodic assessment and far more necessary in a country like India. The Indian Constitution, therefore, settled on the parliamentary system, preferring more responsibility to more stability.

However, the accountability of the legislature to the executive has played out in a manner that is substantially different from what is intended in theory. On the one hand, the legislature has parlayed its power of enforcing the accountability of the executive into a share in executive power, while the executive, on the other hand, has attempted

[3] B.S. Rao, *The Framing of India's Constitution: A Study* (New Delhi: Indian Institute of Public Administration, 1968).

to co-opt the legislature. Some safeguards against this situation were built into the system by preventing legislators from holding 'offices of profit' under the government. It is another matter that these provisions have been so diluted by steadily enlarging the list of offices exempt from this provision as to render this prohibition virtually ineffective. The Constitution has also been since amended to place a ceiling on the total number of legislators as a percentage of the total strength of the legislature. The coalescing of executive and legislative power has happened notwithstanding all these safeguards and without having to appoint legislators formally to any post. The second Administrative Reforms Commission (ARC) characterized this practice as 'the anomaly of legislators functioning as disguised executives'.[4]

Any analysis of accountability and corruption in India often identifies the increasingly large sums of money spent on elections as the main cause of the problem. The need for electoral funding is identified among the most important causes of corruption. As the second ARC puts it, 'abnormal election expenditure has to be recouped in multiples to sustain the electoral cycle ... Cleansing elections is the most important route to improve ethical standards in politics, to curb corruption and rectify maladministration.'[5] Admittedly, state assembly and national parliamentary constituencies are often large, both in terms of area and the number of voters. The minimum expenditure needed to reach out to voters is, therefore, not inconsiderable. Nevertheless, it is common knowledge that far more is being spent than could, by any reasonable standard, be necessary.

While the fact of ballooning election expenditures is undisputed, there is no clear evidence, however, that money is the deciding factor in electoral results. If it were so, it would become very difficult, if not impossible, for a party that has remained out of power for five years to defeat an incumbent, who, having had access to the levers of power over that period, can be expected to be better financed. We see, however, case after case of a badly performing incumbent being thrown out, notwithstanding any shortage of resources on the part of the challengers.

---

[4] Second Administrative Reforms Commission, *Fourth Report on Ethics in Governance* (New Delhi: Government of India, 2008), 8.

[5] Second ARC, *Fourth Report*, 4.

But if the fact remains that three or four or more contestants from a constituency are each willing to spend very large amounts of money, knowing with certainty that only one among them can win, while also being aware that the links between expenditure and victory are tenuous, their behaviour can be considered rational only in the context of the money that can be made by the exercise of the executive power that the victory brings. If this exercise of executive power were effectively disabled, electoral spending would be seen to be a wasted 'investment'. Various mechanisms such as establishment boards, cadre management committees, and transfer guidelines, among others, have been devised and implemented; nevertheless, none of these seem to have substantially addressed the potential for profound misuse of executive power.

As pointed out earlier, the mood in the Constituent Assembly, right from the initial stages of its deliberations, was clearly in favour of a parliamentary democracy. Nevertheless, towards the close of its efforts in 1949, there was an attempt made to reopen the matter. This move was countered with the contention that conditions in the US and India were entirely different; given the nascent stage of democracy in India, the executive and the legislature would need to work in harmony, and that this was possible only under a parliamentary system.[6] Does the enforcement of the executive's accountability to the legislature, however, require a healthy antagonism between the two branches that will be strong enough to prevent their joining together? If so, what would be the essential elements of a system that would achieve this?

CAG in Recent Years

Having to function in this context, it is interesting to examine what—if anything—the CAG has done to improve its impact. As the General Accountability Office (GAO) of the US says, audit effectiveness usually depends on two factors. The first factor is the existence of an institutional mechanism of examination of audit compliance. This greatly increases audit effectiveness, as it not only ensures action on the audit recommendations but also encourages audit in terms of improving its apparatus and instruments. The second factor is the

[6] Rao, *Framing of India's Constitution.*

quality of observations and their perceived utility by the auditee unit/organization.

Measured by the time they devote to a careful examination of the CAG's reports, Parliament and the various state legislatures display a worrying indifference to the very serious issues that the CAG often brings before them.[7] What could be the possible causes for this neglect? One cause that suggests itself is a combination of history, the CAG's own positioning of itself in the larger system, and Parliament's perception of the CAG's role vis-à-vis its (Parliament's) functions.

The auditor general was the pre-Independence predecessor of the CAG. Under the Government of India Act, 1919, the auditor general was appointed by the secretary of state for India. His responsibility was directly to that authority. Under the Government of India Act, 1935, the Crown appointed the auditor general. In addition, his powers and duties were as laid down by the Crown, but these could be modified by the legislature. His reports were to be placed before the legislature. However, the federal legislature envisaged under the Act never materialized. The auditor general, under these enactments, was clearly of an 'executive' type, as contrasted with an auditor of the 'legislative' type that was favoured by some other countries. He was enjoined to report to the home government about the financial transactions of the Government of India. His primary function was to ensure that the local government in India did not stray beyond its powers and transgress into what only the British government was permitted to do.[8] In order to ensure that he did his job of reporting to the home government without fear or favour, the auditor general's independence of the local government was a key feature of the institutional design.

After Independence, the CAG functioned under a 1950 reprint of the original pre-Independence Audit Code. This was clearly a very heavy and enduring legacy, since it was as late as 1971 that a special enactment to define the CAG's powers and role (as contemplated in the Constitution) was finally implemented.

---

[7] See Comptroller and Auditor General of India, *Performance Report 2010–11* (New Delhi: Government of India, 2011).

[8] R.K. Chandrasekharan, *Comptroller and Auditor General of India: Analytical History 1947–1989* (New Delhi: Ashish Publishing, 1990), vol. 1.

Over much of its 150-year history, of which the CAG is justifiably proud, therefore, the concept of the institution serving to aid and assist the legislature in enforcing the accountability of the executive did not exist. Of course, there was no legislature in any meaningful sense for most of this period. However, even after 1950, much the same approach has continued.

The CAG has embodied its aspirations about what it wants to be in a vision of becoming a global leader and initiator of global best practices in public sector accounting and auditing, recognized for independent, credible, balanced, and timely reporting on public finance and governance. In its mission statement, it enunciates its current role and describes what it is doing today as being one mandated by the Constitution, of promoting accountability, transparency, and good governance through high-quality auditing and accounting, while providing independent assurance to its stakeholders, namely the legislature, the executive, and the public, that public funds are being used efficiently and for the intended purposes. In these statements, assistance to parliament figures only incidentally.

What exactly is the constitutional mandate of the CAG? The Constitution is very clear and quite simple in the provisions it makes regarding the CAG. Article 149 merely provides that the CAG's duties would be as prescribed by law made by Parliament, and, as a purely interim and transitional arrangement, says that these would be the same as the duties of the pre-Independence Auditor General. The CAG (Duties, Powers and Conditions of Service) Act, 1971 [henceforth, CAG (DPC) Act], requires the CAG to audit all expenditure of the government to ascertain if the amounts disbursed were available, applicable to the purpose for which they were applied, and were properly authorized (Section 13). Regarding receipts, the CAG is enjoined to verify that the system provides for effective assessment and collection (Section 16). Article 151 provides that the CAG's reports on the accounts shall be submitted to the president or governor for being laid before the legislature.

The CAG, therefore, does not derive any independent mandate directly from the Constitution. Contrary to many statements talking about such a constitutional mandate, the CAG is unambiguously mandated to carry out such tasks as Parliament may, by law, prescribe. The implication is clear that the basic purpose of the CAG is to aid and assist Parliament.

Despite this, Parliament does not seem to have even recognized, leave alone asserted, its position as being the key stakeholder in the CAG. Section 23 of the CAG (DPC) Act doubtless provides that the CAG is authorized to make regulations covering the scope and extent of audit, the broad principles in regard to audit of receipts and expenditure, providing general principles of government accounting for the guidance of government departments. Regulation 9 of the regulations framed under this section clearly specifies that the executive cannot give any directions with regard to the performance of the audit mandate. This is indeed as it should be.

However, this does not derogate in any way the role that Parliament has to play in agenda setting, monitoring, evaluation, and enforcement of accountability from the CAG, all of which have been neglected by Parliament. The CAG's documents talk about a Perspective Plan 2010–15, that focuses on medium to long-term challenges and goals and allocates responsibility and identifies timelines for specific tasks, and a Strategic Plan 2020, that outlines the CAG vision, mission, and core values, emerging patterns of governance in India, organizational goals, and implementation arrangements. This is also said to include a decision to increase the resources devoted to performance audits from 10 to 50 per cent. Apart from the fact that these documents do not seem to be in the public domain, Parliament does not seem to have had any role at all in their preparation. It is not clear as to whether this is because Parliament did not think it necessary to drive this process, or felt constrained by the CAG's constitutional status and 'mandate'.

While seeking to position itself as being independent of the legislature, the CAG, nevertheless, seems to have felt that all the good work it did came to nought in the absence of follow up by Parliament. Initially, parliamentary indifference seems to have led to a sense of resignation, if not of despair. Iyer says that if there is a lack of interest on the part of the legislature to enforce the accountability of the executive, there are no answers left except for perhaps public interest litigation.[9] Recent times have, however, seen the CAG attempting to get over this apathy by directly appealing to the public at large.

---

[9] R.R. Iyer, 'The Role of Audit in Tackling Corruption', in *Corruption in India: Agenda for Action*, eds S. Guhan and S. Paul (New Delhi: Vision Books, 1997), 110.

In public speeches, the CAG has stated that the constitutional mandate of the body places a larger responsibility on it than one of merely preparing reports and placing them before the legislature. The mandate, he argues, is to keep the ultimate stakeholder—the man in the street—apprised of the outcomes of government spending. This is indeed entirely desirable. The CAG explains its case by saying that widespread dissemination of the results of audit 'is being undertaken in the firm belief that an awakened citizenry, once sensitized about the inadequacy of government departments, would exert pressure on these departments and maintain a vigilante [*sic*] thereby ensuring better delivery of government services'. While arguing thus, the CAG positions itself as an important part of a Fifth Estate, of oversight and accountability institutions, that 'should not be subject to the discretion or control of any other person or authority'.[10]

One issue that needs to be disposed of at the outset is the constitutional status of the CAG. This status should be understood as part of the scheme for protecting certain important functionaries of the state from executive domination. Such a constitutional status cannot be considered as creating an additional branch of government over and above the three recognized branches of the legislature, the executive, and the judiciary. In this threefold division of the functions of the state, the CAG serves as an extended outreach agency of the legislature, auditing and appraising the activities of the executive and presenting reports thereon to the legislature, so that the legislature in turn can hold the executive accountable. If the CAG has been provided a special status in the Constitution, this is merely meant to ensure that the CAG is able to function independently of the executive and demand from it documents, records, and explanations necessary for the purposes of its audit. Such a status does not constitute the CAG as a Fifth Estate any more than the special constitutional status provided to other entities such as the Election Commission, the Public Service Commissions, or, indeed, the civil service constitutes them into separate estates or branches of government.

[10] V. Rai, 'Role of Accountability Institutions in a Democracy', Speech at India Today Conclave held on 15 March 2013, downloaded from the website of the CAG on 8 April 2013.

Along with this misconception about what the constitutional status really means is a rather dangerous argument that the institution should not be subject to the control or direction of any other authority. The starting point of sound institutional design should be the premise that the default condition of all power is its misuse; special care must be taken to ensure its proper use. In the memorable words of Dr Ambedkar, the purpose of the Constitution is not so much to create the three branches of government as to place limits on their powers and to restrain their functioning. The CAG cannot be an exception to this rule.

The second set of causes for the neglect of the CAG's findings can be found in its overall approach. That the auditee government departments do their best to thwart the CAG has already been noted.[11] This seems to be a natural response to some of the basic threads that run all through the CAG's reports. Starting with the unstated objective of highlighting only improprieties, or suspicious, or egregiously incorrect, decisions, the CAG invariably ends up in taking a 'damned if you do, damned if you don't' attitude to auditee entities.

Given the long delays in auditing, the CAG always has the benefit of hindsight, and implicitly demands that decisions under review pass this test. Individual decisions that could provide shocking evidence of impropriety or mismanagement are highlighted without providing the overall context, or undertaking a holistic evaluation of performance. Given the sample nature of the CAG's audit coverage, a comprehensive assessment of the performance of key officials of auditing departments cannot be made. Besides, nothing seems to be too inconsequential for an audit report.

Part of the motivation for performance audit is the need to overcome some of these defects noted above, which collectively make the auditing departments position themselves as adversaries and instinctively thwart every attempt of the CAG. As the CAG himself has put it, 'our audits have undergone a culture change. We now engage in positive reporting. Hence from being a bunch of fault finders who are often wiser by hindsight, we now recognise and report good practices that we observe during audit.'[12]

[11] Das, 'Institutions of Accountability'.
[12] Vinod Rai, `Social Obligation of Public Auditors', Speech at the Harvard Kennedy School, Cambridge, MA, 8 February 2013.

For the first time ever, in 2012, the CAG had a peer review conducted of its recent performance audit initiatives. This was conducted by an international team, consisting of representatives of the Supreme Audit Institutions (SAI) of Canada, the Netherlands, Denmark, and the US, with Australia providing the lead. The peer review report was presented in October 2012, and covered performance audit reports presented to legislatures between April 2010 and March 2011.[13] The report shows that the CAG has still a long way to go in the direction of the culture change that has been felt to be desirable.

The review examined 35 CAG performance audits. The report noted that 'the major focus of the performance audit reports was shortcomings in the audited entity's programme administration and implementation, including not meeting or complying with stipulated requirements', and that 'calculations of foregone government revenue, unspent funding, and irregularities in the use of funding as a result of less than effective administration, were prominent features of the reports'.[14] The report went on to further observe that 'a common issue was that the focus on shortcomings meant that there was limited reporting of any programme outcomes and positive findings. In addition, the proportionality of negative findings was often not clear leaving the interpretation to the reader; and on some occasions, SAI India could have more clearly linked audit findings with the broader program level impact of those findings.'[15]

The review concluded that there was scope in around half the reports reviewed to be more balanced in content and tone, by placing the audit findings in the appropriate perspective and reporting more fully against the audit objectives. In such cases, the report said that the recommendations could have been improved by addressing the underlying causes of the identified deficiencies rather than merely restating administrative programme requirements that were not met. The review felt that a regular inclusion of programme outcomes and positive findings would contribute to a balanced presentation of audit reports. The report went on to advise the CAG that 'to achieve a better

[13] CAG, *International Peer Review of the Supreme Audit Institution of India* (New Delhi: Government of India, 2012).

[14] CAG, *International Peer Review*, 35–6.

[15] CAG, *International Peer Review*, 36.

balance, reports could more fully explore and present the challenges faced by audited entities; and include further diagnosis and explanation of any underlying causes of systemic weaknesses in administration and performance'.[16]

While the above deals with the overall approach and conclusions of audit and the manner of presentation of the findings, the peer review also had something to say about the quality of the audit evidence itself. The review considered whether the information, findings, and conclusions in the audit reports were supported by competent and relevant evidence, whose validity was tested and verified. The report found that for about half the audits, there were shortcomings in the evidence. In around one quarter of the reports, the evidence was either not documented at all or inadequately represented in the report.

The CAG operates through an annual quality management framework (AQMF) for the purpose of quality control of its performance audits. The peer review felt that the AQMF had not been clearly communicated to the CAG staff and that the explanatory material that was provided was not aligned with the framework. The review noted that two of the important quality management elements had not been implemented. These are the internal quality assurance review programme for audits, such as quality reviews being conducted by an independent group not directly involved in the performance audits, and the evaluation and dissemination of the lessons learnt from individual audits.

The peer review team reports that it had also interacted with members of the Public Accounts Committee (PAC) and the Committee on Public Undertakings (COPU) of Parliament, who seem to have felt—notwithstanding the various shortcomings pointed out above—that the performance audits provided valuable information, not otherwise available, about the ground-level impact of government programmes and funding, and that the quality of performance reports was good. Overall, the peer review provided 10 specific recommendations. All of these seem to suggest major shortcomings in approach, capabilities, and execution.

Is the strategy adopted recently by the CAG the best response for building an effective and enduring institution that can successfully

---

[16] CAG, *International Peer Review*, 36.

keep the executive under check? Has it done enough by way of internal reorientation and strengthening to be an effective instrument of change? In a few major cases, the efforts of the CAG to directly reach out to the public at large have undoubtedly yielded results that would never have been achieved under earlier practices. Such a strategy, though with several merits, does not seem to be capable of engendering the kind of institutional responses that would lead to a sustained, broad-based improvement in the quality of delivery of government services. Mass movements can be no substitute for the lack of systems. The CAG should not have given up so easily on creating a lasting interest in Parliament in favour of accountability. Public anger is clearly too inadequate a foundation for the kind of systematic and sustained effort that is needed for improved governance.

So what strategy is likely to ensure the broad-based effectiveness of an enduring nature that the CAG aspires for and that is required of the institution under its present set-up? It is instructive to look at comparable institutions in the UK and the US. In the case of the CAG, as in many other cases, we are still stuck to our original British inheritance, while Britain itself has moved on.

The National Audit Act, 1983 of the UK brought about many important changes in the audit mechanism in that country. First, the CAG was formally designated by law as an officer of the House of Commons, while preserving his independence in terms of appointment, removal, power to determine the scope of audit, and so on. The National Audit Office (NAO), therefore, very unambiguously, reckons Parliament and the auditee organizations as its two stakeholders. The long title of the Act makes it clear that it is an Act to strengthen parliamentary control and supervision of expenditure of public money.[17] Second, the CAG is appointed by the sovereign after the Commons

---

[17] The full title states that the National Audit Act is '[a]n Act to strengthen parliamentary control and supervision of expenditure of public money by making new provision for the appointment and status of the Comptroller and Auditor General, establishing a Public Accounts Commission and a National Audit Office and making new provision for promoting economy, efficiency and effectiveness in the use of such money by government departments and other authorities and bodies; to amend or repeal certain provisions of the Exchequer and Audit Departments Acts 1866 and 1921; and for connected purposes'.

has endorsed the jointly agreed recommendation of the prime minister and the chair of the public accounts committee (PAC). Third, the CAG is specifically authorized by law to conduct 'Economy, Efficiency and Effectiveness Examinations' (known as performance audits in India) such that, however, the merits of any policy objectives are not questioned. Fourth, a public accounts commission consisting of Members of Parliament (MPs) has been set up to oversee the functioning of the NAO. Schedule-III of the Act provides for the appointment of an auditor for the NAO (an individual or a firm of chartered accountants) with the power to carry out an examination of the economy, efficiency, and effectiveness of use of resources by the NAO. The report of this auditor is presented to the public accounts commission for further presentation to the House of Commons.

Similarly, the US Government Accountability Office (GAO), whose definition of its mandate the CAG quotes with approval, calls itself an independent, non-partisan agency that works for Congress. It places itself clearly in the legislative branch. The GAO also states that its work is done at the request of congressional committees or subcommittees or is mandated by public laws or committee reports. It is also called the 'congressional watch dog'. The GAO defines its mission as follows:

> To support the Congress in meeting its constitutional responsibility and to help improve the performance and ensure the accountability of the Federal Government for the benefit of American people. It provides Congress with timely information that is objective, fact based, non-partisan, non-ideological, fair and balanced.[18]

Instead of positioning itself as an independent constitutional authority ranged against the executive in enforcing accountability and improving the quality of governance, the CAG would be better placed if it sought to jog Parliament's sense of its duties towards enforcing accountability. The CAG should clearly position itself as an arm of the legislature. The CAG should release a draft agenda of action and actively seek Parliament's comments upon it and, indeed, its approval. Such a process would in no way amount to compromising its independence. It would, while investing the legislature with a sense of ownership of the

---

[18] See, the website of the *U.S. Government Accountability Office*. Available at http://www.gao.gov.

entire audit process, nevertheless allow the CAG to decide the detailed methodologies and scope of audit and maintain its independence in its audit judgements. In fact, the CAG could even point out where exactly the legislature has been remiss in the discharge of its accountability functions and suggest how they could be performed more adequately. The legislature, for its part, must take ownership of the CAG's functions and actively contribute to its agenda. Alongside, the CAG must voluntarily subject itself to being evaluated, according to a mutually agreed framework, by the legislature which, after all, is the key stakeholder in the institution. Such a decision would considerably enhance the credibility of the CAG while strengthening its independence. The NAO works according to a strategy paper approved by the Public Accounts Commission. A firm of chartered accountants reviews the effectiveness with which the NAO utilizes the resources made available to it. The GAO receives a peer review of its operations conducted once every three years. The CAG has gotten a peer review of its performance audit functions conducted for the first time only recently, though even much earlier it had been felt that there was 'an urgent need to substantially reform the audit function in India based on a thorough, comprehensive, and independent appraisal of its performance'.[19] This is an important initiative that needs to be properly institutionalized.

Thus far, the CAG has been helped by its rich legacy and inherited traditions in maintaining the high quality of its output. It is this that has accounted for the high status of the institution. These traditions run the risk of atrophy in the present environment. The constitutional status of the CAG, by itself, cannot account for anything, just as it has not done anything for the functioning or reputation of the public service commissions, or, indeed, that of the civil service. The CAG's independence and status are best ensured by the objectivity, thoroughness, and professionalism of its reporting and by submitting itself voluntarily to public monitoring and evaluation.

CVC, CBI, and the Lokpal

The Central Vigilance Commission (CVC) has been set up under the Central Vigilance Commission Act, 2003 (CVC Act) as an institution

[19] Iyer, 'Role of Audit', 104.

to enquire into alleged offences under the Prevention of Corruption Act, 1988 (PC Act). With respect to Group A officers or their equivalent in government companies and corporations, the CVC can institute an inquiry or investigation on its own. In respect of other employees, the CVC requires a reference to be made by the central government. Apart from this, the CVC is required to exercise superintendence over the CBI in its investigation of offences under the PC Act. The CVC also exercises superintendence over the vigilance administration of the various ministries of the central government and government companies and corporations. In terms of the number of organizations and persons it has to deal with, the CVC's remit is undoubtedly very vast. The CVC has very limited staff strength to discharge this responsibility. The total sanctioned staff strength of the CVC, which was 288 (including 50 senior officers) in 2008, has marginally increased to 296 (including 54 senior officers) in 2013. The number of persons actually in position has, however, remained the same at 230 over this period. The CVC does not have any substantive agency of its own to conduct inquiries and investigations. For this it depends mainly on the CVOs and CBI.

The CVOs function as the extended outreach arm of the CVC. The number of posts of full-time CVOs has increased only slightly in recent years, going up from 186 in 2005 to 197 in 2013. In addition, there are 410 posts of part-time CVOs, who are invariably saddled with other administrative responsibilities. Further, they would also not be as independent as would be desirable because of both their position in the administrative hierarchy and the pressure on them to deliver results in programme implementation. The CVC has, therefore, been arguing for appointing full-time CVOs in so-called sensitive ministries. Regarding smaller ministries, it has suggested that a group of related ministries could be clubbed together and full-time CVOs appointed. For some sensitive major ministries such as railways, and departments such as the Central Board of Direct Taxes and Central Board of Excise and Customs, where insiders have been appointed as full time CVOs, the Commission has argued for posting outsiders in order to ensure greater independence. These recommendations of the CVC are well justified and need to be seriously considered.

The CVC expends considerable effort to deal with the large number of complaints it receives. Of the 9,208 complaints received in 2005, only 641 (6.9 per cent) related to its jurisdiction and required further action. This share stood at 11.3 per cent in 2008 and 12.3 per cent in 2009. The total number of complaints received ballooned to 35,332 in 2013. Only 3.5 per cent of these complaints were found to be requiring further investigation. The Commission had launched a project (vigEYE) to enlist the support of citizens in its fight against corruption. However, we do not have any data on the current status of this initiative.

The CVC has been earlier characterized as an institution that does not rank high in the opinion of either Parliament or the public. This has been attributed to the virtual absence of any control over the two agencies through which the CVC was expected to accomplish its task—the CVOs and the CBI. Furthermore, the very inadequate rules under which disciplinary proceedings are to be conducted has also been identified as a cause for its ineffectiveness. These, it is said, result in delays that are fatal to the effectiveness of the institution.[20]

Administrative vigilance, either of the preventive kind, where systems and procedures are strengthened and transparency enhanced, or punitive vigilance, through examination of files by the CVOs, has its inherent limitations in uncovering and proving malfeasance. This cannot help in cases where money changes hands for officials doing the 'right thing'. With increasing scrutiny of official decisions through mechanisms such as right to information petitions, one can expect a shift to methods of corruption that are not traceable through official files. These developments do pose challenges; nevertheless, careful investigation and inquiry can lead to punitive orders that can withstand judicial challenge, given that the standard of proof required in disciplinary proceedings is of a less rigorous nature than in criminal prosecution.

Substantive and procedural safeguards for accused government employees embedded in the law have drawn the ire of many. It is de rigueur to ask for doing away with the requirement of prior sanction for prosecution, and for repeal of the protection given under Article 311 of the Constitution. A close examination of cases where these factors are claimed to have come in the way is very likely to show that the real culprits are shoddy investigation, imprecise framing of charges, laxness in presentation of the case before the inquiry authority, ill-founded

[20] Das, 'Institutions of Accountability'.

conclusions, and lack of supportive reasoning in the inquiry reports. In short, many of the same factors that lead to poor conviction rates in criminal proceedings lead to ineffective disciplinary proceedings as well.

In order to build capacity, the CVC runs training programmes for CVOs and organizes training programmes for vigilance staff through the CBI Academy. All cases of persons above a certain level are subject to a two-stage advice process by the CVC, which should provide opportunities to remedy some of the defects pointed out above. However, the effectiveness of the departmental enquiry mechanism still remains essentially dependent on the personality and the initiative of the CVO. The CVC has been very conscious of its limited reach and has argued for some time that effectiveness in vigilance work is dependent on the performance of the individual organizations themselves.

A major limitation that leads to the ineffectiveness of the CVC in curbing corruption is traceable to its basic design, which is of taking up enquiries based on files. Such enquiries can tackle malfeasance only where the officers concerned have been so careless or incompetent to leave an incriminating paper trail. While there do occur many such instances, these do not appear by any reckoning to account for any significant proportion of the total quantum of corruption that likely transpires. In order to supplement these efforts based on official records, the CVC has issued guidelines regarding preparing lists of officers of doubtful integrity. In fact, these guidelines are only a reiteration of the administrative instructions that have been in force in government since the mid-1960s. These contemplate keeping a confidential watch, both by the department concerned and the CBI, over officers whose conduct gives rise to suspicion. The list of officers who thus need to be kept under surveillance is supposed to be reviewed and finalized based on mutual discussions and information sharing between the CVOs and the CBI. However, these instructions have not resulted in very effective preventive action. This could be because the persons concerned very often do not appreciate the purpose and spirit of these instructions. Even where this lack of understanding is not the problem, the CBI would be completely over-stretched in delivering results in all the cases that get referred to it under these procedures. A recent case involving a high-level officer in the Indian Railways offers a very clear example of what can be achieved if officers indulging in suspect behaviour are kept under surveillance. This was clearly a case of collusive corruption where there was no likelihood whatsoever of any complaint being given on the basis of which a trap could be laid. Nevertheless, if the persons involved could be trapped red-handed, this speaks volumes of what could be achieved by a proactive investigation agency.

At its core, the CVC possesses only advisory powers; it has been unhappy with this position and has been pressing for changes. For instance, the CVC comments that the effectiveness of its superintendence over vigilance administration is severely curtailed by the proviso to Section 8(1)(h) of the CVC Act, which says that the CVC's superintendence over the vigilance administration of the government will not enable it to either (a) go against directions relating to vigilance matters issued by the Government, or (b) confer upon it any power to issue directions related to policy matters.[21] Quite justifiably, the CVC contends that the government's own directions regarding vigilance matters and its policy decisions often are a source of difficulty.

The CVC has also strongly argued that it should have an adequately resourced mechanism for undertaking direct enquiries. It feels that if the CVC is to play a more proactive and significant role in the eradication of corruption, many important measures have to be taken to provide teeth to the commission. It has asked, among other things, that the two-stage consultation requirement should be included in the rules so that in cases taken up by it, the mandatory consultation with the Union Public Service Commission (UPSC) should be dropped.[22]

One can sense a palpable feeling of fatigue when the CVC says that 'general public apathy towards vigilance activities and a higher tolerance for corruption in society emboldens the corrupt', and goes on to add that 'the CVC's Annual Report to the Parliament does not reach its logical conclusion as there is little debate and discussion for eliciting preventive and corrective actions required on the findings and recommendations of the Commission'.[23]

The CBI has been one of the major institutional mechanisms in the country for combating corruption. Though the work of the CBI extends to other special crimes and economic offences also, the anti-corruption

[21] CVC, *Annual Report, 2005* (New Delhi: Government of India, 2006).
[22] CVC, *Annual Report, 2007* (New Delhi: Government of India, 2008).
[23] CVC, *Annual Report, 2010* (New Delhi: Government of India, 2011).

division (ACD) of the CBI is responsible for the bulk of its cases. Over the last few years, more than 70 per cent of the cases registered in any particular year are accounted for by the ACD.

The CBI categorizes its anti-corruption cases into trap cases, cases of possessing assets disproportionate to income, and 'other cases'. Of these categories, the 'other cases' category is the largest in terms of numbers. In 2011, others as a category accounted for 454 cases out of 711 cases booked by the ACD. In 2012, other cases were 510 out of a total of 790, while in 2013, others were 562 out of a total of 838 cases. Many, if not most, of these presumably pertain to cases registered under Section 13(1)(d)(iii) of the PC Act, which says that a public servant commits the offence of criminal misconduct if he, while holding office as a public servant, obtains for any person, any valuable thing or pecuniary advantage without any public interest. The offence so defined seems to do away with the requirement of *mens rea*. This provision has been widely criticized as being of such a scope that virtually any decision taken by a public servant could fall foul of this. Section 13(1) of the PC Act is sought to be completely substituted with another subsection by the Prevention of Corruption (Amendment) Bill, 2013, which would do away with the above offence.

Like the CVC, the CBI has been constrained by substantial vacancies in its staff strength. The total number of sanctioned posts, which was 5,961 in 2009, grew substantially to 6,526 in 2010. Thereafter, it has remained more or less at the same level, marginally increasing to 6,674 in 2013. At any point of time, vacancies range between 12 and 15 per cent. There are also issues related to the skill sets necessary in the present day and what the CBI actually possesses. Once its investigation process is over and a charge sheet is filed in the appropriate court, the CBI is subject to delays that are inherent in the judicial process. As the CVC notes, it takes five years, on an average, for judicial proceedings in any case under the PC Act to reach its logical conclusion after a charge sheet is filed in court.[24] Over 50 per cent of the cases pending trial have been pending for five years and more. Over 20 per cent of the total pendency has been pending for 10 years and more. Nevertheless, the CBI's success rate, as measured by convictions obtained, has remained quite high at around 67 per cent in the last few years. The CBI has,

[24] CVC, *Annual Report, 2013* (New Delhi: Government of India, 2014).

reportedly, always been the object of an intense effort by the government of the day to ensure control over its processes of investigation and prosecution. There have been reports of instances of alleged use of the CBI to settle political scores.

The recent past has seen a concerted attempt by the civil society organizations to remedy the perceived inadequacies in the present system available for bringing errant public servants to book. This took the form of a Jan Lokpal movement with the objective of setting up an institution that is safeguarded against all interference from, and/or control by, the executive in so far as its regular operations are concerned. The government has also responded to this movement and has enacted not only a bill to provide for a Lokpal at the centre and Lokayuktas in the states, but also has brought forward legislation for other related matters, such as the protection of whistle blowers, the laying down of standards and timelines covering service delivery to citizens, regulation of public procurement, and the provision of services to the citizens through electronic delivery.

The beginnings of the present effort can be traced back to the Supreme Court's orders in the case of *Vineet Narain* v. *Union of India*.[25] In *Vineet Narain*, the Supreme Court was dealing with what it said was a major complaint relating to inaction by the investigating agencies in cases of alleged wrongdoing by those in high and powerful positions. The Supreme Court, therefore, took upon itself the task of directly monitoring the progress of the investigation. It adopted, as explained in its order, a procedure of merely hearing whatever it was that the CBI director or the revenue secretary had to tell the court so as to satisfy itself that the earlier inaction was not persisting. While doing so, the court said, it took care to ensure that no observation of any kind was made by it, nor was any response given which could be construed as the opinion of the court about the merits of the case or of any accusation against the accused. The court explained that its supervision was mindful of, and entirely consistent with, the principle that the investigating agency was answerable only to the law, and that if that duty under the law was not properly discharged by the police, it could be enforced only by a writ of mandamus.

[25] AIR 1996 SC 3386.

At the same time, the court realized that this procedure, being confined to that specific case, was not an adequate answer to the wide-scale problems faced. In its words, 'inertia was the common rule whenever the alleged offender was a powerful person. Thus, it became necessary to take measures to ensure permanency in the remedial effect to prevent inertia of the agencies in such matters.'[26] The court, therefore, virtually accepted the report of the Independent Review Committee (IRC) that had been set up earlier by the Government of India. The only significant difference was with reference to the single directive, or the provision that the CBI must take prior permission from the government if it wants to open an inquiry into the actions of civil servants above the rank of joint secretary. While the IRC was in favour of its continuance, the court disagreed, largely on the grounds that executive directions embodied in the single directive were at variance with the law governing the CBI. The CVC was identified as the agency that would, on a regular and continuing basis, perform the function of supervising the investigations of the CBI that the Supreme Court had taken upon itself in *Vineet Narain*.

Even more importantly, the court laid down that, with the advice of the attorney general, a panel of competent lawyers of experience and impeccable reputation should be appointed, and that their services should be utilized as prosecuting counsel in significant cases. In every prosecution which ended in the discharge or acquittal of the accused, the matter had to be reviewed by a lawyer on the panel to fix responsibility for dereliction of duty, if any, on the concerned officers and for taking strict action against them. It is significant to note that the second ARC has drawn attention to this order of the Court relating to review and taking corrective action in cases of failed prosecutions.[27]

The final orders of the court mandated statutory status for the CVC. The CVC Act now provides that the CVC shall exercise superintendence over the CBI's functioning in respect of investigation of offences under the PC Act. In addition, the CVC can also give directions to the CBI in order to discharge its responsibilities for the superintendence of the investigation. However, this power cannot extend to requiring the CBI to investigate or dispose of any case in any particular manner. The

---

[26] AIR 1996 SC 3386.
[27] Second ARC, *Fourth Report*, Section 4.6.1.

act also empowers the CVC to enquire or investigate either directly or through any other agency any allegation regarding offences committed under the PC Act. It also provides for a participative and transparent procedure for the appointment of the CVC and providing him with security of tenure. The CBI was required to report to the CVC about the cases taken up by it for investigation, the progress of investigations, and cases in which charge sheets were filed and their progress. The CVC was also required to review the progress of all cases where the CBI had recommended sanction of prosecution to publish a separate section on the CBI's functioning in its annual report after the supervisory function was transferred to it.

The provisions in the CVC Act relating to superintendence of the CBI appear to be both widely defined and constrained (by the proviso) at the same time. The actual amplitude of the power would perhaps ultimately depend upon the personality of the CVC. Given that the major motivation behind this legal enablement was described by the Supreme Court as the prevention of inaction or inertia by investigating agencies in the case of offences by powerful persons, the scope of the CVC's superintendence would be best described by what the Court said about the procedure it had itself adopted, as detailed above.

As required by the Supreme Court, the CVC has been reporting on its superintendence of the CBI in its annual reports. However, this section in the annual report merely contents itself with providing statistical details about the number of cases registered, investigated, pending as at the year end, charge sheets filed, judgements delivered, conviction rates, and so forth. As far as the superintendence over the CBI's investigation of corruption cases is concerned, the CVC has pointed out that its power is very limited: the conduct of trials, including the appointment of prosecutors, is outside its purview; all appeals are subject to Law Ministry approval; the director of prosecutions is an officer of the Law Ministry, besides many more such limitations.[28] The CVC lapses into diplomatese when it says that 'the Commission holds regular review meetings with the Director, CBI, at regular intervals, where, apart from a frank exchange of views and ideas, the focus is on the progress and quality of the cases investigated by the CBI'.[29] A study

---

[28] CVC, *Annual Report, 2005* (New Delhi: Government of India, 2005).
[29] CVC, *Annual Report, 2007* (New Delhi: Government of India, 2007).

of these reports does not provide any insight into the real issues that the CVC has had to grapple with in discharging its responsibility of superintendence over the CBI with respect to corruption cases.

We are left with no means, other than the annual reports of the CVC, for understanding how the CVC has ensured that investigations are concluded effectively and speedily while at the same time staying within the legal perimeter outlined in *Vineet Narain*. In fact, the question does arise as to whether there could be any vestigial power of superintendence and any power to issue directions at all, after space for the proviso in Section 8(1)(b) of the CVC Act has been carved out. The general approach adopted by the Supreme Court, as it explained in *Vineet Narain*, would have had a significant impact in the case of direct monitoring of the investigations by the Court, given the stature of the Court. It would perhaps be unrealistic to accept anything near a similar impact in the case of the CVC. In fact, it seems clear that this particular function entrusted to the CVC has not been as effective as necessary. Had it been anything otherwise, there would not have been any need for the Supreme Court to directly monitor the progress of investigations in other important cases such as the 2G case, even though it was the CVC—acting on public complaints filed before it—that had directed the CBI to investigate the case.[30] It was noted earlier that the CVC did not seem to suffer from any particular handicap as a result of not having a statutory status.[31] It is interesting to assess whether the grant of statutory status has, on the other hand, enabled it to improve its effectiveness. Given the limitations on its powers as highlighted above, the conferring of statutory status does not seem to have made any material difference to the effectiveness of the institution.

The Supreme Court had occasion to revisit this issue in the 'Coalgate case' where it took upon itself the job of monitoring the investigations.[32] The Court held that, while the power of the police to investigate cognizable offences is ordinarily not impinged by any fetters, such power

[30] *Centre for Public Interest Litigation* v. *Union of India* [Writ Petition (Civil) no. 423 of 2010]; and *Dr. Subramanian Swamy* v. *Union of India* [Writ Petition (Civil) no. 10 of 2011].

[31] Das, 'Institutions of Accountability'.

[32] *Manohar Lal Sharma* v. *The Principal Secretary* [Writ Petition (Criminal) no. 120 of 2012].

has to be exercised consistent with the statutory provisions and for legitimate purpose. The Court stated further that especially when the facts and circumstances do not indicate that the investigating officer is not functioning bona fide, the Court would not ordinarily interfere. It added that the monitoring of investigations/enquiries is intended to ensure that proper progress takes place without directing or channelling the mode or manner of investigation. It explained the idea as being one of retaining public confidence in the impartial enquiry/investigation into the alleged crime such that the enquiry/investigation into each accusation is made on a reasonable basis irrespective of the position and status of that person and the enquiry/investigation is taken to its logical conclusion in accordance with the law. The Court also made a distinction between supervision and monitoring of investigation. It clarified that supervision implies observing and directing the execution of a task whereas monitoring only means maintaining surveillance. It clarified that 'supervision of investigation by any Court is a contradiction in terms. The Code does not envisage such a procedure and it cannot either.'[33]

In the 2G case, the Supreme Court enlisted the assistance of the CVC in monitoring the investigations being carried out. Copies of the reports of the investigation conducted by CBI and other agencies were ordered to be made available to the CVC in a sealed envelope and the CVC was directed to examine the reports and send its observations/ suggestions within one week to the Supreme Court. In the Coalgate case, the Supreme Court directed that all cases where enquiry officers had recommended filing of regular cases on completion of enquiries but had been overruled by the CBI Head Office should be sent to the CVC for further scrutiny. The CVC, for its part, was directed to send its comments within four weeks to the Court.

How can this inertia or inaction during investigation of the involvement of powerful personalities be avoided? In *Virender Kumar Ohri* v. *Union of India*, the Supreme Court asked for the opinion of the Law Commission of India on how the investigation and trial of criminal cases against influential public personalities could be expedited.[34] The recommendations of the Law Commission essentially are for a proactive

---

[33] *Manohar Lal Sharma* v. *The Principal Secretary.*

[34] Writ Petition (Civil) no. 341 of 2004.

and close monitoring of the progress of such cases by the judiciary at all levels, right up to the high courts.[35] These recommendations amount to a mere reiteration that the existing statutory authorities should all discharge their responsibilities, and beg the question about what is to be done when this does not happen. Does the remedy lie only in a writ of mandamus?

The Lokpal and Lokayuktas Act, 2013 empowers the Lokpal with the power of direction and superintendence over the CBI regarding cases referred by it to the CBI for preliminary enquiry or investigation. However, the same proviso, as now applicable to the CVC, prohibiting the Lokpal from giving specific directions about the investigations, remains. At the same time, the investigation agency (CBI included) will be required to simultaneously submit its investigation report to the Lokpal while filing it before the court. The Lokpal will decide whether a charge sheet or closure report is to be filed. This may provide some assurance that the correct conclusion has, in fact, been drawn from the evidence collected; however, this does not solve the problem of inadequately investigated cases. Given the structure and composition of the Lokpal, it can be reasonably expected that the investigation agencies would be more mindful of, and responsive to, the superintendence of the Lokpal. Nevertheless, the question of what the Lokpal can do in a case where the investigation agency has recommended closure, and the Lokpal feels otherwise, is not clear. If the legal principle is that the investigating agency is supreme, then what would be the practical meaning of this provision?

The annual reports of the CVC or the CBI do not provide any information about the specific orders of the Supreme Court relating to the prosecution agency. Specifically, material about review of cases of discharge or acquittal, and action, if any, taken against officers found guilty of dereliction of duty is not available. The Lokpal is to have its own prosecution wing; this is likely to solve some issues related to prosecution.

---

[35] See Law Commission of India, *Expeditious Investigation and Trial of Criminal Cases Against Influential Public Personalities*, Report no. 239 (New Delhi: Government of India, 2012), submitted before the Supreme Court of India in *Virender Kumar Ohri* v. *Union of India* [Writ Petition (Civil) no. 341 of 2004].

The Supreme Court, in *Vineet Narain*, very clearly laid down that the responsibility of police officers investigating a case was only to the law. It is this principle that has been reiterated by former CBI directors while discussing the issue of whether the Lokpal should be given any role in investigation or filing of charge sheets in courts. They have argued for providing the CBI with financial and administrative autonomy, and made the point that it would be mischievous to say that an autonomous CBI is not accountable to anyone. It has been pointed out that at each stage of a case, the CBI is accountable to the courts. While this may be true in respect of each individual case, such a system does not provide for accountability of the organization as a whole. Accountability in each individual case to a large number of widely dispersed authorities can, by no means, be a substitute for answerability to a single institution that takes an overall view of the organization's performance. As of now, the Lokpal seems to be the organization best suited to play that role.

The Lokpal is an institution that has been long in the making. Many aborted attempts preceded the enactment of the law in 2013. Implementation of the Act has, nevertheless, run into several practical problems. The government has come up with amendments that seem to be essentially ad hoc. In reviewing these amendments, the Parliamentary Standing Committee has made a detailed enumeration of the areas of overlap between the roles of the Lokpal, the CVC, and the CBI. With a full-fledged, high-powered Lokpal, the rationale for continuing with a separate, statutory CVC seems tenuous. The Committee's recommendation for an integrated anti-corruption mechanism, fully within the Lokpal, is well founded. A major objection to this line of argument is the CBI's contention that there are integral connections between corruption cases and other cases investigated by them, and that the division of the organization would lead to a reduced effectiveness in other investigations. This point is doubtless valid. However, on balance, it appears that a fully empowered Lokpal will alone be able to deliver. It would be unproductive to create such an institution and handicap it in investigation.

***

A former Indian prime minister is said to have famously observed that corruption is a global phenomenon. This seems to be largely true even today, with the exception, perhaps, of places like Singapore and the Scandinavian countries. Instances of large-scale corruption have come to light even in developed countries. Why is it, then, that India fares so badly in corruption perceptions as compared to those countries? One reason could be the rampant petty corruption observed in India, which could be absent elsewhere. The more important reason appears to be the virtual failure of our criminal justice system to bring offenders to book, while the advanced countries, of which the US is the prime example, act swiftly to mete out condign punishment to their law-breakers. India, on the contrary, has been satisfied with the process itself serving as the punishment—delivered by agencies whose credibility is often suspect. Investigation, prosecution, and trial have to be rescued from this completely unsatisfactory state of affairs. The legal principles that need to be pressed into service for this purpose need examination.

Kapur and Mehta have highlighted the very inadequate efforts of the Indian Parliament in enforcing the accountability of the executive.[36] Given the composition of the legislature, they are not very optimistic about the prospects of enhanced accountability. Perhaps we need to explore the 'deep structures' undergirding our society and polity to understand the reasons for the present state of affairs, what needs to, and can, be done to remedy it, and the prospects for the future. We need to keep in mind Dr Ambedkar's description of democracy in India as being a mere top dressing on a soil which is essentially undemocratic. Bad governance and lack of accountability in India may have many victims; they certainly have many beneficiaries as well. It is, therefore, very difficult to change the status quo. A complete change in the thinking of society at large is required. That is a comprehensive, long-term project whose details have yet to be worked out.

---

[36] D. Kapur and P.B. Mehta, 'The Indian Parliament as an Institution of Accountability' (UNRISD Programme Paper 23, United Nations Research Institute for Social Development, Geneva, 2006).

8

FOREGROUNDING FINANCIAL ACCOUNTABILITY IN GOVERNANCE

Amitabh Mukhopadhyay

Any kind of trust creates its own vulnerabilities for those who trust. Parliamentary democracy, as a form of popular trust in a framework for responsible government, proliferated in the post–World War era. However, over the last two decades, parliaments have been discredited and pilloried due to an obnoxious lordliness donned by most parliamentarians, as well as widespread corruption among them. A high degree of toleration by people, of both elite capture of state institutions and corruption in societies, has started giving way to a palpable yearning for a culture of accountability across countries.

This *geist* is not limited to a clamour only for managerial and political accountability. It runs deeper, turning inwards from the social domains of everyday life to professional concerns and personal affairs. It poses stark truths about ascribed statuses at offices and within households, demanding structural changes in our very selves, our institutions, and society at large. Deliberative democracies and civic solidarities are the flavour, if not yet the order, of the day.

The disenchantment with institutions that underpin representative government is, to some extent, due to an aversion to ascribed statuses. But it is not without influences emanating from movements within the social sciences that opened up a kaleidoscope of views from the margins.[1] Digital technologies have amplified the challenge by helping us to immediately learn both sides of stories—about political rights, health, education, human rights, women's predicaments, employment, and environmental concerns. Institutional and social mechanisms for securing financial accountability of governments too bear interrogation from these vantage points of the clamour for establishing popular sovereignty in place of the stolid structures of parliamentary supremacy.

This chapter on the Comptroller and Auditor General of India (CAG) studies the institution in four different phases of its evolution and argues that a new legislation to govern his/her duties and powers is essential to reorient the institution for its development needs. The first phase was when the institution gathered its strength, historically, by drawing succor from the concern for responsible government widely debated in social circles in the United Kingdom (UK), after the motion for impeachment of Warren Hastings, the first Governor-General of British India, failed in the House of Commons. In the second phase, the institution relied on its outgoing innovations to fulfil its constitutional role foresightedly envisaged in broad terms by Dr B.R. Ambedkar, the Chairman of the Drafting Committee of the Constitution of India. In the third phase, the agency restructured itself to cope with burgeoning expenditure and runaway deficit financing by government, and in the fourth and final phase (since 1991), the institution stared down the challenges of reinventing itself in the context of financial accountability as a culture-in-the-making in twenty-first century India. After distinguishing between these phases, some of the concerns to be borne in mind in the present context for an urgently necessary new legislation are discussed.

Prior to national Independence and the creation of the Republic of India in 1950, the CAG in India safeguarded the treasury from misuse or abuse by servants of an imperial power. Treasury control, compilation and consolidation of accounts of civil departments of the Union and States, tendering advice on budgetary controls, along with auditing functions, were vested with him. The separation of control of the treasury and accounts from audit functions, naturally, did not feature in such a system of parliamentary financial control.

---

[1] The influences of a Foucault or a Derrida and several others are patently visible in the depths to which 'received disciplines' have been contested by 'insurrections of knowledge'.

In the post-Independence period, the necessary change envisaged, from serving as an institution of a system of control to an institution exclusively for public sector auditing, which is geared to audit as a public service and is not just a service provider for government or parliament (an institution which communicates with citizens at large), has scarcely happened. The framers of the Indian Constitution were keen that it serve as a vehicle of social change and therefore recognized the need for CAG to not stand in the way of development expenditure needs while continuing to serve as a watchdog of the treasury. In their wisdom, they left legislation for weighing the precise balance between the two to be determined by Parliament, resting content with insisting on a change in designation to Comptroller and Auditor General of India and leaving him totally independent—not subsumed under the executive, legislature, or the judiciary. Parliament's law laying down the duties, powers, and conditions of service of CAG saw the light of day two decades later, in the form of the CAG's (Duties, Powers and Conditions of Service) Act, 1971 (henceforth, CAG Act). In the meantime, the CAG hobbled along, relying on the British Government's Audit and Accounts Order, 1936 and on astute innovations that at times annoyed the Executive but survived long enough to become convention due to the extraordinary support of a few public-spirited parliamentarians.

Experience since 1971—pre-eminence gained by the executive vis-à-vis parliament and judiciary, changes in union accounting systems, economic reforms of 1991 and revival of local self-government in 1992–3, and a concerted movement of civil society since 1996 to secure the right to information and the growing dismay of citizens at the weak ineffectuality of parliamentary accountability mechanisms to lend meaning to CAG's reports—have generated impulses for changing the architecture first framed in 1971. And yet, apart from a perfunctory exchange of correspondence between the Ministry of Finance and CAG during 2010–11 on a proposed draft audit law, nothing approaching a public debate has been initiated by any agency thus far.

Meanwhile, due to the appalling state of accounts and audit arrangements for audit of the third tier of government (that is, local self-government), a level to which an increasing quantum of funds have been steadily devolving since 1993, social accountability mechanisms have emerged. These assume great significance not only because they might fill a vacuum but because they focus on the core societal problem of a high level of perceived toleration of corruption. Their potential to transform audit, from an administrative construct of rational-legal systems to an activity that also relates to the moral pragmatism of social concerns and thus becomes a means of public education and deepening democracy, is immense. The recent move by the CAG (March 2015) to accept a relationship with social audit practices that were initially developed by civil society organizations (CSOs) and were then adopted by the Ministry of Rural Development as part of the legislation for the Mahatma Gandhi National Rural Employment Guarantee Scheme (MGNREGS) is a welcome step. Several other practices, such as citizen reports, budget briefs, expenditure tracking, and so on, have also made their mark. We argue that the common weal for responsible government cannot be created in the absence of citizen engagement by CAG—informing citizens, enlisting their participation in auditing and helping them to negotiate solutions with administration.

Given the economic reforms of the early 1990s, constitutional amendments for reviving the place of local bodies in development planning and implementation, introduction of public–private partnerships (PPP) in infrastructure, a rights-based framework for public administration and social sector development with greater devolution of funds to state governments since 2015, fresh legislation to govern the duties and powers of CAG, with cross-cutting practices for citizen engagement by the institution, is necessary. While discussing the importance of legislation for audit that is more in sync with the times, this chapter also examines the influences emanating from the International Organization of Supreme Audit Institutions (INTOSAI), which is the umbrella association for government auditors across the world. The standards set and guidelines issued by INTOSAI since 2010 and its support for Supreme Audit Institutions (SAIs) persuaded the United Nations General Assembly (UNGA) to adopt three successive resolutions in support of the role of SAIs in achieving the post-2015 Sustainable Development Goals (SDGs).

We the People

During his visit to India in November 2010, US President Barack Obama, speaking in the Lok Sabha, called the relationship between

India and the US 'the defining partnership of the twenty-first century. At the heart of this relationship is the fact that the constitutions of both countries begin with the revolutionary words, "We the people"'. And then, marking a departure from addressing the House, he directly addressed the people of India: 'So I want to conclude by speaking directly to the people of India watching today'. He exhorted the people of India to partner with Americans to build 'a world that is more prosperous, more secure, and more just'.

Is the schism between the institution of parliament and the people in India so marked today that one has to turn from the one to the other? Can Indians leave their concerns for equality and fraternity aside and pursue prosperity instead? The similarities between the constitutions of India and the US no doubt go even somewhat beyond their preambles, but differences in the status of popular sovereignty in the two countries and the obvious additional burden of securing social equality in India are obvious too. Indians today hope to rise above the indignity of poverty; some of them aspire to prosperity. Going by popular media reports, however, there is a consensus that the lack of accountability in governance is the major obstacle to development. Foregrounding accountability in governance is essential to revive the trust that people had placed in the institutions of government in India a generation ago.

A change in the nature of relations between parliament and people in India was clearly marked by the movement for *constitutionalism* that social reformer Anna Hazare led, starting in the summer of 2010. This upsurge culminated in the 'Sense of the House' resolution of Parliament of India on 26 August 2011, which resolved that provisions for *lokayukta*s (ombudsmen) for state governments would also be included within the ambit of Parliament's Lokpal Bill for the country as a whole. The movement's importance was evidently discerned by the US Administration as early as November 2010 when the storm had gathered on the streets of New Delhi, much before the Indian Parliament read the writing on the wall and grudgingly passed the resolution. Such an institutional change, from regarding the Constitution as a holy book to a realization that constitutionalism means the efforts of the people to limit the powers of government by giving themselves a constitution and amending it from time to time, is likely to impact governance significantly in the coming years.

A country still encumbered by inequality and appalling poverty needs the State to continue to care for many of the capability-development aspects of the people. While in a formal sense popular sovereignty may be deemed to have been established by constitutions that offered both universal adult franchise and credible electoral processes, it is undeniable that, to the extent that stratification exists in different societies, the insidious emergence of party oligarchies and elite capture of institutions of government vitiate popular sovereignty time and again. Civil society has been persistently tabling the contestations of both individuals and sections of people who find themselves marginalized by the tyranny of stage-managed brute majority politics.

The divergence between political society and civil society in recent times has been a cause of great concern in India. The meteoric emergence of a hastily cobbled together political party called Aam Aadmi Party (AAP) in India in 2013 stunned national parties with its showing in the elections of 2014 to the Delhi State Assembly. As a formation that was not only reminiscent of the volunteers of free India, but one that held out a promise of creating a new causeway between civil society and political society, AAP has been hailed as a precious political development by many observers.

As it panned out, within a year, infantile disorder within the party and the Bharatiya Janata Party (BJP) electoral juggernaut—led by present Prime Minister Narendra Modi—fuelled the rout of AAP in the parliamentary elections of 2014. Nevertheless, what the AAP asserted—that concerns related to public participation in development and good governance be brought centre-stage in national politics—had to be perforce adopted by the BJP, which had sat in opposition for ten long years, to catapult it to a commanding majority in the 2014 parliamentary elections. Such *techne* (craft) deployed by BJP—making the politically correct electoral promises and using media savvy to carve out a majority in parliament—cannot successfully bring about good governance and development, as has become amply evident by the party's first two years in office. The precious concerns of AAP will demand a more sustained praxis in the immediacy of the disaggregated sites of the State (that is, in its various institutions). For our present purposes, it is sufficient to note the fluidity in the status of the parliament in India today and to realize that institutions such as universities or the organization of the CAG cannot really expect much leadership or direction from Parliament in the foreseeable future.

Responsible Government

Prehistory

High-school students in India read about the impeachment in the UK Parliament of Warren Hastings in the late eighteenth century as a milestone in the development of parliamentary oversight of the executive. Few of them learn that the motion for impeachment in the Parliament of UK actually dragged on for seven years (1788–95) and eventually failed, for want of evidence. Witnesses testified to Hastings' good character and denied there was widespread corruption or that Hastings had amassed any illicit wealth or damaged Britain's reputation.

The Regulating Act of 1773 had failed to reign in the British East India Company's nefarious practices. To address its shortcomings, the East India Company Act, 1784 sought to bring the company's rule under the sovereign control of the British Government. It provided for the appointment of a Board of Control for a joint government of British India by both the Company and the Crown with the government holding the ultimate authority. Under the Act, a Calcutta Council was set up, which could veto the Governor-General's proposals. Hastings fell out with the Council, was criticized, and impeached.

Despite the failure, the stirring impeachment by Edmund Burke, upholding the values of his nation—liberty, property, and security— against the rapacity of a trading company that compromised them, remains an inspiring moment in history. It served not only as a precedent for parliamentary oversight to hold government to account, but at a deeper level, provided a powerful argument for government's regulation of business. Though the impeachment failed, it triggered an intense discourse in London, the city of businessmen with considerable investment in the trading company, about responsible government in India.

As a consequence, the Charter Act, 1833, removed the monopoly of the East India Company, instituted a Governor-General of India (replacing Governor-Generals of the presidencies of Bengal, Bombay, and Madras) and introduced a system of open competition for the selection of civil servants. Following the Mutiny of 1857, the Government of India Act, 1858 was passed to establish what became known as the British Raj in India. This Act also initiated a system of an annual budget of Imperial Income and Expenditure. The budgeting system became the reference point for Imperial Audit. Elaborate accounting and internal control and auditing practices evolved from experiences gained with audit of the trading East India Company; the military establishment; railways, posts, and telegraph; and finally, civil administration. The Auditor General provided assurance to the Viceroy in India, and through him to Parliament of UK, that public funds were being accounted for and used efficiently for the intended purposes.

In 1919, the legislative councils in the centre and provinces were expanded and a system of double government was introduced by the Government of India Act (1919) for the provinces of British India. It marked the first introduction of the democratic principle into the executive branch of the British administration of India. The Fundamental Rules to uniformly govern the grades of pay, allowances, and entitlements of the bureaucracy were introduced as rules carrying the force of statutes. These continue to govern the bureaucracy even today. The Public Accounts Committee (PAC) was first constituted in 1922, the year, incidentally, when 'test' audit, instead of a 100 per cent audit, was started in UK.[2] Though created by legislative rules, the PAC was, in effect, an *executive* committee, chaired by the Finance Member of the Viceroy's Council with official and non-official members of the central legislature, and the Auditor General reporting only on delegated subjects like education, health, sanitation but not on the navy or the army, on which reports were submitted through the Viceroy to the UK Parliament. PACs in India, at that juncture, had powers of making disallowances and imposing surcharges on the provincial governments, reflecting their essentially executive nature.

The Government of India Act, 1935, as is well known, ended diarchy and introduced direct elections. Among other things, it strengthened the

---

[2] 'Test audit' refers to an auditor drawing a sample of transactions from any account by first conducting a risk analysis of the accounts to determine the transactions s/he needs to examine in details to provide an assurance or otherwise that inherent and control risks have been satisfactorily dealt with by management.

position of the Auditor General by providing for Provincial Auditors General in a federal set-up. Soon, PACs similar to the central one were set up in the provincial legislatures as well. In 1936, Parliament notified the Accounts and Audit Order. It provided for a unified accounting and auditing arrangement for the whole of British India. While the defence, posts and telegraph (P and T), and railways had their own separate accounts services, the CAG prepared and compiled the accounts of all civil departments (central and state) and also audited the entire government receipts and expenditure, including those of the defence, P and T and railway departments. The then Auditor General in India exercised quasi-judicial powers in interpreting statutory rules like the Fundamental Rules.

History

What could have been on B.R. Ambedkar's mind when, as Chairman of the Drafting Committee, during the Constituent Assembly debates in 1949, he said: 'I am of the opinion that this dignitary or officer is probably the most important officer in the Constitution of India'? Again, why did he insist on the designation 'Comptroller and Auditor General of India' and not simply Auditor General?

The answer lies in the state of the nation at that juncture. While federalism had naturally grown out of the provincial legislatures as well as the requirements of integrating the princely states into the Union, the challenge of deploying armed forces to deal with communal riots had tilted the balance in favour of a centralized government. Ambedkar was acutely aware of the importance of not just setting up institutions, but thinking through the processes of governance. As a Dalit leader, the Constitution he envisaged was one that could serve as a vehicle of social change; Parliament had, therefore, to be unfettered in budgetary devices to support efforts for social change, and yet, it had to be responsible, for which a powerful institution of CAG was needed.

On 4 November 1948, while introducing the Draft Constitution, Ambedkar made a statement on the President in relation to the Council of Ministers and the general character of the executive:

> The presidential system of America is based upon the separation of the executive and the legislature, so that the President and his Secretaries cannot be members of the Congress. *The Draft Constitution does not*

recognize this doctrine. The ministers under the Indian Union are members of Parliament. Only members of Parliament can become ministers. Ministers have the same rights as other members of Parliament.... Under the non-Parliamentary system, such as the one that exists in USA, the assessment of the responsibility of the executive is periodic. It takes place once in several years. It is done by the electorate. In England, where the Parliamentary system prevails, the assessment of responsibility of the executive is both daily and periodic. The daily assessment is done by members of Parliament through questions, resolutions, no-confidence motions, adjournment motions and debates on Addresses. Periodic assessment is done by the electorate which may take place every five years or earlier. The daily assessment system is, it is felt, far more effective than the periodic assessment and far more necessary in a country like India. The Draft Constitution, in recommending the Parliamentary system of Government, *has preferred more responsibility to more stability*.[3] (emphasis added)

Ambedkar's statement had three far-reaching implications. One, participation of private Members of Parliament (MPs) and even of common citizens was ensured (for example, through deliberations parliamentary committees to which they could be invited) in what is often erroneously claimed to be the exclusive domain of the Council of Ministers, namely to determine 'policies'. It is important to dwell on this at some length.

The term 'policy' implies some long-term purpose in a broad subject field (for example, nationalization or privatization of coal mining), not a series of ad hoc decisions. Sometimes, however, we conceive of policy not so much as actively purpose-oriented but rather as a fairly cohesive set of responses to a problem that has arisen (for example, competitive bidding for any procurement). In the sphere of government activities, there are laws, rules, plans, programmes, and projects, each of these in succession being a little more short-term, more specific in place and timing than the previous, and each successively more executive rather than legislative.

In a parliamentary system the Council of Ministers, by themselves, can decide only on matters under the delegated authority of policies that are law, in limited fields of their application like directives, plans,

---

[3] H.R. Khanna, Judge, SC (retd), *Making of India's Constitution*. Eastern Book Company (reprinted 2009). Excerpt from Ambedkar quoted on pages 97–100.

programmes, and projects. For example, in 2012 the Council of Ministers allowed foreign direct investment (FDI) in multi-brand retail through the Foreign Investment Promotion Board, under authority delegated by company law and of the law governing the Reserve Bank of India (RBI). While a minister can suggest and introduce a bill, it is the House that passes it. Not a single rupee can be levied as a tax or spent on any item without the approval of the legislature.

While only Parliament can decide on policy at the level of a law, each and every citizen has the right, and even the duty, to influence it. Therefore, the CAG can and should influence policy, as it has been doing ever since the PAC of the second Lok Sabha requested the CAG to undertake performance audit. This influence grew in magnitude when the systems-based audit of revenues began in the 1960s which, on the recommendations of the PAC, helped the Ministry of Finance to frame amendments to various acts, rules, and procedures. Procedures exist for committees of Parliament to solicit the views of constitutional authorities, individual citizens, and 'publics' in the process of law making or formulating rules. Interpenetration of civil society and the state has been built into the system.

Second, in the parliamentary scheme of things, administrative accountability is limited to the bureaucracy in a narrow sense. Fukuyama naturally equates governance with the actual deployment of power by the bureaucracy because in the presidential form of government of the US (whose orientation to developing countries is his main worry), cabinet secretaries of state are part of the bureaucracy and not the legislature. In India, by contrast, the council of ministers comprises MPs.[4] In India, there is no strict separation of powers between the legislature and the executive; such separation only exists between the judiciary and the other organs. This requires us to exclude the Council of Ministers from the deployment of power (that is, of bureaucracy).

This modified definition of bureaucracy in a parliamentary democracy (as distinct from a presidential one) makes a big difference to the mechanism for transparency and accountability in financial matters. The politicians are left out of the reckoning in the entire process:

[4] F. Fukuyama, *State Building: Governance and World Order in the 21st Century* (Ithaca: Cornell University Press, 2004).

the CAG audits offices, ministries at the level of secretaries approve replies to his observations, and the PAC gathers oral evidence only from secretaries to government while examining CAG's reports. Neither the reports of CAG nor those of PAC, which are tabled in the House, are discussed there. What is more, PAC proceedings are held in camera. Not until a law is violated, in which case matters go to courts of law, does the minister feature. Thus, the responsibility of ministers in financial matters per se is not secured by parliamentary oversight in India. Because members of PAC interact freely with MPs of the ruling party outside committee meetings, this leaves a large space open for financial accountability issues to be negotiated among MPs. The case for an ombudsman (Lokpal), made by Hazare and his colleagues, rested on this basic lacuna in the scheme of financial accountability in India.

Third, only the Auditor General's department, which was already serving both the provincial legislatures and the central one, with expertise gathered over a century, could be an instrument to report to the president on the compliance by the government to the budgetary authorization by Parliament annually, to ensure the transfer of the legitimate share of taxes and grants to the states in a federal system of finance. Thus, CAG's unique and powerful positioning—outside the executive, judiciary, or even the legislature—owed a lot to Ambedkar's astute understanding that the legislature and executive would be intertwined and to the reputation for independent functioning that the institution had built up through the British period.

It would have been foolish to require the CAG to mop the floor with the financial tap on. Ambedkar, therefore, insisted on vesting the powers of a comptroller, along with auditor, to a CAG. The Accounts and Audit Order of 1936, containing the more comprehensive and detailed procedures and directives for audit, was adapted by the Government of India (Provisional Constitution) Order of 1947, and the Constitution in 1950 added Articles 148–151, which declared the independence of the CAG both from the executive and the legislature.

The 1936 Order contained the quasi-judicial powers of *comptrolling*—of exchequer control—which meant that the CAG must annually authorize the RBI to operate the bank accounts of the Union and state Governments, authorize monthly pay slips for salaries to be paid to government servants, check that sanctions supported the correctness of payments by treasuries and the transfers made by the RBI between government accounts, and maintain general provident fund accounts and service particulars of all employees. These functions found no mention in the Articles of the Constitution, but simply flowed from the designation as CAG and the adapting constitutional order of 1947.

Initiatives, 1950–71

Parliament did not enact legislation, as required by Article 149, to govern the duties and powers of CAG for 20 long years. This was partly due to the purposes of accounting being served adequately by CAG's countrywide organization under the 1936 Order, which continued to remain in force till 1971, and partly due to the capture of the parliament by the executive wing of government under a political scenario of one-party dominance. Officers enjoying the personal confidence of the prime minister were appointed as CAG. Despite the lack of a specific legislation, they succeeded in undertaking several far-reaching initiatives between 1950 and 1971, the year CAG's (Duties, Powers and Conditions of Service) Act was passed.

In the 1950s, a socialistic pattern of society, with a mixed economy, was emerging. When the Companies Act was introduced in the House in 1956, the CAG intervened to point out that 'a government company is a fraud on the Constitution' because there was no separation between management and ownership in the public sector joint stock companies envisaged. As a result, it argued, accountability would be seriously hampered. A compromise was struck with the device of providing for supplementary audit by CAG (Section 619 B), over and above the normal audit to be conducted by management-appointed chartered accountants. A new wing for commercial audit was set up to deal with the growing number of public sector companies.

Second, in view of the growing number of massive investment projects (like multipurpose hydroelectric power projects) and community development schemes launched by the central government, the second PAC of the second Lok Sabha requested CAG to report on the efficiency of public utilities and achievements of projects and programmes. This gave birth to the efficiency-cum-performance audits conducted by CAG, beginning in 1958.

Third, to strengthen the system of tax assessment and collection by the central and state revenue departments, a new genre of system-based audit of revenues was introduced. Fourth, the certification of accounts of a host of instrumentalities of State that sprang up—public utilities like state electricity boards (SEBs), transport corporations, housing boards, municipal corporations, universities, major port trusts, and others—wherever separate Acts governing them required audit by CAG. This strained his resources and the task was not rendered any easier by the fact that these institutions adopted various hybrid systems of accounts (cash-based accounts plus features of accrual accounting).

These new spheres of work were added on to the responsibilities for the audit of civil departments, defence establishments, railways, and the P and T departments. Each of these demanded staff deployment and acquiring specific audit expertise in the specific fields.

All these adaptive changes were incorporated in the various sections of the Act of 1971, which also equated the CAG in status and pay to a Supreme Court judge. Instrumentalities of State called autonomous bodies—registered under the Societies Registration Act, 1860, or created by acts governing them individually—were brought under the purview of government audit if substantially financed by government. The most important section introduced at this juncture was the one that related to the powers of the CAG to determine the scope and extent of his audit and make regulations for the same. Another important development was the decision on the recommendations of a task force, to rescind the 1936 Order of government, whereby the comptrolling functions were done away with, without having to change the designation of CAG through a Constitutional amendment.

Restructuring

In 1976, the departmentalized system of accounts was introduced at the Union government level to provide for Pay and Accounts Offices for each department throughout the country, while state governments continued to rely on a district-wise treasury system. This involved the splitting of the cadre of the Indian Audit and Accounts Service, with some of them joining the newly created Civil Accounts Service under a Controller General of Accounts (CGA) who would report to the Secretary (Expenditure) of Government of India (GoI) and maintain accounts with Controllers of Accounts posted to each department of the Union. This was also the juncture (during the brief period of emergency rule under Indira Gandhi) when the function of the CAG, of prescribing the form of accounts at Article 150, was whittled down by the 42nd Amendment and later urgently restored by the 44th Amendment.

By the mid-1970s, the rot in the institution of CAG due to the growth in the strength of staff unions was evident all around. It manifested itself in outright corruption while disbursing pension payments, demands by individual staff members to go on 'more lucrative' audit assignments, in the poor quality of audit certification of public utilities, and in semi-literate Group D employees being promoted to posts of auditors and conducting 'audits' of government offices. Rowdy behaviour of staff within the office premises was a common occurrence and an extortionist orientation while auditing offices of the government sullied the image of CAG.

Two specific aspects of the degeneration bear mention because they had tangible far-reaching effects. One was the certification by the Accountant General in the states of the accounts of SEBs. As is well known, superintending engineers (SEs) manning distribution circles had meters in their power stations which were supposed to indicate the total physical units of electricity flowing to the circle and he was required to account for that physical supply by him, which would be tallied against the total of bills raised and revenue collected from different categories of consumers. The SEs tampered with the meters so that the physical units necessary for rendering accounts were not available. The accounts of physical units supplied by SEs were drawn up by working backwards from the revenues realized and totalled up across all circles without any tallying with the reading of physical units received by each. The difference between the electricity generated by the SEB or purchased from the grid and the number of units for which revenues had been realized was declared to be transmission and distribution losses. Those who stole electricity, ranging from high-tension consumers to farmers and domestic users, paid the electricity workers fair bribes in return, but the SEBs collapsed and were unable to meet their dues to the National Thermal Power Corporation and National Hydroelectric Power Corporation. Through 20 long years, until the power sector reforms began in 1994,

State Auditor Generals (AGs) continued to certify the accounts of SEBs as true and fair.

The cadre of divisional accountants (DAs) who are recruited, posted, promoted by the Accountant Generals in the states but work under the supervision of executive engineers in public works divisions of the state government have always posed a major problem for the CAG's organization. Well versed in public works accounts, they were meant to be the first line of financial control in public works. However, lacking promotional avenues and finding it more profitable to cozy up with the contractors-fed engineers who carry cheque-drawing powers, they are well-connected with political elites and can quickly organize funds (derived from project-estimates) for large public rallies addressed by ministers. The second line of financial control for the divisions is the very AG's office which is their parent department. The original idea was to have an independent DA posted and transferred by the AG to keep control over the large financial powers delegated to engineers at remote locations of projects. But the arrangement never did work, because the AG could never exercise disciplinary control. Even when the vigilance wings of state governments detected signs of corruption and the engineers held preliminary inquiries, when files were sent by engineers to the AG they always lacked complete paperwork, and the delay in disciplinary proceedings helped the bounders to retire before a charge sheet could be issued. There is a strong case for this cadre to be handed over to the state governments but it is a rare AG who would part with the little comforts of guesthouses and vehicles that DAs can arrange for them during their tours in the districts.

By the 1980s, the maintaining of accounts of state governments by the CAG was recognized as a residual function. It no doubt provided a modicum of control over accounting practices of government offices by the CAG and facilitated all vouchers being available centrally for test check as far as the vouching function of audit was concerned, but it did not meet the international standards of audit which required a separation between those maintaining accounts and the auditors. Recognizing the need for separation but persuaded by state governments to continue to discharge the control function for accounts, a restructuring of the state civil audit offices (Accountants General) was carried out, establishing separate offices for the AG (Accounts and Entitlement, A and E) and the AG (Audit) reporting independently to CAG's office in New Delhi. This resulted in a complete break-down of the system for audit vouching for expenditure and ensuring proper accounting of receipts by treasuries. Not until the AG (A and E) offices were strengthened in the mid-1990s with a voucher-level computerization program did this mess get cleared up. A telling piece of evidence that attests to this mismanagement is the fact that no Combined Revenue and Finance Accounts could be produced between 1987 and 1995.

Performance Audit and Information Technology Audit

It is a measure of how comfortable the CAG felt vis-à-vis the government about his power to determine the scope and extent of audit that it took him until 2007 to frame and notify the regulations that were required to be notified by Section 23 of the CAG Act, 1971. Between 1971 and 2007, this power was exercised more to determine if 'special audit', meaning 100 per cent check, was warranted in particular cases referred by the government to CAG or cases he took up of his own volition. The 2007 notification was prompted by renewed interest among the global community of SAIs for performance audit. The regulations followed the framing of a new manual for performance audit in 2005.

Most developed countries deploy about 70 per cent of their resources on performance audits whereas developing countries, with poorer systems of accounting and compliance with laws, keep their SAIs engaged more with financial and compliance auditing. Performance audits can be of two kinds: compliance-oriented (are things being done right?) or research oriented (are the right things being done?). Again, with a few exceptions, only the SAIs of developed countries have ventured so far into research-oriented performance auditing, which contributes to the public discourse. SAIs in developing countries are more attuned to compliance-oriented performance audits. Auditing through computers (called IT Audit) is a means of risk-based audit planning, thereby reducing the staff requirement for financial audits. IT auditing began in earnest by CAG in the mid-1990s and has grown along with the computerization of accounts by government departments. With a training institution called International Centre for Information Systems and Audit established by the CAG in 2002, the Indian Audit and Accounts Department (IAAD) has gained a fair reputation globally in this field. This has yet to show results on a much larger scale of shift of auditors from financial to performance audit, but that is likely to happen as the old auditors retire over the years and younger persons join the organization.

At present, the CAG's organization has about 45,000 employees, audits 50,000 organizational units each year, and submits 135 reports to Union and state legislatures. With all the add-ons, the problem of staffing the department with adequately qualified personnel has been felt acutely at the field levels, but due to the immense clout enjoyed by staff unions, the policy pursued was to create promotional avenues for existing cadres of audit clerks and office-help, even to levels of responsibility for accounting and audit, rather than assert the provisions of Article 148(5) to induct qualified persons into the department. This human resources policy of appeasing staff unions had disastrous consequences for the department's image and performance. It was not until the late-1990s that the unions were finally beaten back and there was a semblance of heads of offices starting to work as such. To meet acute staff shortages at the middle level of audit professionals, periodic recruitments on a very limited scale, through the selection conducted by the Union Public Service Commission (UPSC), have shown encouraging results. Induction of more such officials by reducing the number of clerical staff would help the department to invert the pyramid in its personnel structure.

The training wing in the CAG's organization has been well set up, with two international training centres [International Centre for Information Systems and Audit (iCISA), Noida, and International Centre for Environment Audit and Sustainable Development (iCED), Jaipur], a national academy for IAAS Officers (Shimla), and 13 Regional Training Institutes for audit professionals. Training is also carried on within field offices and by sending staff to training institutions outside the department. A core team of trainers has been created by putting together officers who have undergone an extensive training of trainers' course at IDI (INTOSAI Development Initiative), the training wing of INTOSAI. The IDI training is directed more at livening up the training experience, which is valuable, but it is somewhat weak on professional content. This aspect can be corrected by enlisting support by institutions for private sector audits, or through twinning projects to work with SAIs in developed countries, especially in the area of developing capacity for performance auditing.

No permanent faculty has been installed at CAG's training institutions; all faculty is drawn from the expertise within the department and other government departments. This is administratively wise, but unless visiting faculty members for a course are assembled at least four days in advance to plan their lessons, the courses conducted often lack the professional edge. Fewer but better well-delivered courses are needed for which officers have to devote more time out of their over-crowded schedules, with a greater sense of their leadership role.

However, a change in the training capacity has to follow a re-envisioning of the role of the CAG, a new mandate in the context of the twenty-first century, and strategic planning by the organization.

CAG and Oversight Committees

The government budget is no longer a matter of voting the king's supplies from a stagnant pool of resources to fight wars. What India calls an 'annual financial statement' in its Constitution is not merely a statement of revenues and expenditure classified under different heads. Apart from the finance and appropriation bills, there are other documents—such as the finance minister's speech, outcome/gender budgets, and statements on macroeconomic policy and compliance with the Fiscal Responsibility and Budget Management Act, 2003 (FRBM)—which together constitute what we call the 'Budget'. The Union budget also incorporates the decisions of government on the recommendations of the erstwhile Planning Commission as well as the Finance Commission. It is a macroeconomic intervention in the ever-widening, ever-growing ambit of circulation of goods, services, money, new technologies, and above all, of public opinion related to taxation, borrowing, public spending, and the economy. The macroeconomic budget at the level of the Union combines fiscal, monetary, and pricing policies.

The authorization by Parliament is a performance-linked authorization. The CAG is vested with the responsibility of overseeing the management of the budget by line and finance ministries, from the time it is voted until the annual accounts are reported to legislatures, in accordance with the intent and purposes of the authorization. As per parliamentary rules, the CAG's reports are examined by the PAC, except for the ones prepared on commercial undertakings, which are examined by the Committee on Public Undertakings (COPU). Over time, a convention also developed that the CAG would assist the Estimates Committee whenever required.

Estimates Committee

Parliament established an Estimates Committee in 1950 to examine the budget estimates *prior to its presentation in the House*. By design, the report of the Committee would not be submitted for a discussion in Parliament or subject to a vote, but its recommendations would be implemented by the government as they were. If the government were to find the recommendations impracticable, it would refer that matter back to the Committee and the dispute was to be settled by mutual negotiation.

The role of the Committee was articulated by India's first Finance Minister, John Mathai, in his Budget Speech for 1950–1:

> This Budget is being presented under the new Constitution. From that fact there are two matters that arise to which I would like to invite the attention of the House. The first is this, that the Constitution lays down a somewhat elaborate procedure for the consideration and discussion of the Budget … I would like to say at this stage, that, as far as I am concerned, I would like the Standing Finance Committee to continue at the same time. There is a real distinction between the work of the Standing Finance Committee and the work of the proposed Estimates Committee. The Standing Finance Committee is concerned with specific proposals of expenditure by each Department of Government, but the Estimates Committee's business would be to make a comprehensive examination of expenditure in relation to the resources available to Government. The real business of the Estimates Committee would, therefore, be taking the policy and the objectives of Government (with which they are not concerned) to suggest how this policy and these objectives could be carried out with the least expenditure of public resources. That, Sir, is the first matter to which I would like to refer as arising from the introduction of the Constitution.

Borrowing by government became an increasingly important component of public resources, but became passé under the moral weight of Keynesian economics. Surprisingly, instead of a corresponding enhancement of the importance of the Estimates Committee, the opposite happened, that too, surprisingly, in the post-economic reforms period. In 1993, the Standing Committee on Finance was enlarged and converted into as many as 17 (further, in 2004, into 24) departmentally related Standing Committees that report *only* on Demand for Grants but not on *borrowing by government*. These not only replaced the Standing Committee on Finance but also diminished the importance of the Estimates Committee, which still exists under Rule 311 of the Rules of Procedure and Proceedings of Parliament (and incidentally, is the only committee empowered to review even an existing policy of Parliament) but only reports on the functioning of sundry government organizations, not on changes required in the budget as a whole. The reasons for this curious development are shrouded in mystery and have been held very close to their chest by successive governments.

Financial Responsibility

Prodded by the CAG since 1986, the PAC initiated efforts to convince the government about the need for Parliament to enact a fiscal responsibility and budget management act to operationalize Article 292 of the Constitution, which states that 'the executive power of the Union extends to borrowing upon the security of the Consolidated Fund of India within such limits, if any, as may from time to time be fixed by Parliament by law and to the giving of guarantees within such limits, if any, as may be so fixed'.

At long last, in 2003, Parliament passed the Fiscal Responsibility and Budget Management Act (henceforth, FRBM Act), which grants the Union government the responsibility to ensure inter-generational equity in fiscal management; long-term macro-economic stability; sufficient revenue surplus; prudential debt management through limits on Union government borrowings, debt and deficits; and greater transparency in fiscal operations of the Union government. The act also requires the government to eliminate any fiscal impediments to the effective conduct of monetary policy.

The primary purpose of the FRBM Act, 2003 was to eliminate the government's revenue deficit and bring it down to a manageable 3 per cent of gross domestic product (GDP) by March 2008. However, due to the international financial crisis of 2007–8 that started in the US, the deadline for implementation of the targets in the Act was initially postponed and subsequently altogether suspended in 2009. In 2011, given the process of ongoing recovery, the Economic Advisory Council advised the government to reconsider reinstating the provisions of the FRBM Act. As of the presentation of the budget 2013, this was yet to be heeded. The consequences of the government's cavalier attitude to the fiscal deficit were felt by Indians both on the devaluation of the currency and inflation fronts. With a fall in global oil prices, the Union budget of 1916–17 has finally returned to the path of fiscal correction and aims to bring down the fiscal deficit to 3 per cent of GDP.

A controversy erupted even in 2003 over the wisdom of the FRBM Act. A motley set of Left-oriented economists spread canards about the World Bank having prompted the move, without realizing that it was clearly in pursuance of a longstanding constitutional provision. The criticism gathered steam during and beyond the period of the global economic crisis, when all governments pursued increased spending. Though this issue is beyond the scope of this chapter, readers would find a succinct rebuttal of all the criticism levelled in the stout defence of the FRBM Act by the Chairman and Secretary of the Prime Minister's Economic Advisory Council in Manmohan Singh's UPA government.[5] This chapter underlines the fact that the debate of economists often misses a simple point about budgets: that the deficit is only about a difference between revenues and expenditure; as long as revenue collection is strong, there is no bar to incurring high expenditure.

The ability to collect revenues is one of the best indicators of state strength and India does not score well on this reckoning. Government has been hamstrung by a high level of corruption in the revenue collecting arm. It has not helped that the governments have been scam-ridden and too weak to deny exemptions to influential business lobbies. Unless the leash of an FRBM Act is put on government, populist propensities propel it towards incurring higher deficits instead of improving revenue administration and investing, say, in agricultural development, or by privatizing inefficient public sector companies. What economists tend to forget, but auditors do not, is that the contingent liabilities of government in India are very high. The lending by banks/insurance companies to persistently loss-making public-sector units underwritten by government and the non-performing assets of banks by themselves

[5] D.C. Rangarajan and D. Subbarao, 'The Importance of Being Earnest about Fiscal Responsibility', Working Paper, Madras School of Economics, 2007.

are a major cause for concern over and above the fiscal deficits officially shown in government budgets and accounts. A final point in support of the FRBM legislation is that it is governed by a constitutional provision (Article 292) which wisely includes a far-sighted phrase about the limits of borrowing 'that may be fixed from time to time'.[6] This provides sufficient room for adjustments as and when trade cycles demand it.

In sum, by the time India acquired its FRBM Act, the Estimates Committee for oversight had been dismembered. Instead of progressing, systems for pre-budget scrutiny by the legislature regressed.

Public Accounts Committee

In 1950, a change in the legislative rules transformed the nature of the PAC (first set up in 1922) from being essentially an executive committee to a parliamentary committee that is supervised by the Speaker and assisted by the Lok Sabha Secretariat. The concerns of the PAC expanded in scope over time, successively, from the scrutiny of proper handling of public funds, combating fraud and corruption, getting the most from tax revenue, ensuring effectiveness of public programmes, and improving public financial management systems. Any expenditure incurred in excess of voted budget estimates under any particular head of account (for example, for education) has to be regularized by the PAC. For this, the PAC has the benefit of CAG's reports on appropriation accounts, as well as findings as a result of financial, compliance, and performance audits. After examination of CAG's reports by the PAC, its recommendations are framed and reported to the House. The administration is required to submit action-taken reports on the same.

When the PAC was an executive committee, it enjoyed immense clout. However, when it changed into a parliamentary committee, it had few powers. Shri G.V. Mavalankar, a celebrated parliamentarian and the first Speaker of Lok Sabha, believed that the constituent parts of the state machinery must work together in a spirit of mutual appreciation and cooperation in the service of the people. Several public

---

[6] Article 292 reads: 'The executive power of the Union extends to borrowing upon the security of the Consolidated Fund of India within such limits, if any, as may from time to time be fixed by Parliament by law and to the giving of guarantees within such limits, if any, as may be so fixed.'

spirited secretaries to government and successive CAGs have reiterated the need for different organs of State to realize the importance of this commonness of the national purpose of administrators, audit, and committees of Parliament. However, with fading memories of the national movement and pre-eminence gained by the executive, the triadic functioning was vitiated.[7]

The last straw in tilting the balance towards the executive came in 1980, when a bureaucratic stratagem was rolled out by the Union ministries to bypass the state legislatures and reach development funds directly to registered societies called District Rural Development Agencies (DRDA). Early in their careers, district collectors were exposed to the powers and prestige of being spenders in a system where only a chain of administrative orders, and not a governing law for local self-government, existed. Administrators came to be groomed in the powers of pre-eminence early in their careers. Legislative and administrative mechanisms for safeguarding public monies in a spirit of 'mutual appreciation and cooperation' between administrators, auditors, and committees of legislatures wilted in the face of the pre-eminence of one constituent. The cold fact that has emerged in India is that administration does not care two hoots for accountability because it can be papered over quite easily.

This is not to suggest that the PAC has been totally ineffectual. As already stated, it was instrumental in prodding the government to legislate the FRBM Act. On several occasions, based on the examination of numerous CAG reports, it has suggested refinements in policy. For instance, while examining the CAG report on the Integrated Rural Development Program (IRDP) which offered unsecured soft loans to small and marginal farmers as well as the landless for their self-employment, PAC appreciated the impossibility of converting the landless overnight into entrepreneurs, as pleaded by the government, and recommended that funds be shifted from IRDP to enable the landless to be covered by a much larger quantum of wage-employment. This led up to the transformation of the Employment *Assurance* Program to the Mahatma Gandhi National Rural Employment Guarantee Act (MGNREGA) with its scheme (MGNREGS), as an employment *guarantee* programme.

[7] C. Singh, *Common Property and Common Poverty* (New Delhi: Oxford University Press, 1986).

Annual reports of Lok Sabha Secretariat on the functioning of parliamentary financial committees state that 70 per cent of the PAC's recommendations are acted on by the government. However, what goes unsaid is that this 70 per cent relate to homilies about 'better planning and coordination' or requests to 'reconsider' certain matters. Cases where any punitive action has been taken after fixing responsibility are few and far between. Members of the PAC themselves, during committee meetings, have often expressed complete frustration about the fact that their recommendations are not heeded by the ministries.

Apart from the fact that the PAC enjoys few powers since 1950 other than that of moral suasion, several aspects of its functioning also contribute to its general ineffectuality. For one, if a member of PAC is elected for only one year and not the full term of the House, he or she cannot possibly gain deep knowledge in examining matters before the PAC. Second, there are chinks in a system where the Chairman is free to decide the procedures for its functioning. For example, the annually constituted PAC convenes to select the subjects it wants to examine from among the comments of CAG in its various reports. The subjects carried over from the previous year's PAC (for example, those whose examination could not be taken up or completed) are usually included in the list of matters to be examined by the new PAC.

However, there is no hard and fast rule that is followed. This provides flexibility to the PAC but it also lends itself to abuse. For instance, he can drop the earlier subjects. Or, after deciding on including them, the Chairman can delay the examination of particular subjects till the annual turnover of membership of PAC brings in new members and the subject is subsequently forgotten. The scope for such abuse has increased over time, with the increase in the number of voluminous reports submitted by the CAG. This increase in volume of matters reported to the PAC is a direct measure of the lack of the deterrent power of audits.

Third, the secretaries of the ministries of the Union simply state at PAC hearings that they have written to state governments for action to be taken on objections raised by CAG or comments of CAG on development programmes financed by the Union but implemented by the states, and wash their hands off the matter. This will be corrected to a large extent now that the transfer of most schemes and devolution of funds for development to states has been ushered in by the Fourteenth Finance Commission.

Fourth, chairmen of the PAC often fail to conduct proceedings with a judicial mind. They allow secretaries to approach them over telephone calls outside of official channels, permit witnesses to submit an ever-increasing number of documents confounding the oral hearing stage, allow secretaries to bring along a large number of subordinates to explain specifics enabling them to avoid personally grasping the issues raised in the CAG reports, and—to make matters worse—permit the growing frustration of members to turn to a tendency to humiliate the secretary appearing before them as witness. The asymmetry of power, or 'grilling', as it is called in common parlance, results in major dysfunction. When pressed to take action, the secretary readily agrees, returns red-faced to his office, and issues a circular, reiterating earlier directions. As a result, the compendium of instructions grows fatter, reducing further the chances of anyone other than the dealing clerk to be familiar with the latest instructions.

While there is no taboo on discussion of the PAC's reports in the House, the general practice is not to engage in dialogue. Since the House does not make cash authorizations but increasingly relies on performance-linked authorizations, it is essential that the general practice be reviewed. Furthermore, the proceedings of the PAC are neither open to the press nor to the public. This alienates the PAC from the common citizen who would like to be reassured that probity and accountability indeed exist in the system. These issues have been discussed from time to time by conferences of PACs of both Parliament and state legislatures. Each time, the refrain of the legislators has been that the committee would not retain its bi-partisan spirit if proceedings are open to the public. It is difficult to concede that the double-speak of legislators should be acceptable for any 'larger' public purpose. The steep decline in the prestige of the PAC at the centre has added to the pathetic status of the PACs of the state legislatures, where, it is said, that it is the rare Speaker—let alone the PAC Chairman—who can look the chief minister in the eye.

Challenges for CAG

On several occasions, the CAG's observations and comments appeared to be very critical of the party in power. When a scandal related to the purchase of jeeps broke out in the early 1950s, and the CAG was criticized for compromising the defence of India, Lok Sabha Speaker Ayyangar ruled that no member could criticize the CAG on the floor of the House unless a substantive motion (that is, for impeachment) was brought against him. This ruling has held since then—through various scandals: Bofors, the bundling of good and bad shares for disinvestment of public sector companies, and the Kargil coffins debacle. By and large, the CAG has been accorded due regard by parliamentarians and judges alike.

Even the unseemly attacks by ruling party members in the media in the context of the 2G and coal block allocations reports by the CAG, in 2010 and 2012, respectively, did not succeed in tarnishing the image of Vinod Rai, who headed the institution during this eventful period. In fact, the opposite happened. The responses of the government laid bare the inadequacy of legislative and administrative mechanisms for safeguarding public monies in India. The manner in which PAC members fell out among themselves on partisan lines in examining the 2G report, and the constitution of a joint parliamentary committee (JPC) to superscribe the work of the PAC, with a ruling party member appointed as the JPC Chairman, damaged the dignity of Parliament. Rai, who tabled these very effective reports, injected a combative element in the functioning of the institution by enlisting communicating with citizens through the media.

The agency had, until that point, remained reclusive as far as media was concerned. The new modality of engagement quite naturally opens up the organization to being itself subjected to media trials if the occasion arises. In the opinion of the author, this is a risk well worth taking, because it is only by engaging and opening itself up to whatever criticism might be levelled would the organization be able to improve on its own standards of functioning.

Felt ever more acutely since the 1980s, the lack of credibility of the parliamentary system for accountability occupies the centre-stage in public concerns today. The persistent pleas of citizens that the menace of corruption be fought with laws have gone unheeded thus far. Most Indians are aware that corruption became further entrenched in Indian politics in 1993, when the ruling party of the day bought votes to survive a no-confidence motion in Parliament. Many eminent jurists in India were disappointed when the Supreme Court upheld the challenge to the prosecution of the bribe-takers and the cases against them were dismissed on grounds of Article 105(2) of the Constitution of India, which says that no MP can be made liable to any proceedings in any court in respect of any vote given by him/her in Parliament.[8] Many courts in other parliamentary democracies like Australia and Canada have taken the opposite view; similar provisions in their constitutions cannot be taken to mean that they prohibit inquiry into activities that are incidentally related to legislative affairs but are not part of the legislative process itself.

Again, amendments sought in 2008 to the Prevention of Corruption Act, 1988, to remove the requirement of prior sanction of government for prosecution of public servants, were put in cold storage, where they remain. While the cabinet, in April 2015, approved modifications to the Prevention of Corruption Act Amendment Bill of 2013, Parliament has not yet acted. In the absence of the leadership of the parliament or of the judiciary in combating corruption, the SAI needs to step into a much more proactive role than would be required of the department otherwise. SAIs are organs of the state established to assure legislatures and citizens that the executive has adequately addressed the risks associated with public finances. This general assurance is, of course, subject to their specific comments in reports to legislatures. Historically, these assurances have served governments well; by and large, SAIs have enjoyed regard and respect in the portals of power. However, doubts have been raised about how well founded the assurances are, given the media reports about fraud, corruption, and regulatory failures.

The various reports of the CAG would likely strike an independent observer as highly repetitive in the nature of comments made year after year regarding irregularities noted by audit. This reflects, to a large extent, the persistence of the same type of irregularities in the absence of strict corrective action by government on earlier reports about the same or similar matter. However, to a professional auditor's gaze, this recurrence would also reflect the absence of any serious attempt at audit planning in which a risk-assessment of the entity would take the persistence of the irregularities as information indicating that deeper probe of possible systemic failures in internal controls of the respective offices need to be forcefully reported.

[8] F. Nariman, *The State of the Nation* (New Delhi: Hay House India, 2013), 272.

In a large number of cases, the quality of inspection reports issued to government offices after an audit was concluded leaves much to be desired. Similarly, the quality of performance audits conducted by CAG has been very uneven. Unlike financial and compliance audits, which are part of the assurance that risks have been addressed by government, performance audits are meant to present a report that adds value to the social discourse on the efficiency, economy, and effectiveness in the public sector and contributes to improving the functioning of government. As such, reports on performance audit have to be fair and balanced. A 2011 peer review noted that as many as half the performance reports are not balanced.

With the help of INTOSAI's standards and guidance notes, the office of the CAG is trying to address the problem of low professional standards that have surfaced in the last two decades. The sheer scale and complexity of all-India performance audits by CAG requires that adequate attention be paid to planning, executing, and reporting on them. Placing audit findings in the appropriate perspective and reporting more fully against the audit objectives, more regular inclusion of programme outcomes, and positive findings would contribute to the fair and balanced presentation of audit reports. Focusing a lot more on the design of audits—audit objectives, appropriate criteria, key audit questions related to the audit objectives, and the extent and quality of evidence supporting performance audit findings and conclusions—would help. Seeking comments from third parties on relevant audit findings would help even more in informing audit conclusions and readers of the reports.

Performance auditing spans two different kinds of questions: are things being done right and are the right things being done? While the CAG's organization has accumulated a fair amount of expertise in addressing audits of the first kind, its abilities in planning and executing audits addressing the second type of question are very limited. This is not because CAG officials and auditors deployed on performance audits are not highly qualified or experienced, but because different modalities for learning about the experiences of persons placed in different institutions or as recipients of government services is crucial to deciphering what the key audit questions might be, or where the information to support the lines of enquiry might be available. In many respects, performance audit of the second kind resembles social research and the problem of method in performance auditing is quite as daunting as social research, since it requires establishing cause and effect relationships.

Social Accountability Mechanisms

Across the globe, citizens have grown increasingly despondent about the trust they repose in the architecture of public financial management of their governments. In many countries, civil society has raised serious doubts about the effectiveness of existing mechanisms to provide financial stability with efficient delivery of social services, along with containing corruption.[9]

It is perhaps this growing restiveness of the citizens in many countries that prompted the United Nations General Assembly (UNGA) to adopt three resolutions[10] related to audit institutions—on 22 December 2011, 27 December 2014, and the resolution adopting the Addis Ababa Action Agenda in 2015.[11] Expressing concern for the efficiency, accountability, transparency, and effectiveness of public administration, the resolutions underlined the need for member-states to uphold the principle of independence of SAIs and recognized their important role in promoting the completion of the Millennium Development Goals (MDGs) and furthering the SDGs.

The United Nations works with national governments, and not all of them always comply with whatever they themselves have also been signatories to. Separation of powers in democracy which works through checks and balances in the interplay of institutions is wonderful as long as all of them serve a common public purpose. But when they curl up as insular elite bodies, impervious to public concerns and unassailable by any quarter that falls outside this rarefied circle, then we witness

[9] Department of Economic and Social Affairs, United Nations, *Citizen Engagement Practices by Supreme Audit Institutions* (New York: United Nations, 2013).

[10] United Nations General Assembly, Resolution 66/209, 'Promoting the Efficiency, Accountability, Effectiveness and Transparency of Public Administration by Strengthening Supreme Audit Institutions', 15 March 2012.

[11] Note paragraph 30 of the Resolution on Addis Ababa Action Agenda in particular, which was adopted in the Declaration of the Sustainable Development Goals by UN in 2015.

continuous erosion of the legitimacy of ostensibly democratic states. Alexis de Tocqueville pointed out that in modern democracies, freedom of association is the real safeguard, not only against the authority of the State but also against the tyranny of the majority. A restrictive system of accountability, where public audit is misconstrued as an institutional preserve of SAIs (who are invested with a privileged voice) and the prevalent channel of reporting by SAIs is only to a hierarchy of officialdom and legislatures, leaving direct participation by common citizens or even civil society institutions in the processes out of the framework, is clearly not acceptable in the current 'flat' world.

In the context of an increasing number of countries with democratic form without substance, in the run-up to the UNGA resolutions, the 21st UN/INTOSAI Symposium on Effective Practices of Cooperation between Supreme Audit Institutions and Citizens to Enhance Public Accountability, held in July 2011, assumed importance. The Symposium addressed the values and benefits of cooperation between SAIs, parliaments, and citizens. SAIs are now officially aware of what seemed to have faded from their memories over the last four decades, that they should explore and possibly undertake partnerships for engagement with citizens and civil society out of a common concern for transparency and accountability. At the International Congress of Supreme Audit Institutions (INCOSAI) held in Beijing in October 2013, delegates adopted as an imperative that SAIs move beyond serving as 'just an accountant' and discharge a critical role in good governance. Concerted action by the CAG to orchestrate various initiatives of his organization in this direction is required in India.

The nascent social movement for social audit in India, which dates back to 1996, to enhance public accountability was also discussed at the Symposium. Defining transparency not merely as visibility of whatever might be chosen to be displayed by the State, but more substantively, as the process of seeking correspondence between the registers of experiences/memories in the minds of people and the registers of the State, the decade-long civil society campaign for transparency in India succeeded in finally wresting the Right to Information Act (RTI Act) from the legislature in 2005.[12] The enthusiasm with which individual

---

[12] An earlier version, Freedom of Information Act of 2003, was approved by Parliament, but never notified by the government.

citizens have been using this right since 2005 heralds, some say, the beginning of a transformation in civil administration.

Practices of social auditing organized by civil society organizations or informally by the media have been growing since 1996 and now leverage the RTI Act. The results of social audit practices in unearthing corruption, irregularities, sub-standard work, poor planning, and inefficiency in delivery mechanisms have been encouraging. A specific kind of social audit has been recognized by the government, as an audit it facilitates but is conducted by the citizens, especially by those people who are most affected by or are the intended beneficiaries of the state government schemes under the Mahatma Gandhi National Rural Employment Guarantee Scheme Act, 2005. It enables persons granted an entitlement or benefit by a government programme, scheme, or project to access related accounts and records to verify or question the same at public hearings arranged for the purpose in the presence of local residents, concerned sarpanchs (elected village chiefs), *gram sewak*s (officials of local bodies), facilitators, officials implementing the Scheme, and observers like government officials and persons from other walks of life willing to join the proceedings.

Social audit as a practice has been welcomed by citizens (especially the poor) as the appropriate means of securing the accountability of officials and politicians alike due to its demonstrated ability to gather a diverse array of concerned citizens—conducted on media platforms or in local assemblies—to engage in piecing together evidence of irregularity/corruption, whether in high-tech privatization projects (for example, Dhabol Power Project) or on delivery of simple social services, depending on the matter at hand. What is distinctive about social audit is the fact that *persons investigate the reasons for their own subjugation* (not that of others) in a given predicament and this leads to a voyage of discovery when others join in with their professional or social concerns. It involves speaking truth to power in the presence of the adversary or wrongdoer, which requires immense courage, marshalling of evidence, and communicative action for it to remain a peaceful affair. The value of social audit lies in its ability to pry open the elements involved in collusive corruption and disturbing the conspiracy of silence that surrounds it. This daring to speak out revivifies a moral sphere, without which the notion of financial accountability remains just so much ineffectual paperwork. The administrative framework of mere compliance with a rational-legal set of rules is supplemented (at times even supplanted) by the relatively more pragmatic moral judgement of local residents.

Consultations with advisory groups and professional organizations made up of citizens from all disciplines are another way of involving citizens in an SAI's audit planning. A system of inviting complaints from citizens and monitoring their investigation by all agencies of government has been introduced by SAI of South Korea, with significant results. SAIs of Chile and Argentina have been engaged in a similar manner since 2009. A close collaboration between eminent journalists and the SAI, as being tried out in Poland, is yet another interesting example of the ways in which SAIs are trying to secure accountability in their respective countries.

In the Indian context, the need for the CAG to quickly forge stronger relationships with civil society and media is essential due to the recent trend in national legislation. For one, Parliament passed constitutional amendments for 'local self-government with a development orientation' in 1992–3 but the CAG's responsibilities were not extended to audit of the transactions of local bodies. Since the amendments have emphasized the development orientation more than the regulatory functions, local bodies have continued to serve as mere conduits of finance. State government bureaucracies have been obdurate about not devolving financial and cadre-control powers to local bodies. There are indications that large municipalities, struggling under the sheer weight of coping with the strains of urbanization, are waking up to their increased responsibilities. The devolution by the GoI to the states, of 50 per cent of revenues of Union and state governments, recommended by the Fourteenth Finance Commission and operationalized by Government of India from Fiscal Year Budget 2015–16 onwards, has been a major step towards decentralizing finances. However, the capacity to safeguard good use of the funds is trailing this development, which is being left alarmingly far behind.

The power to arrange for auditors of local bodies (which is not within the purview of the CAG Act, 1971) was left by the constitutional amendments to state governments, with the result that cosmetic changes were introduced in 1994–5 by the states to the archaic Local Fund Audit (LFA) acts of the British Raj. Indeed, the Twelfth Finance Commission, which recommends on sharing of tax proceeds between the Union and states along with grants to local bodies, complained about the disarray of accounting information on local bodies and suggested that powers of technical guidance and supervision (TG and S) of offices of Directors (LFA) be vested with the CAG. The Thirteenth Finance Commission reiterated this and asked for reports of Directors (LFA) and the CAG on TG and S to be tabled in state legislatures. These recommendations were accepted by government and have been complied with in a perfunctory manner, without significant improvements in the accounting practices of rural local bodies, though some of the municipal corporations have undergone remarkable improvement in accounting systems.

Second, since 2005, national legislation conferred various rights to citizens—for employment to rural labour, basic education for children, food at subsidized rates for two-thirds of the population, and of dwelling in forests for original inhabitants. Therefore, the CAG is obliged to report to the president on the economy, efficiency, and effectiveness of programmes to deliver these rights. Third, to actually get these rights, on their part, citizens and civil society need to set up mechanisms for social accountability.

The CAG's obligation translates into a much larger deployment of human resources for performance audits than exists now, which is about 17 per cent of staff strength. In a knowledge economy, the fresh insights he can provide, to all stakeholders, about the reasons for glitches in accounting and service delivery, especially where rights of citizens are concerned, is what will count. As per the guidelines issued by INTOSAI, performance auditing is not related to providing any assurance to stakeholders about systems for programmes/projects being in place, propriety and regularity of expenditure, and so forth. It is simply about contributing to a public discourse by studying topical national issues and reporting on them after examining cause and effect relationships among the findings to arrive at audit conclusions and making constructive recommendations. However, in this scenario of service delivery for entitlement of citizens, performance audits will need to also provide an assurance, in much the same way that financial and compliance audits do. Given the wide spread of operations of government and the fact that the devil lies in the details, with the limited resources at his command, it is unclear how the CAG will meet this expectation.

While there can be no blueprint for building an architecture for social accountability mechanisms for rights-based entitlements of citizens, drawing on the history of the struggles of Mazdoor Kisan Shakti Sangathan (MKSS) leading campaigns for RTI and social audit, helps to delineate its important features. These mechanisms have to be assessed in terms of two parameters: (i) do they improve the efficiency and effectiveness of service delivery by the state?; and (ii) do they impact the socio-economic structure at a deeper level to contribute to social change?

The initial struggles for social audit by MKSS in Rajasthan had begun in 1990 in the face of collusive corruption between rural manual workers and the public works department. Workers had resigned themselves to be contented with payment of part of the wages and the offer by public works departments (PWDs) that they could work for less hours or indifferently. This settlement characterized all of public works projects undertaken by local contractors in the country, to greater or lesser degrees of the intensity of work demanded and proportion of wages paid in different regions. The resultant 'savings' on labour estimates for the works were shared by the PWD officials and the local elite. MKSS persuaded workers to pluck up their courage to demand full payment for work done with measurement up to specifications in the schedule of rates.

This involved an arduous struggle over several years and marked the point of departure for a demand for information and documents like muster rolls. Once the battle was won, the spark lit the prairie fire. With the movement for social audit spreading in various pockets of the country, and then the MGNREGS mounted, the era of collusive corruption on public works—less payment-for-less work—was challenged at the roots by organization of manual labourers. This was *political* change.

One of the remarkable features of the social accountability mechanism set up by the consortium of NGOs and Government of Andhra Pradesh in 2006 (based on the experiences of MKSS) is that it began with a recasting of the schedule of rates for payment of wages based on a work study by the Department of Rural Development to determine how many earth works could be done in a day by a group of workers without the use of heavy machinery like bulldozers. Since the PWD schedule of rates was based on use of machinery and MGNREGS did not allow the use of machinery, a new schedule of rates was drawn up. This raised the fair wage rate, equal to agricultural wage rates, dramatically, in Andhra Pradesh. The strong inputs of training and the diligence with which the audits were carried out, by boys/girls drawn from manual worker households, combined with Information and Communication Technology applications and most importantly, action taken for recoveries for misdemeanours found, have lent the system credibility. Equal wages for men and women are being paid and wage levels for agricultural labour in the districts have risen.

Another problem in public works-oriented programmes was the absence of asset registers maintained by the districts. District collectorates used to maintain them, but ever since DRDAs took over in 1980, they fell into disuse. Nobody knew if the road they were being shown was constructed under a current sanction order or one of yesteryear's. Apparently, asset registers have since been reconstructed in all the districts of the state. If so, at last a government auditor can compare the payment of wages against proof of work done. This is no small achievement in terms of the efficiency and effectiveness of delivery systems.

This is not to say that MGNREGS has become a demand-driven or labour budget-based programme in Andhra Pradesh or anywhere else. The trouble is that when you guarantee 100 days of work for a household and ask them to apply for work, how is the household to decide which dates one or the other family member wants work over the several months of the year, except in situations of extreme distress? The application forms were, until recently, thumb impressed or signed by workers but left blank for young assistants engaged casually by panchayat (village-level local body) offices to fill in as and when work orders were issued. To add to the woes, even when labour budgets are collated and sent to the Union Ministry of Rural Development, funds continue to be released as per the convenience of the financial convenience of government at that point of time. The Supreme Court has recently (2016) taken a serious note of the government's failures to abide by the law and its own commitments even in a situation of drought.[13]

Our concern at present is whether Local Fund Audit Offices of state governments or the CAG's organization on its own can shoulder the responsibility of conducting quality audit of local bodies, given the fact

[13] 'SC to Centre: Provide to Drought-hit States Immediately', *Indian Express*, 7 April 2016.

that there are so many throughout the country. Quite apart from logistics, there are issues about maintaining the ethical standards of auditors involved in such an undertaking. Social accountability mechanisms are gradually filling this space. They are premised on changing the power relations between hapless rural workers and capricious local officials in league with labour contractors and landed interests. In theory, it goes without saying that civil society organizations would be the appropriate agencies for social audit, but in practice, given the enormity of the problems posed by contractors and farmer lobbies, when it comes to implementing rights-based programmes, without the support of the State in India, it is questionable how far civil society organizations would be able to successfully carry forward the audits alongside actually redressing grievances of citizens at different sites along the programme delivery chain.

Due to the specific complementarities possible between the kind of mechanism built in Andhra Pradesh for *internal* audit and external audit by the CAG, it could be thought of as an important model for collaboration. If this works in accordance with the guidance notes issued by INTOSAI (ISSAI 9150: Coordination and Cooperation between SAIs and Internal Auditors in the Public Sector), it could be a creative venture. Other state governments might fruitfully emulate the Andhra Pradesh model. However, social audit, which is founded on struggles of people, must remain *external* to administration in character and not get ensnared into a bureaucratized system of functioning. If, and only if the local influences of a nexus of landed interests, labour contractors, and local officials can be countered effectively by a government-supported structure for social audit, can the Andhra Pradesh model work in other states.

Local Fund Auditors and the CAG would do well to come forward and join efforts at sub-district levels to build capacities of social audit units of the states. They need to take pains to hear the complaints and issues raised by residents/workers at public hearings and take the information into account, while certifying accounts or commenting on performance of local bodies. Another creative avenue of collaborative work could entail the CAG working with the media, not for self-promotion but to add to the depth of findings by following up with investigative reports.

Yet another field for collaboration between the CAG and civil society organizations is sustainable development audits. Public auditors

have traditionally been engaged in commenting on the extent of
the public debt and have gathered considerable expertise. However,
the husbanding of natural resource endowments, which is as critical
for intergenerational equity or sustainable development, has been
neglected. Recently, some audit reports have appeared in the context of
nationalized extractive industries in India, but by and large, the neglect
of the commons as an area of economic concerns by auditors has only
matched that by administrators. Post 2015, the UN's MDGs initiative
has made way for the SDGs. The CAG should play an increasing role
in this space since a distinguishing feature of environmental issues is
that they do not brook territorial boundaries. The CAG will need to
conduct joint audits with SAIs of neighbouring countries like Nepal
and Bangladesh, where major proposed hydroelectric power projects
involve issues related to sharing of waters. To this end, the CAG has set
up the international iCED, which will grow in strength to the extent
that it combines the knowledge flowing through government channels
and through civil society organizations. The CAG's organization will
also need to manage close relationships with NGOs and gather the
counter-currents in information and knowledge needed to interrogate
the government's positions and practices, while maintaining the independence required for objectivity.

The question of allocating responsibilities for the common task of
detection of fraud needs to be debated with renewed vigour among
executive agencies that have the primary responsibility and the means
to better conduct forensic audits, and the auditors, who must review
their risk assessment of controls to focus more on detection of frauds
in their financial audits. The existing procedures, whereby the responsibilities of the various agencies involved in this work (including those
of auditors), bear thorough review.

While the origins of the audit discipline lay in anxieties of people
about fraud and corruption, most SAIs, over time, distanced themselves
from these as core concerns. The Auditing Standards of INTOSAI do
mention checking against fraud as part of 'due care' to be exercised during financial and compliance audits, but this is mere lip service. Other
than in France, few cases of fraud or corruption have been reported by
SAIs working by themselves. It is customary for SAIs to shrug these
off as the responsibility of the executive, best left for investigative and
legal action by them. A separate forensic discipline of fraud detection

has sprung up and offices are being established under the executive wing. Corruption too, requiring investigation to reconcile what is on paper with what is not, is left to vigilance commissions under the executive. The increasing emphasis of SAIs on the distinction between responsibilities of internal (executive) audit and external (statutory) audit and their overemphasis on the need to strengthen internal audit by the executive is symptomatic of their insular formalistic concerns and frustrations about their own weak ineffectuality in handling mis-management and corruption in the public sector through reporting to legislatures. In the wake of computerization of accounts worldwide and electronic data processing techniques of audit, fraud and corruption are being revisited by SAIs. The World Bank's exhortations might revive interest of SAIs in these matters. The UN Convention on Corruption, signed and ratified by almost all countries, might also help to bring these concerns back as expectations of people from their SAIs. However, as of March 2015, INTOSAI's standards and guidance on role of SAIs in detecting fraud and corruption is still awaited. A lot more has been done in unearthing corruption by SAIs in several countries wherever they started up with citizen engagement mechanisms.

Since 2006, statements on gender budgeting have been tabled as part of the Union budget documents but no review of the accountability of government for gender responsive budgeting has been tabled by the CAG. Gender responsive budgeting requires looking at disaggregated data and information on details of activities involved in each and every domain of government activity to arrive at budgetary estimates. For instance, the burden on households to meet out-of-pocket expenses for healthcare of family members or the opportunity cost of the pri-mary care-giver at home foregoing wage-employment opportunities, has become a matter of great concern in the Asian region. Working with women's groups to appreciate issues and costs of care-giving and then examining the government's gender budgeting efforts will require considerable re-orientation. Following the declaration of SDGs, which has shown greater regard for addressing the twin problems of inequal-ity and disempowerment of women than the MDGs did, this area of work will find greater support. UNWOMEN has started collaborating with Asian Organisation of Supreme Audit Institutions (ASOSAI), and hopefully, this forum will be able to gradually influence SAIs in the region.

The audit arrangements for PPPs which are increasingly being deployed in India (for example, in developing ports, highways, and urban transport) require special attention by CAG. In the case of revenue-sharing PPPs, the courts in India have come to the rescue of CAG, who lacked a mandate to audit accounts of the project maintained by private companies, by issuing judgements that regard such projects as 'instrumentalities of the State' and upholding CAG's powers to audit accounts of private companies pertaining to the project and limited to just these accounts, no more. Layers of complexity in accountability arrangements occur when there is more than one agency and, or, more than one government (for example, in a federal system) agreeing to share responsibility for outcomes depending on third parties' service delivery to citizens. The increasingly common situation where third parties deliver services to citizens without direct government provision raises difficult issues of whether or not these third parties share accountability with government for service delivery, and if so, how that operates.

The Office of the Auditor General of Canada developed a definition of accountability that retains the essential features of traditional or hierarchical accountability and responds to the current pressures, such as situations where PPPs are used to deliver services funded by government: 'Accountability is a relationship based on obligations to demonstrate, review, and take responsibility for performance, both the results achieved in light of agreed expectations and the means used'. This definition encompasses different types of accountability relationships: between ministers and agency heads; between departments or agencies of government; between public servants in a hierarchical relationship; between partners in delivery; and between the government and Parliament. The definition claims to enhance the traditional concept of accountability; it 'allows for a shared accountability relationship among partners; encompasses reciprocal accountability of all parties in a delivery relationship; includes both ends and means; and the need for review and adjustment'. Useful as this definition is to further the cause of shared accountability, it does not go far enough. In the arena of public administration and accountability, a PPP is not simply an agreement between two parties to parcel out the control of risks in a project between them. There is a third party—the local community, often galvanized by NGOs—to protect their rights. This triadic interplay often gets stalemated (for example, in many cases related to hydel power projects) in implementation of the project and requires an intervention, quite often an audit by CAG, as a credible impartial observer, to get things moving again.

Towards Greater Transparency and Accountability

This discussion on the frontiers of public sector auditing indicates that a transformed understanding of the role of CAG on our part and major changes in its orientation is necessary to inform any changes to its mandate. While we earnestly wish this happens sooner than later, it is important that the institution of CAG, too, acquires the courage to be as transparent in its procedures as possible. For its own growth and development, it is necessary that it not only respond to applications for RTI as and when made, but proactively disclose on its website the inspection reports issued to offices after conducting an audit. This will have a salutary effect on the quality of the audits it conducts because errors/unsupported comments will be questioned by a wider set than just audit managers. Besides, CAG's website needs a complete overhaul if it is to be user friendly. It has to be understood by the institution that without deployment of knowledgeable persons as administrators of the website, it will remain an inert instrument without facilitating an interactive relation with users.

Likewise, PAC proceedings ought to be open to media coverage. Another measure of the lack of transparency that has shrouded public financial management is provided by the fact that while the first budget was presented in 1860, the Budget Manual of the GoI was publicized for the first time in September 2010. Again, there is no known legal authority except for a commentary by previous secretary-generals of Lok Sabha, Kaul and Shikder, that defines the relationship between the PAC and the CAG in the process of examining CAG reports.[14] The Rules of Procedure and Conduct of Business in the Lok Sabha do not accord him any status such as 'friend, philosopher, and guide' of the committee, which the commentary mentions without quoting any authority for it. Relying on the bric-a-brac of British history is not how

[14] M.N. Kaul and S.L. Shikder, *Practice and Procedure of Parliament*, 6th ed. (New Delhi: Metropolitan Book Co., 2009).

a country with a written constitution should be run. A public financial management law that codifies the budgetary, accounting, audit, and oversight responsibilities is long overdue. It is only after a process of a wide public debate about the reconfiguration and proper mandate for CAG, which takes into account the UN Resolutions, INTOSAI professional practices guidelines, and the imperative for citizen engagement by CAG, can the human resources needs be properly assessed and training functions for the organization be realigned. It is important to remind ourselves that the word 'parliament' simply means discussion among equals and that the governing principle of parliamentary functioning is public reasoning and not mere assertions of power. The plea of securing financial accountability to Parliament, projected as a 'Supreme Being', is often craftily used by ministries and auditors to flex their muscles against persons in institutions where the work of schooling or healthcare or research is done day in and day out. The dysfunctional aspects of audit by CAG or of ministries answerable to Parliament (both intermediaries in the process of securing accountability) flow from this propensity to misuse their intermediate positions. An entire system of governance can be vitiated, as is often the case, by accounts clerks and bureaucrats and financial auditors looming larger than life in the working of an institution.

As mentioned at the outset of this chapter, a societal culture of accountability-in-the-making is what we are looking at in the world today. Increasingly, accountability is losing its character of having been ordained by some superior authority and is finding its meaning in a highly interactive matrix of mutual questioning, discovery of hidden truths, or new knowledge and responses by persons concerned, which is what shapes a better world. Accountability is not only about the long arms of the law, but about people around us frowning at misdeeds, however these may be construed by different publics. This is evident not only in the trending tweets on social media and the writing on Facebook walls, but also in participative assemblies of people at various sites.

9

THE CIVIL SERVICE

*K.P. Krishnan and T.V. Somanathan**

The 'higher' civil services in India, also known as the 'Class I' or 'Group A' services, are of three main types. All India Services (AIS) are those whose members serve both union and state governments. The Union government is also known as the central government or the Government of India (GoI). Central services are those whose members work under the Union government only. State Civil Services are the higher services of state governments. There are three AIS: the Indian Administrative Service (IAS), the Indian Police Service (IPS), and the Indian Forest Service. The IAS and the Indian Foreign Service (IFS), a central service, are considered the most prestigious as judged by preferences of examination candidates and general public perceptions. Their pre-eminence is derived partly from a slight edge in pay scales and slightly faster promotions, but more from their job content—the glamour and travel opportunities of the foreign service and the breathtaking variety of job content of the administrative service.

The IAS is a 'mandarin'-type career civil service, comparable very broadly to the examination-recruited higher services in Britain, France, or Japan. This is contrasted from 'position-based services' where persons

---

* The views expressed are purely personal. The analysis in this chapter is as of July 2013. Subsequent developments have not been considered.

are recruited to a specific post.[1] Where it differs from many other mandarin services is in the vertical and lateral mobility of IAS officers. Not only do they work at several different levels of government—union, state, local, and with public sector corporations—but they also move across ministries and functions to a much larger extent than in most other mandarin civil service systems. In this latter respect, the IAS is closer to the career component of the United States Senior Executive Service (SES).[2] IAS officers do, however, specialize by geographical area—a necessity in a country with such diversity of language, culture, religion, and custom.

Recruitment is primarily through a very stiff competitive examination at a young age, typical of Mandarin-style services. Candidates coming through the competitive examination are referred to as 'regular recruits' or 'direct recruits'. Two other streams of entry exist (known as promotion and selection) which follow less rigorous procedures; these allow state civil servants to be promoted into the IAS. The recruitment examination is conducted by the Union Public Service Commission (UPSC), an apolitical body, and is common across the IAS, IFS, IPS (but not Forest Service), and most non-technical central services. Successful candidates are allotted to services on the basis of their preferences and examination ranks. Most candidates choose the IAS/IFS as their first two preferences (not necessarily in that order) and thus those selected for these services are usually the highest ranked.

IAS officers are allotted to State cadres in which they specialize, learning the state language, customs, laws, and so forth, and clearing examinations in these subjects. They undergo a two-year training, about half of which is spent in the National Academy of Administration, Mussoorie, involving a rigorous multidisciplinary course of examinations and assignments. One year is spent in on-the-job training in the state of allotment, including long stints in rural areas. Part of their career is usually spent in the Union government. The Union government's

[1] R. Mukherjee, 'Senior Public Service: High Performing Managers of Government' (Working Paper, Washington, DC: World Bank, 2004).

[2] B. Nunberg, 'Managing the Civil Service: Reform Lessons from Advanced Industrialized Countries' (Discussion Paper 204, Washington, DC: World Bank, 1995).

Department of Personnel and Training (DoPT) is in charge of the administration of the IAS.

Though the IAS came into existence in 1948, it inherited the mantle of the colonial Indian Civil Service (ICS) and members, especially in the early years, saw themselves as successors of the ICS and its traditions.

Key administrative and police positions in state governments are designated as 'cadre posts', signifying that they may only be held by officers of the IAS/IPS. This is a deliberate feature of the AIS system intended to promote quality, impartiality, integrity, and an all-India outlook. Thus, the Secretaries (equivalent to 'permanent secretaries' in most Commonwealth countries) of most state ministries and the head of the civil service (Chief Secretary) are always IAS officers, and the senior-most police officers (Inspectors-General) and the head of state police (Director-General of Police) are always IPS officers.

The institution of the civil service occupies an important place in India's governance, a fact recognized by the Indian Constitution. This chapter attempts to answer the following questions:

1. How has the civil service changed over the years since Independence?
2. How effective has the civil service been? How have changes from the original institutional design affected civil service effectiveness?
3. What impact have other institutions and social trends had on the civil service and on its effectiveness?
4. What can be done to improve the effectiveness of the civil service?

This chapter is self-contained but draws on, and in some respects summarizes, an earlier paper by the same authors (referred to as Civil Service-I).[3]

Methodology

A few prefatory remarks on methodology are necessary. The study uses and quotes published data and data available in the public realm

---

[3] K.P. Krishnan and T.V. Somanathan, 'Civil Service: An Institutional Perspective', in *Public Institutions in India: Performance and Design*, eds D. Kapur and P.B. Mehta (New Delhi: Oxford University Press, 2007) [referred to as Civil Service-I in this chapter].

wherever possible. In reaching some of its key insights, it relies also on the authors' own knowledge of the institution and responses to structured interviews. However, as loyal civil servants and faithful adherents to the Conduct Rules, the authors have limitations in the degree to which they can use such information. The study, thus, has the advantage of access to insights not available to an outside researcher, but is subject to the corresponding limitation that a full 'citation' of information sources is not always possible.

Definition of Civil Service

The central government alone employs over three million civilians, as can be seen from Table 9.1 (Table A9.1 gives details of the large variety of the Group A central services). In addition, there are the state and local governments and the various public sector authorities and corporations.

Given the large number of services and the many possible definitions, a study of the civil service as very broadly defined would be unwieldy in scope.[4] To make the study manageable, one can narrow down the scope to the leadership positions, since the leadership largely determines the character of the service as a whole. Within the central government, top level 'control' posts are manned partly by the central services and partly by the AIS. Table 9.2 gives details of the share of the

Table 9.1 Number of Civilian Employees in Position (as on 1 April 2014)

Department	Group A	Group B	Group C	Total
Railways	8,493	7283	1,299,912	1,315,688
MHA incl. CAPFs	16,090	60,162	903,862	980,114*
Defence (Civilian)	17,160	59,415	321,847	398,422
Posts	527	6,826	182,418	189,771
Revenue	5,827	40,907	49,078	95,812
Others	43,404	106,299	172,026	321,729
Total	**91,501**	**280,892**	**2,929,143**	**3,301,536**

Source: Report of 7th Central Pay Commission (New Delhi: Government of India, 2015), 29.
Note: *This includes 140,294 employees of Union Territories (including Delhi Police personnel). MHA: Ministry of Home Affairs. CAPF: Central Armed Police Forces.

[4] See Civil Service-I for details.

Table 9.2 Distribution by Service of Senior Officers in Central Government Ministries, 2012

Service (those in *italics* are recruited through generalist civil services examination)	Secretary Level	Additional Secretary Level	Joint Secretary Level	Director Level	Deputy Secretary Level	Total
IAS	81	100	308	136	46	671
IPS	18	10	37	26	9	100
IFS	3	0	4	6	2	15
Indian Forest Service	0	0	11	59	2	72
Indian Audit and Accounts Service	0	1	20	30	9	60
Indian Civil Accounts Service	0	0	0	3	4	7
Indian Defence Accounts Service	0	2	18	28	12	60
Indian Economic Service	0	0	6	16	14	36
Indian Statistical Service	0	0	0	7	12	19
Indian Revenue Service (Customs and Central Excise)	0	1	4	31	2	38
Indian Revenue Service (Income Tax)	0	2	7	49	9	67
Indian Postal Service	1	0	2	23	4	30
Indian Information Service/Broadcasting Engineering Service/Indian Broadcasting Programming Service	0	0	8	5	1	14
Railway Services	1	0	11	49	1	62

(Cont'd)

Table 9.2 (Cont'd)

Service (those in *italics* are recruited through generalist civil services examination)	Secretary Level	Additional Secretary Level	Joint Secretary Level	Director Level	Deputy Secretary Level	Total
Central Power Engineering Service	0	0	0	2	4	6
Indian Defence Estates Service	0	0	0	4	1	5
Indian Legal Service	3	0	0	0	0	3
Central Secretariat Service	0	1	9	*	*	*
Indian Telecom. Service	0	0	0	39	1	40
Indian Ordnance Factory Service	0	0	2	26	1	29
Indian Cost Accounts Service	0	0	0	5	11	16
Central Trade Service	0	0	0	5	0	5
Indian Post & Telecom. Finance & Accounts Service	0	1	2	18	4	25
Others	6	1	0	21	6	34
Total	113	119	449	*	*	*
Percentage of IAS officers	72	84	68	*	*	*
Percentage of AIS officers	88	92	77	*	*	*

Source: Department of Personnel and Training, Ministry of Personnel, Public Grievances and Pensions, Government of India.
Note: *Data for Central Secretariat Service is incomplete.

different services (including the AIS) in the control posts in the central government.[5]

As Table 9.2 shows, the AIS, particularly the IAS, has a pivotal role in terms of its share of top-level policymaking positions across the range of central ministries; the IAS and IPS together account for 88 per cent of Secretary-level posts. Furthermore, while the data are not presented here, they occupy an even larger percentage of the control posts in state governments. Focusing on the IAS presents a manageable yet analytically interesting scope for analysis. Therefore, this chapter primarily concentrates on the IAS but pays some attention to general issues which also affect the lower civil services, and to some areas of interaction between the IAS and other AIS/central services. It does not deal with the IPS.

Criteria of Effectiveness

There are various possible criteria of 'effectiveness' of the civil service as an institution. One perspective is from institutional economics, and from that angle civil service effectiveness would be assessed on the basis of *reducing transaction costs for economic agents and thereby promoting economic development*. However, this approach is too narrowly rooted in economics. Democracy, secularism, and other freedoms have value in themselves regardless of their economic effects. Further, the institutional economics perspective links the effectiveness of the civil service to outcomes which may be the result of deliberate policy choices of others, namely elected politicians. Faithful implementation of policies of an elected executive (insofar as they do not contravene the law or the constitution) is the mark of an effective, not ineffective, civil service even when the policies may increase transaction costs or are perceived as 'wrong' by economists. Also, the preservation of the constitutional order is itself an objective for the civil service in a democracy.

[5] These are primarily the posts in the ministries (contrasted from posts in the operating 'Heads of Department' subordinate to the ministries). However, posts in the Intelligence Bureau and central police organizations are control posts de facto (though within Heads of Department de jure) and hence included in the table in respect of the IPS.

Writing after Civil Service-I (and apparently without reference to it), Alex Matheson *et al.* evolved a framework of four public service behaviours which corresponds quite closely to the criteria in that paper. They went further and argued that the four behaviours (constitutional respect and continuity, impartial and inclusive public service, responsive public service, and performing civil service) are in a hierarchy with *constitutional respect and continuity* as the most important, *impartiality and inclusiveness* as the second and *responsiveness* and *performance* (jointly) in third place in the hierarchy.[6]

Drawing upon that framework, this chapter uses the following criteria to assess civil service effectiveness:

1. Criterion I: Preserving India's constitutional order, including democracy, secularism, national unity, and the rule of law (being 'good' in themselves, regardless of their effect on economic development);
2. Criterion II: Impartial implementation of the rule of law in day-to-day dealings with the citizenry (this is partly connected with Criterion IV because predictability in day-to-day working is crucial for economic development).
3. Criterion III: Faithfully translating the will of elected governments into policies and then implementing those policies effectively.
4. Criterion IV: Promoting economic development by reducing transaction costs and by providing effective and efficient public services.

Criteria III and IV broadly represent the role of the civil service in what Mark Moore calls 'creating public value'.[7]

The traits which civil servants need to be effective vary across these criteria. Criterion I is primarily related to *political neutrality* and a *sense of national spirit and larger purpose*. For Criterion II, *integrity* (lack of corruption) is the most vital trait, though it also requires political neutrality. Criterion III depends considerably on *political neutrality* (so

[6] A. Matheson, B. Weber, N. Manning, and E. Arnould, 'Study on the Political Involvement in Senior Staffing and Delineation of Responsibilities between Ministers and Senior Civil Servants' (OECD Working Papers on Governance 2007/6, OECD Publishing: France, 2007).

[7] M.H. Moore, *Creating Public Value: Strategic Management in Government* (Cambridge: Harvard University Press, 1995).

that civil servants are able to implement policies contrary to their private beliefs and ideologies) and *competence and capacity* (so that they execute policies effectively). It also requires *flexibility and willingness to change, social sensitivity,* and *idealism and empathy* with the public. Criterion IV is primarily an issue of *capacity and competence,* the ability to regulate economic matters effectively, but is also closely related to levels of *integrity.* A civil service that is competent but dishonest may not be conducive to reducing transaction costs, though the experience of East Asian countries including China suggests that the actual effect depends on the manner and nature of the dishonesty.[8]

'Effectiveness' under one parameter does not always mean 'effectiveness' under another since there are often trade-offs between them. A 'committed' civil service, for instance, may score well on Criterion III but end up undermining democracy under Criterion I. A politically neutral and honest but rigid and inflexible civil service may do well under Criteria I and II but, by providing ineffective and incompetent administration, fail under Criteria III and IV.

The Formal Design

This section looks at the formal design features of the AIS and its evolution over time.

Initial Design

The initial design of the AIS had the following key features:[9]

All-India character: The services and its members were designed to be all-India—and not local—in attitude and thinking, for it was intended that the 'common national interest should always prevail over sectional and local claims'. For this reason, the AIS were to occupy key positions at both the national and state levels, and to be a source of objectivity and neutrality rising above regional and local pressures including language, religion, and caste. An explicit objective was that officers should

---

[8] Indeed, corporate executives often seem to suggest that they do not mind corruption so long as 'services' paid for corruptly are delivered quickly and without uncertainty.

[9] For more details, see Civil Service-I.

alternate between the centre and states, so that policymaking at the centre was imbued with a strong sense of practicality gained by actual experience in the field, while policymaking and implementation in the states was informed by a broader national perspective. The cadre allotment rules and central staffing scheme were also designed to serve this objective, by ensuring that a proportion of AIS officers in each state were from other states and that officers alternated between the centre and states.

Dual control: The need for a single service working at central and state level, along with democratic accountability to state governments, led to a design based on 'dual control' of the AIS by both tiers of government.

Merit-based selection: Selection was to be based on merit through a stiff competitive examination with the intent of attracting the best and the brightest to the public service.

Independent selection: Merit-based selection was entrusted to an independent constitutional body (the UPSC).

Protection against arbitrary punishment: The Constitution, under Article 311, made provisions to protect civil servants from arbitrary punishment to ensure their objectivity and neutrality and enable them to function without fear of political reprisal.

Other design elements: These implicitly or explicitly included common training with other services (to build camaraderie), low age of recruitment (for a spirit of idealism), limited number of attempts at the examination (to ensure intellectual calibre), good remuneration and service conditions, and social status and prestige (to attract talent and preserve morale).

Special considerations: These were two special considerations in the initial design which modified the other elements described. The first was promotion from the state civil services and the second was reservation for Scheduled Castes (SCs) and Scheduled Tribes (STs).

The objectives of the initial design and the design features through which they were sought to be achieved are summarized in Figure 9.1.[10] Clearly, most features of the design were conducive to institutional

---

[10] Figure 9.1 is taken from Civil Service-I. This figure from that paper was also cited and reproduced by the 2nd Administrative Reforms Commission in its 10th Report.

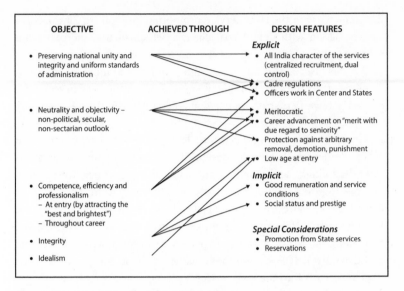

Figure 9.1 Initial Design of the All India Services
Source: Krishnan and Somanathan, 'Civil Service—An Institutional Perspective.'

effectiveness since the design promoted competence (through meritocratic recruitment), integrity (through good remuneration and job security), political neutrality (through security of tenure and protection against arbitrary removal), dynamism (through recruitment at a young age), and flexibility and social sensitivity (through the requirement to work in the states and districts, thereby keeping civil servants firmly connected with grassroots reality).

Explicit Changes to Design

The initial design was modified over the years by explicit changes as well as through the effects of various political, economic, and social forces. The explicit changes, all of them relating to entry into the service, were:

1. An increase in reservations from 22 per cent (only for SCs and STs) to nearly 50 per cent (including Other Backward Classes [OBCs]) after 1995. This was part of the broader change arising from the implementation of the recommendations of the Mandal Commission.

2. An increase in the state service promotion quota from 25 to 33 per cent, along with definitional changes which further increased this quota.
3. An increase in the upper age limit and the number of attempts allowed for the examination along with other changes in examination pattern (a matter discussed in greater detail in the next section).

Changing composition of entrants: The civil service examination was a key element in the initial design. It was to be highly competitive, inter-disciplinary, and taken by graduates at a young age. Restrictions on upper age and the number of attempts (a legacy from the ICS) were intended to ensure that only very bright students (rather than those who 'practised' the examination over many years) would qualify, and the young entry age was also expected to foster a sense of idealism and dynamism. This section looks at the changing composition of the regular recruits into the civil service.

Changes in examination pattern—Age: Table 9.3 summarizes the many changes in the age limit and permitted number of attempts for the Civil Services examination over the years. (The age limit referred to in the table is for general category candidates, that is, those not entitled to reservation.)

As can be seen from Table 9.3, the overall tendency was to raise both the maximum age and the number of permissible attempts.

Changes in examination pattern—English language skills: In the early years, the examination gave significant weight to the writing of an essay in English. The pattern of examination changed in 1979 and this requirement was removed. Instead, English (along with one Indian language) became a qualifying paper of matriculation standard. Candidates were also given the option of using any Indian language as the medium of examination or interview. Later on, in the 1990s, a general essay was re-introduced but could be written either in English or in an Indian language. Thus, proficiency in English no longer was a determinant in the ranking of candidates. This had the positive effect of neutralizing the class and urban bias that English proficiency probably did entail. However, to the extent that English proficiency is important in certain policymaking and international relations roles (remembering that IFS officers are also recruited through the same examination), it may have reduced the competence of the civil service for certain kinds of jobs, particularly at the central level.

Table 9.3 Changes in Eligibility Age and Number of Permissible Attempts for Civil Services Examination

Year	Age (in years)	Number of Attempts
1947	21–6	No restriction
1948	21–5	No restriction
1949 and 1950	21–4 (except for the IRTS for which 21–5 continued)	No restriction
1951–4	20/21–4 (except for IPS for which it was 20–4)	No restriction
1955–60	20/21–4 (IRTS also followed this age limit)	No restriction
1961–1	20/21–4	Number of attempts restricted to two
1972–8	20/21–6 (upper age limit raised based on ARC recommendations)	Two attempts continued
1979–86	21–8 (upper age limit increased)	Number of attempts increased to three
1987–9	21–6	Three attempts continued
1990	21–31 (upper age limit increased)	Number of attempts increased to four
1991	21–8	Four attempts continued
1992	21–33	Number of attempts increased to five
1993–4	21–8	Number of attempts restricted to four again
1995–8	21–8	Number of attempts restricted to four for general category and seven for OBC candidates
1999	21–30	-do-
2000	21–30 (upper age limit of 28 for CISF)	-do-
2003	21–30 (upper age limit relaxed by 5 years for residents of Jammu and Kashmir)	-do-

(Cont'd)

Table 9.3　(Cont'd)

Year	Age (in years)	Number of Attempts
2008	21–30	As above, but seven attempts for the physically handicapped in general category
2014	21–32	Number of attempts increased to six for general category and seven for OBC candidates and the physically handicapped in general category

Source: Department of Personnel and Training, Ministry of Personnel, Public Grievances and Pensions.

Profile of candidates: In writing this chapter, a detailed analysis of civil services examination trends between 1990 and 2010 was undertaken. The study covered the Civil Services Examination as a whole and is thus not confined to the IAS. A detailed presentation of the results would be beyond the scope of this chapter and therefore only a summary of the main findings is given here.

Numbers Selected: Figure 9.2 presents the total number of candidates selected across the years. Males have accounted for about 80 per cent of

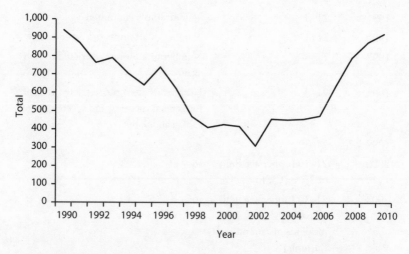

Figure 9.2　Total Candidates Selected in Civil Services Examination, 1990–2010
Source: Krishnan and Somanathan, 'Civil Service—An Institutional Perspective.'

the total candidates recommended and this ratio has been quite steady. The decline between 1998 and 2006 is partly attributable to changes necessitated by a decision of the Central Administrative Tribunal (upheld by the Supreme Court) which re-interpreted the cadre rules to increase the extent of the promotion quota, thereby resulting in a reduced number of direct recruitment vacancies.[11]

Age at entry: Figure 9.3 presents the age profile of the candidates. There is a clear aging of the intake with a steady increase in the share of candidates 26 and above, an increase of more than two years in the average age of those selected. In 1991, 76 per cent of the candidates recommended were below the age of 26, while in 2008 only 33 per cent were. Women entrants are, on average, two years younger. The average age of successful candidates is higher than the overall candidate population, which may reflect the advantage of multiple attempts.

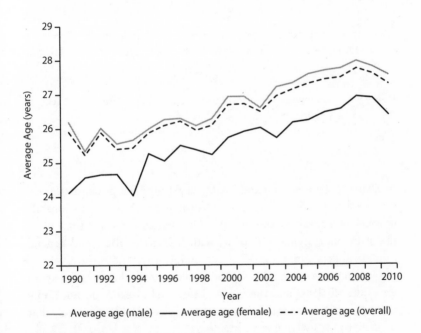

Figure 9.3 Average Age of Candidates Selected in Civil Services Examination, 1990–2010
Source: Krishnan and Somanathan, 'Civil Service—An Institutional Perspective'.

[11] *K.K. Goswamy* v. *Union of India* (TA No. 81 of 1986, Jabalpur Bench).

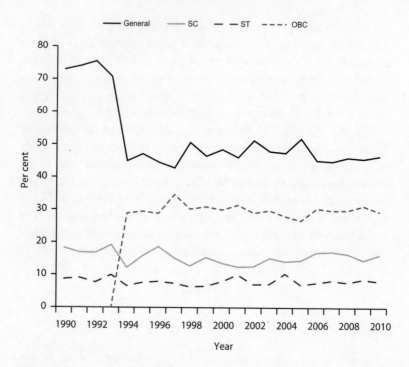

Figure 9.4   Community-wise Distribution of Candidates Selected in Civil Services Examination, 1990–2010
Source: Krishnan and Somanathan, 'Civil Service—An Institutional Perspective.'

Shares of different community categories: Figure 9.4 presents the percentage shares of different community categories. After one major shift in 1994 as a result of the introduction of reservation for the OBCs, the shares have remained stable, with SCs, STs, OBCs, and general candidates accounting for 15, 8, 30, and 47 per cent, respectively, of the recommended candidates. Readers should note that the zero figure for OBCs till 1993 and the fall in the general category do not imply that no one from the former category was selected earlier—merely that separate records were not maintained.

Figure 9.5 shows that all community categories have shown an increase in average age across time. General category candidates have been younger on average than those from other communities, but the

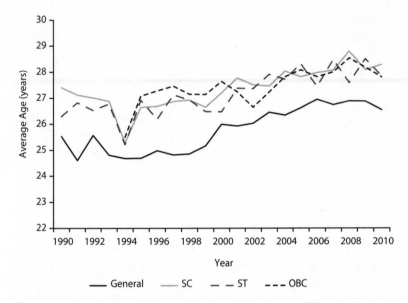

Figure 9.5 Average Age and Community of Candidates Selected in Civil Services Examination, 1990–2010
Source: Krishnan and Somanathan, 'Civil Service—An Institutional Perspective.'

average age of entrants from the other categories are similar and seem to move together.[12]

Attempts taken to clear the civil services exam: The average number of attempts lies between three and four across the time period under consideration. There is a variation by community category, as expected based on the permissible number of attempts.

Qualification: Since 2001, as Figure 9.6 shows, Bachelor's degree holders have outstripped candidates with higher degrees in both appearing for and successfully clearing the examination. Some of these candidates held Bachelor's in Engineering, Technology, or Medicine, courses with a longer duration than other undergraduate courses.

---

[12] This brings into question the logic of age relaxation, particularly additional relaxation for ST and SC candidates, unless the age limit for the general category is reduced to its erstwhile level of 26.

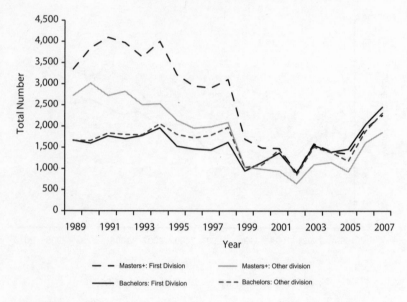

Figure 9.6 Educational Qualifications of Candidates Selected in Civil
Services Examination, 1989–2007
Source: Krishnan and Somanathan, 'Civil Service—An Institutional Perspective.'

Nevertheless, there are grounds for concluding that prima facie there
has been a reduction in quality of entrants.

Medium of examination: As may be seen from figure 9.7, about
95 per cent of the candidates appearing in the Civil Service (Main)
Examination used English or Hindi. This percentage has remained
remarkably stable throughout the period under consideration.
However, the composition of this 95 per cent has changed drastically
over the years. English accounted for over 73 per cent in 1990 while
Hindi accounted for 21 per cent. In 2008, the numbers were 45 and
50 per cent, respectively. Since 2008, the share of English has risen
substantially.

Of the remaining 5 per cent, approximately 3 per cent is accounted
for by five languages (labelled Category A in the figure) which individually are spoken by more than 5 per cent (and collectively by 35 per
cent) of India's population, namely Bengali, Telugu, Tamil, Marathi, and
Urdu. Less than 2 per cent of candidates wrote the examination in all
other languages (labelled category B in the figure).

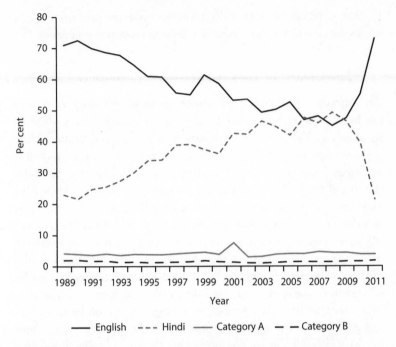

Figure 9.7 Language Used by Candidates for Civil Services Examination, 1989–2011
Source: Krishnan and Somanathan, 'Civil Service—An Institutional Perspective.'

There has been a perception that candidates who take certain languages as an optional subject (not necessarily as medium of instruction), in respect of languages that have a relatively small number of candidates appearing, have a higher success rate. This is sometimes attributed to parochial bias among examiners. The authors studied the success rates for these optional language papers. The data cover many languages and many years and is thus too voluminous to usefully tabulate or summarize within the space limits of this chapter. However, one thing is clear: there is no evidence of any consistent or sustained advantage to any particular optional language paper.

Universities of origin: The top ten universities (Delhi, Jawaharlal Nehru, Indian Institute of Technology—Delhi, Indian Institute of Technology—Kanpur, Panjab, Rajasthan, Allahabad, Pune, Lucknow, Mumbai) together accounted for 50 per cent of selected candidates

in 1998 and 35 per cent in 2010. Over the years, the pool from which
successful candidates have come has become more heterogeneous.

Effectiveness of the Civil Service: An Assessment

On Criterion I (preserving the constitutional order), the civil service
has been quite effective and by developing country standards, out-
standingly so. The preservation of national unity and constitutional rule
through many instances of insurgency, civil disorder, political instability,
and dozens of impositions of President's Rule on the one hand and the
conduct of free and fair elections (in a country not otherwise known for
excellence in governance) on the other, lie at the core of India's success
as a democratic polity. They are achievements for which the IAS and
IPS have been responsible in large measure but for which the services
do not get as much credit as they deserve. It is worth noting that the
Election Commission and the UPSC—both nearly always headed by
officers from the civil service and insulated from direct political control—continue to enjoy a well-deserved high reputation for neutrality
and probity. Persons outside government rarely appreciate the extent
to which the ability to hold India together (as a single political and economic unit), and for the constitutional distribution of executive powers
to operate, has depended, and continues to depend, on the AISs. In a
country of unequalled diversity, the AISs have also played a crucial role
in enabling the central government to understand local pressures and
dynamics and adapt its policies realistically within the constitutional
framework to meet local aspirations without the kind of rigidity often
witnessed when federal governments have civil services unconnected
with the federating units. Without necessarily attributing causality, it is
nevertheless noteworthy that Pakistan made major changes to the civil
service structure and has not been successful in preserving democracy
and constitutionality.[13]

On Criterion II, namely neutrally and fairly implementing rule of
law in dealings with individual citizens, the civil service has been far
less effective. The powerful and the influential have often received
favourable treatment with the poor and the weak often treated

[13] World Bank, 'A Framework for Civil Service Reform in Pakistan', *Report
No. 18386-PAK* (Washington, DC: World Bank, 1998).

shabbily. Enforcement of the law has been erratic. Political interference (see definition in the next section, 'Causes of Poor Performance') has played the major role but the civil service is not free of blame. Corruption by civil servants has become rampant. The civil service has often not put up the level of resistance that its many legal and constitutional protections should have enabled it to. Partly, this is because of the incentive structure under which modern-day civil servants operate. However, to provide perspective, it should be noted that the poor overall record on this issue is mitigated slightly by the impressive work of several distinguished officers who have spent whole careers fighting within the system for the fair treatment of the disadvantaged sections of society. Some like the late (and legendary) S.R. Sankaran became well known while many others have remained in relative anonymity.[14] The number of such officers, while a small proportion, is large enough that the image of 'the crusading honest officer' continues to find a place in popular cinema and in motivating young students to write the civil services examination.

On the third criterion of faithfully executing policy, the assessment is mixed. There is some truth in the perception that the civil service has from time to time obstructed, or at least delayed the implementation of, well-intentioned plans of the political executive. In part, this is an unconscious or indirect result of other problems like corruption and weak law enforcement. In some cases, the resistance to implementation comes not from the senior levels but from the lower levels of civil service.

In the authors' opinion, deliberate obstruction is less common than may be thought by outsiders. Genuine objections to illegal or improper courses of action can also appear or be characterized as 'obstruction'. Some delays and obstructions attributed by the press to the civil service, are (from the authors' own experience) the result of lack of cohesion within the political executive, especially in coalition governments, where what appears to be a civil servant's disagreement is actually a reflection of disagreements among ministers. Also, civil service often lies at the intersection between the political executive's 'publicly proclaimed lofty intentions and privately expressed specific instructions

[14] E.A.S. Sarma, 'S R Sankaran: In Memoriam', *Economic and Political Weekly* 45, no. 3 (23–9 October 2010): 25–7.

(usually less lofty)'. There is a lot of evidence to show that where the political executive has a clear and genuinely-held policy view and expresses it consistently, the civil service does usually deliver.[15] Thus, it is difficult to discern the extent to which the civil service is legitimately to be blamed under this criterion.

On Criterion IV (effectiveness in promoting economic development/reducing transaction costs and providing effective public services), the civil service has not performed well. There is a vast body of facts and evidence which shows that policy uncertainty, inconsistent or arbitrary application of known policy, delays in decision-taking, 'transaction costs' in money and time due to bribery, ineffectiveness in law enforcement, and regional or communal parochialism (impeding the development of all-India institutions and markets) have been widespread characteristics of civil service functioning in the last three decades. In addition, lack of competence has been a problem quite often, though far less so than lack of integrity or neutrality. All of these have reduced the effectiveness of the civil service in promoting economic development.

In sum, the civil service has done well in preserving the overall constitutional order but performed poorly in impartially implementing laws and policies at the individual level. Its record on the third criterion of responsiveness to political will is mixed but on the whole reasonably good, considering that political will has often been unclear or contradictory. It has performed badly in promoting economic growth or providing good public services.

Causes of Poor Performance

The overall conclusion is that the civil service has not met the expectations of the design or the needs of the country. The main causes of the poor performance are discussed here.[16]

---

[15] There are several examples at different points of time, including the successful implementation of the noon meal scheme in Tamil Nadu schools, protection of agricultural tenants under Operation Barga in West Bengal, reliable rural power supply in Gujarat, and the conduct of Kumbh Melas in various states.

[16] A more detailed discussion on many of these trends can be found in Civil Service-I.

The biggest single weakness of the civil service today is its perceived inability to function with integrity and political neutrality. Political interference has become very common over the last three to four decades. Political interference is defined as:

> Acts of politicians—whether formally part of the Executive or not—intended to compel a civil servant, by means of threats or blandishments or both, to follow the course desired by them on decisions which ought to be taken by the civil servant impartially under government policy. It does not refer to the legitimate role of the political executive (ministers and politically-appointed heads of agencies) in exercising powers duly vested in them—a role which may indeed lead them to legitimately overrule advice tendered by civil servants. The distinction is quite easy to observe in practice; political interference is almost always oral, with the civil servant usually pretending that he took the decision of his own volition.

Political interference is currently perceived to occur at all levels: a local Member of the Legislative Assembly (MLA, or state legislator) may interfere with a petty official in the issue of a land title document, a state minister may interfere with a district collector in a personnel decision, a central minister may interfere in the award of a contract or in the enforcement of a penal provision of the law, and so on. Political interference is also felt to be politically and geographically neutral; members of all political parties (national and regional) in all states are perceived to indulge in it, though there may be variations in degree. Often, political interference takes the form of telling a civil servant not to tender advice in the manner the civil servant intended to tender it, which is reflected in a failure to record dissenting views (as legally required under the All India Services [Conduct] Rules).

Popular commentary on the civil service often compares the contemporary civil service adversely with the 'steel frame' of the ICS. It needs to be remembered that the ICS did not function under a democratic framework. Except for a very short and partial interlude, it did not have any elected political executive to deal with; thus a comparison of the IAS with the ICS is not apt. However, a reasonable comparison would be with the civil service in the first three decades after Independence. On that basis, the evidence is clear that the levels of integrity and neutrality were high then and are much lower now.

Many critics (and critiques) of the civil service dwell on the view that that the civil service has only itself to blame for the problem of political interference. 'Spineless', 'crawling when asked to bend', and 'corrupt and self-serving' are among the epithets commonly used. If every officer said 'no' to an improper instruction, and boldly accepted all penal transfers (after all transfers do not affect salaries), political interference would end—so goes a common critique.

Since civil service recruits do not represent an anthropologically different group from the rest of university-educated India, the more interesting analytical question is *why* civil servants behave as they do. The answer to the question lies in a basic change in the structure of career incentives.

The design principle was that civil servants would be secure in terms of pay and perquisites which could not be arbitrarily varied, favourably or unfavourably, by the political executive, so that they would act without fear or favour in accordance with the law. Article 311 of the Constitution provides protection to civil servants against arbitrary dismissal and demotion through a set of strong procedural safeguards. These safeguards have been considerably widened through judicial interpretation. As a result, arbitrary de jure punishment of civil servants is extremely difficult. Promotion is mainly seniority-based and administered largely by the civil service itself, with little political involvement. The All India Service Rules prescribe a fixed age of mandatory retirement and exceptions were extremely rare.[17] Together, they meant that the political executive could not offer special rewards to favoured civil servants.

However, through a combination of the wielding of a stick (at the state level) and the dangling of a carrot (at the central level), the political executive has gradually acquired the power to punish those they dislike and confer special rewards on those they favour.

The 'sticks' of personally disruptive transfer and arbitrary demotion have been acquired and used to telling effect, largely but not exclusively at the state level. The former—frequent transfer to different duty stations, thereby disrupting the personal life of the officer as well as the

[17] The principle has been diluted in recent years with provisions for limited extensions beyond the age of 60 for a small number of posts: six months for chief secretaries of states, two years for five secretary-level posts in the Union (two held by the IAS and three by the IPS), and up to four years for the cabinet secretary.

employment of spouses and the education of children—is well known. Frequent transfers to different duty stations operate as de facto punishments due to the adverse personal consequences for the officer. The lesser known but equally widespread problem is arbitrary demotion. This has happened through the power of transfer combined with the ability to upgrade and downgrade particular posts at will without any semblance of public interest. Thus, by creating a new post with the same pay scale but with clearly lower responsibility or upgrading an existing junior post and making it senior, and then transferring a senior officer to that (junior) post, the government is able to effectively demote an officer. This has primarily been done by the state political executive but the central government and the judiciary have effectively endorsed the right of state executives to behave in this manner. Therefore, while the constitutional protection against arbitrary dismissal remains, the protection against arbitrary demotion does not exist in practice. AIS officers today can be effectively punished by the political executive with no procedural formalities, leave alone procedural fairness.

The 'carrot' of conferment of special reward beyond normal conditions of service has become widespread, largely but not exclusively at the central level. This is through increasing resort to extensions of service and to post-retirement employment in regulatory or quasi-government bodies. Most recent cabinet secretaries have had at least one, if not several, extensions of their service beyond retirement age. The power of extension (for more than six months) rests exclusively with the centre, and hence this is more common at the central level. Apart from de jure extensions, de facto extensions occur through the appointment of retiring officers to regulatory bodies, statutory commissions, and the like. This practice has never been absent and, realistically, can never be completely proscribed in any civil service. However, in the early decades, the number of such posts was very small. As Das has eloquently pointed out, the recent proliferation of regulatory bodies, tribunals, and training institutions has made the practice widespread and the manner of exercise has been perceived to be geared to reward pliability.[18] Even the creation of, or timing of the filling up of posts in, such bodies may be influenced by the retirements of senior officers. The dangling carrot

[18] S.K. Das, *Building a World Class Civil Service for 21st Century India* (New Delhi: Oxford University Press, 2010), Chapter 17.

of an extension or post-retirement job means that officers in the most powerful posts of their careers (Secretaries) are often more pliable than their juniors, since acquiescence or support to political interference may be rewarded with post-retirement 'after-life', and perquisites to boot. Further, whereas those on extension of service cannot draw more than their pensions, those in post-retirement jobs in autonomous bodies are able to double-dip by collecting both pension and the new salaries.

Another facet of political interference is the politicization of promotion of state service officers into the IAS; officers close to particular political parties or personalities are perceived to have an advantage in getting promoted to the IAS/IPS. Officers from the promotion and selection categories form approximately a third of the service.

Other Factors

Other factors that have diminished civil service effectiveness are:

1. Dual control has weakened especially in the last two decades and the centre is perceived as having not protected the AIS officers even where it had the power to do so. The rise of the coalition era at the centre appears to have contributed to this.
2. IAS officers have been reluctant to make full use of the legal protections available to them, because the use of these protections is costly in financial and personal terms. On the few occasions when egregious transfers were contested in the courts, the courts usually did not provide relief and this has deterred others from trying.
3. Arbitrary transfers have led to short tenures in each post. Das has shown that for 2006, 55 per cent of officers had done less than one year in their posts and in no year was this figure less than 48 per cent.[19] This greatly diminishes effectiveness as nearly every incumbent is still on the learning curve in nearly every post. Lakshmi Iyer and Anandi Mani found empirical evidence that 'suggest[s] that the cost of political transfers in terms of longer-term [development] outcomes can be quite high'.[20]

[19] Das, *World Class Civil Service*, Chapter 13.
[20] L. Iyer and A. Mani, 'Traveling Agents: Political Change and Bureaucratic Turnover in India', *Review of Economics and Statistics* 94, no. 3 (August 2012): 723–39.

4. The non-transparency of, and serious weaknesses in, the system of 'empanelment' through which only a minority of IAS officers are made eligible for senior postings at the centre has amplified the power of arbitrary punishment and diminished the all-India character of the service. Empanelment is built on an edifice of performance appraisals over which the political executive has considerable control; a frequently transferred officer may not even have adequate formal appraisals and this counts against him.[21]

5. Through a change in cadre allotment rules in 1985, the vast majority of successful candidates were allotted by a completely random roster system to various states with no reference to their preferences. The purpose was to rectify what was seen as very limited inter-regional movement of candidates. However, the forced social engineering in the new system de-motivated a lot of entrants and has been a major contributor to lowering of morale. For instance, many officers hailing from the Northeast, who wanted to serve in that region, were posted elsewhere while others who did not want to go to the Northeast were forced to go there. For all officers, this would be for the majority of their respective careers and for those who failed to get empanelled for central posts, it would be for virtually the whole of their careers. This system (intended to strengthen the all-India character of the service) had the opposite effect: it led to a large number of officers trying to stay away from their allotted states on central deputation for many years through a variety of means— further increasing their dependence on political favour.

6. Drastic pay compression (that is, reduction in the ratio of senior officers' pay vis-à-vis the junior ranks of the government service) until the 1990s accelerated the loss of morale and created an excuse for corruption.

7. Socio-political trends, particularly spectacular increases in private-sector salaries and the culture of conspicuous consumption have increased corruption, reduced morale, and damaged the social prestige of a civil service career, removing a major 'non-monetary' perquisite.

---

[21] Interestingly, this issue is within the province of the civil service and is largely self-inflicted.

8. Judicial interpretation in widening the protections of Article 311 and considerable judicial leniency to civil servants who perform inefficiently or negligently has reduced efficiency.[22]
9. The dearth of successful prosecutions of the corrupt has made corruption a 'financially efficient' strategy when risks are set against rewards.

A few of the factors mentioned above are indeed attributable to the civil service itself, for instance, the creation of post-retirement posts and the dysfunctions of the empanelment system; most, however, have arisen from factors originating outside the civil services.

Misaligned Incentive Structure

The current incentive structure of the civil service can be summarized as follows in Table 9.4.[23]

Using the analogy of (financial) portfolio theory, the different behaviours can be divided into 'efficient' and 'inefficient' ones in terms of the risk/reward balance. The following kinds of behaviour are 'efficient' and thus encouraged:

1. Acquiring/retaining professional competence;
2. Passive political neutrality;[24]
3. Political alignment;
4. Passive honesty; and
5. Bribery.

The types of behaviour described subsequently are 'inefficient'; and therefore discouraged:

---

[22] For details, see section entitled 'Judicial Interpretation and Judicial Leniency' in Civil Service-I.

[23] As with the rest of the chapter, the analysis is as of 2013.

[24] Defined in Civil Service-I as 'total submission to *whoever is in power without any attachment to that party per se*. ... [carrying] out the bidding of the ruling party even if it is contrary to established rules or procedures but [making] it clear to the "losers" that [one] is simply carrying out "orders" and is not really "committed" to the current ruling group; should the ruling party change, [one] would equally happily carry out the bidding of the new group'.

Table 9.4 The Incentive Structure of the Civil Service

Behaviour	Consequences						Risk/Reward Balance
	Rewards			Punishments			
	Career	Social	From illegal activity	Career	Social	From Illegal Activity	
1. Acquiring/retaining professional competence	Low	Low	N/A	Nil	Nil	N/A	Low Risk/Low reward
2. Political neutrality							
– Active neutrality	Nil	High	N/A	High	Nil	N/A	High risk/Moderate reward
– Passive neutrality	Low	Nil	N/A	Low	Nil	N/A	Low Risk/Low reward
– Political alignment	High	Low	N/A	High	Low	N/A	High risk/High reward
3. Acting independently in enforcing the law and due process	Nil	High	N/A	High	Nil	N/A	High risk/Moderate reward
4. Honesty and Integrity							
– Active honesty	Nil	Low	N/A	High	Nil	N/A	High risk/Low reward
– Passive honesty	Low	Nil	N/A	Nil	Nil	N/A	Low risk/Low reward
– Bribery	Nil	Low	High	Mod.	Low	Mod.	Moderate risk/High reward
5. Innovation	Nil	Low	N/A	Mod.	Nil	N/A	Moderate risk/Low reward

Source: Authors' analysis.

1. Active neutrality;[25]
2. Enforcing the law independently; and
3. Innovation.

This assumes that each of these types of behaviour can be pursued independently of the others. In practice, there are 'synergies' between some of them—for example, between passive neutrality and bribery. An officer who is passively neutral has a better chance of maximizing corrupt opportunities. Likewise, an officer who keeps professionally up-to-date is more likely to be innovative. Active honesty and active political neutrality go together. There are negative synergies too: a corrupt officer has little to gain from acquiring professional skills. Going by this analysis, the theoretical prediction would be that the average IAS officer would tend to be reasonably competent, but politically spineless, incapable of enforcing the law fairly, and corrupt. Iyer and Mani's study provides empirical corroboration to several of these inferences.[26]

This analysis has its limitations, and fortunately, there are still a large number of honest and efficient officers. However, it does show that there is a major misalignment between the actual incentives facing IAS officers and the objectives of the service according to the constitutional design. Without changing the incentive structure, it is futile to expect the majority of civil servants to conform to the behaviours expected in the original design.

Recent Trends Affecting the Civil Service

The preceding section, in analysing the causes of the relatively poor record of the civil services, described a number of long-term trends affecting civil service. This section looks at some more recent trends (negative, positive, and those whose effect is not clear) which have developed over the last decade.

---

[25] Defined in Civil Service-I as 'when taking decisions on individual matters, [the officer] does not favour those belonging to, or recommended by the ruling party, and applies rules and norms impartially'.

[26] Iyer and Mani, 'Traveling Agents'.

Negative Trends

Accelerated Decline in Capacity of the State Civil Services and Lower Ranks: The importance of the State Civil Services (members of whom are eligible for promotion to the IAS) should not be under-estimated. The 2013 case of Durga Shakti Nagpal, a sub-divisional magistrate in Uttar Pradesh who became a cause celebre when she was suspended after taking action against illicit construction and sand mining, indicates how important some of these middle-level posts can be. Yet, of the 1,938 sub-divisional officer/magistrate posts in India (excluding Jammu and Kashmir),[27] only 340 (18 per cent) were held by IAS officers like Mrs Nagpal as of 2013, the rest being held by officers of the State Civil Services. Unfortunately, the State Public Service Commissions have (with honourable exceptions from time to time and state to state) generally not been able to maintain high standards of fairness or probity. There are multiple instances in the last decade where chairmen or members of the Commissions have faced corruption cases.[28] The general public perception is that the processes of selection by these institutions is riddled with corruption and/or political patronage, and this often holds good for the higher state services. This is an institutional problem beyond the scope of this chapter.

The performance of the lower rungs of the government (central and state) is also perceived as having deteriorated. The lower ranks are the points of public interface, so poor performance at this level is a significant contributor to poor civil service performance overall. In the first few decades after Independence, the lower ranks of civil service (that is, Group B and Group C level) held a lot of attraction for graduates of the universities. Good private-sector jobs were rela-tively few, and the stability, decent pay, and conditions of the public service made them the first choice for those not able to compete at the Group A (IAS, etc.) level. Thus, the calibre of entrants was good. At the central level, selection was also largely merit-based. At the state

[27] Data for Jammu and Kashmir was not readily available.

[28] 'DVAC Raids 73 Premises of Candidates; TNPSC Chairman', *Indian Express*, 13 January 2012; 'PPSC Former Chairman Ravi Sidhu Handed Down 6-year Jail', *Times of India*, 16 July 2013.

level, arbitrary selection was more common, but generally not based on outright or widespread corruption. Within the service, the systems of performance appraisal left behind by the British still operated, and so clerical and supervisory levels were also subjected to annual performance appraisals written by their immediate supervisors. The appraisals had some effect on career progression, which meant a fairly high level of discipline.

As already noted, the record of State Public Service Commissions is now very poor. Staff associations have begun to behave in a trade union-like manner and also have grouped themselves across caste categories. They have successfully lobbied for dilution or dismantling of performance appraisal systems, and in many states, most of the non-Group A civil servants have no formal annual appraisals. The combination of security of tenure with non-appraisal of performance has had a strongly negative effect on discipline, quality of work, and the ability of senior officers to get work done. These negative trends have accelerated in the last decade and a half.

The growth of employment opportunities for young graduates in the information technology sector has adversely affected the attractiveness of the lower-level civil service jobs, and anecdotally, appears to have reduced the quality of entrants. Even then, the relative insecurity and lack of work–family balance in the private sector has meant that government jobs still hold some attraction for good graduates. For central government posts, fairly good selection mechanisms have ensured that there is a reasonably fair route for entry, and thus some good candidates are still attracted into the Group B and C levels of the central government. In many state governments, for reasons already mentioned, the good candidates rarely enter the fray.

Large numbers of vacancies: Table 9.5 provides details of the evolution of the size of the IAS. The only period which saw a decline in numbers was from 1991 to 2000. Over the years, the IAS grew for various reasons, both exogenous and endogenous. In the early decades, the growth of the IAS was largely driven by the expanding role of the state. Later, the 73rd and 74th Amendments created a need for civil servants to work in local bodies. Apart from these exogenous factors, the expansion was also apparently driven by the desire of the state political executive to have more 'insiders' in their cadre. Since the cadre allotment policy limited the proportion of outsiders, an increase in cadre

Table 9.5　Total Authorized Strength of the Indian
Administrative Service

Date	Total Authorized Strength
1.1.1951	1,232
1.1.1961	1,862
1.1.1971	3,203
1.1.1981	4,599
1.1.1991	5,334
1.1.2000	5,159
1.1.2010	5,689
1.1.2012	6,154
1.1.2016	6,396

Source: Department of Personnel and Training, Ministry of
Personnel, Public Grievances and Pensions, Government of India.

strength was a way to increase the promotion quota, and thereby to
increase the absolute number of insiders.[29]

Figure 9.8 shows the recent evolution of the authorized and actual
strength: paradoxically, as the authorized strength has grown, the actual
strength has declined, mainly due to retirement of the large cohorts
recruited in the 1970s. The actual number of IAS officers in position
(actual cadre strength) in 2012 was 4,377 vis-à-vis the authorized
strength of 6,154—that is, 29 per cent of the cadre was vacant.

The process of promotion and selection to the AIS has been plagued
by voluminous litigation, and compliance with varying court orders has
been a major reason for the large number of vacancies.

The authors had earlier recommended a reduction in authorized
strength of approximately this magnitude, and in one sense, the fact that
the country is managing for many years within this number appears to
endorse the earlier recommendation.[30] However, while a well-planned
restructuring and elimination of unnecessary posts would be good, an
ad hoc system of vacancies has many negative consequences. It disturbs
orderly succession planning and distorts the ratios of promoted officers

[29] Baswan Committee, *To Take a Comprehensive Look at the Requirement of
IAS Officers over a Longer Timeframe* (Ministry of Personnel, Public Grievances
& Pensions, Government of India, n.d.).

[30] See Civil Service-I.

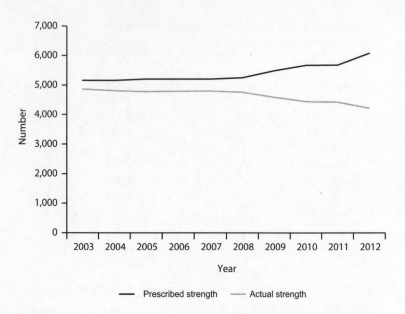

Figure 9.8 Authorized and Actual Strength of Indian Administrative Service, 2003–2012
Source: Krishnan and Somanathan, 'Civil Service—An Institutional Perspective.'

to direct recruits and of officers working in the centre versus the states, all of which have negative implications for civil service effectiveness.

Disproportion in cadre sizes: There are large inter-state variations in the size of cadres vis-à-vis state populations. Table 9.6 shows the extent to which the proportion of IAS officers in each state cadre deviates from that state's share of population.

The table shows that Uttar Pradesh's share of the IAS cadre is about 42 per cent lower than its share of population, while Sikkim has 15 times what would be expected for its size. An interesting trend is that larger states tend to have relatively smaller cadre sizes. To an extent, this is attributable to economies of scale and the special problems of some of the smaller states which may require a larger administrative presence. On the other hand, more developed states may have a larger need for officers in regulatory and project management positions which could offset that. The extreme variation seen in Table 9.6 cannot be explained by these factors. The data lend strong credence to the Baswan Committee's view that cadre expansion has been driven by a

Table 9.6   Cadre Sizes against State Population

Name of Cadre	State(s)'s Share of Population of India (2011)	IAS Cadre Strength (2012)	State's Cadre as Proportion of Total IAS Strength	Excess/ Shortfall as a Proportion of Expected Share
[1]	[2]	[3]	[4]	[4-2/2]
Uttar Pradesh	16.49%	592	9.6%	−42%
Maharashtra	9.29%	350	5.7%	−39%
Bihar	8.58%	326	5.3%	−38%
West Bengal	7.55%	314	5.1%	−32%
Gujarat	4.99%	260	4.2%	−15%
Rajasthan	5.67%	296	4.8%	−15%
Andhra Pradesh	7.00%	376	6.1%	−13%
Karnataka	5.05%	299	4.9%	−4%
Tamil Nadu	5.96%	355	5.8%	−3%
Odisha	3.47%	226	3.7%	6%
Madhya Pradesh	6.00%	417	6.8%	13%
Jharkhand	2.72%	208	3.4%	24%
Kerala	2.76%	214	3.5%	26%
Chhattisgarh	2.11%	178	2.9%	37%
Assam– Meghalaya	2.82%	248	4.0%	43%
Punjab	2.29%	221	3.6%	57%
Haryana	2.09%	205	3.3%	59%
Jammu and Kashmir	1.04%	137	2.2%	115%
Uttarakhand	0.84%	120	1.9%	133%
AGMUT	1.88%	337	5.5%	191%
Himachal Pradesh	0.57%	129	2.1%	270%
Manipur– Tripura	0.53%	207	3.4%	537%

(Cont'd)

Table 9.6   (Cont'd)

Name of Cadre	State(s)'s Share of Population of India (2011)	IAS Cadre Strength (2012)	State's Cadre as Proportion of Total IAS Strength	Excess/ Shortfall as a Proportion of Expected Share
[1]	[2]	[3]	[4]	[4-2/2]
Nagaland	0.16%	91	1.5%	804%
Sikkim	0.05%	48	0.8%	1,453%
Total	100.0%	6,154	100.0%	0%

Source: Website of the Department of Personnel and Training, Ministry of Personnel, Public Grievances and Pensions; Census of India, 2011.

desire in smaller states to ensure adequate 'insider' and/or promotee representation.

Disproportion in the numbers of officers in the central government: Not only do states differ widely in their relative cadre strength, they also differ in the extent to which officers take up central postings. Table 9.7 gives details of the difference between the expected number of IAS officers in the centre from that state and the actual number.

Table 9.7 shows that the Assam–Meghalaya cadre is over-represented by 71 per cent vis-à-vis its expected level while Chhattisgarh is under-represented by 51 per cent.

While Tables 9.6 and 9.7 present a one-time snapshot, analysis was also done over the period 2003 to 2012 using panel data. We used a Spearman's rank correlation coefficient to track the evolving level of disproportion vis-à-vis the expected shares. A rank correlation coefficient of 1 would indicate perfect conformity with the expected distribution; the lower the coefficient, the greater the lack of conformity. Over the period, the coefficient declined from 0.78 in 2003 to 0.72 in 2012 with a low of 0.67 in 2008. The rank correlation was lowest at the Director (middle management) level.

Taking the period as a whole, the over-represented cadres were: Assam–Meghalaya, AGMUT (Arunachal Pradesh, Goa, Mizoram, and Union Territories), Himachal Pradesh, Jammu and Kashmir, Madhya

Table 9.7 Over/Under-representation in the Central Government

Cadre	State(s)' Share of Population of India (2011)	Expected Share of Officers Posted in the Centre (CDR)	Actual Share of Officers Posted in the Centre (2012)	Over-/Under-representation vis-à-vis Population	Over-/Under-representation vis-à-vis Expected Share
Assam-Meghalaya	2.82%	4.06%	6.95%	146%	71%
Kerala	2.76%	3.46%	5.85%	112%	69%
Sikkim	0.05%	0.75%	1.26%	2417%	68%
Himachal Pradesh	0.57%	2.10%	3.32%	486%	58%
Manipur-Tripura	0.53%	3.38%	4.74%	797%	40%
Odisha	3.47%	3.68%	4.42%	28%	20%
Uttar Pradesh	16.49%	9.62%	11.53%	−30%	20%
Jammu and Kashmir	1.04%	2.25%	2.69%	159%	19%
Haryana	2.09%	3.31%	3.79%	81%	15%
AGMUT	1.88%	5.48%	6.00%	219%	9%
Tamil Nadu	5.96%	5.79%	6.32%	6%	9%
Nagaland	0.16%	1.50%	1.58%	865%	5%
Uttarakhand	0.84%	1.95%	1.90%	127%	−3%
West Bengal	7.55%	5.11%	4.90%	−35%	−4%
Madhya Pradesh	6.00%	6.76%	6.00%	0%	−11%
Rajasthan	5.67%	4.81%	4.27%	−25%	−11%
Bihar	8.58%	5.26%	4.11%	−52%	−22%
Andhra Pradesh	7.00%	6.09%	4.58%	−35%	−25%
Karnataka	5.05%	4.88%	3.63%	−28%	−26%

(Cont'd)

Table 9.7   (*Cont'd*)

Cadre	State(s)' Share of Population of India (2011)	Expected Share of Officers Posted in the Centre (CDR)	Actual Share of Officers Posted in the Centre (2012)	Over-/Under-representation vis-à-vis Population	Over-/Under-representation vis-à-vis Expected Share
Maharashtra	9.29%	5.71%	3.95%	–57%	–31%
Gujarat	4.99%	4.21%	2.69%	–46%	–36%
Jharkhand	2.72%	3.38%	2.05%	–25%	–39%
Punjab	2.29%	3.61%	2.05%	–10%	–43%
Chhattisgarh	2.11%	2.85%	1.42%	–33%	–50%
Total	100.00%	100.00%	100.00%		

Source: Authors' compilation.

Pradesh, Manipur–Tripura, Nagaland, Sikkim, Odisha, Uttar Pradesh, Bihar (since changed), and Kerala.

The data, taken with interviews with officers, indicate that the main explanation for over-representation in Delhi relates to the 'fugitive' effect, whereby some officers are very keen to stay away from their cadres. In the case of the Northeast and hill states, this is primarily related to living conditions, including educational opportunities for children, and in some cases, insurgency and consequent lack of normality in the role of a civil administrator. In the case of Uttar Pradesh, Bihar, and Odisha, the explanation is partly related to superior living conditions in Delhi; in the case of Uttar Pradesh it may also be related to the perceived poor career management and frequent penal transfers of officers in the state. The manner in which officers are permanently allotted to cadres with no reference to their preferences (referred to above) has played a major role in this problem.

The over-representation of Kerala is more difficult to explain. Among officers, it is partly attributed to the presence of a cabinet secretary from that cadre (who received several extensions of service) during a large part of the period covered by the analysis—the theory being that there was a 'pull effect' where the cabinet secretary tended to bring in (or attract) people from his cadre, who in turn did the same.

Significant under-representation from Maharashtra, Gujarat, Andhra Pradesh, Karnataka, and (until recently) Tamil Nadu appears to be conversely explained by relatively good living conditions and the presence of metropolitan cities with good educational and other opportunities and thus a reduced incentive to stay in Delhi. The problems of the empanelment process and empanelment delays act as disincentives for officers from these cadres to serve in Delhi.

Another reason for under-filling of the Central Deputation Reserve (CDR) and the under-representation of relatively developed states is the delayed promotions in GoI. According to the guidelines, IAS officers are eligible to be promoted to the super time scale (joint secretary to GoI level), Higher Administrative Grade (assistant secretary to GoI level) and Apex Scale (secretary to GoI level) on completion of 16, 25, and 30 years of service, respectively.[31] In most cadres, these promotions happen largely on schedule. Officers in GoI take three to four years longer to reach each of these levels vis-à-vis their colleagues posted in the states, and this is one of the reasons officers from relatively developed states do not opt for central postings.

Overall, the data show that active management of the numbers to ensure optimal distribution has not happened; the preferences of officers to be (or not to be) in Delhi appear to play a much larger role in their posting to the centre than the design would require.

Adverse effect of disproportionate representation: The data thus show that

1. smaller states tend to have relatively large cadres and correspondingly a relatively large prescribed share of central posts;
2. officers from many of the smaller cadres also tend to take a share of posts at the centre which is even larger than their prescribed share.

This confirms the validity of the perception widely held among officers that the central government has a disproportionate number of officers from the small and less-developed states and too few from the larger, more developed states. The problem this raises is that:

[31] *Office Memorandum No. M 20611.4.92-AIS-II* (New Delhi: Department of Personnel and Training, 28 March 2000).

1. Policymaking is disproportionately led by officers whose experience at state level may not be directly relevant to the governance needs of the states which house the majority of the population;
2. Successful lessons from the more advanced states are transmitted less frequently and less well than if the design proportions were adhered to.

For instance, the problems of managing large cities, large local bodies, or major public–private partnership (PPP) projects, which are key contemporary development challenges, are not present in several states.

Under-representation of the IAS in the central government: The CDR represents the number of posts in the IAS which are meant to be occupied by IAS officers working in the central government. As of 2012, the actual number of officers in the central government (633) was only 48 per cent of the prescribed CDR (1,331). One reason for the shortfall was, of course, the high level of vacancies in the service. Adjusting for the vacancy rate, 946 IAS officers should have been at the centre. Thus, even after adjusting for vacancies, IAS officers at the centre are only 67 per cent of the expected number. Thus, the IAS is under-represented vis-à-vis the central services (who spend their entire career working in the central government). This under-representation is greater at the middle management level. The prognosis is that the top management at the centre will have fewer IAS officers and the IAS officers who will be there will be more of those with limited prior experience in GoI. Both these are problematic—first, the extent to which ground-level experience is reflected in policymaking will be reduced and second, those that are at the centre will be less experienced and hence less able to be effective.

Perception of increased political influence in central postings: Over the last decade, the perception is that the degree of political involvement in postings and transfers at the level of secretary to GoI has increased substantially. Obviously, this is something for which no direct evidence can be obtained, and the authors are basing this observation on interviews with those who have become or are in consideration for the post of secretary to GoI. Officers empanelled as secretary are not necessarily posted as secretary in the order of their seniority or to ministries where they have experience or expertise. The current perception is

that an officer cannot become secretary without the active support of
the minister concerned, and that this support can only be obtained by
personally interacting with the minister, expressing one's interest, and
seeking his support.[32] This is a major change which has taken hold in
the early part of the twenty-first century and is attributed by many
officers to the prevalence of coalition politics. Ministers from parties
other than the principal ruling party often insist on particular officers
being posted in their ministries. It is a fact, for example, that the former
secretary of the Department of Telecommunications who has been
charge-sheeted in the 2G telecom scandal was earlier a joint secretary
in another ministry under the same minister, and many perceive that
he was reputedly made secretary at the minister's request. The authors
cannot vouch for the correctness or otherwise of this perception, but
it illustrates the possible dangers of such an approach. The situation is
in contrast to governments of all parties in the pre-2000 era, where the
posting of secretaries was primarily decided by the cabinet secretary
with the approval of the prime minister, and with political involvement generally being only at the prime minister's level. Exceptions
existed even then, but the exceptions now appear to be the rule. In
recent years, the perceived trend is that political support is sometimes
necessary even to be posted as joint secretary in the more 'prestigious'
ministries.

Officers are presented with a dilemma in this situation: stick to
principles, do not approach anyone, and retire as a special secretary
or secretary of a department with relatively less meaningful work; or
bend, seek political support, and then become less able to act with
independence when on the job. Effectively, this recent tendency has
introduced into the central government a malaise which has long
affected state governments and from which the centre was perceived
as relatively immune.

The result is that India now compares very unfavourably with most
developed countries in terms of civil service independence. Tables 9.8
to 9.10 attempt a comparison of India with certain other countries for
which information is available, on three qualitative dimensions. The

---

[32] There is a further perception that in some cases, such support can only
be obtained by agreeing to do the minister's bidding irrespective of propriety.

Table 9.8   Influence of the Political Executive on Senior Civil Service
Appointments

Rank (1 = Highest Political Power)	India 1995			India 2013	Rank
1	USA	•	•	USA	1
2	Sweden	•	•	IAS—state	2
3	Italy	•	•	Sweden	3
4	South Africa	•	•	Italy	4
5	Mexico	•	•	IAS—centre	5
6	IAS—state	•	•	South Africa	6
7	France	•	•	Mexico	7
8	Belgium	•	•	France	8
9	Poland	•	•	Belgium	9
10	IAS—centre	•	•	Poland	10
11	Korea	•	•	Korea	11
12	New Zealand	•	•	New Zealand	12
13	Denmark	•	•	Denmark	13
14	UK	•	•	UK	14

Source: Authors' analysis.

first table looks at the extent to which top civil service appointments
are based on the political executive, and in this table we have attempted
a subjective time comparison between 1995 (the year before coalition government became the norm) and the current situation. For all
three tables, the data source for countries other than India is Matheson
et al., while data for India is the authors' estimate using the same rating
methodology.[33]

The table shows that the extent of political power over civil service
appointments is higher than in almost all other parliamentary systems
and is now second only to the US, which has a presidential system. It is
generally agreed that in a parliamentary system (where the legislature
is not an effective check on the executive because the executive needs
at all times to have a majority there to survive) an independent civil
service is a crucial element. India's position on this table is thus a matter of concern.

[33] Matheson *et al.*, 'Study on the Political Involvement' chapter.

Table 9.9 Ranking of Turnover of Public Servants Following Elections

Rank	Country	Type of Government
1	USA	Presidential
2	Italy	Parliamentary
3	IAS— State Level	Parliamentary
4	Mexico	Presidential
5	IAS—Central Level	Parliamentary
6	Poland	Parliamentary
7	Korea	Presidential
8	France	Presidential
9	Belgium	Parliamentary
10	UK	Parliamentary
11	New Zealand	Parliamentary
12	Denmark	Parliamentary
13	Sweden	Parliamentary

Source: Authors' estimate (for India); Matheson *et al.*, 'Study on the Political Involvement', Table 13 (for all other countries).

Another measure of politicization is the extent to which civil servants are transferred after an election resulting in a change of government. This is depicted in Table 9.9.

Here India does worse than all parliamentary systems other than Italy, even at the central level.

On another measure, the extent of interference in matters expected to be decided by the civil service, India is ranked the worst of the countries for which information is available (see Table 9.10).

Perception of increased corruption: In 2005, Civil Service-I opined that corruption had crept in and was generally felt to be widespread in the IAS. Over the following decade, the perceived level of corruption has increased further. Given that pay compression has not worsened, and public scrutiny has increased through the Right to Information Act, 2005 (RTI Act) and increased civil society activity, possible hypotheses to explain this are:

1. Continuation of the social pressures referred to in Civil Service-I (high private-sector pay enjoyed by comparators with similar educational background, trend towards conspicuous consumption and away from simple living, weakening of public service values, etc.);

Table 9.10 Tendency of Ministers to Interfere in Management Responsibility of Senior Civil Servants

Rank	Country	Type of Government
1	IAS—State level	Parliamentary
2	IAS—Central level	Parliamentary
3	Italy	Parliamentary
4	Poland	Parliamentary
5	Denmark	Parliamentary
6	USA	Presidential
7	Belgium	Parliamentary
8	Mexico	Presidential
9	Sweden	Parliamentary
10	France	Presidential
11	UK	Parliamentary
12	New Zealand	Parliamentary

Source: Authors' estimate (for India); Matheson *et al.*, 'Study on the Political Involvement', Table 13 (for all other countries).

2. Increased political involvement in both appointments and decision making, bringing civil servants closer to politicians in culture and approach (despite the benefits of security of tenure and lack of need to spend on elections);
3. Increase in the new regulatory powers of the state in areas ranging from utilities to environment (reversing the trend of the 1990s when the licensing system was discontinued).

The effects of the relatively recent events connected with the 2G telecom scandal and other high-profile scams have yet to be fully reflected or understood. However, based on interviews with civil servants, the authors' impression is that the effect has been to change the way in which corrupt officers make money, rather than to reduce corruption, while also reducing, in general, the willingness of officers to offer clear policy advice on potentially controversial issues. Thus, instead of making money on changing a decision, the relatively safer course of holding up routine matters and then clearing the file after receiving illicit gratification is perceived to be more prevalent than earlier.

However, it is very important to emphasize that there are still a large number of honest and dedicated civil servants. The authors (with some colleagues) attempted to estimate an 'integrity perceptions index' for the IAS based on peer opinions. The methodology involved allocating a large sample of officers known to the raters to one of three categories. A limitation of the study was poor coverage of the younger officers, and thus the figures pertain mainly to officers with over 10 years of service. The result of the exercise was:

1. Just over 50 per cent of IAS officers are honest and will not take bribes.
2. About a quarter may engage in consensual corruption but will not harass the unwilling.
3. Another quarter will engage in non-consensual corruption (that is, hold up or change decisions to get bribes) and/or actively collaborate in political corruption.

Obviously, these are extremely worrying figures, but the pleasant surprise is that despite the environment being so adverse, the majority of officers are still honest. This means all is not lost and there is still hope. The regret is that nearly half the officers are perceived to be corrupt.[34]

Perception of reduced competence: There is an increasing perception outside civil service that senior civil servants do not possess the level of competence needed to take good policy decisions or tender good policy advice at state and central levels. The authors have difficulty in assessing this issue. On the one hand, exposure of civil servants to modern management concepts and to training in highly-regarded international academic institutions has definitely increased. The familiarity of senior IAS officers with the latest jargon and buzzwords like 'results frameworks' or 'gender budgeting', among others, and their ability to talk the talk of modern public management has definitely increased. On

---

[34] It is to be noted that competence is not correlated with honesty: they are separate dimensions. There are honest officers who are incompetent and dishonest ones who are competent and vice versa. While an honest-and-efficient officer is obviously the best, it is a matter of much debate among both civil servants and politicians as to whether administration is more effective and public interest better served under a corrupt-but-efficient officer than under an honest-but-inefficient officer.

the other hand, there are many examples of poor civil service advice to ministers. The ability of civil servants to coordinate policymaking between ministries also appears to have deteriorated.

A difficulty with this issue is that the outside perception coincides with a period when public opinion has decisively turned against government in general, to a mood of disenchantment. It is also difficult to estimate the extent of political interference in many questionable policy actions, and therefore to assess whether there was a lack of civil service competence, whether competent advice was over-ruled, or whether advice was not tendered due to political interference. Governance is very often a 'joint product' of the civil service and the political executive, and attribution of competence or incompetence to one or the other is very difficult.

One dimension of 'competence' or 'capacity' is the ability to decide or make specific policy recommendations. This has declined in recent years. It is not clear whether this is because of any change in ability or more due to a change in the incentives. It appears to be partly related to the effects of increased public scrutiny and a feeling that, while a bad decision may lead to adverse consequences, indecision is safe.

Notwithstanding the caveats, the authors, as insiders, do feel that there is a lack of competence in several areas of government, and that many civil servants in key positions do not have the necessary subject-matter and decision-analysis skills. Capacity building is relatively non-controversial and thus an area where reforms may be easier to implement.

Positive Trends

Creation of the Lok Pal: The creation of the Lok Pal, an anti-corruption authority independent of the political executive with wide-ranging powers to investigate and prosecute, holds a lot of promise for more effective detection and prosecution of corruption in civil service.

Recommendations of the 2nd Administrative Reforms Commission (ARC): The 2nd ARC, in its 10th Report, made several recommendations on civil service reform, most of which the authors support. The steps taken by the central government to implement the recommendations have set in motion some positive changes. The recent tendency of the courts to take judicial notice of commission reports increases the chances of their implementation. A full discussion is beyond the scope of this chapter but the most important issues are referred to at the appropriate junctures.

Change in cadre allotment procedure: The cadre allotment procedure was changed with effect from 2008 and is made on the basis of examination ranks and the preferences indicated by candidates. In the long run, this is likely to improve morale, and reduce the extent to which certain cadres are over-represented at the centre. The 2nd ARC has also recommended that, in respect of the north-eastern states, at least one vacancy each year be allotted to insiders. This would be a further improvement.

Marginal improvement in pay compression: Table 9.11 shows the evolution of the ratio of top-level to bottom-level pay without allowances. The minimum salary is for Group D of the government service, while the maximum is the salary of the highest rung of the IAS (cabinet secretary). From 1948 to 1996, there was a continuous and very severe pay compression. Actual compression was worse than shown in the table because of the practice of 'differential DA neutralisation', under which dearness allowance (cost of living indexation, also known as DA) was calculated on only a portion of the salary for those in the higher ranks but on the whole salary for the lower ranks of the government service. Since 1996, differential neutralization has been given up. The ratio has slightly improved through the recommendations of the Sixth Pay Commission. For the first time since Independence, compression was reduced rather than increased, albeit marginally, and the compression ratio was restored to the 1986 level. Thus, changes in pay and perquisites over the last decade have not contributed to any increased incentive for corruption or to a diminution of quality of entry.

However, the ratio remains very low compared to the past and to civil services of most developed countries. The ratio of top civil service pay to top private sector pay (though not analysed in this chapter) has undoubtedly worsened to an even greater degree. While the perquisite value of bungalows in Lutyens' Delhi is large and visible, for a dispassionate analysis of the civil service as a whole, it must be remembered that over 85 per cent of the IAS serves in the states and districts, and of those in Delhi, only the highest ranked get large flats or bungalows.

Proposed changes to examination pattern: Over the years, a perception took hold that those writing the examination in certain languages with a very small number of candidates were advantaged; the unstated

Table 9.11 Pay Compression Ratio, 1948–2006

	1948	1949	1960	1965	1970	1973	1986	1996	2006
Maximum Salary (pre-tax)	3,000	3,000	3,000	3,500	3,500	3,500	8,000	16,580	80,000
Maximum Salary (post-tax)	2,263	2,263	2,281	2,422	2,399	2,331	5,896	12,615	56,000
Minimum Salary (falls below taxable limit and is thus tax free)	55	65	80	103	141	196	750	2,060	7,000
Pre-tax compression ratio	54.5	46.2	37.5	34.0	24.8	17.9	10.7	8.0	11.5
Post-tax compression ratio	41.0	34.8	28.5	23.5	17.0	11.9	7.9	6.1	8.0

Source: Reports of Central Pay Commissions, various years.

presumption was that some subtle bias might operate on the minds of the examiners who might, possibly unconsciously, tend to favour one of 'their own'.[35] The GoI attempted to change the pattern of the examination in 2013:

1. An English comprehension and English précis exam of matriculation level was introduced, carrying a weight of approximately 5 per cent of the total marks.
2. Candidates could only choose an Indian language as one of their optional subjects if they had graduated with the literature of that language as their main subject.
3. Candidates could only use an Indian language (other than Hindi) as medium if they had used that medium in their graduate-level examinations; all other candidates would have to answer the papers in English or Hindi.
4. Papers would only be set in a language if at least 25 candidates opted for that medium of examination.

The changes appear to have been made partly on the basis of the recommendations of a High Level Standing Committee on the issue of language[36] and a separate committee of experts on the examination.[37] According to the chairman of the expert committee, the recommendations were based on the increasing importance of effective communication.[38]

There was opposition to the notified changes by prospective candidates, chief ministers of various states, and also in Parliament,[39] where

[35] As mentioned in the section 'The Formal Design' in this chapter, data does not, however, support that conclusion since the success rate is not significantly different for such candidates.

[36] Response to Parliamentary Question No. 448 in Lok Sabha, answered on 26 February 2013 in the Lok Sabha. The question was by Shri Shivaramagouda Shivanagouda Nalin Kumar Kateel.

[37] 'PM Approves Changes in Civil Services Exam Pattern', *Press Trust of India*, 17 February 2013; the report of the Committee is not publicly available.

[38] 'New UPSC Rules Were to Test Communication Skills', *Press Trust of India*, 17 March 2013.

[39] 'After English Controversy, Changes to UPSC Exam Suspended', *NDTV Cheat Sheet*, 15 March 2013, http://www.ndtv.com/cheat-sheet/after-english-controversy-changes-to-upsc-exam-suspended-516301.

there was almost unanimous condemnation of the notification.[40] Members of Parliament (MPs) across the board stated that the move to make English a compulsory subject was an attack on other regional languages and that the move would disadvantage those from rural areas. The government eventually withdrew the changes.

Apart from the issue of language, the 2nd ARC had recommended an approach where all candidates would take only compulsory papers, with no optional ones.

However, the conduct or content of the examination is hardly the source of the biggest weaknesses in the civil service so these changes—while desirable—will not substantially affect institutional effectiveness, even if implemented.

Proposed changes in IAS appointment by induction and selection: In 2013, the government proposed fundamental changes to the method of entry into the IAS from State Civil Services and other state services.[41] The changes appear to have been made on the basis of the recommendations of the 2nd ARC.[42]

The main change is the introduction of a common written examination to be conducted by the UPSC which would carry a substantial weight (40 per cent for Induction and 55 per cent for Selection).[43] The examination would cover general studies, aptitude, state-specific and service-specific questions, besides an essay.

Some chief ministers and many serving State Civil Service officers have objected to the changes being proposed.[44] Objections include the fact that serving officers' time would be diverted to examination

[40] 'Re: Reported Notification Making English Compulsory in UPSC Civil Services Examinations' (uncorrected debates, Lok Sabha, New Delhi, 15 March 2013), part I.

[41] These proposals introduced the term 'induction' in place of the term 'promotion' for those brought into the IAS from the State Civil Service.

[42] Second Administrative Reforms Commission, *Tenth Report* (New Delhi: Ministry of Personnel, Public Grievances & Pensions, Government of India, 2008).

[43] Other selection criteria would be interview, assessment of service records, and (for induction) length of service.

[44] T.E. Narasimhan, 'Jaya Opposes Change in Induction Method of State Officers into AIS', *Business Standard*, 25 April 2013; 'Continue Present-Day System For Induction of State Officers In IAS, IPS', *The Pioneer*, 31 May 2013.

preparation and that it would be unjust to officers already in the system who have been used to a different method and cannot (at a relatively advanced age) suddenly make the shift.[45]

The proposed changes would go a long way in reducing the politicization of this channel of entry and thus increase the neutrality, independence, and competence of the IAS. If implemented, they would increase merit and make the quality of the service more uniform. The argument about 'wasting' time in examination preparation is weak since continuous learning is a much-needed and desirable quality for a modern civil service.

There is indeed a genuine transitional issue for officers who are on the verge of promotion. A transitional arrangement for those currently affected would be desirable (perhaps by bringing the new scheme into operation after a period of two years), but transitional issues should not stop a desirable reform for the long run.

Other Trends

End of pension with defined benefits: Since 2004, the AIS (like many other central government staff) are no longer eligible for the traditional defined-benefit pension. Instead, they are part of the National Pension Scheme, which is a defined contribution plan where actual pensions will depend on the performance of investments. Without getting into the merits or demerits of defined contribution schemes, it is a fact that the fiscal cost to the government and the financial benefit to the staff are both lower under the new scheme than under the old. The change reduces the overall remuneration package of the civil service at all levels. It is too early to comment on its impact.

Expanding role of local government: The implementation of the 73rd and 74th constitutional amendments over the last decade and a half has meant a change in the role of the civil servant at the district and sub-district level. It took several years for civil servants to adjust to the new reality. On the one hand, the role of the district collector diminished through the introduction of a strong local-elected executive. On the other hand, IAS officers are often posted in the new role of chief

[45] P. Marpakwar, 'Maharashtra Cadre Officials Oppose Exam Plan for IAS Promotion', *Times of India*, 21 May 2013.

executive officers of the local government, working under an elected district administration. In some states, the state political executive encouraged decentralization. In others, it decentralized with reluctance and used the institution of the collector as a means of restricting the extent of decentralized authority. It would be reasonable to say that in a majority of instances, IAS officers did not embrace decentralization as an opportunity to improve local governance and instead largely saw it as a threat to established authority structures.[46] This has gradually changed as the Panchayati Raj (India's tiered system of local government) institutions have become older. The positive effect on their developmental functions has been to strengthen and deepen the exposure of young IAS officers to the needs and aspirations of the population. The negative effect on their regulatory functions has been that it has made them somewhat less willing to enforce the law independently and more conscious of political calculations.

Effect of Right to Information on civil service behaviour: The enactment of the RTI Act in 2005 was an important milestone in Indian public administration. Indeed, without exaggeration, it was a milestone in public administration globally as the Indian RTI law has influenced not only many developed countries, but even the information policy of the World Bank. Much has been said and written about its salutary purpose and effects. This part of the chapter is not an attempt to assess RTI in its entirety; rather, it is a very narrow look at the limited issue of the effects of RTI on civil service behaviour (and in this section the discussion covers both the higher and lower services).

The effects of the RTI Act on the civil service appear to have gone through a series of phases. Most officers, schooled in the British traditions of official secrecy and the default position that everything is restricted, had difficulty in adjusting to the new law. Initially, the reaction was often to find a way—even if contrary to the Act—to deny requests. Many learnt painfully, through orders of the Information Commissions and the courts, that times had decisively changed since they were eventually compelled to provide it and sometimes fined. Then came the various definitional debates about whether one or other type of information was included or not; in every case the battle

[46] T.R. Raghunandan, former Joint Secretary (Rural Development), Government of India, in conversation with the authors.

for restriction was lost and information had to be disclosed. The only institution that successfully waged the battle against disclosure was the Supreme Court and the judiciary.

This led to the second phase: many ills were exposed because the files had been prepared without anticipation of disclosure. Juicy skeletons fell out of many a closet (if one pardons the unsavoury mixed metaphor). The initial impact was to reveal wrong-doing that previously would have remained unknown.

Then came the third phase, where the civil servants realized that they were operating under a different regime. They first began to make sure that the note files were now more carefully written on the assumption that they would be published. While the hope would be that this led to different advice and different decisions, in many cases what it led to was that the same advice was tendered orally; after decisions were taken, the file was written in a defensible manner.

The fourth phase was when civil servants realized that they could harness the power of RTI to further their own career interests. A massive number of RTI applications are now filed by government servants at all levels usually in the name of another (a spouse, friend, etc.). This creates additional work for the offices (in providing details, dealing with appeals, etc.). The extra work is performed either by diversion from other duties (since RTI has a time limit and clear penalty, it takes priority over normal citizen services) or by creating additional staff. In a sense, the establishment matters of government servants—when raised through RTI—take precedence over public service.

An assessment of the effects of RTI on civil service behaviour suggests that:

1. On the positive side, it has made it easier for good civil servants to discourage the taking of egregiously bad decisions, by pointing out that they would be indefensible in the public realm even with the best of reasoning. Civil servants are also taking greater care in thinking through and documenting the rationale for decisions.
2. On the other hand, the pressure on honest officers not to dissent on file appears to have increased because whereas earlier the dissent would only come out rarely, now there is a greater threat of disclosure. RTI has also made it easier for civil servants to leak details that they would like to leak, by getting someone else to file

an RTI application. For this reason, it has made ministers even more suspicious of dissent notes on files because the minister may wonder whether this is purely an internal expression of opinion or is a planned act of sabotage.

3. The disclosure of note files has reduced the recording of internal disagreements on files and made them less interesting and also less reliable for an *ex post* view of what actually happened. Instead, disagreements are aired verbally and only the final 'consensus' view is put in writing. This has often reduced the transparency of the record of decision through the censoring out of some view-points expressed internally. It is likely to be more difficult for historians, researchers, auditors, or courts in the future to find out what really under-pinned a particular decision.

4. Overall, the RTI, in steady state, does not (at least not yet) appear to have had a beneficial effect on honesty and integrity of civil servants.

It is noteworthy that nearly all developed countries and international organizations restrict the disclosure of 'deliberative information' (basically, note files in the Indian context) because disclosure would affect the tendering of frank advice internally and is a communication which deserves 'executive privilege'.[47] The rampant corruption in India and the general mood of suspicion of both civil servants and ministers mean that advocating non-disclosure of anything risks being seen as supporting corruption. However, this is an area which may benefit from dispassionate review. Lawrence Lessig, Professor at Harvard Law School has observed: 'There is no questioning the good that transparency creates in a wide range of contexts ... But we should also recognize that the collateral consequence of that good need not itself be good ... Sunlight may well be a great disinfectant, but as anyone who has waded through a swamp knows, it has other effects as well' [that is, promoting the growth of weeds].[48] Others have observed that the well organized (usually the relatively privileged or the corporate sector) may benefit the most because they can use it the best. The widespread use of RTI

---

[47] Her Mjesty's (HM) Government, *The Civil Service Reform Plan* (London, UK: 2012).

[48] L. Lessig, 'Against Transparency: The Perils of Openness in Government', *The New Republic*, 9 October 2009.

by government servants in service of their career interests is a case in point.

Prosecution without evidence of illegal gratification or enrichment, based on 'conspiracies' or wrongful gain to a private party: Since 1988, the Prevention of Corruption Act has had a section, Section 13(1)(d)(iii), under which a public servant who 'obtains for any person any valuable thing or pecuniary advantage without any public interest' is guilty of corruption. The key element of this offence is that there is no need to establish mens rea on the part of the officer or to establish recklessness, or even negligence. Any order which results in a pecuniary benefit to a private party without public interest is liable to be prosecuted as corruption. Thus, an act of a public servant which—without any prior knowledge on his or her part—ends up benefiting someone can potentially be characterized as an act of corruption.

The intent behind this section was that it is often easy for a corrupt public servant to conceal the act of bribery, and it is often difficult for the prosecution to establish mens rea. Removing the requirement of a guilty mind would make it easier to nail the corrupt.

However, the practical effect of the section has been that innocent and honest officers can now be prosecuted for corruption, with hindsight, on the basis of decisions that ended up unwittingly causing a gain to some party (and even if there were no loss to the exchequer). Second, the relatively poor investigative training, skills, and resources of the anti-corruption agencies in dealing with white collar crime vis-à-vis their counterparts in developed countries means that they generally take the easy route of basing a prosecution solely on a 'criminal conspiracy' supported by notes on a file, without any proof of actual corruption on the part of a civil servant. For instance, where B, a businessman, has done something illegal, and C (a civil servant) has written something on a file favourable to B's application or request, the favourable noting becomes evidence of C conspiring with B and hence makes C liable for the criminal actions of B—even though C might have been acting with no improper motive. For instance, when an industry requests something from the government for a project which has positive economic and employment effects, a well-meaning and honest officer may indeed recommend a favourable decision. If it later turns out that the industry had broken the law in some respect or bribed a minister without any knowledge on the part of the civil servant, the positive recommendation can become a source of suspicion and prosecution.

By way of illustration of the twin effect of these tendencies, in 2001, after an election, a newly elected state government launched a prosecution against a former city mayor (of an opposing political party), alleging corruption in the award of a high-value civil work. Two years earlier, the rules had been amended by delegating enhanced authority to elected local bodies, at the initiative of the Secretary of the Municipal Administration Department, an officer of impeccable integrity and exceptional competence, who had been very serious about implementing the spirit of the 73rd and 74th Amendments. She had written a strong note seeking enhanced delegation for all local bodies and had piloted a bill which was passed by the State Assembly. She was initially named by the prosecution as a co-conspirator since her action of delegating enhanced powers enabled the mayor to proceed with the alleged corrupt transaction which resulted in a wrongful gain to the contractor. The charges against the officer were eventually dropped, but only after she was named as a corruption suspect in the press; she was also never empanelled for posts in GoI as a result.

The result of this tendency of 'investigation by file reading' instead of 'investigation by tracing the money', which has gathered speed in the last decade, is that many officers (of all types) feel it is always best to initially oppose on file any request from the private sector, or indeed a private citizen, even if genuine, as that is the best way to not be accused of conspiring in corruption. Overcoming the negative recommendation would then require a committee which, by its very size and diverse membership, cannot easily be accused of being guilty of conspiracy. This greatly slows down and complicates policymaking and further increases the citizen-unfriendliness of the government. The approach (while possibly deterring some egregious forms of corruption) has also had a deleterious effect on decision-taking, with decisions being made in the interest of self-protection of officers rather than in public interest. Procedural purity has become more important than substantive correctness. There are some 'rules of thumb' which some officers (honest as well as dishonest) follow to minimize the risks of prosecution under these provisions:

1. Initially oppose all requests, however genuine, even if you intend to later accept them; your initial opposition will protect you as the

investigators and courts will presume you were ultimately coerced into changing your mind, either by your superior, a committee, or the cabinet.

2. Accept the lowest tender meeting the minimum specifications on paper, even if the bidder's technical capacity or ability is dubious; hidden costs of delay or bad quality, even if known, are ignored as these will not be apparent on file.

3. If there are any unforeseen situations during contract execution which might require re-negotiation of terms, pursue a legal dispute with the contractor, even if it delays a project and increases the project cost; any cost increase through losing an arbitration or re-tender (even a corrupt arbitration or re-tender) is unlikely to be viewed as corrupt, whereas even an honest exercise of re-negotiation will appear corrupt.

4. Buy from the public sector whenever possible, even if quality or timeliness is poor or the supplier has a bad track record.

5. Do not assess quality on unquantifiable criteria—ignore qualitative aspects which cannot be reduced to numbers on file.

6. Whenever possible, take decisions by committee, even if it is slower and/or subtracts quality by bringing in the inputs of unqualified and inexperienced outsiders—the presence of outsiders is more important than the quality of the decision.

7. Mechanically apply precedent; do not exercise discretion even when the situation calls for it or when hardship will be caused; for any change from precedent, always either promulgate a new rule or create a large committee.

The corrupt (at political and official levels) are quite capable of being corrupt without breaking the formal rules and while adhering scrupulously to procedure, since 'bribery *simpliciter*' need not involve any violation of rules and cannot be detected through file reading. Unfortunately, the investigative and prosecutorial approach often does not recognize this.

Remedial Measures

This section has two parts. The first briefly outlines the remedies proposed in Civil Service-I and comments on their current salience and the extent (if any) to which they have been implemented.

Remedies Proposed Earlier

Reviewing these recommendations nearly 10 years after they were made, nearly all of them appear to be still valid and relevant. While obviously it is not clear to what extent Civil Service-I influenced the debate, there has been some progress on several of them.

Increase in average tenure and prevention of arbitrary penal transfers: Some practical suggestions were made on how to achieve this. These were broadly supported by the 2nd ARC. The issue of minimum tenure in a post has received the attention of the Supreme Court in its judgement in *T.S.R. Subramanian v. Union of India.*[49] The impact of the judgement—which required the central and state governments to notify and adhere to prescribed minimum tenures—remains to be seen as an earlier and similar verdict in respect of the IPS has had only limited effect. Nevertheless, the judgement is a step in the right direction and may herald a turning point in the trend.

Reduction in the size of the cadres/abolition of unnecessary posts: The proliferation of inconsequential posts is a proximate cause of both demoralization and the ability to use transfer as a penalty, as well as a drag on the exchequer. The paper suggested specific steps to eliminate posts that do not deserve to be 'encadred,' or which have ceased to be relevant. This has not been implemented.

Change in the system of near-automatic seniority-based promotion: The current system is meritocratic at the point of entry, but thereafter is largely seniority-based. A system where all officers undergo a rigorous assessment of performance, independent of the political executive through the UPSC, at (say) the 15- and 25-year service marks, was proposed. The 2nd ARC has since recommended enacting a specific provision of law whereby civil servants will be employed for 20 years, and continuation thereafter will depend on the outcome of intensive performance reviews and be decided apolitically.

Change in recruitment and cadre allotment procedures for state service entrants: In keeping with the principles of meritocracy, neutrality, and an All-India character, changes to selection procedure were suggested to ensure that those promoted into the service are the genuinely meritorious among the state civil servants, rather than those who are

---

[49] AIR 2014 SC 263.

politically favoured. This was later also recommended by the 2nd ARC, and the central government has accordingly attempted a change in the procedure for promotion from the state services (discussed earlier in this chapter).

Wider eligibility for the 'selection' category to bring in distinguished non-government candidates: At present, the 'Selection' category of recruitment is used exclusively to bring in state government staff who do not belong to the generalist State Civil Service. A change in the rules to allow distinguished persons from the private sector, universities, and non-governmental organizations (NGOs) was suggested. The 2nd ARC also recommended measures for induction of outsiders into the senior levels of the service, and there has been some progress (see subsequently).

Awards for outstanding civil servants: To improve the self-image of the service and its public image, it was suggested that outstanding civil servants selected by a panel with non-civil servant representation should receive awards for specific achievements of a tangible nature. Such awards have since been instituted.

Reassertion of dual control: It was recommended that the DoPT and corresponding departments for the IPS and IFS should make full *bona fide* use of the central government's extensive powers (including the power to over-rule the state in case of disagreement) in matters relating to compliance with statutory rules, release of officers for central deputation, arbitrary creation/up-gradation/down-gradation of cadre posts, adherence of states to policies like those on duration of tenure, adequacy of field service, and so forth. While there has been no major change, recent trends suggest that the DoPT may be taking this role more seriously.

Review of disciplinary procedures: The time was felt to be ripe for a fundamental review of the approach to disciplinary proceedings. It was recognized that, since the scope and content of disciplinary procedures is now determined largely by the judiciary rather than by the Executive or Legislature, there are limitations on the Executive's ability to change procedures. Nevertheless, a specific reference to the Law Commission was suggested in order to generate a debate and a fresh examination of the judicially interpreted law. The 2nd ARC has recommended major changes to disciplinary procedures and for the removal of the trappings and procedure of criminal trials.

Other Measures

This second part examines other possible remedial measures, some of which the authors recommend, and others which are not recommended but included for comprehensiveness. Those with a question mark in the heading are those which the authors either do not support or have doubts about.

Possible adoption of the principles of 'New Public Management' (NPM)?: The 'NPM' movement was a set of policies for civil service and governance reform adopted initially in several developed Commonwealth countries (Australia, New Zealand, Canada, and United Kingdom) and later in other countries. Some of its key features were:

1. Adoption of private sector managerial techniques;
2. Introducing competition in the provision of public services;
3. Separation of policy and execution, with the latter under specialized autonomous agencies;
4. Separation of purchasers of services from providers of services;
5. Use of performance contracts or memoranda of understanding (MoUs) between Ministries and the autonomous agencies;
6. Performance-linked pay and promotion with bonuses and other such measures for achieving targets set in the contracts/MoUs.

Several of these (performance-linked pay especially) are popular with private-sector commentators in India. The logic of most such commentators usually runs approximately as follows:

1. This is how the private sector operates;
2. The private sector is more efficient and competent than the government;
3. Therefore, logically, those techniques, if applied in government, must necessarily improve efficiency.

The factual basis for (1) and (2) is questionable, but even if one assumes them to be true, both economics and public administration theory indicate that these methods are unlikely to be successful in core public-sector activities (as opposed to commercial activities which happen to be run by the government). From the perspective of economic theory, the economist Oliver Williamson, not exactly a proponent of government intervention in the economy, stated in the context of core sovereign functions: 'Replication of a public bureau by a private firm with or without regulation is impossible'. He goes on to state that 'practices that are widely condemned (low-powered incentives, convoluted bureaucratic procedures, excesses of employment security) actually serve legitimate economizing purposes in this context'.[50] Lant Pritchett, another economist not known for his love of government intervention, stated that 'the provision of key, discretionary, transaction-intensive services through the public sector is the mother of all institutional and organizational design problems' (that is, there are no simple solutions, and certainly not simple market-based ones).[51]

Empirical evidence shows decisively that NPM is not a panacea, and indeed can make things worse.[52] The ability of purchasers and providers to be separated, for purchasers to articulate their preferences in a competitive environment, and the efficacy of decoupling policy from delivery are all questionable, as Janine O'Flynn documents.[53] In respect of introducing competition, she points out that 'evidence shows that [competitive regimes] are usually costly to implement and rarely deliver genuine competition ... such approaches have resulted in increased transaction costs due to the high costs of contract preparation, monitoring and enforcement'. The Organisation for Economic Cooperation and Development's (OECD) own review of NPM stated that the 'reforms produced some unexpected negative results'. The OECD review felt the competitive model 'failed to understand that

[50] O.E. Williamson, 'Public and Private Bureaucracies: A Transaction Cost Economics Perspective', *Journal of Law, Economics and Organization* 15, no. 1 (March 1999): 306–42.

[51] L. Pritchett and M. Woolcock, 'Solutions When the Solution Is the Problem: Arraying the Disarray in Development', *World Development* 32, no. 2 (February 2004): 191–212.

[52] N. Manning, 'The Legacy of the New Public Management in Developing Countries', *International Review of Administrative Sciences* 67, no. 2 (June 2001): 297–312.

[53] J. O'Flynn, 'From New Public Management to Public Value: Paradigmatic Change and Managerial Implications', *The Australian Journal of Public Administration* 66, no. 3 (September 2007): 353–66.

public management arrangements not only deliver public services but also enshrine deeper governance values'.[54]

The early adopters of NPM are now rolling it back. In developing countries, NPM is even more risky because NPM only succeeds if what Nick Manning calls 'OPD' (Old Public Discipline) is present.[55] Heywood points to diminished integrity even in a civil service renowned for probity and political neutrality (UK) through the excessive adoption of NPM.[56] Writing from a continental European perspective, Drechsler identifies the serious flaws inherent in the NPM ideology.[57] If a country suffers from a corrupt and politicized civil service, NPM does not stand much of a chance.

On the specific issue of linking pay to performance, the evidence is very unclear even in developed countries. From an OECD perspective, Bourgon found no evidence that performance-related pay resulted in improvement. He found that 'performance pay may promote behaviours that emphasize success in the short term at the expense of achieving long term results' and 'does not allow enough recognition of the collective and collaborative efforts'. He adds that 'performance rewards would be susceptible to political influence and make public servants too responsive' and points to the Australian move to abolish performance pay for Secretaries.[58] If the case is weak in developed countries with stronger institutions, the case for performance-based pay in the civil service of developing countries appears to be non-existent.[59]

[54] Organisation for Economic Cooperation and Development (OECD), 'Public Sector Modernisation' (Policy Brief, Paris: OECD, 2003).

[55] N. Manning, 'New Public Management'.

[56] P.M. Heywood, 'Integrity Management and the Public Service Ethos in the UK: Patchwork Quilt or Threadbare Blanket? (Paper presented at Conference on Integrity Management and Collaborative Governance, ICAC Centre of Anti-Corruption Studies, Hong Kong, September 2010).

[57] W. Drechsler, 'The Rise and Demise of the New Public Management', *Post-Autistic Economics Review* 33, no. 2 (September 2005): 17–28.

[58] J. Bourgon, 'The Public Service of 2025—Themes, Challenges and Trends: Human Resources Management Trends in OECD Countries', 23 August 2008, Quebec City, http://unpan1.un.org/intradoc/groups/public/documents/un/unpan034107.pdf

[59] Z. Hasnain, N. Manning, and J.H. Pierskalla, 'Performance-Related Pay in the Public Sector: A Review of Theory and Evidence' (Policy Research Working Paper No. 6043, Washington, DC: World Bank, 2012).

Overall, while some NPM practices may indeed play a positive role if applied in the right context, widespread application of NPM will not be the solution to the problems of the Indian civil service.

Abolish the IAS and/or move to a Position-based Specialized Service or Services tied to Specific Ministries?: A reasonable argument can be made that in the modern age, with increased technological sophistication and a knowledge explosion, generalist services are an anachronism. The logical conclusion, if this view is accepted, is to move

1. Either: to a position-based system which prevails in countries like the US and organizations like the World Bank. Staff are hired against specific positions based on qualifications for the particular post. (In the US, most senior level positions are also political appointments.) This would change not only the IAS but also the other central services where, for instance, chartered accountants would form the Indian Audit and Accounts Service, accountants and lawyers would form the Revenue Service, architects would man the Defence Estates service, and so on.
2. Or: to a ministry-based system where generalists start specializing in a ministry or function as soon as they are recruited, as in many countries with mandarin systems. This is a variant of the idea of greater specialization. The key difference is that specialization is by experience, not by qualification. Most central Civil Services are generalists at the point of recruitment, followed by specialization through experience, and thus offer an example of the possible strengths and weaknesses of such an approach.

In both cases, this may be accompanied by a generalist SES at senior levels.

For leadership positions involving coordination across sectors and for policymaking, the question is complex. Subject matter knowledge is obviously important. The central Civil Services officers do possess, on average, better subject matter knowledge of their own specialism than a typical IAS officer who enters a new ministry. Thus, a Commissioner of Income Tax is likely to be more knowledgeable on income tax than the typical IAS officer of equal seniority on the subject to which he is assigned. The weakness of the IAS vis-à-vis services which specialize by experience is lack of contextual knowledge and of specialized skills; vis-à-vis truly specialized services or a position-based system, the difference in specialized knowledge is even greater.

Yet, there is little evidence that taken as a whole, say, the Indian Revenue Service (IRS) is more competent or has higher integrity than the IAS. (The scandal involving a former Union Minister of State for Revenue in 2003 who resigned after his Personal Assistant was arrested for taking bribes from IRS officers, highlighted the extent of corruption in, and politicization of, postings in the IRS).[60] Taking less corruption-prone functions than taxation, there is no evidence that the Postal Department or Defence Estates or Ordnance Factories or even Indian embassies are significantly better administered than the average central ministry.

As regards the real 'specialist' services—the Forest Service, Economic Service, Statistical Service, Cost Accounts Service—there is little evidence that they have higher levels of coordination or policymaking competence. Selections to the post of, say, Chief Economic Adviser—where IES officers have had the opportunity to compete through an open and competitive UPSC process—have rarely gone to officers of that service and rather have gone to outside experts.

Looking at practices in the civil services of developed countries with a parliamentary system, the tendency is actually in the opposite direction: UK and Australia have both moved from greater specialization to greater generalization in recent years and have unwound some of the changes made earlier. The UK is now consciously requiring senior civil servants to acquire wider experience than in a single sector.[61] Australia is moving in the same direction.[62] Singapore's civil service—generally regarded as both honest and effective—is a generalist service.

Even in the private sector, managerial talent is highly fungible across disciplines, to a greater extent than is generally appreciated. The Master's in Business Administration (MBA) is a degree in (business) 'administration' and MBAs are quintessentially generalists. The Tata

---

[60] 'Gingee Ramachandran Resigns from Ministry', *Rediff*, 23 May 2003.

[61] HM Government, *Civil Service Reform Plan*.

[62] PricewaterhouseCoopers, 'Review of the Senior Executive Service: Report to the Special Minister of State for the Public Service and Integrity' (Australian Public Service Commission, 2011). Available at http://www.apsc. gov.au/__data/assets/pdf_file/0004/48559/reviewofses.pdf

Administrative Services, the World Bank's and Asian Development Bank's Young Professional Programs (YPP), are non-governmental examples of managerial cadres which move across the organization. The Chief Executive Officers of all three major US car companies recruited after the crisis in 2008 and credited with rescuing the companies were rank generalists: none of them had previous experience in the automobile industry. One was a former telecom executive, another was from civil aviation, and the third from a customs/trade inspection company. Two other recent Detroit chief executives were also generalists.[63] PepsiCo India hired a chief executive from a mobile phone company.[64]

Agarwal and Somanathan studied this issue in detail, looking at practices across sectors, and concluded that an 'intelligent generalist' (as specifically defined—not necessarily an IAS officer) provided in most situations the best bet. No doubt, they concluded, that currently civil servants are often 'not sufficiently well informed or trained to act in this manner'.[65]

Apart from competence, there are other issues than need consideration. Firstly, a position-based service is very likely to increase politicization by enabling the appointment of chosen persons to specific positions. Second, both position-based and (even more so) ministry-based services have stronger affiliations to their given functions or 'turf' than the IAS, and *ceteris paribus*, this would tend to have a negative impact on inter-sectoral collaboration and coordination.[66] Also, the selection of officers for cross-sectoral coordination posts would be more difficult. Third, a ministry-based service would lack the multi-sectoral experience and perspective which the present system has and which a position-based system could bring (if the right people were chosen for coordinating posts). Fourth, there is the vital issue of the

[63] 'Three Outsiders, Three Styles', *The Economist*, 19 January 2013.

[64] M. Dalal, S.Tandon, and S. Agarwal, 'Leadership Change: New Chief Executives to Steer Consumer Goods Firms in 2014', *Mint*, 3 January 2014.

[65] O.P. Agarwal and T.V. Somanathan, 'Public Policy-Making in India—Issues and Remedies' (Working Paper, Centre for Policy Research, New Delhi, 2005; emphasis in the original).

[66] For instance, disagreements between the Departments of Industrial Policy and Promotion and Environment are likely to be even more difficult to resolve if both of were led by specialists with a strong stake in their respective fields.

all-India (federal) dimension and coordination between three tiers of government. Many proposals for civil service reform ignore this aspect. It is practically impossible to retain the common all-India character of the civil service along with either a position-based or a ministry-based system. The absence of common training, common ethos, and long service at different levels would definitely militate against neutral preservation of the constitutional quasi-federal order, against coordination between the centre and states, and against the modicum of uniformity in administration that the country now has. Table 9.12 summarizes the strengths and weaknesses of the three approaches.

Overall, there can be no easy or a priori conclusion in favour of domain specialization as the predominant method of organization for a federal (All-India) service. Suffice it to say that the evidence is too equivocal to warrant this being a major plank of reform. However,

Table 9.12   Strengths and Weaknesses of Different Civil Service Structures in India

Characteristic	Rating Under		
	Current System	Ministry-based System (Generalist Recruitment, Specialization by Experience)	Position-based System
Subject matter knowledge	Low	Medium	High
Political neutrality of recruitment	High	High	Low
Multi-sectoral experience and perspective	High	Low	High
Collaboration/ coordination across functional boundaries	High	Low	Medium
All India (federal) character, and coordination among tiers of government	High	Low	Low

Source: Authors' analysis.

measures to promote *a degree of specialization in the second half of IAS officers' careers* are likely to have a positive effect while retaining the advantages of the current structure.

Restrict entry to those who have completed a course in public administration?: The 2nd ARC recommended that the GoI should establish new National Institutes of Public Administration to run bachelor's degree courses (broadly on the pattern of the successful National Law Schools). Only graduates of these institutions or those who have completed a bridge course conducted by them would be eligible to write the civil services examination.

It is not clear which problem currently faced by the civil service this ARC recommendation is intended to tackle. In one sense, this approach is similar to the French Ecole Nationale d'Administration (ENA) system where young graduates enter the ENA and then become civil servants. A benefit of this approach would be that candidates would have spent their college years preparing themselves for a public service career and the successful among them might be better skilled in early years of their career. However, this approach would have the serious drawback of removing from the pool many candidates who have an interest in the civil service but feel they should have an alternative career if they are unsuccessful; very promising candidates who are unwilling to spend time on the bridge course which has no value to them would not attempt the examination. It would also produce a 'monoculture' within the civil service and take away one of its big strengths—the broad and multi-disciplinary character. Also, graduates of the new public administration institutes who fail to pass the civil service examination would reach a dead end; since their qualification would be largely worthless in the private sector; they may eventually 'demand', through political or judicial means, absorption in government. On the whole, this proposal is not a good one.[67]

---

[67] S.K. Das had proposed recruitment at the end of higher secondary school, as an alternative to examinations for entry to medical colleges, IITs, and the likes. He argued that this would widen the pool by bringing in bright students who might otherwise enter the private sector and not take the examination later, remove issues of age relaxation, and increase the degree of idealism and dynamism among the recruits. This would be a fundamental change whose consideration is beyond the scope of this paper. Das, *World Class Civil Service*, 172–4.

Creation of civil services board/enacting a civil services Act?: The 2nd
ARC and others have recommended creation of a Civil Services Board
under a Civil Services Act, which would be in charge of personnel
management at central and state levels. It is unlikely that this will be
an effective solution; there is already a statutory framework and the
record of such boards and committees (especially at state level) does
not create confidence that they would function without political interference. However, they will probably do no harm. Also, taken together
with the increased willingness of courts to intervene, they may possibly
become more effective in the long run.

Curb post-retirement opportunities by aligning retirement ages: A
simple but highly effective solution to the problem of top civil servants seeking post-retirement opportunities is to amend all the statutes
relating to tribunals, regulatory bodies, and training institutions to bring
their retirement age to exactly the same level as the civil service retirement age. Thus, these opportunities should be taken up before, not
after, retirement. This should also apply to judicial members whose
retirement age should be identical to the retirement age of High Court/
Supreme Court judges (as the case may be).

Induction of outsiders into the civil service: The inherent constraints
of a generalist service have been addressed in several countries by lateral induction of outsiders into senior positions. This offers a valuable
addition to the talent pool without entailing all the disadvantages of a
full-fledged position-based service.

In the Indian context, the risk is that appointments would be made
on wrongful or political considerations, and those recruited might not
work in public interest, but in the interest of particular lobbies or vested
interests. Civil Service-I advocated systematic induction of outsiders by
a transparent method involving the UPSC so as to achieve the objective
without politicization or corruption. This corresponds with practices in
Australia and New Zealand, which have been in the vanguard of the
induction of outsiders within a parliamentary system.[68] The Sixth Pay
Commission made a similar recommendation as did the 2nd ARC. The

[68] G. Duncan and J. Chapman, 'New Public Management, New
Millennium, New Zealand' (Paper presented at the Public Policy Network
Conference, The Australian National University, Canberra, January 2009);
PricewaterhouseCoopers, 'Review of the Senior Executive Service'.

GoI appears to be moving in this direction. In 2008, the Department of Expenditure approved in principle the hiring of outsiders on contract basis against regular central government posts.

The DoPT has prepared draft guidelines in 2013 for making these contract appointments. Under them, officers already in government service can apply for these posts, but only if they agree to resign from the service. The guidelines allow for a differentiated pay scale subject normally to a consolidated all-inclusive ceiling, and for selection to be done by the UPSC. Each ministry will have to identify the number and nature of posts involved. This change, if implemented, would represent a major step forward towards inducting outsiders of competence in to the public service at the central level. The entrustment of the selection to the UPSC represents a good and practical safeguard. The level of remuneration is not competitive with the private sector, but sufficient to attract those who may have already earned well in the private sector and are interested in making a contribution to public welfare; it is calibrated in a manner that is unlikely to cause internal comparative problems with the mainstream civil service. The ceiling will have to be indexed to inflation since it is all inclusive. Overall, the proposal has been well designed and, if implemented, is likely to mark a new beginning in Indian public administration.

E-governance: Experience has demonstrated that e-governance has potential, but is not a panacea. The repeated references to railway reservations paradoxically illustrate how few the known success stories are. E-governance in the policy and regulatory sphere (as distinct from service delivery, where it has more potential) presents a greater degree of difficulty. However, even in policy advice there are some key facets where there is scope for quick and major improvement. Conversion of a plethora of orders, precedents, and rules into comprehensive and self-contained 'master circulars' available online to all staff and/or to the public, and updating thereof whenever a change is made can reduce the 'power of the clerk' and increase consistent application of policy. A systematic effort to consolidate all internal instructions and guidelines in each central and state department and make them available on an intranet would be a major qualitative improvement to the functioning of the civil service. The key is that the compilation should be definitive and comprehensive and any instruction not there should be deemed to be withdrawn. Electronic work flow for file decisions is another promising area. It does present some challenges in design, as it is crucial that electronic work flow preserves the record of advice tendered at different levels, without allowing any level to obliterate previous recommendations.

Increased delegation of authority: A very widespread tendency in Indian public administration, across departments and tiers of government, is a high degree of centralization of authority on financial and other matters at higher levels. While this is an old tradition, a recent change has been that more and more decisions are taken by large inter-departmental committees chaired by very senior officers. The logic is usually as follows:

1. the lower levels are less competent;
2. the lower levels are more corrupt;
3. committees will bring collective wisdom (more heads are better than one);
4. central authorities can better resist improper local pressures;
5. since even senior officers may be corrupt, committees will reduce the risk of corruption; and
6. therefore in the interest of quality of administration and to reduce fraud and corruption, decisions must be taken at higher levels and by committees.

There is some truth in these considerations, although with the prevailing levels of corruption at high levels, the assumption that lower levels are more corrupt is probably no longer valid. However, centralization also has disadvantages. First, it removes the locus of the decision further from the locus of the problem; by making the decision-taker more remote it reduces empathy, knowledge of field reality, and the ability of the citizen to be heard by the actual decision-taker. Second, it makes decision-taking slower. Third, it facilitates centralized corruption: if, say, transfers of teachers or award of contracts were handled at block level, a corrupt minister or secretary (either acting on his own or in response to political interference) would not be able to fully 'control' the transfers or contracts, and hence may not be as successful in extracting bribes. Local politicians may be corrupt, but the amounts involved are likely to be much lower and decisions would be taken much faster and with greater voice for the affected parties. Committees, instead of preventing corruption, may provide the corrupt with 'safety in numbers' and embolden the taking of a corrupt decision which (if it was left to an individual officer) one may not have been willing to take.

Given that corruption and fraud are no longer lower-level problems but also exist at the top, it is time to do away with the automatic preference for centralization of financial, personnel, and procurement powers. The benefits of greater delegation of authority will outweigh the drawbacks in many circumstances. Therefore, a systematic 'zero-base' review of delegation of powers across a wide range of functions is recommended with a bias towards increasing delegation.

Training in specific skills using modern online learning technology: Instead of expensive visits and residential courses at, for instance, Duke University or Harvard's Kennedy School of Government—which are currently part of in-service training programmes—the DoPT and the National Academy of Administration should, in collaboration with leading Western universities, commission, develop, and use very carefully designed and updated online courses. These would be of three types. The first would be targeted and subject-specific modules to provide each joint secretary/director with an up-to-date curriculum giving the latest trends (in the sector the officer is assigned to) in India and abroad, with an overview of the laws and regulations applicable, the key pending policy issues, and so forth. Such courses should be made compulsory, with officers posted in a particular ministry or sector (at the centre or even in the states) required to complete the online course with a pass mark within, say, two months of joining—failing which they will not be qualified for their next increment. About 200–400 such modules may need to be developed, with at least one for each department, and not more than one per division. Courses could be updated systematically once a year. This represents a quick and feasible way of improving competence, and should neither face political resistance nor require additional funding.

The second area where targeted training can improve capacity across a variety of sectors is training in procurement and financial procedures. Many officers (from generalist or specialist services) have a poor understanding of the rules and principles of good public procurement and of the financial code. Quite apart from deliberate malfeasance, many officers make mistakes purely out of ignorance. Furthermore, their ignorance creates undue fear of these matters, which leads to slower decisions, the appointment of unnecessary committees, the prompting of repeated queries, and so on—all of which slows down administration and reduces quality. The UK Civil Service has recently started a capacity-building effort aimed at procurement and certain other targeted common skills.[69] A set of modules on procurement and financial rules should be built as an online training tool using the best modern content and delivery techniques, updated regularly, and tailored to Indian rules and regulations.

A third area would focus on good decision-taking processes. The traditional civil service rules have strong procedural safeguards against bad decisions, but these are mostly through wide consultation. They do not adequately address the typical cognitive mistakes made in decision-taking. A targeted training module for senior officers at the level of joint secretary and above should be developed on techniques like those advocated by Nobel Laureate Daniel Kahnemann in his recent practical note on 'quality control for decisions' (which is content-neutral and applicable to all sectors).[70]

Overall, a re-deployment of training funds spent on the IAS to develop tailored and very specific on-line training content from the best providers is strongly recommended.

Evaluation of selections: The UPSC should undertake periodic aggregate evaluations of the performance of cohorts of recruits (without individual names) vis-à-vis various selection and performance parameters, after lags of, say, 10 years. This may provide useful insights which can be used to improve the selection process. While there may be methodological issues with such an exercise, they are not insurmountable.

Improved Matching Processes: Currently, postings are generally done without formal involvement of the officer posted. This should be modified to allow for internal advertisement and applications among those within the zone of consideration without affecting government's unfettered right to appoint any officer to any post. It would help minimize unintentional mismatches and encourage a greater proportion of win-win outcomes, better matching of competence with need, and increased motivation.

[69] HM Government, *Meeting the Challenge of Change: A Capabilities Plan for the Civil Service* (London, UK: 2013).

[70] D. Kahneman, D. Lovallo, and O. Sibony, 'The Big Idea: Before You Make That Big Decision … ', *Harvard Business Review* 89, no. 6 (2011): 51–60.

Introduce performance appraisals for the lower civil services and integrate them into promotion decisions: Indiscipline and poor work culture at lower levels is difficult to remedy and a major obstacle to governance reform. There are several levels, especially in state governments, where there is no formal performance evaluation. Some form of performance evaluation needs to be present at all levels, even for 'Multi-Tasking Staff' (office assistants) and drivers. This will, if nothing else, help discipline and productivity. At clerical levels, it could be an input into promotion decisions. For example, if promotions from one clerical level to the next were based on, say, 80 marks for seniority and 20 marks for appraisals, there might be a greater degree of responsiveness; at the same time, the scope for arbitrariness and favouritism would be constrained since the weight of performance would only be 20 per cent.[71]

Re-creation of a positive professional identity: Esprit de corps is rare in the real world. The ICS and the IAS had it in their early years.[72] It does not exist now due to contradictory political, social, and legal expectations; constant and voluble criticism of the bureaucracy by the media, civil society, private industry, politicians and judiciary (often for mutually conflicting reasons); erosion of social standing; widespread corruption; and a confusing admixture of colonial, regulatory, developmental, and welfare orientations.

The civil service needs a new and clear professional identity and cogent sense of mission that will engender strong public support. Key elements would be commitments to:

1. Act in accordance with the law and the constitution, observe high standards of conduct, personal probity, intellectual integrity, and political neutrality and refuse individually and collectively to submit to political interference (that is, political will contrary to the law);
2. Faithfully carry out the legitimately expressed will of the elected government regardless of personal preferences;
3. Provide the elected executive at the central, state, and local levels with competent, efficient, and effective public administration

---

[71] Strengthening performance appraisals of senior civil servants has been touched upon earlier as part of the discussion on changing promotion policy.

[72] Das, *World Class Civil Service*, Chapter 15.

through fair and consistent law enforcement, managerial excellence, and high-quality policy advice; and

4. Provide citizens with responsive, courteous, and cost-effective public services.

India would benefit immensely from a resurrection of civil service esprit de corps around such an identity.

APPENDIX

Table A9.1   List of Central Civil Services Group A (Technical and Non-technical) with Authorized Strength*

Non-Technical	
Office of The Comptroller and Auditor General of India	
1. Indian Audit and Accounts Service	875
Ministry of Commerce and Industry	
2. Indian Trade Service	184
Ministry of Communications and Information Technology	
3. Indian P and T Accounts and Finance Service.	1,723 (as on 1 July 2005)
4. Indian Postal Service	574
Ministry of Defence	
5. Indian Defence Accounts Service	660
6. Indian Defence Estates Service	134
Ministry of External Affairs	
7. Indian Foreign Service	706
Ministry of Finance	
8. Indian Civil Accounts Service	208
9. Indian Custom & Central Excise Service	2,310
10. Indian Revenue Service	4,184
Ministry of Information and Broadcasting	
11. Indian Information Service	475
Ministry of Railways	
12. Indian Railway Accounts Service	855
13. Indian Railway Personnel Service	448
14. Indian Railway Traffic Service	1,148
15. Railway Protection Force	295

Technical		
Ministry of Commerce and Industry (Supply Division)		
1.	Indian Inspection Service	94
2.	Indian Supply Service	99
Ministry of Communications and Information Technology		
3.	Indian Telecommunication Service	8,335 (as on 1 July 2003)
4.	P and T Building Works Service (Architectural, Electrical, and Civil Wing)	89
Ministry of Defence		
5.	Border Roads Engineering Service (E&M Cadre)	502 (as on 1 July 2006)
6.	Indian Naval Armament Service	108
7.	Indian Ordnance Factories Service	1,718
8.	Indian Defence Service of Engineers.	1,488 (as on 1 July 2006)
Ministry of Power		
9.	Central Power Engineering Service	486
Ministry of Information and Broadcasting		
10.	Indian Broadcasting Service (Engineering)	1,448 (as on 1 July 2006)
Ministry of Railways		
11.	Indian Railway Service of Electrical Engineering	990
12.	Indian Railway Service of Engineers	2,040
13.	Indian Railway Service of Mechanical Engineers	1,253
14.	Indian Railway Service of Signal and Telecommunication Engineers	958
15.	Indian Railway Stores Service	656
Ministry of Road Transport and Highways		
16.	Central Engineering Service (Roads)	208
Ministry of Urban Development & Poverty Alleviation		
17.	Central Architects Service (CPWD)	173 (as on 1 July 2006)
18.	Central Electrical and Mechanical Engineering Service (CPWD)	263 (as on 1 July 2006)
19.	Central Engineering Service (CPWD)	860 (as on 1 July 2006)

	Ministry of Water Resources	
20.	Central Water Engineering Service	775
	Health	
	Ministry of Defence	
1.	Indian Ordnance Factories Health Service (CDMO Cadre)	221
	Ministry of Health and Family Welfare	
2.	Central Health Service	7,465
	Ministry of Home Affairs.	
3.	Border Security Force Health Service	415
4.	Central Reserve Police Health Service	297
5.	Indo Tibetan Border Police Health Service	272
	Ministry of Railways.	
6.	Indian Railway Medical Service	2,538
	Others	
	Ministry of Corporate Affairs	
1.	Indian Company Law Service	231
	Ministry of Defence	
2.	Defence Aeronautical Quality Assurance Service	262
3.	Defence Quality Assurance Service	528
4.	Defence Research And Development Service	7,256
	Ministry of Finance	
5.	Indian Cost Accounts Service	163
6.	Indian Economic Service	501
	Ministry of Home Affairs	
7.	Border Security Force	3,125
8.	Central Industrial Security Force	1,076
9.	Central Reserve Police Force	3,385
10.	Indo Tibetan Border Police	596
	Ministry of Information and Broadcasting	
11.	Indian Broadcasting (Programme) Service	1,109 (as on 1 January 2001)

	Ministry of Labour	
12.	Central Labour Service	343
	Ministry of Law and Justice	
13.	Indian Legal Service	152
	Ministry of Coal and Mines	
14.	Geological Survey Of India	
	(i) Geological Stream	2,300
	(ii) Mineralogical stream	40
	(iii) Mechanical stream	29
	(iv) Chemical Stream	328
	(v) Drilling Stream	61
	(vi) Geophysical Stream	325
	(vii) Geophysical (Instt) Stream	64
	Total	3,147
	Ministry of Science and Technology	
15.	Indian Meteorological Service	453 (as on 1 July 06)
16.	Survey of India Group 'A' Service	391
	Ministry of Statistics and Programme Implementation	
17.	Indian Statistical Service	800

Source: Available at http://persmin.gov.in/DOPT/CSWing/CRDivision/Authorised_strength_Group_%20A.htm.

Note: (*Duty posts as on 1 January 2007, unless otherwise stated).

10

ELECTION COMMISSION OF INDIA

E. Sridharan and *Milan Vaishnav*

The eminent historian Ramachandra Guha has referred to India as 'the most recklessly ambitious experiment in history'.[1] With disregard for past precedent, following the British colonialists' departure, India's founding fathers took the bold decision to establish an independent republic which would abide by democratic principles and procedures. Crucially, India's post-Independence republic guaranteed universal franchise for all adult citizens at a time when the vast majority of the country was living in abject poverty.

While elections, of course, do not make a democracy, they are unquestionably the sine qua non of each and every democracy. Following the birth of independent India, the successful execution of participatory elections faced—and, in many ways, still faces today—a host of cumbersome challenges: profound ethnic, religious, linguistic, and cultural diversity; significant geographic variation and a predominantly rural electorate; rampant poverty and illiteracy; and deeply ingrained forms of inequality. Any one of these challenges is large enough to vex election authorities in advanced democracies, so their compound effect in a nascent democracy cannot be overstated.

Against these considerable odds, the Election Commission of India (ECI) has proven to be a model of election management, earning

<hr>

[1] R. Guha, 'Democratic to a Fault?', *Prospect*, 25 January 2012.

plaudits both at home and abroad. Thanks to the wisdom of India's founders, the Commission was given a solid foundation from the outset, having been established as a permanent, independent constitutional body. This is not to suggest that the Commission has not had to adapt to changing circumstances; the broad nature of its constitutional framework not only gave the Commission a solid underpinning, but also allowed for flexibility in interpreting and enforcing its mandate.[2]

What has emerged over the past six-and-a-half decades is an Election Commission that has significant powers, far greater than what its counterparts in many democracies have at their disposal.[3] However, a powerful ECI need not have been an effective or prudent one, yet for the most part—and with due respect to its occasional detractors—scholars and average Indians hold the institution in high regard. According to a 1996 poll conducted by the Centre for the Study of Developing Societies, the ECI was the most respected public institution in all of India with 62 per cent of respondents favourably disposed.[4] A 2008 study found that an even higher percentage—nearly 80 per cent—of Indians surveyed expressed a high degree of trust in the Commission, second only to the army among state institutions.[5]

The high regard for the Election Commission also points to a more general paradox concerning India's public sector institutions, or what Lant Pritchett calls India's 'flailing state'.[6] The state in India appears to undertake highly complex tasks with relative efficacy—such as running an atomic weapons programme or regulating monetary policy—while

---

[2] A. McMillan, 'The Election Commission of India and the Regulation and Administration of Electoral Politics', *Election Law Journal: Rules, Politics, and Policy* 11, no. 2 (2012): 187–201.

[3] D. Gilmartin and R. Moog, 'Introduction to "Election Law in India"', *Election Law Journal: Rules, Politics, and Policy* 11, no. 2 (2012): 136–48.

[4] P.R. deSouza, 'The Election Commission and Electoral Reforms in India', in *Democracy, Diversity and Stability: 50 Years of Indian Independence*, eds D.D. Khanna, L.L. Mehrotra, and G.W. Kueck (New Delhi: Macmillan India, 1998), 51.

[5] SDSA Team, *State of Democracy in South Asia: A Report* (New Delhi: Oxford University Press, 2008).

[6] L. Pritchett, 'Review of *In Spite of the Gods: The Strange Rise of Modern India*, by Edward Luce', *Journal of Economic Literature* 47, no. 3 (2009): 771–80.

struggling to perform more ordinary governance tasks—such as delivering basic health and education.

While the commission has overcome daunting challenges beginning with the first general election in 1952, its future course is by no means pre-determined. Indeed, there remain serious concerns about the conduct of elections in India, namely the disconcerting influence of 'money' and 'muscle' power. Furthermore, while scholars Lloyd and Susanne Rudolph have rightly praised the Commission for serving as an effective 'bulwark of free and fair elections',[7] its status as regulator has not been free from controversy. As Alistair McMillan has pointed out, the commission has had to carefully balance the pressures of robust party politics with preserving what *it* views to be in the national interest.[8] Its role as a neutral 'referee' cannot so easily be disassociated from the normative implications of its decisions.

The remainder of this chapter is organized as follows. In the next section, we briefly review the ECI's background, its constitutional and legal frameworks, and basic organizational structure. In the third, we discuss the Commission's regulatory expansionism in the wake of India's dramatic social and political changes since Independence. In the fourth section, we discuss the organizational capacity and capabilities of the Commission, paying special attention to the organizational and technological innovations the ECI has pioneered in an effort to police the conduct of elections. In the penultimate section, we discuss two areas where electoral reform is most pressing but has been slow in the making: election finance ('money') and the criminalization of politics ('muscle'). Finally, we conclude with some parting thoughts on the changing role of the ECI and its relative position in India's democratic system in the twenty-first century.

Institutional Origins and Structure

India's experience with elections began much before Independence. As Rama Devi and Mendiratta explain, there is historical evidence to

---

[7] S.H. Rudolph and L.I. Rudolph, 'New Dimensions in Indian Democracy', *Journal of Democracy* 13, no. 1 (January 2002): 52–66.

[8] A. McMillan, 'The Election Commission', in *The Oxford Companion to Politics in India*, eds N.G. Jayal and P.B. Mehta (New Delhi: Oxford University Press, 2010), 98.

suggest that in ancient times many parts of India had experimented with various forms of republican governance.[9] Much better known, of course, is the record of local elections occurring under British rule in the late nineteenth century with limited, but consequential, provincial-level elections being instituted following the Indian Councils Act of 1909 (for example, Morley–Minto Reforms) and the Montagu–Chelmsford reforms of 1919.[10] Although Parliament in Britain had been 'gradually inching' towards constitutional reforms with regard to India's governance throughout the late colonial period, the reforms it instituted were highly uneven, partial in nature, and extremely circumscribed with respect to franchise.[11]

As the road to Independence grew clearer and India's founders commenced their discussions about India's post-Independence constitution, they consciously built on certain principles of colonial law, while understandably rejecting myriad others.[12] Importantly, under British rule, there had been no provision made for an independent election commission to regulate the conduct of elections across the country. In debating the virtues of establishing such a body, the framers were guided by three cardinal principles: equality, independence, and representation.[13] The framers believed that all adult Indians should be vested with the same rights to participate—as voters and aspirant candidates—in the democratic process, irrespective of caste, creed, gender, or social status. Furthermore, to ensure its arms-length distance from the rough-and-tumble of party politics, the members of India's Constituent Assembly placed a premium on the independence of any future election body. The third and final principle—representation—refers to the concern that the country's electoral supervisory body adequately balances the need to ensure the representative quality of India's democracy with the desire to check electoral malpractice.

---

[9] V.S. Rama Devi and S.L. Mendiratta, *How India Votes: Election Laws, Practice and Procedure* (New Delhi: Butterworths, 2000).

[10] Gilmartin and Moog, 'Introduction to "Election Law in India"', 136.

[11] Rama Devi and Mendiratta, *How India Votes*, 6.

[12] Gilmartin and Moog, 'Introduction to "Election Law in India"', 137.

[13] DeSouza, 'Election Commission,' 98.

Constitutional Provisions

The cornerstone of the ECI's mandate derives from Article 324 of the Constitution, which grants it the authority over the 'superintendence, direction and control of the preparation of the electoral rolls' for all elections to the national parliament, state assemblies, presidency, and vice-presidency. Article 324 also clarifies that the Commission is to be led by a single Chief Election Commissioner (CEC), although it gives the President the authority to appoint additional commissioners. It is important to note, with regard to this last proviso, that the framers explicitly rejected the idea of decentralized state-wise election commissions in favour of a centralized authority that—to their minds— would be less susceptible to parochial influence.[14] While this decision is at odds with many of the founders' other federalist tendencies, it was seen as crucial in insulating the Commission from local influence.[15]

With Article 324 as the cornerstone, several additional articles delineated the Commission's mandate and authorities in greater detail. Article 325 grants the Commission the authority to prepare a unified election roll with the additional guidance that it must ensure the roll protects equality under the law and does not discriminate on grounds of religion, race, caste, or sex. Article 326 states the right to universal adult suffrage.[16] Articles 327 and 328 provide the commission with the power to make provisions for elections to the national parliament as well as the state assemblies. Finally, Article 329 bars the interference of the judiciary during the electoral process.[17] While these articles

---

[14] Gilmartin and Moog, 'Introduction to "Election Law in India"', 138.

[15] U.K. Singh, 'Institutions and Democratic Governance: A Study of the Election Commission and Electoral Governance in India', *NMML Monograph* (New Delhi: Nehru Memorial Museum and Library, 2004), vol. 9. According to Singh, B.R. Ambedkar introduced an amendment to create a unified commission as opposed to separate commissions for the Union and the various states. Ambedkar apparently believed that a decentralized set-up would be more vulnerable to discrimination at the local level.

[16] The voting age, originally set at 21, was later revised to 18 in 1988 through a constitutional amendment.

[17] A. Roy, 'Identifying Citizens: Electoral Rolls, the Right to Vote and the Election Commission of India', *Election Law Journal: Rules, Politics, and Policy* 11, no. 2 (June 2012): 170–86.

constitute the core of the Commission's constitutional authority, several other articles elaborate technical issues relating to the mode of elections, the structure of the parliament and state assemblies, and the role of the commission in advising the president on the disqualification of elected representatives.

Soon after the Constitution was adopted in 1949, and in advance of the first general election, Parliament moved swiftly to pass implementing legislation that effectively put meat on the relatively bare bones of the Constitution's electoral provisions. Two acts—the Representation of the People Acts (RPAs) of 1950 and 1951—spelled out in greater detail the specifics of electoral administration, and they remain the bedrock of India's election law to the present day. The 1950 Act provides guidance on the preparation and revision of electoral rolls, the drawing of electoral boundaries (to be handled by an independent agency established by Parliament rather than the ECI), and the qualification and eligibility criteria of voters. The foremost pre-occupation of the 1951 Act, in turn, is the actual conduct of elections (election administration, eligibility of candidates, regulation of parties, and campaign processes).[18] Furthermore, the Act also provides for a system of citizen-driven post-election 'petitions' to be adjudicated by the judiciary. The 'post-election' nature of these petitions needs to be underscored; as outlined in the Constitution and subsequent election law, when elections are ongoing, the commission enjoys primacy over the judiciary and other branches of government. While this primacy has not gone unchallenged, it remains largely intact even today, as we discuss subsequently.

Organizational Structure

Article 324 of the Constitution states that the ECI 'shall consist of the Chief Election Commissioner [CEC] and such number of other

---

[18] Under the Constitution, the jurisdiction of the ECI as it relates to political parties was highly ambiguous. A subsequent order of the commission, the Election Symbols (Reservation and Allotment) Order of 1968 clarified matters. The ECI stipulated that all parties were to formally register with the commission. The commission, in turn, would allocate and regulate the use of election symbols by parties. See Gilmartin and Moog, 'Introduction to "Election Law in India"', 141. While this did clarify some hotly contested issues, as we will see below, it did not fully resolve them.

Election Commissioners, if any, as the President may from time to time fix'. The appointment of the CEC and other election commissioners (EC) is made by the President, and Article 5 of Section 324 states that the CEC can only be removed from his office in 'like manner and on the like grounds' as a judge of the Supreme Court. The article also allows for the President, after consultation with the ECI, the authority to name regional commissioners to assist with elections, if deemed necessary.

For the first several decades after Independence, the ECI was guided by a single CEC, although since 1993 (for reasons elaborated below), the ECI has operated as a three-member body with decisions taken on the basis of consensus. Although there is no formal provision of law that stipulates ECs should be drawn from the Indian Administrative Service (IAS), this has become customary. After some controversy, the terms of service of the commissioners were fixed by Parliament so that all commissioners would be treated equivalent to judges of the Supreme Court (in terms of salary, perquisites, retirement, etc.). Commissioners are appointed to six-year terms and are subject to a mandatory retirement age of 65.

Although the Constitution gives the President the authority to appoint regional commissioners in consultation with the ECI, this has only happened once (in the very first general election). Instead, the ECI has relied on chief electoral officers (CEOs) located in each of the states. The state-level CEOs were given statutory backing by an amendment to the RPA passed in 1956, which also gave the ECI power to name and supervise these officials (typically a civil servant belonging to the IAS from that state's cadre) in consultation with the state governments. These state-level CEOs are the point people for state and national elections and they function as the Commission's eyes and ears on the ground.[19]

In addition, the work of the ECs is supported by a secretariat based in New Delhi. According to former Deputy Election Commissioners R.P. Bhalla, the ECI began its life with a skeletal staff comprising a handful of officers working for the Constituent Assembly who were rendered unemployed once the Assembly concluded its work.[20] The staff has grown

[19] U.K. Singh, 'Institutions and Democratic Governance', 21.
[20] R.P. Bhalla, *Elections in India (1950–1972)* (New Delhi: S. Chand and Co., 1978).

significantly since then; as of the early 2000s, more than 300 people toiled in the secretariat.[21] The administrative expenditure for the ECI, unlike other constitutional authorities, is a voted expenditure rather than a 'charge' on the Consolidated Fund of India—a change the Commission has long advocated for.[22] The Commission's fiscal year 2013–14 budget stood at 68.5 crore rupees (or roughly 11.2 million dollars).[23]

The administrative machinery related to India's electoral system is intricate and multilayered. At the top, of course, sits the ECI, which is the apex body for administering elections. The ECI itself has no full-time staff in the field; it relies heavily on state and local governments to provide personnel for preparing the rolls and administering elections. Thus, when either the rolls are being revised or elections are being held, the ECI's 'staff' is augmented by millions of additional workers (typically government or quasi-government employees) deputized to work under its aegis. For example, in carrying out India's 2009 general election, the ECI oversaw roughly 11 million personnel across the country. Crucially, and at times controversially, these millions working on behalf of the ECI are subject to the Commission's disciplinary control.

At the top level of the 'field machinery' sit the 36 state CEOs. Within states, each of India's 684 administrative districts is served by a district election officer (DEO), who is typically the district magistrate/collector. The DEO, typically dual-hatted as the returning officer (RO), is the 'kingpin' for all election activities taking places in his/her district.[24] Below the DEO, there are electoral registration officers (ERO) who are government employees deputized to oversee the voter registration process and revision of the electoral rolls for each of the 4,120 state assembly and 543 national parliamentary constituencies.[25] Finally, at

[21] McMillan, 'Election Commission'. Further, while officers serving at the deputy commissioner, principal secretary, or director level typically consist of individuals on deputation from the IAS, officers below this rank come from within the secretariat's own ranks. See Rama Devi and Mendiratta, *How India Votes*, 186.

[22] Rama Devi and Mendiratta, *How India Votes*, 187.

[23] Government of India, *Union Budget 2013–14* (New Delhi: Ministry of Finance, 2014).

[24] Rama Devi and Mendiratta, *How India Votes*, 211

[25] EROs are assisted in this task by Assistant Electoral Registration Officers (AEROs).

the lowest level sit booth level officers (BLO), a relatively new administrative innovation, who are in charge of individual polling booths.
To ensure that this process functions smoothly, the ECI also appoints
observers of two types—general observers (drawn from the IAS) and
expenditure observers (drawn from the Indian Revenue Service)—to
monitor election proceedings in all constituencies.[26]

The ECI's writ does not extend to elections that take place below the
state level. The 73rd and 74th Amendments to the Constitution, which
established new local-governance structures in rural and urban India,
authorized the creation of autonomous State Election Commissions
(SECs) to oversee the conduct of elections to rural panchayat and
urban local bodies. In recent years, analysts have raised concerns about
political interference and the overall lower quality of the SECs when it
comes to their conduct of local elections. To the extent these concerns
are valid, the underlying reasons likely rest with the variation across
states in terms of bureaucratic capacity and the quality of the judiciary.

Another issue that has remained outside of the formal purview of
the ECI is delimitation, or the drawing of electoral boundaries. Under
Article 81 of the Constitution, Parliament has the authority to make
laws related to delimitation, which they have typically outsourced
to an independent agency set up after each decennial census.[27] The
ECI, however, has played a supporting role in assisting the various
Delimitation Commissions, although it lacks any legal or supervisory
authorities in this regard.[28]

Regulatory Expansionism

The ECI was fortunate to have been established as a constitutional
body, one whose independence and standing was fiercely protected by

---

[26] In special cases, the ECI also deputizes special observers from the Indian
Police Service (IPS) in sensitive areas.

[27] For various reasons, Parliament did not establish a delimitation commission between 1972 and 2001. When a delimitation commission was finally
established to redraw boundaries, it did so under certain constraints (namely an
inability to change the overall number of seats or their state-wise distribution
in either Parliament or the state assemblies).

[28] McMillan, 'Election Commission', 107.

India's founders and frequently by the courts. Having said that, there was a great deal of ambiguity in both the Constitution, as well as in subsequent legislation, about crucial aspects of the Commission's mandate. Over the past six decades, India has changed in ways impossible to foresee. In response, the commission has had to adjust accordingly, often without clear statutory guidance.

In the initial period following the promulgation of the Constitution, the Commission was not a subject of significant controversy and was focused on building an autonomous electoral agency from scratch. It was aided in its initial institution-building phase by a leader of tremendous capacity in the form of Sukumar Sen, a little remembered but incredibly important figure in Indian democracy, who served as the first CEC.[29] Jawaharlal Nehru, as the country's first prime minister and a true believer in the Commission's role in integrating India, also took it upon himself to bolster the stature of the Commission in the early years, granting it ample latitude in organizing polls.[30]

After Nehru's death, the political scenario in India became more complex. Internal fissures developed within the Congress, the party's dominance slowly eroded (especially at the state level), and a new host of competitors to the Congress gradually began asserting themselves. During Indira Gandhi's prime ministership, in particular, the Commission was increasingly drawn into difficult, often highly politicized battles. First came the ECI's role in deciding which faction of the Congress to officially recognize after the party's split in 1967. Soon after came the Allahabad High Court decision in 1975 to nullify Mrs Gandhi's 1971 successful election to Parliament in response to allegations of corrupt electoral practices. This controversy, of course, in turn led to Gandhi's decision to declare a state of national emergency.

[29] R. Guha, 'The Biggest Gamble in History', *The Hindu*, 27 January 2002. Guha recalls that Nehru pressured Sen to hold India's first general elections as quickly as possible following the promulgation of the Constitution. Sen, a mathematician by training, understood the logistical complexities involved and stood his ground. In the end, Sen appears to have been vindicated; the Commission's painstaking preparations for the first national polls resulted in remarkably successful elections in 1952.

[30] Gilmartin and Moog, 'Introduction to "Election Law in India"', 140.

The end of the emergency and the restoration of the democratic process led to a rejuvenation of the Commission and redoubling of its assertiveness. Indeed, this was one of the positive, though unanticipated, effects of India's brief detour from democracy.[31] Yet, this was also a period when India's electoral system was placed under great stress, thanks to heightened levels of political competition and the growth of money and muscle power.

In the early 1990s, the Commission entered a new period of regulatory activism intended to protect the sanctity of democratic elections. The growing assertiveness of the ECI was not just the product of the inexorable pressures of dirty elections, a strong opposition, and an increasingly mobilized public and media during the 1990s, but also due to the personality of then CEC T.N. Seshan. It was a case of both structure as well as agency. Former Prime Minister Rajiv Gandhi warned his successor, Chandra Shekhar, about appointing Seshan to the post of CEC in December 1990, stating he would forever rue the day. Seshan was reportedly a strong personality, but also someone who revelled in political intrigue. He tried to push the envelope on the broad constitutional remit given to the CEC by trying to control the timing and conduct of elections, enforce the Model Code of Conduct, and regulate political parties.

In this section, we briefly review some of the societal pressures on election administration, how the Commission attempted to respond to them, and the subsequent controversies that emerged in light of the agency's contested authority. We end with a detailed discussion on an important innovation in the conduct of elections in India, the Model Code of Conduct.

Social and Political Pressures

In order to understand the Commission's regulatory expansionism over the last few decades, one needs to have a proper appreciation of the changing nature of elections in India. In the immediate post-Independence era, the Congress party dominated the Indian political imagination. It is too simplistic to say it had a monopoly over political competition; after all, there were a total of 55 political parties that

---

[31] Gilmartin and Moog, 'Introduction to "Election Law in India"', 142.

contested the inaugural general elections. But when the results of the 1952 general election were announced, Congress emerged victorious in 364 of 489 seats, earning 45 per cent of the popular vote. Furthermore, across the political spectrum, control over parties, and the candidate pool itself, was still dominated by the upper-caste Hindus. In many parts of the country, lower and backward castes did not enjoy political or social emancipation.

Over the next several decades, the 'Congress system' gradually broke down, giving way to new and emerging political parties, many of whom were grounded in regional politics. Figure 10.1 plots the increase in the number of political parties contesting national elections, while Figure 10.2 documents the growth in the number of candidates contesting national elections. Whereas 55 parties participated in India's first general election in 1952, that number increased by several orders of magnitude after 1989. By 2014, as many as 464 parties fielded candidates in India's fifteenth general election. The number

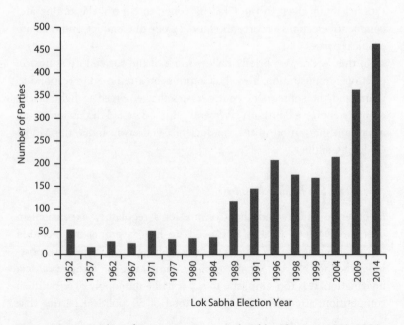

Figure 10.1 Number of Parties Contesting Lok Sabha Elections, 1952–2014
Source: Election Commission of India.

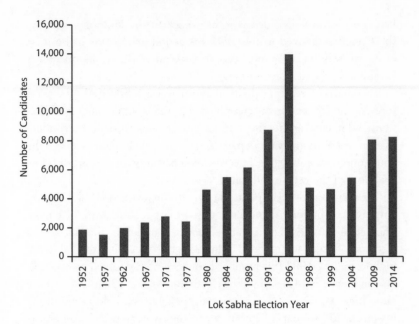

Figure 10.2   Number of Candidates Contesting Lok Sabha Elections, 1952–2014
Source: Election Commission of India.

of candidates has also increased significantly: from 1,874 in 1952 to 8,251 in 2014.[32]

Further complicating this picture was the transition from an era of single-party majority to coalition government in New Delhi, an attribute that has firmly become a part of Indian political life post-1989. Indeed, coalition government became a reality not only at the centre, but also in the states, leading one observer to refer to the present period of Indian politics as an 'era of coalitions of coalitions'.[33] The decisive victory of the Bharatiya Janata Party (BJP) in the 2014 general election, in which the party earned an outright majority in Parliament for the

[32] The increase in the cost of deposits, or the price of standing as a candidate, was dramatically increased in1996, which explains the sudden drop-off in 1999.

[33] C. Jaffrelot, 'A Blur of Identities', *Outlook India*, 19 March 2002.

first time in three decades, is a throwback to the kind of hegemony the Congress enjoyed in the 1947–89 period. It remains to be seen, of course, whether this most recent electoral verdict is anomalous or heralds a return to a previous era.

The sharp increase in political competition introduced new pressures on the ECI and vastly complicated its role as implementer of elections and neutral arbiter. In addition to managing the smooth conduct of elections with many more parties in the fray, it also had to 'check the abuse of power not by one, but by several parties who are part of ruling coalitions at the centre and states'.[34]

The increasing level of political competition proceeded hand in hand with a sharp popular democratic upsurge. At a basic level, of course, population growth triggered an exponential uptick in the size of the electorate, as seen in Figure 10.3. In 1952, the electorate stood at 173.2 million, and by 1984 this number had more than doubled to 400 million. In India's 2014 elections, the electorate stood at 834 million. At the same time, a process of democratic deepening took hold as politically marginalized segments of society found their voice—often through the express of caste or ethnic identities—in the democratic discourse.

As Jaffrelot documents, in 1952, nearly two-thirds of Members of Parliament (MPs) from the northern Hindi belt were from the Hindu upper castes, and fewer than 5 per cent from the Other Backward Classes (OBCs).[35] By 2004, the upper caste share fell to just one-third while the OBC share stood at 25 per cent. This 'silent revolution', to borrow a phrase from Christophe Jaffrelot, posed serious challenges to the conduct of elections because the Commission had to protect the democratic rights of the newly mobilized communities, while guarding against the tensions that naturally arise when competing social identities clashed.[36]

[34] M. Katju, 'Election Commission and Changing Contours of Politics', *Economic and Political Weekly* 44, no. 16 (18–24 April 2009): 8–12.

[35] C. Jaffrelot, 'Introduction', in *Rise of the Plebeians? The Changing Face of the Indian Legislative Assemblies*, eds C. Jaffrelot and S. Kumar (New Delhi: Routledge, 2009).

[36] C. Jaffrelot, *India's Silent Revolution: The Rise of the Lower Castes in North India* (New York: Columbia University Press, 2003); M. Katju, 'Election Commission and Functioning of Democracy', *Economic and Political Weekly* 41, no. 17 (29 April–5 May 2006): 1635–40.

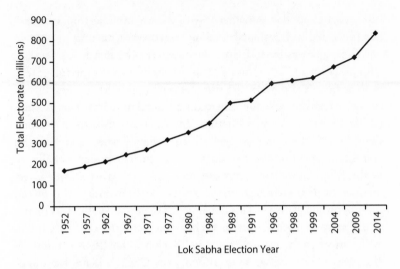

Figure 10.3 Size of the Electorate in Lok Sabha Elections, 1952–2014
Source: Election Commission of India.

This process of democratic deepening was, on balance, a profoundly positive development. Yet at the same time, this democratic deepening also produced many sub-optimal outcomes. Two, in particular, proved especially vexing for India's election guardians: criminalization of politics, and the increasing role of money in elections. The implications for elections were stark: increasing election-related violence, instances of outright vote rigging ('booth-capturing') and a steady inflow of undeclared, 'black money' used for elections.[37] We return to these twin themes in the penultimate section.

Executive–Agency Political Context

While the constitution gave the CEC and the Commission very broadly defined powers of superintendence, direction, and control, it was the unstated assumption and expectation on the part of the ruling party that the CEC (always a retired civil servant) would be 'cooperative', manage elections according to their wishes (and time-table) of the

---

[37] 'Black money' is the term applied to funds on which taxes have not been paid or to money raised through illegal activities.

ruling party, and look the other way in the event of electoral malpractice (provided such instances were not overly egregious).

While this was by and large the case over the first three decades, with successive CECs refusing to assert themselves to the full extent of their potential powers, the rise of strong opposition parties, first in the states, and then at the centre during the late 1970s, changed the political balance. Along with this came increasingly strong electoral challenges to the ruling party. Both the ruling parties as well as the opposition began to resort to dirty electoral tricks, posing a challenge to the ECI. This, in turn, put pressure on successive CECs to assert themselves in the context of increasing media exposure and public and opposition pressure. This dynamic led to repeated attempts by the ruling party of the day to try and check the authority of the ECI. The evolution of an increasingly assertive ECI since the 1990s is the story of a seesaw battle between assertion by the CEC, and later the three-member ECI as a whole, and attempts by the ruling party to constrain the CEC/ECI. Over the long run, however, a much more powerful ECI has emerged and been accepted by the political class.

The calls to establish a multi-member commission date back to at least the 1970s. Finally, in October 1989, just a month before the general election, Prime Minister Rajiv Gandhi exploited the provision for additional ECs by appointing two: V.S. Saigal (retired Indian Police Service) and S.S. Dhanoa (retired IAS). This move was widely perceived as an attempt to limit the absolute powers of then CEC R.V.S. Peri Sastri, who was reputed to oversee elections strictly by the book.[38] The opposition fought the appointments tooth and nail, Dhanoa and Saigal fell afoul of Haryana Chief Minister (and key power broker) Devi Lal during the election, and soon the latter emerged as deputy Prime Minister under V.P. Singh. The V.P. Singh government subsequently removed the two ECs by abolishing the posts by presidential amendment of the notification, a move later upheld by the Supreme Court. However, in that judgement, the Court did find that multiple heads are better than one, in principle, when it comes to the ECI.

---

[38] Indeed, Dhanoa later admitted to a senior ECI official that he was sent there with a 'mandate'; in fact, the two new ECs often called on then Home Minister Buta Singh at his residence before coming to work.

Later, when CEC T.N. Seshan's star was on the rise, Prime Minister Narasimha Rao appointed two additional ECs in 1993, M.S. Gill and G.V.G. Krishnamurthy, to check Seshan's power, as he was seen as a loose cannon. Although Seshan resisted the move, in 1995 a Supreme Court bench ruled in a 5–0 decision that the appointment of two additional ECs was legal, that the CEC was only *primus inter pares* (first among equals), and that the two could overrule the CEC.[39] From that point on, the ECI has consistently been a three-member body. And when Seshan's term ended in December 1996, M.S. Gill was named the new CEC.

Gill also thwarted, through judicious informal advice, by a move contemplated by Prime Minister Vajpayee to appoint two more ECs, taking the number to five, to check the existing ECI. On Gill's part, this was an act of deft political management. However, Vajpayee's National Democratic Alliance (NDA) government did contemplate another attempt to engineer a cooperative ECI. The BJP was not happy with the assertiveness of CEC Lyngdoh when he delayed the Gujarat state assembly election of 2002, disallowing BJP Chief Minister Narendra Modi to hold an early election in the summer following the post-Godhra riots. In January 2004, just before the impending national elections and before Lyngdoh was to retire, it was rumoured that the retiring cabinet secretary T.R. Prasad would be brought in as CEC directly, superseding the two ECs, T.S. Krishnamurthy and B.B. Tandon (who eventually became CECs in that order). However, the move was abandoned when the two ECs threatened to resign. This anecdote indicates the consolidation of a new phase in executive–ECI relations: by now, it had become very important for the ruling party of the day to *not* be seen as attempting to undermine the ECI's authority. Since M.S. Gill's tenure, the tradition in the three-member ECI has been to follow the seniority principle, and a later CEC (Quraishi) has suggested that this be made law.

The setting up of protocols for the smooth functioning of the three-member Commission after the 1995 Court judgement was crucial to its consolidation and subsequent evolution. Then Deputy Election

---

[39] Seshan's resistance was so complete that for about two years Seshan did not give substantial work to the two ECs and the ECI staff offered little cooperation since rank-and-file officers feared the wrath of the CEC.

Commissioner Subas Pani (1995–2002) played a key role in the setting up of such protocols between November 1995 and Seshan's exit in December 1996. These systems included those for movement of files between the members, convening of meetings, media briefings (including appointing an official spokesman), writing of annual confidential reports of officers, recruitment of entry-level staff through staff selection boards instead of employment exchanges (to ensure good support staff were available), computerization of electoral rolls and identity cards, setting up a professional website, and so on. These systems and protocols considerably facilitated efficient and smooth functioning of the Commission, while at the same time minimizing actual and potential friction between Seshan and the other two members.[40]

Regulatory Response

Faced with a series of new challenges brought on by India's social, political, and economic changes, the ECI's response was to engage in a sustained pattern of regulatory expansionism. The broad construction of the Commission's legal and constitutional framework, coupled with its reputation for integrity and the popular support it enjoyed, allowed it to take on a much broader role in terms of regulating elections than it had enjoyed at the outset. In part, this transformation was also facilitated by a weakness demonstrated by other institutions of the state. As McMillan writes, 'A weak legislative framework and the slow and imperfect functioning of the judiciary have created a vacuum of authority into which the Election Commission has frequently been drawn'.[41] This expansionism has frequently raised questions about whether the ECI has breached its constitutional remit, inviting criticism by many political actors and leading to numerous disputes that have often ended up in the courts. To explore these issues, we divide them into two clusters: pre-election activities, such as voter registration and the nomination of candidates, and the actual conduct of elections.

Voter registration: One of the foremost challenges facing the Commission involved voter registration, which gets to the heart of

[40] It should be noted that it was not always the CEC versus the others, and that the three largely agreed on most substantive issues.
[41] McMillan, 'Administration of Electoral Politics', 199.

the participatory democratic process. In practice, the Commission interpreted its mandate as an affirmative responsibility to enrol voters rather than place the burden on the voters for ensuring their place on the electoral rolls.[42] Thus, the default setting is for the Commission to perform a good faith effort in ensuring that every eligible voter's name is found on the electoral rolls, while it is merely the duty of the voters to check the agency's work.

To carry out this task, the Commission dedicates considerable resources to conducting a thorough house-to-house canvass of eligible voters every five years (it also conducts summary revisions on an annual basis), making the resulting lists available for public scrutiny. The ECI's decision to place the burden of registration on itself, rather than on the voter, has been fraught with practical challenges. Indeed, the Commission has found itself in the uncomfortable position of taking decisions on matters related to citizenship. As the political scientist Anupama Roy explains, the Commission—backed by the courts—was granted the 'power to decide ... whether those who laid claims to being eligible to vote were in fact citizens'.[43] In a landmark judgement stemming from a case filed in the aftermath of the 1983 elections, the Supreme Court ordered the ECI to ensure the accurate revision of electoral rolls, taking into account the citizenship status of voters (to ensure that any would-be voters included on the rolls were in fact citizens of India).

The ECI, reluctant to wade into such murky waters, responded by placing the burden on voters to disclose their citizenship status, but the precedent of blurring the lines between citizenship and voter eligibility had been established.[44] A series of controversial orders in the early 1990s by the ECI directing staff to purge voter lists of 'foreigners' resulted in several court cases which ultimately made their way to the Supreme Court, which ruled that there must be limits on the ECI's efforts to ensure the citizenship status of voters. In the cases in question, entire neighbourhoods comprised largely of Muslims saw their residents' names purged from the lists, raising concerns about the 'sweeping' nature of the ECI's powers.[45]

---

[42] Roy, 'Identifying Citizens', 174.

[43] Roy, 'Identifying Citizens', 176.

[44] Roy, 'Identifying Citizens', 175–81.

[45] Roy, 'Identifying Citizens', 179–81.

Still today, controversies about voter registration remain, with urbanization posing a particular challenge to the work of election authorities. Due to rapid urbanization, maintaining up-to-date voter lists in urban areas is an immense challenge. As several experts warned in a 2012 column: 'This is not about bureaucratic neglect or administrative incompetence, but rather the early warning signs of a new order: a dynamic, mobile urban citizenry'.[46] In the 2014 general election, several thousand Mumbai residents, including many prominent personalities, were inadvertently left off the voter rolls—resulting in a minor embarrassment for election authorities.[47]

Nomination of candidates: As part of its superintendence function, the ECI has also been forced to define parameters relating to the nomination of candidates standing for election. Two issues merit mention here. The first relates to the proliferation of candidates and parties contesting elections. Here, once again, the ECI has been forced to balance the promotion of democratic principles with ensuring relative efficiency. In an attempt to regulate entry, candidates have been required to submit a security 'deposit', which they forfeit if they obtain less than one-sixth of the vote share in their respective constituency. As Figure 10.2 demonstrated, the number of candidates contesting elections has sharply increased over the years; in an effort to deter 'non-serious' candidates from entering the fray, the ECI raised the security deposit from Rs 500 to Rs 10,000 in 1997 (or from $13 to $267).[48] This had an immediate effect on the quantum of candidates, with the number of contestants falling dramatically after this decision was taken, before rebounding in subsequent years.[49]

[46] R. Ramanathan, S. Ramanathan, T.S. Krishnamurthy, and N.R. Narayana Murthy, 'The Urban Voter, Not on a Roll', *Indian Express*, 1 August 2012.

[47] B. Jaisinghani, 'Thousands of Voters' Names Go Missing in Mumbai', *Times of India*, 25 April 2014.

[48] McMillan, 'Administration of Electoral Politics', 192.

[49] L.L. Linden, 'Could Have Been a Contender? The Effects of Limiting the Number of Candidates in Indian State Parliamentary Elections', (Working Paper, Department of Economics, University of Texas-Austin, December 2005), 17. The author found that the increase in deposits decreased the number of new candidates in each constituency by an average of six candidates, but only marginally increased the electoral prospects of the average existing candidate.

A second issue relates to the criminalization of politics. For many years, the ECI had been agitating for either new powers to bar candidates facing serious criminal cases from standing for elections or, at the very least, the authority to make transparent the criminal and financial details of nominated candidates. In response to public interest litigation (PIL) filed by the Association for Democratic Reforms (ADR), a good governance non-governmental organization (NGO), the Supreme Court in 2003 clarified that the ECI could require that all candidates standing for election at the state and national levels must submit, at the time of nomination, a judicial affidavit declaring the candidate's criminal, educational, and financial records. With the court's backing, the ECI framed new guidelines for disclosure, which have improved the level of transparency voters can access about the candidates in the fray.[50] As we discuss in greater detail subsequently, these new guidelines have had mixed success, and the larger issue of candidates under serious criminal scrutiny being barred from standing remains a distant hope.

Regulation of parties: The 1951 RPA grants the authority of registering political parties to the ECI, which requires that parties furnish the agency with a copy of its party constitution. This authority was further fleshed out through the ECI's 1968 ordinance on election symbols. Owing to high rates of illiteracy, the ECI reserves and allocates election symbols to parties based on a series of intricate rules having to do with the parties' past performance. This means parties can gain or lose symbols (including to other parties, who can adopt those symbols in subsequent elections) and that the ECI, by default, has been saddled with the unenviable task of deciding which faction retains the symbol in the case of party splits.[51] Furthermore, based on a party's performance, the ECI categorizes parties as either 'national' or 'state' parties.

The ECI has, in recent decades, sought to extend its writ when it comes to regulating parties. A major issue facing India's democracy is the lack of democratic norms and procedures within political parties, a practice that openly flouts the ECI's requirement that parties adhere to

---

[50] As CEC, Gill also asserted his authority to disqualify candidates for 'corrupt practices' under Section 8A of the RPA; the president has to act on the ECI's opinion. However, courts very rarely upheld the corrupt practices charge.

[51] As we mentioned before, this was a major issue when the Congress party split in 1969 under Indira Gandhi.

such practices.[52] The lack of intra-party democracy means that parties often operate as little more than family-dominated fiefdoms or cliques where a handful of elites (though often in practice just the party president) control the party apparatus, including the selection of candidates and the content of its platform.

In an attempt to rectify this, the ECI under Seshan declared that the Commission can, and would, deregister any party that did not adhere to its internal constitution.[53] The genesis of this practice was that Rajiv Gandhi, in the wake of the Anti-Defection Law (52nd Constitutional Amendment of 1985), made parties submit copies of their constitutions to the ECI. Later, in 1988, section 29A was added to the RPA by which parties submitted their constitutions to the ECI and committed themselves to upholding democracy.

Seshan, and later Gill, interpreted this to mean that parties would have to hold internal elections. Subsequent ECs stuck to this line, although they eventually backed off once it became clear that withdrawing recognition on such grounds would likely be challenged in the courts.[54] While the ECI still supports such powers, it has made clear that a constitutional amendment to augment its existing authorities would be necessary.[55] The politics behind this move were more subtle. Forcing parties to hold internal elections was intended to weaken the hold of party leaderships, which had been made all-powerful by the anti-defection law, and thereby reduce the threat from such leaders to the authority of the ECI.

Conduct of elections: Perhaps the most notable innovation championed by the ECI has been the Model Code of Conduct (MCC), a voluntary set of principles that guide the conduct of candidates and parties, as well as incumbent governments, during election time. While the 1951 RPA established detailed procedures about petitions by

[52] P.B. Mehta, 'Is Electoral and Institutional Reform the Answer?' *Seminar* 506 (October 2001).

[53] McMillan, 'Administration of Electoral Politics', 193.

[54] However, Seshan did succeed in getting Shiv Sena leader Bal Thackeray banned from contesting elections for six years, a victory only in principle since Thackeray never actually stood for election.

[55] N. Bath, 'Role of the Election Commission of India in Strengthening Democracy in India', Paper presented at the Annual Meeting of the International Political Science Association, Montreal, 2006.

aggrieved parties after the elections were held, it did not contain provisions for interference while elections were ongoing. This is the gap the ECI hoped to fill with the MCC.[56]

The intent behind the MCC is to provide a normative framework for speech, electioneering, election manifestos, Election Day conduct, and the overall behaviour of campaigns. What is remarkable about the code is that the ECI's power to enforce it relies primarily on moral suasion; the code does not have the force of law and exists merely as a set of voluntary minimum standards. The code, whose original impetus came from civil society groups, was first adopted in Kerala in 1960. It stipulated best practices for participants in the election in an effort to minimize corruption, vote buying, and sectarian or other possible anti-democratic behaviour. Importantly, it also outlined norms for the government of the day to follow so that it would not use its enormous powers of incumbency to sway the electorate.[57]

The ECI first utilized the MCC at an all-India level in the late 1960s, although it made several substantial revisions to the code along the way to adapt to changing circumstances. However, it was not until 1982 that all parties accepted the Model Code, allowing it to fully take root. Until the 1990s, the MCC was largely a set of norms the ECI championed, but did not actively police. This changed in the 1990s for a few reasons.[58] First, the electoral context was much more intense in

---

[56] The ECI defines the MCC as 'a set of norms which has been evolved with the consensus of political parties who have consented to abide by the principles embodied in the said code and also binds them to respect and observe it in its letter and spirit'. Election Commission of India, *Model Code of Conduct for the Guidance of Political Parties and Candidates* (New Delhi: Election Commission of India, 2007): 7.

[57] R. Majeed, 'Implementing Standards without the Force of Law: India's Electoral Conduct Code, 1990–2001', *Innovations for Successful Societies Case Study* (Princeton, NJ: Princeton University, 2011).

[58] U.K. Singh, 'Between Moral Force and Supplementary Legality: A Model Code of Conduct and the Election Commission of India', *Election Law Journal: Rules, Politics, and Policy* 11, no. 2 (June 2012): 149–69. As Singh points out, the emphasis on the 1990s as a critical juncture is possibly overstated. Following emergency rule, the ECI did engage in a bout of activism in order to restore its constitutional role and reinforce democratic procedures with respect to elections. Both had taken a hit during this period from 1975 to 1977.

the late 1980s and early 1990s, with competition, insecurity, election fraud, and violence all on an upswing. Second, the ECI had grown tired of promoting the code only to then see political parties and other actors openly flout it. And third, Seshan was seized with the fear that ordinary Indians were losing faith both in the institution of the ECI specifically and the democratic process in general.

Beginning in the 1990s, the ECI transitioned from championing the code to actually implementing it. This entailed a huge devotion of human and financial resources to ensure that the relevant parties actually followed the letter and spirit of the code throughout the country. In practically enforcing the code, the ECI's power 'was derived from its constitutional position as the apolitical arbiter' of a unique form of morality.[59] Politicians, parties, many citizens, and occasionally, the courts have not fully accepted the notion of the ECI's unique morality. Indeed, one particular bone of contention relates to what Gilmartin refers to as 'electoral time'—an idealized conception of a period in which the ECI (in service of free and fair elections) was *the* law, if not above it.

One practical issue that grew out of this was a dispute over when the MCC is actually operative. The ECI contended that the MCC comes into force as soon as the ECI announces elections (as opposed to when the ECI formally notifies elections, which happens at a later date). The dispute ended up before the courts, with the ECI eventually brokering a settlement with political parties that the MCC would come into force at the time of 'announcement', and compromising that the gap between 'announcement' and 'notification' would not exceed three weeks.[60]

The issue of 'electoral time' has several additional aspects. One has to do with the length of the campaign period. Under a 1996 Amendment to the RPA, Parliament (with the ECI's consent) agreed to reduce the campaign period from three weeks down to two. While the campaign period has shrunk, ironically, elections now unfold over a greater length of time. This has to do, in part, with the security requirements modern elections entail, which means that in many big states (and in national

---

[59] D. Gilmartin, 'One Day's Sultan: T.N. Seshan and Indian Democracy', *Contributions to Indian Sociology* 43, no. 2 (May/August 2009): 247–84.

[60] Singh, 'Moral Force', 165.

elections) elections last several weeks or occasionally a few months, taking place in phases. For instance, the 2014 general election unfolded over nine phases, spanning five weeks.

Another has to do with the actual timing of elections itself, or 'time-tabling'. While the basic parameters of scheduling elections are detailed under existing statute, the ECI does have significant latitude in determining the precise timing and sequencing of elections. This issue came to a head on multiple occasions, though two are especially noteworthy. The first was during Bihar's 1995 assembly elections, when Seshan tormented then Chief Minister Lalu Prasad Yadav by forcing the rescheduling of polls on multiple occasions due to a perceived inadequacy on the part of the state government in making provisions for elections. In this case, the Supreme Court was forced to intervene and roll back some of Seshan's excited activism. The second critical event took place in 2002 in Gujarat, which had just suffered some of the worst communal violence between Hindus and Muslims in decades. There, the ECI intervened to delay the ruling BJP's attempt to hold early elections, which it worried would further inflame communal tensions. Although the BJP swept back to power, the ECI emerged victorious in the battle over the timing and elections were delayed—an important legal and moral victory from the Commission's perspective.[61]

Although Seshan played a central role in re-asserting the ECI's authority, it was under Gill's stewardship and deft political, as well as internal management within the ECI, that the new three-member ECI came to be institutionalized over 1997–2001, a period of political flux followed by a relatively stable BJP-led National Democratic Alliance (NDA) government. Gill continued Seshan's practice of asserting control over the timing of elections, the appointment and transfer of civil servants and police officers connected to the conduct of free and fair elections, enforcement of the Model Code, forcing of political parties to hold internal elections, and the proposal first mooted by the ECI in 1997 to bar candidates with criminal antecedents. It was Gill who initiated the practice of transferring all district-level civil servants and police officers, down to *tahsildars* (sub-district revenue officers), who had been in their posts for four or more years at the time of announcement of elections. This process has since become customary, with the

---

[61] Roy, 'Identifying Citizens', 182.

modification under CEC Quraishi that those who had served in the same posts at those levels for three of the preceding four years would be automatically transferred. By Quraishi's appointment in 2010, this practice gave the ECI appointment and transfer powers during elections over roughly 40 per cent of the state bureaucracy.

There are at least two broader concerns, however, concerning the MCC. The first has to do with the restrictions the code places on the conduct of government. Because the MCC is intended to create a level playing field, it places serious constraints on government policymaking (such as the announcement of government programmes or sanctioning of new investments) in advance of elections. In a given state government term, separate national, state, and local elections—each governed by the MCC—take up a significant amount of policymaking time.

The second concern is related to a kind of technocratic efficiency by the ECI that appeals to the Indian middle classes. For all of his democratic crusading, Seshan was dubbed a 'middle-class hero,' but his many critics believed he was a power-hungry, anti-democratic force. His supporters felt his actions were necessary to clean up India's democracy, while opponents lamented his 'Orwellian power'.[62] As Gilmartin writes, Seshan's critics viewed him as a man 'ready to wield the Model Code not just as an instrument of political and legal restraint but as an instrument of power, and one that could potentially threaten not only the corrupt politicians ... *but* all real politics'.[63] In effect, they argued, Seshan believed (mistakenly, in their view) that he could 'hold the election process to a higher morality than existed in "normal" political life'.[64]

Elections in India have long been celebrated for their carnival-like quality, when the nation is transformed into a large fairground to commemorate the largest public festival in the country.[65] Yet critics maintain that the ECI, thanks to the efforts of Seshan and his successors, has slowly chipped away at this celebratory sentiment thanks to its hyperactive regulation of public displays, rallies, public meetings, and

[62] Singh, 'Moral Force', 165.

[63] Gilmartin, 'One Day's Sultan', 262.

[64] Gilmartin, 'One Day's Sultan', 271.

[65] M. Banerjee, 'Elections as Communitas', *Social Research* 78, no. 1 (Spring 2011): 75–98.

other election-related paraphernalia in an effort to guarantee a level playing field. The ECI, as a May 2014 editorial in *Economic and Political Weekly* observed, is often-times caught between accusations that it is overstepping its mandate and the need to manage overly inflated expectations placed upon it by politicians, parties, and the citizenry.[66]

Over the past decade, what were once seen as assertions of the CEC against the ruling party about the timing, conduct, and reporting of elections, the control of the administration at election time, and the regulation of parties and candidates, have all become normal practices. Transparency measures like those of 2003, forcing candidates to declare their criminal records, family financial assets and liabilities, and educational qualifications, have been aided by legal transparency laws like the Right to Information Act, 2005 (RTI Act).[67]

Organizational Capacity and Coordination

One of the lamentable aspects of India's post-Independence record has been the relative inattention, particularly in recent decades, to the health and status of India's public sector institutions. The ECI, while certainly imperfect, does represent a case of relative institutional rejuvenation and even innovation. This section provides a brief review of the composition of the ECI, its organizational culture, and the way in which it has innovated to keep pace with India's changing electoral environment.

Composition of the ECI

In the previous section, we detailed the evolution of the ECI from a single-member commission to the current 'troika' set-up. One remaining issue which merits discussion is the stability of the current configuration. Has the three-member CEC stabilized itself as an independent

---

[66] 'The Election and Its Commission', *Economic and Political Weekly* 49, no. 20 (10–17 May 2014): 7.

[67] As one recent CEC privately remarked to the authors, the actions of Seshan and his successors encouraged later CECs to be more assertive and, in fact, raised the bar for them to maintain their image, particularly in the light of intense media scrutiny in which every utterance makes news.

institution, or can it still be undermined? In the opinion of several former CECs, the ECI is still vulnerable on these grounds for at least four reasons.

First, it is still possible for a government to appoint additional ECs and enlarge the size of the ECI while adhering to the letter of the law. Thus, in theory at least, 'packing' of the ECI is still possible. Second, the tenure of the two additional ECs is less secure than that of the CEC, a constitutional lacuna that, according to one former CEC, should have been addressed, but was left inadvertently unaddressed in the 1995 Supreme Court judgement upholding the three-member commission. But the question remains: how can the remaining two ECs be truly equal if they do not enjoy equal security of tenure? Third, while the current tradition is that one of the two ECs will be promoted to CEC in order of seniority, this is only convention. The lack of clear rules potentially renders the ECs vulnerable to government pressure. One former CEC has suggested making the seniority principle law. Fourth, conflict among the three commissioners could possibly create an opening for political interference and manipulation. And, of course, there remains the risk of partisan or political appointments made by the government of the day.

The second and fourth lacunae mentioned came out sharply in the conflict that had been brewing since 2007 and erupted in public between CEC N. Gopalaswamy and EC Navin Chawla in January 2009, when Gopalaswamy asked the President to remove Chawla and the latter refused.[68]

There were two related issues involved here on which there was no constitutional clarity. One was whether under Article 324(5), the CEC had *suo motu* powers to recommend the removal of an EC.[69] The second was whether the CEC could ask an EC for an explanation of his conduct, in this case of Chawla's allegedly biased conduct—stemming

---

[68] 'Election Commission in Tatters', *Economic and Political Weekly* 44, no. 9 (21–8 February 2009): 5. For the account in this section, we are grateful to Navin Chawla for interviews granted on 7 July and 2 October 2013. For a detailed account of the sequence of events discussed here, see Harish Khare, 'Restoring Order at Nirvachan Sadan Statecraft', *Hindu*, 26 February, 2009.

[69] S. Panchu, 'Free and Fair Election Commissioners?', *Economic and Political Weekly* 44, no. 9 (28 February–6 March 2009): 10–12.

from the BJP's contention—that he was a close associate of the Gandhi family.

The BJP initially complained to the President and then to the CEC, asking for Chawla's removal. Chawla, in turn, accused Gopalaswamy of meeting secretly with BJP leaders in his chamber.

Soon, the debate moved to whether the CEC could require that Chawla furnish an explanation for certain actions he had taken on the ground, given that there is no clear legal provision supporting the notion that the CEC has the authority to demand an explanation from an EC of equal status. Chawla maintained this position in his replies to Gopalaswamy of 12 September 2008 and 10 December 2008, and was supported by the Union Law Secretary T.K. Viswanathan in his letter of 7 November 2008 (which was in response to Chawla's formal letter to the Union Law Ministry seeking clarification of his powers).[70]

Gopalaswamy retorted that, as CEC, he had *suo motu* authority to recommend the removal of one of his fellow commissioners, something that neither Seshan nor his predecessor B.B. Tandon had claimed in the past, and wrote to the president on 12 January 2009, asking for Chawla's removal.[71] The president sent it to the prime minister who sent it to the Law Ministry, which issued a point-by-point rebuttal. Eventually, the matter was resolved in March 2009, just before the general election, and Chawla became CEC in April. However, from the point of view of the stability and viability of a three-member ECI of equals, the root cause of this dispute was the lacuna under Article 324(5) that left ECs less secure in their tenure than the CEC. The ECI, just before Chawla's tenure ended in 2010, wrote to the prime minister recommending the correction of this lacuna by making the tenure of the ECs as secure as that of the CEC.[72] This uncertainty persists to the present day.

[70] Viswanathan maintained that the removal of an EC cannot be initiated by the CEC without the reference or concurrence of the government and that the three members are equal, and no response to the CEC's demand for an explanation is due from an EC.

[71] Panchu, 'Free and Fair Election Commissioners?', 10–12.

[72] This letter was drafted in consultation with the other two ECs, but signed only by CEC Chawla as it was felt by the two ECs that their signature might be read as indicating a concern for their security of tenure, whereas the point being made was one of principle, so as to render the functioning of the three-member ECI harmonious.

In sum, while it is unlikely that any party would try to blatantly undermine the ECI, its autonomy is still not entirely secure for the above four reasons. Past committees have recommended that the ECs be chosen by a committee to minimize the threat of political or partisan appointment, but this remains a mere proposal.

Organizational Culture

Interviews with former CECs and officers of the ECI make clear that one of the strongest attributes of the ECI is its esprit de corps, a characteristic which can be attributed to its constitutional independence, its exceptional leadership, beginning with Sukumar Sen, as well as the deference paid to the Commission by the judiciary, which has often stepped in to protect the organization's autonomy.[73] As with the selection of the ECs, there is always the danger of politics creeping into the organization. To date, the ECI has been fortunate insofar as politicization has not often been a headline issue. However, as the political scientist Manjari Katju reminds us, the commission must endeavour to ensure it is a politically 'non-committed' institution. But it also must not allow the pendulum to swing too far to the other extreme: 'it has to ensure that it does not become socially rigid or politically *status quoist*' (emphasis added).[74]

Technological Innovation

An important channel by which the ECI has been able to maximize its capacity has been the adoption of technology. There is no better example of this than the fact that India is one of the earliest adopters of electronic voting technology. As McMillan explains, the Commission first experimented with the use of electronic voting machines (EVMs) in 1982, though the Supreme Court disallowed their use in 1984.[75] An amendment to the RPA, in 1951, paved the way for their reintroduction; since 2003, the ECI has used them for all state and national

---

[73] Of course, the courts have at times stepped in to check the Commission's authority when it has deemed it overstepped its mandate.

[74] Katju, 'Election Commission and Functioning of Democracy', 1639.

[75] McMillan, 'Election Commission', 104.

elections. For the 2014 general election, the ECI employed more than 1.7 million such voting machines. This is all the more impressive when one considers the fact that many advanced industrial countries, such as the US, have struggled mightily in their efforts to implement electronic voting.[76] Chance has also played a role in technological changes helping the evolution of the ECI's capabilities and reputation. The computerization of electoral rolls for the 1998 election was crucial for the 1999 election being smoothly conducted only a year later, an unforeseeable development, and this further buttressed the drive to adopt information technology.

On this front, the ECI did a considerable amount of work following the 1996 general election, which proved crucial to the successful execution of two national elections in quick succession in 1998 and 1999. The introduction of professional management systems with extensive and intensive use of information and communication technology (ICT) and vastly improved systems and procedures in electoral management enhanced the ECI's 'event management' function. Central to this was a massive training exercise to ensure that election officials could adapt to the new ICT systems. The ECI also took the initiative to install critical ICT infrastructure in place at the national, state, and district levels.

The success of the strategy is evident from the complete transition to EVMs for national elections within a few years and the fact that nearly two million EVMs being used for such an event is hardly commented upon today. The use of EVMs has contributed significantly to addressing the plague of electoral malpractice India witnessed in prior decades. In more recent years, the Commission has used technology to tackle electoral malpractice in other ways as well.

First, beginning in 2007, the ECI conducts a 'vulnerability mapping' exercise prior to every election in order to determine which polling booths face the greatest likelihood of violence or unrest.[77] Using data

[76] The ECI's reliance on EVMs is not without its detractors. See Hari K. Prasad, J. Alex Halderman, Rop Gonggrijp, Scott Wolchok, Eric Wustrow, Arun Kankipati, Sai Krishna Sakhamuri, and VasavyaYagati, 'Security Analysis of India's Electronic Voting Machines', Proceedings of the 17th ACM Conference on Computer and Communications Security, Chicago, 2010.

[77] M. Scharff, 'Policing Election Day: Vulnerability Mapping in India, 2006–2009', *Innovations for Successful Societies Case Study* (Princeton, NJ: Princeton University, 2011).

on violent incidents, past election outcomes, and voter trends, the Commission classifies polling booths based on their 'sensitivity'. This, in turn, directly informs the Commission's decisions about how and where to most effectively deploy police and paramilitary personnel. As part of the mapping exercise, district officials are tasked to draw up lists of potential troublemakers residing or operating in these sensitive areas, who are then subject to monitoring and/or preventive detention. For the 2014 general elections, according to the ECI, 75,237 hamlets were identified as potentially 'vulnerable' and 250,892 individuals were tagged as 'possible intimidators'. To monitor and inventory potential security threats, in 2009 the ECI hired nearly 75,000 videographers to assist its officers.[78]

Another technological innovation relates to communications for election monitoring. The ECI has regularized the practice of deploying communications technology to ensure direct connectivity between the ECI and booth-level officers overseeing individual polling stations. Using text messaging technology, the ECI can receive real-time updates on the status of elections, including the status of the polling party, the presence of security forces and micro-observers, and any instances of voting disruption. Furthermore, this same technology has been used to provide information to voters, such as announcing information about Election Day and providing electronic voter slips. In recent elections, the ECI has also installed webcams so that election officers can get real-time, first-hand information from polling booths and monitor possible irregularities.

This is not to suggest that all of the ECI's technological innovations have been successful. Although the incidence of electoral malpractice has diminished considerably with time, there were several worrying instances of blatant electoral fraud in the 2014 general election. Many of these prompted the ECI to mandate re-polls.[79] A second instance where technology has not been a panacea relates to the registration of voters. Because the task of registering voters and ensuring updated rolls

[78] S.Y. Quraishi, 'Conducting Elections in the World's Largest Plural Society', Lecture delivered at the Centre for the Advanced Study of India, University of Pennsylvania, Philadelphia, 25 February 2011.

[79] See, inter alia, J. Joseph, 'A Month after Election, 8 Gurgaon Booths Set For Repoll', *Times of India*, 14 May 2014.

is so burdensome, technology has the potential of improving efficiency. But the ECI's efforts in this area have been uneven. During his tenure as CEC, T.N. Seshan was particularly seized by the issue of voter registration, viewing any shortcomings in the electoral rolls as a blemish on India's democracy itself. According to McMillan, Seshan pursued a 'quixotic' campaign to solve the problems of registration and verification through the provision of voter identification cards.[80] The process was both administratively complex and expensive, and Seshan's willingness to delay elections until all voters had photo-accompanied ID cards raised questions about the ECI's ability to hold elections hostage to a personal crusade carried out by a single individual. In 1997, the Commission shifted gears, investing instead in the computerization of the electoral roll. This has reduced the administrative burden on the Commission, although it is perhaps of limited relevance to voters who lack internet access. Voters' photos have now been integrated with the electoral rolls.

Organizational Innovation

With a limited staff, the ECI has developed a complex system of election management, relying largely on deputizing officials from the central and state governments. This mobilization of government staff has, on balance, acted as an effective force multiplier. This is not to imply that the system is without its flaws, since an inherent principal–agent problem still remains. In other words, a relatively small ECI leadership must supervise a sprawling bureaucracy of deputized officials ('agents') who may have incentives to engage in corruption or shirk their responsibilities at the local levels, out of sight of the ECI brass (the 'principal').[81]

To counteract such misaligned incentives, one critical measure the ECI has relied on is the ability to discipline officials operating under its aegis. In practical terms, this means that the ECI can exert effective control over any official who is serving on special election duty. This

---

[80] McMillan, 'Administration of Electoral Politics', 191.
[81] Indeed, one of the authors heard accounts of parties and politicians paying off officials on election duty in Andhra Pradesh during the 2014 general elections in order to avoid Model Code and other violations.

authority has been challenged in various ways by the central and state governments, and while it is subject to future reversals, a broad consensus exists today over the Commission's ability to suspend officials for dereliction of duty, request transfer of government officials, and even directly order the transfer (or the prevention of transfer) for officials on election duty.[82]

The creation of the BLO position at the electoral booth level represents a second important organizational innovation. The BLO serves as the frontline functionary of India's election authorities, in essence a contract employee who is hired by the ECI to verify and revise the electoral rolls in a particular polling catchment area.[83] To fill this position, the ECI selects an actual voter from a given polling area, which means s/he has valuable local knowledge and is able to effectively interact with residents to ensure the rolls are updated based on deaths, changes in residency, and so on. In addition to aiding in the preparation of the electoral rolls, the BLO also plays a role in monitoring the conduct of elections. The BLO is effectively a custodian for one particular voting booth and is accountable for the 1,000–1,500 voters who live in the immediate polling area.[84] The creation of this position is especially important given the rapid increase in the number of polling stations with the increase in population and the ECI's mandate that no voter should have to travel more than 2 kilometres to reach a polling station (Figure 10.4 charts the increase in the number of polling stations from 1952 to 2014).

The ECI has also invested new resources in educating voters to get involved in the political process. Through its Systematic Voters' Education and Electoral Participation (SVEEP) programme, the Commission has ramped up its voter mobilization and registration efforts. While causal

---

[82] Rama Devi and Mendiratta, *How India Votes*, 217; McMillan, 'Election Commission', 103.

[83] The ECI first experimented with a BLO position in 2007 and, by 2009, had scaled it up to the entire country.

[84] N. Chawla, 'The Importance of Being a Booth Level Officer', *Hindu*, 28 May 2013. The ECI describes the BLO as 'a friend, philosopher and guide of the local people in matters relating to the [electoral] roll'. See Election Commission of India, *Handbook for Booth Level Officers* (New Delhi: Election Commission of India, 2011): 1.

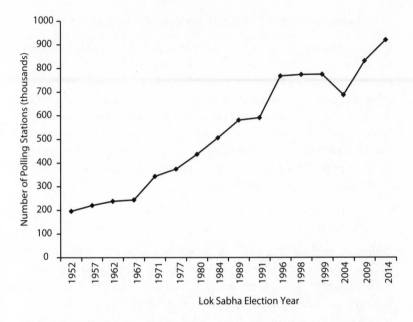

Figure 10.4 Number of Polling Stations in Lok Sabha Elections, 1952–2014
Source: Election Commission of India.

attribution is difficult, these efforts appear to be paying off. In the 2014 general election, India recorded an all-time high voter turnout: 66.4 per cent. Furthermore, the gap between male and female turnout has slowly been disappearing over time. In 2014, the gap narrowed to just 1.5 percentage points, a significant improvement even from the prior general election in 2009 (when the gap stood at 4.2 percentage points).

Finally, of more recent vintage is the ECI's recent move to institutionalize its election expertise through its India International Institute of Democracy and Election Management (IIDEM), described as 'an advanced resource centre of learning, research, training and extension for participatory democracy and election management'. Established in 2011 with support from the GoI, the United Nations, and other international partners, the goal of IIDEM is to serve as both a national as well as international hub for debating and exchanging best practices in election management. This institution, it is hoped, will not only strengthen India's election management capacities, but also serve to do the same for other developed and developing democracies.

Looking Ahead: The Challenges of Money and Muscle

In the previous sections, we have documented how the ECI has adapted when faced with numerous challenges to the conduct of free and fair elections. This adaptation has sometimes been calculated, though in other instances compelled by the failure of other public institutions to act or the direction and guidance of the courts. Projecting into the future, there are two looming concerns which the ECI has repeatedly grappled with (with mixed success), but whose impact will only continue to grow. These concerns are the influence of money and 'muscle' in elections. We review each in turn.

Money Power

Although hard numbers are scarce, existing research and anecdotal evidence suggest that elections in India are among the most expensive in the world.[85] Despite strict limits on candidate expenditures, qualitative and quantitative reports indicate that the actual sums spent are in orders of magnitude larger than what candidates and parties report to authorities.[86] Much of this expenditure comes from undocumented sources, and is a direct result of poor regulation that is outmoded and ridden with loopholes and an economy in which the state retains enormous regulatory power that it can often wield with significant discretion in exchange for kickbacks or side payments.[87] The quest for money, including 'black money', has a number of adverse downstream effects: it constrains the talent pool of candidates who are able to contest elections, entrenches top-down, internally undemocratic party structures,

[85] S. Sukhtankar and M. Vaishnav, 'Corruption in India: Bridging Research Evidence and Policy Options', *India Policy Forum* 11 (2015): 193–276.

[86] For instance, an independent survey of election expenditure carried out in 1999 found that for the Congress and the BJP, the two major national parties, the actual spending by all sources was between four and six times the then existing ceiling. More recent evidence collected suggests this multiple has grown in recent years. See Milan Vaishnav, *When Crime Pays: Money and Muscle in Indian Politics* (New Haven, CT: Yale University Press, 2017).

[87] Indeed, research suggests that the overwhelming bulk of party funds are from corrupt payments in return for contracts or clearances, according to politicians across parties as well as bureaucrats.

and incentivizes politicians to engage in corruption while in office in order to recoup election expenses (and/or raise funds for the future).

The evolution of India's legal framework with respect to how political parties can raise funds and expend resources on election campaigns can be divided into roughly two phases, 1947 to 2003 and 2003 to the present.[88] In the initial post-Independence period, parties in India financed themselves through private donations and membership dues. Corporate contributions to political parties were legal, subject to certain restrictions, and had to be declared in the company's accounts. While the RPA, 1951 introduced strict limits on the amount that could be spent on election campaigns, legal loopholes and the absence of credible monitoring rendered these limits ineffectual. A particularly egregious shortcoming was the lack of attention given to third-party expenditure on behalf of individual candidates, which provided a ready channel through which undocumented (and unlimited) money could flow.

By the 1960s, there were concerns in policy circles about an emerging nexus between black money and political fund-raising. The issue of black money infiltrating the political system was a prominent feature of the reports issued by two government-sponsored commissions: the Santhanam Committee on Prevention of Corruption (1964) and the Wanchoo Direct Taxes Enquiry Committee (1971).

In 1969, Prime Minister Indira Gandhi convinced Parliament to ban corporate donations to political parties, a critical decision from which India's political economy has not yet recovered. The ostensible reason for the ban was to prevent large business groups from exerting undue

---

[88] This section draws heavily on E. Sridharan and M. Vaishnav, 'India', in *Checkbook Elections? Political Finance in Comparative Perspective*, eds P. Norris and A. Abel van Es (New York: Oxford University Press, 2016), 64–83; M.V.R. Gowda and E. Sridharan, 'Reforming India's Party Financing and Election Expenditure Laws', *Election Law Journal: Rules, Politics, and Policy* 11, no. 2 (June 2012): 226–40; E. Sridharan, 'Parties, the Party System and Collective Action for State Funding of Elections: A Comparative Perspective on Possible Options', in *India's Political Parties*, eds P.R. deSouza and E. Sridharan (New Delhi: Sage, 2006), 311–40; and E. Sridharan, 'Electoral Finance Reform: The Relevance of International Experience', in *Reinventing Public Service Delivery in India: Selected Case Studies*, ed. V.K. Chand (New Delhi: Sage, 2006), 363–88.

influence on politics. However, it is clear from historical records that this was largely a pretext; Gandhi introduced this measure because she feared that corporate interests would fund right-wing opposition parties, namely the Swatantra Party and the rising Jan Sangh. Indeed, this action was part and parcel of a range of policy decisions taken by Gandhi to cover her right flank. However, the ban was enacted without substituting corporate funding with state funding, as had been introduced in a range of Western democracies in the 1950s and 1960s. Parties found themselves faced with a shortage of adequate, legal sources of funding to enable them to run their organizations and election campaigns. In retrospect, this situation gave them little choice but to openly embrace illicit sources of funds or black money.

Over time, the supply of black money has grown in the broader economy, in parallel with a high-tax, tightly regulated economic policy framework. The highly regulated economy or 'license-quota-permit raj' mandated that government licenses and permits were required for all manners of economic activity. Of course, bureaucrats and politicians could often allocate licenses and permits on a discretionary and ad hoc basis in exchange for kickbacks.[89] This led to a corrupt fund-raising nexus between business groups and ruling parties in the centre and the states, and the Congress party was in many ways the single biggest beneficiary.

In 1974, the Supreme Court ruled that party and supporter expenditure not authorized by the candidate would count towards the calculation of a candidate's election expenses, plugging the earlier loophole on third-party expenditure. Parliament quickly passed an amendment to the law, effectively negating the court's ruling. This once again gutted the effectiveness of placing any monetary limits on a candidate's election expenditure, largely since the party and the candidate's supporters could spend without any limit. India now witnessed electoral spending arms races in which parties tried to outspend each other and tried to attract voters with inducements of various sorts (for example, providing free liquor or freebies during election campaigns).

The main development in the 1980s was the amendment of the Companies Act in 1985 under then Prime Minister Rajiv Gandhi,

[89] D. Kapur and M. Vaishnav, 'Quid Pro Quo: Builders, Politicians, and Election Finance in India', Center for Global Development Working Paper 276, 29 March 2013.

which once again allowed corporate donations to political parties under certain conditions. Unfortunately, the re-legalization of corporate donations to political parties did not have its intended effect of reducing party dependence on black money and increasing transparency of political contributions. In part, this was because it did not provide tax incentives for political contributions. More importantly, in our view, by that time the system of contributions in black money had become so entrenched that there was no incentive for business groups to come above board. Businesses had to deal with a range of parties and politicians in power at the centre and in various states. Therefore, the secrecy of political contributions became paramount so that those not so favoured would not penalize donors for supporting their political rivals. Since political donations would have to be made public in a company's annual reports, companies tended to stay with the by-then customary practice of secret political donations.

Aside from a few changes at the margins—shortening the campaign period from 21 to 14 days, introducing a partial state subsidy in the form of allocation of free time for major state and national parties on state-owned television and radio networks, and instituting minimal financial audit requirements for parties—the 1990s largely witnessed a successive series of reform proposals emerge from civil society, government, and industry, only to get lost in the political morass.

And there reformist plans would rest until a series of small breakthroughs were achieved, beginning in 2003, which marks the start of the second phase of India's political finance evolution. Three specific changes transpired that have made some headway in improving the level of transparency.

First, in September 2003, the NDA government passed the Election and Other Related Laws (Amendment) Act, which made company and individual contributions to a political party 100 per cent tax-deductible.[90] For the first time, this created incentives for companies and individual donors to donate openly by check. While this law creates incentives for donors to contribute by check, it is not clear whether the incentive of a tax exemption on donations will outweigh the possible

---

[90] However, company contributions are still subject to the limit of 5 per cent of average net profit over the past three years.

disadvantages of loss of anonymity.[91] The law also made it mandatory for companies as well as parties to disclose any political contributions in excess of Rs 20,000. While this is a step in the right direction, most parties report receiving only a small share of contributions from larger contributions.[92]

Second, the United Progressive Alliance (UPA) government passed the RTI Act in 2005, which allowed for ordinary Indians to petition public entities for information about the operation of political parties. Using this new law, ADR urged India's Central Information Commission (CIC) to mandate political parties disclose their income tax returns and make public their income and expenditures as a matter of public interest.[93] All parties resisted this attempt at forcing transparency but were forced to relent after the CIC accepted the legitimacy of the petition in 2008. These 'audited' statements provide at best a loose approximation of the true state of party finances, given that the audit is done by someone hand-picked by the parties themselves rather than an independent outfit. During this timeframe, the ECI (assisted by the Supreme Court) also began mandating that candidates to state and national office disclose judicial affidavits that detail their criminal, educational, and financial details. While these affidavits are self-reported, they do contain useful information about the private dealings of aspirants to elected office.[94]

[91] Further, the donations are tax deductible only if they are made to political parties rather than to individual candidates. This is likely to affect the magnitude of contributions because there is no guarantee that the political party would distribute contributions to the donors' choice of candidates in a transparent manner.

[92] Indeed, one of the best-known workarounds is for donors to give multiple donations of Rs 19,999 so as to avoid the mandatory disclosure requirement.

[93] As a factual matter, parties have been obligated under law to privately disclose their tax returns since 1980, although in practice have actually been doing so after a 1996 Supreme Court order. In 2008, the CIC ruled that these should be made public.

[94] In 2014, the ECI issued new transparency guidelines to parties, but it lacks the legal authority to make these new rules binding. Hence, if parties choose not to comply with them, there is little recourse (other than moral suasion) the ECI has to take action against them.

Finally, this period also witnessed the rise of 100 per cent tax-exempt electoral trusts that companies can set up to make political contributions in a transparent and regulated manner. Many of these trusts employ formulas (based on past electoral performance) to allocate their donations to various parties, thereby reducing the political content of their decision to fund one party over another.

In sum, laws and regulations governing political finance in India, whether regulating party funding or limiting campaign expenditure, have tended to have unintended, counterproductive, and perverse effects on the electoral system. The State's interventionist role in the economy further compounds the situation. Thanks to a series of decisions taken in the initial decades after Independence, a corrupt equilibrium has taken hold and now perpetuates itself. There is no incentive to break out of the corrupt nexus that has resulted from the working of the present electoral and campaign finance laws. It is how 'the system' works.

If the ECI is to chip away at this sub-optimal equilibrium, it requires enhanced powers. At present, existing statute does not give the Commission unambiguous authority to sanction candidates or parties who provide false or misleading information. This requires changes to the RPA which only Parliament can approve. Insisting that parties submit audited accounts and issuing transparency 'guidelines' is a welcome move, but only when these audits are truly independent will they break open the corrupt nexus between money and politics. Third, the ECI must be granted greater powers to regulate political parties. India's major political parties are fighting a ruling by the CIC that they are 'public entities' and, hence, subject to the provisions of the RTI Act. Several reform proponents agree that while greater transparency is imperative, it should be the ECI, not the CIC, that is entrusted with supervisory authority. Finally, there have been innumerable proposals for state funding of elections. In our view, state funding should only be on the table if parties are willing to submit to greater transparency; without such a quid pro quo, there is nothing to stop parties from racking up state and private monies.

Muscle Power

A second looming challenge facing the ECI relates to the criminalization of politics. This is not a new issue. Since the early days of the

458   **Rethinking Public Institutions in India**

republic, a nexus of crime and politics has operated within India's borders. In the earliest elections, many Congress politicians regularly employed *goondas* (thugs) during election time to engage in voter mobilization, vote buying, and often voter suppression and/or voter fraud in exchange for patronage and protection. However, the balance of power between politicians and *goondas* shifted in favour of the latter in the 1970s. During that period, individuals who had previously engaged in criminal activity on behalf of politicians began to directly contest elections, no longer content to concede the spotlight to traditional party elites.[95] This issue came into much sharper focus, thanks to the government-commissioned Vohra Committee report, which was released in 1995. The report concluded:

> The nexus between the criminal gangs, police, bureaucracy and politicians has come out clearly in various parts of the country ... [T]hese gangs enjoy the patronage of local level politicians, cutting across party lines and the protection of Government functionaries. Some political leaders become the leaders of these gangs ... and ... get themselves elected to local bodies, State Assemblies and the National parliament. Resultantly, such elements have acquired considerable political clout.[96]

The entry of criminals into politics was facilitated by many factors: the breakdown of the Congress party's dominance and the decay of its vertical patronage networks,[97] a general deterioration in law and order, and the politicization of the state overseen by Prime Minister Indira Gandhi,[98] a 'demand overload' facing state institutions prompted by

[95] For instance, political scientist Atul Kohli quotes a Bihari MLA as saying, '[Before 1977] criminal elements used to help politicians. Sooner or later they realized, why not run ourselves'. See A. Kohli, *Democracy and Discontent: India's Growing Crisis of Governability* (New York: Cambridge University Press, 1990), 218. Other sources too have noted that while criminals were once content to engage behind-the-scenes in the service of politicians, at some point they decided to step into the political foreground. See, inter alia, C. Jaffrelot, 'Indian Democracy: The Rule of Law on Trial', *India Review* 1, no. 1 (January 2002): 77–120; J. Manor, 'Changing State, Changing Society in India', *Journal of South Asian Studies* 25, no. 2 (2002): 231–56.

[96] Ministry of Home Affairs, *Report of the Vohra Committee* (New Delhi: Government of India, 1995).

[97] Jaffrelot, 'Indian Democracy'.

[98] Kohli, *Democracy and Discontent*.

lower-caste political mobilization,[99] as well as rising uncertainty, thanks to intensifying political competition.[100] Put simply, as the quality of governance declined in a situation where social divisions are deep seated, candidates with criminal reputations could successfully parlay their criminality as a signal of their credibility to 'get things done' for their narrow community (often defined in ethnic or religious terms). A final critical factor which merits particular mention is the deterioration in the election finance regime. Armed with access to liquid financial resources and the ability to transfer money undetected, many criminal elements became invaluable assets to political parties. In this way, money and muscle are inexorably linked. Drawing on affidavits submitted to the ECI by candidates contesting the 2004, 2009, and 2014 national parliamentary elections, recent research shows that the poorest 20 per cent of candidates, in terms of personal financial assets, had a one per cent chance of winning parliamentary elections. The richest quintile, in contrast, had greater than 23 per cent likelihood.[101]

As the situation worsened, the ECI agitated for a crackdown on the criminalization of politics. One of the most tangible reforms to be implemented was greater transparency around the criminal antecedents of candidates, thanks to the new affidavit regime instituted in 2003.[102]

It is these data that have brought to light the cold, hard facts about the criminal antecedents of MPs and the various state assemblies. For instance, of the 543 members of the 16th Lok Sabha elected in 2014, 186 (or 24 per cent) face pending criminal cases while 112 (or 21 per cent) face cases of a 'serious' nature. The numbers at the state level are equally disconcerting: 31 per cent of elected MLAs face pending

[99] Manor, 'Changing State'.

[100] The uncertainty induced by the political transition from one-party dominance to genuine, robust multi-party competition forced criminals to vertically integrate their operations. By directly contesting elections, criminals could cut out the politician-cum-middleman and take matters into their own hands, in the hopes of reducing the uncertainty and costs associated with negotiating (and renegotiating) contracts with parties who might or might not capture power.

[101] M. Vaishnav, *When Crime Pays*.

[102] R. Sen, 'Identifying Criminals and Crorepatis in Indian Politics: An Analysis of Two Supreme Court Rulings', *Election Law Journal: Rules, Politics, and Policy* 11, no. 2 (June 2012): 216–25.

criminal cases. While these are cases, not convictions, candidates must only disclose those cases where a judge has taken cognizance of the case (as opposed to the mere filing of charges).

The ECI publishes these individual affidavits on its website prior to the election. With the assistance and ingenuity of civil society, these affidavits are compiled, translated, and standardized to facilitate dissemination. Groups like ADR and National Election Watch have harnessed technology, such as SMS/text-messaging, to inform voters of the precise backgrounds of all candidates standing in a given constituency election. In spite of this information and related awareness campaigns, there is some evidence to suggest the problem is getting worse, rather than better. Whereas one-quarter (24 per cent) of MPs elected in 2004 were under criminal indictment, that share increased (to 30 per cent) in 2009 and 34 per cent in 2014.

There are several underlying factors driving the criminalization of politics, and only a package of reforms that deals comprehensively with all of them will succeed in cleansing Indian politics. When it comes to voter demand, there are no quick fixes: nothing short of improving the quality of governance will be able to dissuade voters from providing political support for candidates who are able to demonstrate, by whatever means necessary, their ability to adequately mediate the relationship between citizens and the State. Until and unless the State is seen as an actor that can adequately deliver services, provide security, and dispense justice, many voters will find it in their self-interest to back a 'strongman' who will. The only real solution to the 'demand' side lies outside of the remit of the ECI: curtailing the salience of identity politics and strengthening core public institutions so that the state is seen as an ally of the common man, rather than an antagonist.

However, there are a number of steps the ECI could take, in conjunction with Parliament, especially when it comes to regulating parties and candidates. For starters, the Commission requires new authorities to regulate political finance and punish non-compliers more rigorously. To reduce the supply of 'tainted' candidates, there are potentially two sets of reforms the ECI could pursue. The first involves placing limits around who can stand for election. As part of a package of electoral reforms the ECI drew up prior to the transition from CEC Quraishi to his successor V.S. Sampath, the Commission specifically argued for barring candidates facing serious criminal cases.[103] To guard against politically motivated charges, it has proposed that this would only apply to candidates facing charges that have been framed by a judge, filed at least one year prior to election, and carry a potential sentence of five years or more. This would need legislative authorization, but it is an idea that should be debated by elected officials. The second involves post-election action against candidates who win election and face serious pending cases. Many civil society groups have recommended that cases against sitting MLAs and MPs be subject to a fast-track judicial process.

Addressing the twin issues of money and muscle will not be easy, but the recent past abounds with several examples of incremental progress. In July 2013, the Supreme Court issued an important ruling in response to a PIL suit. Under Section 8(4) of the RPA, 1951, sitting MPs and MLAs can serve in office even if they are convicted of a crime until their appeals are exhausted. A suit filed by Lily Thomas and Lok Prahari claimed this latter clause advantages elected politicians over aspirant candidates, for whom a conviction merits disqualification, appeal or no appeal. In siding with the plaintiffs, the Court stated that this special exception afforded to elected representatives is beyond Parliament's constitutional powers. So as to not penalize current incumbents, who won office under the prior regime, the ruling will only apply prospectively. The first elected representative to fall victim to this new ruling was none other than Lalu Prasad Yadav, the powerful former chief minister of the state of Bihar, who was convicted in a 2013 case related to the fodder scam.[104] The precise impact of this ruling remains to be seen and there is good reason to be sceptical. Very few of India's criminally suspect legislators are likely to be convicted, given the weakness of India's justice system. Regardless of the defendant's guilt or innocence, in India the wheels of justice move in slow motion—it

---

[103] S.Y. Quraishi, *An Undocumented Wonder: The Making of the Great Indian Election* (New Delhi: Rupa, 2014).

[104] Immediately following the ruling, the government introduced a bill in Parliament to supplant the court's judgement, but its move was heavily criticized by the opposition, civil society, and the media. To circumvent Parliament, the government briefly considered introducing an executive ordinance but wisely reversed course.

can take years, if not decades, for criminal cases to reach their logical conclusion. One study found that cases filed against MPs in the 15th Lok Sabha (2009–14) had been pending for seven years, on average.[105]

Judicial remedies can cut both ways, however. The courts can sometimes overstep their remit. In another decision in response to a separate PIL suit, the court ruled that a person who is in jail or in police custody cannot contest legislative body elections even if that individual was not formally charged with committing a crime. Prior to this ruling, candidates in jail awaiting trial or those convicted but not granted bail were free to contest elections. And, indeed, in many notable cases they did exactly that—often winning without ever setting foot on the campaign trail. In this case, the court ruled that ordinary voters in India must forfeit the right to vote if they are imprisoned or in police custody and, hence, the same standard should apply to politicians. The court largely based its decision on Sections 4 and 5 of the RPA, which state that in order to be elected to the legislature, a candidate must be an elector. If said candidate is in jail, s/he can no longer be an elector. However, Parliament quickly moved to pass a bill, later signed by the president, which negated the court's ruling. As Kapur and Vaishnav have argued, the court's ruling was somewhat problematic, given the incentive it created for crafty politicians to manipulate the police to punish political rivals.[106]

***

Over the past seven decades, the ECI has been relatively successful compared to other public institutions due to the crucial role played by a combination of structure and agency in its evolution. The structure consists of the Constitution, particularly the broad remit of article 324, and the multi-polar distribution of power in the post-1989, post-Congress party system. Agency was provided by the actions of CEC T.N. Seshan in the first half of the 1990s, continued by his successors building on his legacy that normalized the use of discretionary powers.

---

[105] Quraishi, *Undocumented Wonder*.

[106] D. Kapur and M. Vaishnav, 'Strengthening Rule of Law', in *Getting India Back on Track: An Action Agenda for Reform*, ed. B. Debroy, A. Tellis, and R. Trevor (Washington, DC: Carnegie Endowment for International Peace, 2014).

However, four dangers still lurk that can possibly derail the autonomy of the ECI in the future. First, the government can 'pack' the Commission by appointing additional members. Second, the two ECs enjoy less security of tenure than the CEC and are thus vulnerable to pressure. Third, the tradition of civil servants being appointed to the Commission in order of seniority (by convention, not by rule) and the fact that the two ECs will hope to succeed the CEC opens up the possibility of manipulation by the government of the day. Fourth, conflict among the three members could create an opening for political interference and manipulation. However, any of these developments are most unlikely, given the continuing multi-polar distribution of power, intense media scrutiny, and massive public support for the ECI as an independent institution. To these institutional challenges, one must add the looming twin threats of money and muscle in Indian electoral politics. Dogged activism by civil society, an interventionist judiciary, and strong ECI have helped manage these threats, but the struggle remains an uphill one.

11

RE-ENERGIZING DEMOCRATIC
DECENTRALIZATION IN INDIA

T.R. Raghunandan

Strengthening India's system of local government (LG) is a vital aspect of institution building for a more efficient, participative, and accountable government. Until the advent of constitutionally mandated LGs in 1993, India's boast of being the world's largest democracy sounded specious in the face of its low intensity of public representation at the national and state levels. Just 800 Members of Parliament (MPs) and about 4,500 legislators in state legislative assemblies and councils represented a population that grew in the 40 years after Independence from 350 to 800 million. The 73rd and 74th Amendments to the Constitution, which mandated urban and rural LGs, created the space for nearly 3.2 million representatives elected to village, intermediate, and district panchayats (DP) in rural areas and nagar panchayats (urban local government), municipalities, and municipal corporations in urban areas, thus improving the intensity of representation dramatically.[1]

[1] Each rural local government member represents about 340 citizens and each urban representative, about 560. These high intensities are due to the large number of members in gram (village) panchayats in rural and nagar panchayats in urban areas. Larger agglomerations such as municipal corporations have relatively lower intensities, in the range of one ward member for about 15,000 to 50,000 people.

However, these elected representatives and the LGs to which they are elected are still perceived to be shadowy outliers in India's governance system, extras in the Bollywood-style national democratic spectacle. Unfortunately, the discourse on good governance largely ignores them. While there is some genuflection in their direction, LGs are not considered very relevant to the process of pursuing national progress. Higher-level politicians, bureaucrats, and non-governmental organizations (NGOs) who influence policy consider LGs—at best—as institutions that might perform a few tasks at their bidding but cannot be trusted unless placed under the close supervision of government officials.

LGs are nearly universally decried as lacking capacity, and efforts to decentralize are scoffed at as 'decentralising corruption'. The 'lack of capacity' argument ironically flies in the face of the fact that nearly all staff posted at the local level are recruited centrally by state governments and placed on secondment with LGs, open to being withdrawn at the will of the state government. In nearly all states, fiscal stresses (when they occur) have resulted in reductions in the recruitment of staff placed at the local level, rendering LGs even more hampered in their institutional capacities to deliver services for which they are responsible and accountable. While several LGs overcome these impediments that are placed in their path by government inaction and function well, there is a conspiracy of silence about their good work. The narrative of governance, scripted by the higher-level politician–bureaucrat combine, tends towards decentralization of the blame for misgovernance to LGs and centralization of the credit for good governance to higher-level governments.[2]

This chapter describes the current state of play in the practice of democratic decentralization in India. It then explores the possible steps that could be taken to strengthen the intergovernmental design of decentralization, so that LGs might perform more effectively.

[2] This was the trenchant comment of a local government elected representative to the author in a conference of Panchayats in a state, in 2006. He continued thus, 'We do the good work, and the District Collector collects awards and makes PowerPoint presentations at Vigyan Bhavan (India's national convention centre at Delhi)'.

Robust LGs: An Unfulfilled Dream[3]

Modern India's approach to strengthening and empowering LG systems has been fitful. There has been no concerted, pan-national pressure in India to strengthen LGs. While there have been—and still are—a few flag-bearers who steadfastly believe in the ideal of people governing themselves, pro-decentralization intent in political speeches, manifestos, and policy pronouncements have not been followed by effective action.

India's lukewarm approach to democratic decentralization has its roots in its constitutional design of being a 'holding together' federation, where the states comprising the Indian union are constructs of the very union they constitute. As India is not a 'coming together' federation, where once independent and sovereign states consent to transform themselves into subnational units and devolve upward some of their powers to the national federal government,[4] Indian federalism has strong centralizing overtones. The Indian union determines how much power ought to be vested in the states and not vice versa. Residual powers vest in the Union. This ethos of centralization pervades the design of the LG system and conditions their behaviour in practice. LGs tend to see themselves as institutions at the bottom of a tiered government structure and are indifferent to, and possibly unaware of, the possibility that governments can be organized as autonomous within their spheres of functioning.

The flip side of the disinterest in seeking self-governing rights is the acquiescence to the idea of being ruled by higher levels of government. The fact that many modern Indians tend to accept centralized power without question might be traced back to the emphasis, particularly in the early years of the republic, on national integration as a commanding priority. Given the background of the partition and the efforts at

---

[3] Paragraphs 1 to 7 have been abstracted from T.R. Raghunandan, ed., 'Introduction', in *Decentralisation and Local Governments, the Indian Experience: Essays from Economic and Political Weekly* (New Delhi: Orient BlackSwan Publishers, 2012), with the kind permission of *Economic and Political Weekly*.

[4] This distinction is drawn from P. Bardhan, 'Decentralization of Governance and Development', *Journal of Economic Perspectives* 16, no. 4 (Fall 2002): 185–205.

integrating princely States into independent India, there was an emphasis on the need for Indians to cement themselves together into a nation. Phrases such as 'joining the national mainstream' went uncontested, with hardly any debate as to what constituted a 'national mainstream'. The oft-used slogan 'unity in diversity' was more interpreted as 'unity, over diversity'.

Popular pressure to decentralize was channelized through political means into demands for statehood, rather than to devolve more powers and responsibilities to LGs. The political and social ethos that favours a strong centre has resulted in most Indians accepting the notion that government is a hierarchy of tiered institutions. Even when Indians militate against bad governance, we prefer to demand that our existing rulers govern better, rather than seek the right to govern ourselves. These reasons perhaps explain why the constitutional provisions concerning LGs have not been effective—largely, Indians have not sought that they be effectively implemented.

The strongest argument in favour of decentralization worldwide has not been that it will improve higher technocratic efficiency in the short term, but that decentralization will radically change the nature of politics, unleashing hitherto unfelt energies. However, in India, emboldened by the absence of pressure from below to decentralize, the LG system has been designed in an atmosphere suffused with the notion that it ought to be insulated or protected from politics.[5] Democratic decentralization has been stunted in practice by the discourse being framed within the narrow context of improving service delivery; this has been the foundational weakness with the debate over its merits. Higher-level politicians and bureaucrats balk at the suggestion that a strong LG system that functions autonomously within its sphere will improve the vigour of practice of democracy. To the contrary, they stress that public service delivery is so bad that LG must be designed so as to first address that priority.[6] There are not many takers for the argument that

[5] Many states prohibit the formal entry of political parties into the local government sphere. Only three states—West Bengal, Kerala, and Tripura—permit them to participate in village panchayat elections.

[6] This is a familiar and oft repeated argument that pro-decentralization policymakers hear from more conservative elements. Lord Ripon, in one of the earliest policy initiatives on strengthening decentralization, unequivocally

the complementarity between the ideal of local self-governance and the imperative of improving public service delivery should organically emerge from the political construct, and not be artificially created and driven through a technocratic command and control system. Indeed, the cumulative legacies of all the institutions studied in this volume stand in the way of opening up a discourse on whether the emphasis should shift from the service delivery benefits that might accrue, to the political implications of a strong and empowered LG system.[7]

In 'holding together' federations and unitary countries worldwide, effective LG empowerment has largely taken place through big-bang devolution. A leap of faith is usually taken or forced upon a politician or a political group and substantive functions are assigned to LGs, along with sufficient resources to perform these effectively. Such accelerated drives for devolution are prompted by deep political imperatives, which might be a desire to break away from an unsavoury past of discrimination and domination (such as South Africa), fear of balkanization (such as Indonesia), or as a strategy for seeking political legitimacy.[8] However, in India, given the circumstances described above, LG empowerment has ebbed and flowed, with only a few examples of accelerated evolution. States have had diverse experiences with decentralization so far, spanning the periods before and after the 73rd and 74th Amendments to the Constitution of India (1993).[9]

---

emphasized that he did not want the idea of self-governance to be sacrificed at the altar of efficiency. While admitting that, in the first instance, district boards—comprising nominated individuals—would fare better, he had no doubts that LGs would gradually improve in their functioning with the presence of elected representatives.

[7] This was drawn from the perceptive comments of Pratap Bhanu Mehta when the initial draft of this chapter was discussed.

[8] Many military dictators have good records in empowering LGs. Examples in the region include: in Pakistan, General Ayub Khan's 'Basic Democrats' effort of the 1950s and General Pervez Musharraf's Local Government Ordinance of 2001. In Bangladesh, Lieutenant General H.M. Ershad created the middle tier of LGs, the *upa zila parishads*, in the 1980s.

[9] The latter did bring about some standardization, particularly with respect to the establishment of rural LGs at three levels, the conduct of regular elections, seat reservations, leadership positions in LGs, and the establishment of independent authorities mandated in the amendments, such as the state finance and election commissions.

While only a few examples are well publicized, most states have gone through brief periods of strongly believing in decentralization. West Bengal's approach in the early seventies combined the strengthening of panchayats as political institutions and the undertaking of land reforms. Both efforts were aimed to give political space to the local cadres of the Left Front, which ousted the Congress from power. Karnataka, in 1987, de-concentrated responsibilities to powerful district-level rural LGs (*zilla parishads*) and in a step considered radical at that time, cleaved the state budget to provide nearly a quarter of the financial resources to these bodies. However, Karnataka simultaneously centralized village-level governance to some extent by replacing over 20,000 village level LGs (gram panchayats, henceforth GP) with 3,300 elected mandal panchayats, in a two-tier system.[10] Mandals were, however, not considered 'spheres' of government, but were placed under the hierarchical control of the zilla parishad. Kerala, a late bloomer in contemporary decentralization, focused on a more grassroots-level approach, empowering and strengthening its village panchayats. In Kerala, due to the high population sizes of the village panchayats, they were positioned more as rural municipalities covering a larger number of habitations as compared to their counterparts in other states. What made Kerala's approach unique was the placement of nearly a third of the state budget with the panchayats, largely as block grants, with flexibility to choose projects that is, even today, much beyond that given in any other state. Reforms in the grant system were backed by a 'Peoples' Planning Campaign' which brought nearly one hundred thousand volunteers together with the village panchayats in order to promote peoples' participation in neighbourhood meetings and prepare a grassroots-level perspective plan.

In 2001, Madhya Pradesh went a step further, to create communitarian spaces below the village level panchayats to facilitate micro-planning. This was based on the political belief that the village panchayats had deteriorated into one-man shows, dominated by the elected chief (sarpanch). Powers were divested from the panchayats and vested in communitarian subcommittees. Bihar re-enacted its Panchayati Raj (the rural local government system) law in 2006, becoming the first state to reserve 50 per cent of elected panchayat positions for women.

[10] The gain was that elections were held to the mandals; they had not been held for the village panchayats for more than a decade, previously.

However, the one common feature among both self-proclaimed champion states and those with records assessed to be indifferent, is that the periods of reform have alternated with longer periods when the pace has slackened and rhetoric replaced action.

This trend has been a result of several factors. First, where devolution to LGs has momentarily occupied centre-stage, progress has been critically dependent on a few individual political champions, backed by bureaucrats committed to the idea. In India's competitive political system, pursuing an agenda of decentralization is not a frontline strategy for ambitious political leaders seeking to climb the political ladder. Established politicians, too, are not motivated to make decentralization their political mission; they do not see how pushing for power to the people can bring them more political benefit, especially when voters themselves do not demand such changes. Similarly, ambitious bureaucrats do not see the pursuit of a decentralization agenda as beneficial for career growth. Thus, even when political signals have favoured decentralization, actual progress has always been hamstrung by weak administrative action. This is why political initiatives have often quickly dissipated and powers, given to LGs with much fanfare through legislative changes, have been clawed back through executive fiat, without meeting with resistance from people.

Second, because of the stop-start nature of the devolution of functions, funds, and functionaries to LGs, many decentralization efforts slackened much before the stated vision was achieved. What remains stable—if it can be termed as 'stability'—is an uneasy limbo where centralizers and decentralizers creep up on each other to further their respective agendas. In this limbo, typically, the functions devolved to LGs are imprecise and overlap with state activities, expenditure responsibilities are either unfunded or restricted by tied funds, and staff is inadequate, poorly trained, and owe greater allegiance to the state than LGs.

The Grounding of a Few Successes

Over the past two decades of constitutionally mandated LG functioning, one aspect of the LG system that has been institutionalized is the conduct of regular elections to them. Recent events even embolden one to claim that democratic representation to LGs is now free of the risk of reversal.

The system of representation to LGs is a complex one and its design reflects the dichotomy between the political imperative for their creation and the service delivery expected through their functioning. The constitutional vision of the political structure of LGs is of giving everybody a fair chance to represent the people through the local electoral process. This is operationalized in five design precepts. First, elections to LGs are to be held regularly, every five years, so that there is uninterrupted succession of elected bodies. Second, all LG elections are based upon territorial constituencies, though states can choose whether these are single or multi-member constituencies. Third, the Constitution mandates an elaborate system of reservation. Women are to be provided not less than 33 per cent of the total number of elected seats. Scheduled Castes (SCs) and Scheduled Tribes (STs) are to be provided reservation in the proportion of their population shares in the LGs in which their reservations are to be reckoned. Women belonging to the SC and ST groupings are provided a minimum of 33 per cent reservation within their respective categories. Similarly, states can extend reservations to other backward communities.[11] Fourth, to ensure that different territorial constituencies receive the benefit of these arrangements, reserved seats are assigned to them on a rotating basis. Fifth, control and superintendence of elections to LGs is vested in independent State Election Commissions (SECs), rather than the Election Commission of India (ECI). These constitutional arrangements, often criticized for being too detailed, are further elaborated through a welter of state-specific laws and rules that govern the manner in which constituencies are delimited and reservations reckoned and rotated. That these provisions, intended to boost the inclusion of marginalized groups in electoral representation, are valued by them is also evident from the fact that that the majority of court disputes relating to decentralization relate to the reservation arrangements.[12]

[11] The Supreme Court of India has placed an upper limit of 50 per cent on reservations. See the Supreme Court verdict in *Dr. K. Krishna Murthy* v. *Union of India*, (2010) 7 SCC 202.

[12] In a compilation of litigation cases undertaken by the Rural Litigation and Entitlement Kendra, Dehra Dun, for the Ministry of Panchayati Raj in 2005, it was estimated that more than 75 per cent of all cases pertaining to panchayats concerned election and reservation-related disputes.

Even as court decisions over the past two decades have clarified how these arrangements are to be interpreted, there are a few downstream consequences of the reservation design on the accountability of local representatives and the effectiveness of the LGs to which they are elected. A key shortcoming of the election system is the one of rotation of constituencies every five years. This practice, while aiming to serve the objective of bringing in more excluded groups and individuals into the electoral fold, also diminishes the re-election chances of representatives who obtain the benefit of reservation. This, in turn, leaves little incentive for them to seek re-election, which in turn results in disinterest in effective performance on the service delivery responsibilities of LGs. Another weakness is that determining the reservation matrix is often not left with an impartial SEC, but is retained by state governments with themselves, where it is subject to manipulation by vested interests, in order to dent the electoral chances of potential rivals. Some design strategies could mitigate, if not eliminate such problems. For instance, the interval between one rotation and the next can be lengthened, to enable LG representatives from the reserved categories to gain experience.[13] A system of multi-member constituencies can also render rotation unnecessary.

In the overall analysis, the reservation arrangements have largely fulfilled their purpose. A large number of women and SC and ST representatives have been elected to the LGs and are making their presence felt. Besides, in terms of institutional weaknesses that require design solutions to be set right, the reservation system is possibly easier to unravel and correct, as compared to other aspects of the LG architecture.

A more sinister matter has been the persistent efforts by state governments to postpone elections to LGs and appoint state officials as administrators to run them. The Constitution mandates that elections to each term of LGs shall be completed before the completion of the earlier term,[14] so that the next LG can take over on the completion of

---

[13] This has been done in Tamil Nadu and, more recently, in Karnataka, where reservations of certain territorial constituencies for women are unchanged for two five-year terms in succession.

[14] Article 243E(1) and (3) are applicable to panchayats and 243U(1) and (3) pertain to municipalities.

the term of the sitting body.[15] However, states ignored these provisions and proceeded to postpone elections on several occasions.[16] Alibis for delays have included the delimitation of LG boundaries, determining the seat reservation matrix, and natural calamities. Efforts undertaken by SECs to block election postponements were often blunted, typically through three strategies. First, they were sometimes denied the finances to hold elections. Second, on occasion, states have appointed pliable officers who can be pressured to toe the state's political line to lead SECs. Third, certain key activities, such as determining the seat reservation matrix or the discretion to obtain additional security forces to supervise elections, have been retained with the government, diluting the constitutional intent that SECs are to be assigned functions of control and superintendence of elections.

Fortunately, in an effort to prevent election postponement, over the past eight years courts have taken an increasingly strict view of various practices intended to weaken SEC intervention. In the case of *Kishan Singh Tomar*, a five-judge Constitution Bench of the Supreme Court held that elections shall be held within the five-year period mandated in the Constitution as the term for each LG. The court held that '... it is clear that the State Election Commission shall not put forward any excuse based on unreasonable grounds that the elections could not be completed on time ... The Election Commission shall complete the election before the expiration of the duration of five years' period as stipulated in Clause (5) and not yield to situations that may be created by vested interests to postpone elections from being held within the stipulated time.'[17]

Despite judicial action, state governments continued to postpone LG elections through devious strategies. One common mode has been

[15] These articles further elaborate that, in case the elected body is superseded within its five-year period, fresh elections are to be held for the remainder of the term within six months from the date of supersession.

[16] For example, since the ratification of the 73rd and 74th Constitutional Amendments, local elections have been postponed in Tamil Nadu, Odisha, Bihar, Uttarakhand, Jharkhand, Puducherry (on two occasions), Karnataka [for zilla (district) and *taluk* (intermediate-level) panchayats], Goa (for gram panchayats), and Assam.

[17] *Kishan Singh Tomar* v. *Municipal Corporation of Ahmedabad*, (2006) 8 SCC 352.

to delay the declaration of the reservation matrix.[18] The other has been to announce a matrix that is manifestly defective and then wait passively as warring parties obtain court stays on the elections, questioning defects in the matrix.[19] The beneficiaries of such delays were legislators and officials appointed as administrators; the legislators were able to influence local administrators of LGs to do their bidding. Officials believed that the nuisance of the LG-elected representatives 'interfering' in their work was out of the way. For corrupt officers, the absence of LG-elected representatives also meant that there was no need to share the spoils with a large number of the latter.

It was only a matter of time before courts began to realize that the Kishan Singh Tomar decision was being bypassed. Matters came to a head when the Government of Karnataka attempted to postpone municipal elections in 2013. The state ignored repeated pleas by the SEC to complete the reservation matrix well in advance of the elections. Finally, exasperated with the interminable delay by the state, the SEC directed the district deputy commissioners to conduct elections, based upon the earlier reservation matrix. This prompted ruling party and opposition Members of the Legislative Assemblies (MLAs) to join hands and swiftly pass a law to enable postponement. What was worse, they hauled up the SEC for breach of privilege of the legislature. The Karnataka High Court, when approached by the SEC, directed the government to conduct elections without postponement. When the state approached it for setting aside this directive, the Supreme Court's reply was blunt. While rejecting the state's plea, the court directed it to extend full cooperation to the SEC in holding municipal elections.[20] What was more, the court also observed that in case the state government was delaying the determination of the reservation matrix,

[18] Examples include Jharkhand, Karnataka, Goa, Assam, and recently Andhra Pradesh and West Bengal.

[19] For example, Karnataka managed to run the Bruhat Bangalore Mahanagar Palika through administrators between 2008 and 2010 on the pretext that the body was being reorganized and its boundaries enlarged. Similarly, Andhra Pradesh postponed their local body elections from 2011 to 2013, on the ground that the state's reservation matrix was stayed by the High Court.

[20] Supreme Court order in *State of Karnataka* v. *State Election Commission* [Special Leave Petition (Civil) no. 877 of 2013].

the SEC was free to conduct the elections based upon the matrix for the previous election. Soon thereafter, the Supreme Court vacated the Andhra Pradesh High Court's stay on LG elections in Andhra Pradesh and directed that elections be conducted. It has, since then, thwarted similar efforts by the West Bengal government to postpone panchayat elections.

The pronouncements in the Karnataka, Andhra Pradesh, and West Bengal cases might dissuade states from undertaking clumsy efforts to postpone LG elections by delaying one or the other activities in the chain of events leading up to the election. Election postponements in the future are, hopefully, too fraught with risk for *malafide* political and bureaucratic interests to attempt.

Thus, it is clear that 20 years after the 73rd and 74th Amendments, a system of elected LGs is here to stay, forever. But what these elected bodies will do remains an open question.

Functional and Fiscal Decentralization: A Worsening Situation

A sound intergovernmental system is built on a foundation of assigning clearly defined roles to each level of government. Clarifying the roles of government levels greatly facilitates efficient delivery of services, because people can hold each tier accountable for the performance of its responsibilities. In turn, enhanced accountability drives governments to acquire the necessary capacities, such as staffing and stronger organizational arrangements, for effective performance.[21]

In India, the Constitution lays down the broad framework for the assignment of functions to LGs with broadly similar clauses applicable to panchayats and municipalities, respectively (Table 11.1).

Articles 243G and 243W use the word 'may' five times in each of them. At first sight, this indicates that states have wide latitude to determine the scope of functional decentralization. Subject to state

---

[21] Paragraphs 1 to 6 extract ideas presented by this author (T.R. Raghunandan) in the State of the Panchayats Report, 2010, in Theme Report 7, on Expenditure Assignments to Panchayats. See Ministry of Panchayati Raj, *Annual Report on the State of the Panchayats* (New Delhi: Government of India, 2010).

Table 11.1 Constitutional Assignment of Functions to Local Governments

Clause 243G	Clause 243W	
Powers, authority, and responsibilities of		
Panchayats	Municipalities, etc.	
Subject to the provisions of this Constitution, the Legislature of a state may, by law, endow		
the Panchayats	(a) the Municipalities	(b) the Committees
with such powers and authority as may be necessary to enable them to function as institutions of self-government		with such powers and authority as may be necessary to enable them to carry out the responsibilities conferred upon them including those in relation to the matters listed in the Twelfth Schedule.
and such law may contain provisions for the devolution of powers and responsibilities upon		
Panchayats at the appropriate level,	Municipalities	
subject to such conditions as may be specified therein, with respect to—		
(i) the preparation of plans for economic development and social justice;		
	(ii) the performance of functions and	
the implementation of schemes		
for economic development and social justice		
as may be entrusted to them including those in relation to the matters listed in the		
Eleventh Schedule	Twelfth Schedule	

Source: Authors' analysis.

discretion, these articles enable three separate and distinct operational processes of functional decentralization. The first is the 'endowment' of 'powers and authority' to LGs, so that they can function as self-governments' (the scope of which is not further defined in the Constitution). The second is the 'devolution' of 'powers and responsibility' to prepare plans for economic development and social schemes, and the third— intertwined with the second—is the 'entrustment' of 'schemes for implementation'. This means that LGs would have certain functions

that constitute their core authority and responsibilities as self-governments, drawn from endowed and devolved powers. In addition, they
would also have agency functions of scheme implementation.

In practice, ascertaining and comparing the range of functional
decentralization between states is not easy, as all states do not articulate their laws and rules in the same way. States also make misleading
reports and false claims on devolution, typically couched in political
rhetoric. The findings of research work undertaken in this regard by this
author with respect to rural LGs (panchayats) reveal a few patterns.[22]

First, devolution through law needs to be followed up with delegated legislation and executive orders, which map out the devolution
of functions, finances, and functionaries to panchayats. However, even
if delegated legislation and executive orders might make department
employees accountable to the panchayats concerned, if no changes are
made in long-established codes, circulars, and transfer orders prescribing technical standards and approval processes, implementation might
still de facto continue to vest with state-level line departments.[23]

Second, state laws express the mandate on the functions and activities devolved to the panchayats in different modes. Some states have
classified devolved functions into 'mandatory' and 'discretionary', or
'optional', functions. Others resort to precise clauses that devolve
specific, clear tasks and responsibilities to the panchayats and a broad
enabling clause that empowers the state to grant (and by implication,
take away) more powers and responsibilities to the panchayats. The law
might contain elaborate provisions laying out the details of functions
assigned to panchayats, or undertake it through an appended schedule, or through a combination of both approaches. These variations in
legislative practice results in non-standardized reporting of the extent
of devolution. Thus, some states tend to report a high range of devolution by counting individual activities assigned under law separately as
'subjects' devolved. Others tend to give reports in terms of departments devolved. It is important, both from a point of view of assuring
conceptual clarity as well as permitting comparisons between states,
to maintain the distinction between 'activities', 'subjects', and 'departments' when analysing functional devolution.

[22] Raghunandan, Theme Report 7.
[23] The Public Works Department (PWD) Code is a good example of this.

There is also considerable variation in the range of devolution of matters to the panchayats, with the least variation between states on the extent of powers of the village panchayats and the highest variation in respect of the district panchayats.[24] There is also considerable variation in the depth of devolution within each subject matter: a state that might seem to have, at first glance, a weak approach to devolution,

[24] Studies show that in respect of gram panchayats, all 16 states studied have readily devolved activities relating to social and farm forestry, drinking water, roads, culverts, bridges, ferries, waterways, and other means of communication, markets and fairs, health and sanitation, including hospitals, primary health centres, and dispensaries and maintenance of community assets. They are also least inclined to devolve fuel and fodder, the Public Distribution System (PDS), minor forest produce, small-scale industries (including food processing industries), and technical training and vocational education to this level. With respect to the intermediate panchayats, a 100 per cent consensus on devolution exists only with respect to social welfare, although there is near-consensus on the devolution of agriculture, including agricultural extension, animal husbandry, dairying and poultry, health and sanitation (including hospitals, primary health centres, and dispensaries), minor irrigation, water management and watershed development, fisheries, poverty alleviation programmes, education, including primary and secondary schools, markets and fairs, social welfare, including welfare of the handicapped and mentally retarded, women and child development, and maintenance of community assets. States also generally tend not to devolve activities relating to the matters of technical training and vocational education, libraries, minor forest produce, PDS, and small-scale industries to the intermediate panchayats. With respect to DPs, there is a clearly discernible reluctance to devolve. There is not even one subject on which all the states show agreement on devolution. The closest is education and social welfare, which 13 of the 16 states (81 per cent) have devolved to the DPs. This is followed by agriculture, including agricultural extension and minor irrigation, water management, and watershed development. In the case of roads, culverts, bridges, ferries, waterways, and other means of communication, health and sanitation, including hospitals, primary health centres, and dispensaries and family welfare, 12 states have devolved certain powers and responsibilities. With the exception of five states, other states have shown a marked reluctance to devolve activities relating to non-conventional energy sources and fuel and fodder. Similarly, six states only devolved the 'matters' of PDS, technical training and vocational education, and rural electrification. Only seven states have devolved the 'libraries' to the DPs.

might actually display greater precision and depth of devolution when the details are examined.

Next, many matters devolved through the law result in different tiers of government sharing the same responsibility. The result of such vague legislative drafting is diffused accountability. In addition, there are several unfunded mandates that arise from vague legal provisions transferring functions to panchayats. Most states claim that devolution in the constitutional sense has been done, while in reality confining and controlling the panchayats and denying them the powers required to function as institutions of self-government through some frequently observed practices, such as: (a) conditional devolution, where states reserve to themselves the powers to amplify or withdraw powers and responsibilities from the panchayats through executive orders; (b) open-ended devolution through sweeping clauses, without providing for enabling rules to actually operationalize such devolution; and (c) vague devolution, through using operative words such as 'promotion' or 'advise', when describing the role to be played by the panchayats concerned.

There are also several good legislative practices—for example, where laws have transferred public assets from state departments to the panchayats and mapped out their responsibilities.[25]

The situation with respect to the devolution of powers and responsibilities to urban LGs is probably worse. Here too, there is wide variation in the extent of powers devolved or responsibilities entrusted to LGs. Urban spatial planning, which is a critical service that ought to be provided by LGs, is often retained in powerful parastatals such as the urban development authorities. Public utilities, such as those engaged in water and sanitation, are vested with utility companies or authorities, which operate outside the control and superintendence of the LGs. Another pervasive arrangement in the urban context is the positioning of parastatals as service providers to the municipalities, without providing any scope for the municipalities to hold parastatals accountable for their performance.

Probably, the greatest weakness in the urban design of LGs is the limited scope for the direct participation of people in governance. The Constitution defines a gram sabha in rural areas as a body comprising

---

[25] Kerala is one such example.

the voters relating to a village within a panchayat and permits states to define the scope of their powers and responsibilities.[26] In urban areas, there is no equivalent institution, which automatically enables urban voters to be part of a citizens' assembly. Instead, the constitution enjoins upon states to constitute ward committees in the manner as determined by it. To make matters worse, ward committees are not mandated for municipalities with populations less than 300,000 people. Predictably, while states have passed relatively strong laws endowing gram sabhas in rural areas with extensive powers, in urban areas, ward committees are yet to be constituted, or are configured as nominated bodies, with little power and scope for participation.

Steps have been taken to better clarify the functional ambit of LGs. Since its constitution in 2004, the Ministry of Panchayati Raj (MoPR) has promoted the idea of activity mapping, a process of unbundling functions devolved upon panchayats into their component activities and their assignment to various stakeholders in accordance with the principle of subsidiarity. However, its efforts have not met with much success.

Recently, an Expert Committee appointed by the MoPR undertook a thorough review of both central- and state-level efforts to promote the idea and undertake activity mapping.[27] It made the unflattering observation that MoPR efforts, even though backed by instructions from the prime minister, were blunted and ignored by the Planning Commission and central ministries. The committee noted that when the MoPR approached the cabinet secretariat for support, it refused

[26] In tribal areas delineated in the Fifth Schedule of the Constitution, the powers to be endowed to LGs are mandated directly by a central law—the Panchayats (Extension to Scheduled Areas) Act, 1996, which gives traditional communities rights over common property resources and the duty to protect traditional customs and practices.

[27] This is the Expert Committee on Leveraging Panchayats for Efficient Delivery of Public Goods and Services. The Committee was chaired by the former Union Panchayati Raj Minister, Mr. Mani Shankar Aiyar. Its report, *Towards Holistic Panchayat Raj, Twentieth Anniversary Report of the Expert Committee on Leveraging Panchayats for Efficient Delivery of Public Goods and Services,* was released in April 2013. This author was the principal consultant to the Expert Committee.

to help. In the words of the committee, 'the question is deadlocked because the Ministry of Panchayati Raj cannot move and the Cabinet Secretariat will not move. That is where matters stand: at a standstill.'[28]

The committee also observed that strenuous efforts to pursue states to undertake activity mapping have gone in vain. It observed that deadlines for completion of activity mapping were extended and, in spite of regular review, actual progress was not significant. In state after state, the issue was sidestepped in a variety of ways: resurrecting long-dormant generic orders for activity mapping issued in the past and claiming to have completed the process; releasing statements of intentions, crafted more to meet the need to release these at political summit meetings, rather than as clear forward policy steps; or issuing orders that withdrew powers and responsibilities from the panchayats. On the bright side, the committee observed that there have also been painstaking efforts in some states at starting a process of real devolution in which activity mapping was followed by budget analysis and rear-ranging budget heads to match the functions proposed to be devolved, even though this was slow and incomplete.[29]

The committee noted that there was poor ownership to the idea of activity mapping; only state departments of Panchayati Raj were com-mitted to it. Even if generic orders on activity mapping were issued by the Panchayati Raj department, they did not have much effect; other departments continued to issue centralizing orders as before. Since in most states activity mapping was issued in the form of executive instructions and not through legislation, they could be easily overruled by subsequent orders. Besides, central government ministries often mandated the setting up of parallel structures, ignoring the legisla-tive arrangements and activity mapping orders of states. These direc-tives provided alibis for their departmental counterparts in states to withdraw powers from the panchayats; often in violation of state laws mandating devolution. This diluted MoPR efforts as well; they could not persuade states to undertake activity mapping if central ministries themselves were remiss.

Based upon this analysis, the committee suggested that activity map-ping should be done by all states, as a prior exercise for devolution of

---

[28] Expert Committee, *Holistic Panchayat*, vol. 1, paragraph 3.18, 50.

[29] Kerala is often quoted as a good example.

the major areas of service delivery, such as health, education, nutrition, water supply, sanitation, civic services, employment generation, poverty alleviation, local economic development, livelihoods, agriculture and allied sectors, social security, and disaster management. Activity mapping should also clearly state whether the function is a devolved core function, or where the panchayats function as agencies and where they have a mediating role. In respect of agency functions, the committee suggested that higher-level governments, parastatals, or others entrusting any function on panchayats must enter into enforceable contracts that lay out the roles and responsibilities of both the panchayats as an agency as well as that of the entity that entrusts such agency function. Such contracts should also provide for meeting completely the costs of carrying out the agency function by the LG concerned.

The committee suggested that activity mapping should be linked to budget envelopes with a separate statement of funds allocated to Panchayati Raj Institutions, or PRIs, in an annexe to the budget. It also noted the need to dispel line department misgivings that activity mapping disempowers them; indeed, their role might increase, though they would not be doing the same things that they were doing before. State governments would need to be responsible for setting standards of services to be delivered by the panchayats and monitoring whether the same is being met. Finally, the committee prepared model activity maps covering eight sectors to serve as frameworks that the centre and states might follow.

Apart from the exhortation that both the centre and states should pursue activity mapping with a sense of purpose, the committee's recommendations draw attention to two serious matters that would still impede meaningful activity mapping if not addressed. The first is the issue of parallel structures. Parallel bodies are those set up as directed by the state or central governments to plan and execute development projects in areas that are in the functional domain of LGs, using funds provided by the state or central governments or donors.[30] They are

[30] Paragraphs 4.12 to 4.14 have been abstracted from Raghunandan, 'Introduction', with the permission of the *Economic and Political Weekly*. These ideas were first expressed in a paper presented by S.M. Vijayanand (then the Principal Secretary, Department of Local Self-Government Institutions, Government of Kerala and later Chief Secretary, Government of Kerala) and

typically established, structured, and operated in accordance with executive fiat and are not mandated to be established through any constitutional provision.[31] They typically have a system of decision-making on resource allocation and execution of projects that is independent and removed from the LG set-up. They have considerable autonomy and include bureaucrats, elected representatives, non-officials, and community representatives in their governing structure. Examples of parallel bodies include district rural development agencies, forest and watershed development agencies, and societies set up for implementing specific programmes such as the Sarva Shiksha Abhiyan (SSA), the National Rural Health Mission, and the National Horticultural Mission.

Parallel bodies originated before the constitutional recognition of LGs. They were to provide professional support, often of a multi-disciplinary and supra-departmental nature, for implementation of programmes. They facilitated easy and accountable funds management through being able to receive funds directly and deposit them in interest-drawing accounts in commercial banks outside the government treasury system, thus avoiding the risks of restrictions on fund flow. This, in turn, enabled better tracking of fund utilization, provided utilization details, proper accounting, and better follow-up on releases. They also provided flexible organizational systems for quick decision-making and easy procurement of goods and services. Finally, they also enabled non-official participation in decision-making, especially of MPs and MLAs, which was appropriate in the pre-constitutionally mandated LG era.

---

this author at the second Round Table of State Ministers of Panchayati Raj, organised by the Union Ministry of Panchayati Raj at Mysore, Karnataka in July 2004.

[31] The most powerful parallel bodies are the District Rural Development Agencies (DRDAs) constituted by the Ministry of Rural Development of the Union government. These are described as 'pre-Panchayati Raj institutions in the sense that they were set up as professional units with non-official participation, before the constitutional mandate of economic development and social justice was vested in the Panchayati Raj institutions'. See Department of Rural Development, Ministry of Rural Development, Government of India, *Report of the Committee on Restructuring of DRDA* (New Delhi: Government of India, 2012).

While parallel bodies were successful in ensuring non-diversion of funds, there was no commensurate improvement in ensuring better planning, transparency, and participation. Their existence is incongruous following the 73rd and 74th Amendments. They not only usurp the legitimate functional space of LGs, but also challenge the idea of a functional domain for them. By dominating the implementation process, they question the idea of LGs; indeed, they mock them through superior resource endowments and visible patronage systems. Higher-level authorities continue to park tied funds in programme-specific parallel structures that supplant LGs because of their persistent belief that the latter do not have the capacities to implement their programmes. These problems are worsened by serious gaps in staffing within the parallel structures themselves, particularly at the cutting edge.

Perhaps the most serious indictment of parallel bodies was delivered by a Committee appointed by the Union government. The Report of the Committee on Restructuring of DRDA[32] offers several reasons[33] for the need to restructure these parallel structures, concluding that 'in the constitutional context created by the amendments, political context brought in by functioning of elected bodies, development context giving primacy to participatory development, and administrative context giving importance to transparency and accountability there is a need for revisiting the raison d'être of bodies like DRDAs'. It observes that states like Madhya Pradesh, Chhattisgarh, Rajasthan, West Bengal, and Kerala went further and abolished DRDAs as separate legal entities

[32] Department of Rural Development, Ministry of Rural Development, Government of India, January 2012.

[33] The reasons given by the Committee are summarized as follows. First, the Constitution mandates that planning for economic development and social justice, and implementation of such plans, should be the responsibility of the PRIs, and it further provides for transferring schemes in the functional domain of PRIs to them. In this context, it is necessary to examine the role and relevance of bodies like DRDAs. Second, the Constitution envisages harmonization not only of laws, but also of institutional mechanisms with the Panchayati Raj system. The principle of concomitance cannot be limited to just laws but it extends to institutional arrangements as well. Viewed in this sense, such institutions have to be harmonized with the PRI setup or else they become *ultra vires* of the Constitution.

and merged them with the zilla parishads following the example of Karnataka, which did so as far back as 1987—without any negative effect on the flow of funds from the GoI, their proper utilization, and timely submission of accounts.

The report goes on to assert that 'as parallel bodies pose a serious threat to the growth and maturation of PRIs as institutions of Local Self Government as envisaged in the Constitution, it is necessary that they are fully harmonised with the Panchayat Raj set up'. It draws a distinction between the professional component and the autonomous-institutional component of institutions such as the DRDA. While opining that the former is absolutely indispensable, particularly taking into account the fact that PRIs have relatively weak professional support, it asserts that the latter has no relevance when democratically elected bodies are in existence. In conclusion, it recommends that 'DRDAs are suitably restructured by changing their institutional structure and character as charitable societies and converting them into a high quality professional group, preferably placed in the District Panchayats, but with the specific mandate to service the District Planning Committees'. Unfortunately, in spite of the Union government's declaration of having accepted the report of the Committee, the DRDAs continue unhindered as parallel bodies.

The second serious impediment to meaningful activity mapping is the poor level of fiscal decentralization to LGs. The constitutional design of the intergovernmental transfer system enables LGs to receive and appropriate funds through five main sources. First, in an indirect fashion, they can receive a share of central revenues. Article 280(3)(b)(ii) mandates that the Union Finance Commission recommends a share of the central revenues to 'augment the resources of the states' to 'supplement the resources of LGs'. Second, a similar mechanism is put in place at the state level, where state finance commissions are to recommend the share of state revenues that ought to be devolved upon LGs. Third, LGs can receive funds through the entrustment of central and state schemes. Fourth, states can, through law, enable LGs to levy taxes and appropriate the funds collected. Finally, LGs can—typically with permission from the state—obtain loans to undertake their development work.

In practice, receiving revenue shares from the central government on the basis of Union Finance Commission recommendations has turned out to be the most robust arrangement. Initially, finance commissions recommended ad-hoc grant allocations to the LGs, but the Thirteenth Finance Commission broke new ground by allocating a percentage of the central revenues for them. Earlier, states also used to divert these funds for their own purposes, but the Twelfth Finance Commission recommended strict measures to prevent such practices. The Thirteenth Finance Commission also imposed conditionalities on better accounting measures and local revenue collection in order for states to avail of topping up grants.[34] The Fourteenth Finance Commission[35] has increased the share of the LGs allocated from the divisible pool of taxes from Rs 861.61 billion to Rs 2,874.36 billion, an increase of 234 per cent over the grants recommended by the Thirteenth Finance Commission, and representing a rise from 2.3 to over 4 per cent of the central divisible pool of taxes, to the LGs.[36]

In sharp contrast, the system of revenue sharing between states and LGs, as recommended by state finance commissions, has not been well grounded. State Finance Commission reports have been ignored or shelved in most states. Some states have followed the good convention of constituting these institutions regularly and following their recommendations, but this is more the exception than the rule (Kerala is one such example).

One of the curious trends in the intergovernmental financial arrangement has been the tendency to use Article 282 of the Constitution as the preferred route to make specific-purpose fiscal transfers to states and LGs. This clause, which comes under the chapter 'Miscellaneous Financial Provisions' in the Constitution, states that 'the Union or a State may make any grants for any public purpose, notwithstanding that the purpose is not one with respect to which Parliament or the

[34] The only blip is the tendency for states to impose conditionalities that restrict the use of these funds by LGs, even though the Thirteenth Finance Commission recommends that this ought not to be done.

[35] The recommendations of the Commission have been accepted completely by the Union government and will be implemented from 2015 to 2020.

[36] The basic grants have been raised from Rs 563.35 billion to Rs 2,499.78 billion, a 344 per cent increase. In the case of performance grants, which, as a proportion of the total grants has been brought down to 10 per cent and 20 per cent in the case of rural LGs and urban LGs, respectively, the increase is from Rs 298.26 billion to Rs 374.58 billion.

Legislature of the State, may make laws'. The positioning of this clause outside the chapter that relates to fiscal transfers suggests that it is to be considered an exception clause under which fiscal transfers can be made in emergencies, say, for example, in the case of a natural disaster. Yet, over time, this exception clause has become the window for the transfer of a considerable volume of discretionary and specific-purpose grants, in the form of 'schemes'. By 2012–13, central fiscal transfers made under this clause constituted about 75 per cent of the level of funds transferred through the provisions of Article 280 (Table 11.2).[37]

Most significant is the fact that transfers under Article 282 need not be dependent upon the recommendation of a Finance Commission. This has enabled the Union government to make considerable fiscal transfers through parallel structures, which not only bypass LGs at the field level, but also bypass state budgets. These allocations are off budget and handled largely by banks, which benefit from the use of the interest-free 'float' provided by these pass-through allocations. In 2013–14, the number of central fiscal transfers through this discretionary window totalled more than 150, comprising centrally sponsored schemes (CSSs) and 'additional central assistance' programmes. Most of these were designed and managed by the Planning Commission, a non-constitutional and non-statutory body chaired by the prime minister, which wielded considerable power and authority because of the hold it had on such transfers. The funds transferred through Article 282 of the Constitution also fuelled schemes entrusted to the LGs, such as the Mahatma Gandhi National Rural Employment Guarantee Programme Scheme (MGNREGS). Until 2014–15, efforts to rationalize these transfers largely failed.[38] In the 2014–15 interim budget, the outgoing finance minister announced the restructuring of the CSSs into 66 programmes for greater synergy and claimed that such funds will be released into state consolidated funds as central assistance to state plans.[39] As a result, central assistance to state

[37] T.R. Raghunandan, 'Issues in Federalism and Decentralization', in Ashima Goyal, ed., *The Oxford Handbook of the Indian Economy in the 21st Century* (Oxford: Oxford University Press, 2014), 450.

[38] Reports that were not considered when presented included that of the Arvind Verma Committee (2007) appointed by the Planning Commission and the Second Administrative Reforms Committee.

[39] This was in line with the recommendations of the B.K. Chaturvedi Committee suggesting reduction in the number of CSSs.

Table 11.2 Centre–State Fiscal Transfers

Centre to State Fiscal Transfer made under Article 280 and 275

Sl.	Items	Amount (Rs Billion)			
		2009–10	2010–11	2011–12	2012–13
1	States' Share of Taxes and Duties [Art. 280(3)(a)]	1,648.32	2,193.03	2,554.14	3,019.21
2	Non-Plan Grants and Loans [includes Grants under Art. 275(1)]	460.29	498.75	553.97	642.96
3					

Centre to State Fiscal Transfers Made Under Article 282

Sl.	Item	Amount (Rs Billion)			
		2009–10	2010–11	2011–12	2012–13
1	Central Assistance for State and UT Plans (Planning Commission)	844.90	930.793	1,051.99	1,299.98
2	Assistance for Central and Centrally Sponsored Schemes (Planning Commission)	244.75	306.06	371.26	415.92
3	Direct Release to State/UT Implementing Agencies (MPLADS)	15.32	15.33	29.5	39.55

4					
4	Direct Release to State/ District Level Autonomous Bodies/ Implementing Agencies	905.21	1,187.4	1,128.03	1,333.59

Source: T.R. Raghunandan, 'Issues in Federalism and Decentralization.'

and union territory plans was announced to grow substantially from Rs 1,362.54 billion in 2013–14 to Rs 3,385.62 billion in 2014–15. The announcement that central funds would be sent into the consolidated account of the state did, in theory, remove the justification for parallel structures—namely, that they could insulate central fiscal transfers from the vagaries of state finances and politicians. However, this new pattern of central funding through the consolidated fund alone did not result in the dismantling of parallel structures at the state and district levels.

Following the acceptance of the report of the Fourteenth Finance Commission by the Union government, the vertical share of the states in the divisible pool of union taxes was increased from 32 to 42 per cent. This has resulted in cuts in CSSs. Overall, while preliminary studies show that there has been a net gain across all states in terms of the volume of intergovernmental fiscal transfers from the Union government, whether the greater autonomy given to states through the replacement of specific purpose transfers such as the CSSs by revenue shares will result in a more generous devolution to LGs from the State, remains to be seen.[40]

With respect to own revenues, property tax collection in urban areas has improved considerably due to many reforms covering the estimation system, citizen interphase, and enforcement, though there is still slack to be pulled in. State laws list out the assigned taxes and also set out the broad policy of how taxes are to be estimated, levied, and collected, besides stating out punitive measures to curb defaults.[41]

[40] The 'State of Social Sector Expenditure' report of the Accountability Initiative of the Centre for Policy Research traces the trends in 13 states, following the change in the nature of fiscal transfers as described earlier. Preliminary findings are that there is no significant reduction in the overall fiscal space available to state governments. The report states, 'based on current data available, despite cuts in CSS, most states do have the required fiscal space to maintain current levels of social sector expenditure, if they so choose'. See A. Kapur, V. Srinivas, P.R. Choudhury, *State of Social Sector Expenditure in 2015–16* (New Delhi: Centre for Policy Research, 2016).

[41] Typically, these taxation powers include property taxes, user charges for water supply and sanitation services, professional taxes, taxes on advertisement boards, ferries, parking fees, and entertainment tax on non-cinematographic shows.

Some of the states and LGs have innovated, with information technology (IT)-based databases for estimation and collection of taxes. Institutional measures also include self-assessment of taxes, with random inspections and punitive measures as a back-up to ensure compliance. Tax collection in rural areas has been patchy in comparison, with states in the south and the west having a much better track record. Rural LGs, as they are generally poorly staffed, do not have the institutional capacities to levy taxes and collect them, except in a few states. This usually results in no taxes being collected, or arbitrary lump sum amounts being collected.

The Thirteenth Finance Commission made the imposition of property taxes a condition for receiving incentive grants, from 2013 onwards. It suggested that states should establish a valuation board in order to standardize property assessment and valuation and that states should institute a geographic information system (GIS) platform for mapping all properties in cities to prevent leakage. Furthermore, it suggested that the Union government's urban renewal mission should introduce a specific conditionality aimed at reducing the gap between the assessed and market value of properties. With these measures, it estimates that property tax revenues could increase eight fold, merely by bringing all cities to an 85 per cent coverage level and 85 per cent collection efficiency, without increasing tax rates.

Borrowings by LGs have largely remained confined to urban areas. Some good practices have developed over time, including the pooling of municipal requirements on borrowing into municipal bonds, which are negotiated and obtained by bodies such as urban finance corporations, set up in a few states. However, in the final analysis, while these sources can be potentially quite substantial, the actual extent of fiscal devolution is abysmally low.

A connected matter of concern is the gradual positioning of LGs as agents of the Union and state governments, who use their considerable financial clout to drive large mega-schemes that marginalize and curb the fiscal independence of LGs. While there has been a considerable increase of funds flowing through this route to LGs, performing these agency functions has had its deleterious effects. Most LGs are not compensated for the additional administrative expenditure that is entailed by performing such agency functions. Moreover, governance functions get neglected in the rush to perform agency functions. In addition, local

revenues do not get collected as LGs substitute specific-purpose transfers for their own revenues.[42]

To compound the high degrees of fiscal centralization, there is a
confusing array of mechanisms of transfer of funds from higher to
LG levels. Funds can move, on the basis of several triggers such as
submission of utilization certificates and approval protocols, through
treasuries or bank accounts. Projects such as the PAISA project of the
Accountability Initiative exist,[43] but a study by the Centre for Policy
Research has exposed how lumpy and opaque these can be.[44] If studies
reveal the extent of these bottlenecks in the fiscal transfer system in
just one scheme, one can imagine the extent of confusion when all
fiscal transfers meant for the LGs are considered.

If one pauses to examine the ethos, design, and functioning of the LG
system against the background of theories of fiscal federalism, its weaknesses are readily apparent. Fiscal federalism has evolved considerably
beyond the thoughts of its early proponents, who considered it to be a
vehicle for better political negotiation, to a means of more efficiently
and responsively delivering services, to stating that it essentially is a
means of managing spill-over externalities of services whose footprints
do not match the boundaries of political structures. Second-generation
theorists studied how decentralization and empowerment of LGs in
Latin America had triggered macro-economic failure. LGs there, when
empowered to raise resources, prepared inflated plans and borrowed
heavily; in the absence of any hard budget constraints at the local level,
LGs ran up huge expenditure liabilities that the state eventually had
to underwrite. The first insight that emerged from a study of these failures was that, contrary to the assumption inherent in first-generation
approaches, elected public officials did not necessarily act in further-
ance of the common public good (or as put more elegantly, 'benevolent

[42] This is a predictable response. Local revenues strengthen accountability
measures to a higher proportion than higher-level transfers because citizens are
more vigilant over expenses incurred from the taxes that they pay. They see that
connection more proximately with respect to local taxes.

[43] PAISA stands for 'Planning, Allocations and Expenditures, Institutions:
Studies in Accountability'.

[44] The PAISA project undertakes the public expenditure tracking in the
funds going to Schools under SSA. See Accountability Initiative, *PAISA Report*
(New Delhi: Centre for Policy Research, 2012).

maximisers of the social welfare'[45]) but behaved with an eye on their future election prospects.

Second, in the absence of controls to the contrary, every institution made attempts to reduce its budget constraints by exporting its tax burden. Subnational and LGs faced with a soft budget constraint had a strong incentive to spend beyond their means, because they always veered to the expectation that they would be bailed out by the central government. What can be derived from the observations of second generation fiscal federalism (SGFF) proponents is that much stronger disincentives need to be incorporated into institutional design of intergovernmental arrangements, to ensure that LGs function within their financial means and efficiently perform their responsibilities, without compromising on the essential reason for decentralization, which is greater responsiveness to local heterogeneity and greater voice for the people.

Tested against these viewpoints drawn from both political and fiscal federalism literature, India's institutional design for decentralization is intriguing. The discourse surrounding decentralization indicates a broad consensus that LGs should be empowered to do what they can handle most responsively and what is most efficiently delivered at their levels. However, at second glance, we also see that India's fiscal decentralization is resource-poor; local tax collections are next to nothing, very little money filters down to the local government via intergovernmental fiscal transfers, and LGs are shackled with strict administrative, financial, and audit controls. While this tight-fisted approach to fiscal decentralization might give the impression that India has imbibed the lessons that emerge from SGFF, at second glance, this is not so. These controls are not rollbacks as a reaction to fiscal profligacy of LGs; our stinginess is the result of a reluctance to decentralize. The blunt fact is that behind the smokescreen of a de jure commitment to political decentralization, we have been very conservative when it comes to funding LGs through tax assignments and fiscal transfers. In spite of the constitutional provisions, our system does not amount to anything more than delegation of certain agency functions to LGs, with low levels of fiscal decentralization, further curtailed by strict expenditure

---

[45] B. Weingast, 'Second Generation Fiscal Federalism: Political Aspects of Decentralization and Economic Development', *World Development* 53 (January 2013), 14–25.

controls. Taken together, these do impose a hard budget constraint regime on LGs, but it is of the nature of controls that a principal would impose upon an agent and does not comprise a generic institutional check inherent on irresponsible local spending. Furthermore, that in our system, it is always open to individual LGs to seek and obtain specific doles and concessions, depending upon the political equation that it has with higher levels of governments, is further evidence that ours is not a model for SGFF—there is hardly any evidence of a normative hard budget constraint regime for LGs being in place.

In conclusion, the lack of progress in activity mapping, the proliferation of parallel structures, high degrees of centralization in financing, and the confusing methods of fiscal transfers are four knockout punches that lay low any possibility that LGs can function effectively. Together, they also send an unequivocal message: that the momentum is clearly towards centralization. LGs are a forgotten constitutional heirloom in the governance cupboard, to be occasionally taken down, dusted, admired, and then locked up again. We seem condemned to suffer the consequences of hazy functional allocations. New parallel structures continue to be established and there seems no way that the current momentum toward fiscal centralization will slow down. No political party goes beyond mouthing the empty rhetoric of decentralization. Voters also do not consider the absence of decentralization as an election issue. Bureaucrats are more enamoured of techno-managerial solutions and do not see LGs as anything more than places where they might be posted, from where they can exercise their executive power, without being accountable to the locally elected body. The results of excessive centralization are there for everyone to see: abysmal local service delivery systems and the virtual absence of any effective regulation over civic and other essential services. Yet, the obvious opportunity to reverse the tide by strengthening LGs through sustained institutional reforms is ignored.

If higher-level governments continue to deny LGs their rightful place in governing the country, what is the way out?

A Killer Application from the Supply Side: Building an Allocation, Release, and Expenditure Information Network

The obvious result of the confusing array of fiscal transfers is that LGs, indeed, all grassroots-level implementing institutions, do not know the level of funds to which they are entitled, when they will receive these, what triggers their releases, and who else is spending public funds in their jurisdictions. Greater accountability over public expenditure can be achieved by building an allocation, release, and expenditure information network (EIN). Doing so would produce a transparent, efficient, outcome-oriented, and participatory system all the way from the centre to each LG. A standardized coding of expenditure entities will enable allocations and expenditure at project locations to be provided. Every entity or individual involved will gain real-time visibility into fund utilization and outcomes. If all line ministries dovetail their information systems into an EIN, they could improve their response and even provide fast-track funding for best performers. At the grassroots level, LGs will obtain greater awareness on entitlements under programmes of various line agencies. They will also benefit from instant disbursement of funds upon reporting of utilization and can also sound the alarm if bottlenecks are encountered in disbursals. Most important, they will be able to closely watch and present to the gram sabhas details of the expenditure of other agencies of the government in their respective jurisdictions. A grant, release, and expenditure information network could be run by a central agency, which runs the technology platform on the Internet. Based on standardized templates, workflows, and a database that preserves the entitlements of various entities, it can enable users to drill down to collect information on utilization, feedback, knowledge of entities, interactions, and performance and forecast future performance. For those who send funds down, it could enable the detection of best-performing institutions and establish outcome-based, fast-track fund release. For fund recipients, including LG users, it will provide space to track their entitlements and enable regular utilization certificate filing. It can also provide a window into the fiscal flows of other entities operating in a specific area or sector, and thus facilitate greater vigilance.

Currently, there might be bottlenecks of connectivity, and lack of hardware, electricity, and IT literacy in implementing such a system right down to the last stakeholder (which would include the members of nearly 250,000 LGs), but these are likely to diminish rapidly. Even as they do, last-mile connectivity could be provided to them through face-to-face interaction, mobile networks, and community radio.

Pulling Up by the Bootstraps—Capacity Development through Peer Learning and Self-help[46]

A simplistic and narrow viewpoint on kick-starting a process of strengthening LGs starts with the premise that they require capacity building to better undertake their responsibilities. Pointing to the large number of poor, illiterate, and SC/ST members elected to LGs, most sceptics believe that capacity building should precede devolution. However, equating capacity with the ability to read or write is simplistic and ignores the value of local knowledge that LG representatives possess. By not realizing the innate skills and drive of 3.2 million elected representatives, the enormous potential that exists within the LG structure is allowed to dissipate.

The Expert Committee's findings on supply-driven capacity development underscored the point that higher levels of government were not capable of delivering anything more than homilies to LGs, through training programmes. The MoPR had developed a framework for capability development of LGs, the National Capability Development Framework, and for its implementation, made available Rs 2,500 million every year to states.[47] The Expert Committee's findings on the utilization of these allocations revealed that after six years of implementation, only 55 per cent of the funds had been drawn. States that ended up in the bottom of the list were those that required the funds the most.[48] Regarding the quality of implementation, the report observed that none of the evaluation studies commissioned by the Ministry had actually studied in sufficient depth the implementation of

---

[46] This section has been abstracted from Raghunandan, 'Introduction', and Chapter VI of the Twentieth Anniversary Report of the Expert Committee on Leveraging Panchayats, *Towards Holistic Panchayat Raj, Twentieth Anniversary Report of the Expert Committee on Leveraging Panchayats for Efficient Delivery of Public Goods and Services* (New Delhi: Government of India, 2013),

[47] Under the Backward Regions Grant Fund, from 2008 to 2013.

[48] The bottom five states are Uttar Pradesh, Gujarat, Assam, Bihar, and Jharkhand. One hundred and eight of the Backward Regions Grant Fund's (BRGF's) 250 districts are located in these states.

the capacity development activities in juxtaposition to the perspective plans prepared by the state concerned.[49]

It is clear that supply-driven initiatives in training panchayat representatives suffer from serious shortcomings. The notion that panchayat members need training is itself of doubtful validity. The Expert Committee comments are relevant in this regard:

> It is a paradox that at higher levels of government, it is more easily accepted that an elected representative is not expected to have the levels of technical and administrative knowledge that the bureaucracy has. On the other hand, it is understood that a generalist political leader who is assigned to perform the role of a minister would necessarily depend upon the aid and advice given to her by an experienced and knowledgeable secretariat comprising experts well versed in the task of running a government. Thus individuals, who may or may not have the 'capacity' to govern, are supported by institutions that have the organisational capacity required to run administrations and governments. Yet, quite often, this simple precept is forgotten when it comes to Panchayats. A high expectation is set by the bureaucracy-led administration from the Panchayat elected representative in terms of ability to perform. Much of these double standards arise from the contrasting grammar of engagement between the bureaucracy and the higher and local levels of elected representatives, respectively. While the bureaucracy accepts the position that they are subordinate to central- and state-level political executives, they see local elected representatives as their subordinates, who are to do as commanded, as a substitute for the lower bureaucracy itself.

Clearly, if any approach to capacity development is to be useful, it first needs to distinguish organisational capacity from individual capacities and have distinctly different strategies in place for making up shortcomings in both these areas. Tackling organisational lack of capacities requires radically different approaches as compared to strengthening individual capacities. Training, competency building and capacity development can be visualised as ever widening circles. Training is merely one component of developing competencies, which in turn is part of

---

[49] This is an important deficiency, because the NCBF allowed State to customize their training programmes within the overall standards set, depending upon the election cycle for the conduct of Panchayat elections.

the larger universe of capacity development. For example, even in the absence of conventional training of elected representatives, the capacities of Panchayats to perform their duties can be enhanced if competent staff is posted in adequate measure to the Panchayats and made accountable for their performance to them. Even if the government in unable for whatever reason to recruit and post staff, it could rapidly enable Panchayats to improve their competencies by enabling them to obtain technical expertise such as engineers and accountants through outsourced arrangements.[50]

Given these deficiencies in the current training methodologies for LGs and acknowledging the fact that higher-level governments have no incentive to genuinely build capacities in LGs, there seems to be no other alternative but for LGs to pull themselves up by their bootstraps. Happily, the critical bottleneck is not finding innovators or visionaries within the LG system, but enabling them to upscale. There are several initiatives across the country that demonstrate that a culture of self-help and innovation is developing among LGs. Sympathetic and sensitive approaches to capacity development are being designed and implemented, albeit at a small scale. If LG champions across the country could get in touch with each other, indeed, facilitate the documentation of each other's work, these numerous but isolated initiatives could be transformed into a groundswell of networked capacities, which in turn could propel that long-awaited demand for decentralization emerging from the grassroots. A few of these promising innovations, which have the potential to set off a chain reaction of institutional strengthening of LGs, is described below.[51]

The Kutch Nav Nirman Abhiyan's Unique Training Initiative

In 2010, through a Swiss development corporation-supported initiative, an innovative training programme was conducted in Kutch, Gujarat, for panchayat representatives. The programme was also conducted in Pratapgarh and Udaipur districts of Rajasthan in 2011. The programme,

[50] Expert Committee, paragraphs 6.1.3 and 6.1.4 from *Holistic Panchayat*.

[51] This author has been associated with some of these initiatives in several capacities and written about all of them in various publications. The following paragraphs have been extracted and abridged from Expert Committee, *Holistic Panchayat*, Chapter VI, to which these accounts were contributed by the author.

run in six modules over three months, comprised three technology-related sessions (abbreviated as TELPE, or Technology Enhanced Learning Process Enabler) and alternated with content sessions [named *Prajatantra* (democracy), *Aayojan ka Adhikar* (the right to plan), and *Bhavishya* (the future)]. All participants were provided laptops and high-speed wireless Internet facilities during the programme. In the intervening periods between two course sessions, the laptops were lodged in a laptop library, from where the participants could borrow the machines for revising lessons and taking up inter-modular assignments. The designing and rolling out of these programmes brought together experts in panchayati raj and experienced learning technologists.[52]

The initial vision was to design and implement a knowledge support system for panchayat representatives and those who work with them. The programmes in Kutch and Rajasthan exposed participants not only to the core content related to grassroots democracy and panchayati raj, but also to Internet-based techniques that would enable them to network better, collaborate on tasks, surf the web for information, and most important of all, create their own content by sharing their grassroots-level experiences and skills. The aim of the programme was to equip participants to link with the world, and equally, for the world to link with them, without any intermediaries or trainers.

Following the programme where both panchayat raj-related core content and familiarization with technological tools were intermeshed, panchayat members began to routinely use Skype for conference calls. They also recorded their experiences using videos and photos and discussed them through social media tools, such as Facebook. The panchayat associations in Kutch and panchayats covered in the training programme in Udaipur and Pratapgarh developed their own blogs, regularly updating these websites with content vetted and cleared by their editorial boards. The programme revealed the enormous power of the Internet, which, when linked with sensitively designed content that encourages panchayat representatives to exchange information with each other, could dramatically change the way in which they network

[52] Parimala Inamdar, Principal Consultant of Aquarians Management Consultancy Pvt. Ltd., was involved in developing the pedagogy and roll-out strategy. Sushma Iyengar, from the *Kutch Nav Nirman Abhiyan*, and this author assisted in designing the content of the programme.

between themselves, link with resource persons, and provide knowledge support to one another.

Improving the Organizational Capacity of Gram Panchayats: The Arghyam Experiment in Karnataka

Arghyam is an NGO that primarily works in the area of water and sanitation. In 2010, Arghyam conducted a survey on the implementation of water and sanitation activities at the GP level.[53] The survey discovered serious gaps and shortfalls in performance by the GPs. When Arghyam set out to disseminate the survey results, they found that while GPs were conscious of these shortfalls and desired to take action, they did not look like organizations that could address urgent issues such as water quality, let alone take over effective execution of multiple government programmes. Arghyam began to study the organizational structure of two panchayats in Karnataka in order to understand their institutional shortcomings, to develop a step-by-step, replicable framework for developing a strong GP organization, and to initiate a process of real-time change. The gram panchayat organizational development (GPOD) project worked closely with the panchayats to develop their internal vision statement and then prepared detailed process maps for the key services to be delivered by them. Close interaction with the panchayats revealed that, quite contrary to the common perception, GP members were involved in numerous activities. Moreover, they were pressured by citizen expectations and held themselves accountable to them. Another revelation was that often, members spent money out of their pockets to address public problems because fund flows from government were unpredictable. Reimbursements of such bridge financing by members were grievously delayed. In addition, well-functioning GPs evolved fairly nuanced solutions to local problems, with no support and help from higher-level governments.

Following extensive discussion with panchayat representatives, the project established detailed organizational structures that clarified responsibilities of various members, including those of standing committees. Since there are more sectors than standing committees, the

[53] More information about the Ashwas Survey, conducted in the period 2008–9, is available at: http://ashwas.indiawaterportal.org/.

concept of an elected representative taking charge as 'head' for a particular sector was conceived. Thus, for example, the head in charge of education was tasked to liaise and facilitate the coordination between the relevant panchayat standing committee and the school management committees (which would number around 10 in each panchayat). This arrangement proved to be a success, as the heads performed much in the manner of cabinet ministers, and took their sectoral responsibilities seriously. These organizational tweaks, which aimed at encouraging elected representatives to take on sectoral responsibilities, had widespread and significant impacts. Due to the development of distributed leadership, ownership and confidence increased among members. More members sought information on funds received and spent and, in turn, leveraged free floating and discretionary grants available with other institutions better. These funds were allocated more responsively, based upon discussions and consultations within the panchayat. That led to the creation of standard processes for key services to be delivered in the GP, such as provision of drinking water and street light maintenance, and so forth. Effective performance by the panchayats triggered a greater climate of trust between people and their representatives, which emboldened one panchayat to revise local tax rates, after a gap of 22 years.

The Arghyam experiment underscored the significance of a systems approach when dealing with improving panchayat organizational capacities. When panchayat members chose to perform specific sectoral responsibilities, fixed targets for themselves, discussed these with the public, and made themselves responsible for delivery, their relationship with parallel structures such as the school development management committees became collaborative rather than combative. Besides, the next natural demand was for portfolio-wise, targeted training. Since they had a stake in learning, they participated in the design of the training programmes too.

However, the most significant outcome of the Arghyam experiment was the realization that service Memoranda of Understanding (MoUs) are desirable between panchayats and line departments, based on the panchayats' perspective and annual plans. Echoing the observation of the Expert Committee that agency arrangements between panchayats and higher-level organizations should formally state out mutual rights and obligations, the Arghyam experiment emphasized that such service

MOUs should clarify the roles of both parties, performance metrics, and mutual expectations on the flow of funds. Above all, it should clearly state the resources earmarked by the line department both in terms of staff support and money, to enable the panchayat to perform its agency function effectively.

The Green Kerala Express Social Reality Show[54]

The Kerala government, in collaboration with the centre-owned television channel, Doordarshan, employed a novel method to activate competition among panchayats and showcase the best performing panchayats through a television social reality show called 'The Green Kerala Express', which aired on Doordarshan in 2010.

All GPs, municipalities, and municipal corporations in the state were invited to provide a short video showcasing their sustainable development projects. More than 200 LGs responded with interesting stories of local development, covering aspects such as water and land management, sanitation, environment, health, energy, education, social welfare, MGNREGS, women empowerment projects taken up under the Kudumbashree programme, agriculture, and food security. Of these, 152 were shortlisted and the production teams visited each of them to interact with the people; this interaction was captured in two short films, one on the cultural and historic profile of the village and the other on the developmental initiative. These LGs were then invited to the studio, where the films were screened, and they interacted with a five-member jury. Based on the percentage of the marks awarded to the LGs, which depended upon citizen votes collected through SMS, 15 LGs were eventually selected for the second round. The jury visited each of the 15 LGs and evaluated their performance on the ground.

Based on a final, on-screen jury interaction, the best three panchayats and two municipalities were selected (with additional help from the audience). The best three panchayats were awarded prizes by the chief minister of Kerala in the final live telecast.[55] These panchayats

---

[54] Extracted and abridged from M.G. Rao and T.R. Raghunandan, *Panchayats and Economic Development* (New Delhi: National Institute of Public Finance and Policy, 2010).

[55] These were Elappully, Akathethara (both from Palakkad district), and Adatt (Thrissur district), which won the first, second, and third prizes, respectively.

had undertaken several innovative programmes involving agricultural production, anti-poverty programmes, tourism facilities, senior citizens' clubs, deforestation, and e-governance.

Several factors contributed to the success of the TV programme. The popular social reality show format and slick production quality attracted and held the attention of viewers.[56] The shows, starting on 1 March 2010 ran continuously, with daily 40-minute episodes, culminating in the grand show finale on 27 July. The daily episodes ensured audience interest and involvement in the voting for selecting the best performers. The credibility and non-partisan nature of the jury, which comprised renowned literary, journalistic, and academic figures respected in Kerala was an important factor, given the state's strong political polarization even at the LG level. The generous financial awards offered created interest as well.[57]

The analysis of the winners, as also the well-performing panchayats that reached the second round, revealed that all winners focused on promoting larger local development issues and not the provision of local public services alone. This was possible because Kerala made available block grants for the panchayats, which provided scope for innovation. The panchayat winners also understood the intricate economic linkages between different kinds of complimentary activities needed to strengthen the developmental effort. Thus, in Elapully, dairying was linked to paddy cultivation and the marketing of agricultural products. The winners were innovative, both in the way that they have run conventional programmes (deliberately slowing down MGNREGS to prevent artificial shortages of labour in Elapully) and also in starting new ones (Adatt's tourism project). They were also versatile; while promoting local economic development, they did not neglect their core responsibilities of improving civic services or providing social services (such as the senior citizens club in Akathethara). Quite often, the confidence and credibility built up through effectively managing core responsibilities played a large part in the successful implementation of development programmes.

[56] There was plenty of glamour in the form of good anchors and popular stars from the Malayalam film industry also anchoring some shows.

[57] The best three panchayats received prizes of Rs 10 million, Rs 5 million, and Rs 2.5 million, respectively. The remaining LGs participating in the final round received Rs 1 million each.

There were many facilitators that contributed to the success of the programme. First, the state government played an important enabling role in providing the right environment for the panchayats to undertake such innovations. The provision of a block grant with only broad conditionalities on its use was an important contributor. Second, the decentralized planning methodology in the state, which promoted a cooperative rather than an adversarial relationship between the different tiers of LGs, made convergence of programmes and innovation easier. Third, linkages with the state's self-help group programme for women, Kudumbashree, played a great part in the success of the development initiatives taken up in these panchayats. The Kudumbashree groups provided flexibility, acted as outreach agents of the panchayats, and served as important links in the marketing system that is essential to making economic development initiatives successful and sustainable.

A Multi-pronged Strategy for the Future

What then, does the future hold in store for achieving a vision of strong LGs? Currently, both political and systemic initiatives towards decentralization seem to have weakened. Bureaucrats and higher-level politicians have a stranglehold on public finances and are not likely to relinquish their powers easily. For that reason, activity mapping and fiscal decentralization might or might not happen, because they require a change of heart in the powers that be. Parallel bodies, though criticized, will continue to proliferate, given the current trends. Moreover, other more fashionable strategies to reaching out seem to be gaining centre-stage, such as banking inclusion and direct cash transfers.[58]

To the author, even as efforts do not flag on the political and policy design side, the tide can be turned if practices such as those detailed earlier are grounded, if necessary, by slipping them below the political and bureaucratic radar. The most effective supply-side initiative in this regard could be the implementation of an EIN from the centre down to the last mile. A few dedicated bureaucrats are quietly working on this and some elements of such a network are already in place, but that is

[58] The relationship of these forms of reaching out and democratic decentralization has not been debated in depth here. This author has some points to suggest, but for reasons of brevity, these have been left out of this chapter.

not enough.[59] Higher-level governments have privileged access to key financial data, but they are not good at communication. What could change the game is if supply-side initiatives on making fiscal data available are supported by rising demands (from the local level) in search of financial transparency. Such local demands, when coupled with quick dissemination of information through the social media networks of LGs, could result in a tsunami of requests from local stakeholders about where, by whom, and for what reason money is allocated and spent.[60]

The second strategy that could change the perspective on LG institutional strengthening is the recognition, as revealed by the GPOD project, that elected representatives are already functioning as quasi-executives. Funding them through increased honoraria would probably be a better way of bringing in implementation capacities, than pursuing the conventional hiring of expensive government servants, deputing them to LGs, and then monitoring them to see if they work. Enhanced own revenues collected by LGs could fund these honoraria.[61] While

[59] Central government reforms in this regard have been suggested in the Report of the Technology Advisory Group for Unique Projects, Ministry of Finance, New Delhi, 2011 (The TAGUP report). Adopting some of the recommendations in the report, the central government is putting in place a Central Sector Plan Monitoring System (CSPMS), which addresses a part of the problem. However, the CSPMS is not an open network. It only addresses the GoI's schemes and it does not consider the needs of the LGs.

[60] A pilot study conducted by Accountability Initiative in Mulbagal Taluk, Karnataka reveals that the amount spent by all entities, devolved or otherwise, in the jurisdiction of an average village panchayat would be in the range of Rs 60 to 80 million per year. However, the amount that is directly spent by the village panchayat directly might not exceed 5 per cent of this amount. Thus, while the local area is awash with funds, the village panchayat—in spite of its wide array of formal powers and responsibilities—has little control over expenditure incurred in its area by State entities. See T.R. Raghunandan, S. Iyengar, and T. Bhatikar, *PAISA for Panchayats—Tracking Fiscal Devolution to Local Governments: A Case Study from Kolar District, Karnataka* (New Delhi: Centre for Policy Research, 2016).

[61] Providing reasonable compensation to elected representatives is standard operating procedure in most democracies. For example, in Switzerland communes can negotiate the compensation they pay to their elected representatives based upon the extent of time they spend on working for the commune. Thus, members are classified as either full time or part time and compensated for

this upsets the conventional, strongly held notion in India that implementation ought to be vested with a remotely recruited permanent bureaucracy that carries out the decisions of the people articulated through elected representatives, the current situation (where there are a large number of staff vacancies at the local level) does not leave any option. The Weberian ideal of the bureaucracy as an enlightened outsider has already collapsed in India and there is no likelihood of it being restored to its former glory. There is often no counterfactual to the approach that the LGs might have to fend for themselves in sourcing capacity to perform their devolved functions effectively; more often than not, the state simply does not have the capacity to provide adequate capacity to them. From an accountability perspective too, the recognition that local elected representatives perform quasi-executive functions, monetizing that effort, and compensating them might be a better option than hiring and placing a permanent bureaucracy at the local level which, with each passing year and pay commission recommendation, becomes more expensive to maintain. Removing a bad performer in the government is difficult. However, the LG system—via elections—provides an arrangement where the representative's performance is directly reviewed by voters.

The experience of the GPOD project holds great promise because it highlights the potential that a local remaking of the LG organizational structure offers. It provokes thinking that one could go beyond simplistic organizational design strategies imposed from the top, such as the formation of standing committees and the integration of user committees into the LG system by labelling them as standing committees. These are simplistic solutions that have failed to bring about collaboration between LGs and parallel structures. It also lays bare the fact that local administration, whether decentralized or otherwise, involves an expense that must be covered from somewhere. Indeed, if these are not met through legitimate channels, then LGs justify corruption as necessary to lubricate the wheels of the government. Once corruption

---

their work, with such arrangements being captured in consultancy contracts entered into with the elected representative concerned. While such compensation is not considered as a source of profit, they adequately cover the expenses incurred by the elected representative on behalf of the local government.

is condoned on the ground that it is need-based, it can provide safe alibis for the greedy to operate as well.

Activity mapping, often claimed to be the magic bullet that introduces precision in the assignment of functions to LGs, is eminently desirable but also presents the danger of over-engineering the relationships between LGs as well as between LGs and the state. Over-specifying the ambit and scope of their responsibilities could inhibit LGs from experimenting with and evolving their own arrangements. Instead, freeing LGs to enter into contracts for defining their inter-relationships would enable decentralization to evolve and be enriched through local innovation. This would be an extension of the arrangement of inter-agency contracts, described earlier.

Finally, the experiments with horizontal learning and use of social media to share panchayat-level peer learning could surge in the face of the current top-down, supply-side initiatives for training. Social media does not burn money. Network development is cheaper than cascading face-to-face lecture programmes that deliver homilies to disinterested elected representatives. The galloping spread of the Internet and the availability of cheaper phones and web-enabled devices can spread this strategy faster than one can think. This is also an area where neither age nor experience count. Higher levels might scoff at these scenarios being futuristic, but they could be seriously wrong.

In a situation where messiah-led decentralization is well and truly dead, the realization that crafting an intergovernmental system that addresses decentralization effectively is better initiated from below, will hopefully gain ground. In strengthening LGs, we do not require many big single rejigs, though they might help as well. What we require are many tiny reforms and the capability to spread their effects virally. We need to realize that the big picture indeed comprises many small ones: the greater the number of pixels, the better the definition. In this scenario, the issue is to realize that capacity gaps really are at the highest level, which is unable to manage the transition to a decentralized, multi-level government system. There are serious mindset challenges that the higher-level politician and the senior bureaucrats suffer from. Even as they struggle with these, they must realize that decentralization represents an opportunity for them and not a threat. And as long as they do not sense the energy at the grassroots and respect it, they are the losers.

INDEX

Aam Aadmi Party (AAP) 302
Aayojan ka Adhikar 499
Abdul Kalam, A.P.J. 55–6, 63
accountability 25, 102–3, 110,
191, 214–15, 222–3, 269–72,
275–6, 295–7, 326–9, 335–8;
external 13, 22, 25, 184, 191–2;
institutions of 13–14, 277;
internal 13, 25, 191, 223, 269;
restrictive system of 327; types of
191, *see also* social accountability
mechanisms
Accounts and Audit Order of 1936
308
Action taken report (ATR) 90
Addis Ababa Action Agenda 326
administration 371–2; modernism
of 222; vigilance and 285; civil
administration 304, 328
Administrative Reforms Commission
(2008) 272, 290, 348, 384–5,
388, 396–7, 405–6
Adult franchise 211
Advocates Act (1961) 117
Agarwal, O.P. 192, 222
agriculture 1, 100, 174, 183, 205,
216, 478, 482, 502

Ahmed, Fakhruddin Ali 37, 41;
declaring emergency 57
All India Services (AIS) 339, 342,
345, 347–8, 358, 361, 371, 389
Ambedkar, B.R. 271, 278, 296, 298,
305, 308
Amendment 24, 69, 83, 100–1, 103,
131, 175, 310–11, 432, 438, 454;
42nd Amendment 64, 311; 44th
Amendment 37–8, 64, 311; 52nd
Constitutional 438, (*see also* Anti-
Defection Law); 73rd and 74th
Amendment 25, 184, 209, 370,
394, 425, 464, 468, 475, 484;
99th Amendment 111–12, 114; to
RPA 423, 440
Annual quality management
framework (AQMF) 280
anti-corruption division (ACD) 288
anti-defection law 68, 85, 97–9,
102–3, 438
Appellate Tribunal 117–18
Appellate Tribunal for Electricity
(APTEL) 240–1
Arbitration and Conciliation Act
(1996) 123
Arghyam experiment 500–1

Estimates Committee 88, 316–17, 319
European Central Bank (ECB) 153
Expenditure information network (EIN) 494–5, 504

fast-track courts 128
favouritism 135, 411
federal institutions 2, 12–13, 16
Federal Open Market Committee (FOMC), US 153
Federal Reserve System, US 150, 166
federal system 34, 36, 46, 57, 185, 308, 336
Federalism 29, 305
Finance Commission 13, 21, 198, 200, 206, 217, 315, 486–7; Eleventh 198, 213; Twelfth 329, 486; Thirteenth 330, 486, 491; Fourteenth 22, 198, 200–1, 203, 206, 213, 217, 321, 329, 486, 490
Financial Sector Legislative Reforms Commission (FSLRC) 18, 140, 149–52, 154, 158, 161, 176
financial: crisis 140, 147, 164–6, 170, 177; institutions 140, 164–5, 171; markets 146, 160, 163, 171, 178; stability 140, 146–7, 149, 164–6, 168–9, 174–8, 326; system 140, 160, 164, 166, 174
Fiscal Responsibility and Budget Management Act (FRBM Act 2003) 141, 315, 317–20
fiscal: deficits 140, 143, 145, 150, 162, 318–19; monetization of 144; policy 140, 145, 162–3, 178; transfer system 492
Fixed Income Money Market Dealers Association of India 176
foreign direct investment (FDI) 307

formal institutions 36–7, 174, 221; regeneration of 38

Gandhi, Indira 37, 41–2, 311, 426, 453, 458
Gandhi, Rajiv 42–3, 60, 427, 432, 438, 454
General Accountability Office (GAO) 273, 282–3
geographic information system (GIS) 491
German Reichsbank 166
Gill, M.S. 433, 441
Gopalan, A.K. 107
Gopalaswamy, N. 445
governance 8, 12–13, 167, 227–8, 235–6, 253, 275–6, 301–2, 419–20, 465, 467–9; accountability in 337–8; CAG and 315–16, 322–6; by coalition 36; estimates committee 316–17; financial responsibility 317–19; and government 303–13; information technology audit 313–15; public accounts committee 319–22; social accountability mechanisms 326–37
Government of India (Provisional Constitution) Order of 1947 308
Government of India Act (1858) 304
Government of India Act (1919) 67, 274, 304
Government of India Act (1935) 304
government: debt by 140, 144, 159–62; expenditures of 162, 177, 183, 202, 209; formation of 19, 36, 38; securities and 141, 144, 160–2, 168, 171, 177–8
Govinda Rao, M. 160, 200
Goyal, Piyush 21

EDITORS AND CONTRIBUTORS

Editors

Devesh Kapur is the Madan Lal Sobti professor for the Study of Contemporary India and the director of the Center for the Advanced Study of India at the University of Pennsylvania, Philadelphia, and non-resident fellow at the Center for Global Development, Washington, DC, USA. His publications include *The World Bank: Its First Half Century* (1997); *Diaspora, Democracy and Development: The Domestic Impact of International Migration from India* (2010); *Defying the Odds: The Rise of Dalit Entrepreneurs* (2014); and *The Other One Percent: Indians in America* (2016). Prior to joining the University of Pennsylvania, he held appointments at the Brookings Institution, Harvard University, and University of Texas at Austin.

Pratap Bhanu Mehta is the president and chief executive of the Centre for Policy Research in New Delhi, India. He has published widely on political theory, law, and Indian politics. He has co-edited *The Oxford Companion to Politics in India* (with Niraja Gopal Jayal, 2010) and *The Oxford Handbook of the Indian Constitution* (with Sujit Choudhry and Madhav Khosla, 2016). He is the winner of the 2011 Infosys Prize for Social Sciences.

Milan Vaishnav is a senior fellow in the South Asia Program at the Carnegie Endowment for International Peace in Washington, DC, USA. His primary research focus is the political economy of India, and he examines issues such as corruption and governance, state capacity, distributive politics, and electoral behaviour. He is the author of *When Crime Pays: Money and Muscle in Indian Politics* (2017). Previously, he worked at the Center for Global Development, Washington, DC, where he served as a postdoctoral research fellow; the Center for Strategic and International Studies, Washington, DC; and the Council on Foreign Relations, Washington, DC. He has taught at Columbia, Georgetown, and George Washington universities. He holds a PhD in political science from Columbia University School of General Studies, New York.

Contributors

Errol D'Souza is a professor of economics and the Dean of Faculty at the Indian Institute of Management, Ahmedabad. He has held appointments as the India chair professor at Sciences Po in Paris, visiting professor of the Indian Institute of Advanced Study, Shimla, honorary senior fellow at the National University of Singapore, and visiting professor at the Turin School of Development of the International Labour Organization. He was a member, Technical Advisory Committee on Monetary Policy, of the Reserve Bank of India. His main areas of interest are macro-economics, public policy, and labour markets.

Navroz K. Dubash is a senior fellow at the Centre for Policy Research, New Delhi. His research and policy interests include climate change policy and governance, the political economy of energy and water, the regulatory state in the developing world, and the role of civil society in global environmental governance. His publications include *Tubewell Capitalism: Groundwater Development and Agarian Change in Gujarat* (2002), which was awarded the S.R. Sen Prize in 2006, and edited volumes *A Handbook on Climate Change and India: Development, Politics, and Governance* (2012) and *The Rise of the Regulatory State of the South: Infrastructure and Development in Emerging Economies* (with Bronwen Morgan, 2013). In 2015 he was awarded the T.N. Khoshoo Memorial Award for his work on climate change. In addition to his academic work, he actively engages government and civil society on these topics.

Madhav Khosla is the inaugural Dr B.R. Ambedkar academic fellow at Columbia Law School and a PhD candidate at the Department of

Government, Harvard University. Prior to Harvard, he studied at Yale Law School and the National Law School of India University, Bangalore. Khosla's books include *The Indian Constitution* (2012), *Letters for a Nation: From Jawaharlal Nehru to His Chief Ministers* (2014), *Unstable Constitutionalism: Law and Politics in South Asia* (with Mark Tushnet, 2015), and *The Oxford Handbook of the Indian Constitution* (with Sujit Choudhry and Pratap Bhanu Mehta, 2016).

K.P. Krishnan is a member of the Indian Administrative Service and at present working in the (union) Government of India. He has held a number of senior positions in the Government of India, Government of Karnataka, and the World Bank. He is a trained economist and lawyer with a PhD in Economics from the Indian Institute of Management, Bangalore.

M.R. Madhavan is the president of PRS Legislative Research, New Delhi. His interests are in improving the processes of legislative bodies in three broad dimensions: strengthening the mechanisms for legislators to take decisions in a better informed manner, increasing the transparency of the system to enable citizens to know more about the work of legislators and legislatures, and working towards law-making in a more participatory manner by catalysing engagement between citizens and their elected representatives.

James Manor is the Emeka Anyaoku Professor Emeritus of Commonwealth Studies in the School of Advanced Study, University of London. He has previously taught at Yale, Harvard, and Leicester universities; IDS Sussex; and ISEC, Bangalore. His most recent books are *Politics and State: Society Relations in India* (2016) and *Politics and the Right to Work: India's Mahatma Gandhi National Rural Employment Guarantee Act* (with Rob Jenkins, 2016).

Amitabh Mukhopadhyay is the former director general in the Office of the Comptroller and Auditor General of India. He is currently an international consultant for citizen engagement by state institutions. He has helped the United Nations Department of Economic and Social Affairs to enlist the support of the International Organization of Supreme Audit Institutions for strengthening the means of implementation of the Sustainable Development Goals. He has also worked intensively with state audit offices in the Republics of Nepal, Georgia, and Sri Lanka, and with the financial oversight committees of Parliaments in India, Tunisia, Egypt, and Morocco. Since the early 1990s, he was associated actively with public campaigns for the Right to Information as well as social audits of anti-poverty programmes in India.

Ananth Padmanabhan is a fellow at Carnegie India, New Delhi, and an SJD candidate at the University of Pennsylvania Law School. He is the author of a leading treatise, *Intellectual Property Rights: Infringement and Remedies* (2012). Prior to his doctoral work, he graduated from Penn Law's LLM Program, where he was awarded the Karin Lest Award for Excellence, and the National Law School of India University, Bangalore, where he won the H.M. Seervai Gold Medal for the best essay on constitutional law.

T.R. Raghunandan is a consultant on decentralized public governance and anti-corruption. Formerly a member of the Indian Administrative Service, he served as the joint secretary, Government of India, Ministry of Panchayati Raj (2004–9) and secretary, Rural Development and Panchayat Raj, Karnataka (2001–4). He is part of the advisory board of the Accountability Initiative, Centre for Policy Research, New Delhi, and the Swiss Cooperation Office, New Delhi. He has co-founded a non-profit organization, Avantika Foundation in Bangalore, which works in the area of decentralized public governance.

Nirvikar Singh is distinguished professor of economics and Sarbjit Singh Aurora Chair of Sikh and Punjabi Studies at the University of California, Santa Cruz, where he also directs the Center for Analytical Finance. He has been a member of the Advisory Group to the Finance Minister of India on G-20 matters, and has served as a consultant to the chief economic advisor, Ministry of Finance, Government of India. His current research topics include entrepreneurship, information technology and development, political economy, Indian-Americans, and the Indian economy. He has authored over 100 research papers and has co-authored and co-edited five books. He has also served as an advisor for several start-ups and knowledge services firms in Silicon Valley and India.

T.V. Somanathan is a member of the Indian Administrative Service who has held a number of senior positions in the union and state governments in India. He was also director, manager, and earlier a young professional at the World Bank, Washington, DC. He has a PhD in Economics, is a member of the Institute of Chartered Accountants in England and Wales and other professional bodies, has completed the Executive Development Program at Harvard Business School, and is the author of two books and numerous published papers to his credit.

E. Sridharan is the academic director of the University of Pennsylvania Institute for the Advanced Study of India, New Delhi. He is a political scientist with research interests in Indian and comparative politics, political economy of development, and international relations. He has 9 books and nearly 70 articles to his credit. He is the editor of *India Review*, a pan-social science refereed quarterly on India, and is on the editorial board of the UK-based journal *Commonwealth and Comparative Politics*. He has held visiting appointments at the University of California, Berkeley; London School of Economics; Institute for Developing Economies, Tokyo; Institute of South Asian Studies, National University of Singapore; and the Center for the Advanced Study of India, University of Pennsylvania, Philadelphia. He received his PhD in political science from the University of Pennsylvania.

R. Sridharan is a member of the Indian Administrative Service. He has worked with the Government of Karnataka for considerable periods in the finance and power sectors and also in the Government of India. He has also been the chief vigilance officer of the Food Corporation of India.